MULTI-DISCIPLINARY APPROACHES TO MEDIEVAL BRITTANY, 450–1200

MEDIEVAL TEXTS AND CULTURES OF NORTHERN EUROPE

General Editor
Rory Naismith, *University of Cambridge*

Editorial Board
Elizabeth Boyle, *Maynooth University*
Aisling Byrne, *University of Reading*
Carolyne Larrington, *University of Oxford*
Erik Niblaeus, *University of Cambridge*
Emily V. Thornbury, *Yale University*
Victoria Turner, *University of St Andrews*

Previously published volumes in this series are listed at the back of the book.

VOLUME 36

Multi-disciplinary Approaches to Medieval Brittany, 450–1200

Connections and Disconnections

Edited by

Caroline Brett, Paul Russell, and Fiona Edmonds

BREPOLS

British Library Cataloguing in Publication Data

A catalogue record for this book is available from the British Library.

© 2023, Brepols Publishers n.v., Turnhout, Belgium

All rights reserved. No part of this publication may be reproduced,
stored in a retrieval system, or transmitted, in any form or by any means,
electronic, mechanical, photocopying, recording, or otherwise,
without the prior permission of the publisher.

D/2023/0095/216
ISBN: 978-2-503-60110-6
e-ISBN: 978-2-503-60111-3
DOI: 10.1484/M.TCNE-EB.5.130466
ISSN: 1784-2859
e-ISSN: 2294-8414

Printed in the EU on acid-free paper

CONTENTS

List of Illustrations   vii

Acknowledgements   x

Abbreviations   xi

1. Introduction
CAROLINE BRETT, FIONA EDMONDS, and PAUL RUSSELL   1

2. The 'Late Roman Military Migration':
A Historiographical Myth
PATRICK GALLIOU   9

3. The Settlement of Brittany in Light of
a Migration Period Archaeology
JOHN HINES   27

4. The Archaeology of Early Medieval Rural Societies in Brittany —
Settlements, Landscapes, Legacies, and New Influences:
Interdisciplinary Research
ISABELLE CATTEDDU and JOSEPH LE GALL   57

5. Espace et pouvoirs en Bretagne aux premiers siècles
du Moyen Âge (vi^e–ixe siècle)
MAGALI COUMERT   81

6. Alain de Bretagne, l'exil d'un Prince
JOELLE QUAGHEBEUR   109

7. *Memoria*, Memorialization, and the Monks
of Mont-Saint-Michel, *c.* 960–1033
K. S. B. KEATS-ROHAN — 141

8. Présence d'une culture celtique insulaire
chez les anciens hagiographes bretons
JOSEPH-CLAUDE POULIN — 179

9. Cross-Channel Intercourse in the Earliest Breton *Vitae*
KAREN JANKULAK — 207

10. Explaining the Origins of Brittany in the
Twelfth Century: St Cadog's Solution
BEN GUY — 239

11. Generic Place-Name Elements in the Three Brittonic Regions
O. J. PADEL — 263

12. Facing Different Ways: The Onomastics of People
in Medieval Brittany
PAUL RUSSELL — 311

Index — 359

LIST OF ILLUSTRATIONS

2. The 'Late Roman Military Migration' — *Patrick Galliou*

Figure 2.1. Distribution of finds of Late Romano-British
pottery in Brittany...14

Figure 2.2. The *Tractus armoricanus et nervicanus*. 16

Figure 2.3. Late Roman wall at Alet. 17

Figure 2.4. Late Roman gate at Le Yaudet. 17

Figure 2.5. Plan of the Brest *castellum*..18

Figure 2.6. Wall and Tower 2 of the Brest *castellum*............................18

Figure 2.7. Late Roman belt-fitting, Bosseno *villa* (Carnac, Morbihan).....20

Figure 2.8. Late Roman belt-fitting, Etel (Morbihan).........................21

Figure 2.9. Quoit Brooch Style buckle and glass
from the Pont-de-Buis (Finistère) grave............................22

**3. The Settlement of Brittany in Light of a Migration Period Archaeology
—** *John Hines*

Figure 3.1. Two distribution maps representing different forms of archaeological evidence for population movement in the fifth century..........29

Figure 3.2. Mucking, Essex: the distribution of Early Anglo-Saxon
sunken feature buildings (SFBs) in primary settlement zone A
with relatively high frequencies of Late Roman pottery. 39

Figure 3.3. Examples of bracelets and anklets of forms derived from
Romano-British models in Early Anglo-Saxon children's graves
(up to the age of approximately twelve years old)......................41

Figure 3.4. Specimens of Quoit Brooch Style metalwork from Brittany.....44

Figure 3.5. The locations of Quoit Brooch Style finds in Brittany. 45

Figure 3.6. The development of the Quoit Brooch Style in England........46

viii LIST OF ILLUSTRATIONS

4. The Archaeology of Early Medieval Rural Societies in Brittany — *Isabelle Catteddu and Joseph Le Gall*

Figure 4.1. Map of the early medieval sites excavated in Brittany. Development of archaeological research in 2005 and in 2018. 59

Figure 4.2. Graphic rendering of the rural settlement of Montours 'le Teilleul' (Ille-et-Vilaine) during the eighth and ninth centuries....... 61

Figure 4.3. Map of Châteaugiron, site A: the rural settlement during the eighth and ninth centuries................................ 61

Figure 4.4. Ring-forts excavated in Brittany.............................. 63

Figure 4.5. The ringwork of Bressilien in Paule (Côtes-d'Armor).......... 64

Figure 4.6. View of the main stone building of the elite site of Bressilien in Paule.. 67

Figure 4.7. View of the excavation of silos on the early medieval Bressilien elite site in Paule (Côtes-d'Armor)................. 67

Figure 4.8. Corn-drying kilns at the Bressilien site. 68

Figure 4.9. Gilt bronze ornament uncovered in the chapel of Saint-Symphorien... 70

6. Alain de Bretagne, l'exil d'un Prince — *Joelle Quaghebeur*

Figure 6.1. Arbre généalogique du lignage d'Alain II de Bretagne. 132

7. *Memoria*, Memorialization and the Monks of Mont-Saint-Michel, *c.* 960–1033 — *K. S. B. Keats-Rohan*

Table 7.1. 'The Fleury List', Orléans, Bib. mun., MS 127 (103), p. 361 160

Table 7.2. Abbots evidenced in the Necrology and Martyrology-Necrology of Mont-Saint-Michel. 163–64

Figure 7.1. Opening page of the Mont's Necrology 166

Figure 7.2. Eulogy of Abbot Maiol of Cluny, died 11 May 994 167

Figure 7.3. Monastic renewal and reform *c.* 920–1020 172

LIST OF ILLUSTRATIONS

11. Generic Place-Name Elements in the Three Brittonic Regions — *O. J. Padel*

Figure 11.1. Cornwall: place-names in *Tre-*............................266

Figure 11.2. Wales: place-names in *Tre-* (modern)......................268

Figure 11.3. Eastern Brittany: names in *Tre-*..........................270

Figure 11.4. Cornwall: names in *Bod-*, *Bos-*..........................275

Figure 11.5. Cornwall: names in *Car-* (Old Cornish *Caer-*)............277

Figure 11.6. Cornwall: names in *Lis-*, *Les-*, *-lis* and *Hen-lys*....281

Figure 11.7. Cornwall: manors with names in *Lis-*, etc.
showing hundredal boundaries...283

Figure 11.8. Eastern Brittany: names in *Les-* and *Lis-*...............284

Figure 11.9. Cornwall: parish churches and parochial chapels
with names in *Lann-*, *-lann*...289

Figure 11.10. Parishes in Brittany with names in *Plou-*, etc...........295

Figure 11.11. Cornwall: Pelynt and Luxulyan. 297

Figure 11.12. Cornwall: place-names in *Eglos-*.. 301

Acknowledgements

This book consists of the papers given at a conference on 1–2 December 2017 at the Department of Anglo-Saxon, Norse and Celtic, University of Cambridge, as part of the project 'Brittany and the Atlantic Archipelago' funded by the Leverhulme Trust through their Research Project Grant scheme between 2015 and 2019, based at the Department of Anglo-Saxon, Norse and Celtic, with Paul Russell as principal investigator, Fiona Edmonds as co-investigator, and Caroline Brett as research associate.

The editors would like to thank all the contributors for making this volume possible, for their punctilious efficiency in preparing their papers for publication and their patience at editorial delays, and the anonymous readers of the draft version of this volume for their helpful and constructive comments. Thanks are also due to all those who chaired sessions and particularly to Professor Thomas Charles-Edwards and Professor Wendy Davies for providing the opening and closing remarks and for the valuable advice that they, together with Dr Oliver Padel, provided throughout the project. We also thank the staff and students of the Faculty of English and the Department of Anglo-Saxon, Norse and Celtic for organizing the conference and welcoming the attendees, and Girton College, St John's College, and Hughes Hall for offering accommodation to speakers.

Abbreviations

AASS	*Acta Sanctorum*
ABPO	*Annales de Bretagne et des Pays de l'Ouest*
AnBoll	*Analecta Bollandiana*
ASC	Anglo-Saxon Chronicle
BBCS	*Bulletin of the Board of Celtic Studies*
BHL	Bibliotheca Hagiographica Latina
BSAF	*Bulletin de la société archéologique du Finistère*
CC CM	*Corpus Christianorum Continuatio Mediaevalis*
CC SL	*Corpus Christianorum Series Latina*
CL	*Cartulary of Landévennec*, ed. R.-F.-L. Le Men and E. Ernault, *Cartulaire de Landévennec*, in *Mélanges historiques: choix de documents*, vol. 5 (Paris: Imprimerie Nationale, 1886), pp. 533–600
CMCS	*Cambridge/Cambrian Medieval Celtic Studies*
CR	*Cartulary of Redon*, ed. A. de Courson, *Cartulaire de l'Abbaye de Redon en Bretagne* (Paris: Imprimerie Impériale, 1863)
EHR	*The English Historical Review*
ÉC	*Études celtiques*
INRAP	*Institut national de recherches archéologiques préventatives*

JMH	*Journal of Medieval History*
KCD	J. M. Kemble, *Codex Diplomaticus Ævi Saxonici*, 6 vols (London, 1839–1848)
MA	*Medieval Archaeology*
MGH	*Monumenta Germaniae Historica*
MGH AA	*Monumenta Germaniae Historica Auctores Antiquissimi*
MGH Epp.	*Monumenta Germaniae Historica Epistolae*
MGH LL	*Monumenta Germaniae Historica Leges*
MGH SS RG	*Monumenta Germaniae Historica Scriptores rerum Germanicarum*
MGH SS RG in us. schol. s. e.	*Monumenta Germaniae Historica Scriptores rerum Germanicarum in usum scholarum separatim editi*
MGH SS RM	*Monumenta Germaniae Historica Scriptores rerum Merovingicarum*
MSHAB	*Mémoires de la Société historique et archéologique de Bretagne*
NMS	*Nottingham Medieval Studies*
S (+ number)	P. H. Sawyer, *Anglo-Saxon Charters: an Annotated List and Bibliography* (London, 1968) <www.esawyer.org.uk>
SC	*Studia Celtica*
SCH	Studies in Celtic History

1. Introduction

Caroline Brett, Fiona Edmonds, and Paul Russell

The history of Brittany, the north-western Atlantic peninsula of France, has always been hard to characterize in terms of the nation states and linguistic regions that make up modern Europe. Brittany's prehistoric archaeology shows it to have been a zone of high connectivity with the islands beyond and with other Atlantic-facing coasts of Europe. Yet within the centralized states that have incorporated it in historic times — from the Roman Empire to modern France — it has often seemed remote. Compared to England and metropolitan France, it generated little written source-material until the modern era (original sources produced in Brittany itself before the year 1100 are limited to saints' lives and two valuable, but geographically circumscribed, collections of charters). The temptation for historians of the Middle Ages has often been either to leave Brittany on one side, or to write its history by analogy, assuming its general parity with one or other of the zones it bridged: Celtic Britain or continental France. Our title emphasises 'disconnections' as well as 'connections' to indicate the need to move beyond such assumptions, to be prepared to discard our models, and to return regularly to what the sources, limited as they are, can actually tell us.

It is easier to ask than to answer questions about Brittany and its origins. How did it acquire its British Celtic language, place-names and saints' legends? Did this occur in a sudden spate of turmoil following the fall of Rome, or in a long-term process of osmosis? At what point did its Continental connections come to predominate over its Insular heritage in politics, social organization and culture? Or are these questions simply the wrong ones to be asking, harking back to a nineteenth- and early twentieth-century template of scholarship that obscures as much as it reveals?

KEYWORDS archaeology, interdisciplinarity, hagiography, language, names, territoriality

Multi-disciplinary Approaches to Medieval Brittany, 450–1200: Connections and Disconnections, ed. by Caroline Brett, Fiona Edmonds, and Paul Russell, TCNE 36 (Turnhout: Brepols, 2023) pp. 1–7   BREPOLS PUBLISHERS   10.1484/M.TCNE-EB.5.132306

Brittany offers the opportunity to write a different kind of early medieval history, relieved of the hindsight imposed by seeking for the 'origins' of nations or kingdoms: the history of an area that was geographically well defined, yet often politically amorphous, receiving a multiplicity of influences but seldom dominated for long by any one neighbour: a hybrid society that was in some respects unique.

The wish to study this region in greater depth, in the context of recent developments in medieval studies, prompted the editors of this volume to apply for Leverhulme Trust funding for a four-year project at the Department of Anglo-Saxon, Norse and Celtic, Cambridge, between 2015 and 2019. The main outputs of the project are a monograph, *Brittany and the Atlantic Archipelago, 450–1200: Contact, Myth and History*, published by Cambridge University Press in 2021, and the present volume, consisting of the papers presented at a conference held in Cambridge on 1–2 December 2017. The papers here are published to a large extent as originally given, with minimal updating of references to include publications which have appeared since that date. The leading theme of the monograph is the interplay between Brittany's actual, evolving relationship with the Insular world, and Bretons' developing ideas about their history and identity. Various kinds of source-material are used including language, archaeology, and manuscripts, but the principal connecting thread is historical and the discussion is dominated by the representation of Brittany and its inhabitants in literary texts. The intention in organizing the conference was to widen the perspective of the project by bringing together a variety of disciplinary expertise. As well as historians, we invited archaeologists, scholars of language, personal names and place-names, literary history and prosopography, in the hope that directions for future research would emerge. Some of the contributors were long-term specialists in Brittany, others approached it from a wider background in Celtic or early medieval studies: these variations in focus helped to build up a multi-layered picture with a wealth of spatial and inter-disciplinary connections.

To take archaeology first, the contributions by Patrick Galliou and John Hines focus on updating the interpretation of Brittany's scanty late antique and early medieval archaeological record in the light of wider developments in the archaeology of the 'migration period' in Europe. Galliou dissects the archaeological underpinning of the theory, originally derived from medieval literary sources, that the British settlement of Brittany was a military movement organized by Roman authorities in the third and fourth centuries. Hines takes up the argument where Galliou leaves it, showing that a comparison of the early medieval archaeology of Brittany and western Britain currently offers little to show

1. INTRODUCTION

convergence: a rare artefact type that obviously links post-Roman Brittany to Britain, the fifth-century 'Quoit Brooch Style' material, is found in south-eastern Britain rather than in the south-west, long regarded as the point of origin of most migrants to Brittany. He concludes by suggesting that 'becoming Breton', rather than being an incidental product of migration and colonization, was a deliberate choice on the part of the inhabitants of Armorica and as such should be seen as a central test case for the relative importance of population-movement and ethnogenesis in post-Roman Europe as a whole.

The rather emphatic severing of one kind of postulated connection between Britain and Brittany in these papers paves the way for the contribution by Isabelle Catteddu and Joseph Le Gall, which broadens the focus from the search for evidence of migration to investigation of settlement and society more generally. Drawing on a wealth of new evidence from developer-led archaeology, Catteddu and Le Gall demonstrate that early medieval Breton material culture, while appearing relatively modest, contains great diversity and reveals multiple, sometimes unexpected, external connections. All these papers add scope and detail, and the authority of their authors' long experience in primary research, to the necessarily rather general treatment of archaeological evidence in the monograph.

The historical contributions by Magali Coumert, Joëlle Quaghebeur and Katharine Keats-Rohan likewise touch on issues treated in the project monograph, but with added detail grounded in their individual specialisms. They too perform the complementary tasks of questioning anachronistic assumptions and introducing new perspectives. Magali Coumert's paper is inspired by her interest in epistemology and the weight of inherited assumptions in the writing of Breton history, and also reflects the current interest among French medieval historians in territoriality and its comparative lack of definition in the early Middle Ages. Re-examining the contemporary source-material of the sixth and early seventh centuries, she points out that, shorn of the retrospective view imposed by sources of the Carolingian period and after, the existence of 'Brittany' as a unit — combining a political territory, a language, and an ethnic group, *Brittones* or Bretons — cannot be substantiated before *c.* 800. Joëlle Quaghebeur has done more than any other researcher to elucidate the little-known political history of western Brittany from the Carolingian period to the central Middle Ages. With her paper we move forward to the Viking Age when Brittany's belatedly created territorial integrity threatened to fall apart, and the region was temporarily an important counter in the post-Carolingian configuration of north-west Europe. The installation of the Breton duke Alan II by the English king Æthelstan has long been known as an historic episode, but is here framed in the broader context of connections between the courts of Francia, Wessex, and Wales in the 930s, as rulers attempted to contain the Vikings. Katharine Keats-Rohan is known for her authoritative work on the prosopography of England after 1066 and especially on the role of Bretons in what she has termed the 'non-Norman Conquest'. Her paper too pivots on the Viking Age and on the period of ecclesiastical reform and reconstruction that followed. Using the narrative and commemorative records of the monastery of Mont-Saint-Michel on the Breton/Norman border as a point of departure, she shows that eastern Brittany in the tenth and eleventh centuries was part of a continuum of reformist initiatives that stretched from Burgundy through Lotharingia, Flanders, Neustria, and beyond: regardless of political fragmentation, here was an intimate web of connections that counterbalances the idea of a beleaguered and isolated Brittany in the decades preceding the Gregorian reform.

'Disconnection' and reconnection likewise characterize the three contributions that are aimed at placing Brittany's heritage of early medieval Latin hagiography in its Insular and Continental context. These are the contributions that are closest in subject-matter to the monograph, but they offer a complementary perspective and differ from it in some details of interpretation. Saints' Lives are the most extensive cultural productions that survive from early medieval Brittany, and have long been scrutinized by those in search of a 'Celtic' heritage; but it is necessary to distinguish between the different senses in which Brittany may, or may not, have belonged to a shared Brittonic or wider 'Celtic' cultural sphere in the centuries following the fall of Rome. Joseph-Claude Poulin, from a position of unparalleled expertise in the textual history of Breton saints' Lives, points out the ways in which it is *not* meaningful to categorize these texts as 'Celtic', in the sense of forming a distinctive and homogenous grouping with similar texts from early medieval Ireland and Wales. Most of their tropes and stylistic traits were also popular in the Frankish realms and in the Western Church in general. However, Karen Jankulak, bringing to bear her experience with the varied evidence for the diffusion of saints' cults, shows in her survey of 'Cross-Channel Intercourse in the Earliest Breton *Vitae*', that the substantive information shared between Breton and Welsh *Vitae* 'tell[s] of regular, if not continuous, intellectual exchanges [between the Celtic-speaking regions] across the later first millennium'. Ben Guy, whose recent work has revolutionized the understanding of medieval Welsh genealogy, focuses his study more closely on the hagiography and genealogy emanating from the monastery of Llancarfan in Glamorgan in the late eleventh and early twelfth centuries. He demonstrates how its literati, prompted by the proximity of Breton settlers at

1. INTRODUCTION

Monmouth after the Norman Conquest, experimented with successive theories about the foundation of Brittany that culminated in the overwhelmingly successful inventions of Geoffrey of Monmouth.

These contributions show how a simultaneously long and short focus, placing texts under the microscope of close reading while also broadening the context in which they are read, can elicit substantial new understanding from material that has long been familiar to scholarship. The search for historical insights from linguistic and onomastic material from Brittany, by comparison, has received less attention since the pioneering work of K. H. Jackson, with exceptions such as the place-name studies of the late Professor Bernard Tanguy. This lends special importance to the two contributions to this volume by linguists: Oliver Padel, the acknowledged expert on Cornish place-names, and Paul Russell, who specialises in the language interface between Latin and British in the early Middle Ages. Padel's essay is an exploratory comparison of a range of sacred and secular place-name elements in Brittany, Cornwall, and Wales, which concludes that the variation in usage points to real and intriguing social and administrative differences between these regions. Paul Russell's similarly broad survey of the development of personal names in early medieval Brittany includes a comparison with Welsh and Cornish names and makes important methodological points about the role of semantic meaning, fashion, and social change in their evolution. Further study in this field may clarify the similarities and differences between Brittany and other Insular and Continental societies in the significance of names, clarifying how they may be used in the kind of reconstruction of familial and social relationships that forms the substance of regional medieval studies in many parts of France.

The study of language and names, alongside archaeology and possibly genetics, holds out the promise of adding substantially to the knowledge base on early medieval Brittany. So does the study of manuscripts and their contents — texts, script, and glosses — together with inscriptions. At least one hundred and fifty to two hundred ninth- and tenth-century manuscripts with Breton connections are extant, greatly exceeding the survival rate from the other Celtic-speaking regions. The absence of a contribution specifically on manuscripts in the present volume is regrettable but we hope that the gap may be partially filled by the chapter on manuscript-culture in the monograph by the editors, cited above, pending the full publication of the project 'Ireland and Carolingian Brittany: Texts and Transmission' (IRCABRITT) at NUI Galway, which promises to transform understanding of Brittany's cultural connections.

All these disciplines offer the possibility of mitigating one of the greatest problems in the early history of Brittany: the chronologically discontinuous coverage of the source-material. A problem that our series of papers could not altogether avoid, on account of their varied subject matter, was the tendency to focus attention on the separate periods for which source-material does exist, or for which compelling problems present themselves — the post-Roman period, the ninth century, the 'Viking crisis', and the eleventh and twelfth centuries. Inevitably it is difficult to tackle the lengthy blanks in between, and this in turn obscures questions of longer-term historical development. Only certain papers, for instance the language papers and those by Catteddu, Keats-Rohan, and Jankulak, had the opportunity to take a more longitudinal view, an approach which we hope to see continued in future work. Some informed guesses, at least, on what transpired in Brittany during the evidentiary blank of the mid-seventh to eighth centuries, are overdue, as is a reassessment of the transition from Carolingian Brittany, with its unusual, independent village communities (so vividly elucidated by Wendy Davies), to eleventh-century Brittany with its typically northern French knightly aristocracy and dependent peasantry. More generally, a true *longue durée* approach that makes full use of various disciplines will allow Brittany to emerge as an important indicator, on a European scale, of the slow shifts between centralization and decentralization of power, between land-based and maritime economic systems, that determined whether it was pulled towards the Continent or faced the sea. Barry Cunliffe's extensive scholarship is notable for a *longue durée* approach to these questions, as seen most recently in his book *Bretons and Britons: The Fight for Identity* (Oxford University Press, 2021). The wide variety of disciplines and the detailed case studies encompassed in this volume have additional insights to contribute.

We offer this collection of essays in the hope of setting Brittany closer to the centre of early medieval studies: neither an anomaly that needs specialized treatment in an airtight 'Celtic' chamber, nor a remote but typical region to which historical models developed elsewhere can be mechanically applied, but an example, to be set alongside others, of the sheer variety of social adaptations that arose in response to the general conditions of the early medieval world — political shrinkage, economic abatement, the sacralization of space. We hope, too, that scholars working on this field in a variety of languages will continue to collaborate and to learn from one another's approaches — inspired by the often anonymous medieval pioneers who forged those connections which we now study.

1. INTRODUCTION

Caroline Brett is Affiliated Lecturer in the Department of Anglo-Saxon, Norse and Celtic at the University of Cambridge. She was Research Associate on the Leverhulme-funded project 'Brittany and the Atlantic Archipelago' and author, with Fiona Edmonds and Paul Russell, of *Brittany and the Atlantic Archipelago, 450–1200: Contact, Myth and History* (2021).

Fiona Edmonds is Professor in History and Director of the Regional Heritage Centre at Lancaster University. She is the author of *Gaelic Influence in the Northumbrian Kingdom: The Golden Age and the Viking Age* (2019), which won the 2021 Frank Watson Book Prize.

Paul Russell is Professor of Celtic in the Department of Anglo-Saxon, Norse and Celtic at the University of Cambridge. His research interests include Medieval Latin in the Celtic-speaking world, learned texts in Celtic languages, Celtic philology and linguistics, and medieval Welsh law. He has recently published *Reading Ovid in Medieval Wales* (2017) and *Vita Griffini filii Conani: The Medieval Latin Life of Gruffudd ap Cynan* (2005), which won the 2004 Legonna Prize.

Caroline Brett est maître de conférences associée au Department of Anglo-Saxon, Norse and Celtic à l'Université de Cambridge. Elle fut associée de recherches de l'entreprise de recherche 'Brittany and the Atlantic Archipelago' financié par le Leverhulme Trust et est auteur, avec Fiona Edmonds et Paul Russell, de *Brittany and the Atlantic Archipelago, 450–1200: Contact, Myth and History* (2021).

Fiona Edmonds est professeure en histoire et directeur du Regional Heritage Centre à l'Université de Lancaster. Elle est auteur de *Gaelic Influence in the Northumbrian Kingdom: The Golden Age and the Viking Age* (2019), ouvrage qui gagna le Prix Frank Watson en 2021.

Paul Russell est professeur en celtique au Department of Anglo-Saxon, Norse and Celtic à l'Université de Cambridge. Ses recherches englobent l'usage du latin dans le monde celtique médiéval, philologie et linguistique celtiques, et la loi médiévale du Pays de Galles. Il a publié *Reading Ovid in Medieval Wales* (2017) et *Vita Griffini filii Conani: The Medieval Latin Life of Gruffudd ap Cynan* (2005): ce dernier ouvrage gagna le Prix Legonna en 2004.

2. The 'Late Roman Military Migration': A Historiographical Myth

Patrick Galliou

ABSTRACT At the end of the twentieth century it had become an accepted tenet of Breton history that the earliest migration of Britons to Brittany was organized by the Roman imperial authorities in the late third and fourth centuries, to repopulate the peninsula and defend it against sea-borne raids. However, new discoveries and re-evaluation of archaeological evidence have cast doubt on the reality of the phenomena which the 'military migration' was designed to explain. Small-scale 'Saxon piracy' did not destroy late antique Armorica's economy and trade links; symptoms of 'barbarization' are seen in settlement archaeology throughout northern Gaul and cannot be ascribed to the arrival of 'non-Romanized Britons'; even specific artefact types such as fifth-century metalwork in the 'Quoit Brooch Style' indicate contact between Britain and northern Gaul, but not necessarily migration. It is necessary to develop and test new models to account for the implantation of British language and identity in Brittany.

RÉSUMÉ À la fin du xxᵉ siècle, l'hypothèse d'une première vague migratoire de la Bretagne insulaire vers l'Armorique dans les iiiᵉ et ivᵉ siècles, organisée par les autorités romaines pour repeupler la péninsule et en renforcer la défense contre les pirates, était devenue 'la vulgate de l'historiographie régionale'. Des nouvelles découvertes archéologiques, et les réinterprétations de ces données ont cependant mis en doute la réalité des phénomènes qu'entendait expliquer l'hypothèse d'une migration militaire. Les raids des Saxons, Frisons et autres n'avaient détruit ni l'économie interne ni les échanges externes de l'Armorique dans l'Antiquité tardive. Les symptômes de 'barbarisation' attribués naguère à l'arrivée de Bretons 'non-romanisés' se rencontrent dans l'archéologie de tout le nord de la Gaule. Même des objets très spécifiques aux parallèles britonniques comme les boucles de ceinture du style 'Quoit Brooch' ne prouvent pas la migration. Il faut développer et vérifier de nouveaux modèles pour expliquer l'implantation de la langue et de l'identité bretonne en Armorique.

KEYWORDS Armorican peninsula, belt fittings, Brest, brooches, *laeti*, Le Yaudet, military migration, pirates, pottery, Quoit Brooch Style, *Tractus Armoricanus*

Multi-disciplinary Approaches to Medieval Brittany, 450–1200: Connections and Disconnections, ed. by Caroline Brett, Fiona Edmonds, and Paul Russell, TCNE 36 (Turnhout: Brepols, 2023) pp. 9–26   BREPOLS 🖳 PUBLISHERS   10.1484/M.TCNE-EB.5.132307

The theory according to which a 'first Breton migration' was organized, in the fourth or even the late third century, by Roman authorities acting within the administrative and military framework of the Empire so as to defend the coasts of Gaul, and more particularly the west of the Armorican peninsula, threatened by Saxon/Frankish raids, was first put forward in 1947 by the French historian Ferdinand Lot — 'Furent-ils installés [the Bretons], étant encore juridiquement sujets de l'Empire, par les autorités romaines, désireuses de repeupler les côtes armoricaines, dévastées par les pirates saxons?'[1] — and repeated, some twenty years later (1965), by Nora Chadwick in her 'Colonization of Brittany from Celtic Britain'.[2] Before the end of the century, it had become the *doxa* among French historians. In his 1972 PhD on the *Osismi* (published in 1978), Louis Pape judged that

> Dans une Armorique affaiblie par la crise du IIIe siècle les autorités romaines favorisent, dès le IVe siècle, une implantation de populations en provenance du Sud-Ouest de la Bretagne et les installent dans une situation proche de celle des *laeti*, avec mission de participer à l'organisation défensive du pays: ces *laeti* reçoivent, en particulier, la charge de construire des routes stratégiques et reçoivent en échange des terres le long de ces voies, les plus fréquentées au Bas Empire. Ces groupes sont d'abord très minoritaires; puis, lorsque les menaces irlandaises se font plus fortes, le mouvement de migration se renforce par petites vagues successives à partir des années 350–360 ...[3]

In 1979, in a paper given to the Stirling conference on Roman frontiers, I — much to my regret — argued that late 'military style' copper alloy brooches and belt fittings found on a small number of rural sites — mostly villas and temples — bore witness to the presence of military contingents, probably coming from the least Romanized parts of Britain, i.e. Cornwall and Wales,

---

[1] 'Were they [the Bretons], still juridically subjects of the Empire, established by the Roman authorities, desirous of re-populating the Armorican coasts which had been devastated by Saxon pirates?', Lot, *La Gaule*, p. 483.

[2] Chadwick, 'The Colonization of Brittany from Celtic Britain'.

[3] 'In an Armorica weakened by the crisis of the third century, the Roman authorities encouraged, as early as the fourth century, an implantation of immigrants from the south-west of Britain whom they installed in a position similar to that of *laeti*, with a mission to participate in the defence of the region: these *laeti* were tasked, in particular, with the construction of strategic roads and in exchange were granted land adjacent to those roads, which were most heavily used in the late Empire. These groups were at first very much in the minority but, as the threat from Ireland grew, the migratory movement increased in small successive waves from the 350s and 360s onwards ...' Pape, *La Civitas des Osismes*, p. 227.

2. THE 'LATE ROMAN MILITARY MIGRATION'

as the villas and temples in which they were found showed obvious signs of what was then believed to be a 'barbarianization' of Roman settlements due to incoming Britons.[4] Léon Fleuriot in his *Origines de la Bretagne* (1980) and Soazick Kernéis in her *Celtiques* (1998) offered similar analyses and the idea of an early British military migration to the west of the Armorican peninsula gradually took root among Breton historians, to such an extent that, as late as 2012, Bernard Merdrignac could write unhesitatingly that the supposed third- or fourth-century British migration to Armorica was 'a central tenet of Breton history' ('la vulgate de l'historiographie régionale').[5]

Like all historical dogmas, this needed to be re-examined and reassessed in the light of new archaeological discoveries and the re-evaluation of old finds, all the more so as, as Caroline Brett had rightly pointed out in her seminal 2011 article, 'the study of the Breton migrations has become "stuck" with old-fashioned models from which the study of Late Antiquity has otherwise moved on'.[6] In 2015 I therefore chose to open our analysis of the Late Roman *castellum* at Brest onto a more comprehensive approach to Late Roman Armorica, thus reaching very different findings from our 1979 conclusions.[7]

As a matter of fact, the 'early military migration' theory rests on three postulates:

(a) In the 270s and during the whole fourth century, 'pirates' sailing down from the North Sea raided the coasts of Gaul;

(b) The Armorican peninsula was almost entirely depopulated, whole communities having fled from the Saxon raids, the few which had remained being unable to protect their lands or urban and rural settlements;

(c) The solution to this quandary found by the Roman authorities was to build massive coastal defences to contain Saxon/Frankish inroads, while moving groups from other provinces, mostly from *Britannia*, and settling them as *laeti* in the peninsula. They were given lands against the promise of defending them, of building 'strategic' roads and fighting back incoming raiders.

---

[4] Galliou, 'The Defence of Armorica', pp. 398–411.

[5] Fleuriot, *Les Origines de la Bretagne*; Kerneis, *Les Celtiques*; Merdrignac, *D'une Bretagne à l'autre*, p. 45.

[6] Brett, 'Soldiers, Saints, and States?', p. 3.

[7] Galliou and Simon, *Le Castellum de Brest*.

Let us re-examine these three postulates in the same order:

(a) The presence of 'Saxon/Frankish pirates' — the expression should be defined more accurately — in the North Sea and the northern half of the Channel is well attested at the end of the third century, compelling Roman authorities to entrust the Menapian, Carausius — the future usurper (AD 286–293) — with the defence and safety of the Channel seaways.[8] But such 'pirates' do not seem to have seriously raided the coasts of western Gaul before the second half of the fifth century, when they are mentioned by Sidonius Apollinaris, and their possible attacks have left no recognizable impact on the archaeological landscape.[9] Nowhere can be seen the traces of the massive destruction and conflagrations so dear to the hearts of nineteenth-century Breton romantic historians. Late third-century and fourth-century coin hoards, so common in Gaul and Britain, were long believed to bear direct witness to such incursions, as terrorized individuals would bury their savings to keep them from the preying hands of Saxon/Frankish raiders and, having been slaughtered by the latter, would never be able to recover them. But, as a matter of fact, though some of these hoards may well correspond to some latent fear and to some degree of social and economic insecurity, most were left in the ground not because their owners had been killed, but simply because the minting of new types of coins and the demonetization of the previous coinage turned their buried savings into mere scrap metal, not worth digging up.[10]

Besides, the importance of such incursions into the western seaways has probably been largely exaggerated. Like the Viking raids of a later period, such attacks must have involved a small number of boats and a few dozen men. They would have been aimed at isolated, undefended sites and not at towns or nucleated settlements, where resistance could prove too strong for the taste of marauders. Local militias, such as the strong native force gathered on the coast of Galicia in 456 to oppose the landing of four hundred Herules, could also turn into another business risk for Saxon raiders.[11] But they could, of course,

---

[8] Aurelius Victor, *De Caesaribus*, pp. 39–40; Eutropius, *Breviarium ab urbe condita*, IX, 21, pp. 125–26.

[9] Sidonius Apollinaris, *Carmina*, VII, l. 369, trans. pp. 150–51; *Epistolae*, VIII, 6, trans. pp. 428–33.

[10] Estiot, 'Une campagne germanique', p. 225 n. 44; Huvelin, 'Le trésor de Saint-Colombier en Sarzeau', p. 59.

[11] Hydatius, *Chronicon*, AD 456, in *Chronique/Hydace*, I, 152–53.

2. THE 'LATE ROMAN MILITARY MIGRATION'

board vessels at sea or, like Ammianus's Isaurian pirates, they could have used stealth rather than frontal assault, i.e.:

> hide themselves there in pathless lurking-places and defiles as the dark nights were coming on — the moon being still crescent and so not shining with full brilliance — and watched the sailors. And when they saw that they were buried in sleep, creeping on all fours along the anchor-ropes and making their way on tiptoe into the boats, they came upon the crew all unawares, and since their natural ferocity was fired by greed, they spared no one, even of those who surrendered, but massacred them all and without resistance carried off the cargoes, led either by their value or their usefulness.[12]

(b) The second postulation is based on the idea, forcefully expressed by La Borderie in his 1905-1914 *Histoire de la Bretagne*, and by his followers, that the Armorican peninsula, a large part of which was then believed to have been covered by a dense and almost impenetrable forest, was sparsely peopled in the Early Roman Empire, and, having been deserted by its inhabitants in the Later Empire was mostly left empty and fallow.[13] But intensive fieldwork and air surveys have shown literally thousands of Iron Age and Roman enclosed farms, spread all over the peninsula in open landscapes where deforestation activities had begun a few millennia before, and have revealed no clear break in the overall distribution of population between the Roman period and the High Middle Ages, Early or Late Roman cemeteries, like those of Saint-Urnel (Plomeur, Finistère) and probably Lostmarc'h (Crozon, Finistère), also continuing in use well into the Middle Ages.[14]

Finds of fourth- and early fifth-century pottery in rural and urban settlements, such as black burnished ware from Dorset or New Forest vessels from the vicinity of Southampton,[15] Argonne rouletted Samian from the environs of

---

[12] '[A]viis latebrosis sese convallibusque occultantes cum appeterent noctes – luna etiam tum cornuta ideoque nondum solido splendore fulgente nauticos observabant quos cum in somnum sentirent effusos per ancoralia, quadrupedo gradu repentes seseque suspensis passibus iniectantes in scaphas eisdem sensim nihil opinantibus adsistebant et incendente aviditate saevitiam ne cedentium quidem parcendo obtruncatis omnibus merces opimas velut viles nullis repugnantibus avertebant', Ammianus Marcellinus, *Res gestae*, XIV.2.2, trans. I, 13–14.

[13] De la Borderie, *Histoire de Bretagne*, I, 42–43.

[14] Giot and Monnier, 'Le cimetière des anciens Bretons de Saint-Saturnin ou Saint-Urnel en Plomeur, Finistère'; Galliou, 'Un conservatoire archéologique méconnu'.

[15] Tuffreau-Libre, Mossmann-Bouquillon, and Symonds, 'La céramique dite *black-burnished* dans le Nord de la France'.

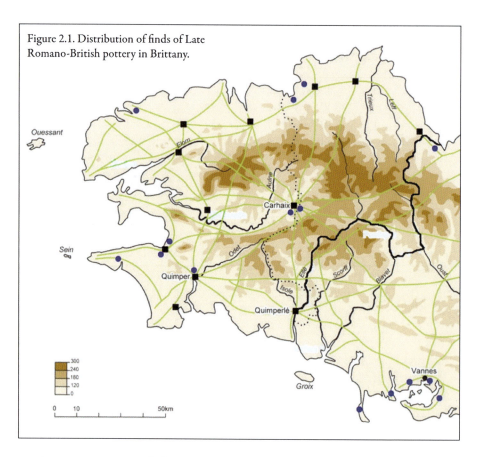

Figure 2.1. Distribution of finds of Late Romano-British pottery in Brittany.

Verdun, in eastern Gaul,[16] marbled wares from Aquitaine,[17] and wine amphorae from a variety of Gaulish and Mediterranean sources are certainly proof that ships were still plying the age-old Atlantic and Channel maritime routes between the estuaries of the Garonne, Loire, Seine, Rhine, and Thames and putting in at Armorican ports (Fig. 2.1). The presence of such imports on many sites also indicates that Armorican communities were still far from being economically inactive and had not been cut off from their traditional trading connections. The sudden and complete demise, in the last quarter of the third century, of the fish-processing industry which had developed on the coasts of the *Osismii* and the *Veneti* from the 150s, and which I had ascribed, in 1979,

[16] Gazenbeek and Van der Leeuw, 'L'Argonne dans l'Antiquité'; Blaskiewicz and Jigan 'Le problème de la diffusion'.
[17] Galliou, Fulford and Clément, 'La diffusion de la céramique "à l'éponge"'.

2. THE 'LATE ROMAN MILITARY MIGRATION'

to a general economic collapse of these western *civitates*, may be due to simpler causes, completely unrelated to supposed military difficulties, among which a sudden disappearance, for climatic reasons, of the shoals of sardines exploited by this industry, is the most likely.[18] In the early twentieth century, Breton fishing ports and canning units were hit hard by similar events, which generated very serious economic and social disruption.[19]

(c) There is no trace, insofar as archaeology is concerned, of any population movement from Britain to Armorica in the Later Roman period, though, of course, one can never be sure that ethnic and political identity would necessarily be reflected in material culture. The British pottery found in western and northern Gaul was thus certainly not brought overseas by British immigrants but distributed by standard, though undoubtedly complex, trade networks. One can also wonder about the legal/administrative construct which would have downgraded peaceful Roman citizens — all free inhabitants of the Empire were Roman citizens since Caracalla's edict of 212 — into *laeti* or *deditices* and allowed them to be transported *en masse* to western/northern Gaul.

The British contingents, brought across the Channel by Magnus Maximus in 383 in his unsuccessful attempt to seize imperial power, and subsequently given land in Gaul (according to a famous passage in the *Historia Brittonum* by pseudo-Nennius)[20] are totally elusive, both in late third- or fourth-century settlements and in the nearby inhumation cemeteries, though it must be noted

---

[18] Sanquer and Galliou, '*Garum*, sel et salaisons en Armorique gallo-romaine'; Galliou, *L'Armorique romaine*, pp. 125–35; Galliou, 'The Defence', p. 399.

[19] Durand, 'La crise sardinière française', p. 29.

[20] 'Septimus imperator regnavit in Britannia Maximianus. Ipse perrexit cum omnibus militibus Brittonnum a Brittannia, et occidit Gratianum, regem Romanorum, et imperium tenuit totius Europae, et noluit dimittere milites, qui perrexerunt cum eo, ad Brittanniam, ad uxores suas et ad filios suos et ad possessiones suas, sed dedit illis multas regiones a stagno quod est super verticem Montis Iovis usque ad civitatem quae vocatur Cant Guic, et usque ad cumulum occidentalem, id est Cruc Ochidient. Hi sunt Brittones Armorici, et nunquam reversi sunt hac usque in hodiernum diem. Propter hoc Brittanniam occupata est ab extraneis gentibus et cives expulsi sunt, usque dum Deo auxilium dederit illis' (The seventh [Roman] emperor to reign in Britain was Maximianus. He went forth from Britain with all the troops of the British and killed Gratian, the king of the Romans, and held the empire of all Europe. He refused to send the soldiers who had gone forth with him back to Britain, to their wives and children and lands, but gave them many districts from the lake on top of Mount Jove to the city called Quentovic, as far as the Western Mass, that is, the Western Ridge. They are the Armorican British, and they never came back, even to the present day), *Historia Brittonum*, § 27, trans. pp. 24–25. On *Historia Brittonum*, see also the discussion in this volume by Ben Guy, 'Explaining the Origins of Brittany', pp. 241–42.

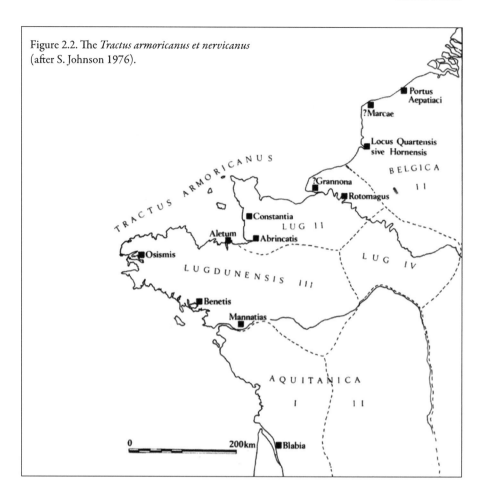

Figure 2.2. The *Tractus armoricanus et nervicanus* (after S. Johnson 1976).

that few of the latter have been excavated so far. Similarly, the forces garrisoning the forts of the *Tractus Armoricanus* (Fig. 2.2) in the late fourth and early fifth centuries — the *Martenses* at Alet, the *Mauri Osismiaci* at Brest and *Mauri Veneti* at Vannes — were certainly not drawn from Britain but from other provinces of the Empire, or may even have been, at least in part, recruited locally, as the *-aci* Gaulish ending of the *Mauri Osismiaci* tends to show.[21]

The forts themselves, built in the late third and early fourth centuries along the British North Sea coast and on both sides of the Channel (Alet (Fig. 2.3), Le Yaudet (Fig. 2.4), and Brest (Figs 2.5–2.6) for Brittany) have long been

[21] Galliou and Simon, *Le Castellum de Brest*, pp. 91–97.

2. THE 'LATE ROMAN MILITARY MIGRATION'

Figure 2.3. Late Roman wall at Alet (Centre régional archéologique d'Alet).

Figure 2.4. Late Roman gate at Le Yaudet (author).

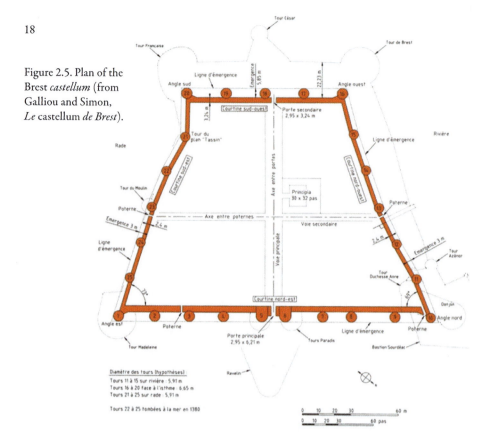

Figure 2.5. Plan of the Brest *castellum* (from Galliou and Simon, *Le* castellum *de Brest*).

Figure 2.6. Wall and Tower 2 (partly destroyed in the seventeenth century) of the Brest *castellum* (author).

seen as elements of a defensive chain meant to protect British and Gaulish shores from Saxon raids.[22] Most were located on the estuaries of short tidal rivers (Rance, Léguer, Elorn/Aulne) and would certainly have prevented enemy boats from sailing inland and crews from pillaging to their hearts' content. But this so-called 'defensive chain' was actually far from being comprehensive, as it left a number of other estuaries (the Jaudy and Trieux of Côtes-d'Armor, for instance) totally unprotected and as there is no trace of military contingents which would have been posted in between the forts to complete the so-called 'defensive chain'. Therefore, many historians now tend to think that such fortresses were not static defences but elements of a safety net, fortified ports, in which goods from the hinterland were concentrated and in which wine and oil from further south were brought before being shipped to the legions stationed in Britain and along the Lower Rhine. Besides, some of these forts (Alet, Le Yaudet, possibly Brest) were actually built on the very site of Late Iron Age defended settlements, which, before the Roman conquest, played a similar role in cross-Channel trading networks. They admittedly give credence to the reality of a Saxon/Frankish menace along the western seaways, which, however must have been kept at a fairly low level of intensity.

As no indisputable proof of population movement from Britain to Armorica in that early period can be put forward, how can one then account for the supposed 'barbarianization' of Armorican communities and the presence of 'military' artefacts in Late Roman civilian settlements? Though some villas, often close to *civitas* capitals, such as Kerran, near *Darioritum/Venetis* (Vannes), were undoubtedly extended and embellished in the fourth century,[23] most had their bath-houses and living quarters, often decorated with painted plaster and *opus sectile* floors, turned into rough-and-ready workshops, while masonry buildings were often abandoned in favour of wooden structures. Now, this phenomenon, which, in 1979, I believed was strictly Armorican and due to the settlement of hardly 'civilized' Britons, has since been shown to be common to the whole of northern Gaul and totally unrelated to an influx of barbarian immigrants.[24] What it expresses is a growing and generalized discontent with Roman ways and mores, a falling out of love with what Rome had brought in terms of com-

---

[22] For Alet, see Langouët, *Les Coriosolites, un peuple armoricain*, pp. 221–44; for Le Yaudet, Cunliffe and Galliou, *Le Yaudet en Ploulec'h*; for Brest, Galliou and Simon, *Le Castellum de Brest*.

[23] Galliou, *Les Vénètes d'Armorique*, pp. 419, 427–28.

[24] Galliou, 'The Defence', pp. 410–11; Van Ossel, *Établissements ruraux*.

Figure 2.7. Late Roman belt-fitting, Bosseno *villa* (Carnac, Morbihan) Cliché: M. Pérez-Bleuzen, Musée de Carnac.

fort and leisure, and a switch in the modes of display of the elite, away from the *otium* of a leisurely lifestyle and the architectural affirmation of wealth and power. This also shows in the gradual dereliction of urban centres and the abandonment and destruction of major temples (Corseul), aqueducts (Carhaix), *fora* and theatres (Vannes).[25] The inhabitants of villas and 'native' settlements, of *civitas* capitals and small towns, had clearly not fled and been replaced by foreign communities: most continued living in the same place — this was particularly true of rural settlements — till the end of the Roman period and sometimes even later, but in reduced circumstances and a very different environment.

If so, how can one explain the presence, in rural settlements, of Late Roman copper alloy brooches and belt buckles generally believed to be part of the uniform of high-ranking soldiers and administrators — how the expressions *cingulum ponere* and *cingulum deponere* came to mean to enter and to leave the civil service (Figs 2.7–2.8)?[26] Similar finds, in other parts of Gaul unexposed to Germanic incursions or the raids of Saxon/Frankish pirates, tend to show that such metalwork was worn, not only by soldiers or imperial administrators, but also by landowners, *curiales*, who had been entrusted with police and administrative functions by the senate of their *civitas* and proudly displayed their badges of social rank, or, in a later and probably more degraded context, where the established *civitas* framework had slowly disintegrated and power was fragmented, had forcibly seized such roles, defending their lands as best they could with the help of their — probably small — private armies and, preserving some degree of law and order in the fifth-century turmoil, held up what was left of *romanitas*.

---

[25] Provost, Mutarelli, and Maligorne, *Corseul*, pp. 219–25; Provost, Leprêtre, and Philippe, *L'aqueduc de* Vorgium, pp. 305–06; Galliou, *Les Vénètes d'Armorique*, pp. 412–13.

[26] Jones, *The Later Roman Empire*, p. 566.

2. THE 'LATE ROMAN MILITARY MIGRATION'

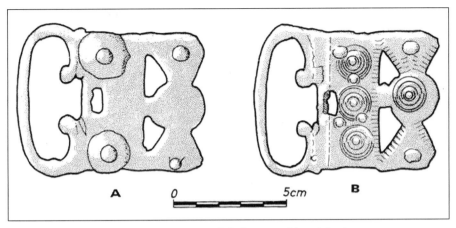

Figure 2.8. Late Roman belt-fitting, Etel (Morbihan)
(after Sanquer, 'Chronique d'archéologie antique', fig. 18, A & B).

No proof of such a state of things exists, in so far as Armorica is concerned, but, in the late fifth century, the Life of St Daniel the Stylite mentions 'a certain Titus, a man of vigour who dwelt in Gaul and had in his service a number of men well trained for battle', while Sidonius Apollinaris, in a letter to his brother-in-law Ecdicius, a wealthy landowner from Auvergne, congratulated him for having brought his 'following of barely eighteen mounted comrades ... through several thousands of Goths'.[27] In 468, emperors Leo I and Anthemius strictly forbade individuals to have armed slaves and *bucellarii* at their service, and landowners were similarly forbidden to keep armed retainers (*armata mancipia*), thereby implying that such arrangements were far from uncommon throughout the Empire.[28]

Though some foreign mercenaries may possibly have been recruited to beef up these private militias, one must conclude that no trace whatsoever of a massive late third- to fourth-century military migration from Britain to Armorica appears in the archaeological landscape and that the supposed movement is nothing but a historiographical myth, based on an inadequate evaluation of available data. What used to be called the 'second migration' of the late fifth and sixth centuries has also, as a matter of fact, left precious few indisputable archaeological vestiges. Among them, the so-called Quoit Brooch Style metalwork — mostly belt-fittings — is a matter of dispute as to its geographical ori-

---

[27] *Three Byzantine Saints*, p. 43; Sidonius Apollinaris, *Epistolae*, III, 3, trans. pp. 14–15.
[28] *The Codex of Justinian*, IX.12,10, trans. III, 2321–22.

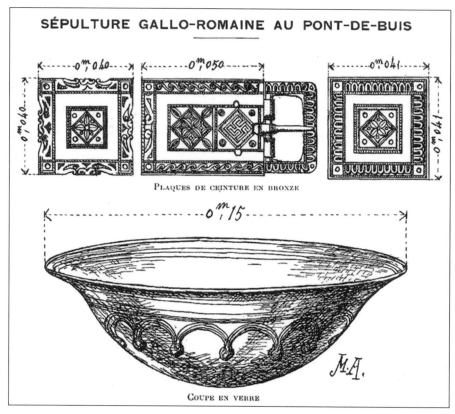

Figure 2.9. Quoit Brooch Style buckle and glass from the Pont-de-Buis (Finistère) grave (after Abgrall 1911).

gin. Decorated with animal heads in the Germanic style, it is generally believed to have been fashioned, in the second half of the fifth century, mostly in Kent and Sussex, for the Germanic mercenaries of Romano-British authorities.[29] A few such artefacts have been found in Brittany, in a lime-kiln reused as a tomb in Pont-de-Buis (Finistère) (Fig. 2.9), in a small inhumation cemetery in Saint-Marcel (Morbihan) and in larger inhumation cemeteries at Rennes (La Cochardière) and La Mézière (Ille-et-Vilaine), where they were reckoned to have belonged to British immigrants of the 'second wave'.[30] However, this attri-

---

[29] Suzuki, *The Quoit Brooch Style*. For further discussion of Quoit Brooch Style in this volume, see Hines, 'The Settlement of Brittany', pp. 43–47.

[30] Abgrall, 'Sépulture romaine découverte à Pont-de-Buis'; Le Boulanger and Simon, 'De la ferme antique', pp. 240–42; Labaune-Jean, 'Deux fibules'.

bution remains highly problematic, as, in the first two cases, they were associated with glass vessels of the late fifth to early sixth centuries and are therefore not quite contemporary with the corresponding inhumations, but had probably been kept as heirlooms in local families for at least one generation. Their association with British immigrants seems dubious at best if these elements were made in south-eastern England, which is obviously not the part of Britain immigrants to Armorica are supposed to come from. One cannot be sure, either, that they were actually made in Britain or were part of a wider cultural complex, similar objects being fashioned, in the fifth century, on both sides of the Channel, and some of the Saint-Marcel pieces, for instance, having, so far, no equivalent in England.[31] One can only hope that future archaeological investigations and re-examination of the available evidence will help solve what, to a large extent, remains a wide-open question.

Patrick Galliou, FSA [P.Galliou@wanadoo.fr] is Emeritus Professor, Université de Bretagne occidentale (Brest). He has published extensively on Late Iron Age and Roman Armorica.

[31] Ager, 'A Late Roman Buckle'.

Works Cited

Primary Sources

Ammianus Marcellinus, *Res Gestae*, I: *Books 14–19*, trans. by J. C. Rolfe, Loeb Classical Library, 300 (Cambridge, MA: Harvard University Press, 1935, repr. 1950)

Aurelius Victor, *Liber de Caesaribus* (*Livre des Césars/Aurelius Victor*), ed. and trans. by P. Dufraigne (Paris: Les Belles Lettres, 1975)

Eutropius, *Breviarum ab urbe condita* (*Abrégé d'histoire romaine/Eutrope*), ed. and trans. by J. Hellegouarc'h (Paris: Les Belles Lettres, 1999)

Historia Brittonum, in *Nennius: British History and the Welsh Annals*, trans. by J. Morris, History from the Sources (London: Phillimore & Co., 1980), pp. 9–43, 50–84

Hydatius, *Chronicon* (*Chronique/Hydace*), ed. and trans. by A. Tranoy, Sources chrétiennes, 218–19, 2 vols (Paris: Éditions du Cerf, 1974)

Justinian, *The Codex of Justinian: A New Annotated Translation with Parallel Latin and Greek Text, Based on a Translation by Justice Fred H. Blume*, ed. by B. W. Frier, 3 vols (Cambridge: Cambridge University Press, 2016)

Life of St Daniel the Stylite, in *Three Byzantine Saints: Contemporary Biographies of St Daniel the Stylite, St Theodore of Sykeon and St John the Almsgiver*, trans. by E. Dawes, introductions and notes by N. H. Baynes (Oxford: Blackwell, 1948)

Sidonius Apollinaris, *Carmina*, trans. by W. B. Anderson, in *Poems. Letters: Books 1–2*, Loeb Classical Library, 296 (Cambridge, MA: Harvard University Press, 1936), pp. 1–327

——, *Epistolae*, trans. by W. B. Anderson, in *Letters: Books 3–4*, Loeb Classical Library, 420 (Cambridge, MA: Harvard University Press, 1965)

Secondary Works

Abgrall, J.-M., 'Sépulture romaine découverte à Pont-de-Buis', *BSAF*, 38 (1911), 188–93

Ager, B., 'A Late Roman Buckle- or Belt-Plate in the British Museum said to be from Northern France', *MA*, 40 (1996), 203–11

Blazkiewicz, P., and C. Jigan, 'Le problème de la diffusion et de la datation de la céramique sigillée d'Argonne décorée à la molette des IVe–Ve siècles dans le Nord-Ouest de l'Empire', in *Société Française d'étude de la céramique antique en Gaule. actes du Congrès de Cognac. 8–11 mai 1991*, ed. by L. Rivet (Marseille: Société Française d'étude de la céramique antique en Gaule, 1991), pp. 385–415

Brett, C., 'Soldiers, Saints, and States? The Breton Migrations Revisited', *CMCS*, 61 (2011), 1–56

Chadwick, N., 'The Colonization of Brittany from Celtic Britain', *Proceedings of the British Academy*, 51 (1965), 235–99

Cunliffe, B., and P. Galliou, *Le Yaudet en Ploulec'h, Côtes-d'Armor. Archéologie d'une agglomération (IIe siècle av. J.-C. – XXe siècle apr. J.-C.)*, 3 vols (Rennes: Presses universitaires de Rennes, 2015)

De la Borderie, A., and B. Pocquet, *Histoire de Bretagne*, 6 vols (Rennes: Plihon et Hommay, 1896–1914), i [1905]

Durand, M.-H., 'La crise sardinière française: les premières recherches scientifiques autour d'une crise économique et sociale', in *Pêcheries ouest-africaines: variabilité, instabilité et changement*, ed. by P. Cury and C. Roy (Paris: Orstom, 1991), pp. 26–36

Estiot, S., 'Une campagne germanique de l'empereur Probus: l'atelier de *Ticinum* en 277–278', in *H. G. Pflaum, un historien du xxᵉ siècle*, ed. by S. Demougin and P. Cosme (Geneva: Droz, 2006), pp. 207–47

Fleuriot, L., *Les origines de la Bretagne* (Paris: Payot, 1980)

Galliou, P., *L'Armorique romaine* (Brasparts: Les Bibliophiles de Bretagne, 1983)

——, 'Un conservatoire archéologique méconnu: Lostmarc'h en Crozon', *Les Cahiers de l'Iroise*, 205 (2007), 27–38

——, 'The Defence of Armorica in the Later Roman Empire', in *Roman Frontier Studies 1979. Papers presented to the 12th International Congress of Roman Frontier Studies*, ed. by W. S. Hanson and L. J. F. Keppie, BAR International Series, 71 (Oxford: British Archaeological Reports, 1980), pp. 397–422

——, *Les Vénètes d'Armorique* (Spézet: Coop Breizh, 2017)

——, M. Fulford and M. Clément, 'La diffusion de la céramique "à l'éponge" dans le Nord-Ouest de l'Empire romain', *Gallia*, 38 (1980), 265–78

——, and J.-M. Simon, *Le* castellum *de Brest et la défense de la péninsule armoricaine au cours de l'antiquité tardive* (Rennes: Presses universitaires de Rennes, 2015)

Gazenbeek, M., and S. Van der Leeuw, 'L'Argonne dans l'antiquité: étude d'une région productrice de sigillée et de verre', *Gallia*, 60 (2003), 269–317

Giot, P.-R., and J.-L. Monnier, 'Le cimetière des anciens Bretons de Saint-Saturnin ou Saint-Urnel en Plomeur, Finistère', *Gallia*, 35 (1977), 141–71

Huvelin, H., 'Le trésor de Saint-Colombier en Sarzeau', *Trésors monétaires*, 2 (1980), 59–102

Johnson, S., *Later Roman Britain* (London: Routledge, 1980)

Jones, A. H. M., *The Later Roman Empire (284–602): A Social, Economic and Administrative Survey* (Oxford: Oxford University Press, 1964)

Kerneis, S., *Les Celtiques. Servitude et grandeur des auxiliaires bretons dans l'empire romain* (Clermont-Ferrand: Presses universitaires de la Faculté de droit, 1998)

Labaune-Jean, F., 'Deux fibules du *Quoit Brooch Style* datant du vᵉ s. en Ille-et-Vilaine (Bretagne)', *Cahiers LandArc*, 9 (2015), 1–8

Langouët, L., *Les Coriosolites, un peuple armoricain* (Saint-Malo: Centre régional archéologique d'Alet, 1988)

Le Boulanger, F., and L. Simon, 'De la ferme antique à la nécropole de l'antiquité tardive (milieu du iiᵉ s.– fin du vᵉ s. apr. J.-C.). Étude archéologique du site de Saint-Marcel (« le Bourg », Morbihan)', *Gallia*, 69 (2012), 167–307

Lot, F., *La Gaule. Les fondements ethniques, sociaux et politiques de la nation française* (Paris: Arthème Fayard, 1947)

Merdrignac, B., *D'une Bretagne à l'autre: les migrations bretonnes entre histoire et légendes* (Rennes: Presses universitaires de Rennes, 2012)

Pape, L., *La Civitas des Osismes à l'époque gallo-romaine* (Paris: Klincksieck, 1978)

Provost, A., B. Leprêtre, and É. Philippe, *L'aqueduc de Vorgium/Carhaix (Finistère). Contribution à l'étude des aqueducs romains*, Supplément *Gallia*, 61 (Paris: Éditions du CNRS, 2013)

Provost, A., V. Mutarelli, and Y. Maligorne, *Corseul: le monument romain du Haut-Bécherel, sanctuaire public des Coriosolites* (Rennes: Presses universitaires de Rennes, 2010)

Sanquer, R., 'Chronique d'archéologie antique et médiévale', *Bulletin de la Société archéologique du Finistère*, 105 (1977), 62–67

——, and P. Galliou, '*Garum*, sel et salaisons en Armorique gallo-romaine', *Gallia*, 30 (1972), 189–223

Suzuki, S., *The Quoit Brooch Style and Anglo-Saxon Settlement* (Woodbridge: Boydell, 2000)

Tuffreau-Libre, M., A. Mossmann-Bouquillon, and R. P. Symonds, 'La céramique dite *black-burnished* dans le Nord de la France', in *Société française d'étude de la céramique antique en Gaule. Actes du congrès de Rouen, 25–28 mai 1995*, ed. by L. Rivet (Rouen: Société française d'étude de la céramique antique, 1995), pp. 91–112

Van Ossel, P., *Établissements ruraux de l'antiquité tardive dans le Nord de la Gaule* (Paris: Éditions du CNRS, 1992)

3. THE SETTLEMENT OF BRITTANY IN LIGHT OF A MIGRATION PERIOD ARCHAEOLOGY

John Hines

ABSTRACT The proposition that a major Migration Period involving parts of Asia and much of Europe was correlated with the demise of the Roman Empire in the West and the start of the Early Middle Ages is a long-standing one. For more than half a century, there has been much emphasis on the importance of considering explanations for the cultural diffusions and changes of that time alternative to population movement and colonization. It is argued here that there is no need for a particularly sceptical approach to the traditional view, and that Britain, with *Armorica*-Brittany, provides distinctive and informative evidence in a European perspective. British identity in Britain was subject to radical reconstruction in and around the fifth and sixth centuries, and the introduction of a proto-Breton identity on the Continent is to be seen as a dimension of the same process. The archaeological evidence from Brittany to compare with the well-studied historical notices is slender, but especial attention is due to the presence of Quoit Brooch Style metalwork that represents a connection with the already anglicizing south-east of Britain rather than the south-west as otherwise usually inferred.

RÉSUMÉ Il existe une idée, longtemps établie, qu'une période migratoire importante, qui impliqua des régions de l'Asie et la plus grande partie de l'Europe, porta sur la fin de l'Empire romaine en l'Ouest et les commencements du Moyen Âge. À présent, et pendant plus qu'un demi-siècle, les historiens ont mis l'accent sur d'autres explications que les mouvements de populations et la colonisation pour les changements et diffusions culturels de cette époque. Ici, je propose qu'un scepticisme excessif envers le point de vue traditionnel n'est pas de mise, et que la Grande-Bretagne et la Bretagne armoricaine fournissent des preuves distinctifs et informateurs à l'échelle européenne. L'identité britonnique en Grande-Bretagne fut reconstruite en profondeur dans les ve et vi^e siècles, et l'introduction d'une identité bretonne sur le Continent doit être vue comme une dimension du même processus. Les preuves archéologiques provenant de la Bretagne continentale sont tenues, en comparaison avec les notices historiques bien étudiés, mais il faut porter l'attention sur les objets ornés de style 'Quoit Brooch', qui représentent des relations avec la région déjà anglicisante du sud-est de la Grande-Bretagne, plutôt que le sud-ouest comme on est habitué à supposer.

KEYWORDS Anglo-Saxon England, artefacts, Britons, Brittany, Early Middle Ages, ethnogenesis, Late Antiquity, material culture, migration, Quoit Brooch Style, theoretical archaeology

Multi-disciplinary Approaches to Medieval Brittany, 450–1200: Connections and Disconnections, ed. by Caroline Brett, Fiona Edmonds, and Paul Russell, TCNE 36 (Turnhout: Brepols, 2023) pp. 27–55   BREPOLS ⬚ PUBLISHERS   10.1484/M.TCNE-EB.5.132308

The Migration Period Controversy

The concept of a Migration Period (*Âge de grandes migrations*; *Völkerwande-rungszeit*) in Europe is historically deeply rooted. A phase of widespread and large-scale demographic convulsions and relocations of population appears not only to mark the transition from the end of the Roman-ruled and culturally dominated 'Ancient' world to the Early Middle Ages,[1] but has been claimed to explain it. Few areas were unaffected by these events. The populations indicated to have been on the move by contemporary or near-contemporary documentary records came predominantly from Turkic-speaking areas of the Eurasian steppe zone or from the Germanic language-family heartland of northern Europe. Iberia and Italy were reportedly invaded and settled by Langobards, Ostro- and Visigoths, Alans and/or Vandals — some of whom would move on into Roman North Africa. Pannonia and Dacia appear to have been major transit zones over and again, and were especially open to invasions from the east: successively from Huns, Avars, Bulgars, and eventually the Magyars.[2] In eastern Europe, Goths, Gepids, and Heruli appear to have moved in both directions along or within a north-west/south-east axis between the southern Baltic and Black Sea, although the conclusive final emigration was in the form of a Gothic federation that moved southwards in the fifth century. Franks and Burgundians, and Angles, Saxons and Jutes, are the principal further groups to whom the conquest and settlement of the provinces of Gaul and Britain are attributed.[3] Outline narratives can be gleaned from a number of documentary sources, both in the form of records from within the decaying and shrinking Roman Empire and the traditions of those claiming descent from the migrant peoples. Typically, these sources are cursory, and often indirect.

---

[1] Conventional English-language terminology will be used in this paper. While there is an essentially common framework of periodization for nearly all of Europe, the terminology differs hugely, so that direct lexical equivalents of 'medieval', 'early-medieval', or 'high-/late-medieval' can mean very different things in the historical and archaeological traditions of the various European languages. The problem of profound confusion extends to large-scale terms such as what 'Iron Age', 'Migration Period', and 'Merovingian Period' refer to within different, precisely defined, chronological systems.

[2] With the Golden Horde and the Ottoman Empire, the pattern recurs through to the Early Modern Period. See, for example, Halsall, *Barbarian Migrations*; Bierbrauer, 'Gepiden im 5. Jahrhundert'; Curta, *Southeastern Europe*; Rácz, 'Zwischen Hunnen- und Gepidenzeit'; Jackson, *The Mongols*.

[3] Discussed further, with appropriate bibliographical references, below esp. pp. 35–40.

3. THE SETTLEMENT OF BRITTANY

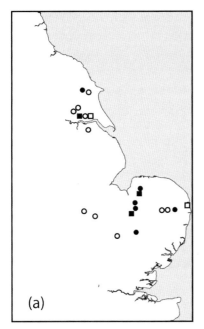

Figure 3.1. Two distribution maps representing different forms of archaeological evidence for population movement in the fifth century. (a) Artefactual distribution of early Class B wrist-clasps in eastern England, showing archetype forms introduced from Scandinavia and their immediate typological derivatives. (b) Finds of human skeletal remains with artificially elongated skulls of a 'Hunnic' type in Europe: after Hakenbeck, 'Infant Head Shaping in Europe'. Only adult skulls with this form of modification occur west of the C-shaped line on the map.

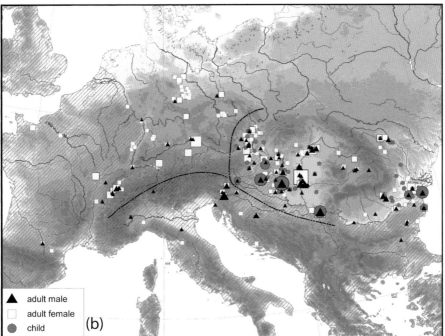

There are various forms of archaeological evidence which appear to support this general model, with its major components of crisis, repopulation, and politico-ethnic reconstruction that meant that the fall of the Roman Empire in the West was part of a process that led to the emergence of new population groupings which one may call 'nations', strongly associated with certain territories and often becoming organized as kingdoms, which in some cases are directly ancestral to the states of modern Europe. The diffusion of artefacts typical in primary stages of particular regions within Europe or central Asia over wider areas in chronologically subsequent stages, or even the expansion or relocation of whole cultural complexes of consistent material practice (in simple terms, a typical 'way of life'), has in many cases been argued either to corroborate migrations identified in historical sources, or in no small number of cases to provide additional examples of large-scale population movement otherwise unrecorded in the selective documentary evidence (Fig. 3.1, above).[4]

Although the long-established building blocks of artefact and stylistic typologies and distribution maps of material culture remain valid and important in archaeology, with regard to northern Europe in particular, in and around the supposed Migration Period greater attention has been concentrated recently on further fields of data and analysis in the form of palaeo-environmental and settlement-site studies. There prove to be extensive areas — especially along and in the hinterlands of the southern shores of the North Sea and the Baltic — where the evidence cumulatively reveals a major wave of de-intensification in agriculture and apparently therefore a level of depopulation that could amount to the total cessation of human occupation and the abandonment of large areas of land.[5] The use of the word 'wave' here is to be emphasized, because it is by no means clear that this was a single, synchronized event across the Continent and into southern Scandinavia — such as might, conceivably, be attributed to a devastating plague or an intense natural disaster. In Frisia, for instance, the principal settlement hiatus is assigned to the fourth century, with the apparent abandonment of much of the northern part of the Netherlands by what

---

[4] The available literature on suggested archaeological corroboration of historically documented migrations is so vast that to attempt to offer a bibliographical guide is unrealistic. For the inference of unrecorded migrations, relevant examples can be found in Hines, *The Scandinavian Character of Anglian England*, and Bursche, Hines, and Zapolska, eds, *The Migration Period between the Oder and Vistula*.

[5] Knol and IJssennagger, 'Palaeogeography and People'; Dreibrodt and Wiethold, 'Lake Belau and its Catchment'; Nösler and Wolters, 'Kontinuität und Wandel'; Gebühr, 'Angulus desertus'; Pędzisweska and others, 'Pollen Evidence'.

3. THE SETTLEMENT OF BRITTANY

is thought to have still been a Celtic-speaking population before the area was resettled by a population using both material culture and language very similar to other North Sea Germanic populations, and in particular those designated the early Anglo-Saxons. Further east in Lower Saxony, however, the settlement hiatus seems rather to fall in a period of about a hundred years from the later fifth to the later sixth century: that in itself would fit with this population having removed itself to Frisia and England, although it is a good question why it should have chosen to do so in the former case. A point of not only great interest but indeed of fundamental importance in relation to the apparently concurrent phenomena of depopulation and geographical cultural change is that practically nowhere in this period does depopulation in one area appear to be correlated with a growth in population somewhere else, such as implies that the population *numbers* were simply redistributed. The sixth, seventh, and even much of the eighth centuries continue to form a startling void for much of the southern trunk of the Jutland peninsula in Schleswig-Holstein. In Poland, new metal-detector finds of archaeological evidence point to the survival of Germanic ethnic groups (associated with specific 'Cultures') through to the sixth century and in some cases later, while Slavic cultural features do not appear until the seventh century. Perhaps the only part of Europe where the evidence would naturally be interpreted in terms of steady and marked population growth through this period is Ireland, where no migratory influx would be argued, although a new settlement and Gaelicization of areas of western Scotland may also be as a result of the redistribution of the Irish population.[6]

In recent years, biomolecular and biochemical evidence from human skeletal remains in the form of a[ncient]DNA and stable isotopes of oxygen and strontium ingested via groundwater and plants in the areas where people have lived has shed some convincing light on demographic mobility too,[7] although many would agree that these scientific techniques and the scope for interpreting the data are yet at an early stage of development. A parameter that has inexcusably been neglected in arguments over whether force of numbers or social and cultural power best explain the expansion of cultural practices to new areas is the question of absolute population levels. It is one thing for one region to be depopulated because of emigration to somewhere else; another

---

[6] Scott, 'Socioeconomic Change in Early Medieval Ireland' (and refs); Campbell, 'Were the Scots Irish?' (cf. n. 16, below); Charles-Edwards, *Wales and the Britons*, pp. 174–91.

[7] Amorim and others, *Understanding Sixth-century Barbarian Organization*; Schiffels and others, 'Iron Age and Anglo-Saxon Genomes'.

because of a general demographic crisis. Nearly all discussions trying to reconstruct what was going in these 'Dark Ages' of transformation in Europe have silently assumed an effective steady-state of overall population. If, however, population levels were falling both widely and severely in north-west Europe at this time, the dynamics are fundamentally different from those in stable conditions. In the simplest terms, the quantity of colonists required to outnumber and replace an indigenous population and that required to provide a dominant elite could converge to a point at which the distinction becomes meaningless. But considerably more significant is that, in a situation of competitive contact between populations, a marked decline in numbers — or alternatively, presumably, strong growth — would render the interactions both within and between those populations considerably more complicated than with a simple bilateral (or hierarchical) relationship. Circumstances of either progressive failure or uncontrolled success would themselves catalyse the loss or weakening of a sense of identity or promote it; thus the demographic facts must be vital to the theories that in isolation have been argued over inconclusively for decades. Estimating population figures in Britain before the High Middle Ages is a fraught and uncertain matter, but it remains doubtful that the population recorded in the Domesday Survey of 1086–1087 was any higher than that estimated for fourth-century Roman Britain,[8] and what one might call puddles of evidence — extrapolated burying population figures for Early Anglo-Saxon cemeteries, and the Tribal and Burghal Hidages[9] — point to lower levels in between. But, when and how far the population in Britain fell, and when and how steeply numbers rose again, are as yet imponderable.

Despite the sheer volume and diversity of evidence that the ethnic, cultural, and linguistic map of Europe changed profoundly during the two to three centuries from the late fourth to the early seventh century AD, however, the idea that a simple causative explanation could be found in mass migrations, conquests and recolonization targeted particularly upon poorly defended but attractive lands in the old Roman Empire has been the object of determined dissent for more than half-a-century now. The attack was led in the 1960s, in English-language scholarship. Grahame Clark, then Disney Professor of Archaeology in Cambridge, in what is recognized to be the founding text of this doctrine published in 1966, in fact explicitly recognized that 'even the last 2,000 years

[8] Millett, *The Romanization of Britain*, pp. 181–83; Hinton, 'Demography'.

[9] Malim and Hines, *Edix Hill*, pp. 325–27; Caruth and Hines, *RAF Lakenheath* (forthcoming), ch. 10.

3. THE SETTLEMENT OF BRITTANY

[in Britain] have witnessed three major phases of invasion and numerous small infiltrations': events which he did not trouble to identify, although he presumably meant the Roman and Norman conquests and the *adventus Saxonum*.[10] The positive contents of his paper, emphasizing empirical evidence of autochthonous factors in the prehistoric transitions in Britain from neolithicization to the early Iron Age, must be acknowledged. However, Clark's supercilious reference to the alleged naivety and intellectual laziness of 'British archaeologists of the era from Kipling to Winston Churchill' embodies the preconceptions of his own generation and circumstances every bit as much as the writings of his late Victorian or early twentieth-century predecessors do.

Here, one should focus on the historical contingency of Clark's paper, to account for its immense impact. Clark's position captured an iconoclastic *Zeitgeist* of the 1960s — backed up, in Cambridge, by the mathematical security and material positivism represented by his younger colleague David Clarke's *Analytical Archaeology* of 1968. With particular reference to the Early Middle Ages, doubts about the value of the sparse historical sources, which Edward Gibbon roundly dismissed as 'rubbish of the Dark Ages' in the eighteenth century,[11] had continued throughout the two centuries from Gibbon to this 'New Archaeology'. Archaeological scholars from the middle of the nineteenth century onwards were aware of the need to compare archaeological data critically with what should seem to be the relevant textual evidence and to be wary of making simplistic assumptions.[12] Before the First World War, E. T. Leeds was publishing detailed arguments on how precise archaeological study might rewrite the history of the Anglo-Saxon settlements, admittedly without simply dismissing what was reported in the Anglo-Saxon Chronicle wholesale.[13] Following him with specific reference to the origins of the Early Anglo-Saxon Period, and preceding Clark's paper, both J. N. L. Myres and Vera Evison had published revisionary and at the time influential research wherein the archaeo-

---

[10] Clark, 'The Invasion Hypothesis', p. 173. Did he just forget the Viking Age? It seems unlikely that in 1966 he would have supposed that could have been regarded as a 'small infiltration' without reference to Peter Sawyer's controversial thesis downplaying the Viking impact on England in *The Age of the Vikings* (1962).

[11] Gibbon, *Decline and Fall*, chs XXXVII and XXXIX.

[12] See Hines, 'The Archaeological Study of Early Anglo-Saxon Cemeteries', for a relatively sympathetic overview and references.

[13] Leeds, 'The Distribution of the Anglo-Saxon Saucer Brooch'; Leeds, *The Archaeology of the Anglo-Saxon Settlements*.

logy of the very early Anglo-Saxon Period and culture was treated as a basis for rewriting the history of the transition.[14]

Although from the later 1970s to the 1990s the anti-migrationist position was elevated to the status of a new orthodoxy, it eventually came under attack from two quite different sides. One was from scholars who were primarily theoreticians, who needed to keep introducing new theoretical perspectives and for whom the value of an innovation was measured in terms of how radical a change it represented. The other was empiricists who did not find that critical evaluation of the evidence — textual, archaeological, and often linguistic too — erased migration events from serious consideration at all. Followed by the unforeseen, rapid collapse of the Soviet bloc in eastern Europe in the years 1989–1991 and the unleashing of ferociously nationalist movements, these positions found constructive common ground in studies of the symbolic use of material culture, and of the construction, appropriation, and strategic deployment of ethnic identity, in both history and the archaeological record.[15]

The story of Archaeology for about the last quarter-century has in reality abundantly shown how profoundly the discipline is still led and shaped by practical external developments, and particularly by rapid advances in electronic micro-technology, allowing on the one hand ever more sophisticated metal-detectors to be used to generate quantities of archaeological finds hitherto unimagined, and on the other hand providing readily accessible and rapidly searchable databases of sorted evidence, as well as programmes and computing power for complex statistical analyses and exploration of digital 'big data' to be undertaken. The advances in bioscientific study of early-medieval demography outlined above represent this particularly well. The dependency of archaeology upon empirical evidence and inductive methods rather than theoretical predispositions can itself now be regarded as an empirically and historically proven fact. What that also means is that there is no greater justification now than there ever was for supposing that the conditions and course of events of the 'age of the great migrations' were essentially simple. Without ruling out considerable demographic movement on the one hand, or the extensive population mixing and presumed consequential re-definition of ethnic identities which tends to be labelled 'ethnogenesis' as a leading phenomenon of Early Medieval European history on the other, the past five decades' willingness to explore

[14] Evison, *Fifth-Century Invasions*; Myres, 'Romano-Saxon Pottery'; Myres, *Anglo-Saxon Pottery and the Settlement of England*.

[15] Jones, *Archaeology of Ethnicity*.

alternative explanations and complex patterns of cause and effect, stimulus and response, have indeed placed us in a much stronger position to discuss the Migration Period as a phenomenon in a mature and meaningful manner than was available even a generation ago.

Britannia and Armorica, England and Brittany, from the Fourth to Sixth Centuries AD

The Migration Period thus has been a complex and a hotly debated topic for far more than a generation in European archaeology. This is of course crucial to any assessment of the evidence for a British settlement of Armorica to create Brittany in the fifth and sixth centuries. The corollary is also true, and equally important: the evidence from Brittany, which is by no means negligible, is highly pertinent to the continuing themes of analysis and debate, both theoretical and empirical, concerning the Migration Period *per se*. This area on the north-west point of the Continent and the topic of its cultural transformation in the Late Antique Period/very Early Middle Ages has much to contribute to a conceptualization of the Migration Period as a European phenomenon and thus on a continental scale. The two areas of western Europe that had been within the Roman Empire where, through the fifth and earlier sixth centuries, a change of identity and language took place so thorough that it has survived to the present day, are England and Brittany.[16]

As many, no doubt, would assume to be an *a priori* truth, and as indeed will be corroborated empirically below, the British colonization and appropriation of the Armorican peninsula cannot be discussed separately from the events in Britain that led to the emergence of Anglo-Saxon England. These cases concern the former Roman provinces of Gallia and Britannia, and especially what is now northern France and southern England. A key question — again one that has been discussed for a very long time — is how far one should suppose or infer that the situations and course of events on either side of the Channel were significantly similar, or whether, conversely, there was a fundamental cleft between the Continental landmass and Britain as the Western Roman Empire fell. A valid characterization of fourth-century, Later Empire, Armorica and

[16] Beyond the Empire, the extent to which the Gaelicization of western Scotland was due to new settlement in the fourth to sixth centuries has been questioned (Campbell, 'Were the Scots Irish?'); in the case of the northern Netherlands, a settlement hiatus in the fourth–fifth centuries AD apparently saw the demise of a Celtic-speaking population and its replacement, eventually, by a West Germanic-speaking one.

Britannia could well conclude, summarily, that the island to the north was in practical terms dominant then: for instance on the evidence of the imports of Dorset, New Forest and Oxfordshire pottery in Brittany, and not least the evidence of a striking fall-off in Imperial coinage in Armorica after the extinguishing of the Gallic Empire of the late third century AD.[17] In that light, it is justifiable to regard the events of the early fifth century, with the near total de-Romanization of the area that would become England, in terms of 'the higher they stand, the further they fall': the disintegration of a greater, but weakly rooted, Imperial superstructure in Britain was all the more ruinous when it finally came about. In terms of the northern island leading the way, note also Zosimus' claim that it was the inhabitants of Britannia who first took their military defence against barbarian incursions into their own hands, and that they were swiftly followed by the Armoricans.[18]

Panegyrics from the time of Constantius Chlorus and Constantine, and the text of *Notitia Dignitatum* about a century later, indicate that northern Gaul — as well as *Germania Secunda* and *Inferior* — saw the presence of groups of Germanic *laeti*, known probably both as *Franci* and *Saxones*, in the fourth century.[19] Cemetery evidence of the burial of women in distinctly Germanic forms of costume, and of men with both weaponry and typically provincial-Roman official military and administrative costume fittings, points to the concomitant shifts in material practice and a change in the overall cultural complexion of this region that might be expected as a consequence of their settlement there,[20] even if — as has been emphasized *ad tedium* — attaching a specific ethnic label to any one individual on the basis of what they were buried with, or indeed because they were buried in a grave containing artefacts at all, is inappropriate and simply unhelpful. It remains unclear how far the subsequent ceding of considerable areas of south-western and eastern Gaul respectively to populations of Visigothic and Burgundian *foederati* in the first half of the fifth century represents the Western Empire surviving through ever greater pragmatic concessions in terms of transfer of land, or is no more than a difference in termino-

---

[17] Galliou and Simon, *Le castellum de Brest*, pp. 128–29 and 162–63; Galliou, *La Bretagne romaine*, esp. pp. 113–16; cf. Reece, *Coinage of Roman Britain*.

[18] Zosimus, *New History*, trans. VII, 5; Zosimus was not a contemporary historian, and the information was probably derived by him from Olympiodorus.

[19] James, *The Franks*, pp. 38–52; Springer, *Die Sachsen*, pp. 32–46.

[20] Böhme, *Germanische Grabfunde*; Böhme, 'Migrants' Fortunes'.

logy between the fourth and fifth centuries.[21] Those are, strictly, questions for the historian — to say which is by no means to sideline them, for this is a time and place in relation to which the archaeologist simply *is* also a historian, and no historian can ignore the archaeological evidence. What is particularly striking in an archaeologically informed perspective, however, is the unmistakable fact that a barbarization of elite material culture (I use the term 'barbarization' in a precisely Roman sense), involving both Germanic and Hunnic elements albeit combined with Roman ones, is especially clear across northern Gaul and *Germania Secunda* by the late fifth century in contrast to the evidence from Aquitaine and Burgundy.[22]

As Vera Evison showed in *The Fifth-Century Invasions South of the Thames* of 1965, these material developments on the adjacent Continent left their mark in southern Britain too, in the form of metal artefacts ranging from armaments to dress-accessories, and both ceramic and glass vessels.[23] Even without her 'Francophile' inference of Frankish invasion and a Frankish rather than a Saxon or a Jutish settlement of southern Britain in this obscure period, it is important to ask, even if rhetorically, whether one should *in any way* expand the reification of that material into evidence of the presence of folk called 'Franks' in Britain in the fifth century. The fact that 'Frankish' is a valid, pragmatic label for specific features of material culture, and that it represents a meaningful term in fifth-century ethnic discourse itself, should actually discourage us from making unnecessary assumptions about how the people who were directly associated with these objects in southern Britain would have referred to themselves, or were categorized by others. It is a valid position to be satisfied with quantifiable data on the substance, range, and character of evidence for cross-Channel contact and exchange. Without ignoring the truism that objects which cross an area of sea between landmasses must have been carried by someone for some reason, speculation on an unrecorded level and form of migration and settlement associated with those data may be valid in some perspectives but an unnecessary distraction in others.

Nominally 'Frankish' material forms characteristic of a zone of the northwestern Continent from Normandy to the Rhineland are not the only finds

---

[21] Kaiser, *Die Burgunder*, pp. 26–74; Heather, 'The Creation of the Visigoths'; Kaiser, *The Fall of the Roman Empire*, esp. pp. 415–25, and cf. p. 490 for the author's comments on the concepts of *foedus* and *foederati*.

[22] James, *The Merovingian Archaeology of South-West Gaul*.

[23] See now especially Soulat, *Le mobilier funéraire*.

that represent similarities either side of the Channel.[24] In light of the histori-cal divergences between the two areas from this time (with the only partial exception of Brittany), one may, however, be justified in suggesting that overall, the differences are more significant than the similarities. By the middle of the fifth century, and in most cases long before then, the demise of the culture that characterized Late Roman Britain was practically total. Most towns, from west to east and north to south, show complete abandonment.[25] The story is the same at villa sites: at Shakenoak in Oxfordshire, for instance, highlighted in the 1970s as ostensibly a leading example of adaptation and continuity into the Anglo-Saxon Period, it is now possible to focus in greater detail on the spo-radic and variable evidence of activity from the fourth century to the eighth. There is a visible sequence of activity in the fifth century, but characterized by the profound decay of the principal structure, Building A, a build-up of dark earth with very worn coins from up to and around the year 400 and cut-up fit-tings from a couple of Late-Roman military-style belt-sets, followed by twenty-two inhumation graves of the mid- to late fifth century.[26] Pottery and one local brooch from a ditch-fill attest to the new style of settlement in the near vicinity, but the sequence is one of change and dislocation not evolution.

New work is also bringing the origin of the sites and material culture recog-nized as Anglo-Saxon in Britain into better focus, but without the fifth century yet falling open to us in a well-lit and comprehensive picture, and with huge lacunae remaining. Fuller publication of the evidence from the extensive gravel-ridge site at Mucking in Essex enables us to *describe* a near-continuous sequence of material, including a Roman pottery series apparently extending into the early fifth century; typically early to mid-fifth-century belt fittings; and the presence of distinctly Anglo-Saxon metalwork and pottery from the mid-fifth century to the seventh.[27] What remains a matter of uncertainty or contention is whether or not we have completely lost the primary structural contexts of the latest Roman material, so that what is observed of it is only that which came

---

[24] See, e.g., Soulat, *Le mobilier funéraire*, pp. 369–88; Deckers, 'Cultural Convergence in a Maritime Context', esp. pp. 174–76.

[25] Esmonde Cleary, 'The Ending(s) of Roman Britain', esp. pp. 17–19; Henig, 'The Fate of Late Roman Towns'.

[26] Brodribb and others, *Shakenoak*. The six radiocarbon-dated skeletons are all from the courtyard area between Buildings A and C, not within Building A. The fifth-century dating is suggested by a single-phase Bayesian model constructed by the present author using OxCal 4.4.2. Blair and others, 'Shakenoak revisited', forthcoming.

[27] Lucy and Evans, *Romano-British Settlement and Cemeteries*.

3. THE SETTLEMENT OF BRITTANY

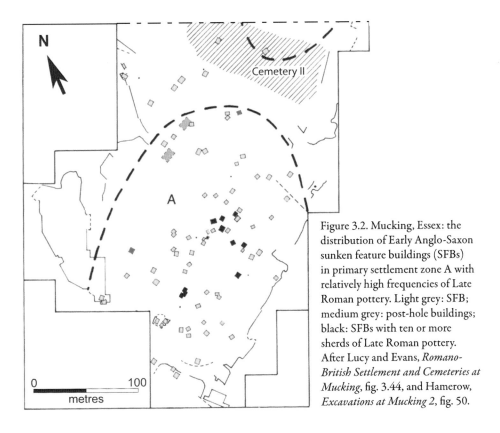

Figure 3.2. Mucking, Essex: the distribution of Early Anglo-Saxon sunken feature buildings (SFBs) in primary settlement zone A with relatively high frequencies of Late Roman pottery. Light grey: SFB; medium grey: post-hole buildings; black: SFBs with ten or more sherds of Late Roman pottery. After Lucy and Evans, *Romano-British Settlement and Cemeteries at Mucking*, fig. 3.44, and Hamerow, *Excavations at Mucking 2*, fig. 50.

to be residually re-deposited alongside, but not homogeneously mixed with, other early Anglo-Saxon material in the earliest Anglo-Saxon layers — located in *Grubenhäuser* at the southern end of the site (Fig. 3.2).

A clear sense of the nature of the evidence for the introduction of a new 'Anglo-Saxon' cultural order to southern and eastern Britain is vital to any case for continuity and overlap or for radical discontinuity between the population and culture of Late Roman Britain and the Anglo-Saxon Period. This is equally true if one argues that continuity is prominent in some contexts while disjunction is the dominant theme in others. While Mucking, and indeed other sites in Essex such as the small town of Heybridge and the villa at Rivenhall, provide evidence of an Early Anglo-Saxon presence contiguous with the latest phases that may be described as Late or sub-Roman,[28] a strong feature of the cultural and historical shift around the fifth century in Britain is the abandonment of

---

[28] Drury and Wickenden, 'Heybridge'; Rodwell and Rodwell, *Rivenhall*.

old sites and the appearance of quite new locations at which the dead were buried or people lived. The chronological analysis of the large cremation cemetery at Spong Hill in Norfolk shows that this site was used intensely for burial in a distinctly Germanic and indeed largely Anglian style in the middle quarters of the fifth century, presumably as the common burial ground of a population settled at different places across a district or region.[29] From the late fifth to mid-sixth century, inhumation was practised here alongside cremation, but at a much lower frequency, implying a smaller burying population. In Lincolnshire, Caitlin Green has argued attractively that such major early cremation cemeteries form a ring around the Roman city of Lincoln, conceivably reflecting regional settlement of *laeti* or *foederati* settlement, but the distribution pattern in East Anglia is different.[30]

Also in different forms in different areas, one can identify transitional and hybrid phenomena between the Late Roman and the Early Anglo-Saxon cultures even within the context of this apparent dislocation. A strong example is the adoption into the Anglo-Saxon suite of costume accessories of slip-knot wire bracelets: a common Romano-British form for adult female costume but unknown in the Continental Germanic zones (Fig. 3.3). Interestingly these were functionally repurposed as children's wear from the evidence of Anglo-Saxon cemeteries — such as Great Chesterford in north-western Essex;[31] admittedly an unusual site, adjacent to a Roman small town, for the amount of Roman material appearing in the Anglo-Saxon grave-assemblages, and for the number of children's graves identified, but still in most respects thoroughly typical of the period, and of a coherent region comprising southern Cambridgeshire as well.

Even more critical for a realistic reconstruction and understanding of the British settlement of Armorica, although fundamentally inter-related with the gradual introduction and flourishing of an Anglo-Saxon culture and identity in eastern and southern Britain, are the key features of development in the western areas that remained under the control of and whose language and cultural character were determined by the Britons. The evidence for this zone is notoriously elusive. The one substantial documentary source available, Gildas'

---

[29] Hills and Lucy, *Spong Hill*.

[30] Green, *Britons and Anglo-Saxons*.

[31] Evison, *Great Chesterford*, p. 18; Caruth and Hines (forthcoming), *RAF Lakenheath*, ch. 5.5. In respect of the derivation of the type, it was misleading of Evison to describe the slip-knot anklet from Great Chesterford grave 34 as a 'typical Anglo-Saxon' item.

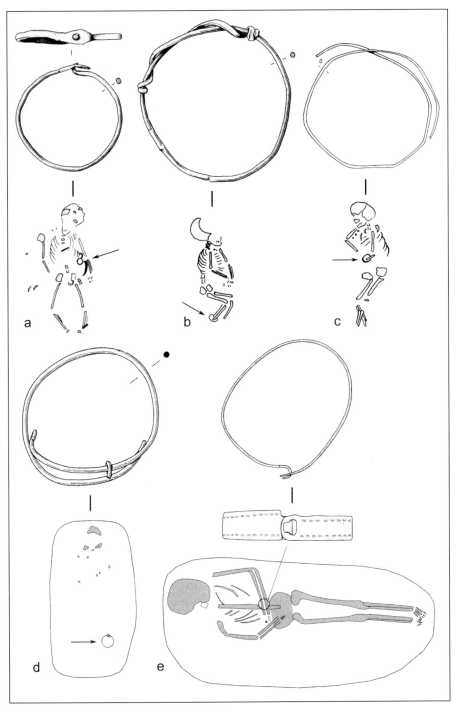

Figure 3.3. Examples of bracelets and anklets of forms derived from Romano-British models in Early Anglo-Saxon children's graves (up to the age of approximately twelve years old). (a)–(c) Great Chesterford, Essex, graves 31, 34, and 154; (d)–(e) RAF Lakenheath, Eriswell, graves 023, 156 and 334. (a)–(c) after Evison, *Great Chesterford*; (d)–(e) after Caruth and Hines, *RAF Lakenheath*.

De excidio Britanniae, is uncertain in date, although in the current author's view, the absence of any clear reference to the extreme climatic dust-veil event of AD 536 must mean this was composed no later than the start of that year, while the balance of the relationship between the Britons and the 'Saxons' that Gildas attributes to his whole life time of forty-three years seems to fit best if the source is assigned a date as close to AD 536 as possible.[32] The representation of the recent history and current state of Britannia in the text is massively shaped by Christian learning and polemical presumptions. Yet the source is manifestly direct evidence of the survival of a Latin/Roman culture in Britain in more than just a linguistic sense: it provides information on the political structure of post-Roman Britain; and it also provides an understanding of recent demographic and military events in Britain which cannot be sheer fiction, however inaccurate it is.

Archaeologically our view of immediately post-Roman Britain is skewed because of the limited amount of durable and identifiable material attributed to this period and cultural group. But it is significant that there were continued contacts with the Mediterranean world, via the Atlantic seaways, represented by imported pottery: both red-slipped high-quality tablewares and amphorae that would have contained other commodities such as oil, wine, or dyes.[33] Demonstrably, western 'British' Britain had maintained overseas connections and exchange of a range that contrasts absolutely with the cross-channel and North Sea links of the Anglo-Saxon East, noted above.[34] The largest collections of this imported pottery are at what appear to have been elite sites such as Tintagel and the Cadbury hillforts of Somerset, as well as at trading sites such as Bantham in Torbay, Devon. What are classified as 'single finds' of Byzantine coins around the coasts of western Britain increasingly suggest a rather more diffuse distribution of items imported from the eastern Mediterranean.[35] In a straightforward manner, the emergence of a more local or regional, militarized elite making use of defensive strongholds fits completely with Gildas' evidence

[32] Woods, 'Gildas and the Mystery Cloud', argues that Gildas' use of the imagery of an extremely dense cloud and references to the darkness of night was inspired by the situation in these years, but the similes are too general for this to be really persuasive. See also Dumville, 'Gildas and Maelgwn', for a generally sceptical view of the possibility of dating.

[33] Alcock, *Arthur's Britain*; Campbell, *Continental and Mediterranean Imports*; Duggan, 'Ceramic Imports'.

[34] Dark, ed., *External Contacts*; Wickham, *Framing the Early Middle Ages*, pp. 700–20 and 794–824.

[35] Moorhead, 'Early Byzantine Copper Coins'.

3. THE SETTLEMENT OF BRITTANY

for the development of a class of kings that he saw as 'tyrannical' and immoral. Christianity took root in a remarkable way across the west and north of Britain and in Ireland in this context, and this is widely represented in material form by inscribed stones — with a mixture of Latin and Irish epigraphy — that also reflect the interwoven character of secular and ecclesiastical power within society.[36] Humbler and numerically more representative rural communities remain difficult to detect. Poundbury by Dorchester in Dorset can serve as a fair example. Materially, the nature of the settlement, with its buildings and material culture (pottery) is not strikingly different from what one would classify as contemporary Anglo-Saxon sites of this nature. The burial practices of this population, however, continuing to use a Roman extra-mural burial place, and also to inter the dead without artefacts although with hobnailed footwear, do represent a distinct tradition.[37]

One of the most prominent products of the survival and adaptation of Late Roman traditions in Britain, certainly in relation to the archaeological evidence for the settlement of Brittany at that time, is the metalwork of the 'Quoit Brooch Style'. This metalwork had been discussed as metalwork of 'Gallo-Roman' style before Egil Bakka dubbed it the Quoit Brooch Style in 1958, around the same time as Sonia Chadwick Hawkes was proposing to identify it as 'Jutish Style A'.[38] Bakka's name for the style has become conventional, but in fact the linkage of the style (such as it is) to a few fine ring-shaped brooches misses the point that it must have been developed primarily on belt-fittings, deriving directly from Late Roman military and civil administrative, quasi-uniform costume fittings. Within the whole range of these dress-accessories found in the former provinces of Britannia, there are some types which would appear more probably to have been manufactured on the Continent, some types which are distinctly British in distribution, and even some types that have been

[36] Edwards, *The Archaeology of Early Medieval Ireland*, pp. 99–104; Charles-Edwards, *Wales and the Britons*, pp. 116–73.

[37] Sparey Green, *Excavations at Poundbury*; Farwell and Molleson, *Poundbury*, II. It is useful in this context also to note the strong conclusions of the *Fields of Britannia* project (Rippon, Smart, and Pears, *Fields of Britannia*) about a high level of survival of the physical infrastructure of the Late-Roman agrarian landscape into the Anglo-Saxon period.

[38] Leeds, *Early Anglo-Saxon Art and Archaeology*, pp. 3–19; Bakka, *On the Beginning of Salin's Style I*; Chadwick Hawkes, 'Jutish Style A' (see 'Postscript', p. 73, for an explanation of why her paper does not address Bakka's study and terminology directly); Suzuki, *The Quoit Brooch Style*.

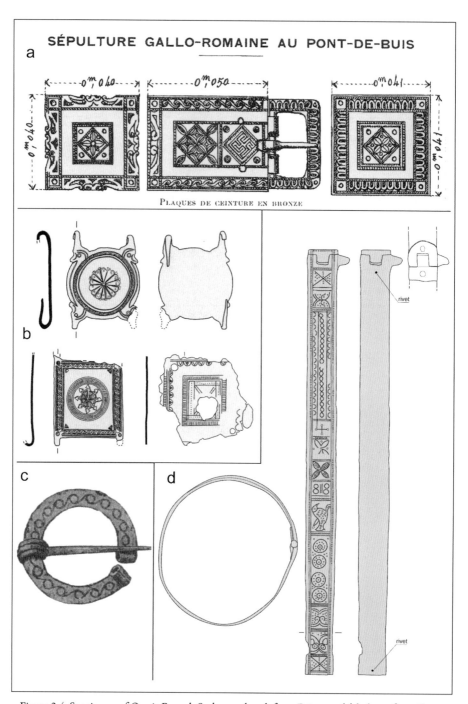

Figure 3.4. Specimens of Quoit Brooch Style metalwork from Brittany: (a) belt-set from Goas-an-Eyec, Pont-de-Buis-lès-Quimerch, Finistère; (b) belt-fittings from Saint-Marcel, Morbihan, grave A; (c) penannular brooch from Carnac, Morbihan; (d) strip bracelet from Saint-Marcel, Morbihan, grave 106. Scale approximately 2:3. (a) After Abrgall, 'Sépulture Gallo-Romaine à Pont-de-Buis', following p. 192; (b) and (d) drawn by S. Jean, reproduced with permission; (c) drawing published by Miln, *Fouilles faites à Carnac*.

3. THE SETTLEMENT OF BRITTANY

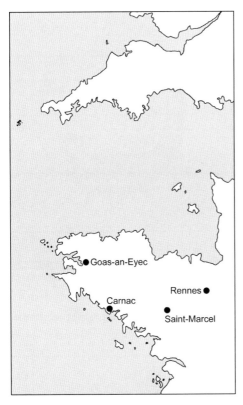

Figure 3.5. The locations of Quoit Brooch Style finds in Brittany. Map by author.

found exclusively in Anglo-Saxon burial contexts.[39] Within Britain, metalwork representing the Quoit Brooch Style belongs to the latter category. The Quoit Brooch Style is represented in Brittany in the form of related belt fittings in a belt-set from Goas-an-Eyec, Pont-de-Buis-lès-Quimerch, and mounts from three graves in a cemetery at Saint-Marcel (Figs 3.4–3.5).[40]

In Britain, the distribution of the material collectively referred to as Quoit Brooch Style very clearly points to a centre of gravity in the south-east; typologically, indeed, the earliest specimens cluster around London in the form of buckles from Mitcham, Croydon and Orpington (Fig. 3.6, overleaf). The extension of the style to ring-shaped brooches, which may be of the broken-ring 'penannular' form, or 'quoit'/'pseudo-penannular' brooches with terminal stops and a notch within the ring, is a secondary development. It remains unresolved whether this development was due to the expansion of the range of the decorative style to a Germanic annular brooch-type in south-eastern England, or its combination with a penannular form that had historical roots in Roman Britain.[41] Whichever the case, it is clearly a matter of particularly close relationship between south-eastern England and Brittany that there are two specimens of Quoit Brooch Style

---

[39] Chadwick Hawkes and Dunning, 'Soldiers and Settlers'.

[40] Galliou and Simon, *Le castellum de Brest*, pp. 152–63; Saint-Marcel graves A, 67 and 145: Le Boulanger and Simon, 'La nécropole de Saint-Marcel', esp. figs 72 and 74–76, and pp. 240–42 (a note on the objects decorated in the Quoit Brooch Style by Barry Ager).

[41] Ager, 'The Smaller Variants of the Anglo-Saxon Quoit Brooch'; Suzuki, *The Quoit Brooch Style*, esp. pp. 85–93.

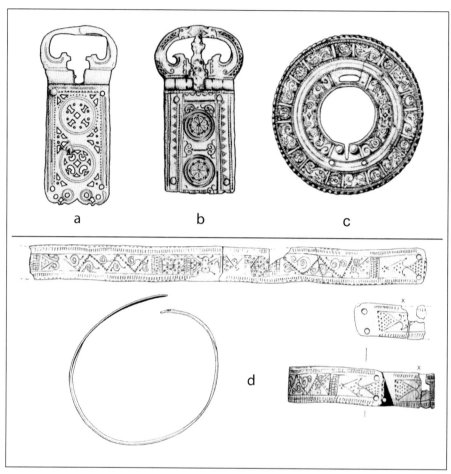

Figure 3.6. The development of the Quoit Brooch Style in England: (a)–(b) early buckles from (a) Mitcham and (b) Orpington, Greater London; (c) quoit brooch from Howletts, Kent; (d) strip bracelet from Mucking, Essex, grave 631. Scale approximately 2:3.
(a)–(c) Drawn by Peter Inker (Inker, 'Technology as Active Material Culture');
(d) from Hirst and Clark, *Excavations at Mucking 3*, reproduced with permission.

penannular brooch from the latter area: from a villa site at Carnac, and a recent find from Rennes.[42] Although this is altogether a relatively small corpus of metalwork, what is referred to as one 'style' is in fact diverse in both form and decorative repertoire. One may readily concur, therefore, with Patrick Galliou and Jean-Michel Simon, that not only could one see it as the product of development

---

[42] Galliou and Simon, *Le castellum de Brest*, pp. 157–59, fig. 148; INRAP, 'À Rennes'.

3. THE SETTLEMENT OF BRITTANY

from multiple sources, but that it is possible that northern Gaul independently contributed to that in some measure.[43] Nonetheless, the buckles really are critical, especially if one also notes Ellen Swift's valuable work on this material from an object-biography perspective, indicating that amongst the more widely dispersed representatives of Quoit Brooch Style metalwork are several pieces that show considerable re-use and adaptation.[44] One piece in Saint-Michel grave A appears to be a further instance. Quoit Brooch Style metalwork is also represented at Saint-Marcel by strip-metal bracelets in two graves (graves 106 and 129), closely paralleled at Mucking, Essex, grave 631.[45]

Typology and distribution maps are still of fundamental value in archaeological study, and the Quoit Brooch Style belt fittings are a shining example. They associate fifth-century Armorica, the embryonic Brittany, with southern Britain: but, contrary to what the linguistic closeness of Breton and Cornish have led many to postulate, this particular link is with south-eastern Britain, and with contexts that were already embryonically Anglo-Saxon, not with a resolutely independent south-west.[46] Indeed, contrasts between Brittany and fifth- to seventh-century south-west Britain remain substantial. There are demonstrable parallels in the tradition of inscribed stone monuments.[47] However the imported Mediterranean and later Atlantic Coast ceramics that were high-status consumables in western Britain and Ireland are extremely rare in Brittany. Finds have been recorded at a couple of sites on the northern coast of Brittany where quantitatively they appear to represent redistribution from Britain.[48]

---

[43] Galliou and Simon, *Le* castellum *de Brest*, pp. 162–63. To underline the heterogeneity of the material identified as 'Quoit Brooch Style', it can be noted that in British archaeological terms, the fixed plate buckle from the Étel dunes and the belt mount from the villa site at Carnac which Galliou and Simon (figs 145 and 149) attribute to this style would usually be considered 'sub- or late-Roman' rather than put in this category, while they do not label the penannular brooch from Carnac thus. For further discussion of Quoit Brooch Style in this volume, see Galliou, 'The "Late Roman Military Migration"', pp. 9–26 above.

[44] Swift, 'Re-evaluating the Quoit Brooch Style'.

[45] Le Boulanger and Simon, 'La nécropole de Saint-Marcel', pp. 271–75 and 284–86; Hirst and Clark, *Excavations at Mucking 3*, p. 102 (fig. 55) and pp. 495–96. Also comparable as strip-metal bracelets are an example from East Shefford, Berkshire, grave 5 (British Museum accession no. 1891,0323,14; no published image) and a newly found fragment from Borden, Swale, Kent, on the Portable Antiquities Scheme database: KENT-06B559.

[46] Cf. Guy, 'The Breton Migration'.

[47] Davies and others, *The Inscriptions of Early Medieval Brittany*.

[48] Campbell, *Mediterranean and Continental Imports*, pp. 125–39, esp. fig. 83.

Brittany appears never to have seen any systematic reoccupation of hillforts as high-status citadels. Le Yaudet might appear an exception, but really that is a case of change of use of a Roman fortification not the recommissioning of an Iron-age *oppidum*.[49] There is also intriguing evidence of activity of this date from a small hill fort at Plésidy, Côtes-d'Armor, including the finds of gold solidi of Julius Nepos (473–475) and Zeno (474–491), but that evidence derives, unfortunately, from poorly recorded excavations of the 1860s.[50] Coins of those emperors are extremely rare in Britain, and effectively unknown in the non-Anglo-Saxon west of the island.[51] Equally distinctive in terms of the Breton economy, then, is the evidence from the tin-production site at Abbaretz-Nozay just north of Nantes, where two Merovingian gold coins and a probably broadly contemporary small bronze ten-nummi coin of Maurice Tiberius struck in Carthage have been found.[52]

In the University of Wales O'Donnell Lecture series of 1997, I stressed how strongly the British identity in early post-Roman Britain was a construct, and was something actively created under the stimulus of the pressure and the practices of the incoming Germanic culture.[53] Post-Roman Britishness drew on its own heritage in the form of models, certainly, but it was far more than just a tradition in the form of some ineradicable heritage that found itself able to flourish again in conditions of independence from the Roman Empire. Armorica, infrastructurally a far more Romanized region than the south-west peninsula of Britain, either *bought in* or was *brought in* — probably both — to this production of a British identity. This is the really key concept to emphasize for the nature of British influence on Brittany. That influence certainly involved contacts, population movement, and a form of resettlement one can call colonization, but the language-change, and the adoption of a new identity, are not merely accidental clues to those as the core historical processes. Rather, becoming *Breton* served a purpose, as it supported regional autonomy for Brittany, both within the decaying Empire in the West and from the powerful Merovingian kingdoms. Thus without dismissing the evidence gleaned from Sidonius Apollinaris, Gildas, Gregory of Tours, and later saints' lives, of migra-

---

[49] Cunliffe and Galliou, 'Britons and Bretons'.

[50] Monteil, 'Les agglomérations', pp. 27–28.

[51] Bland and Loriot, *Roman and Early Byzantine Gold Coins*, esp. pp. 86–88, tab. 33. The only recorded coin of Zeno (Cat. 772) is of dubious credibility as a British find.

[52] Champaud, 'Abbaretz-Nozay', pp. 64–72.

[53] Hines, 'Welsh and English'.

tion from Britain to Brittany, this is an exemplary case-study of how population movement — whether as a numerical tsunami or as an irresistible elite — can be incorporated as a factor into our reconstruction and explanation of changes within the controversial Migration Period but cannot stand or indeed fall as the sole explanatory cause. In that way, actually, the history and archaeology of early Brittany, which have been much overlooked in the pan-European view, are truly important in the context of a Migration Period archaeology of Europe as a whole. If one approaches the question of the concrete evidence for the British settlement of Armorica in terms of a simple of checklist of what phenomena one could expect to represent the 'original' Britons, one finds relatively little that is either unambiguous or truly links the areas. If, however, one considers what such phenomena as we can observe amount to altogether, as evidence of cultural process in the different contexts they come into contact with, then a far more dynamic representation of relationships between Britain and Brittany can be seen.

Acknowledgements

Thanks are due to many colleagues for advice, information and encouragement in the preparation of this paper, but especially to Dr Susanne Hakenbeck (Cambridge) for supplying the distribution map of Hunnic elongated skulls in Fig. 3.1b, and to Mme. Françoise Le Boulanger of INRAP (Cesson-Sévigné) for both kindly and promptly supplying a pdf copy of her publication of the Saint-Marcel, Morbihan, cemetery site, and to M. Stephane Jean, INRAP, for copies of his illustrations with permission to reproduce them.

John Hines is Professor emeritus of Cardiff University. He is a former President of the Viking Society for Northern Research, and is currently Vice-President of the Society of Antiquaries of London. From 1997–2006 he was editor of *Medieval Archaeology*, and is General Editor of the monograph series Anglo-Saxon Studies for Boydell & Brewer. His research interests lie in the integrated study of material, linguistic and textual history of northern Europe, centring upon the Early Middle Ages.

Works Cited

Primary Sources

Procopius, *History of the Wars*, in *Procopius: History of the Wars, Secret History, and Buildings*, trans. by A. Cameron (New York: Washington Square Press, 1967)

Zosimus, *New History*, trans. by R. T. Ridley (Leiden: Brill, 1982)

Secondary Works

Ager, B., 'The Smaller Variants of the Anglo-Saxon Quoit Brooch', *Anglo-Saxon Studies in Archaeology and History*, 4 (1985), 1–58

Abrgall, J.-M., 'Sépulture Gallo-Romaine à Pont-de-Buis', *BSAF*, 38 (1911), 188–92

Alcock, L., *Arthur's Britain: History and Archaeology A.D. 367–634* (Harmondsworth: Penguin, 1971)

Amorim, C. E. G., S. Vai, C. Posth, A. Modi, I. Koncz, S. Hakenbeck, M. C. La Rocca, B. Mende, D. Bobo, W. Pohl, L. Pejrani Baricco, E. Bedini, P. Francalacci, C. Giostra, T. Vida, D. Winger, U. von Freeden, S. Ghirotto, M. Lari, G. Barbujani, J. Krause, D. Caramelli, P. J. Geary, and K. R. Veeramah, 'Understanding 6th-century Barbarian Social Organization and Migration through Paleogenomics', *Nature Communications*, 9 (2018), Article 3547

Bakka, E., *On the Beginning of Salin's Style I in England*, Universitetet i Bergen Årbok: Historisk-antikvarisk rekke, 3 (Bergen: Grieg, 1959)

Bierbrauer, V., 'Gepiden im 5. Jahrhundert – Eine Spurensuche', in *Miscellanea Romano-Barbarica*, ed. by V. Michăilescu-Bîrliba, C. Hriban, and L. Munteanu (Bucharest: Academiei Române, 2006), pp. 167–216

Blair, J., J. Hines, K. Tait, and R. Madgwick, 'Shakenoak Revisited: Post-Roman Occupation and Burial at a Cotswold-Edge Villa in the Light of New Evidence and Approaches', forthcoming

Bland, R., and X. Loriot, *Roman and Early Byzantine Gold Coins found in Britain and Ireland*, Royal Numismatic Society Special Publication, 46 (London: Royal Numismatic Society, 2010)

Böhme, H. W., *Germanische Grabfunde des 4. und 5. Jahrhunderts zwischen unterer Elbe und Loire*, Münchner Beiträge zur Vor- und Frühgeschichte, 19 (Munich: Beck, 1974)

——, 'Migrants' Fortunes: The Integration of Germanic Peoples in Late Antique Gaul', in *Foreigners in Early Medieval Europe: Thirteen International Studies on Early Medieval Mobility*, ed. by D. Quast (Mainz: Verlag des Römisch-Germanischen Zentralmuseums, 2009), pp. 131–47

Brodribb, A. C. C., A. R. Hands, and D. R. Walker, *Excavations at Shakenoak Farm, near Wilcote Farm, Oxfordshire*, 5 parts (Oxford: British Archaeological Reports, 1968–1978)

Bursche, A., J. Hines, and A. Zapolska, eds, *The Migration Period between the Oder and the Vistula*, 2 vols (Leiden: Brill, 2020)

3. THE SETTLEMENT OF BRITTANY

Campbell, E., *Continental and Mediterranean Imports to Atlantic Britain and Ireland, AD 400–800*, CBA Research Report, 157 (York: Council for British Archaeology, 2007)

——, 'Were the Scots Irish?', *Antiquity*, 75 (2001), 285–92

Caruth, J., and J. Hines, *The Anglo-Saxon Burial Grounds at RAF Lakenheath (Eriswell), Suffolk*, East Anglian Archaeology, 179, 2 vols (forthcoming)

Chadwick Hawkes, S., 'The Jutish Style A: A Study of Germanic Animal Art in Southern England in the Fifth Century A.D.', *Archaeologia*, 98 (1961), 29–74

——, and G. C. Dunning, 'Soldiers and Settlers in Britain, Fourth to Fifth Century', *MA*, 5 (1961), 1–70

Champaud, C., 'L'exploitation ancienne de cassitérite d'Abbaretz-Nomay (Loire-Inférieure): contribution aux problèmes de l'étain antique', *Annales de Bretagne*, 64 (1957), 46–96

Charles-Edwards, T., *Wales and the Britons 350–1064* (Oxford: Oxford University Press, 2013)

Clark, G., 'The Invasion Hypothesis in British Archaeology', *Antiquity*, 60 (1966), 172–89

Crawford, B. E., and B. Ballin-Smith, *The Biggings, Papa Stour, Shetland: The History and Excavation of a Royal Norwegian Farm*, Society of Antiquaries of Scotland Monograph Series, 15 (Edinburgh: Society of Antiquaries of Scotland, 1999)

Cunliffe, B., and P. Galliou, 'Britons and Bretons: Some New Evidence from Le Yaudet', *The Archaeological Journal*, 157, 200–28

Curta, F., *Southeastern Europe in the Middle Ages 500–1250* (Cambridge: Cambridge University Press, 2006)

Dark, K. R., ed., *External Contacts and the Economy of Late Roman and Post-Roman Britain* (Woodbridge: Boydell, 1996)

Davies, W., J. Graham-Campbell, M. Handley, P. J. E. Kershaw, J. T. Koch, G. Le Duc, and K. Lockyear, *The Inscriptions of Early Medieval Brittany* (Oakville, CN: Celtic Studies Publications, 2000)

Deckers, P., 'Cultural Convergence in a Maritime Context: Language and Material Culture as Parallel Phenomena in the Early-Medieval Southern North Sea Region', in *Frisians and their North Sea Neighbours from the Fifth Century to the Viking Age*, ed. by J. Hines and N. IJssennagger (Woodbridge: Boydell, 2017), pp. 173–92

Dooley, A., 'The Plague and its Consequences in Ireland', in *Plague and the End of Antiquity: The Pandemic of 541–750*, ed. by L. K. Little (Cambridge: Cambridge University Press, 2002), pp. 215–28

Dreibrodt, S., and J. Wiethold, 'Lake Belau and its Catchment (Northern Germany): A Key Archive of Environmental History in Northern Central Europe since the Onset of Agriculture', *The Holocene*, 25 (2015), 296–322

Drury, P. J., N. P. Wickenden, D. B. Harden, R. M. Luff, A. Mainman, and R. Reece, 'An Early Anglo-Saxon Settlement within the Romano-British Small Town of Heybridge, Essex', *MA*, 26 (1982), 1–40

Duggan, M., 'Ceramic Imports to Britain and the Atlantic Seaboard in the Fifth Century and Beyond', *Internet Archaeology*, 41 (2016) <https://doi.org/10.11141/ia.41.3/> [accessed 15 February 2019]

Dumville, D. N., 'Gildas and Maelgwn: Problems of Dating', in *Gildas: New Approaches*, ed. by M. Lapidge, and D. N. Dumville, Studies in Celtic History, 5 (Woodbridge: Boydell, 1984), pp. 51–59

Eagles, B., *From Roman Civitas to Anglo-Saxon Shire: Topographical Studies on the Formation of Wessex* (Oxford: Oxbow, 2018)

Edwards, N., *The Archaeology of Early Medieval Ireland* (London: Batsford, 1990)

Esmonde Cleary, S., 'The Ending(s) of Roman Britain', in *The Oxford Handbook of Anglo-Saxon Archaeology*, ed. by H. Hamerow, D. A. Hinton, and S. Crawford (Oxford: Oxford University Press, 2011), pp. 13–29

Evison, V. I., *An Anglo-Saxon Cemetery at Great Chesterford, Essex*, CBA Research Report, 91 (York: Council for British Archaeology, 1994)

——, *The Fifth-century Invasions South of the Thames* (London: Athlone Press, 1965)

Farwell, D. E., and T. I. Molleson, *Poundbury*, II: *The Cemeteries*, Dorset National History and Archaeological Society Monograph Series, 11 (Dorchester: Dorset National History and Archaeological Society, 1993)

Galliou, P., *La Bretagne romaine: de l'Armorique à la Bretagne* (Paris: Jean-Paul Gisserot, 1991)

——, and J.-M. Simon, *Le* castellum *de Brest et la défense da la péninsule armoricaine au cours de l'antiquité tardive* (Rennes: Presses universitaires de Rennes, 2015)

Gebühr, M., 'Angulus desertus?', *Studien zur Sachsenforschung*, 11 (1998), 43–85

Gibbon, E., *The Decline and Fall of the Roman Empire*, 6 vols (London: Strahan and Cadell, 1776–1789)

Green, C., *Britons and Anglo-Saxons: Lincolnshire AD 400–650*, Studies in the History of Lincolnshire, 3, 2nd edn (Lincoln: The History of Lincolnshire Committee, 2020)

Guy, B., 'The Breton Migration: A New Synthesis', *Zeitschrift für celtische Philologie*, 61 (2014), 101–56

Hakenbeck, S., 'Infant Head Shaping in Eurasia in the First Millennium AD', in *Oxford Handbook for the Archaeology of Childhood*, ed. by S. Crawford, D. M. Hadley, and G. Shepherd (Oxford: Oxford University Press, 2018), pp. 483–504

Halsall, G., *Barbarian Migrations and the Roman West, 367–568* (Cambridge: Cambridge University Press, 2007)

Hamerow, H., *Excavations at Mucking*, II: *The Anglo-Saxon Settlement* (London: English Heritage, 1993)

Heather, P., 'The Creation of the Visigoths', in *The Visigoths from the Migration Period to the Seventh Century*, ed. by P. Heather (Woodbridge: Boydell, 1999), pp. 41–92

——, *The Fall of the Roman Empire* (London: Macmillan, 2005)

Henig, M., 'The Fate of Late Roman Towns', in *The Oxford Handbook of Anglo-Saxon Archaeology*, ed. by H. Hamerow, D. A. Hinton, and S. Crawford (Oxford: Oxford University Press, 2011), pp. 515–33

3. THE SETTLEMENT OF BRITTANY

Hills, C. M., and S. Lucy, *Spong Hill, Part IX: Chronology and Synthesis* (Cambridge: McDonald Institute for Archaeological Research, 2013)

Hines, J., 'The Archaeological Study of Early Anglo-Saxon Cemeteries', in *Anglo-Saxon Graves and Grave Goods of the 6th and 7th Centuries AD: A Chronological Framework*, ed. by J. Hines and A. Bayliss, Society for Medieval Archaeology Monograph, 33 (Leeds: Society for Medieval Archaeology, 2013), pp. 13–32

——, *The Scandinavian Character of Anglian England in the Pre-Viking Period*, BAR British Series, 124 (Oxford: British Archaeological Reports, 1984)

——, 'Welsh and English: Mutual Origins in Post-Roman Britain', *SC*, 34 (2000), 81–104

Hinton, D. A., 'Demography: From Domesday and Beyond', *Journal of Medieval History*, 39 (2013), 146–78

Hirst, S., and D. Clark, *Excavations at Mucking*, III: *The Anglo-Saxon Cemeteries*, 2 vols (London: MOLA, 2009)

Inker, P., 'Technology as Active Material Culture: The Quoit Brooch Style', *MA*, 44 (2000), 22–52

INRAP, 'À Rennes, le quartier gallo-romain de l'Hôtel-Dieu mis au jour' <https://www.inrap.fr/rennes-le-quartier-gallo-romain-de-l-hotel-dieu-mis-au-jour-11693> [accessed 18 February 2019]

Jackson, P., *The Mongols and the West, 1221–1410* (Harlow: Pearson, 2005)

James, E., *The Franks* (Oxford: Blackwell, 1988)

——, *The Merovingian Archaeology of South-West Gaul*, BAR International Series, 25, 2 parts (Oxford: British Archaeological Reports, 1977)

Jones, S., *The Archaeology of Ethnicity: Constructing Identities in the Past and Present* (London: Routledge, 1997)

Kaiser, R., *Die Burgunder*, Kohlhammer Urban-Taschenbücher, 586 (Stuttgart: W. Kohlhammer, 2004)

Keller, M., M. A. Spyrou, C. L. Scheib, G. U. Neumann, A. Kröpelin, B. Haas-Gebhard, B. Päffgen, J. Haberstroh, A. R. i Lacomba, C. Raynaud, C. Cessford, R. Durand, P. Stadler, K. Nägele, J. S. Bates, B. Trautmann, S. A. Inskip, J. Peters, J. E. Robb, T. Kivisild, D. Castex, M. McCormick, K. I. Bos, M. Harbeck, A. Herbig, and J. Krause, 'Ancient *Yersinia pestis* Genomes from across Western Europe Reveal Early Diversification during the First Pandemic (541–750)', *bioRxiv* <https://doi.org/10.1101/481226> [accessed 18 February 2019]

Knol, E., and N. IJssennagger, 'Palaeogeography and People: Historical Frisians in an Archaeological Light', in *Frisians and their North Sea Neighbours from the Fifth Century to the Viking Age*, ed. by J. Hines and N. IJssennagger (Woodbridge: Boydell, 2017), pp. 5–24

Le Boulanger, F., and L. Simon, 'De la ferme antique à la nécropole de l'Antiquité tardive (milieu du II. s.–fin du Vᵉ s. apr. J.-C.): Étude archéologique du site de Saint-Marcel « le Bourg» (Morbihan)', *Gallia*, 69 (2012), 167–307

Leeds, E. T., *The Archaeology of the Anglo-Saxon Settlements* (Oxford: Clarendon Press, 1913)

——, 'The Distribution of the Anglo-Saxon Saucer Brooch in Relation to the Battle of Bedford, AD 571', *Archaeologia*, 63 (1912), 159–202

——, *Early Anglo-Saxon Art and Archaeology* (Oxford: Clarendon Press, 1936)

Lucy, S., and C. Evans, *Romano-British Settlement and Cemeteries at Mucking: Excavations by Margaret and Tom Jones, 1965–1978* (Oxford: Oxbow, 2016)

Maddicott, J., 'Plague in Seventh-Century England', in *Plague and the End of Antiquity: The Pandemic of 541–750*, ed. by L. K. Little (Cambridge: Cambridge University Press, 2002), pp. 171–214

Malim, T., and J. Hines, *The Anglo-Saxon Cemetery at Edix Hill (Barrington A), Cambridgeshire*, CBA Research Report, 112 (York: Council for British Archaeology, 1998)

Malim, T., K. Penn, B. Robinson, G. Wait, and K. Welsh, 'New Evidence on the Cambridgeshire Dykes and Worsted Street Roman Road', *Proceedings of the Cambridge Antiquarian Society*, 85 (1997), 27–122

Millett, M., *The Romanization of Britain: An Essay in Archaeological Interpretation* (Cambridge: Cambridge University Press, 1990)

Miln, J., *Fouilles faites à Carnac (Morbihan)* (Paris: Didier, 1877)

Monteil, M., 'Les agglomérations de la province de Lyonnaise Troisième (Bretagne et Pays-de-Loire)', *Gallia*, 74 (2017), 15–37

Moorhead, S., 'Early Byzantine Copper Coins Found in Britain – A Review of New Finds Recorded with the Portable Antiquities Scheme', in *Ancient History, Numismatics and Epigraphy in the Mediterranean World*, ed. by O. Tekin (Istanbul: Ege Publications, 2009), pp. 263–74

Myres, J. N. L., *Anglo-Saxon Pottery and the Settlement of England* (Oxford: Clarendon Press, 1969)

——, 'Romano-Saxon Pottery', in *Dark-Age Britain*, ed. by D. B. Harden (London: Methuen, 1956), pp. 16–39

Nösler, D., and S. Wolters, 'Kontinuität und Wandel – Zur Frage der spätvölkerwanderungszeitlichen Siedlungslücke im Elbe-Weser-Dreieck', in *Dunkle Jahrhunderte in Mitteleuropa?*, ed. by O. Heinrich-Tamaska, N. Krohn, and S. Ristow (Hamburg: Verlag Dr Kovač, 2009), pp. 367–88

Pędziswewska, A., M. Latałowa, J. Święta-Musznicka, M. Zimny, M. Kupryjanowicz, A. Noryśkiewicz, and K. Bloom, 'Pollen Evidence of Change in Environment and Settlement during the 1st Millennium AD', in *The Migration Period between the Oder and Vistula*, ed. by A. Bursche, J. Hines, and A. Zapolska, 2 vols (Leiden: Brill, 2020), I, pp. 137–98

Portable Antiquities Scheme database, <www.finds.org.uk>

Rácz, Z., 'Zwischen Hunnen- und Gepidenzeit: Frauengräber aus dem 5. Jahrhundert im Karpatenbecken', *Acta Archaeologica Academiae Scientiarum Hungaricae*, 67 (2016), 301–60

Reece, R., *The Coinage of Roman Britain* (Stroud: Tempus, 2002)

Rippon, S., C. Smart, and B. Pears, *The Fields of Britannia: Continuity and Change in the Late Roman and Early Medieval Landscape* (Oxford: Oxford University Press, 2015)

Rodwell, W., and K. A. Rodwell, *Rivenhall: Investigations of a Villa, Church, and Village, 1950–1977*, Chelmsford Archaeological Trust, 4 (London: Chelmsford Archaeological Trust, 1985)

Schiffels, S., W. Haak, P. Paajanen, B. Llamas, E. Popescu, L. Loe, R. Clarke, A. Lyons, R. Mortimer, D. Sayer, C. Tyler-Smith, A. Cooper, and R. Durbin, 'Iron Age and Anglo-Saxon Genomes from East England Reveal British Migration History', *Nature Communications* 7 (2016), Article 10,408 <https://doi.org/10.1038/ncomms10408> [accessed 28 October 2022]

Scott, R. E., 'Socioeconomic Change in Early Medieval Ireland: Agricultural Innovation, Population Growth, and Human Health', in *European Archaeology as Anthropology*, ed. by P. J. Crabtree and P. Bogucki (Philadelphia: University of Pennsylvania Museum of Archaeology and Anthropology, 2017), pp. 161–93

Soulat, J., *Le mobilier funéraire de type franc et mérovingien dans le Kent et sa périphérie*, Europe Médiévale, 13 (Drémil-Lafage: Éditions Mergoil, 2018)

Sparey Green, C., *Excavations at Poundbury*, II: *The Settlements*, Dorset National History and Archaeological Society Monograph Series, 7 (Dorchester: Dorset National History and Archaeological Society, 1987)

Springer, M., *Die Sachsen*, Kohlhammer Urban-Taschenbücher, 598 (Stuttgart: Kohlhammer, 2004)

Suzuki, S., *The Quoit Brooch Style and Anglo-Saxon Settlement* (Woodbridge: Boydell, 2000)

Swift, E. D., 'Re-evaluating the Quoit Brooch Style: Economic and Cultural Transformations in the 5th Century AD, with an Updated Catalogue of Known Quoit Brooch Style Artefacts', *MA*, 63 (2019), 1–55

Wickham, C., *Framing the Early Middle Ages: Europe and the Mediterranean, 400–800* (Oxford: Oxford University Press, 2005)

Woods, D., 'Gildas and the Mystery Cloud of 536–7', *Journal of Theological Studies*, 61 (2010), 226–34

4. The Archaeology of Early Medieval Rural Societies in Brittany — Settlements, Landscapes, Legacies, and New Influences: Interdisciplinary Research

Isabelle Catteddu and Joseph Le Gall

ABSTRACT Over the past thirty years developer-led archaeology, has provided an enormous amount of new data, unprecedented in the history of our discipline. Numerous large-scale excavations have made it possible to observe a great variety of early medieval sites. In Brittany, they highlight regional but also microregional specificities, between eastern, western, and central parts of the region.

Multi-disciplinary research multiplied the available evidence for close and obvious links between the Breton peninsula and the British Isles, Ireland, and the Frankish world. Moreover, architecture, artefacts, and agropastoral practices show the wide range of outside influences and clues of acculturation. What is mainly demonstrated by recent excavations is the porosity between multicultural societies and multi-faceted Atlantic connections. New scenarios invite us to rethink the early Middle Ages.

RÉSUMÉ Au cours des trente dernières années, l'archéologie préventive a été à l'origine d'un nombre de découvertes sans précédent dans l'histoire de notre discipline. Les sites altomédiévaux mis au jour renouvellent en profondeur notre connaissance des sociétés de cette période. En Bretagne, les occupations rurales témoignent d'une grande diversité régionale mais également de spécificités microrégionales.

La recherche transdisciplinaire multiplie également les témoins de liens étroits entre la Bretagne continentale et insulaire, ainsi qu'avec l'Irlande, le monde anglo-saxon en général mais aussi le monde germanique franc. L'architecture, le mobilier, les pratiques agropastorales, montrent à la fois la multiplicité des influences extérieures et des témoins d'acculturation. Mais ce que nous montre plus largement les découvertes récentes, c'est une importante porosité entre des sociétés multiculturelles. De nouveaux scénarios nous invitent à repenser la période du premier Moyen Âge et à déconstruire d'anciens paradigmes.

KEYWORDS *avena strigosa*, Bressilien, ceramics, elite sites, grain processing, Châteaugiron, Gouesnac'h, Guipavas, Kergoutois, Langoëlan, Montours, Plouedern, preventive archaeology, rural settlement, Saint-Martin-des-Champs, sunken-featured buildings

Multi-disciplinary Approaches to Medieval Brittany, 450–1200: Connections and Disconnections, ed. by Caroline Brett, Fiona Edmonds, and Paul Russell, TCNE 36 (Turnhout: Brepols, 2023) pp. 57–80   BREPOLS PUBLISHERS   10.1484/M.TCNE-EB.5.132309

Over the past thirty years, 'preventive archaeology' (developer-led archaeology) has provided an enormous amount of new data, unprecedented in the history of our discipline. The early Middle Ages is probably the period which has benefitted most from this increased rate of discovery. These excavations, combined with the results of several major field surveys, enable a much more detailed picture of early medieval settlements to be drawn than was possible thirty years ago. Moreover, it is a picture of far greater complexity and diversity than could have been imagined (Fig. 4.1).

Because of the broad extent of some projects, preventive archaeology allows large open area excavation, which often highlights not one, but several diachronic settlements, allowing us to study a territory over the *longue durée* and to open new fields of research: not only the built-up settlement itself — the living areas — but also the surrounding landscapes.

These new scales of time and space also highlight mobility and change in the forms of settlements and landscapes. They refine our understanding of how rural space was exploited by human communities, thus making us sensitive to the rhythms of occupation, better able to recognize ruptures here, continuities there, transformations elsewhere. It opens new clues about legacies and new influences. That means new methodologies but also a multiplication of angles of vision to study the data and then conduct cross-disciplinary research.[1]

Furthermore, numerous large-scale excavations have made it possible to observe a great variety of early medieval sites. Whereas some settlements consist of just a few scattered farmsteads, others include areas with specialized activities, enclosures, and trackways, sometimes a larger farm or a manor and even cemeteries and a church. This can be observed from as early as the seventh and eighth centuries.

The diversity of settlement forms appears not only in functional (for instance pottery workshops or metalworking sites), chronological (evolution between the sixth and twelfth centuries), or social (elite sites), but also in regional terms.[2] Thus, within Brittany, regional and microregional specificities may be seen in rural settlements, funerary sites, and in material culture (artefacts).

---

[1] Catteddu, 'Move On! There is Nothing to See Here'; Catteddu, 'Archéologie des sociétés rurales', pp. 57–78.

[2] Catteddu, *Archéologie médiévale en France*, p. 177; Catteddu, 'Insediamenti rurali', pp. 13–36.

4. THE ARCHAEOLOGY OF EARLY MEDIEVAL RURAL SOCIETIES IN BRITTANY

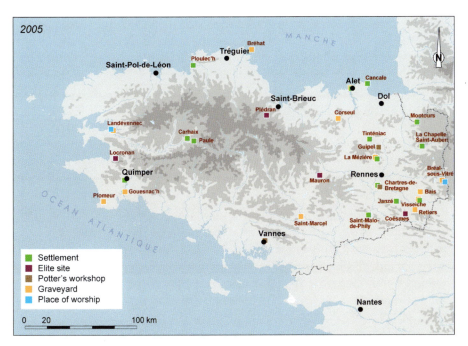

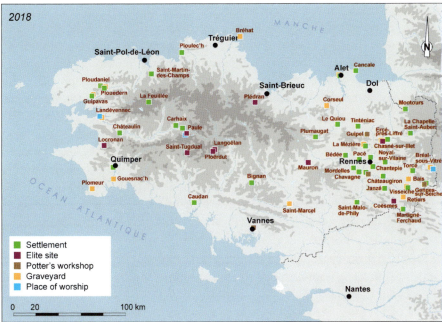

Figure 4.1. Map of the early medieval sites excavated in Brittany. Development of archaeological research in 2005 and in 2018 (from Ah-Thon and others, eds, *Formes, natures et implantations des occupations rurales*, I (2019), figure 1).

Rural Settlements in Eastern Armorica

Recent excavations conducted in Ille-et-Vilaine in Eastern Brittany show microregional specificities in early medieval settlement forms. The great majority yield farm units, isolated or grouped, are organized into regular parcels of land, divided by ditches, with paths providing access. Living areas and agropastoral activities were located within the enclosed parcels, much as they would be in a hamlet made up of a few farms (Fig. 4.2). Radiocarbon dating and the relative chronology of ditches and artefacts show that these areas and living environments underwent dynamic changes during this period, and occasionally changes in function.

Farms that at first stood alone in one or several parcels of land subsequently grew and multiplied, with their access lanes merging with the dividing lines of the network. Several farms could exist simultaneously or even come together, share the land, and form a hamlet. It was a self-organizing process of gradual land appropriation, rather than one generated by a predefined network. Each land parcel would wedge itself into an area left by the adjacent land parcels, on the simple basis of what already existed. Restructuring of this kind took into account the roads, the inherited Gaulish and Gallo-Roman landscape, as well as topography and physical features.[3]

The archaeological sites of Montours excavated in Ille-et-Vilaine in 1996 and the more recently excavated site of Châteaugiron offer very good examples of this process. At Châteaugiron, the excavation over an area of twenty-four hectares yielded settlements that dated from the third millennium BC to the present day. The earliest land organization was that of two Late Iron Age farms situated within a network of land parcels and roads bounded by ditches. The farm to the south was also occupied and transformed during the Gallic and Roman eras and abandoned during the third century. During the sixth century, the area was re-occupied by two important early medieval settlements (sites A and B), which lasted into the tenth century. On site A (Fig. 4.3), where over ten hectares (twenty-five acres) were excavated, ditches mark out thirty enclosed land-parcels with regular sizes. Several pathways facilitated circulation between the residential plots and those devoted to growing crops, to grazing animals or to specialized activities such as cooking, food storage, or grain-threshing and blacksmithing. Chronological study suggests that the first farm with attached plots of land-parcels developed during the sixth century. By the eighth and

---

[3] Catteddu, ed., *Châteaugiron ZAC de la Perdriotais*; Catteddu, 'Archéologie des sociétés rurales', p. 123.

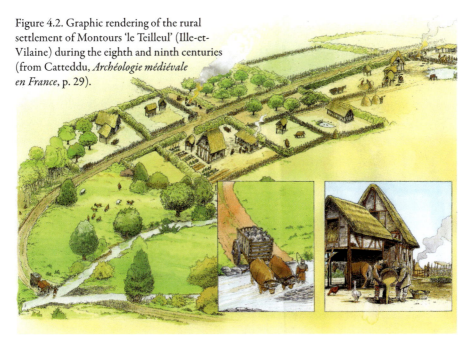

Figure 4.2. Graphic rendering of the rural settlement of Montours 'le Teilleul' (Ille-et-Vilaine) during the eighth and ninth centuries (from Catteddu, *Archéologie médiévale en France*, p. 29).

Figure 4.3. Map of Château-giron, site A: the rural settlement during the eighth and ninth centuries. Three farm units were organized within quadrangular plots, delimited by ditches. The earliest, shown in red, was established from the sixth century, the second (green) between the seventh and ninth centuries, and the third (blue) was the only one to be enlarged, lasting from the seventh to the tenth century (from Catteddu, 'Insediamenti rurali della Francia settentrionale', p. 25, figure 15).

ninth centuries, this same area seems to have been subdivided into three farm units. By the end of occupation in the tenth century, however, these had been replaced by a single unit which expanded further to the north, towards the current town. On site B, 200 m (650 feet) away, a contemporary early medieval settlement grew within a new network.[4]

The same regular organization of settlements has been identified on the site of Montours and elsewhere in Brittany, as in the Rennes Basin.[5] All these sites were built in the course of the seventh century, or in a few cases at the end of the sixth, and abandoned around the tenth century. The eighth and ninth centuries seemed to be the period best represented, with a major extension of the sites and considerable economic dynamism. Very good examples of this organization are visible on the sites of Chantepie (sixth to eighth centuries),[6] Chavagne (end of sixth to tenth century),[7] Ercé-près-Liffré (end of fifth to tenth century),[8] Mordelles (sixth or seventh to ninth century),[9] Noyal-sur-Vilaine (sixth to eighth century), and Torcé (seventh to ninth century).[10]

This system of ditched and rectilinear enclosures is well known in Anglo-Saxon England, with an emergence during the Middle Saxon period in Eastern England, at the latest.[11] It is also found at several sites in south Normandy and in the Pays-de-Loire region, that is, along the Western Atlantic coast and in the vicinity of the Channel. But these last sites, where only smaller areas have been excavated, do not allow us to see such regular organization.[12]

Rural Settlements in Western and Central Brittany

Research on the western side of a line from Saint-Brieuc to Vannes has recently revealed new settlements whose characteristics and layouts are different from the sites of eastern Brittany (Fig. 4.4). In these areas, spatial analysis again dem-

---

[4] Catteddu, 'Archéologie des sociétés rurales', pp. 120–23.

[5] Catteddu, ed., *Les habitats carolingiens*.

[6] Bethus, *Chantepie*.

[7] Le Gall and Lemée-Demontfaucon, *Chavagne « La Touche, tranche 2 » (Ille-et-Vilaine)*.

[8] Ah-Thon, *Ercé-près-Liffré*.

[9] Le Boulanger, *Mordelles, « Val de Sermon » (Ille-et-Vilaine)*.

[10] Cahu, *Noyal-sur-Vilaine « La Primaudière » (Ille-et-Vilaine)*; Cahu, *Torcé « Vassé » (Ille-et-Vilaine)*.

[11] Hamerow, *Rural Settlements*.

[12] Catteddu, 'Archéologie des sociétés rurales'; Carpentier and Hincker, 'L'habitat rural'.

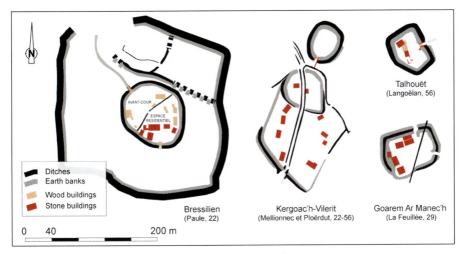

Figure 4.4. Ring-forts excavated in Brittany
(from Le Gall and Leroy, 'Le haut Moyen Âge', p. 130).

onstrates the re-use of Gaulish and Gallo-Roman territorial organization. But the organizational process of gradual appropriation of parcels of land is absent or less visible.

These enclosed settlements show a certain disparity of plan and form, especially in the type of enclosures — sometimes quadrangular, but more often circular, oval, or horseshoe enclosures — which delimited individual dispersed farms in the countryside, more often along pre-existing roads. A main enclosure with deeper or shallower ditches included buildings for one or several families, agricultural outbuildings, and craft activities. On the main sites, other enclosures were added.

Along the line of the Roman aqueduct of Carhaix, the settlement of Kergoutois, dating to the eighth and ninth centuries, was organized in three areas separated by ditches and with a gate for access: a first area for grain processing, a second with a sunken-featured building, a firepit, silos and ovens, and a third area with another building.[13] The site of Caudan in Morbihan, dating between the end of the seventh and the tenth centuries, offers the same characteristics.[14]

However, the most recent excavations give a more nuanced picture, as we can see in Saint-Martin-des-Champs, in the Finistère region, where enclosed

---

[13] Le Boulanger, 'L'habitat de Kergoutois'.

[14] Le Boulanger, *Caudan, « ZAC de Lenn Sec'h, lot 2 » (Morbihan)*.

Figure 4.5. The ringwork of Bressilien in Paule (Côtes-d'Armor) (from Le Gall and Leroy, 'Le haut Moyen Âge', p. 135).

4. THE ARCHAEOLOGY OF EARLY MEDIEVAL RURAL SOCIETIES IN BRITTANY

parcels contained buildings, ovens, and silos. This system of enclosed parcels looks like the sites in Eastern Brittany, but is less regular.[15] In Guipavas near Brest, a site occupied between the seventh and eighth centuries, and again in the thirteenth century, the landscape was structured during the Gaulish and Gallo-Roman periods and the early medieval settlements re-used these antique limits.[16] In Guipavas, an initial large enclosure housed two spaces. One space contained residential buildings and outbuildings, ovens and silos grouped around a courtyard. Two hundred metres south, another settlement was divided into regular parcels of antique origin in which buildings, sunken-featured buildings, and an area for outbuildings, craft, and rural activities were aligned along the ditches of the enclosures and along pathways. If the layout of these last settlements reminds us of the regular grid of ditches of Eastern Brittany, the architecture and material culture are different, a point that we are going to develop in the following pages.[17]

Elite Sites

Another type of site has been evidenced. Characterized as high-status settlements, they are all located in central Brittany, on hillsides or on the edge of plateaus, close to Gaulish or Gallo-Roman routes. Some of them were already centres of power in pre-Roman times. All these sites were built during the course of the seventh or eighth centuries and abandoned during the tenth century. They are surrounded by imposing, deep ditches (Fig. 4.5) and systems of earth banks, as in La Feuillée, Ploërdut-Mellionnec, Langoëlan, and Saint-Tugdual.[18]

At Bressilien in Paule commune (Côtes-d'Armor), a large oval enclosure of five hectares delimited by a deep ditch contains a second oval enclosure of 6500 m^2 (Fig. 4.4). Access is along a path lined by low walls, dominated by a gatehouse, as at Langoëlan. The second enclosure is protected by a timber-reinforced earth bank and a ditch 2.6 m in depth and divided by another substantial ditch into two courtyard areas. One courtyard contains evidence for craft and agricultural activities: large wooden buildings — some of them sunken-featured — grain pro-

---

[15] Mentele, *Saint-Martin-des-Champs (Finistère)*.

[16] Simier and Cavanillas, *ZAC de Lavallot Nord (Bretagne Finistère)*, p. 130; Blanchet, *Plouedern, « Leslouc'h » (Finistère)*.

[17] Catteddu and Le Gall, 'Archéologie du premier Moyen Âge'.

[18] For Langoëlan, see Leroy, *Langoëlan « Talhouët » (Morbihan)*; for Saint-Tugdual, Quillivic, *Saint-Tugdual (Morbihan)*.

cessing facilities, corn-drying ovens, rotary querns for flour-grinding, and silo-pits for storage. The second courtyard, at a higher level, is the residential zone, with an early phase of earthen and wooden buildings and signs of craft and agricultural activities (silos and a smithy). At the end of the eighth century and the beginning of the ninth, the wooden buildings were replaced by large stone buildings (Figs 4.6 and 4.7). Small fragments of decorated window glass, silver coins, and a large volume of storage space are indications of a high-status site. Inside the large external enclosure, trenching revealed more silos, ironworking waste, and a large iron-smelting workshop.[19] 300 m to the north-east, the chapel of Saint-Symphorien has also been studied, while another small oval enclosure with additional farm-buildings has been found to the west.[20]

Some of the characteristics of these elite sites can be seen in the ringwork of Locronan which dates to the ninth and tenth centuries (excavated in the 1980s by Philippe Guigon), and in the Camp de Péran in Plédran (partially excavated in the 1980s by Jean-Pierre Nicolardot).[21]

In Eastern Brittany, contemporary elite settlements offer a different pattern, and their architecture can be more modest. In Coesmes (Ille-et-Vilaine), dating from the sixth century, a substantial palisade, a long wooden fence, a monumental entrance, and ostentatious artefacts provide clues of a high-status site.[22] Further evidence of an elite presence has been identified in Chavagne (Ille-et-Vilaine),[23] with the presence of chain-mail, and in Noyal-sur-Vilaine, where a pile of arrowheads has been uncovered: both examples of military material associated with ostentatious architecture and the presence of a central court.

The first occupation of Chasné-sur-Illet, excavated in the centre of the present village in Ille-et-Vilaine, near the present church, dates back to the sixth or seventh century.[24] It developed from the eighth century with the construction or the arrangement of inhabited plots or parcels of land, and quickly became a seigneurial domain before the year 1000. A large quadrangular enclosure delimitated by deep ditches was divided into two areas. The smaller of the two (3500 m^2) included large residential buildings and silos with a high storage

[19] Le Gall, *L'habitat aristocratique de Bressilien à Paule*; Le Gall, 'Une résidence aristocratique des VIIIe–IXe siècles'.

[20] Le Gall and Menez, *La Chapelle de Saint-Symphorien à Paule*.

[21] Guigon, 'La résidence palatiale'; Nicolardot and Guigon, 'Une forteresse'.

[22] Leroux, *L'habitat du haut Moyen Âge*.

[23] Le Gall and Lemée-Demontfaucon, *Chavagne « La Touche, tranche 2 » (Ille-et-Vilaine)*.

[24] Beuchet, *Chasné-sur-Illet « ZAC du Champ des Buttes » (Ille-et-Vilaine)*.

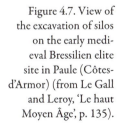

Figure 4.6. View of the main stone building of the elite site of Bressilien in Paule (from Le Gall and Leroy, 'Le haut Moyen Âge', p. 137.).

Figure 4.7. View of the excavation of silos on the early medieval Bressilien elite site in Paule (Côtes-d'Armor) (from Le Gall and Leroy, 'Le haut Moyen Âge', p. 135).

Figure 4.8. Corn-drying kilns at the Bressilien site (from Le Gall and Leroy, 'Le haut Moyen Âge', p. 135).

capacity (15 m³), as well as an enormous oven and a sunken-featured building dedicated to craft activities. They yielded decorated ceramics and a fragment of a spur, dating to the eleventh century. A moated site was built over the Carolingian settlement in the twelfth century.

A Focus on the Individual Vestiges and Archaeological Structures

Several regional but also micro-regional peculiarities can also be highlighted through the study of some specific remains, such as the large sunken-featured buildings and the ovens. Only a few years ago, sunken-featured buildings were completely unknown in Brittany and even in western France, while they were numerous in northern and eastern Gaul and in Germany.

4. THE ARCHAEOLOGY OF EARLY MEDIEVAL RURAL SOCIETIES IN BRITTANY

But this was without taking into consideration the recent excavations. Sunken-featured buildings have now been uncovered in early medieval settlements in our region, even if they are less numerous. Surprisingly, they are more numerous in central and western Brittany. Some of them cover a large area (of 30 m²), have stone foundations or are built in a combination of wood, stone and earth, as at Carhaix, Paule, Guipavas, Saint-Martin-des-Champs, Ploudaniel, Plouedern, the Talhouët site in Langoëlan, Bressilien and Quehelen in Paule.

Another regional Breton peculiarity is corn-drying ovens. These take the form of trenches whose edges were inset with rough stones, supporting a wooden or wicker platform on which the grain was spread. Embers were deposited at the bottom of these trenches to warm the air and dry the grains. This type of oven is virtually unknown in Gaul, except in Brittany; however, it is well known in England and in Ireland.[25] Still more interesting, in western and central Brittany the ovens are faced with stone and are larger than in the eastern part of the region (Fig. 4.8) (as in Guipavas, Châteaulin, Paule, Kergoutois, Bressilien, Saint-Martin-des-Champs).

A Focus on the Artefacts

Material culture also belongs to this debate about regional specificities. Ceramic and metallic vessels represent significant evidence of influences and economic relationships. In general, and in comparison with other French regions, ceramic vessels are rather rare on Breton sites. Nevertheless, micro-regional peculiarities can be identified, as in eastern Brittany, thanks to early medieval pottery workshop sites and numerous excavations. On the other hand, in central Brittany pottery is extremely rare. Its scarcity is probably linked to a more privileged use of wood, basketwork, leather, or metal, as seen on western British sites and in Ireland. Even more interesting, on the west coast, in Plouedern and Guipavas, the few pottery items found have nothing in common with northern Gaulish pottery production. Instead, they show the same typology as products from eastern English settlements. They are made from local clay, but the shapes conform to Anglo-Saxon typology.[26]

Another interesting link with the Insular world is the find of a church or liturgical artefact in the chapel of Saint-Symphorien in Paule, very close to the Bressilien site. A small handbell (ninth-century) and a gilt bronze frag-

[25] O'Sullivan and others, *Early Medieval Dwellings*.

[26] Soulat, *Le matériel archéologique de type saxon*.

Figure 4.9. Gilt bronze ornament uncovered in the chapel of Saint-Symphorien. It is probably a fragment of a cross or reliquary. The design of the 'triskel', the interlacings and the technique are datable to the eighth or ninth centuries (from Le Gall and Leroy, 'Le haut Moyen Âge', p. 138).

ment of a reliquary or of a cross (Fig. 4.9), are identical to Irish productions.[27] A third example is a chance discovery made in 2013 in Tredarzec (Côtes-d'Armor), where a deposit of metal dishes from the sixth century again shows similarities with other examples found in northern and eastern France and across the Channel in the southeast of England.[28] Cauldrons correspond to the Westland type, well known in Western Scandinavia. A production site has been identified on the east coast of Norway. Another possible area of production of these vessels is in the valley of the Meuse in Belgium between Dinant and Namur. But the main areas of production seem to be in Scandinavia and in England. Some cemeteries have yielded the same artefacts: Saint-Dizier (eastern France), Bifrons (Kent), Great Chesterford (Essex), Empingham (Rutland), and Finglesham (Kent).[29]

Paleoenvironmental Studies

Environmental studies are also essential to our understanding of how ecosystems and rural areas evolved in the region. One of the principal contributions relates to the changes in agropastoral practices in the early Middle Ages. Plant and ecosystem diversity indicates that oats and rye were grown as crops in both western and eastern Brittany. Two kinds of oats were grown. The most common, *Avena sativa*, is not as a rule the dominant grain crop on early medieval sites,

---

[27] Le Gall and Menez, *La Chapelle de Saint-Symphorien à Paule*, p. 4. These artifacts seem to have been made between the years 700 and 900 in Ireland, Scotland, and Wales: Bourke, 'Les cloches à main'.

[28] Menez, ed., *Trédarzec (Côtes d'Armor)*, pp. 20–33; study by Labaune, 'Étude préliminaire', pp. 20–33.

[29] Menez, ed., *Trédarzec (Côtes d'Armor)*, pp. 20–33; study by Labaune, 'Étude préliminaire', pp. 20–33.

4. THE ARCHAEOLOGY OF EARLY MEDIEVAL RURAL SOCIETIES IN BRITTANY

but it is all over Brittany. We also found here the other species, *Avena strigosa*, which is practically unknown elsewhere in medieval France, but is common in Frisia, Holland, and northern Germany right up into Scandinavia. It remains unclear whether the use of *Avena strigosa* represents a particular local practice or a more general alignment of agricultural practice in Brittany with that of northern Europe.[30] Moreover, such diversity of plants signals a large increase in livestock farming in conjunction with changes in land use, and the increased area of moorland and meadows, both wet and dry, as is well-known in Anglo-Saxon England.[31]

What about the Funerary Sites?

As in other regions of France, very few fourth- and fifth-century settlements have been identified in Brittany. However, some recently excavated funerary sites yield very specific funerary practices, material deposits, and grave goods. They also show links with the British Isles and Northern Gaul.

The site of Gouesnac'h (in Finistère) highlights the juxtaposition of two kinds of funerary structures: quadrangular enclosures and inhumation pits.[32] The grave goods (ceramics and glass) are well known in Carhaix, in the *civitas* of the Osismi, and the metallic buckle and knife found in two tombs have parallels in the German world, in northern Gaul, and also in other cemeteries excavated in Brittany dating from the end of the fourth century and from the fifth century.

Similar graves in the centre of quadrangular enclosures (five metres wide) are also known in Châteauneuf-du-Faou, in Plouescat (Finistère), and in Wales.[33] If burials and associated artefacts find chronological equivalents, the square enclosures which form contiguous units placed between tombs were until now totally unknown in the funerary landscape of Late Antique Brittany.

---

[30] Catteddu, 'Archéologie des sociétés rurales', pp. 139–41; Catteddu ed., *Châteaugiron « la Perdriotais » (Ille-et-Vilaine)*, pp. 424–25; Catteddu, 'Habitat, structuration de l'espace rural et pratiques agropastorales'.

[31] Hamerow, *Rural Settlements*, p. 145; Catteddu, 'Archéologie des sociétés rurales', pp. 104, 141–44.

[32] Colleter, Labaune-Jean, and Hinguant, 'Le cimetière de Ty Korn', pp. 311–13, 320–24.

[33] Roy, *Châteauneuf-du-Faou « Kroas Lesneven »*, pp. 73–77; Nicolas, *Cléder/Plouescat, Créac'h ar Vrenn (Finistère)*, pp. 91–133.

Despite the lack of data — limited excavation, eroded structures, very few bone remains, and few datable deposits — it is possible to compare Gouesnac'h with other sites in western Brittany, but also with northern and eastern sites in Gaul, dating from the end of the fifth century, even in eastern and northern Britain and within Wales, for instance Tandderwen (north Wales). There, however, each enclosure surrounds an inhumation pit, and these are later, dating to a period between 600 and 900 AD or 550 and 750 AD.[34]

In Plouedern (Finistère), a group of three small circular funerary enclosures dating to the seventh century has been uncovered. Their external diameter is four metres, and their internal diameter two and a half metres. This kind of funerary monument is well known in Anglo-Saxon contexts and in Merovingian graves in north-eastern France.[35] Pottery found in the graves is made from local clay, but in form is comparable with Insular types (Late Roman 'Black Burnished' and 'Cranbeck' wares dating from the fourth and fifth centuries, but also ninth- to eleventh-century pottery found at Mawgan Porth, Cornwall). Other pottery finds show similarities with Saxon vessels from the West Riding of Yorkshire.[36]

Further south and east, in the oldest burial site of Saint-Marcel (Morbihan), a rectangular enclosure was surrounded by forty-five inhumation burials in use between the second half of the fourth and the end of the fifth century or even the beginning of the sixth. Finds uncovered in five graves allow us to establish a comparison with the Quoit Brooch Style, found in military graves in northern Gaul and in Anglo-Saxon settlements.[37]

In the early Middle Ages, as in Antiquity, it was usual to equip the deceased with grave-goods, most probably as a reflection of social position. This custom ceased at approximately the same time as the abandonment of extra-mural cemeteries. The date of this fundamental transition varies widely. In the Mediterranean it took place during the fifth century, and it can be dated to the later seventh century in western Europe, later still in the north. This change of burial custom coincides strikingly with the consolidation of Christianity in the respective regions and may thus express a general change in attitude towards death and the dead.[38]

---

[34] Colleter, Labaune-Jean, and Hinguant, 'Le cimetière de Ty Korn', pp. 318–23, fig. 19.

[35] Blanchet, *Plouedern, « Leslouc'h » (Finistère)*, p. 268.

[36] Blanchet, *Plouedern, « Leslouc'h » (Finistère)*; study of the ceramics by Labaune, pp. 296–97.

[37] Le Boulanger and others, 'De la ferme antique à la nécropole'.

[38] Catteddu, *Archéologie médiévale en France*, pp. 140–50.

4. THE ARCHAEOLOGY OF EARLY MEDIEVAL RURAL SOCIETIES IN BRITTANY

In Brittany, however, an exception can be made for the examples given above. We find a very high proportion of unfurnished graves. Unfortunately, bad skeletal preservation also prevents accurate study. The deceased are buried in sarcophagi (an antique tradition) made from shelly limestone, or laid directly in the earth.[39]

In Eastern Brittany, very few settlements dated between the fifth and ninth centuries have been excavated together with associated cemeteries or even small groups of tombs. But the presence of graves from the sixth century under chapels or churches that have been parish centres since the eleventh century suggests a very early stabilization of the villages in the region. Recent excavations give new data in this field of research, as in the centre of the village of Bréal-sous-Vitré, in Chasné-sur-Illet, Bais and Visseiche.[40]

In the western part of the region, in Guipavas, near Brest (Finistere), a cemetery with 251 graves, close to two early medieval settlements, has been excavated but cannot be dated.[41]

The study of the hearts of present-day villages will also provide new opportunities to analyse religious sites, little excavated in the last few years. Following the excavation of the abbey of Landévennec new sites are reinforcing the data, as in Chasné-sur-Illet, Bréal-sous-Vitré in Ille-et-Vilaine, and the chapels of Saint Symphorien and Saint Tugdual in central Brittany.

Conclusion

Recent years have seen the excavation of numerous early medieval sites, often on an impressive scale. We now have evidence of sufficient quantity and quality to begin to examine settlements as dynamic social arenas rather than passive agglomerations of archaeological features.

One of the main themes that archaeology has evidenced is probably the great diversity of early medieval rural settlements. Another is that in place of the old model of rupture around the year 1000, the archaeological data now encourages us to look for new and more subtle rhythms in the development of rural landscapes, breaking the spell of the old academic chronology. The period

---

[39] Guigon, *Les sépultures*.

[40] Le Boulanger, Colleter, and Pichot, *Église, cimetière et paroissiens*; Beuchet, *Chasné-sur-Illet « ZAC du Champ des Buttes » (Ille-et-Vilaine)*, pp. 85–101; Guigon and Bardel, 'Les nécropoles mérovingiennes de Bais et de Visseiche (Ille-et-Vilaine)'; Le Boulanger, *Bais (Ille-et-Vilaine)*; Le Boulanger ed., *Visseiche Le Bourg, Nécropole et habitat du haut Moyen Âge*.

[41] Simier and Cavanillas, *ZAC de Lavallot Nord (Bretagne Finistère)*, III, 13–49.

from the mid-seventh to the mid-eighth century now appears as a decisive turning point in many places, before the new transformations in the tenth century, which it does make sense to connect with the rise of local elites and the multiplication of centres of domination in the countryside. What is probably the next greatest transformation takes place in the twelfth century. Our analysis must, of course, take into account local and regional geographical or geomorphological specificities, and historicocultural traditions. The diversity of early medieval settlements, which is often regional and indeed microregional, encourages us to think more about scenarios than models.[42]

In Brittany, archaeological studies on early medieval sites primarily highlight regional specificities, common to the whole peninsula, while being different from the other French regions. Numerous features are similar to characteristics found in the British Isles:

- the scarcity, even the absence of burial deposits;
- the presence of numerous corn-drying kilns on rural settlements, which are very rare further east;
- regional agropastoral practices such as the over-representation of the culture of *Avena* as a privileged crop, the integration of a new cereal (*Avena strigosa*), and the development of livestock breeding;
- as in Britain, we can observe a 'long eighth century' when new farming regimes emerged, with changes in settlement configuration. These include the introduction of complexes of enclosures and droveways, often maintained over long periods, as well as the establishment of hay meadows, developments which seem to be associated with new, more intensive animal and crop husbandry regimes;
- new types of building such as buildings on an oval plan and large sunken-featured buildings.

Archaeology also stresses microregional specificities. These include differences between the eastern and western part of the peninsula and new signs of extra-regional contacts:

- in the shape and organization of settlements between the eastern and western part of the region (even if this has to be qualified);

[42] Catteddu, 'Archéologie des sociétés rurales', pp. 61, 150–56; Catteddu, 'Insediamenti rurali', p. 34.

4. THE ARCHAEOLOGY OF EARLY MEDIEVAL RURAL SOCIETIES IN BRITTANY

- in the types of ovens (corn drying kilns);
- in the shape of ceramics and artefacts;
- in architecture.

All these specificities taken together — although, taken independently, they are not exclusive to Brittany — presumably reflect a way of living, of building and organizing settlements, of funerary practice, specific to Brittany, and in some cases to the western Armorican peninsula. Regional context and the important migration of people from insular Britain from the fourth century encourages us to consider external influences reflected in these practices, including British influences, but also Anglo-Saxon, German, and others. During much of the early Middle Ages, but also earlier still, as our proto-historian colleagues have shown, local people seemed to privilege their relationship with the British Isles.

In the same way, trade and exchanges were not limited to Britain, as shown by several artefacts such as the fragment of decorated glass uncovered at Bressilien, linked to Swedish production. Other interesting data include the agricultural practices and the use of *avena strigosa* as a witness to contacts with Scandinavian countries in the eighth and ninth centuries.

Recent research also reveals important relations between the Breton kingdom and the Carolingian empire, as shown by the emergence of stone buildings similar to Carolingian aristocratic residences, and the discovery of Carolingian coins (as on the Bressilien site). This reflects an elite's acculturation to the Frankish way of life and organization.[43]

Lastly, the recent excavations of Saint-Martin-des-Champs and Guipavas in Finistère show again the new shape of settlements, offering some comparison with sites in eastern Brittany. But they also yield artefacts (and architecture) typical of Britain. This reminds us of the need to take into account the social status of the site, the legacies, the topography, the scale of analysis, and also the chronology. It is now important to enlarge this first analysis with data and synthesis collected in the Normandy region and the whole Atlantic coast.

Research has multiplied the available evidence for close and obvious links between Brittany and the British Isles, Ireland, and also with the Germanic and Frankish worlds. Architecture, artefacts, and agropastoral practices show at once the wide range of outside influences and the clues of acculturation. Above all, what is demonstrated by recent excavations is the important porosity

---

[43] Catteddu and Le Gall, 'Archéologie du premier Moyen Âge'.

between multicultural societies and multi-faceted Atlantic connections. These new scenarios invite us to rethink the early Middle Ages.

In France, archaeology has radically revisited its methodology and its perspectives, improving results and opening the way to dynamic research programmes throughout the country. We initiated a new collective research programme about early medieval settlements in Brittany.[44] The random, opportunistic aspect of rescue archaeology has allowed us to renew our approach, deconstruct or undo paradigms, test our methods, and create new ones.[45]

Dr Isabelle Catteddu is an archaeologist who obtained her PhD at the University of Paris 1 Panthéon-Sorbonne. She works at INRAP (National Institute of Preventive Archaeological Research) in Brittany and has been in charge of a number of major excavations and projects since 1990. She has also organized exhibitions (*What's New in the Middle Ages*, La Villette – Cité des Sciences et de l'Industrie, Paris 2016), edited collaborative publications and produced syntheses of recent research. She specializes in the early Middle Ages, in early medieval rural societies, settlement, landscape, and societies' relations with their environments. She prioritizes multidisciplinary research and works with international teams through congress participation and publications.

Joseph Le Gall is an archaeologist working for the INRAP (National Institute of Preventive Archaeological Research). He has been in charge of a decade of excavations in Brittany since 2008. He is a specialist in the Iron Age and the Early Middle Ages, and is interested in different diachronic themes, from the architecture of buildings to the evolution of terroirs and territories.

---

[44] Ah Thon and others, *Formes, natures et implantations rurales en Bretagne du IVe au XIe siècle.*

[45] Catteddu, 'Archéologie des sociétés rurales', pp. 156–63; Catteddu, 'Move On! There is Nothing to See Here'.

Works Cited

Ah Thon, E., *Ercé-près-Liffré, « ZAC du Bocage de l'Illet » (Ille-et-Vilaine). Un cercle funéraire du Bronze final et un habitat enclos du haut Moyen Âge*, Rapport final d'opération (Cesson-Sévigné: Inrap Grand Ouest, 2014)

——, I. Catteddu, F. Le Boulanger, L. Beuchet, D. Cahu, F. Labaune-Jean, J. Le Gall, and P. Poilpré, eds, *Formes, natures et implantations des occupations rurales en Bretagne du IVe au XIe siècle. Projet collectif de recherche*, Rapport d'activités, 2019, 2020, 2021, 3 vols (Cesson-Sévigné: Inrap Grand Ouest, 2019, 2020, 2021)

Bethus, T., *Chantepie, « Les rives du Blosne » (Ille-et-Vilaine). Un habitat enclos du haut Moyen Âge (VIe–IXe siècle)*. Rapport final d'opération (Cesson-Sévigné: Inrap Grand Ouest, 2011)

Beuchet, L., *Chasné-sur-Illet « ZAC du Champ des Buttes » (Ille-et-Vilaine)*, Rapport final d'opération (Cesson-Sévigné: Inrap Grand Ouest, 2016)

Blanchet, S., *Plouedern, « Leslouc'h » (Finistère). Une longue occupation de la protohistoire au Moyen Âge*, Rapport final d'opération (Cesson-Sévigné: Inrap Grand Ouest, 2013)

Bourke, C., 'Les cloches à main de la Bretagne primitive', *BSAF*, 110 (1982), 339–53

Cahu, D., *Noyal-sur-Vilaine « La Primaudière » (Ille-et-Vilaine). Enclos (funéraire) du premier âge du Fer. Habitat rural du VIe–VIIe siècle au IXe–Xe siècle*, Rapport final d'opération (Cesson-Sévigné: Inrap Grand Ouest, 2014)

——, *Torcé « Vassé » (Ille-et-Vilaine). Habitat enclos fin VIIe–IXe siècle*, Rapport final d'opération (Cesson-Sévigné: Inrap Grand Ouest, 2014)

Carpentier, V., and V. Hincker, 'L'habitat rural du haut Moyen Âge en Basse-Normandie. Arrêt sur vingt années de recherches archéologiques', in *La Gaule, le monde insulaire et l'Europe du Nord au haut Moyen Âge. Actualité de l'archéologie en Normandie (V^e–Xe s.). Actes des XXVIIe journées internationales d'archéologie mérovingienne*, ed. by C. Lorren (Saint-Germain-en-Laye: Association française d'archéologie mérovingienne), pp. 183–209

Catteddu, I., 'Archéologie des sociétés rurales altomédiévales dans la moitié nord de la France: modes d'habitats, gestion de l'espace, pratiques agropastorales et milieux (études de cas d'archéologie préventive)', 3 vols (doctoral dissertation, Université de Paris 1 Panthéon-Sorbonne, 2012)

——, *Archéologie médiévale en France. Le Premier Moyen Âge (V^e–XIe siècles)* (Paris: Éditions la Découverte, 2009)

——, ed., *Châteaugiron « la Perdriotais » (Ille-et-Vilaine). Archéologie et environnement d'un terroir sur la longue durée et histoire de l'aménagement d'un territoire*, Rapport final d'opération, 3 vols (Cesson-Sévigné: Inrap Grand Ouest, 2013)

——, 'Habitat, structuration de l'espace rural et pratiques agropastorales au premier Moyen Âge. Exemple d'une collaboration interdisciplinaire autour de deux fouilles archéologiques préventives en Ille-et-Vilaine à Montours et Châteaugiron', in *Penser la paysannerie médiévale, un défi impossible? Volume d'hommage à Jean-Pierre Devroey*, ed. by A. Dierkens, N. Schroeder, and A. Wilkin (Paris: Éditions de la Sorbonne, 2017), pp. 335–46

——, ed., *Les habitats carolingiens de Montours et de la Chapelle-Saint-Aubert (Ille-et-Vilaine)* (Paris: Documents d'archéologie française, 2001)

——, 'Insediamenti rurali della Francia settentrionale fra VI e IX secolo. Forme, tipologie, funzioni ed economia', in *Città e campagna. Culture, insediamenti, economia (secc. VI–IX). Atti del II Incontro per l'Archeologia barbarica (Milano, 15 maggio 2017)*, ed. by C. Giostra (Milan: SAP, 2017), pp. 13–36

——, 'Move On! There is Nothing to See Here. Reflections of a Rescue Archaeologist on the Archaeology of the Invisible', in *Clashes of Time. The Contemporary Past as a Challenge for Archaeology*, ed. by J.-M. Blaising, J. Driessen, J.-P. Legendre, and L. Olivier (Louvain: Presses Universitaires de Louvain, 2017), pp. 183–93

——, 'Archéologie du premier Moyen Âge en Bretagne : nouveaux objets et nouveaux scénarios pour « repenser » le premier Moyen Âge', in *Quel Moyen Âge ? La recherche en question*, ed. by H. Gouget and M. Coumert, Histoires des Bretagnes, 6 (Brest: CRBC, 2019), pp. 483–99

——, and J. Le Gall, 'Archéologie du premier Moyen Âge rural en Bretagne. État des lieux et perspectives', in *L'habitat rural du haut Moyen Âge en France (V^e–XIe s.). Dynamiques du peuplement, formes, fonctions et statut des établissements. Actes du colloque AFAM Montpellier, 36èmes Journées d'Archéologie Mérovingienne de l'AFAM 2015 (Montpellier-Lattes), Archéologie du midi médiéval supplément*, ed. by J. Hernandez, L. Schneider, and J. Soulat (Carcassone: Centre d'archéologie médiévale du Languedoc, 2020), pp. 199–209

——, F. Le Boulanger, E. Ah Thon, L. Beuchet, D. Cahu, F. Labaune-Jean, J. Le Gall, and P. Poilpré, ed., *Formes, natures et implantations des occupations rurales en Bretagne du IVe au XIe siècle. Projet collectif de recherche*, Rapport d'activités, 2019 (Cesson-Sévigné: Inrap Grand Ouest, 2019)

Colleter, R., F. Labaune-Jean, and S. Hinguant, 'Le cimetière de Ty Korn à Gouesnac'h (Finistère). Un ensemble funéraire original de l'Antiquité tardive en Bretagne', *Gallia*, 69 (2012), 309–44

Guigon, P., 'La résidence palatiale de Locronan', in *Saint Ronan et la Troménie. Actes du colloque international 28–30 avril 1989* (Bannalec: Imprimerie Régionale, 1995), pp. 71–108

——, *Les sépultures du haut Moyen-Âge en Bretagne* (Rennes: Institut culturel de Bretagne, 1994)

——, and J.-P. Bardel, 'Les nécropoles mérovingiennes de Bais et de Visseiche (Ille-et-Vilaine)', *MSHAB*, 66 (1989), 299–353

Hamerow, H., *Rural Settlements and Society in Anglo-Saxon England* (Oxford: Oxford University Press, 2012)

Labaune, J. F., 'Étude préliminaire de récipients découvertes à Trédarzec', in *Trédarzec (Côtes d'Armor), Crec'h Choupot. Le dépôt de récipients du haut Moyen Âge. Sondage à l'emplacement d'un dépôt de récipients métalliques du haut Moyen Âge*, ed. by Y. Menez, Rapport final d'opération de sondage (Cesson-Sévigné: Inrap Grand Ouest, 2013)

Le Boulanger, F., ed., *Bais (Ille-et-Vilaine). Places de l'église et de l'Ancien Marché et voieries autour de l'église Saint-Marse. Des tombes du haut Moyen Âge auprès de l'église*, Rapport

4. THE ARCHAEOLOGY OF EARLY MEDIEVAL RURAL SOCIETIES IN BRITTANY 79

final d'opération de diagnostic archéologique (Cesson-Sévigné: Inrap Grand Ouest, 2011)

——, *Caudan, « ZAC de Lenn Sec'h, lot 2 » (Morbihan). Un établissement rural du haut Moyen Âge*, Rapport final d'opération (Cesson-Sévigné: Inrap Grand Ouest, 2015)

——, 'L'habitat de Kergoutois', in *Archéologie en centre Bretagne*, ed. by Y. Menez, T. Lorho, and E. Chartier-Le Floch (Spézet: Coop Breizh, 2015), pp. 126–40

——, *Mordelles, « Val de Sermon » (Ille-et-Vilaine). Des Champs au Hameau (du Ier siècle ap. J.-C. à nos jours)*, Rapport final d'opération (Cesson-Sévigné: Inrap Grand Ouest, 2016)

——, *Visseiche Le Bourg, Nécropole et habitat du haut Moyen Âge*, Document final de synthèse de prospection thématique (Cesson-Sévigné: Inrap Grand Ouest, 2004)

——, R. Colleter, and D. Pichot, *Église, cimetière et paroissiens: Bréal-sous-Vitré (Ille-et-Vilaine), étude historique, archéologique et anthropologique (VIIe–XVIIIe siècle)* (Arles: éditions Errance, 2012)

——, L. Simon, S. Jean, H. Paitier, B. Ager, P.-A. Besombes, S. Blanchet, G. Le Cloirec, and P. Naas, 'De la ferme antique à la nécropole de l'Antiquité tardive (milieu du IIe s.–fin du Ve s. apr. J.-C.). Étude archéologique du site de Saint-Marcel « Le Bourg » (Morbihan)', *Gallia*, 69 (2012), 167–307

Le Gall, J., *L'habitat aristocratique de Bressilien à Paule (Côtes-d'Armor)*, Rapport intermédiaire d'opération biannuelle, 2011–2012 (Rennes: Service Régional de l'Archéologie de Bretagne, 2008)

——, 'Une résidence aristocratique des VIIIe–IXe siècles au cœur de la Bretagne. L'enceinte de Bressilien à Paule (Côtes d'Armor)', in *Les élites et leurs résidences en Bretagne au Moyen Âge. Actes du colloque de Guingamp et Dinan (28 et 29 mai 2010)*, ed. by P.-Y. Laffont (Rennes: Presses universitaires de Rennes, 2014)

——, and M. Lemée-Demontfaucon, *Chavagne « La Touche, tranche 2 » (Ille-et-Vilaine)*, Rapport final d'opération (Cesson-Sévigné: Inrap Grand Ouest, 2017)

——, and B. Leroy, 'Le haut Moyen Âge', in *Archéologie en centre Bretagne*, ed. by Y. Menez, T. Lorho, and E. Chartier-Le Floch (Spézet: Coop Breizh, 2015), pp. 126–40

——, and Y. Menez, *La Chapelle de Saint-Symphorien à Paule*, Rapport de fouille annuelle, 2008 (Rennes: Service Régional de l'Archéologie de Bretagne, 2008)

Leroux, G., *L'habitat du haut Moyen Âge des Rochettes à Coësmes (Ille-et-Vilaine)*, Rapport final d'opération de fouille (Cesson-Sévigné: Inrap Grand Ouest, 2004)

Leroy, B., *Langoëlan « Talhouët » (Morbihan) – Bretagne. Évaluation de l'enceinte de Talhouët, Er Hastel*, Rapport de sondage, Arvales (Rennes: SRA Bretagne, 2013)

Menez, Y., ed., *Trédarzec (Côtes d'Armor), Crec'h Choupot. Le dépôt de récipients du haut Moyen Âge. Sondage à l'emplacement d'un dépôt de récipients métalliques du haut Moyen Âge*, Rapport final d'opération de sondage (Cesson-Sévigné: Inrap Grand Ouest, 2013)

Mentele, S., *Saint-Martin-des-Champs (Finistère). Les occupations du « Haut Launay » (Finistère)*, Rapport final d'opération (Cesson-Sévigné: Inrap Grand Ouest, 2017)

Nicolardot, J.-P., and P. Guigon, 'Une forteresse du Xe siècle: le camp de Péran à Plédran (Côte-d'Armor)', *Revue archéologique de l'Ouest*, 7 (1991), 123–57

Nicolas, É., *Cléder/Plouescat, Créac'h ar Vrenn (Finistère). Des bâtiments de la transition entre le Néolithique final et l'Âge du Bronze ancien et une nécropole du Bas-Empire*, Rapport final d'opération (Cesson-Sévigné: Inrap Grand Ouest, 2015)

Quillivic, M., *Saint-Tugdual (Morbihan). L'enceinte de Talvern-Panner*, Rapport d'opération archéologique, Arvales (Rennes: SRA Bretagne, 2015)

Roy, E., *Châteauneuf-du-Faou « Kroas Lesneven ». Le petit cimetière du IVᵉ siècle après J.-C. de Châteauneuf-du-Faou dans le Finistère*, Rapport de diagnostic archéologique (Cesson-Sévigné: Inrap Grand Ouest, 2010)

Simier, B., and J. Cavanillas, *ZAC de Lavallot Nord (Bretagne Finistère). Évolution d'un terroir entre la Préhistoire et le Moyen Âge*, Rapport final d'opération, 3 vols (Cesson-Sévigné: Inrap Grand Ouest, 2017)

5. Espace et pouvoirs en Bretagne aux premiers siècles du Moyen Âge (VIᵉ–IXᵉ siècle)

Magali Coumert

RÉSUMÉ Cet article présente une enquête sur les Bretons installés sur le continent pour montrer qu'avant le IXᵉ siècle, il existe bien un groupe ethnique appelé *Britanni* par ses voisins, mais que celui-ci n'agit ni comme une communauté politique unifiée, ni comme une communauté religieuse spécifique. Les Bretons avaient divers chefs, avec leur propre stratégie et étaient en rapport avec des évêques liés à l'Église des royaumes francs. Leur domination s'étendait sur un espace mouvant de la péninsule armoricaine, allant jusqu'à Vannes et Bayeux, qui ne possédait pas de limites fixes. Les informations sur une implantation bretonne en Galice ne permettent que d'y déceler une éphémère communauté religieuse liée à la Grande-Bretagne, mais qui disparut trop vite pour nous permettre d'en identifier le fonctionnement.

ABSTRACT This paper investigates the Bretons who settled on the Continent and shows that before the ninth century, in what became Brittany, there was an ethnic group who were called *Britanni* by their neighbours, but they did not act either as a unified political community nor as a specific religious community. The Bretons had various leaders, each with a particular strategy, and had relationships with bishops linked to the churches of the Frankish kingdoms. Breton domination was exerted over a fluid space in the Armorican peninsula, as far east as Vannes and Bayeux, without fixed boundaries. Information on a British settlement in Galicia allows us to discern only an ephemeral religious community linked with Britain which disappeared too quickly to allow us to assess how it worked.

MOTS-CLÉS Britons, Catihern, citoyens, évêques, Frédégaire, Galice, Grégoire de Tours, Lovocat, *Parochiale Suevum*, Riotime, Samson, territoire, Venance Fortunat

---

Multi-disciplinary Approaches to Medieval Brittany, 450–1200: Connections and Disconnections, ed. by Caroline Brett, Fiona Edmonds, and Paul Russell, TCNE 36 (Turnhout: Brepols, 2023) pp. 81–108   BREPOLS 🖳 PUBLISHERS   10.1484/M.TCNE-EB.5.132310

En Grande Bretagne, la notion romaine d'une frontière linéaire était concrétisée par le mur d'Hadrien, qui séparait le territoire de l'Empire des barbares du nord. Son existence et son rôle symbolique étaient rappelés par Gildas au VIᵉ siècle de notre ère.[1] Il a donc pu paraître logique, en s'interrogeant sur la formation de la Bretagne du haut Moyen Âge, de rechercher, sur ce modèle, l'emplacement d'un territoire défini par des limites linéaires identifiables.[2] Ce type d'enquête se fondait sur l'équivalence supposée entre:

- un groupe ethnique de *Britanni*. J'utiliserai ici pour traduire leur nom le terme de Britons lorsqu'il semble arbitraire de déterminer si la référence des *Britanni* restait la Grande Bretagne ou si elle était devenue la Bretagne continentale. Je ne choisirai le terme de Bretons que si la référence continentale est sans ambiguïté;

- une communauté linguistique. Suivant une hypothèse commune, la présence des Britons apparaitrait à travers des toponymes spécifiques en langue bretonne, comme ceux en 'plou';

- un territoire unifié et délimité, dénommé *Britannia*;

- une organisation religieuse spécifique, liée à l'installation des Britons et à l'action de saints qui en sont issus et se seraient consacrés à leur christianisation: Samson, Guénolé.

Une telle perspective est par exemple synthétisée dans l'ouvrage intitulé *Les premiers Bretons d'Armorique*, publié en 2003.[3] P.-R. Giot va jusqu'à y évoquer une 'colonisation rationnelle réussie'.[4] Une approche de ce type permettait le croisement des données des rares sources écrites, notamment de l'hagiographie bretonne, dont les premières rédactions, si on excepte la question de la Vie ancienne de Samson, sont datées du IXᵉ siècle, et de la toponymie pour arriver à retracer le territoire des Britons après la migration.[5]

---

[1] Gildas, *De excidio Britanniae*, 15.3 et 18.2, pp. 21–22, 93–94.

[2] J.-P. Brunterc'h cherchait ainsi 'le *limes* breton avant le VIIIᵉ siècle', dans Brunterc'h, 'Le duché du Maine', p. 31. Son enquête ne peut pas être utilisée car les centaines ne sont pas attestées à l'époque mérovingienne.

[3] Giot, Guigon, et Merdrignac, *Les premiers Bretons d'Armorique*, principalement pour les articles de Giot, 'Histoire naturelle des hommes d'Armorique et de Bretagne', pp. 31–74, Merdrignac, 'La chrétienté bretonne des origines au VIᵉ siècle', pp. 75–91, et Merdrignac, 'Les saints et la "seconde migration bretonne"', pp. 93–120.

[4] Giot, Guigon, et Merdrignac, *Les premiers Bretons d'Armorique*, p. 57.

[5] Olson, 'Introduction', pp. 1–18; Poulin, 'Présence', dans ce volume. Voir la synthèse de ces approches par A. Chédeville dans Chédeville et Guillotel, *La Bretagne des saints et des rois*,

5. ESPACE ET POUVOIRS EN BRETAGNE AUX PREMIERS SIÈCLES DU MOYEN ÂGE

L'équivalence supposée entre espace d'implantation des Britons au haut Moyen Âge et zone marquée par une toponymie en langue bretonne est explicite dans les travaux de B. Tanguy, notamment dans son enquête, qui part de la lettre envoyée par les évêques de Rennes, Tours et Angers aux prêtres Lovocat et Catihern au début du VIe siècle, pour retrouver un toponyme qui pourrait être lié à Catihern.[6] Fondée sur le présupposé que seul le Catihern évoqué par la lettre aurait pu entrainer l'existence d'un toponyme, son enquête ne retenait que la toponymie en langue bretonne, malgré l'association des évêques de Rennes, d'Angers et de Tours pour la rédaction de la lettre, ce qui renvoie expressément à des espaces non-bretonnants.[7] Or les populations de Gaule de l'ouest comme de la Grande-Bretagne romaine maîtrisaient, dans une certaine mesure, le latin. L'émergence d'une population utilisant la langue brittonique sur le continent résulte donc de choix, car quels qu'aient été les reliquats du gaulois, le latin et le brittonique permettaient un certain degré d'intercompréhension entre insulaires et continentaux.[8] L'implantation de la langue brittonique correspond donc, comme l'a remarqué B. Guy, non pas à une zone d'émigration — l'usage du latin rendant invisibles certains migrants — mais à un espace socio-économique où la langue bretonne a pu prendre un rôle spécifique, en dehors des structures et des élites héritées de l'époque romaine.[9]

Je voudrais ici remettre en question l'existence d'un espace fixe et délimité, dominé par les Britons et décrit par leurs voisins comme tel, avant 800, en montrant qu'il existe alors un groupe ethnique de *Britanni* sur le continent, dénommés par rapport à la Grande Bretagne, mais que celui-ci ne correspond alors ni à une communauté politique, ni à une communauté religieuse spécifiques et qu'il est impossible de lui attribuer un territoire fixe, notamment par la toponymie. Pour cette enquête, je n'utiliserai pas l'ensemble de la production hagiographique postérieure à 800, en considérant *a priori* qu'elle projette sur le passé les préoccupations particulières au IXe siècle et notamment la recomposition des différents pouvoirs après la fondation de Redon et la guerre des fils de Louis le Pieux.[10]

---

pp. 89–151. Les localisations des éléments de la *Notitia Dignitatum* et de l'*Historia Brittonum* retenues par Camby, 'Limites politiques oubliées', viennent des travaux de L. Fleuriot et S. Kernéis et n'apparaissent pas suffisamment fondées.

[6] Mise en cartes dans Tanguy et Lagrée, *Atlas d'Histoire de Bretagne*; Tanguy, 'De l'origine des évêchés bretons'.

[7] Sur cette tentative, voir Mazel, *L'évêque et le territoire*, p. 392, n. 141.

[8] Brett, Edmonds, et Russell, *Brittany and the Atlantic Archipelago*, pp. 17–31.

[9] Guy, 'The Breton Migration', surtout pp. 130–34.

[10] Voir l'écart ainsi creusé avec Chédeville, 'Francs et Bretons', et Le Gall-Tanguy, 'La forma-

La transformation des cités épiscopales

Dans la province de Lyonnaise IIIe, créée entre 383 et 388 ap. J.-C.,[11] les changements de l'organisation religieuse et urbaine furent importants puisque les cités de Corseul, Carhaix et Jublains perdirent de l'importance au cours du ve siècle, ne laissant plus que des évêques à Nantes, Rennes, Vannes, Angers, et Le Mans, ainsi que le métropolitain à Tours, tels qu'ils apparaissent au concile de Vannes qui eut lieu entre 461 et 491.[12] La lettre du pape Nicolas I à l'évêque de Dol en 866, lui refusant la création d'une province ecclésiastique, note quant à elle la présence de sept évêchés *apud Britannos*, chez les Bretons.[13] Mais ces changements doivent-ils être directement mis en rapport avec la migration de britanniques, associés à leurs saints, ou peuvent-ils être pensés dans le cadre plus large des transformations continentales du pouvoir épiscopal et de son rapport à l'espace entre le ve et le XIIIe siècle?[14]

L'appropriation de l'espace du point de vue de l'évêque, pour la projection de son pouvoir sur le diocèse, fut le résultat d'un long processus depuis le ve siècle. Dans la lettre des évêques de Tours, Rennes et Angers à Lovocat et Catihern, entre 509 et 521, apparait un groupe chrétien allogène.[15] L'ensemble de la lettre se présente comme une correspondance entre des autorités religieuses responsables de deux groupes différents: *cum ad uos nostrae pervenerunt pagina litterarum*, 'quand les pages de nos lettres vous sont parvenues'. 'Nous', ce sont les deux évêques de Rennes et d'Angers, Melaine et Eustochius, associés à Licinius archevêque de Tours, leur métropolitain de la province de Lyonnaise IIIe. Les évêques décrivent une situation dans les Gaules, *intra Gallias*, sur le témoignage d'un prêtre nommé Sparatus. Ils définissent la communauté de l'Église catho-

---

tion des espaces diocésains'. Sur les recompositions du IXe siècle, voir Smith, '*Aedificatio sancti loci*'; Lunven, 'L'espace du diocèse', et Garault, 'La *Vita Sancti Machutis*'.

[11] La grande province de Lyonnaise du Haut Empire a été partagée une première fois en deux sous Dioclétien (284–305), puis une deuxième fois en quatre, sans doute sous Maxime (383–388). Voir Ferdière, *La Gaule Lyonnaise*, pp. 126–27.

[12] Monteil, 'Les agglomérations'; *Concile de Vannes*, dans *Concilia Galliae A. 314–506*, pp. 150–57. Voir Brett, 'Soldiers, Saints and States?', pp. 19–21.

[13] Nicolas I, *Lettres*, 127, p. 648. Sur la logique du pape, voir Noble, 'Pope Nicholas I and the Franks'.

[14] Lunven, *Du diocèse à la paroisse*.

[15] Munich, Bayerische Staatsbibliothek 5508, fol. 102[r], col. 2, l. 4–33 à fol. 102[v], col. 1, l. 1 à col. 2, l. 23. Le manuscrit est consultable en ligne: urn:nbn:de:bvb:12-bsb00036890-3. Édition dans Duchesne, 'Lovocat et Catihern'. Voir Rudelt, *Action et Mémoire*.

5. ESPACE ET POUVOIRS EN BRETAGNE AUX PREMIERS SIÈCLES DU MOYEN ÂGE

lique (*communio ecclesiastica, unitas ecclesiae, fides catholica*) et se rapportent à la tradition du christianisme universel, ici à propos d'une supposée hérésie orientale méconnue et mal comprise (*pepondiana*).

Leurs correspondants, 'vous', sont simplement désignés comme des prêtres, mais la précision du fait qu'ils célèbrent la messe *per diversorum ciuium uestrorum capanas*, permet de préciser l'origine interne à l'empire romain des contrevenants et leur association à une communauté. En effet, le terme de citoyens, *cives vestri*, vient désigner l'existence de deux communautés différentes, héritières de l'empire romain. D'un côté, les évêques de Gaule et leurs ouailles. De l'autre, un groupe observé par un prêtre, composé lui aussi de citoyens, mais différents. Or ce terme de *cives* est précisément celui par lequel Gildas désigne les *Britanni* dans son *De excidio Britanniae*.[16] Ce terme correspond au groupe auquel il s'identifie: les Britons comme des héritiers des Romains par la langue latine et par la christianisation dans l'île de Bretagne, désormais délaissés par l'empire et livrés à leur propre destin.[17] Les prénoms des prêtres Lovocat et Catihern nous portent vers une tradition onomastique celtique, mais celle-ci n'est pas mise en avant comme porteuse de sens ou de prestige dans cette lettre.[18] Il est probable que le groupe désigné soit des Britons, mais il est notable qu'il ne vienne pas à l'idée des rédacteurs de les désigner comme tels: le cadre de l'empire romain reste la référence commune.[19] Il n'est donc pas possible de mettre en avant une démarcation idéologiquement significative entre les deux groupes, comme entre chrétiens et païens, ou barbares et civilisés.[20]

Les occupations, les raisons de la présence de ce groupe de citoyens avec leur propre organisation chrétienne, ne sont pas évoquées dans la lettre qui ne retient que le caractère impropre de leur organisation religieuse, et surtout divers mauvais usages liés à l'espace. Tout d'abord, l'usage d'autels portatifs: 'les tables que nous ne doutons pas avoir été consacrées par des prêtres, comme vous le dites', *antedictas tabulas quas a presbyteris non dubitamus, ut dicitis consecratas*. Ici paraitrait l'argument des prêtres, ce qui indique qu'il y eut un dialogue, peut-être par l'intermédiaire du prêtre Sparatus: leurs autels furent consacrés. Mais les évêques entendent faire respecter leur rôle de premier dispensateur du

---

[16] Gildas, *De excidio Britanniae*, 26.1, pp. 28, 98.

[17] Gildas, *De excidio Britanniae*, 23.3, pp. 26, 97.

[18] Russell, 'Old Welsh Dinacat, Cunedag, Tutagual'.

[19] Coumert, 'Les relations entre Grande et Petite Bretagne'.

[20] Pohl, 'Frontiers and Ethnic Identities'.

sacré, et leur privilège:[21] les autels doivent être en pierre et la consécration par de simples prêtres est interdite, comme le rappellent les conciles tenus en Gaule à Épaone en 517, qui lient saint chrême et consécration, ainsi que le concile d'Orléans en 549 qui rappelle qu'il ne peut y avoir de consécration d'autel sans évêque.[22]

Outre l'intervention de femmes dans la distribution de l'eucharistie, la messe serait célébrée dans des endroits impropres, des *capanas*, associées à des citoyens dont *diversis* vient indiquer le nombre, l'absence de qualification particulière, ou la dispersion spatiale. Isidore de Séville († 636) considère que *capana* est une appellation courante pour des cabanes, un habitat temporaire, lié aux travaux des champs.[23] La même idée d'un habitat inconvenant est développée par les évêques à propos de la cohabitation des hommes et des femmes, qui pourrait se faire, sans lien familial, sous le toit de leur cellule, *intra tectum cellolę suae*.

Nous voyons ainsi les évêques de la province ecclésiastique de Tours défendre leur juridiction épiscopale contre un groupe, défini par une tradition romaine et catholique, capable de reconnaitre l'autorité des évêques et de comprendre leur lettre en latin, mais caractérisé par une pratique impropre de l'espace (et des rôles genrés, mais je ne l'étudierai pas particulièrement ici), pour l'habitat et la célébration de la messe.[24] Ces autres citoyens ne respectaient pas le territoire des évêques, comme ce fut souvent le cas au cours des Vᵉ–VIᵉ siècles.[25]

Ce groupe de 'vos concitoyens', *cives vestri*, n'est défini ni par une désignation ethnique, ni un lieu, ou une langue. Il se distingue par une organisation chrétienne et spatiale impropre, mobile et temporaire, dans un espace indéfini de la Lyonnaise IIIᵉ, peut-être aux confins des diocèses de Rennes et d'Angers. Ce groupe participait aux mutations des structures ecclésiastiques aux Vᵉ et VIᵉ siècles, et ne se différenciait pas autrement des autres chrétiens héritiers de l'empire, car les évêques pouvaient supposer une origine orientale de ses pratiques déviantes. Le cadre administratif laissé par l'empire romain, connu en Gaule par la Notice des Gaules, composée entre 386 et 450, ne nous fournit

---

[21] Basdevant-Gaudemet, 'L'évêque'.

[22] Concile d'Épaone, c. 26, Vᵉ concile d'Orléans, c. 8, in *Les canons des conciles mérovingiens*, I, 112–13, 306–07.

[23] Isidore de Séville, *Étymologies*, Livre XV.xii.2, pp. 76–77.

[24] De façon générale, voir Coumert, 'Les marqueurs de masculinité'.

[25] Mazel, *L'évêque et le territoire*, autres exemples pp. 35–39. Les conciles sous l'autorité des rois mérovingiens rappellent sans cesse l'importance de la juridiction épiscopale, comme le IIIᵉ concile d'Orléans (538), c. 16, in *Les canons des conciles mérovingiens*, I, pp. 244–45.

5. ESPACE ET POUVOIRS EN BRETAGNE AUX PREMIERS SIÈCLES DU MOYEN ÂGE

qu'un point de départ des transformations des cités et des diocèses.[26] Les évolutions sont d'autant plus difficiles à suivre que le terme de *civitas* ne désigne plus alors que la ville abritant un siège épiscopal, et non plus son territoire.[27] Néanmoins, le pouvoir politique semble lui aussi s'être appuyé sur les cités, comme le montrent les partages entre les rois mérovingiens qui se les répartissent.[28] Parfois même, comme ce fut le cas du siège éphémère de Rezé, en 511, il semble que des évêchés soient apparus de façon éphémère pour correspondre à des partages politiques au sein de la famille royale franque.[29]

La géographie du pouvoir épiscopal était ainsi mouvante et disputée aux ve–vi^e siècle et les évêques tentaient de résister aux modifications, comme le montre le concile de Tours, en 567: 'Nous ajoutons cela que personne ne doit se permettre d'ordonner évêque en Armorique un Briton ou un Romain sans le consentement ou les lettres du métropolitain ou des comprovinciaux.'[30] Pour situer le problème posé par ces *Britanni* qui voudraient devenir évêque, les évêques rassemblés à Tours choisissent un terme spatial, Armorique, qui depuis l'antiquité désigne les provinces occidentales de la Gaule, mais avec un certain flou. Si nous nous basons sur le *Tractus Armoricanus*, nous voyons désigner par l'adjectif 'armoricain' un littoral qui va au moins de Nantes à Rouen.[31] Les rares autres mentions des vi^e–viie siècles ne permettent pas, à mon avis, de restreindre *a priori* l'espace d'installation des Britons, et donc l'étendue éventuelle d'une *Britannia*, avant l'époque carolingienne.

Jordanès décrit le débarquement des Britons sur le continent avec Riotime à Bourges, vers 468: 'Le roi de ceux-ci [les Britons], Riotime, vint avec 12000 hommes dans la cité de Bourges et y fut reçu après avoir débarqué des bateaux, au sortir de l'Océan.'[32]

---

[26] *Notitia Galliarum.*

[27] Mazel, *L'évêque et le territoire*, p. 32.

[28] Par exemple dans le pacte d'Andelot, Grégoire de Tours, *Libri Historiarum X*, IX.20, p. 439. Lienhard, 'Remarques à propos des partages territoriaux'.

[29] Mazel, *L'évêque et le territoire*, pp. 35, 36, 183 et 413.

[30] *Concile de Tours* (567), c. 9: 'Adicimus etiam, ne quis Brittanum atque Romanum in Armorico sine metropolis aut comprouincialium uoluntate uel literis episcopum ordinare praesumat': *Les canons des conciles mérovingiens*, II, pp. 354–55.

[31] Galliou et Simon, *Le Castellum de Brest*, pp. 69–114.

[32] '[Brittonum] quorum rex Riotimus, cum duodecim milibus veniens in Biturigas civitatem, oceano e navibus egressus susceptus est': Jordanès, *De Origine Actibusque Getarum*, XLV. 237, p. 97; trad., p. 91. La traduction proposée par Camby, 'Limites politiques oubliées'oubliées », p. 96 me semble erronée.

Ce passage de Jordanès, qui écrivait son œuvre à Constantinople vers 552, montre son peu de maîtrise de la géographie gauloise, car il est proprement impossible de débarquer de l'océan à Bourges, ou même à proximité.[33] Il faut au moins remonter la Loire jusqu'à Orléans, sur plus de trois cents kilomètres, puis une marche s'impose. Mais le terme de Britons reste associé pour lui à la grande île voisine, et il souligne l'appel à des combattants d'outre-mer. La présence de ces Britons aux environs de Bourges vers 468 semble confirmée par la correspondance de Sidoine Apollinaire, qui demande le soutien de Riotime.[34] Cela ne permet pas d'affirmer une présence plus durable dans cette région, ni un lien direct avec le peuplement de l'Armorique.[35]

Cette communauté était à la fois ethnique — ses membres sont désignés comme Britons —, professionnelle — ce sont des mercenaires — et politique — les Britons sont commandés par un roi. Il a toujours été tentant de relier ce groupe à l'évêque Mansuetus des Britons, présent au concile de Tours en 461, mais qu'il y ait eu, ou non, un encadrement religieux spécifique pour ce groupe, il n'est plus mentionné après sa défaite militaire.[36] Cette communauté éphémère de Britons près de Bourges montrait donc une certaine unité, mais disparut sans laisser de trace.

La grande mobilité de ce groupe ethnique le met en parallèle avec d'autres groupes de combattants au Ve siècle, comme les Vandales, qui traversèrent l'Europe jusqu'en Afrique, ou les Francs, qui firent des funérailles grandioses à leur roi Chilpéric, enterré à Tournai en 481, puis abandonnèrent la Belgique II[de] et choisirent Paris, pour enterrer, catholiquement cette fois, son successeur.[37] Dans le cas des Francs, leur diversité religieuse initiale ne s'appuyait pas sur un encadrement spécifique et si un espace fut associé au pouvoir du roi franc, c'est dans le cadre hérité des cités, dont il réunit les évêques en 511 à Orléans.[38]

[33] Coumert, *Origine des peuples*, pp. 45–59.

[34] Sidoine Apollinaire, *Lettres*, I.7 et III. 9, pp. 22–23, 98. Voir Fahy, 'When did Britons become Bretons?'; Pietri, 'Grégoire de Tours et les Bretons d'Armorique'; Charles-Edwards, *Wales and the Britons*, pp. 66–74, 86–88 et 238–41.

[35] Brett, 'Soldiers, Saints and States', p. 12. Charles-Edwards, *Wales and the Britons*, pp. 57–60.

[36] Brett, 'Soldiers, Saints and States', p. 19; Fahy, 'When Did Britons Become Bretons?'; Grégoire de Tours, *Libri Historiarum X*, II.18, p. 65.

[37] Steinacher, *Die Vandalen*; Perin, 'La tombe de Clovis'.

[38] Habituellement, une lettre de Rémi de Reims est interprétée comme indiquant la domination de Clovis sur la Belgique Seconde, mais l'article de Barrett et Woudhuysen, 'Remigius', rappelle les fragiles hypothèses dont dépend cette lecture de l'unique manuscrit conservé.

5. ESPACE ET POUVOIRS EN BRETAGNE AUX PREMIERS SIÈCLES DU MOYEN ÂGE   89

Bien que la défaite militaire ait privé les Britons de Bourges de toute ins-cription dans la durée, quelques auteurs de la deuxième moitié du VIe siècle évoquent une *Britannia* continentale, marquant l'ancrage de Britons à l'ouest de la Gaule. Néanmoins, la comparaison des témoignages montre la très grande amplitude de cette désignation.

Les Bretagnes des VIe–VIIe siècles

Les premiers usages de *Britannia* pour désigner un espace continental appa-raissent chez Grégoire de Tours, qui rédigea ses *Histoires* entre 573 et 594.[39] Mais s'il emploie bien ce terme par quatre fois au singulier, il faut relativiser l'apparente unité de cette désignation par les neuf fois où il emploie cette expression au pluriel.[40] Par exemple, l'évêque de Tours rapporte comment: 'Cependant le roi Clotaire, furieux contre Chramne, se porta avec une armée contre lui dans les Bretagnes'.[41] En revanche, il relate comment l'armée de Chilpéric s'est rendue en Bretagne pour combattre: 'Ensuite, les Tourangeaux, les Poitevins, les Bajocasses, les Manceaux et les Angevins et bien d'autres par-tirent pour la Bretagne sur l'ordre du roi Chilpéric et campèrent le long de la Vilaine pour combattre contre Weroc, fils de feu Maclou'.[42]

Il considère deux fois plus souvent qu'il y a des Bretagnes continentales qu'une seule, ce qui peut illustrer sa perception de la fragmentation politique de cette domination venue de la grande île: il décrit ainsi longuement les com-

---

[39] Coumert, 'Le peuplement de l'Armorique'; Merdrignac et Plouchart, 'La fondation des évêchés bretons', p. 156; Murray, 'The Composition of the *Histories* of Gregory of Tours', défend l'hypothèse d'une rédaction commencée après 585.

[40] Singulier: Grégoire de Tours, *Libri Historiarum X*: *Britannia*, v.16, p. 214, l. 15; v.26, p. 232, l. 12; v.29, p. 235, l. 1; titres du ch. X.9, p. 476, l. 1. Pluriel: *Britanniae*, IV.20, p. 152, l. 12 et p. 153, l. 5; titre du ch. v.26, p. 191, l. 22; v.21, p. 229, l. 4; v.48, p. 258, l. 19; x.9, p. 493, l. 4 et 5; x.11, p. 495, l. 3. Il me semble qu'il faut ici ajouter v.16, p. 214, l. 10, même si le terme peut désigner les Bretagnes ou les Bretons. La variation entre singulier et pluriel est négligée par les traducteurs Buchner et Giesebrecht, *Zehn Bücher Geschichten*, Latouche, *Histoire des Francs*, et Thorpe, *History of the Franks*.

[41] Grégoire de Tours, *Libri Historiarum X*, IV.20, p. 153: 'Chlotarius autem rex contra Chramnum frendens cum exercitu adversus eum in Brittanias dirigit'.

[42] Grégoire de Tours, *Libri Historiarum X*, v.26, p. 232: 'Dehinc Toronici, Pictavi, Baio-cassini, Caenomannici et Andecavi cum aliis multis in Brittania ex iussu Chilperici regis abierunt et contra Varocum, filium quondam Macliavi, ad Viciloniam fluvium resedent'.

bats entre les chefs bretons Maclou et Budic.[43] Néanmoins, il semble difficile de donner un sens précis à ces variations, dans la mesure où un même épisode est désigné dans la table des chapitres par: 'De l'armée de Gontran qui quitta la Bretagne',[44] puis donne lieu à une description de la façon dont cette armée a quitté les Bretagnes:

> Lorsque l'armée quitta les Bretagnes, les plus robustes traversèrent le fleuve; mais les plus faibles et les pauvres qui étaient avec eux ne purent le traverser en même temps et comme ils étaient restés sur la rive de la Vilaine, Weroc, oublieux de son serment et des otages qu'il avait donnés, envoya Canaon son fils avec une armée.[45]

Lorsque Grégoire de Tours rédige ses *Histoires*, la domination des Britons permet l'emploi du terme de *Britannia* pour désigner des régions continentales. Mais le terme est le plus souvent mis au pluriel, pour désigner différentes zones associées à un pouvoir venu d'Outre-Manche. Une seule d'entre elle semble faire l'objet d'une localisation précise, lorsque Grégoire de Tours multiplie les indications sur les lieux des différentes batailles entre les armées franques et bretonnes, sur la Vilaine et sur l'Oust.[46] Ces délimitations sur la Vilaine et l'Oust sont redondantes avec ses indications, suivant lesquelles la domination des Britons ne concerne que le diocèse de Vannes. Celui-ci est bien décrit comme soumis, à moins d'être, brièvement, libéré du joug breton par l'intervention du roi franc:

> Quant à Ebrachaire, il s'avança jusqu'à la ville de Vannes et l'évêque Regalis envoya au-devant de lui ses clercs avec leurs croix et leurs chantres qui l'escortèrent jusqu'à la ville. [...] Nous ne sommes en rien fautifs à l'égard des rois nos maitres, dit l'évêque, et jamais nous n'avons eu la présomption de nous opposer à leurs intérêts, mais conquis par les Britons, nous avons été soumis à un dur joug.[47]

---

[43] Grégoire de Tours, *Libri Historiarum X*, v.16, p. 214. Voir Pietri, 'Grégoire de Tours'.

[44] Grégoire de Tours, *Libri Historiarum X*, liste des chapitres du livre x.9, p. 476: 'De exercitu Gunthchramni regis, qui in Brittaniam abiit'.

[45] Grégoire de Tours, *Libri Historiarum X*, x.9, p. 493: 'Egrediente autem exercitu a Brittaniis ac transeuntibus amnem robustiores, inferiores et pauperes, qui cum his erant, simul transire non potuerunt. Cumque in litus illud Vicinoniae amnis restitissent, Warocus, oblitus sacramenti atque obsedum, quos dederat, misit Canaonem filium suum cum exercitu'.

[46] Grégoire de Tours, *Libri Historiarum X*, v.26; x.9, pp. 232, 493. Voir Riché, 'Grégoire de Tours et l'Armorique'.

[47] Grégoire de Tours, *Libri Historiarum X*, x.9, p. 492: 'Ebracharius vero usque Venetus urbem accessit. Miserat enim ad eum obviam episcopus Regalis clericos suos cum crucibus et psallentio, qui eos usque ad urbem deduxerunt. [...] Nihil nos dominis nostris regibus culpabe-

5. ESPACE ET POUVOIRS EN BRETAGNE AUX PREMIERS SIÈCLES DU MOYEN ÂGE

Grégoire de Tours applique donc aux Britons un classement des individus en fonction de leurs évêques. Helmut Reimitz a pu montrer combien la vision de Grégoire de Tours d'une 'genealogy of pastoral power' lui était spécifique, s'inscrivait dans une réaction à l'égard des changements politiques contemporains et fut, après sa mort, l'objet de multiples actualisations.[48] L'évêque poursuit son œuvre d'ordonnancement du monde en attribuant à la domination des Bretons un diocèse précis, dont il se garde bien de préciser comment il était réparti entre les différents chefs bretons. La référence à l'organisation administrative et religieuse de la Gaule romaine permet de souligner la continuité, par les évêques, de l'histoire du Salut.

D'un autre côté, Grégoire souligne que les diocèses de Rennes et Nantes ne font absolument pas partie de la *Britannia*. Certes, il mentionne plusieurs expéditions de pillage aux alentours de ces deux villes:

> Les Britons dévastèrent aussi la région de Rennes en l'incendiant, la pillant et faisant des prisonniers. Ils progressèrent en bataillant jusqu'au village de *Cornutium*.[49]

Pendant cette année les Britons firent d'importants ravages aux alentours de la ville de Nantes et de celle de Rennes. Ils emportent un immense butin, dévastent les champs, dépouillent les vignes de leurs fruits et emmènent des prisonniers.[50]

> Cette même année les Britons soumirent les territoires de Nantes et de Rennes à un sévère pillage; ils vendangèrent les vignes, dévastèrent les cultures et emmenèrent en captivité la population des domaines sans rien tenir des promesses antérieures et non seulement ils ne tinrent pas leurs promesses, mais en outre ils dénigrèrent nos rois.[51]

---

lis sumus nec umquam contra utilitatem eorum superbi extitimus, sed in captivitate Brittanorum positi, gravi iugo subditi sumus'.

[48] Reimitz, *History, Frankish Identity and the Framing of Western Ethnicity*, pp. 27–43; Reimitz, 'The Early Medieval Editions of Gregory of Tours' *Histories*'.

[49] Grégoire de Tours, *Libri Historiarum X*, v.29, p. 234: 'Brittani quoque graviter regionem Redonicam vastaverunt incendio, praeda, captivitate. Qui usque Cornutium vicum debellando progressi sunt'. Monteil, 'Les agglomérations', p. 29, rappelle que l'identification avec Corps-Nuds reste hypothétique car aucun vestige antique n'y a été trouvé.

[50] Grégoire de Tours, *Libri Historiarum X*, v.31, p. 236: 'Brittani eo anno valde infesti circa urbem fuere Namneticam atque Redonicam. Qui inmensam auferentes praedam, agros pervadunt, vineas a fructibus vacuant et captivus adducunt'.

[51] Grégoire de Tours, *Libri Historiarum X*, ix.24, p. 444: 'Brittani eo anno graviter terraturium Namneticum Redonicumque praedae subiecerunt, vindimiantes vineas, culturas devastantes ac populum villarum abducentes captivum, nihilque de promissis superioribus costodi-

Mais ces raids ne correspondent pas à une implantation durable, qui n'est évoquée que dans le pays de Vannes, *in Vinitico*, où est rapporté le butin:

> Quant à Weroc, oublieux de son serment et de son engagement, il négligea tout ce qu'il avait promis, dévasta les vignes des Nantais et cueillant la vendange, transporta le vin dans le pays vannetais.[52]

Plusieurs fois, Grégoire de Tours mentionne que les cités de Rennes et de Nantes reviennent sous l'autorité des rois francs, comme à propos de 586:

> Comme le duc Beppolène était constamment gourmandé par elle (Frédégonde) et qu'elle ne lui rendait pas les honneurs dus à sa personne, lui se voyant méprisé s'en alla auprès du roi Gontran. Ayant obtenu de lui le pouvoir ducal sur les cités qui appartenaient à Clotaire, fils du roi Chilpéric, il s'y rendit pourvu d'une grande autorité; mais il ne fut pas accueilli par les habitants de Rennes.[53]

L'autorité remise en question est ici disputée entre les différents rois francs, et leurs représentants, dont la guerre civile dure depuis 575. Mais Rennes semble échapper à toute domination durable des Britons. De même, Nantes peut être ravagée, mais les chefs des Britons reconnaissent qu'il ne s'agit pas de leur domination légitime:

> Les Britons, ayant alors envahi le territoire nantais, y firent des ravages; ils pillèrent des domaines et emmenèrent des gens en captivité. [...] Ces personnages, s'étant rendus dans le pays nantais, exposèrent à Weroc et à Vidimaclus ce que le roi leur avait prescrit. Mais ceux-ci répliquèrent: nous savons nous aussi que ces cités reviennent au fils du roi Clotaire et que nous devons leur être soumis, nous n'hésitons donc pas à payer une composition pour tous les délits que nous avons commis.[54]

---

entes, et non solum non costodientes promissa, verum etiam detrahentes regibus nostris'.

[52] Grégoire de Tours, *Libri Historiarum X*, ix.18, p. 432: 'Warocus vero oblitus sacramenti et cautionis suae, omnia postposuit, quae promisit, vineas Namneticorum abstulit et vindimiam colligens, vinum in Vinitico transtulit'.

[53] Grégoire de Tours, *Libri Historiarum X*, viii.42, p. 408: 'Per quam cum Beppolenus dux valde fatigaretur nec iuxta personam suam ei honor debetus inpenderetur, cernens se dispici, ad Guntchramno regem abiit. A quo accepta potestate ducatus super civitates illas, quae ad Chlotharium, Chilperici regis filium, pertinebant, cum magna potentia pergit, sed a Rhedonicis non est receptus'.

[54] Grégoire de Tours, *Libri Historiarum X*, ix 18, pp. 431–32: 'Brittani quoque inruentes in termino Namnitico, praedas egerunt, pervadentes villas et captivus abducentes. [...] Qui euntes in termino Namnitico, locuti sunt cum Warocho et Vidimacle omnia quae rex praeciperat. At illi dixerunt: "Scimus et nos civitates istas Chlotharii regis filiis redebere et nos ipsis debere esse subiectus; tamen quae contra rationem gessimus cuncta componere non moramur"'.

5. ESPACE ET POUVOIRS EN BRETAGNE AUX PREMIERS SIÈCLES DU MOYEN ÂGE

Ainsi, Grégoire de Tours ne nie pas que ces cités soient à portée d'une attaque des Britons, mais il affirme que lorsqu'ils y pénètrent, c'est un acte de guerre et de provocation envers les rois francs.[55]

Grégoire de Tours envisage donc selon les cas une Bretagne ou des Bretagnes continentales, pour laquelle il ne décrit comme limites que celles du diocèse de Vannes, sur la Vilaine et l'Oust. En dehors de ce diocèse, il considère que les diocèses de Rennes et Nantes peuvent être pillés par les Britons, mais qu'ils ne peuvent y prétendre à une implantation durable en raison du pouvoir des rois francs.

Dans le cas de Nantes, son extériorité par rapport au pouvoir des Britons parait confirmée par la Vie d'Ermeland, fondateur du monastère d'Indre: composée entre la fin du VIIIe siècle et le début du IXe siècle, elle relate des événements supposés se dérouler vers 700 et ignore tout des Britons, qu'elle ne mentionne jamais.[56] B. Judic en déduit qu' 'une aristocratie gallo-franque tenait alors fermement l'estuaire de la Loire et pouvait ignorer les menaces des Bretons ou *a fortiori* les menaces lointaines et encore inconnues des Normands'.[57] Néanmoins, les descriptions de Grégoire de Tours rentrent dans son système de représentation de la fonction épiscopale, et de l'économie du Salut, où les limites héritées des diocèses jouent un rôle idéologique structurant, ce qui ne correspondait pas forcément aux perceptions de ses contemporains.

L'emploi du terme de *Britannia*, au singulier ou au pluriel, ne semble pas s'imposer à tous dans la seconde moitié du VIe siècle. Ainsi, Marius d'Avenches peut décrire les mêmes événements de l'année 560 que Grégoire sans mentionner ce terme, en indiquant simplement que les événements eurent lieu 'chez les Britons'.[58] Néanmoins, l'usage de *Britannia* pour décrire un espace continental n'est pas une exclusivité de Grégoire de Tours, car il apparait aussi dans la *Vie de saint Pair* par Venance Fortunat, presque contemporaine, car elle fut rédigée entre 565, date de son arrivée en Gaule et 591, date à laquelle s'arrêta sa production littéraire, en lien avec son élévation peu après sur le siège épiscopal de Poitiers.[59] Venance mourut avant 614. Les auteurs de la *Prosopographie chrétienne de la Gaule* envisagent plus précisément une rédaction vers 573, en rai-

---

[55] Grégoire de Tours, *Libri Historiarum X*, IX.24, p. 444, cité *supra*, p. 91.

[56] Commentaire dans Brett, 'In the Margins of History?', p. 38. *Vita Ermenlandi*.

[57] Judic, 'Quelques réflexions sur la *Vita Ermelandi*'.

[58] Marius d'Avenches, *Chronique*, p. 237: 'ad Brittanos'.

[59] Venance Fortunat, *Vita S. Paterni*; Pietri et Heijmans, éd., *Prosopographie chrétienne*, pp. 801–22.

son de la rencontre avec Romacharius, évêque de Coutances, à l'occasion d'une dédicace célébrée ensemble à Nantes avant 573, peu après la mort de Paterne/ Pair.[60] Cet évêque de Coutances aurait pu être l'intermédiaire entre Venance Fortunat et Martianus, abbé du monastère fondé à Sesciacus par Pair, qui lui demanda de rédiger la vie de son fondateur.

L'usage de *Britannia* par Venance Fortunat diverge de celui de Grégoire de Tours, bien que les deux auteurs aient été liés et que leurs écrits soient presque contemporains.[61] Il décrit ainsi l'action de Pair: 'Enfin, de nombreux monastères sont par lui dédiés à Dieu dans les cités de Coutances, Bayeux, Le Mans, Avranches et Rennes en Bretagne (*Britanniae*).'[62]

À travers le terme de *civitates*, il semble bien qu'il soit possible ici de comprendre les diocèses de Coutances, Bayeux, Le Mans, Avranches et Rennes. La prégnance de la Bretagne de la seconde moitié du Moyen Âge est telle que l'on considère le plus souvent que la précision géographique en Bretagne ne concerne que le diocèse de Rennes.[63] B. Krusch ponctue pour limiter la précision au dernier diocèse évoqué, mais il s'est ici contenté de collationner un manuscrit du XIIIe siècle et l'édition de Mabillon, ce qui nous prive de tout retour à la version manuscrite pour, éventuellement, établir la ponctuation.[64]

Pourtant, comme nous l'avons vu, aucune des cités ci-dessus désignées ne correspond à l'espace attribué par Grégoire de Tours à la *Britannia*, ni Rennes ni aucune des autres. C. Brett a suggéré qu'il s'agissait d'une extension de l'implantation bretonne, au moment où Fortunat rédige sa *Vie*, mais la proximité des rédactions de Grégoire de Tours et de Venance Fortunat, qui rédigent tous deux dans le dernier tiers du VIe siècle des récits concernant des événements vingt à dix ans antérieurs, ne permet pas de lever la contradiction pour leurs

---

[60] Pietri et Heijmans, éd., *Prosopographie chrétienne*, p. 810. Venance Fortunat, *Vita S. Patern*, éd. et trad. Santorelli, p. 11 et suivantes, envisage une rédaction entre 566 et 576, en raison de la succession des vies de saint rédigées par Venance.

[61] Reydellet, 'Tours et Poitiers'; Roberts, 'Venantius Fortunatus and Gregory of Tours'.

[62] Venance Fortunat, *Vita S. Paterni*, § 33, éd. Krusch, p. 36: 'Denique per civitates Constantiam scilicet, Baiocas, Cinomannis, Abrincas, Redones Britanniae multa monasteria per eum domino sont fundata'.

[63] Voir les remarques d'A. Y. Bourgès, 'La *Vita Paterni* de Venance Fortunat'.

[64] Voir la description de Krusch dans Venance Fortunat, *Vita S. Paterni*, éd. Krusch, pp. xv–xvi. Venance Fortunat, *Vita S. Paterni*, éd et trad. Santorelli, se contente de traduire le texte de Krusch et n'apporte rien sur ce point.

lecteurs.[65] Ceux-ci devaient être capables de comprendre que 'Britannia' désignait un espace dominé par des Bretons où, suivant les cas, se trouvait ou ne se trouvait pas intégré le diocèse de Rennes.

Suivant son hagiographe, Paterne/Pair mène son action entre Coutances, Bayeux, Le Mans, Avranches, et Rennes.[66] Cet espace ne correspond pas aux divisions héritées de l'empire romain, car il est à cheval entre la province ecclésiastique de Rouen et celle de Tours, les Lyonnaises seconde et troisième. Or pour Venance Fortunat, le diocèse de Rennes est un élément central et structurant du parcours du saint. Ainsi, ce sont les évêques Melaine (de Rennes), Leontianus (de Coutances) et Vigor (de Bayeux) qui lui apparaissent pour le faire ordonner évêque (avant 560).[67] De même, quand il opère un miracle dans la villa non identifiée de Teudeciaco, il soigne une femme de Rennes, *femina civis Redonica*.[68] En revanche, à sa mort, avant 573, ne sont présents que les évêques de Coutances (Lauto) et de Bayeux (Leucadius).[69]

L'espace désigné par Venance comme *Britannia* ne correspond pas à une zone reproduisant exclusivement des toponymes brittoniques, qu'il s'agisse seulement de Rennes ou de toutes les autres cités. La toponymie, en relevant les toponymes en *plou* ou en *gui*, ou la ligne de parler du breton établie par J. Loth ne permettent pas non plus d'établir des limites sur l'Oust et la Vilaine telles que les mentionne Grégoire de Tours.[70] L'étude attentive des premiers usages continentaux de la *Britannia* ou des *Britanniae* nous porte donc à nous affranchir des limites toponymiques qui ne sont perceptibles, au plus tôt, que pour l'époque carolingienne, et de nous contenter de constater la fluidité des appellations dans la seconde moitié du VIe siècle.[71] Avant le IXe siècle, le terme de *Britannia* ne semble renvoyer ni à un espace précis, bien que Grégoire de Tours veuille le cantonner au diocèse de Vannes, ni à une aire linguistique repérable par la toponymie. Il ne correspond pas non plus à un espace politique et religieux particulier, car Pair évolue en *Britannia*, mais fonde des monastères jusqu'au Mans et à Bayeux, rencontre le roi franc Childebert et participe au concile de Paris de 561. Bref, il semble qu'au VIe siècle, aucun territoire fixe lié

---

[65] Brett, 'The Hare and the Tortoise?', p. 88.

[66] Voir 'Paternus' dans Pietri et Heijmans, éd., *Prosopographie chrétienne*, pp. 1430–32.

[67] Venance Fortunat, *Vita S. Paterni*, § 46, éd. Krusch, pp. 36–37.

[68] Venance Fortunat, *Vita S. Paterni*, § 49, éd. Krusch, p. 37.

[69] Venance Fortunat, *Vita S. Paterni*, § 53, éd. Krusch, p. 37.

[70] Tanguy, 'La limite linguistique'.

[71] Voir l'hypothèse défendue par Lunven, 'L'espace du diocèse'.

à une communauté particulière ne semble pouvoir être définie derrière l'appellation de *Britannia*.[72]

Un dernier point d'étude de l'usage de *Britannia* aux VIIe–VIIIe siècles pourrait être la *Vie ancienne de Samson*.[73] J'avais proposé que le terme de *Britannia*, à propos de l'intervention en Domnonée (1.59), y désigne la Grande-Bretagne, mais je me rallie au contre argument, développé par R. Sowerby et J.-C. Poulin, en lien avec l'usage opposé de *Romania*, qui désigne une autre partie du continent.[74] Après les avoir lus, il me semble que l'on peut retenir la divergence de l'usage du terme de *Britannia*, employé deux fois pour décrire le continent, au contraire du reste de la *Vita*, comme l'une des traces des différentes étapes de rédaction de l'œuvre, entre la *Vita primigenia* et le remanieur dolois. Pour les questions de désignation d'un territoire des Bretons, cela revient à supposer que cette désignation était négligée par le rédacteur de la *Vita primigenia* en Cornouailles au VIIe siècle, mais employée sur le continent, à la fin du VIIe ou au VIIIe siècle par le rédacteur de la *Vie* qui nous est parvenue.[75] Dans celle-ci, *Britannia* et *Romania* désignent deux espaces continentaux différenciés, mais où Childebert apparait comme une autorité de référence commune et où intervient Samson. Cette *Britannia* était donc disputée entre différents chefs bretons, ici Conomor et Judual, et perméable aux influences religieuses insulaires et franques.

Comme l'a fait remarquer C. Brett, au concile de Chalon, rassemblé sous l'autorité du roi de Neustrie entre 647 et 654, se trouvaient réunis cinq évêques sur les sept de la province de Rouen, où il ne manquait que les évêques d'Avranches et d'Évreux, et quatre évêques (Tours, Nantes, Le Mans et Rennes) sur les huit de la province de Tours.[76] L'espace où avait évolué Pair, associé à la *Britannia* par Venance, était donc d'une certaine manière, au moins par la présence aux conciles, intégré à l'Église franque moins d'un siècle après ses écrits.

---

[72] Contrairement aux communautés rurales bretonnes du IXe siècle, telles que les évoque Davies, 'Population, Territory and Community Membership', pp. 298–99.

[73] Vie ancienne de Samson de Dol.

[74] Sowerby, 'The Lives of St Samson', p. 6, n. 28; Poulin, 'La circulation de l'information', pp. 58–59 et 73.

[75] Les arguments avancés par Poulin, 'La circulation de l'information', pp. 67–71, pour une datation tardive me semblent intéressants, mais la tradition de Julien Pomère ou du Pseudo-Bède est trop peu connue pour être dirimante.

[76] Brett, 'In the Margins of History?', p. 34; Concile de Chalon, in *Les canons des conciles mérovingiens*, pp. 550–63.

5. ESPACE ET POUVOIRS EN BRETAGNE AUX PREMIERS SIÈCLES DU MOYEN ÂGE   97

Un jalon chronologique important de l'usage du terme de *Britannia*, après le singulier et le pluriel employés par Grégoire de Tours, est alors la *Chronique* dite de Frédégaire, composée entre environ 660 et 714.[77] Elle décrit seulement les événements de 590 comme une guerre entre Francs et Bretons sur les rives de la Vilaine, sans mentionner de *Britannia*. Néanmoins, elle emploie ce terme pour mentionner la soumission du roi des Bretons Judicaël, et celle du 'royaume qu'il gouvernait en Bretagne', *regnum quem regibat Brittaniae*, ce qui sous-entend qu'il aurait existé plusieurs royaumes dans l'espace alors désigné comme *Britannia*.[78]

Ainsi, pour les auteurs des royaumes francs des VIe et VIIe siècles, il existe un espace que l'on peut nommer la Bretagne ou les Bretagnes, en lien avec la domination de Britons qui s'y sont installés depuis l'île voisine. Mais ces territoires, fractionnés entre différents chefs, ne donnent lieu qu'à des indications géographiques floues et contradictoires. La Vilaine en constitue parfois la limite, Rennes est parfois située en Bretagne, mais le plus souvent en dehors. À l'exception du diocèse de Vannes, le terme est mentionné en lien avec des manifestations du pouvoir royal franc, en Domnonée pour saint Samson, dans le diocèse de Rennes, ou dans les diocèses de Rennes à Coutances pour saint Pair, dans le royaume de Judicaël pour la *Chronique de Frédégaire*. Si les noms de la plupart des princes bretons renvoient à une langue brittonique, seule la *Vie ancienne de Samson* mentionne l'usage d'une *Brittanica lingua*.[79] Néanmoins, de nombreux lieux d'action de Samson, comme le palais de Childebert (1.54) ou les bords de Seine (1.38 et 58) ne peuvent correspondre à une toponymie bretonne et montrent son action en dehors de cette communauté linguistique.

Il faut donc renoncer à associer *Britannia* à un espace politique délimité de domination des Bretons en Armorique avant le IXe siècle. Celui-ci restait mobile, au gré de fragmentations politiques mouvantes, probablement négociées, et ne correspondait pas à une organisation religieuse à part. À la même époque, un évêque de Britons, en Galice, aurait évolué d'un évêque ayant autorité sur une communauté ethnique vers un évêque ayant une autorité territo-

---

[77] Sur ce point, voir en dernier lieu Collins, *Die Fredegar-Chroniken*, pp. 25–26, ainsi que l'introduction à leur traduction par Devillers et Meyers, *Frédégaire, Chronique des temps mérovingiens*, pp. 5–38.

[78] Frédégaire, *Chronique des temps mérovingiens*, IV.11, IV.78, pp. 75 et 179.

[79] Vie ancienne de Samson de Dol, 1.46, pp. 212–14.

riale suivant une hypothèse formulée par S. Young dont il me semble nécessaire de reprendre l'argumentation.[80]

Implantation des Britons en Galice

En Galice, les Suèves furent tout d'abord indépendants de la hiérarchie catholique, à la suite du choix de l'arianisme par le roi Remismond, allié au roi wisigothique Théodoric II (453–466).[81] C'est le roi suève Théodemir qui organisa le premier concile catholique de Braga, en 561, puis le concile de Lugo, en 569, pour définir l'organisation catholique du royaume, dont le *Parochiale Suevum*, rédigé entre 572 et 582 reproduit la liste diocésaine.[82] Cette organisation fut éphémère, car le roi wisigoth Léovigild conquit le royaume suève en 585. Le *Parochiale Suevum*, liste de provinces ecclésiastiques, de diocèses et de communautés religieuses, ne nous est parvenue que par diverses copies tardives, notamment par l'intermédiaire de l'évêque Pélage d'Oviedo au XIIe siècle, et fut sujette à de nombreuses interpolations. Le passage final, qui concerne des Britons ne fournissait cependant aucune base de revendication médiévale, et ne semble pas avoir été interpolé. Il indique, après douze provinces ecclésiastiques: 'au siège des Britons, les églises qui sont au sein des Britons, avec le monastère de Maxime, et celles qui sont dans les Asturies'.[83]

L'identification classique de ce monastère est le monastère Santa Maria de Bretoña à côté de Mondoñedo.[84] Elle apparait pour la première fois chez dom Plaine, en 1885: il identifie ce lieu sans autre argument que la toponymie, et l'associe à une charte de 830, qui rappelle un siège abandonné, *sedes Britoniensis*, ainsi qu'aux mentions d'un évêque Théodesindus de Britonia en 871–872.[85] Dans son article paru au début du XXIe siècle, S. Young reconnait que la charte est au moins en partie interpolée et que les mentions de Théodesindus résultent de forgeries du scriptorium d'Oviedo, dans la deuxième moitié du IXe siècle. Il reprend l'association avec Bretoña et suppose la transformation de ce siège en raison de la forme prise dans la tradition manuscrite.

---

[80] Young, 'The Bishops'. Ces suggestions ne sont pas discutées par Olson, 'Introduction', pp. 14–15.

[81] Dumézil, *Les racines chrétiennes de l'Europe*, pp. 270–74.

[82] Díaz, 'El *parrochiale suevum*'; Güisan, 'Lugo en los tiempos oscuros'.

[83] *Parochiale Suevum*, XIII.1, p. 420: 'Ad sedem Britonorum ecclesias que sunt intro Britones una cum monasterio Maximi et que in Asturiis sunt'.

[84] Voir par exemple, Koch, 'Britonia', p. 291.

[85] Plaine, 'L'ancien évêché de Britonia en Galice'.

Le deuxième concile de Braga, en 572, a conservé les souscriptions des participants, contrairement au concile de 561. La dernière est celle-ci: *Mailoc Britonensis ecclesiae episcopus his gestis subscripsi.*[86] Cette souscription et le *Parochiale Suevum* nous montrent ainsi vers 572 un groupe dont le nom évoque la *Britannia*, et dont l'organisation religieuse est distincte du reste de l'Église du royaume suève. Ici, leur présence a pu aboutir, à ce moment-là, à une reconnaissance de leur organisation religieuse et d'un espace à part, défini par des églises et à un monastère.

Après la conquête wisigothique, les souverains cherchèrent l'unité religieuse à travers l'arianisme, sous Léovigild, puis le catholicisme à la suite de la conversion de son fils Reccared, en 586.[87] Durant son règne, le catholicisme fut tout d'abord favorisé, sans interdire l'arianisme, puis le catholicisme devint seule religion officielle au concile de Tolède III (589).[88] La spécificité des Britons n'a pourtant pas été supprimée dans le contexte général d'affirmation du pouvoir territorial des évêques du royaume wisigothique.[89] Elle dura jusqu'à l'intervention du roi Recceswinth, que rappellent les évêques réunis au concile de Mérida en 666, qui décida que 'les limites de la province de Lusitanie, avec ses évêques et leurs églises, seront restaurées et ramenées sous l'autorité de la province et du siège métropolitain [de Mérida], conformément aux anciens canons.'[90]

Un siège spécifique est mentionné parmi les signataires du 4e concile de Tolède (633), du 7e et 8e concile de Tolède (646 et 653), et du 3e concile de Braga (675).[91] S. Young croit pouvoir relever dans ces mentions le passage d'un

---

[86] Édition du deuxième concile de Braga dans *Martini episcopi Bracarensis opera omnia*, p. 123.

[87] Dumézil, *Les racines chrétiennes de l'Europe*, pp. 275–83.

[88] Dumézil, *Les racines chrétiennes de l'Europe*, pp. 641–54.

[89] Martin, 'Les évêques visigothiques dans leur espace'; Díaz, 'Monasteries in a Peripheral Area', ne mentionne pas le monastère de Maxime, mais montre une particulière résistance au changement dans cette province.

[90] Martin, 'Les évêques visigothiques dans leur espace', p. 218. *Concile de Mérida*, VIII, in *Concilios visigóticos e hispano-romanos*, p. 331: 'ut terminos huius provinciae Lusitaniae cum suis episcopis eorumque parrochiis iuxte priorum cannonum sententias ad nomen provinciae et metropolitanam hanc sedem reduceret et restauraret'.

[91] 4e concile de Tolède, in *La colección canónica Hispana*, v, 270: 'Metopius in Christi nomine ecclesiae Brittaniensis episcopus subscripsi', 7e concile de Tolède, in *La colección canónica Hispana*, v, 361: 'Sonna ecclesiae Brittaniensis etsi indignus episcopus hoec statuta definiens subscripsi'. 8e concile de Tolède, in *La colección canónica Hispana*, v, 446: 'Mactericus presbyter Sonanni episcopi ecclesiae Brittaniensis'. 3e concile de Braga, in *Concilios visigóticos e hispano-romanos*, p. 379: 'Bela Britaniensis ecclesiae episcopus his constitutionibus interfui et subscribsi'. Young, 'The Bishops', p. 2, n. 4, indique qu'il n'a pas retenu une note de Fleuriot,

évêché ethnique à un évêché territorialisé, car les formes changeraient de *ecclesia Brittanorum* (dans le *Parochiale Suevum*) pour les formes *ecclesia Britonensis* (dominantes ensuite). Ainsi, serait désigné non plus un évêque des Britons mais un évêque de Britonia. Or, les collections canoniques qui nous ont transmis les souscriptions épiscopales ont connu trop de vicissitudes pour ne pas avoir été transformées au cours de la transmission manuscrite. S. Young ne l'a pas vu car son édition de référence ne proposait que la transcription d'un seul manuscrit pour ces conciles: le manuscrit D. I. 2 de la bibliothèque de l'Escorial.[92] Or, les souscriptions se présentent à chaque fois dans une liste formatée, et la forme des noms propres peut-être plus ou moins standardisée suivant les copistes, voire les choix de l'éditeur.

Pour le *Parochiale Suevum*, F. Glorie a repris l'édition de Pierre David de 1947, qui repose sur des manuscrits des XIIᵉ–XIIIᵉ siècles et des éditions modernes.[93] Les formes fluctuent entre A: *Britonnorum*, B, C: *Britoniorum*, D: *Britanorum*, mais aussi F: *Bretonicam*, H: *Bretunicam* et G: *Britonacensis teneat*.[94] Que retenir d'une telle fluctuation, si ce n'est la diversité des choix des copistes? Si l'on compare avec la tradition de la liste du concile de Braga, dont l'édition par C. Barlow reprend 11 manuscrits différents, du IXᵉ au XIIᵉ siècle, la forme parait très variable. Seuls cinq manuscrits donnent la forme *Britonensis*, retenue par l'éditeur, alors que six varient entre A: *brittono*, W: *britunorum*, VNO: *brittanorum*, M: *brittinorum*. La répartition de ces différentes formes dans le *stemma* proposé par l'éditeur n'apparait pas cohérente: les variantes viennent ici probablement davantage des copistes, qui ont plus ou moins lissé la diversité de la liste initiale, que des modèles manuscrits.[95] Les variantes font

---

Les origines de la Bretagne, p. 137, n. 36, sur un évêque Metonius qui viendrait du manuscrit Paris, BnF, latin 4280. Ce manuscrit du XIIᵉ siècle (voir la notice du site de *BnF*), désormais consultable en ligne en noir et blanc (sur Gallica: ark:/12148/btv1b9068478s), reprend des extraits de canons. On y trouve au fol. 115ᵛ, *Metonius de Britonnia episcopus* dans une liste des souscripteurs du concile de Tolède de 633 qui, curieusement, ne comporte qu'un souscripteur sur deux à partir des métropolitains. Il s'agit d'une copie défectueuse, où une colonne sur deux n'a pas été retenue. Les variations des noms propres sont importantes et il s'agit bien, *a priori*, de l'évêque Metopius retenu sous ce nom par l'édition la plus récente.

[92] *Concilios visigóticos e hispano-romanos*, pp. viii–ix. Sur cette édition, voir Dumézil, *Les racines chrétiennes de l'Europe*, p. 641 et suivantes. Sur le codex Vigilanus, de 974–976, voir la notice du site de Köln, Universitätsbibliothek, *Bibliotheca Legum*.

[93] David, *Études historiques*.

[94] *Parochiale Suevum*, p. 420.

[95] *Martini episcopi Bracarensis opera omnia*, p. 95.

ainsi penser que la forme 'Britonensis' pourrait résulter d'une standardisation par les copistes, sur le modèle de la liste des différents sièges qui précèdent, alors que la mention initiale leur était peu claire.

La forme du nom du diocèse en Galice parait plus stable dans les manuscrits de la *Collectio canonum Hispana*, qui transmet les conciles de Tolède. Mais si la plupart des manuscrits retiennent *ecclesiae Brittaniensis episcopus* pour le Metopius du quatrième concile de Tolède, avec des orthographes différentes, un manuscrit du IXe siècle propose *de Britonia*, tout comme il propose *de Oreto* pour l'évêque précédent et *de Tude* pour le suivant.[96] Les diversités initiales des listes épiscopales ont donc été lissées et standardisées suivant les différentes traditions manuscrites, et nous ne pouvons plus les reconstituer.

Le cas de la Galice nous fournit donc l'exemple d'une éphémère communauté chrétienne, associée à la présence de Britons, vers 572. Mais ce groupe fut rapidement intégré dans la hiérarchie religieuse au sein de la province ecclésiastique de Lugo, et les éventuelles spécificités de départ n'étaient plus rappelées que par le nom du siège épiscopal, qui disparut au siècle suivant. Les copistes, puis les éditeurs, ont hésité dans la transcription du nom de cet évêché, ce qui montre leur perplexité, mais ne nous indique pas comment interpréter ces mentions. Notre documentation ne nous permet pas d'associer ce groupe à un ensemble politique, social ou linguistique.[97] Son intégration semble avoir été très rapide. Nous pouvons donc seulement retenir le cas de la Galice pour illustrer l'existence éphémère d'un évêque briton sans siège précis, mais associé à certaines églises et à un monastère.[98] Il y eut plusieurs successeurs de cet évêque, sur un siège qui fut intégré dans le système épiscopal local après quelques générations.

Nous avons donc repéré, à travers l'étude de l'emploi du terme de *Britannia*, la désignation d'espaces différents et d'usages contradictoires entre deux auteurs de la deuxième moitié du VIe siècle. Les limites de ces *Britanniae* paraissent

---

[96] 4e concile de Tolède, in *La colección canónica Hispana*, v, 270. Le manuscrit Π, Paris, BnF, latin 3846, du début du IXe siècle, est utilisé dans l'édition pour représenter l'ensemble de la tradition α de cette collection canonique. Voir l'introduction de l'édition, pp. 12–13, et la description de ce manuscrit dans Mordek, *Bibliotheca capitularium regum Francorum manuscripta*, pp. 439–42.

[97] Seul le premier évêque, Mailoc, porte un nom brittonique, contrairement aux affirmations de Fleuriot, *Les origines de la Bretagne*, p. 137. Le nom de Sonna n'est pas spécifique, car il est aussi porté par un évêque d'Orense qui souscrit au 8e concile de Tolède, en 653 (*La colección canónica Hispana*, v, 443), et un évêque d'Osma au 13e concile de Tolède, en 683 (*La colección canónica Hispana*, VI, 259).

[98] En ce sens, Olson, 'Introduction', pp. 12–13.

floues, et elles ne sont associées ni à des communautés religieuses spécifiques, ni à des pouvoirs politiques indépendants, ni à des zones repérables par la toponymie bretonne postérieure. Elles ne peuvent donc directement expliquer ni les reconfigurations territoriales qui eurent lieu durant le premier siècle du pouvoir carolingien, marquées par le capitulaire de Herstal pour la création de diocèses territoriaux, ni les négociations des délégations de pouvoir lors de la guerre civile, à partir de 830.[99]

Les revendications des princes bretons du IXe siècle, qui acquirent des Carolingiens un titre royal et un territoire, sont, à mes yeux, à mettre davantage en rapport avec les équilibres transformés au sein du royaume franc qu'avec des communautés ou des territoires brittoniques structurés autour d'un héritage insulaire dont j'ai essayé de démontrer la plasticité. Nous avons ici entr'aperçu des communautés linguistiques, des espaces religieux éphémères, des territoires politiques mouvants, mais jamais ces trois éléments n'ont été unifiés dans la durée. À propos de l'Espagne wisigothique, M. Kulikowski a défendu l'idée que la corrélation entre la culture, l'identité ethnique et les limites géographiques nécessitait une force politique durable, que seuls purent exercer les Arabes et les Carolingiens au haut Moyen Âge.[100] En suivant cette voie d'explication, la naissance d'une Bretagne continentale ne serait pas à chercher avant le IXe siècle. Rien ne témoigne auparavant de la constitution de communautés brittoniques séparées, établies sur des territoires marqués par une toponymie en langue bretonne, soudées autour de pratiques religieuses spécifiques.

Peut-être ce silence est-il le fruit de notre documentation, qui s'arrête aux confins des diocèses de Vannes et de Rennes. Mais peut-être ce silence est-il aussi significatif du fait qu'il existait dans la péninsule armoricaine des populations employant un langage brittonique et des chefs fiers de leurs origines d'outre-Manche, mais que ces groupes n'avaient pas constitué un territoire particulier. Ils exerçaient leur pouvoir sur des espaces fragmentés et éphémères, qui furent recomposés lors des affrontements et des fondations religieuses des VIIIe–IXe siècles.

Magali Coumert a soutenu en 2005 à l'université de Nanterre une thèse portant sur les *Récits d'origine des peuples au haut Moyen Âge (550–830)*, publiée en 2007 dans la collection des Études Augustiniennes, et en 2020, une habilitation à diriger les recherches dont le mémoire inédit portait sur les manuscrits de la loi salique. De 2006 à 2021, elle était maître de conférences à l'université de Brest et depuis 2021, elle est professeur d'histoire médiévale à l'université de Tours.

---

[99] *Capitulaire de Herstal* (779), 1, in *Capitularia regum Francorum* I, 20, p. 47.

[100] Kulikowski, 'Ethnicity, Rulership, and Early Medieval Frontiers'.

5. ESPACE ET POUVOIRS EN BRETAGNE AUX PREMIERS SIÈCLES DU MOYEN ÂGE — 103

Bibliographie

Sources

Bibliotheca Legum, El Escorial, Real Biblioteca de San Lorenzo D. I. 2 <http://www.leges. uni-koeln.de/mss/handschrift/el-escorial-rb-d-I-2/> [consultée le 30 octobre 2018]

BnF, Latin 4280 <https://archivesetmanuscrits.bnf.fr/ark:/12148/cc630723 [consultée le 30 octobre 2018]

Les canons des conciles mérovingiens (VIe–VIIe siècles), éd. Ch. De Clerq, trad. J. Gaudemet et B. Basdevant, 2 vols (Paris: Éditions du Cerf, 1989)

Capitularia regum Francorum I, éd. A. Boretius, *MGH LL* (Hanover: Hahn, 1883)

La colección canónica Hispana, V et VI, éd. G. Martínez Díez et F. Rodriguez (Madrid: Consejo Superior de Investigaciones Científicas, Instituto Enrique Flórez, 1992, 2002)

Concilia Galliae A. 314–506, éd. Ch. Munier (Turnhout: Brepols, 1963)

Concilios visigóticos e hispano-romanos, éd. J. Vives (Barcelone: Consejo Superior de Investigaciones Científicas, Instituto Enrique Flórez, 1963)

Frédégaire, *Chronique des temps mérovingiens (Livre IV et continuations)*, éd. J. M. Wallace-Hadrill, trad. O. Devillers et J. Meyers (Turnhout: Brepols, 2001)

Gildas, *The Ruin of Britain and Other Works*, éd. et trad. M. Winterbottom (London: Phillimore, 1978)

Grégoire de Tours,, *Libri Historiarum X*, éd. B. Krusch et W. Levison, *MGH SS RM* I.1 (Hanover: Hahn, 1951); trad. W. Giesebrecht et R. Buchner, *Zehn Bücher Geschichten. Gregor von Tours*, 2 vols (Darmstadt: Wissenschaftliche Buchgesellschaft, 1955–1956) (allemand); trad. R. Latouche, *Histoire des Francs. Gregoire de Tours*, 2 vols (Paris: Les Belles Lettres, 1963–1965) (français); trad. L. Thorpe, *The History of the Franks. Gregory of Tours* (Harmondsworth: Penguin, 1974) (anglais)

Isidore de Seville, *Étymologies, Livre 15, Les constructions et les terres*, éd. et trad. J.-Y. Guillaumin (Paris: Les Belles Lettres, 2016)

Jordanes,, *De Origine Actibusque Getarum*, éd. Fr. Giunta et A. Grillone (Rome: Istituto storico italiano per il Medio Evo, 1991); trad. O. Devillers, *Histoire des Goths* (Paris: Les Belles Lettres, 1995)

Marius d'Avenches, *Chronique*, éd. Th. Mommsen, in *Chronica Minora saec. IV. V. VI. VII* II *MGH AA* XI (Berlin: Weidmann, 1894), pp. 225–39

Martin de Braga, *Œuvres,* éd. C. W. Barlow, in *Martini episcopi Bracarensis opera omnia* (New Haven: Yale University Press, 1950)

Nicolas Ier, *Lettres*, éd. E. Perels, in *Epistolae Karolini aevi* IV, *MGH Epp.* VI (Berlin: Weidmann, 1925), pp. 257–690

Notitia Galliarum, éd. Th. Mommsen, in *Chronica Minora saec. IV. V. VI. VII* II, *MGH AA* IX (Berlin: Weidmann, 1892), pp. 552–612

Parochiale Suevum, éd. F. Glorie, in *Itineraria et alia geographica*, *CC SL* CLXXV (Turnhout: Brepols, 1965), pp. 411–20

Sidoine Apollinaire, *Lettres*, éd. et trad. A. Loyen, 2 vols (Paris: Les Belles Lettres, 1970)

Venance Fortunat, *Vita S. Paterni* (BHL 6477), éd. B. Krusch, *MGH AA* iv.2 (Berlin: Weidmann, 1885), pp. 33–37; éd. et trad. P. Santorelli, *Vite dei santi Paterno e Marcello. Venanzio Fortunato* (Naples: Loffredo, 2015)

Vie ancienne de Samson de Dol (BHL 7478), éd. et trad. P. Flobert, Sources d'histoire médiévale (Paris: CNRS, 1997)

Vita Ermenlandi (BHL 3851), éd. W. Levison, *Passiones vitaeque sanctorum aevi Merovingici III, MGH SS RM* v (Hanover: Hahn, 1910), pp. 674–710

Études

Barrett, G. D., et G. Woudhuysen, 'Remigius and the "Important News" of Clovis Rewritten', *Antiquité Tardive. Revue Internationale d'Histoire et d'Archéologie (IVe–VIIe siècle)*, 24 (2016), 471–500

Basdevant-Gaudemet, B., 'L'évêque, d'après la législation de quelques conciles mérovingiens', in *Clovis. Histoire et mémoire*, i: *Clovis et son temps, l'événement*, éd. M. Rouche (Paris: Presses de l'université Sorbonne, 1997), pp. 471–94

Bourgès, A. Y., 'La *Vita Paterni* de Venance Fortunat', disponible sur <http://hagio-historiographiemedievale.blogspot.fr/2012/06/la-vita-paterni-de-venance-fortunat-et.html> [consulté le 28 novembre 2017]

Brett, C., 'The Hare and the Tortoise? *Vita Prima Sancti Samsonis, Vita Paterni* and Merovingian Hagiography', in *St Samson of Dol and the Earliest History of Brittany, Cornwall and Wales*, éd. L. Olson, SCH, 37 (Woodbridge: Boydell, 2017), pp. 83–101

——, 'In the Margins of History? The Breton March from Dagobert to Charlemagne', in *Histoires des Bretagnes 5. En Marge*, éd. H. Bouget et M. Coumert (Brest: CRBC, 2015), pp. 31–46

——, 'Soldiers, Saints and States? The Breton Migrations Revisited', *CMCS*, 61 (2011), 1–56

——, avec F. Edmonds et P. Russell, *Brittany and the Atlantic Archipelago 450–1200: Contact, Myth and History* (Cambridge: Cambridge University Press, 2021)

Brunterc'h, J.-P., 'Le duché du Maine et la Marche de Bretagne', in *La Neustrie. Les pays au nord de la Loire de 650 à 850*, éd. H. Atsma, Beihefte der Francia, 16 (Sigmaringen: Thorbecke, 1989), pp. 29–127

Camby, C., 'Limites politiques oubliées: Armorique et Bretagne – Critique de sources', *MSHAB*, 86 (2008), 89–105

Charles-Edwards, T., *Wales and the Britons 350–1064*, The History of Wales, 1 (Oxford: Oxford University Press, 2014)

Chédeville, A., 'Francs et Bretons pendant la première moitié du VIe siècle: avant la rupture', in *Clovis. Histoire et mémoire i. Clovis et son temps, l'événement*, éd. M. Rouche (Paris: Presses de l'université Sorbonne, 1997), pp. 899–915

——, et H. Guillotel, *La Bretagne des saints et des rois V^e–Xe siècle*, Histoire de la Bretagne, 6 (Rennes: Ouest-France, 1984)

Collins, R., *Die Fredegar-Chroniken*, MGH Studien und Texte, 44 (Hanover: Hahn, 2007)

5. ESPACE ET POUVOIRS EN BRETAGNE AUX PREMIERS SIÈCLES DU MOYEN ÂGE

Coumert, M., 'Les marqueurs de masculinité entre Antiquité et Moyen Âge en Occident (IVe–VIIe siècle)', in *Une histoire sans les hommes est-elle possible? Genre et masculinités*, éd. A.-M. Sohn, Sociétés, espaces, temps (Lyon: ENS Éditions, 2013), pp. 96–108

——, *Origine des peuples. Les récits du haut Moyen Âge occidental (550–850)* (Paris: Institut d'études augustiniennes, 2007)

——, 'Le peuplement de l'Armorique', in *Histoires des Bretagnes. Les mythes fondateurs*, éd. M. Coumert et H. Tetrel (Brest: CRBC, 2010), pp. 15–42

——, 'Les relations entre Grande et Petite Bretagne au premier Moyen Âge', *MSHAB*, 91 (2013), 187–202

David, P., *Études historiques sur la Galice et le Portugal du VIe au XIIe siècle*, Collection portugaise, 7 (Lisbonne: Livraría Portugália, 1947)

Davies, W., 'Populations, Territory and Community Membership: Contrasts and Conclusions', in *People and Space in the Middle Ages, 300–1300*, éd. W. Davies, G. Halsall, et A. Reynolds, Studies in the Early Middle Ages, 15 (Turnhout: Brepols, 2006), pp. 295–307

Díaz, P. C., 'Monasteries in a Peripheral Area: Seventh-Century Gallaecia', in *Topographies of Power in the Early Middle Ages*, éd. M. De Jong et F. Theuws, Transformation of the Roman World, 6 (Leiden: Brill, 2001), pp. 329–59

——, 'El *parrochiale suevum*: organización eclesiástica, poder político y poblamiento en la *Gallaecia* tardoantigua', in *Homenaje a José Maria Blázquez*, éd. J. Alvar, 6 vols (Madrid: Ediciones Clásicas, 1998), VI, 35–47

Duchesne, L., 'Lovocat et Catihern, prêtres bretons du temps de saint Melaine', *Revue de Bretagne et de Vendée*, 7 (1885), 3–19

Dumézil, B., *Les racines chrétiennes de l'Europe. Conversion et liberté dans les royaumes barbares, V[e]–VIIIe siècle* (Paris, Fayard, 2005)

Fahy, D., 'When Did the Britons Become Bretons? A Note on the Foundation of Brittany', *Welsh History Review*, 2 (1964–1965), 111–24

Ferdière, A., *Les Gaules, IIe s. av. J.C. – Ve s. ap. J.C.* (Paris: Colin, 2005)

——, *La Gaule Lyonnaise* (Paris: Picard, 2011)

Fleuriot, L., *Les origines de la Bretagne*, Bibliothèque historique (Paris: Payot, 1980)

Galliou, P. et J.-M. Simon, *Le castellum de Brest et la défense de la péninsule armoricaine au cours de l'Antiquité tardive*, Archéologie et culture (Rennes: Presses universitaires, 2015)

Garault, C., '*La Vita Sancti Machutis* par Bili: reflets des enjeux territoriaux liés au pouvoir épiscopal dans les années 870 en Haute Bretagne', in *Genèse des espaces politiques (IXe– XIIe siècle). Autour de la question spatiale dans les royaumes francs et post-carolingiens*, éd. G. Bührer-Thierry, S. Patzold, et J. Schneider, Haut Moyen Âge, 28 (Turnhout: Brepols, 2017), pp. 189–95

Giot, P.-R., P. Guignon, et B. Merdrignac, *Les premiers Bretons d'Armorique* (Rennes: Presses universitaires, 2003)

Güisan, J. M. N., 'Lugo en los tiempos oscuros. Las menciones literarias de la ciudad entre los siglos V y X (III)', *Boletín do museo provincial de Lugo*, 8 (1997–1998), 177–94

Guy, B., 'The Breton Migration: A New Synthesis', *Zeitschrift für celtische Philologie*, 61 (2014), 101–56

Judic, B., 'Quelques réflexions sur la *Vita Ermelandi*', *Revue du Nord*, 86 (2004), 499–510

Koch, J. T., 'Britonia', in *Celtic Culture. A Historical Encyclopedia*, éd. J. T. Koch, 5 vols (Santa Barbara, CA: ABC-CLIO, 2006), I, 291

Kulikowski, M., 'Ethnicity, Rulership, and Early Medieval Frontiers', in *Borders, Barriers and Ethnogenesis. Frontiers in Late Antiquity and the Middle Ages*, éd. Fl. Curta (Turnhout: Brepols, 2005), pp. 248–54

Le Gall-Tanguy, R., 'La formation des espaces diocésains en Léon, Cornouaille et Trégor (Vᵉ–XIIIᵉ siècle)', in *Ériger et borner diocèses et principautés au Moyen-Âge. Limites et frontières II*, éd. N. Baron, S. Boisselier, Cl. François, et Fl. Sabaté (Villeneuve d'Ascq: Presses universitaires du Septentrion, 2017), pp. 21–44

Lienhard, T., 'Remarques à propos des partages territoriaux mérovingiens dans la seconde moitié du Vᵉ siècle', in *Coopétition: Rivaliser, coopérer dans les sociétés du haut Moyen Âge (500–1100)*, éd. R. Le Jan, G. Bührer-Thierry, et S. Gasparri (Turnhout: Brepols, 2018), pp. 92–102

Lunven, A., *Du diocèse à la paroisse. Évêchés de Rennes, Dol et Saint-Malo (Vᵉ–XIIIᵉ siècle)* (Rennes: Presses universitaires, 2014)

——, 'L'espace du diocèse à l'époque carolingienne: l'apport des formules de datation des actes du cartulaire de Redon', in *Genèse des espaces politiques (IXᵉ–XIIᵉ siècle). Autour de la question spatiale dans les royaumes francs et post-carolingiens*, éd. G. Bührer-Thierry, S. Patzold, et J. Schneider, Haut Moyen Âge, 28 (Turnhout: Brepols, 2017), pp. 167–87

Martin, C., 'Les évêques visigothiques dans leur espace: de l'autonomie à l'intégration', in *Les élites et leurs espaces. Mobilité, rayonnement, domination (du VIᵉ au XIᵉ siècle)*, éd. Ph. Depreux, F. Bougard, et R. Le Jan, Haut Moyen Âge, 5 (Turnhout: Brepols, 2007), pp. 207–23

Mazel, F., *L'évêque et le territoire. L'invention médiévale de l'espace (Vᵉ–XIIIᵉ siècles)* (Paris: Éditions du Seuil, 2016)

Merdrignac, B., et L. Plouchart, 'La fondation des évêchés bretons: question de l'histoire religieuse à la géographie sociale', in *L'espace du diocèse. Genèse d'un territoire dans l'Occident médiéval (Vᵉ–XIIIᵉ siècle)*, éd. F. Mazel (Rennes: Presses universitaires, 2008), pp. 143–63

Monteil, M., 'Les agglomérations de la province de Lyonnaise Troisième (Bretagne et Pays de la Loire). Entre abandon, perduration et nouvelles créations (IIIᵉ–VIᵉ s. ap. J.-C.)', *Gallia*, 74 (2017), 15–37

Mordek, H., *Bibliotheca capitularium regum Francorum manuscripta: Überlieferung und Traditionszusammenhang der fränkischen Herrschererlasse* (Munich: Monumenta Germaniae Historica, 1995)

Murray, A. C., 'The Composition of the *Histories* of Gregory of Tours and its Bearing on the Political Narrative', in *A Companion to Gregory of Tours*, éd. A. C. Murray, Brill's Companions to the Christian Tradition, 63 (Leiden: Brill, 2015), pp. 63–101

Noble, T., 'Pope Nicholas I and the Franks: Politics and Ecclesiology in the Ninth Century', in *Religious Franks. Religion and Power in the Frankish Kingdoms. Studies in Honour of Mayke de Jong*, éd. R. Meens, D. van Espelo, B. van den Hoven van Genderen, J. Raaijmakers, I. van Renswoude, et C. van Rhijn (Manchester: Manchester University Press, 2016), pp. 472–88

Olson, L., 'Introduction', in *St Samson of Dol and the Earliest History of Brittany, Cornwall and Wales*, éd. L. Olson, SCH, 37 (Woodbridge: Boydell, 2017), pp. 1–18

Perin, P., 'La tombe de Clovis', in *Media in Francia. Recueil de mélanges offert à Karl Ferdinand Werner à l'occasion de son 65ᵉ anniversaire par ses amis et collègues français* (Maulévrier: Hérault-Éditions, 1989), pp. 363–78

Pietri, L., 'Grégoire de Tours et les Bretons d'Armorique: la chronique d'un double échec', *Britannia Monastica*, 17 (2013), 121–32

——, et M. Heijmans (éd.), *Prosopographie chrétienne du Bas-Empire 4. La Gaule chrétienne* (Paris: Association des amis du centre d'histoire et civilisation de Byzance, 2013)

Plaine, F., 'L'ancien évêché de Britonia en Galice', *Bulletin archéologique de l'Association bretonne: 28ᵉ congrès tenu à Saint-Malo du 1ᵉʳ au 6 septembre 1885 (Classe d'archéologie, 3ᵉ série, tome 5)* (1886), 47–53

Pohl, W., 'Frontiers and Ethnic Identities: Some Final Considerations', in *Borders, Barriers and Ethnogenesis. Frontiers in Late Antiquity and the Middle Ages*, éd. Fl. Curta, Studies in the Early Middle Ages, 12 (Turnhout: Brepols, 2005), pp. 255–65

Poulin, J.-C., 'La circulation de l'information dans la vie ancienne de s. Samson de Dol et la question de sa datation', in *St Samson of Dol and the Earliest History of Brittany, Cornwall and Wales*, éd. L. Olson, SCH, 37 (Woodbridge: Boydell, 2017), pp. 37–82

——, *L'hagiographie bretonne du haut Moyen Âge: répertoire raisonné*, Beihefte der Francia, 69 (Ostfildern: Thorbecke, 2009)

Reimitz, H., 'The Early Medieval Editions of Gregory of Tours's *Histories*', in *A Companion to Gregory of Tours*, éd. A. C. Murray, Brill's Companions to the Christian Tradition, 63 (Leiden: Brill, 2015), pp. 519–65

——, *History, Frankish Identity and the Framing of Western Ethnicity, 550–850*, Cambridge Studies in Medieval Life and Thought 4 ser., 101 (Cambridge: Cambridge University Press, 2015)

Reydellet, M., 'Tours et Poitiers: les relations entre Grégoire et Fortunat', in *Grégoire de Tours et l'espace gaulois: actes du congrès international, Tours, 3–5 novembre 1994*, éd. N. Gauthier et H. Galinié (Tours: Revue archéologique du centre de la France, 1997), pp. 159–67

Riché, P., 'Grégoire de Tours et l'Armorique', in *Grégoire de Tours et l'espace gaulois: actes du congrès international, Tours, 3–5 novembre 1994*, éd. N. Gauthier et H. Galinié (Tours: Revue archéologique du centre de la France, 1997), pp. 23–26

Roberts, M., 'Venantius Fortunatus and Gregory of Tours: Poetry and Patronage', in *A Companion to Gregory of Tours*, éd. A. C. Murray, Brill's Companions to the Christian Tradition, 63 (Leiden: Brill, 2015), pp. 35–59

Rudelt, A., 'Action et Mémoire de l'évêque et saint Melaine de Rennes', mémoire de recherche de Master 2 sous la direction de Magali Coumert (Université de Bretagne Occidentale, Brest, 2018)

Russell, P., 'Old Welsh *Dinacat, Cunedag, Tutagual*: Fossilized Phonology in Brittonic Personal Names', in *Indo-European Perspectives. Studies in Honour of Anna Morpurgo Davies*, éd. J. H. W. Penney (Oxford: Oxford University Press, 2004), pp. 447–60

Smith, J. M. H., '*Aedificatio sancti loci*: The Making of a Ninth-Century Holy Place', in *Topographies of Power in the Early Middle Ages*, éd. M. de Jong et F. Theuws, Transformation of the Roman World, 6 (Leiden: Brill, 2001), pp. 361–96

Sowerby, R., 'The Lives of St Samson. Rewriting the Ambitions of an Early Medieval Cult', *Francia*, 38 (2011), 1–31

Steinacher, R., *Die Vandalen. Aufstieg und Fall eines Barbarenreichs* (Stuttgart: Klett-Cotta, 2016)

Tanguy, B., 'De l'origine des évêchés bretons', *Les débuts de l'organisation religieuse de la Bretagne armoricaine, Britannia Monastica*, 3 (1994), 5–33

——, 'La limite linguistique dans la péninsule armoricaine à l'époque de l'émigration bretonne (IVᵉ–VIᵉ siècle) d'après les données toponymiques', *ABPO*, 87 (1980), 429–62

——, et M. Lagrée, *Atlas d'Histoire de Bretagne* (Morlaix: Skol Vreizh, 2002)

Young, S., 'The Bishops of the Early Medieval Spanish Diocese of Britonia', *CMCS*, 45 (2003), 1–19

6. ALAIN DE BRETAGNE, L'EXIL D'UN PRINCE

Joelle Quaghebeur

RÉSUMÉ Attestés depuis le règne d'Alfred le Grand (871–899), les contacts entre les nobles bretons et la cour de Wessex n'allèrent qu'en s'amplifiant. Ils aboutirent au début du xe siècle, au départ en exil Outre-Manche du gendre du roi Alain le Grand, le comte de Poher Matuedoi et de son fils. Tous deux partirent rejoindre le roi Edouard; le fils de ce dernier, Æthelstan, étant le parrain du jeune Alain. La situation chaotique de la Bretagne — l'assassinat de deux de ses rois au IXe siècle avait ébranlé cette royauté subordonnée aux Carolingiens, ces derniers connaissant eux-mêmes des successions dynastiques difficiles — et l'ampleur grandissante des attaques scandinaves avaient donc amené à ce que les liens se renforcent 'des deux côtés de la mer'. Partis se réfugier en Wessex, les Bretons y retrouvèrent des hommes qu'ils connaissaient, mais les princes gallois présents à la cour pratiquaient une langue qui leur était familière. Des affinités se créèrent, aussi le *nomen* d'*Houuel* donné par Alain Barbe-Torte à son fils aîné, au début des années 930, ne doit-il pas nous faire comprendre qu'en ces années l'héritier royal breton avait perdu l'espoir de retrouver sa terre et ses droits…?

ABSTRACT Contact between the Breton nobility and the court of Wessex is attested from the reign of Alfred the Great (871–899) and intensified in the following decades. In the early tenth century it culminated in the departure of Matuedoi, count of Poher (son-in-law of King Alan the Great), and of his son Alan, into exile beyond the English Channel. They took refuge with King Edward the Elder, whose son, Æthelstan, was the young Alan's godfather. The chaotic situation in Brittany — the assassination of two of its rulers in the ninth century had shaken this sub-kingdom of the Carolingians, who were themselves experiencing dynastic difficulties — and the ever-increasing scale of Scandinavian attacks had led to the strengthening of ties between 'the two shores of the sea'. In Wessex the Bretons met rulers whom they already knew: moreover, the Welsh princes present at the West Saxon court spoke a language familiar to them. Relationships were forged: thus the name of *Houuel* given by Alan Barbe-Torte to his elder son in the early 930s may give us to understand that during those years the Breton royal heir had given up hope of regaining his rights over his homeland.

MOTS-CLÉS Æthelstan, Alain II 'Barbe-Torte', Alain le Grand, alliances, Asser, Carolingien, *Chronique anglo-saxonne*, Chronique de Nantes, diplomatie, exil, Flodoard, haut Moyen Âge, Matuedoi, noblesse, *nomina*, Pascweten, Pays de Galles, roi, Scandinaves, Wessex

---

Multi-disciplinary Approaches to Medieval Brittany, 450–1200: Connections and Disconnections, ed. by Caroline Brett, Fiona Edmonds, and Paul Russell, TCNE 36 (Turnhout: Brepols, 2023) pp. 109–140   BREPOLS PUBLISHERS   10.1484/M.TCNE-EB.5.132311

La Chronique de Nantes, en quelques lignes, indique la fuite, au début du xe siècle, d'une grande partie des nobles bretons, titulaires d'*honores*, vers la Francie, la Bourgogne et l'Aquitaine. L'un d'entre eux, comte de Poher, Matuedoi, prit une autre route, maritime celle-ci: il traversa la mer pour rejoindre le roi des Angles, Æthelstan. La Chronique justifie implicitement ce choix par le fait que le roi Æthelstan avait soulevé le fils de Matuedoi, Alain, sur les fonts baptismaux, cette cérémonie ayant fait naître des liens de *familia* et d'*amicitia*, le roi 'avait une grande foi en lui'.[1] Cette dernière phrase soulève une question: comment se fit-il qu'un représentant de la noblesse bretonne ait pu choisir Outre-Manche, pour son fils qui avait pour grand-père le roi de Bretagne, un père spirituel?

Ce baptême, qui ne put que s'effectuer dans le royaume de Wessex, témoigne donc de liens existant entre ce dernier et le royaume de Bretagne. Disparu en 952, Alain naquit probablement à l'aube du xe siècle, en des temps terribles pour la Bretagne, désormais une proie privilégiée pour les Scandinaves. Car le roi franc Charles le Simple, occupé à développer une politique lotharingienne, n'apportait plus aucune aide aux Bretons. Ces derniers furent-ils donc amenés à aller chercher auprès d'un autre royaume dont ils se sentaient proches, sinon des contingents de *milites*, au moins des conseils pour la mise en défense des côtes de leur royaume?

Les sources parvenues jusqu'à nous ne permettent pas de saisir aisément la nature des relations entre les deux royaumes. Aussi l'exil de l'héritier royal breton en Wessex mérite-t-il d'être étudié de façon très précise car il témoigne de la confiance sensible entre deux lignages royaux européens, dans une période de grande incertitude pour l'avenir.

Pour ce faire, il apparaît nécessaire de dresser un tableau de ce qui contribua au départ des élites bretonnes et de mesurer l'emprise viking au début du xe siècle. Puis de réfléchir sur le choix du lieu d'exil, un royaume d'Outre-Manche, du jeune prince breton, Alain, porteur de tous les espoirs d'une royauté fidèle aux Carolingiens. Enfin, de mesurer si Alain ne perdit pas un temps l'espoir de voir rétablir ses droits sur la terre bretonne, envisageant alors un exil définitif.

Le royaume de Bretagne, une proie pour les 'hommes du Nord'

La Chronique de Nantes fut rédigée bien postérieurement et était donc par sa sensibilité ou ses réalités, très éloignée de la fin de l'époque carolingienne. Le Chroniqueur travailla, selon Pierre le Baud, à partir des chroniques de l'Église

---

[1] *La Chronique de Nantes*, pp. 82–83.

6. ALAIN DE BRETAGNE, L'EXIL D'UN PRINCE

de Nantes, des sources ayant disparu. Il en tira des informations objectives, comme, par exemple, les notions de comtes, vicomtes, *machtierns* qui ainsi formulées, établissaient une hiérarchie administrative au service du roi, gérant sous son autorité le royaume. Si le comte et le vicomte relevaient d'un ordre administratif carolingien, il n'en était pas de même du *machtiern*. Un courant historiographique y a vu une survivance d'institutions celtiques.[2] Si ce terme linguistiquement celtique témoigne d'une réalité ancienne, non romaine (à la différence du *comes*), il apparaît, à lire la Chronique, qu'au Xe siècle, les détenteurs de ce titre héréditaire ayant pour charge majeure de rendre la justice, avaient intégré pleinement le service du Prince. Leur place dans cette liste les mettait sous l'autorité du vicomte, par là du comte et donc du roi de Bretagne. Cette énumération atteste que s'était alors accomplie une fusion d'institutions d'origines probablement différentes. Cette évolution institutionnelle avait débuté sous le gouvernement de Nominoe, soit à partir de 831. Les *machtierns* et leurs attributions juridiques disparurent des actes à partir du milieu du Xe siècle.

Le Chroniqueur mentionna d'autres réalités comme les lieux où la noblesse de Bretagne partit se réfugier, la Francie, la Bourgogne, l'Aquitaine. Ces deux dernières constituaient deux principautés héréditaires apparues à la fin du IXe siècle. Si la Bourgogne apparaissait 'continentale' car éloignée des côtes, l'Aquitaine souffrait comme la Bretagne d'une situation géographique qui la plaçait sur la route des pirates. L'alliance que fit Nominoe avec Pépin d'Aquitaine après 840, fit-elle que des liens (parfois matrimoniaux) s'étaient créés entre les deux territoires? En gagnant l'Aquitaine, les nobles bretons rejoignaient peut-être une partie de leur famille. La Francie recouvrait, elle, le domaine carolingien mais aussi celui de la Maison robertienne. Ce secteur était donc compris comme relativement sûr, celui où les attaques scandinaves paraissaient être jugulées.

Le rédacteur de la Chronique indiqua également que le comte de Poher Matuedoi emmena avec lui en exil son fils Alain, plus tard surnommé Barbe-Torte, né de son union avec une fille d'Alain le Grand; il avait ouvert son texte par la destruction de 'toute la Bretagne' par les Scandinaves, ce qui avait amené le départ de la noblesse de Bretagne. Il voulut utiliser une notion, répétée, pour qualifier ce départ: *fugientes* et *fugit*, il voulait ainsi insister sur la notion de 'fuite'. Était-ce la description d'une réalité — un départ précipité, dans la peur — ou un jugement qu'il portait (et son époque avec lui) sur l'événement relaté? Car l'image était forte et délibérément. Dans le monde carolingien les titulaires d'*honores* étaient nécessairement des hommes de guerre, par l'éducation reçue

---

[2] Sheringham, 'Les machtierns'.

et dans l'exercice de la charge confiée par le Prince. Les nobles bretons étaient donc montrés ici comme contrevenant au code de l'honneur auquel les liait leur *honor*. Cela voulait donc montrer la violence extrême qui régnait alors.

Cette façon de relater ce qui se déroula montrait également que la Bretagne perdit tous ceux qui en assuraient l'administration. Un vaste territoire fut livré à lui-même, le Chroniqueur ayant une pensée pour ceux qui ne purent fuir et eurent un sort terrible. *Pauperes vero Britanni terram colentes sub potestate Normannorum remanserunt absque rectore et defensore* 'les pauvres Bretons cultivant la terre restèrent sous la *potestas* des Normands, sans chef et défenseur'.[3] La compassion de celui qui écrivait ces lignes s'accompagnait, sans doute, de la critique des *potentes* abandonnant les populations dont ils avaient la charge, les *pauperes*, sans armes; ils perdaient ainsi pour lui, leur *honor* dans tous les sens du terme. Mais l'époque de rédaction de ce texte, était profondément pénétrée des valeurs chevaleresques de bravoure et de protection des faibles, aussi le chroniqueur ne pouvait qu'être choqué de cette attitude de la noblesse de Bretagne.

Il est de bon ton actuellement, dans une historiographie minimisant l'ampleur de la violence scandinave, de nier les souffrances occasionnées par le phénomène viking. L'image d'un petit royaume dont tous les cadres choisirent la fuite (même si on peut la juger peu glorieuse) doit donc amener à nuancer ces propos quasi révisionnistes. Car le tableau dressé par la Chronique de Nantes est corroboré par Flodoard qui écrivait à l'année 919: *Nordmanni omnem Britanniam in Cornu Galliae in ora scilicet maritima sitam depopulantur, proterunt atque delent, abductis, venditis, ceterisque cunctis ejectis Britonnibus* 'Les Normands ravagent, écrasent et ruinent toute la Bretagne située à l'extrémité de la Gaule, celle qui est en bordure de mer, les Bretons étant enlevés, vendus et autrement chassés en masse'.[4] Le sort de la Bretagne marqua donc visiblement les esprits par son caractère extrême, Flodoard décrivait lui aussi le destin de tous ceux qui ne purent 'fuir'. La disparition du roi Alain le Grand en 907, avait permis un déchaînement final de violence. Mais depuis les années 830, la présence scandinave n'avait cessé de s'affirmer, aidée par une situation politique bretonne souvent chaotique. Faute de sources (la présence scandinave ayant pour corollaire des incendies de *scriptoria*) nous ne pouvons qu'égrener quelques dates, suffisantes pour mesurer une aggravation constante de la situation: 837, 843, 847, les années 850, 913, 921 et 927.

---

[3] *La Chronique de Nantes*, p. 83.

[4] *Les annales de Flodoard*, p. 1.

6. ALAIN DE BRETAGNE, L'EXIL D'UN PRINCE

La première mention d'une attaque scandinave en Bretagne apparaît dans les Annales de Saint-Florent de Saumur en 837, *Normanni vastant Britanniam*, 'les Hommes du nord dévastent la Bretagne'.[5] Nominoe, *missus* de l'empereur était occupé à combattre certains milieux francs désireux de s'emparer de la terre dont il avait la charge.[6] La Bretagne était donc, dans certains secteurs, vide d'hommes en armes, cela aida à l'attaque des Scandinaves, parfaitement renseignés sur les difficultés bretonnes. Ce ne pouvait être en réalité la première attaque. Qu'auraient indiqué les chroniques bretonnes (celle de Landévennec, par exemple) si elles étaient parvenues jusqu'à nous ...? Sans doute est-ce l'ampleur des destructions qui impressionna le moine ligérien, car il savait combien son propre monastère pouvait être menacé, la Loire constituant un enjeu stratégique et économique pour les Scandinaves. Leur volonté de maîtriser ce secteur fluvial se matérialisa lorsqu'ils tuèrent, le 24 juin 843, l'évêque de Nantes Gunhard, alors qu'il disait la messe.[7] Une façon de signifier aux populations locales combien la charité prônée par les chrétiens leur était étrangère.

Les incursions des pirates ne firent que s'aggraver. En 847, Nominoe perdit trois batailles, fut contraint de fuir et d'acheter leur départ.[8] Le récent vainqueur des armées franques à Ballon s'avoua donc vaincu. Car familier des champs de bataille, Nominoe n'avait pas suffisamment de troupes pour maîtriser des attaques côtières, sporadiques, sur tout son territoire.

---

[5] *Annales Sancti Florentii Salmurensis*, p. 113.

[6] Cette expédition est mentionnée, entre autres, dans les *Annales de Saint-Bertin*, p. 22, mais ses raisons sont explicitées dans un texte émanant de l'abbaye Saint-Sauveur de Redon, *The Monks of Redon*, I.11, p. 140: 'In tempore igitur Lodovici imperatoris discordia facta est inter Francos et Britones. Nam Franci volebant per vim totam Britanniam occupare, sicut antea solebant facere' (au temps de l'empereur Louis, il y eut une discorde entre les Francs et les Bretons. En effet, les Francs voulaient s'emparer par la violence de toute la Bretagne, comme ils avaient coutume de le faire auparavant'). Nominoe adressa alors une ambassade à l'empereur, qui se trouvait à Aix-la-Chapelle, afin de savoir si cette guerre était déclenchée sur son ordre. Sur ces événements et leurs conséquences, Brunterc'h, 'Le duché du Maine', pp. 62–63.

[7] Une copie fragmentaire du Xᵉ siècle d'une annale nantaise sans doute contemporaine des événements, provenant de l'abbaye Saint-Serge d'Angers, mentionne 'capta est a Normannis paganis [...] civitas Nannetis. In qua violatum et templum sanctum et Gunhardus sumus sacerdos [...] trucidatus more fuit gladii' (la cité de Nantes a été prise par les hommes du Nord païens. Dans celle-ci, le temple saint fut violé et Gunhard pontife suprême égorgé par le glaive), Lot et Halphen, *Le règne de Charles le Chauve*, pp. 79–80, n. 3. Ces annales ont été publiées pour partie dans *La Chronique de Nantes*, pp. 14–18.

[8] *Annales de Saint-Bertin*, p. 54.

Le monastère de Saint-Sauveur de Redon (accessible à des marins, car au bord d'un fleuve) fut attaqué en 854, il fut préservé par un miracle.[9] Dédié au Sauveur du monde, sa Maison ne pouvait, pour l'auteur du texte, que bénéficier d'une protection privilégiée; mais le moine ne marquait-il pas également l'incapacité du roi Erispoe, fils de Nominoe, à accomplir son devoir de Prince: la défense des *pauperes*, des sans-armes, auxquels appartenait le monde monastique? Comme si l'incurie du Prince avait contraint Dieu à intervenir ... Le moine rendait-il ainsi discrètement hommage au roi Salomon (ou Alain le Grand) qui lui s'illustra contre les Scandinaves?[10]

Le comté de Vannes semblait une proie privilégiée pour ces derniers. Ainsi le 11 mars 854, dans un acte d'Erispoe, venu jusqu'au palais épiscopal de Courantgen, à Vannes, apprend-on que l'évêque était captif des hommes du Nord.[11] La présence du roi avait-elle une raison militaire? Aida-t-il à la libération de l'évêque? L'abbaye n'eut, semble-t-il, pas à intervenir de la même façon que pour le noble Pascweten, par la suite comte de Vannes. En 857, Saint-Sauveur acheta, en effet, sa liberté en échange d'un calice et d'une patène d'or. Remerciant la communauté monastique, car revenu à la liberté, Pascweten céda une saline et un domaine.[12] Le monastère avait eu ici un rôle de 'banque' à qui on empruntait ce qui était nécessaire à sa libération, mais il s'entremettait également dans des négociations avec les Scandinaves. Les moines suppléaient déjà les manques ou incapacités des titulaires d'*honores* et en ce sens témoignaient d'une désorganisation qui s'aggravait.

Car les rivages du sud du *regnum* breton apparaissaient particulièrement exposés aux attaques: par la présence d'îles, Groix ou Belle-Île, commodes bases d'attaques et de repli, mais également par de longues grèves où les navires pouvaient s'échouer aisément, après des navigations souvent rudes. De même le secteur du monastère de Landévennec souffrit-il certainement de visites précoces.[13] Vers 870, l'abbé Uurdisten, paraphrasant une homélie de Grégoire le

---

[9] Dép. d'Ille-et-Vilaine; le moine décrivit la colère du Ciel et la peur des pirates comblant de cadeaux le sanctuaire: *The Monks of Redon*, III.9, pp. 212–18.

[10] La date de rédaction de ce texte fait l'objet de discussions entre érudits, Ferdinand Lot datait le texte de 868–875 et en attribuait la paternité à Ratvili, moine de Redon et futur évêque d'Alet. Une hypothèse à laquelle se rallièrent Hubert Guillotel et Jean-Claude Poulin. Caroline Brett, sa dernière éditrice, doute de cette attribution et propose une datation plus large, entre 868 et les environs de 919/920.

[11] *CR*, *Appendix*, XL, p. 369.

[12] *CR*, XXVI, pp. 21–22, 857, 8 juillet.

[13] Dép. du Finistère; l'archéologie y a trouvé des murailles, du côté de la mer, élevées au

6. ALAIN DE BRETAGNE, L'EXIL D'UN PRINCE

Grand, où était mentionnée Rome assiégée par les Lombards, fit un parallèle avec la terre où s'élevait sa Maison. *At nunc pressa jacet, heroum orbata potentum cede, gemens, victa, externo sub fasce reflexa*: 'Elle gît maintenant écrasée, privée de ses puissants héros, gémissante, vaincue, ployant sous le fardeau de l'étranger'.[14] Le contexte politique dramatique du royaume de Bretagne avait aidé à cela, l'assassinat d'Erispoe en 857, par son cousin Salomon, entraîna des fractures au sein de la noblesse. La mort en 874, dans des conditions tout aussi dramatiques, de Salomon, acheva de briser la société bretonne. Et ce qui fut compris par certains contemporains comme une juste vengeance, arriva dans un contexte marqué par une présence scandinave désormais permanente.

La noblesse de Bretagne eût donc du se consacrer à défendre le *regnum*, elle se perdit en luttes pour le contrôle du pouvoir breton. Réginon de Prüm — avec une chronologie jugée souvent fantaisiste par H. Guillotel — devient pour la fin du IXe siècle notre source majeure. Relatant les luttes opposant Judicael et Alain le Grand, il écrivit à l'année 889, qu'elles permirent aux païens de leur arracher leur territoire en totalité jusqu'à la rivière du Blavet.[15] La brièveté de la mention ne permet pas de comprendre ce qui était là décrit, quelle région, à l'est ou à l'ouest du Blavet (la Cornouaille ou le Vannetais) passa-t-elle sous contrôle scandinave? Mais soulignons le terme de *possessio* qualifiant le contrôle scandinave, il pourrait avoir un sens institutionnel, une cession de territoires faite par la puissance publique. Y eut-il donc accord écrit? Quoi qu'il en soit, il s'agissait bien d'une installation scandinave désormais pérenne.

Réginon décrivant les combats opposant les compétiteurs au pouvoir breton, indiqua quatre *nomina* majeurs: Uurvand, Pascweten, Judicael et Alain. Nous ne savons rien de Uurvand, ni du secteur géographique de Bretagne dominé par son lignage. Sans doute, si l'on suit la géographie politique dessinée par ceux à qui il s'opposa, s'agissait-il, du nord de la Bretagne. Au regard de ses ambitions à dominer le *regnum*, il ne pouvait qu'être issu de la haute noblesse bretonne. Pascweten fut, lui, mentionné à plusieurs reprises dans diverses sources, parce qu'il joua alors un rôle majeur. Il apparaît pour la première fois en 851, dans un acte de donation d'Erispoe, en faveur de Saint-Sauveur de Redon, le roi cédait

---

début du IXe siècle. *Cartulaire de Saint-Guénolé de Landévennec*, p. 139.

[14] *Cartulaire de l'abbaye de Landevenec*, p. 82.

[15] Rivière du centre Bretagne, le Blavet se jette dans la mer à la hauteur de Lorient (dép. du Morbihan); *Reginonis abbatis Prumensis Chronicon*, p. 135 '[...] ceduntur passim et usque ad Blavittam fluvium omnis eorum possessio dirigitur'.

la paroisse de Caer (actuelle Locmariaquer) dans le comté de Vannes.[16] Erispoe était entouré de ses hommes de confiance. Sans doute était-ce en qualité de représentant de la noblesse locale que le roi avait donc fait appel à Pascweten alors qu'il concédait un secteur vannetais relevant de la puissance publique.[17] En 857 et 859, Pascweten fit des donations à l'abbaye, dans le secteur de Caden et de Guérande, soit dans le sud du Vannetais et au nord du Nantais.[18] Il n'était investi d'aucun titre, mais suffisamment connu pour que l'abbaye ait alors acheté sa libération aux Scandinaves par un calice et une patène d'or, deux objets précieux par leur valeur marchande mais surtout symbolique et marquant l'importance de Pascweten pour la région. Sa place auprès de Salomon s'affirma durant ces années, en 862, il était ainsi aux côtés du *princeps* qui faisait une donation dans le secteur de La Turballe, il était cité, parmi les témoins, en première position.[19] Cette place était-elle due au fait que l'on se trouvait là dans un secteur dominé par son lignage, un secteur porteur de grandes richesses par le commerce du sel? C'est, en effet, une saline située à Guérande, à quelques kilomètres de La Turballe, qu'il abandonna à Saint-Sauveur en contrepartie du règlement de sa rançon, évoquée plus haut. En dotant l'abbaye, il remerciait les moines mais également le Sauveur, qui l'avait sauvé des Hommes du Nord; donner un riche bien 'familial', auquel son lignage était particulièrement attaché, correspondrait donc bien à une démarche de piété et de gratitude. Sa capture par les Scandinaves pourrait ainsi s'expliquer par le fait que, possessionné dans ce secteur du comté de Nantes, il avait eu à s'opposer à eux.

Le titre de comte ne lui fut donné dans le cartulaire de Redon que le 22 mai 865: *comes provinciae Broweroch*.[20] Il dut donc cet *honor* à Salomon. Ses droits patrimoniaux étaient en quelque sort reconnus: *Bro Weroch* ('le pays de Waroch') rappelait le chef breton investi par le roi mérovingien, au VIe siècle, du comté de Vannes. Le frère de Pascweten, le futur Alain le Grand donna ce *nomen* à l'un de ses fils, marquant ainsi la détention de ce nom par son lignage et donc un contrôle très ancien de ces territoires. Mais ce lignage noble doit être également compris comme ayant pour ambition de contrôler le Nantais, soit un secteur tout à la fois prospère et dangereux car convoité. Pascweten avait-il participé à l'assassinat d'Erispoe? Son innocence est vraisemblable, sinon il eût

---

[16] Dép. du Morbihan; *CR*, LXX, pp. 55–56, 851.

[17] Quaghebeur, 'Puissance publique, puissances privées'.

[18] *CR*, XXVI, pp. 21–22 et XXIII, pp. 19–20.

[19] *CR*, XXX, pp. 24–25.

[20] *CR*, CCXLVIII, p. 208.

été 'récompensé' bien plus rapidement. Mais il devint si proche du *princeps* que ce dernier l'envoyât auprès de Charles le Chauve en 867 et 868. *Missus* du *dux* Salomon, il était également précisé qu'il était le 'gendre de Salomon', comme si cette proximité 'familiale' valait pour un titre supplémentaire. Enfin en 868, il vint chercher pour Salomon le vestiaire royal à Compiègne.[21]

Les textes à notre disposition ne nous précisent pas les ancêtres, les parents, de Pascweten, juste qu'il avait un frère cadet, nommé Alain. Ce dernier accéda au titre royal, investi par le carolingien Charles le Simple, à qui il avait promis sa *fides*.[22] Alain apparaît aux côtés de son frère dans un acte de 866, cité en 5e position.[23] En 862, Alain était absent alors que Pascweten abandonnait *de sua hereditate* un bien en Plélan-le-Grand relevant du patrimoine familial et qui aurait donc justifié la présence de son frère.[24] Alain n'avait peut-être pas alors atteint l'âge nécessaire pour être témoin.

Les annales franques eurent, un peu plus tard, à mentionner Pascweten. Car en 874, il figurait avec Uurvand parmi les *primores* des Bretons qui mirent à mort Salomon.[25] L'annaliste de Saint-Bertin voulut rappeler la mort d'Erispoe, assassiné alors qu'il s'était réfugié dans une église et qu'il invoquait Dieu. La colère engendrée par la mort du roi breton n'était donc pas éteinte dans le monde franc. La prudence de Salomon à ne pas rencontrer 'physiquement' Charles le Chauve provenait certainement de sa crainte d'un juste châtiment. N'avait-il pas tué son cousin et roi? En outre, Charles le Chauve se disait *compater* d'Erispoe lors des fiançailles de leurs enfants en 856, Salomon s'était donc en quelque sorte attaqué à la *familia* de Charles, d'où la réticence (voire la répugnance) de ce dernier à l'investir du titre royal.

Nobles de Bretagne, entre alliances politiques et fidélités personnelles

Après la mort de Salomon, les *primores* de Bretagne se déchirèrent pour la maîtrise du pouvoir. Pascweten, dont le mariage avec Prostlon, la fille de Salomon, n'avait pu qu'accentuer les ambitions entama alors des combats contre son allié Uurvand, allant jusqu'à s'allier à des Scandinaves.

---

[21] *Annales de Saint-Bertin*, p. 151.

[22] Chédeville et Guillotel, *La Bretagne des saints et des rois*, p. 370.

[23] *CR*, XLIX, pp. 39–40, 13 juillet 866.

[24] Département d'Ille-et-Vilaine; *Cartulaire de l'abbaye de Redon*, LXXXV, pp. 64–65, 17 janvier 862.

[25] *Annales de Saint-Bertin*, p. 196.

Pascweten et Uurvand disparus,[26] les combats s'engagèrent entre Judicael et Alain. Ce dernier avait succédé à son frère aîné à la tête du comté de Vannes en 876, en 878 il était donné comme *provinciae Uuarroduae comes gratiae (sic) Dei*.[27] Alain s'était placé sous l'autorité de Louis le Bègue à qui il s'était commendé à Tours en mai 878.[28] Il est vraisemblable que lui avait été confirmé son pouvoir sur les comtés qu'il contrôlait, le Vannetais, le Nantais, le Rennais, l'Avranchin et le Cotentin, soit la *Nova Britannia*, 'réserve étant faite de la présence des Normands en Basse-Loire'.[29]

Judicael, quant à lui, s'était vu reconnaître ses droits sur le Poher, dont son lignage était issu. Un acte de Redon le qualifiait, en effet, de *princeps Pochaer*, soulignant ainsi le lignage qui était sien, celui du roi Erispoe.[30] Salomon, investi du titre royal par le Carolingien, avait donc voulu satisfaire Charles le Chauve, en rendant à un héritier légitime les droits qui étaient siens. Soulignons que la mère de Judicael était la filleule du carolingien. Ce dernier, après l'assassinat tragique d'Erispoe, dut ainsi assumer, en qualité de père spirituel, les responsabilités d'un père à l'égard de la très jeune orpheline. Le mariage qu'elle contracta ensuite ne put se faire qu'avec l'accord du roi. Choisit-il même le futur époux? Car il s'agissait nécessairement d'un choix aux résonnances politiques pour une région en situation délicate. Judicael, fils de sa filleule, ne put donc que bénéficier, jusqu'en 877, lui aussi du regard attentif du roi carolingien. Cette 'présence' en Bretagne, ne fut-ce que dans des obligations de nature spirituelle, du roi carolingien doit être soulignée car elle eut alors nécessairement des incidences sur lesquelles il conviendrait de réfléchir.

---

[26] Pascweten mourut dans les premiers mois de 876: Chédeville et Guillotel, *La Bretagne des saints et des rois*, p. 357.

[27] *CR*, CCXXXV, pp. 182–83.

[28] C'est ce qu'avait démontré H. Guillotel, en s'appuyant sur divers documents: une mention des *Annales de Saint-Bertin*, p. 140, où il est mentionné: 'Tunc Gozfrid partem de Brittonibus ad regis fidelitatem convertit' (Gauzfrid fit passer dans la fidélité de Louis une partie des Bretons), ainsi que sur les diplômes royaux de Louis qui attestent sa présence à Tours de mai à juillet 878, enfin sur les concessions faites, à la même période, par le prince breton à l'abbaye de Redon. Pour la première fois, la formule de datation de l'acte CCXXXV du Cartulaire de Redon (*CR*, pp. 182–83), comporta, en effet, entre autres formules de datation 'la première année du roi Louis'. Entre le 3 mai et le 12 juin 878, Alain se rendit donc à Tours où il se vit reconnaître son autorité sur les territoires en sa main, Chédeville et Guillotel, *La Bretagne des saints et des rois*, pp. 359–61.

[29] Chédeville et Guillotel, *La Bretagne des saints et des rois*, pp. 359–61.

[30] *CR*, CCXLVII, pp. 198–99.

6. ALAIN DE BRETAGNE, L'EXIL D'UN PRINCE

Alain le Grand et Judicael, initialement rivaux, furent amenés à cesser de se combattre afin d'unir leur forces contre les Scandinaves. En 889, un acte d'Alain le montre restituant un bien à l'église cathédrale de Nantes.[31] La présence de Judicael signifie qu'une réconciliation était intervenue entre les chefs bretons.[32]

Mais une donation faite à Nantes, justifiait-elle la présence du *princeps de Poher*? La venue de Judicael avait un autre sens: Aourken-Orgain, l'épouse d'Alain, elle aussi présente, était issue du lignage de Judicael, très probablement sa sœur. Elle était donc une descendante d'Erispoe.[33] À ce titre elle avait été une héritière convoitée car ses enfants seraient de sang royal et auraient légitimité à gouverner la Bretagne. Pascweten avait obtenu d'épouser Prostlon, fille du roi Salomon, son frère dût avoir des ambitions identiques en s'alliant à la première lignée royale bretonne.

Ce qui a été souligné il y a quelques lignes, de la permanence carolingienne en Bretagne au travers de parrainages spirituels, pourraient donner également un autre sens à cette union. Car Alain savait par ce mariage satisfaire le parti carolingien. Épouser Aourken-Orgain était aussi marquer sa *fides* à la lignée carolingienne, elle qui avait reconnu la royauté confiée à Erispoe. Plus loin encore, c'était s'allier à une puissance royale ancienne, car Nominoe, père d'Erispoe, était selon toute vraisemblance, fils du roi Morvan décapité sur l'ordre de Louis le Pieux en 818.[34] Appartenir désormais à la parentèle de Judicael[35] était donc un acte politique qui liait un peu plus sa récente royauté à l'autorité carolingienne voire à sa *familia*.

Lors de cette donation, Alain promit d'offrir à Dieu et à Saint-Pierre de Rome, la dixième partie de ses biens en échange de la victoire sur les Normands. Alain était le premier à formuler pareille promesse en Bretagne, s'inspirait-il de l'exemple donné l'année précédente, par le roi Alfred qui avait fait parvenir à Rome, par le biais de sa sœur, ses aumônes ainsi que celles des Saxons de l'ouest?[36]

---

[31] *La Chronique de Nantes*, pp. 68–72.

[32] Chédeville et Guillotel, *La Bretagne des saints et des rois*, p. 366.

[33] Quaghebeur, *La Cornouaille du IXe au XIIe siècle*, pp. 61–68.

[34] Quaghebeur, 'Landévennec, l'abbaye des rois de Bretagne'.

[35] Dans ce texte, Alain qualifiait ceux qui l'entouraient d'amis, de parents, de proches et de consanguins: *La Chronique de Nantes*, p. 70.

[36] *Anglo-Saxon Chronicle*, p. 53.

Le royaume de Wessex connut aux IXe–Xe siècles trois règnes importants dans l'histoire de l'Angleterre, ceux d'Alfred le Grand (871–899), d'Edouard l'Ancien (899–924) et d'Æthelstan (924–939). Le Wessex se trouvant sur la route des Scandinaves, ces rois eurent tous trois à les affronter. Il convient donc de mesurer les ressemblances avec ce qu'endurait le royaume de Bretagne.

Le règne d'Alfred le Grand est considéré comme un moment important dans la constitution du royaume d'Angleterre, le roi étant regardé comme un unificateur et détenteur d'un pouvoir en pleine affirmation.[37] Sa capacité à rassembler ses sujets autour de lui avait pour origine son rôle dans la défense de l'île de Bretagne contre les Scandinaves. Car il s'illustra à de multiples reprises dans des combats victorieux, comme en 870, où il gagna neuf batailles. Cela suggère combien le sud de l'île était menacé. Cette activité militaire parcourut tout son règne et en 885–86, il reprit Londres aux Danois. Mais les velléités de conquête des hommes du Nord ne s'apaisaient pas. Son règne fut donc un moment de résistance, le roi entreprenant une politique de mise en défense du territoire par des forteresses. La *Chronique anglo-saxonne* relate qu'il fit également construire de nouveaux navires. Le roi avait compris que la lutte contre les Scandinaves devait se faire sur mer. Car une terre maritime, comme l'île de Bretagne, ne pouvait être surveillée efficacement. Or le roi ne disposait pas de suffisamment d'hommes pour les disséminer le long des côtes. La stratégie du roi fut efficace car la pression scandinave fut indéniablement maîtrisée. Pareils choix et réussites militaires ne pouvaient-il pas inspirer les souverains d'autres terres, tout aussi menacées, comme la Bretagne?

L'autorité du roi, à même d'enrayer un 'processus scandinave', contribua à ce que certains princes gallois se soumettent à lui. Ainsi en 885, le roi de Dyfed, avec d'autres rois, prêta serment de fidélité. Celui qui relata cette soumission de princes, jusqu'alors rétifs au pouvoir anglo-saxon, est un moine gallois, Asser.

Membre de la cour d'Alfred, il rédigea en 893, une biographie du roi, source précieuse pour les événements de cette époque mais également pour le portrait spirituel et moral du roi.[38] Originaire du royaume de Dyfed, il voulait témoigner de l'œuvre pacificatrice et unificatrice d'Alfred. Asser apparaît représentatif des lettrés de l'époque carolingienne, défenseur des conceptions politiques de leur Prince. Mais le moine gallois avait choisi de servir le roi de Wessex. Il voulut laisser à la postérité l'image de 'son' roi, celui d'un redoutable guerrier

---

[37] Molyneaux, *The Formation of the English Kingdom*, pp. 25–27.

[38] Asser, *Histoire du roi Alfred*.

6. ALAIN DE BRETAGNE, L'EXIL D'UN PRINCE

et d'un protecteur des pauvres, l'image donc du bon roi au haut Moyen Âge. Cette vision quasi-carolingienne du pouvoir royal ne doit pas surprendre. Car si l'une des sources majeures du moine gallois fut la *Chronique anglo-saxonne*,[39] il s'inspira également des biographies royales rédigées dans le monde carolingien. Asser avait côtoyé à la cour d'Alfred des érudits francs. Le royaume de Wessex entretenait, en effet, des liens profonds avec le monde carolingien. Le roi Æthelwulf, revenant d'un pèlerinage à Rome, avait reçu Judith de son père, le roi Charles.[40] La fille de Charles le Chauve, Judith fut, en effet, donnée en mariage au roi de Wessex et sacrée en 856 par l'archevêque Hincmar, avant de gagner son royaume. Le mariage, outil politique pour cette époque, créait alliances diplomatiques et liens du sang; ces derniers étant un gage supplémentaire de la force des liens politiques désormais existants. Les Carolingiens entendaient donc se gagner de nouveaux alliés mais ils reconnaissaient également la dynastie de Wessex comme digne de 'diffuser' par ses héritiers le sang carolingien. La *Chronique anglo-saxonne* indique qu'Alfred, envoyé à Rome par son père, le pape Léon IV (847–855) le reçut comme son fils adoptif et lui administra la confirmation. La réalité de cette cérémonie a été remise en cause.[41] Mais de la même façon, le futur Charlemagne et son frère Carloman avaient été 'adoptés' par le pape Étienne, lors de sa venue dans le royaume des Francs, en 754. Un exemple que l'on voulut peut-être reprendre donc outre-Manche. Car Rome créant ces liens 'familiaux' avec les royautés européennes, entendait influer sur le gouvernement futur de ces princes: fils spirituels du pontife ces jeunes gens recevaient implicitement un modèle de comportement pour la charge qui serait leur. Et Alfred se sentit bien investi d'une responsabilité particulière dans la défense des chrétiens et donc la lutte contre les païens.

Mais Asser le Gallois nous renseigne également sur d'autres réalités politiques de son temps. Ainsi, il désignait toujours les Gallois par le terme de *Britanni* et leur territoire par celui de *Britannia*.[42] Il faut souligner qu'à la même époque les habitants du royaume de Bretagne se disaient également être des *Britanni*. Pour différencier ces derniers des Gallois, Asser les qualifiait d' 'Armoricains'. Ainsi, relatant l'accession au titre impérial de Charles le Gros, en 885, écrivit-il 'Charles, roi des Alamans, reçut par l'approbation et le consentement de tout le royaume de Francie et tous les royaumes situés entre

---

[39] Asser, *Histoire du roi Alfred*. Elle fut produite sous les auspices de la cour, aux années 890.

[40] Asser, *Histoire du roi Alfred*, ch. 13, p. 23.

[41] Nelson, 'The Franks and the English'.

[42] Asser, *Histoire du roi Alfred*, p. 14, n. 46.

la mer Tyrrhénienne et le golfe marin qui se trouve entre les vieux Saxons et les Gaulois, à l'exception du royaume armoricain.'[43]

Il décrivait ici une situation institutionnelle tout à fait étonnante. Le royaume de Bretagne n'aurait pas prêté allégeance au nouvel empereur, à Ponthion en juin 885. Faut-il comprendre ici la trace de revendications bretonnes à une liberté politique à l'égard des Carolingiens? Cela est peu vraisemblable. Rappelons qu'en ces années, la royauté bretonne était 'vacante', Salomon disparu en 874, personne n'avait été investi par le Carolingien du titre royal. Et entre 907 et 913 — date à laquelle il trouva la mort — Uurmaelon, *comes* de Poher, était dit *regere* la *monarchia* de Bretagne.[44] Cette brève mention témoigne du strict respect des institutions qu'avait alors la noblesse de Bretagne: elle se devait d'avoir un chef, coordonnant les opérations militaires nécessaires, mais elle ne s'octroya pas le droit de le faire roi, car elle savait que seul le Carolingien pouvait investir un nouveau titulaire de la royauté subordonnée bretonne. L'homme le plus puissant de la *Britannia* était, aux années 880, Alain le Grand, mais disposait-il de la légitimité nécessaire pour engager la *fides* du peuple de Bretagne à l'égard de l'empereur? Il ne le semble pas. Ou estimait-il que le roi légitime dont les Bretons dépendaient était le tout jeune Charles le Simple, fils de Louis le Bègue à qui il avait prêté hommage?

Asser livrait donc ici une information inédite au regard des rares sources bretonnes à notre disposition et nous permet de saisir la situation institutionnelle complexe dans laquelle se trouvait alors le *regnum* breton. Privé d'un représentant légitime auprès des puissances européennes, il était 'absent' du jeu politique important qui avait cours, les Bretons ne pouvant adresser aucun représentant légitime à l'assemblée tenue lors de l'investiture de Charles le Gros. Le futur Alain le Grand avait engagé sa fidélité, en mai-juin 878, à Tours, auprès de Louis le Bègue. Mais si son contrôle d'un vaste territoire (la *nova Britannia*) avait été autorisé, il n'avait pas obtenu alors pour autant l'investiture royale.

Enfin, soulignons la bonne information d'Asser quant à la situation des 'Armoricains', résultait-elle d'un intérêt particulier du Gallois qu'il était, pour un peuple qu'il ne pouvait que considérer que comme 'frère' et dont il avait sans doute côtoyé des représentants ...?

Car nous décrivant la générosité, voire la munificence, de son roi, Asser fut amené de nouveau à citer les Armoricains. Il expliqua, en effet, comment Alfred entendit partager ses richesses. Une part étant réservée aux monastères de tout

---

[43] Asser, *Histoire du roi Alfred*, p. 103.

[44] *CR*, CCLXXVI, pp. 223–24.

6. ALAIN DE BRETAGNE, L'EXIL D'UN PRINCE

le pays, de Mercie, mais aussi, 'certaines années, tour à tour, et selon ses possibilités', il faisait des dons aux 'églises et aux serviteurs de Dieu du pays des Bretons, de Cornouaille, de Gaule, d'Armorique et de Northumbrie et même à l'occasion d'Irlande'.[45] Ce bref passage, indique donc clairement des liens entre le royaume de Bretagne et le Wessex entre 871 et 899. Des sanctuaires bretons bénéficièrent des largesses du roi. Gageons que la disparition tragique du roi Salomon en 874, en 'Armorique', amena la compassion du roi et donc sa générosité, voire sa vigilante protection à l'égard de certaines églises 'armoricaines'. Le roi étant par essence protecteur de l'Église de son royaume, selon les conceptions carolingiennes bien connues dans le Wessex.

Un peu plus loin, Asser indiqua la générosité d'Alfred, 'en faveur d'étrangers de toutes origines, venue de pays lointains ou proches qui lui demandaient de l'argent ou pas, il donnait à chacun en fonction de ses besoins et de son rang'.[46] Ce dernier terme évoque la présence de nobles. Une générosité matérielle n'était pas peut-être la plus attendue par ce milieu, en revanche avoir l'honneur de jurer sa *fides* au Prince de Wessex était certainement convoité. En ces années d'incertitude politique en Bretagne (Alfred accéda au titre royal trois ans avant l'assassinat du roi Salomon) certains nobles bretons commencèrent-ils de se tourner vers le roi de Wessex, le protecteur de monastères qu'ils dotaient eux-mêmes?

Cet article s'est ouvert par le départ en exil, au royaume de Wessex, de Matuedoi comte de Poher et de son fils Alain, donné comme ayant été porté sur les fonts baptismaux par le roi Æthelstan. La réalité de ce parrainage spirituel ne peut guère être mise en doute et elle correspond bien aux mentalités de ce temps. Mais le baptême avait ici rôle d'entrée en fidélité, le filleul jurant ainsi implicitement sa *fides* à son puissant parrain. Ce qui peut étonner, est que ce parrainage émanait d'un royaume autre que franc, tant on est habitué pour la Bretagne, depuis l'exemple de Nominoe, à établir un lien de fidélité à l'égard du Carolingien.

Car comment les Carolingiens purent-ils admettre cette sorte de 'fidélité multiple' de la part de nobles issus d'un royaume qui leur était politiquement subordonné? Alain Barbe-Torte naquit sans doute alors que la Bretagne connaissait un flou politique, qui la voyait désormais sans roi investi par le

---

[45] Asser, *Histoire du roi Alfred*, ch. 102, pp. 170–73.
[46] Asser, *Histoire du roi Alfred*, ch. 101, pp. 170–71.

Carolingien, soit entre 878 et 898.[47] Le mariage de la fille de Charles le Chauve avec Æthelwulf avait indéniablement amené le monde carolingien à regarder ce royaume comme 'ami'. Aussi, pour les Bretons, ce fut aussi faire preuve d'une forme de fidélité à l'égard des choix carolingiens que de se tourner, à leur tour, vers le Wessex pour y contracter des alliances, matrimoniales ou spirituelles. Mais si Æthelstan fut indéniablement le maître d'œuvre majeur de la restauration du pouvoir d'Alain Barbe-Torte en 936, il paraît difficile d'admettre qu'il put être le roi qui l'accueillit en exil. Car Æthelstan régnant à partir de 924, en 936, Alain eût été âgé de 12 ans, bien jeune pour achever militairement la reconquête de son pays! Ce furent donc les rois Alfred (871–899) ou Edouard l'Ancien (899–924) qui accueillirent les fugitifs. Ce que l'on sait de l'état de la Bretagne incline à pencher pour le roi Edouard. L'entrée en fidélité de Matuedoi put amener le roi à accepter que l'un de ses fils devienne le parrain du nouveau-né qu'était encore Alain. Ce lien de nature spirituelle, était compris comme une manière de sceller les relations futures des deux royaumes. Car Alain, comme Æthelstan, était destiné à devenir roi. Mais l'exil de la famille royale bretonne n'était pas encore envisagé, à l'aube du Xe siècle, le roi Alain le Grand se battait alors pour sa *patria* — la 'terre de ses pères'. Aussi le voyage de Matuedoi en Wessex devait signifier qu'il y était venu en émissaire du roi breton. Ce qui justifia que l'on voulut créer des liens 'personnels' entre les deux lignées, le fils du roi de Wessex devenant le père spirituel d'un petit-fils de roi. Le parrain devrait guider et protéger son filleul dans sa vie future. Ce lien très fort, pour des chrétiens, contribua nécessairement à ce que Matuedoi ait amené son filleul à Æthelstan alors que la Bretagne était en proie à la furie des Hommes du Nord, quelques années plus tard. Mais ce baptême pouvait-il ne pas avoir également un sens politique? Car ne plaçait-il implicitement la Bretagne, en qualité de royaume, sous la protection du royaume de Wessex? Certains nobles bretons envisageaient donc, en ces temps si difficiles, des alliances politiques nouvelles, non plus seulement continentales et carolingiennes mais 'des deux côtés de la mer'.

Succédant à son père, le roi Alfred, en 899, Edouard consacra le début de son règne à lutter contre les Scandinaves et fit entrer la Mercie dans son royaume. Né au milieu des années 870, il commença à se battre du vivant d'Alfred. Marié vers 893, il eut un fils, Æthelstan, né vers 894 et une fille qui épousa le roi scan-

---

[47] La cérémonie d'hommage entre Alain le Grand et Louis le Bègue ne valait pas pour une investiture royale. En revanche, très vite après être devenu pleinement roi, en 898, Charles le Simple investit Alain le Grand du titre de roi subordonné. Disparu en 952, Alain Barbe-Torte dut naître plutôt à la fin de ce moment politique délicat pour la Bretagne.

6. ALAIN DE BRETAGNE, L'EXIL D'UN PRINCE

dinave Sihtric Cáech. À la fin de sa vie, Alfred avait organisé une cérémonie d'investiture au titre royal pour son petit-fils Æthelstan. Les raisons exactes de cette cérémonie sont inconnues. Edouard dut lutter contre son cousin Æthelwold qui revendiquait également le trône, ce dernier s'alliant aux Danois d'East-Anglia. En 906, Edouard conclut une paix avec les Danois. Mais il reprit l'offensive militaire et à partir de 911, il entama une campagne de fortifications des secteurs repris aux Vikings. Edouard fonda des forteresses, parfois directement au contact des Scandinaves.[48] En 914, une flotte venue de Bretagne entra dans la Severn et attaqua le sud-est du pays de Galles. Sans doute s'agissait-il des Scandinaves qui avaient attaqué et embrasé l'abbaye de Landévennec.[49] En 917, il obtint des victoires décisives, reçut la soumission des Scandinaves de Northampton, de Cambridge et d'East-Anglia. Son autorité s'étendait alors sur toute l'Angleterre au sud du Humber. Les princes gallois prêtèrent alors serment à Edouard.

Rappelons le terrible constat dressé par Flodoard pour la Bretagne en 919. Ne peut-on comprendre que le vainqueur des Scandinaves qu'apparaissait être Edouard, occupé non plus à la défense mais aussi à la reconquête de territoires, put fasciner une noblesse armoricaine qui entretenait déjà des relations avec le pouvoir royal de Wessex ...?

La proximité existant entre les élites des deux royaumes est peut-être sensible dans le fait que construisant, en 901, un monastère d'hommes à côté de la cathédrale de Winchester, vraisemblablement conçu pour devenir un mausolée royal,[50] le roi voulut acquérir les reliques du saint breton Judoc. Ce dernier était fils de roi et frère du *rex* Judicael qui rencontra le roi Dagobert aux années 630. Judicael, comme le mentionnent divers documents, avait préféré, lors de sa venue à Clichy, aller parler spiritualité avec le référendaire Dadon, plutôt que de partager le repas du roi, il abdiqua quelques années plus tard et se retira au monastère de Saint-Méen de Gaël.[51] Judoc eût du succéder à son frère mais il

---

[48] Ainsi à Bedford, où dominait le comte Thurketil, chef des Danois.

[49] Quaghebeur, 'Norvège et Bretagne', pp. 121–22.

[50] Rumble, 'Edward and the Churches of Winchester and Wessex'; Marafioti, 'The King's Body: Burial and Succession', pp. 26–29.

[51] Dép. d'Ille-et-Vilaine; la *vita* de Judicael se trouve dans le ms latin 9889 de la Bibliothèque nationale de France, une édition partielle en a été faite par Fawtier, 'Ingomar, historien breton'. Ce monastère avait bénéficié d'un diplôme d'immunité de Charlemagne, renouvelé par Louis le Pieux, ce qui montre son importance au regard de l'Empire (texte publié par Morice, *Mémoires*, I, cols. 225–27). Il fut détruit par les Scandinaves, à un point tel que l'on ne sait rien de son emplacement initial, sans doute à proximité du monastère élevé à partir de 1024. La *vita*

refusa cet *honor* suprême et choisit également une vie de prières. La présence de ses reliques, soit celles d'un saint homme de Bretagne, de sang royal, dans ce qui devait devenir la nécropole royale de Wessex était donc pleine de sens, elle marque également la grande proximité existant alors entre les pouvoirs royaux d' 'Armorique' et de Wessex. Et le monastère de Saint-Méen de Gaël où reposait peut-être le roi Judicael, n'avait-il pas été au nombre des églises qui avaient bénéficié de la générosité du roi Alfred?

Cette dimension spirituelle, qui liait la terre de Wessex à celle de Bretagne, est de même sensible dans une lettre adressée, en 926, par le clergé de Dol au roi Æthelstan. Il y était rappelé que son père Edouard, appartenait à confraternité de prières de Saint-Samson de Dol.[52] Car amoureux des reliques, Æthelstan s'en procura également en Bretagne. Tous en Occident connaissait la particulière dilection du roi anglo-saxon pour ces saints objets, ainsi Radbod, prévôt de l'évêque de Dol lui adressa-t-il en 926 celles de saint Senier, saint Paterne et saint Scubilion. Il joignit à cet envoi cette lettre.

À l'année 936, Flodoard nota le décès du roi Raoul, le comte Hugues adressant des ambassadeurs outre-mer pour rappeler Louis fils de Charles et lui confier le pouvoir souverain. Après avoir reçu le serment des ambassadeurs francs, le roi Æthelstan, le dirigea sur la Francie avec quelques évêques et plusieurs autres de ses fidèles. Flodoard indiquant que les Bretons s'en vont des régions d'outre-mer et avec le soutien du roi Æthelstan regagnent leur terre.[53] Le retour d'Alain Barbe-Torte apparaît, en outre, mentionné dans deux textes postérieurs à ces événements, la Chronique de Nantes, déjà citée, et l'ouvrage de Dudon de Saint-Quentin, *De moribus et actis primorum Normanniae ducum*.[54] Ces deux textes, moins elliptiques, sont tous deux critiquables car tardifs. Mais il faut comprendre que le rôle d'Æthelstan fut majeur dans les tractations nécessaires au retour du prince breton en sa terre. Æthelstan, né vers 894, disparut le

---

de Judicael fut alors écrite par le moine Ingomar, qui disait que le roi, ami du sanctuaire, y prit la robe. Si cela était vrai, on peut avancer qu'il y fut inhumé. Outre des intérêts stratégiques et politiques, la présence de ce roi saint amena-t-elle Charlemagne puis son fils à particulièrement protéger ce monastère?

[52] Cette lettre nous a été transmise par Guillaume de Malmesbury, dans William of Malmesbury, *Gesta Pontificum Anglorum*, v.249, 1, 597–99. Si l'on peut mettre en doute le témoignage du chroniqueur du XIIe siècle sur les règnes des souverains des IXe–Xe siècles, on voit mal pourquoi il aurait forgé pareil document, qui doit donc être fiable. H. Guillotel avance pour la date de rédaction de cette lettre, l'année 926, Guillotel, 'L'exode du clergé breton', p. 297.

[53] *Les annales de Flodoard*, p. 63.

[54] *De moribus et actis primorum Normanniae ducum*.

6. ALAIN DE BRETAGNE, L'EXIL D'UN PRINCE   127

27 octobre 939. Ce cadre chronologique peut être rapproché de la vie d'Alain Barbe-Torte, disparu lui en 952; ces deux hommes, proches par leur âge, furent à même de nouer des relations d'amitié, même si pour Æthelstan s'ajoutait en sa qualité de parrain une dimension 'paternelle'. Les contacts existants entre leurs royaumes respectifs, de façon ancienne permettaient, en outre, qu'ils ne se regardent pas comme des étrangers. Et le fils de roi qu'était Æthelstan, ayant côtoyé Alain avant même qu'il ne monte lui-même en 924 sur le trône de Wessex, ne pouvait que compatir à la douleur de l'exil du jeune breton, comme lui petit-fils de roi et sans doute déjà regardé comme l'héritier d'un *regnum* disparu. Cette dimension très humaine, cette amitié, entre deux jeunes princes, ne doit pas être oubliée. Car Alain, ne pouvant relever l'*honor* familial, était désormais également sans terres, soit sans aucun revenu et donc soumis à la bonté et à la générosité de ceux qui l'avaient accueilli avec son père.

Comme son père Edouard, Æthelstan (924–939) a longtemps pâti de la figure de son grand-père, le roi Alfred. Il est désormais considéré comme l'un des grands rois d'Angleterre. Il connut toutes les difficultés, entre autres militaires, liées à la présence scandinave mais il sut aussi attirer à sa cour les souverains gallois et écossais, donnant à son royaume, dans la première moitié du Xe siècle, une dimension politique remarquable.

Il eut une activité militaire importante, mais la période à laquelle il vivait pouvait-elle l'en dispenser? Sacré roi en septembre 925, il conquit le royaume viking d'York en 927,[55] faisant ainsi que son autorité s'étende à toute l'Angleterre. Son autorité affermie, il amena le roi d'Écosse, Constantin et le Gallois Hywel Dda à venir lui prêter hommage. En 934, il envahit le royaume d'Écosse, de nouveau insoumis, accompagné de quatre rois gallois dont Hywel.[56] Depuis le règne d'Æthelred (865–871), des rois du pays de Galles venaient à la cour de Wessex. *Subreguli*, rois subordonnés, ils furent présents de 928 à 956.[57] Leur statut peut naturellement être rapproché de celui des rois bretons (depuis Erispoe en 851) eux aussi 'rois subordonnés' au pouvoir carolingien. À la différence, peut-être, qu'en Bretagne les nobles de sang royal ne pouvaient qu'être investis officiellement de leur charge royale (de leur *honor*) que par le roi carolingien. Celui-ci leur était donc 'supérieur' et les 'nommait' comme il le faisait pour

---

[55] L'année précédente il avait donné sa sœur en mariage au viking Sihtric d'York, ce dernier disparu, Æthelstan se sentit autorisé à passer à l'attaque.

[56] Foot, *Æthelstan: the First King of England*, pp. 87–88, 122–23, 165–67; les rois gallois fêtèrent Noël à la cour en 935, pp. 88–89.

[57] Davies, *Wales in the Early Middle Ages*, pp. 113–14.

tous ses représentants. Mais cette grande proximité institutionnelle entre les pratiques du Wessex et celles du monde carolingien (monde qui était celui de la Bretagne) ne pouvait que rendre familier le milieu anglo-saxon aux Bretons en exil, car il était donc un peu le leur.

C'est sa politique diplomatique qui fit aussi d'Æthelstan un roi particulièrement remarquable, le roi de Wessex usant là de façon majeure de l'outil matrimonial. Æthelstan sut par ce biais accroître le prestige de son lignage. Il 'donna' ainsi ses sœurs (parfois demi-sœurs) aux représentants des grandes puissances continentales du moment: Eadgifu épousa le roi de Francie Charles le Simple, à la fin des années 910, Eadhild convoitée par le *dux* des Francs Hugues le Grand (soit alors l'homme le plus puissant du royaume franc) lui fut donnée après que le robertien ait adressé une ambassade chargée de très précieux cadeaux (outre les épices, les bijoux, elle apportait l'épée de Constantin, la lance de Charlemagne et une relique, un fragment de la Sainte-Couronne). Mais l'alliance la plus prestigieuse fut conclue par le don de Eadgyth qui épousa, vers 929–930, l'empereur Otton, fils de Henri l'Oiseleur. Ces mariages témoignaient d'une intense activité diplomatique car le roi était désireux de se rapprocher des pouvoirs royaux et impériaux continentaux. Mais ces derniers étaient flattés de nouer une alliance avec le royaume de Wessex. Ce prestige était attaché au rôle politique considérable que le Wessex jouait, en cette période de guerre avec le monde scandinave. Car ce royaume et ses rois pouvaient apparaître comme étant au contact de tous les mondes du nord de l'Europe, sans exclure aucune de leurs composantes et donc comme ayant une connaissance fine de ces réalités lointaines; en outre, en lutte (ou allié, rappelons le mariage de la sœur d'Æthelstan avec le roi d'York) lui aussi depuis des décennies contre la menace scandinave, il était à même de donner de précieux conseils.

Les fréquents contacts entretenus par le roi avec le continent avaient également pour cause le fait qu'Æthelstan était un grand collectionneur de livres et de reliques. Il attira à sa cour érudits, bretons et irlandais, comme Israël le Grammairien, peut-être un breton.[58]

Son règne s'inscrivait dans la période la plus sombre connue par la Bretagne, désormais aux mains des Scandinaves,[59] les élites d'encadrement partaient ou

---

[58] Foot, *Æthelstan: the First King of England*, pp. 94, 99–107, 190–91; Brett, 'A Breton Pilgrim in England', pp. 44–45.

[59] H. Guillotel entrevoyait deux principautés, l'une en Poher-Cornouaille, l'autre à Nantes, 'Le premier siècle du pouvoir ducal breton'.

6. ALAIN DE BRETAGNE, L'EXIL D'UN PRINCE

étaient parties en exil, les monastères et les églises cathédrales étaient désertés.[60] Les érudits bretons, qui étaient auprès d'Æthelstan étaient donc des réfugiés, venus à la cour de Wessex, leurs monastères étant détruits ou inaccessibles.[61] Le roi n'accueillit donc pas que l'héritier royal et son père et la présence en Wessex, de ces hommes de Dieu et de l'héritier royal n'attira-t-elle pas des nobles bretons dispersés hors de leur pays?

La lettre que Radbod, prévôt de l'évêque de Dol lui adressa en 926, lui rappelant la proximité spirituelle entretenue par son père Edouard avec un sanctuaire breton, s'achevait en demandant qu'on ne les oubliât pas, lui et ses clercs, et se terminait par une formule énigmatique.[62] Une inquiétude était là perceptible.

En 911, le roi Charles le Simple avait concédé au scandinave Rollon plusieurs comtés de la Basse-Seine, en échange de son baptême et d'un serment de fidélité. En 921, Robert de Neustrie 'conseil et secours du royaume' aux dires même du roi, ayant assiégé durant plusieurs mois les Scandinaves de la Loire, reçut d'eux des otages et leur céda la Bretagne qu'ils avaient dévastée.[63] Herbert de Vermandois et Robert, après ce siège infructueux conclurent, en effet, une paix en échange de la concession du *pagus* de Nantes (soit le territoire du comté).[64] Cette cession fut faite pour le roi et fut renouvelée en 927, après un autre siège infructueux.[65] Peu après le fils de Rollon, Guillaume Longue-Épée se commendait à Charles le Simple et lui assurait son *amicitia*.[66] Cette cession de la Bretagne par le pouvoir robertien aux Scandinaves, ne laissa-t-elle pas un goût amer aux Bretons en exil ...? Le comté de Nantes avait été concédé aux Scandinaves, à l'image de ce qui avait été fait en Neustrie en 911. Pour les contemporains, la comparaison apparaissait d'ailleurs naturelle, car Flodoard écrivait à l'année 921 que les Hommes du Nord 'de Bretagne' commencèrent de recevoir la foi du Christ, or la conversion avait été une condition préliminaire

---

[60] Sur ce que les textes laissent entrevoir de la situation difficile de la Bretagne, Guillotel, 'L'exode du clergé breton', pp. 299–300: 'Ce long examen des sources confirme le témoignage de l'annaliste de Redon qui plaçait en 920 l'exode général du clergé breton [...] les moines de Landévennec exceptés, les clercs se dirigèrent vers la *Francia*, les régions dominées par les Robertiens [...] les chefs nationaux bretons faisant défaut'.

[61] Comme les moines de Saint-Gwénolé de Landévennec, réfugiés à Montreuil-sur-Mer (dép. du Pas-de-Calais), probablement depuis la destruction de leur monastère en 913.

[62] Cf. *supra*, p. 126.

[63] *Les annales de Flodoard*, p. 6.

[64] *Les annales de Flodoard*, p. 38.

[65] *Les annales de Flodoard*, p. 6.

[66] *Les annales de Flodoard*, pp. 39–40.

pour que fut conclu le traité de 911.[67] L'avenir, à la fin des années 920, pouvait donc apparaître aux Bretons en exil, bien sombre. Car les pouvoirs, robertien et carolingien — tous deux royaux depuis 888 — semblaient prêts à pactiser avec les Scandinaves et donc à sacrifier le royaume de Bretagne. C'est alors que se dessinaient ces projets funestes pour la Bretagne que le prévôt de Dol, Radbod écrivait au roi Æthelstan, *Igitur, rex gloriose ... deprecamur atque humiliter imploramus qui in exulatu atque captivitate nostris meritis atque peccatis in Francia, ut non obliviscatur vestrae felicissimae largitatis magna misericordia* 'C'est pourquoi, roi glorieux ... nous vous supplions et implorons humblement, nous qui séjournons en Francie dans l'exil et la captivité pour notre punition et nos péchés afin que la grande miséricorde de votre très heureuse largesse ne nous oublie pas'.[68]

Aussi que pouvait demander implicitement Radbod en écrivant au roi de Wessex, sinon d'aider les Bretons à regagner leur terre? Le roi apparaissait, alors, être au cœur, sinon le cœur, de négociations diplomatiques complexes au niveau européen. Car aux années 930, il contribua à ce que trois jeunes princes, en exil à sa cour, retrouvent leurs droits et leur royaume: Louis de France, son neveu, Alain de Bretagne, son filleul, et Hakon de Norvège. Ce dernier apparaît, en effet, donné dans les sources norroises comme son filleul et fils adoptif.[69] 'L'histoire de Hakon le Bon' relate dans son chapitre premier la façon dont 'Hakon, le pupille d'Æthelstan fut fait roi'. Avant de mourir en 939, ce dernier lui procurant une troupe et de bons navires, l'équipa magnifiquement pour son voyage et l'aida à retrouver son trône.[70]

Alain et Louis revinrent eux en leur terre en 936. Ces restaurations de pouvoir, quasi simultanées, ne peuvent être fortuites et attestent un véritable jeu géopolitique à l'échelle européenne, jeu dont le roi de Wessex était le maître.[71] Rappelons, en effet, la présence aux années 930 à la cour du roi de trois héritiers

[67] Guillot, 'La conversion des Normands à partir de 911'.

[68] Guillotel, 'L'exode du clergé breton', p. 297.

[69] Ce que rappela Snorri Sturluson vers 1230, en rédigeant *l'Histoire des rois de Norvège*, pp. 159–60. Le poète et historien islandais avait une vaste connaissance des sources orales et écrites relatives aux IXe–XIe siècles. Ainsi raconte-t-il au 39e chapitre de l''Histoire de Harald à la belle chevelure' l''adoption' forcée de Hakon par Æthelstan, car 'posé sur genoux du roi', et au chapitre suivant, le fait que le roi le fit baptiser et lui enseigna 'la vraie foi ainsi que les bonnes mœurs et toutes sortes de manières raffinées'. Il fut d'ailleurs appelé 'Hakon, le pupille d'Athelstan', *Histoire des rois de Norvège*, p. 160.

[70] Snorri Sturluson, *Histoire des rois de Norvège*, pp. 164–65.

[71] Quaghebeur, 'Norvège et Bretagne aux IXe et Xe siècles', p. 129.

royaux en exil. La cour d'Æthelstan était donc à cette époque (et était regardée comme telle) un 'creuset' où se côtoyaient des hommes aux intérêts divergents et qui auraient été ennemis sur d'autres territoires. Pour ce qui concerne la Bretagne, les trois 'partis' intéressés à la dévolution du pouvoir en cette terre étaient, en effet, représentés: les Bretons avec Alain, les Francs par l'héritier du roi Charles le Simple (ce dernier avait concédé le titre royal au grand-père d'Alain), les Norvégiens enfin avec Hakon, Norvégiens qui occupaient alors la Bretagne. L'exil des Bretons pouvait donc préparer l'avenir, faisant se côtoyer tous ceux qui pouvaient contribuer à ce qu'il prenne fin. Et Æthelstan, plus que quiconque apparaissait comme celui à même d'aider l'héritier qu'était Alain à recouvrer sa terre et ses droits.

Britanni des 'deux côtés de la mer'

Au haut Moyen Âge, les *nomina*, masculins comme féminins, relevaient pleinement des biens patrimoniaux des lignages nobles et à ce titre on ne pouvait se les approprier indûment, seule l'alliance matrimoniale (et éventuellement une prestation de *fides*-foi) pouvait amener l'adoption d'un *nomen* jusqu'alors inconnu dans une lignée.[72]

Aussi le matériau onomastique est-il un moyen d'approche très précieux pour les spécialistes de l'époque altomédiévale. En l'absence de sources, ou en raison des aspects lacunaires de celles existantes, l'étude des noms de personne permet de saisir les politiques matrimoniales de la noblesse et ainsi d'approcher autant les réalités historiques et sociales que les mentalités des hommes de cette époque. Depuis une cinquantaine d'années, l'école historiographique allemande, avec, entre autres, les travaux remarquables de K.-F. Werner, a porté une particulière attention aux *nomina* donnés aux nobles du haut Moyen Âge. Car le patronyme d'un noble proclamait son appartenance à un lignage mais était également un projet politique et/ou spirituel et relevait du patrimoine familial. Le *nomen* prédisposait à l'exercice d'une charge, civile ou ecclésiastique et donnait des droits à celle-ci. Aussi y avait-il nécessité de relever les *nomina* d'ancêtres qui avaient exercé les *honores* — charges convoitées. Cela faisait que lors d'un mariage hypergamique on adjoignait, avec fierté et empressement, à l'héritage onomastique familial de nouveaux *nomina* porteurs d'une puissance

---

[72] Cf. à ce sujet les travaux fondamentaux de Karl-Ferdinand Werner, entre autres 'Liens de parenté et noms de personne', et Settipani et Keats-Rohan, éd., *Onomastique et parenté dans l'Occident médiéval*.

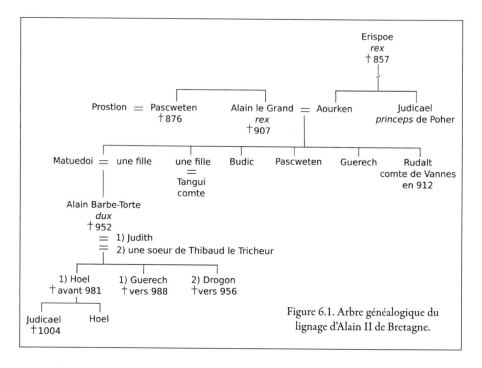

Figure 6.1. Arbre généalogique du lignage d'Alain II de Bretagne.

nouvelle car légitimes sur des territoires et des fonctions. En utilisant cet outil onomastique, que peut-on entrevoir pour Alain Barbe-Torte et les siens?

Soulignons tout d'abord le *nomen* donné à Alain. Si l'on ne sait rien de son origine (il apparaît absent de l'onomastique lignagère noble bretonne antérieure à l'époque carolingienne), il devint grâce au roi Alain le Grand, un patronyme royal, à ce titre donc rare. Or Alain Barbe-Torte, son petit-fils, n'était qu'un héritier en ligne féminine, lui donner ce *nomen* était étonnant car il lui ouvrait des droits éminents. Le roi Alain ayant eu plusieurs fils, il faut en conclure que sa fille était leur aînée et détentrice à ce titre de ce *nomen* prestigieux qu'elle donna donc à celui qui devait succéder à son grand-père (Fig. 6.1). Le droit politique des femmes nobles en terre bretonne est ici sensible et rappelons que l'on vit, quelques siècles plus tard, deux duchesses de plein droit, Constance et Anne. Cette situation amenant à considérer le mariage de Prostlon, fille du roi Salomon, avec Pascweten comme ouvrant peut-être la porte au titre royal, ce qui expliquerait que Pascweten ait assassiné son beau-père. De même les prétentions à diriger la Bretagne d'Alain le Grand étaient-elles étayées par l'épouse qu'il avait choisie, Aourken-Orgain, petite-fille du roi Erispoe. Les nobles bretonnes de haute naissance furent donc particulièrement convoitées au IXe siècle, car elles pouvaient être, semble-t-il, un 'moyen d'accès' à l'*honor* royal.

6. ALAIN DE BRETAGNE, L'EXIL D'UN PRINCE

Mais que peut nous livrer une enquête onomastique plus approfondie, de l'avenir que se comprit Alain Barbe-Torte, devenu un homme?

Trois fils d'Alain apparaissent mentionnés dans les sources. Drogon, au nom carolingien naquit peu avant la disparition d'Alain en 952, de son union avec la sœur de Thibaud le Tricheur; ce dernier, chef de la Maison de Blois était un allié des Robertiens. Drogon était le fruit d'un mariage légitime et à ce titre était considéré par son père comme celui qui devait lui succéder à la tête de la Bretagne. Aussi, sur le point de mourir, le *dux* appela à lui les Grands de Bretagne afin qu'ils s'engagent à le servir.[73] Par ce mariage, Alain s'était lié à une héritière au sang carolingien, il voulut donc marquer par un *nomen* bien éloigné des traditions de son lignage que le futur *dux* de Bretagne avait dans ses veines du sang impérial. Alain fut probablement amer que le Carolingien ne lui ait pas accordé le titre royal mais avait-il oublié pour autant la fierté de ses ancêtres à servir la grandeur carolingienne ...?

Drogon avait deux frères aînés, Hoel et Guerech, nés d'une première union avec Judith, femme noble.[74] Cette dernière était encore vivante aux années 980, Guerech étant sur le point de mourir, elle veillait sur ses petits-enfants Judicael et Hoel.[75] Elle ne fut pas qualifiée d'*uxor* d'Alain, c'est-à-dire d'épouse légitime. Durant l'époque carolingienne de nombreux nobles, avant de contracter un *legale connubium*, prenaient une 'épouse de jeunesse', souvent une femme noble.[76] Mais le cas de Judith, concubine du prince breton, est un *hapax* dans la lignée des princesses bretonnes de l'époque carolingienne, car ces dernières furent toujours qualifiées du titre *uxor*.[77] Alain rompait donc avec une tradition ancienne car en Bretagne on respectait les strictes règles du mariage chrétien élaborées par l'Église. Alain donna aux deux fils nés de cette union les *nomina* d'Hoel et Guerech. Ce dernier patronyme avait été celui de l'un des fils d'Alain le Grand.[78] Variante du *nomen* Waroch, il rappelait l'assise patrimoniale du lignage dans le Vannetais et voulait conserver la *memoria* de l'homme qui avait combattu le roi franc au VIe siècle puis obtenu l'investiture comtale. Guerech,

---

[73] *La Chronique de Nantes*, p. 105, Drogon y était donné comme *parvulus*, un tout jeune enfant.

[74] *La Chronique de Nantes*, p. 113.

[75] *La Chronique de Nantes*, pp. 126–27.

[76] Le Jan, *Famille et pouvoir dans le monde franc*.

[77] Marmorhec, Wembrit, Aourken, épouses d'Erispoe, de Salomon et Alain le Grand.

[78] Guerech souffrant, le roi abandonna des biens à l'abbaye de Redon, *Cartulaire de l'abbaye de Redon*, Appendix, LI, pp. 373–74.

fils cadet, portait donc un *nomen* à forte valeur symbolique, conservé car marquant l'ancienneté des droits du lignage en Bretagne-Sud. Mais Alain choisit de donner à son fils aîné un *nomen* qui apparaissait être une rupture onomastique: Hoel. Ce patronyme était jusqu'alors inconnu en Bretagne, parmi les humbles et les nobles.[79] Le premier homme à porter ce *nomen* fut donc le fils aîné d'Alain Barbe-Torte, celui à qui aurait pu échoir une responsabilité royale, car son sang lui en donnait le droit.[80] Pourquoi cette 'innovation' et ce non-respect des règles onomastiques, qui plus est dans un grave contexte de crise politique car d'exil?

Ce *nomen* était-il issu de la dot onomastique de Judith? L'adoption de *nomina* 'nouveaux' se justifiait au haut Moyen Âge lors d'une union matrimoniale. Nouvellement apportés par l'épousée, ils étaient adoptés pour les héritiers car porteurs de prestige et de pouvoirs. Alain voulut donc semble-t-il parer son premier né de ce *nomen* qu'il comprenait comme un ajout à la gloire de sa Maison. Une fierté qui se perpétuait encore au XIe siècle: l'arrière-petite-fille de Judith portait le nom de son aïeule et donnait à son premier né, le futur comte de Cornouaille, le *nomen* d'*Houuel*.

Ce patronyme doit être rapproché de celui de Hywel, connu aux IXe–Xe siècles dans plusieurs royaumes du Pays de Galles, son détenteur le plus célèbre étant le roi Hywel Dda (mort vers 950). Alain et Judith, vivant Outre-Manche jusqu'en 936, auraient-ils pu s'approprier ce *nomen* royal? Cela est difficilement concevable. En outre, Alain avait dû côtoyer à la cour d'Æthelstan, le roi gallois, car *subregulus*, il y fut régulièrement présent de 927 à 949. Et la *Chronique anglo-saxonne* nota bien à l'année 927 qu'Hywel 'roi des Gallois de l'ouest' se soumit à Æthelstan.[81]

Trois hypothèses peuvent donc être envisagées: le roi gallois Hywel fut le parrain, au sens chrétien, du fils d'Alain et à ce titre consentit à ce que le prince breton lui donnât son *nomen*; ou Hywel était devenu le *dominus* d'Alain, à l'image du lien qui unissait sans doute son père Matuedoi au roi Edouard; enfin dernière possibilité, Judith était une princesse galloise. Car le nom de Judith était lui-même particulier, il s'agissait d'un *nomen* féminin carolingien, porté par la fille aînée de Charles le Chauve donnée en mariage en 856 au roi Æthelwulf; cette carolingienne fit donc que ce *nomen* 'traversa' la Manche. Judith, à la mort du roi, fut mariée au fils de ce dernier, ce qui causa un grand trouble, car pour l'Église il s'agissait d'un inceste. Le mariage rompu, Judith

---

[79] Le *Cartulaire de Redon*, formidable 'réservoir' onomastique en témoigne.

[80] Quaghebeur, 'Alain Barbe-Torte ou le retour improbable d'un prince en sa terre', p. 159.

[81] *Anglo-Saxon Chronicle*, p. 68.

6. ALAIN DE BRETAGNE, L'EXIL D'UN PRINCE

revint sur le continent. Mais ses mariages anglais restèrent-ils vraiment sans aucun héritier ...? Car on voit mal, au regard du prestige du nom de Judith (carolingien et porté par une reine de Wessex sacrée) une appropriation indue en Wessex. La Maison royale de Wessex, afin de sceller plus étroitement la paix avec les rois de Galles, ne leur donna-t-elle pas une jeune fille qui emporta avec elle les *nomina* attachés à son sang?

Il faut souligner que si nous connaissons, à l'heure actuelle, le roi gallois sous le nom d'Hywel, les documents contemporains adoptaient la graphie *Howael*, comme d'ailleurs sur le penny d'argent frappé au nom de Hywel et conservé au British Museum. Le Gallois Asser, mentionnant Hywel ap Rhys, écrivait *Houil*, une transcription proche, pour le Gallois qu'il était, de la manière de prononcer ce nom[82] ou de celui figurant dans la liste des comtes de Cornouaille du Cartulaire de Landévennec, Houuel.[83]

Hoel, à la mort de son père Alain Barbe-Torte, en 952, était en âge de lui succéder car la *Chronique de Nantes* indique que les Nantais se tournèrent vers lui après que son demi-frère Drogon eut disparu.[84] Il avait assisté à l'importante donation faite par son père à l'abbaye de Landévennec. Alain y disait combien 'inlassablement' l'abbé Jean s'était fait le messager de la paix des deux côtés de la mer, aidant à son retour en sa terre,[85] l'acte fut dressé entre 944–952, mais au regard du rôle joué par l'abbé de Landévennec, il faut envisager qu'il fut dressé plutôt en 944–945. Hoel y apparaissait investi de l'*honor* comtal de Nantes, il était donc âgé d'au moins quinze ans. Il était bien né outre-mer et le scribe écrivait son *nomen, Houuel*.

De lignée royale, le fils d'Alain Barbe-Torte était appelé à avoir un rôle important en Bretagne, son *nomen* devant permettre à son peuple de le 'reconnaître' avec les droits qui étaient siens. Aussi le fait que son père ne lui ait pas donné un nom qui lui ouvrirait le cœur des Bretons, doit être compris comme le fait qu'Alain Barbe-Torte, lors de la naissance de son premier né, avait perdu tout espoir de voir rétablir ses propres droits dynastiques. Voulant assurer un avenir à son héritier, le *nomen* d'*Howael-Houuel* lui attirerait toute la sympathie et le respect dont bénéficiait Hywel Dda-le Bon, dans les terres où il était connu et respecté.

---

[82] Asser, *Histoire du roi Alfred*, éd. et trad. Gautier, chapitre 80, pp. 130–31.

[83] *Cartulaire de Landévennec*, éd. le Men et Ernault, 54, pp. 576–77.

[84] *La Chronique de Nantes*, éd. Merlet, pp. 112–13; Drogon mourut entre 952 et 957.

[85] Cet acte a été étudié par Guillotel, *Actes des ducs de Bretagne*, 2, pp. 152–54.

Ce lien établi avec le Pays de Galles est étayé par un autre indice. Était présent lors de la donation ducale à Landévennec, le vicomte Diles, or un autre document le dote du surnom *Heirguor Chebre* — l'exilé de Cambrie.[86] Ce texte fut élaboré au milieu du XIe siècle à Landévennec, il s'agit d'une liste de dix-neuf noms d'hommes, les quatre derniers ayant été comtes de Cornouaille de la fin du Xe siècle et au milieu du XIe siècle; le *nomen* de Diles les précède immédiatement, il vécut donc au Xe siècle. Or *Chebre* est la forme bretonnisée de *Cambria*, soit l'actuel Pays de Galles.[87] Cet homme était donc représentatif de la communauté bretonne qui avait entouré le jeune prince lors de l'exil. Diles appartenait à un lignage de machtierns vannetais, présent depuis les années 830 dans les actes du Cartulaire de Redon, en 852, l'un de ses membres dotait ainsi l'abbaye en présence de *nobiles viri* au sein desquels se trouvait Pascweten.[88] Le lignage parvint à installer l'un des siens sur le siège épiscopal de Vannes. Mentionné comme évêque le 5 février 870, Diles était probablement le *presbyter*, présent auprès de Pascweten, dans un acte légèrement antérieur.[89] La proximité, entretenue par ce lignage vannetais, depuis plusieurs décennies, à l'égard de la Maison de Pascweten et donc d'Alain Barbe-Torte amena donc à ce que leurs chemins d'exil soient identiques. Et cette fidélité, jamais démentie, fut récompensée au retour en Bretagne par un titre vicomtal.[90] Mais le surnom donné à Diles par les moines de Landévennec nous donne deux informations: Diles entendait être reconnu de cette façon, ce que respectèrent les moines de Landévennec qui le connaissaient bien. Or revendiquer un statut d'ancien exilé apparaît étonnant sauf à ce que cela marque la fidélité indéfectible à son Prince, en ne le quittant même dans un exil outre-mer. Cela nous indique donc que le duc Alain avait été lui aussi exilé en Cambrie. La présence envisagée d'Alain Barbe-Torte au Pays de Galles n'est-elle pas ici confirmée?

Le jeune prince et son père avaient sans doute constitué autour d'eux une communauté d'exilés et comme Alain ils durent choisir, eux qui se disaient *Britanni*, de rejoindre des territoires où l'on pratiquait la langue qui était la leur, où certains paysages leur rappelaient ceux de leur terre, atténuant ainsi la douleur de l'exil.

---

[86] *Cartulaire de Landévennec*, 54, pp. 576–77.

[87] Loth, *Chrestomathie bretonne*, pp. 115–16.

[88] *CR*, xx, pp. 17–18.

[89] *CR*, ccxxxiv, pp. 181–82, et lxxii, pp. 57, 858 × 862, un premier lundi de novembre.

[90] Alain Barbe-Torte, confiant à Diles le Poher-Cornouaille.

6. ALAIN DE BRETAGNE, L'EXIL D'UN PRINCE

Car les Bretons ne perdirent-ils pas, un temps, l'espoir de retrouver leur pays ...? Aux années 930, la situation évolua, en effet, de façon inquiétante. Cela amena Alain à venir en Bretagne en 931 et à y mener une révolte, le jour de la Saint-Michel. Comme si le Breton demandait à l'Archange de l'aider à vaincre la présence démoniaque qu'était pour lui celle des Scandinaves. S'il tua le *dux* scandinave Felecan, il dut pourtant quitter de nouveau la Bretagne. Le patronyme celtique de Felecan ainsi que son *honor* ducal, marque d'une reconnaissance institutionnelle, suffisent à mesurer les évolutions en cours et qui livraient la Bretagne à un pouvoir scandinave.[91] Le *princeps* Guillaume Longue-Épée en profita pour dévaster le territoire rebelle, ramenant à lui le *dux* Berenger, descendant d'Erispoe et en 933, le normand se commendant au roi Raoul il reçut le Cotentin et l'Avranchin, amputant ainsi le territoire du *regnum* breton disparu. Depuis le milieu des années 920, le sud de la Bretagne, dont le Nantais, apparaissait abandonné aux Scandinaves, le début des années 930 voyait donc la situation bretonne s'aggraver encore. Les exilés ne pensèrent-ils pas alors ne plus jamais revenir en leur terre c'est-à-dire retrouver leurs *honores* et leurs possessions patrimoniales ...?

Dès le règne d'Alfred le Grand, des contacts s'établirent entre les 'Armoricains' et le royaume de Wessex. Ils ne purent que s'affermir lors des événements tragiques connus par le royaume de Bretagne dans les décennies qui suivirent. La noblesse bretonne, sembla alors se tourner vers les souverains anglo-saxons, faute d'obtenir des Carolingiens et des Robertiens, aide et conseil. Des liens de nature spirituelle se créèrent, ils auguraient peut-être d'un avenir politique différent, certains nobles bretons, au plus haut niveau, n'envisagèrent-ils pas de créer des liens politiques novateurs? Car la fidélité promise aux Carolingiens

---

[91] Il faut souligner que Flodoard, *Les annales de Flodoard*, pp. 51–52 qualifie simplement Incon (chef des Normands de la Loire) de *Nordmannus* 'homme du Nord'. Probablement parce que Flodoard ne lui savait aucune légitimité institutionnelle à contrôler la Bretagne. En revanche, l'érudit rémois donna à Felecan le titre de *dux*, *Les annales de Flodoard*, éd. Lauer, p. 50. Felecan voyait donc son pouvoir reconnu par une instance que nous ne pouvons pas saisir. Le Poher-Cornouaille, lieu de la révolte menée par Alain Barbe-Torte et qui fut précédée de la mort de Felecan, connaissait-il, comme le Nantais, une installation 'officielle' des Scandinaves? Cela fut l'une des hypothèses d'Hubert Guillotel, 'Le premier siècle du pouvoir ducal breton'. Mais soulignons le *nomen* de Felecan: il apparaît être d'origine celtique, irlandais pour Lucien Musset, écossais pour Gillian Fellows-Jensen, gallois pour le très regretté Bernard Tanguy, de *ffelaig-* 'brillant, chef', information non publiée dont nous l'avions vivement remercié. Musset, 'Participation des Vikings venus de pays celtes'; Fellows-Jensen, 'Les noms de lieux d'origine scandinave'.

par Nominoe depuis 831, voire de façon plus ancienne, n'apparaissait-elle pas remise en question par l'affirmation de la puissance robertienne qui, avant 936, semblait triompher en Francie? Le royaume de Wessex était un royaume proche de l'idéologie carolingienne, les Bretons, abandonnés par les Robertiens qui cédèrent, le comté de Nantes voire la Bretagne aux Scandinaves aux années 920, répugnèrent-ils à leur engager leur *fides* ...?

Si ces considérations existaient bien au début du xe siècle, le fait que l'héritier royal, Alain, en exil jusqu'en 936, n'ait pas voulu donner à son fils aîné un *nomen* relevant de son lignage était significatif d'une nouvelle fracture. Les 'Armoricains' du royaume de Bretagne avaient sans doute rejoint ceux qui se disaient comme eux *Britanni*, les Gallois. Comme si les Bretons, alors que leur monde s'effondrait, avaient fait à rebours le voyage de certains de leurs ancêtres et avaient choisi désormais de retrouver les territoires qui avaient été leurs.

Joëlle Quaghebeur, maître de conférences en histoire médiévale (Université de Bretagne-Sud, France, 1996–2021, E. R.) a soutenu à l'université de Paris-Sorbonne une thèse de doctorat ayant pour titre *La Cornouaille du IXe au XIIe siècle. Mémoire, pouvoirs, noblesse* (P.U.R., Rennes, 2002). Ayant eu pour Maîtres des historiens du Droit, ses travaux de recherche et ses publications ont continué de porter sur l'histoire des institutions, le pouvoir du Prince, la noblesse, du VIe au XIIe siècle, dans un territoire particulier, la Bretagne.

Bibliographie

Sources

The Anglo-Saxon Chronicle. A Revised Translation, éd. et trad. D. Whitelock, D. C. Douglas, et S. I. Tucker (London: Eyre, 1961)

Annales de Saint-Bertin, éd. F. Grat, J. Vielliard et S. Clemencet, Société de l'Histoire de France, 470 (Paris: Klincksieck, 1964)

Les annales de Flodoard, éd. Ph. Lauer (Paris: Alphonse Picard et fils, 1905)

Annales Sancti Florentii Salmurensis, in *Recueil d'annales angevines et vendômoises*, éd. L. Halphen (Paris: Picard, 1903), pp. 111–26

Asser, *Histoire du roi Alfred*, éd. et trad. A. Gauthier, Classiques de l'histoire du Moyen Âge, 52 (Paris: Les Belles Lettres, 2013)

Cartulaire de l'abbaye de Landevenec, éd. A. de La Borderie (Rennes: Catel, 1888)

Cartulaire de l'abbaye de Redon en Bretagne, éd. A. de Courson (Paris: Imprimerie Impériale, 1863)

Cartulaire de l'abbaye Sainte-Croix de Quimperlé, éd. L. Maitre et P. de Berthou, Bibliothèque bretonne armoricaine, 4 (Rennes: Plihon et Hommay, 1904)

6. ALAIN DE BRETAGNE, L'EXIL D'UN PRINCE

Cartulaire de Landévennec, éd. R.-F.-L. le Men et E. Ernault, in *Mélanges historiques: choix de documents*, Collection de documents inédits sur l'histoire de France, 5 (Paris: Imprimerie Nationale, 1886), pp. 533–600

Cartulaire de Saint-Guénolé de Landévennec, dir. S. Lebecq, Collection Sources médiévales de l'histoire de Bretagne (Rennes: Presses universitaires, 2015)

La Chronique de Nantes (570–1049), éd. R. Merlet (Paris: Picard, 1896)

Dudon de Saint-Quentin, *De moribus et actis primorum Normanniae ducum*, éd. J. Lair (Caen: Le Blanc-Hardel, 1865)

Mémoires pour servir de preuves à l'histoire de Bretagne, éd. H. Morice, 3 vols (Paris: Osmont, 1742–1746)

The Monks of Redon: Gesta Sanctorum Rotonensium and Vita Conuuoionis, éd. et trad. C. Brett, SCH, 10 (Woodbridge: Boydell, 1989)

Reginonis abbatis Prumiensis Chronicon cum continuatione Treverensi, éd. F. Kurze (Hanover: Hahn, 1890)

William of Malmesbury, *Gesta Pontificum Anglorum = The History of the English Bishops*, éd. et trad. M. Winterbottom avec l'assistance de R. M. Thomson, 2 vols (Oxford: Clarendon Press, 2007)

Snorri Sturluson, *L'Histoire des rois de Norvège,* introd. et trad. par F. X. Dillmann (Paris: Gallimard, 2000)

Études

Brett, C., 'A Breton Pilgrim in England in the Reign of King Æthelstan', in *France and the British Isles in the Middle Ages and Renaissance*, éd. G. Jondorf et D. N. Dumville (Woodbridge: Boydell, 1991), pp. 43–70

Brunterc'h, Jean-Pierre, 'Le duché du Maine et la Marche de Bretagne', in *La Neustrie. Les pays au nord de la Loire de 650 à 850*, éd. H. Atsma, Beihefte der Francia, 16 (Sigmaringen: Thorbecke, 1989), pp. 29–127

Chédeville, A. et H. Guillotel, *La Bretagne des saints et des rois V^e–Xe siècle*, Histoire de la Bretagne, 6 (Rennes: Ouest-France, 1984)

Davies, W., *Wales in the Early Middle Ages*, Studies in the Early History of Britain (Leicester: University Press, 1988)

Fawtier, R., 'Ingomar, historien breton', in *Mélanges d'histoire du Moyen Âge offerts à M. Ferdinand Lot par ses amis et ses élèves* (Paris: Champion, 1925), pp. 181–203

Foot, S., *Æthelstan: First King of England* (New Haven, CT: Yale University Press, 2011)

Guillot, O., 'La conversion des Normands à partir de 911', in *Arcana imperii* II, éd. O. Guillot, Cahiers de l'Institut d'anthropologie juridique de Limoges, 23 (Limoges: Presses universitaires, 2010), pp. 63–92

Guillotel, H., 'Le premier siècle du pouvoir ducal breton (936–1040)', in *Principautés et territoires et Études d'histoire Lorraine (Actes du 103e Congrès national des sociétés savantes, Nancy-Metz, 1978)*, Section de philologie et d'histoire jusqu'à 1610, 103 (Paris: Bibliothèque nationale, 1979), pp. 63–68

——, 'L'exode du clergé breton devant les invasions scandinaves', *MSHAB*, 59 (1982), 269–315

——, *Les Actes des ducs de Bretagne (944–1148)*, éd. Ph. Charon, Ph. Guigon, C. Henry, M. Jones, K. Keats-Rohan, et J.-C. Meuret, Sources médiévales de l'histoire de Bretagne, 3 (Rennes: Presses universitaires, 2014)

Le Jan, R., *Famille et pouvoir dans le monde franc (VIIIe–Xe siècle). Essai d'anthropologie sociale*, Histoire ancienne et médiévale, 33 (Paris: Publications de la Sorbonne, 1995)

Marafioti, N., *The King's Body: Burial and Succession in Late Anglo-Saxon England* (Toronto: University Press, 2014)

Molyneaux, G., *The Formation of the English Kingdom in the Tenth Century* (Oxford: University Press, 2015)

Nelson, J. L., 'The Franks and the English in the Ninth Century Reconsidered', in J. Nelson, *Rulers and Ruling Families in Early Medieval Europe: Alfred, Charles the Bald, and Others* (Aldershot: Ashgate, 1999), p. VI

Quaghebeur, J., *La Cornouaille du IXe au XIIe siècle: Mémoire, pouvoirs, noblesse* (Rennes: Presses universitaires, 2002)

——, 'Norvège et Bretagne aux IXe et Xe siècles: un destin partagé', in *Les fondations scandinaves en Occident et les débuts du duché de Normandie, Actes du colloque de Cerisy-la-Salle (25–29 septembre 2002)*, éd. Pierre Bauduin (Caen: Publications du CRAHM, 2005), pp. 113–31

——, 'Puissance publique, puissances privées sur les côtes du comté de Vannes (IXe–XIIe siècle)', in *Pouvoirs et littoraux du XVe au XXe siècle*, éd. G. Le Bouëdec et F. Chappé (Rennes: Presses universitaires, 2000), pp. 11–28

——, 'Alain Barbe-Torte ou le retour improbable d'un prince en sa terre', *Bulletin de l'Association bretonne*, 112 (2003), 143–68

——, 'Landévennec, l'abbaye des rois de Bretagne', in *Landévennec 818–2018. Une abbaye bénédictine en Bretagne, Actes du colloque de Landévennec des 6, 7 et 8 juin 2018*, éd. Yves Coativy (Brest: Centre de recherche bretonne et celtique, 2020), pp. 97–109

Rumble, A. R., 'Edward and the Churches of Winchester and Wessex', in *Edward the Elder, 899–924*, éd. N. J. Higham et D. H. Hill (London: Routledge, 2001), pp. 230–47

Settipani, C., et K. S. B. Keats-Rohan (éd.), *Onomastique et parenté dans l'Occident medieval*, Prosopographica et Genealogica, 3 (Oxford: Linacre College, 2000)

Sheringham, J. T., 'Les machtierns. Quelques témoignages gallois et cornouaillais', *MSHAB*, 58 (1981), 61–72

Werner, K.-F., 'Liens de parenté et noms de personne. Un problème historique et méthodologique', in *Famille et parenté dans l'Occident médiéval: Actes du colloque de Paris (6–8 juin 1974)*, Publications de l'École française de Rome, 30 (Rome: École Française de Rome, 1977), pp. 13–18, 25–34

7. *MEMORIA*, MEMORIALIZATION, AND THE MONKS OF MONT-SAINT-MICHEL, *c.* 960–1033

K. S. B. Keats-Rohan

ABSTRACT An otherwise unknown bishop of Avranches, Autbert, established a community of canons on Mont-Saint-Michel in 708. A Benedictine abbey existed by 966. Numerous shadowy references in the intervening period do not permit a definitive history on their own, but do show that this Neustrian community was strongly linked to Brittany. Two narrative foundation texts survive; contrasting with these memorializing texts are liturgical texts which incorporate the obits of monks from *c.* 960 to 1212, with later additions. Analysis of the obits, contextualized by reference to confraternities with other monasteries, and to recent revisionist views of the tenth-century revival of Benedictinism, is highly revealing. It points to an eclectic early community, partly inspired by Odo of Cluny, who established themselves with the support of Archbishop Hugh of Rouen. The first to adopt the reforms of William of Volpiano, they introduced them to Brittany in the time of Mainard II, also abbot of Redon, and Hildebert I, *c.* 1000–1017.

RÉSUMÉ En 708, un évêque d'Avranches inconnu par ailleurs, Autbert, établit une communauté de canons sur le Mont-Saint-Michel. Dès 966, il y existait une abbaye bénédictine. Dans les années intermédiaires, les références historiques nombreuses mais obscures ne permettent pas la construction d'une histoire définitive, mais indiquent que cette communauté neustrienne avait des liens forts avec la Bretagne. Les textes qui nous sont parvenus comprennent deux récits de fondation: ces textes narrateurs contrastent avec les textes liturgiques voués à la *memoria*, qui intègrent les obits de moines d'entre 960 et 1212, avec des additions postérieures. L'analyse des obits, comparés avec les listes de confraternité d'autres abbayes, et mis dans le contexte d'études récentes révisionnistes du renouveau monastique du xe s., s'avoue révélatrice. Elle met en relief une communauté aux origines éclectiques, inspirée en partie par Odon de Cluny, établie avec l'aide de l'archevêque Hugues de Rouen. Les premiers à adopter les réformes de Guillaume de Dijon, les moines les introduisirent à la Bretagne à l'époque de Mainard II, abbé du Mont et de Redon, et de Hildebert I, *c.* 1000–1017.

KEYWORDS Alet, Conwoion, Dol, exodus of Breton clergy, Fécamp, Hildebert I, Landévennec, liturgy, Mainard I, Mainard II, martyrology, commemoration, monastic reform, necrology, Odo and Maiol of Cluny, Redon, Saint-Bénigne de Dijon, Saint-Jacut-de-la-Mer, Saint-Jouin, Saint-Méen-le-Grand, Saint-Taurin d'Évreux, Saint-Wandrille, William of Volpiano.

Multi-disciplinary Approaches to Medieval Brittany, 450–1200: Connections and Disconnections, ed. by Caroline Brett, Fiona Edmonds, and Paul Russell, TCNE 36 (Turnhout: Brepols, 2023) pp. 141–177   BREPOLS PUBLISHERS   10.1484/M.TCNE-EB.5.132312

The sanctuary of Saint Michael the Archangel at Mont Tumba was founded in 708, in the late Merovingian period. The existence of the founder, a bishop of Avranches, is nowhere attested outside the community's foundation history, an early ninth-century text known as *Revelatio*. At the turn of the eleventh century, a list of monks living and dead was written into a sacramentary intended for use at the abbey of Fleury. The mid-eleventh century saw the production of the Mont's Sacramentary, now MS New York, Morgan Library 641. Among a series of short, but important, documents of the same period are two sets of annals, from around 1048 and 1116. About 1075 a text known as *Introductio monachorum* was compiled from earlier tenth- and eleventh-century material, including a forged papal bull and a royal diploma, plus a collection of *Miracula*. Subsequently, an official history of the abbey was confected by welding together the *Revelatio* and the *Introductio*. The earliest surviving version of this *Historia* is found in the Cartulary, which was written (though not quite finished) around 1149/1150.[1] The early thirteenth century saw the compilation of the Martyrology-Necrology and a much larger Necrology, eventually bound with other related material into the surviving Chapter Book, now Bibliothèque patrimoniale d'Avranches, MS 214. For the earlier periods, all we have are fragments.

Given this exiguous documentary survival from the early history of one of the most famous monasteries of western Europe, it is important to find ways to maximize the benefit from what does survive. This will be a complex and multi-faceted exercise, and one that can be undertaken here in only the broadest terms. The community's texts can have not only a practical purpose or function — liturgical, administrative, etc. — but also a programme, a more or less overt intention to project a message from within the community to an external audience. A good deal of what survives, including the Cartulary, concerns the right to elect their own abbot, based on Chapter 64 of the Rule of St Benedict.

The texts are also about recording the past for the benefit of present and future members of the community, which is not to say that they are histories. Where such texts are also programmatic, i.e., intended to reach an external audience, we may expect to find that the idea of history as what actually happened parts company with a record of what we are required to believe happened. Not infrequently, we shall be in the presence of a writer imposing anachronistic ideas upon his attempts to explain to himself obscure aspects of

---

[1] See Bouet and Desbordes, *Chroniques Latines*, pp. 9–14; *Cartulary of Mont-Saint-Michel*, pp. 63–76.

his community's past. Even the annals show some of these symptoms. Some of the more substantial texts relate to *memoria* in the sense of the liturgical remembrance of the dead as individuals; others are concerned with memorialization, by which, somewhat paradoxically, is meant the creation of memorials to the community at different stages of its living. These distinctions provide crucial guides as to how these texts can be used and interpreted as sources for the abbey's history. None of these features is unique to this abbey, but this is a propitious moment for another look at the Mont material, the subject of much controversy in recent years, thanks to the launch of the Virtual Library of all 248 surviving manuscripts now at Avranches, which is spurring new research and new interpretations.[2]

The Ninth-century Monastic Reform

The *Revelatio* and other texts were published with extensive commentary by Pierre Bouet and Olivier Desbordes in 2009. *Revelatio* is shown to be a product of the first Carolingian renaissance, written around 820 by a well-schooled canon who was a member of the community whose origins he described.[3] An early magnet for hermits, we are told, the first formal community on the Mont was the work of an otherwise unknown Bishop Autbert of Avranches, who, according to the later Annals, in 708 under Childebert III, instituted twelve canons and a provost to serve a sanctuary of St Michael modelled on Monte Gargano in Apulia. The narrative of *Revelatio* closely resembles that of the *Liber de apparitione sancti Michaelis in Monte Gargano*.[4] A grant of revenues from the episcopal vills of Genêts and Itier in the Avranchin was allocated to provide maintenance for the community. At the time of writing, the number of canons was reduced, which the author saw as a failure on the part of Autbert's successors. Whether the community failed at any point in the ninth century is unknown, but canons would remain in service at the Mont, alongside monks, although in 1179 Robert of Torigny petitioned the pope to reduce their number to three.[5]

---

[2] *Bibliothèque virtuelle du Mont Saint-Michel.*

[3] For this paragraph see Bouet and Desbordes, *Chroniques latines*, pp. 29–87, and, for the text itself, pp. 90–103.

[4] Printed in *Chroniques latines*, pp. 123–35.

[5] Bouet and Desbordes, *Chroniques latines*, pp. 162–65.

The writing of *Revelatio* coincided with the launch of Louis the Pious's initiative, in alliance with St Benedict of Aniane, to better organize under uniform rules the communities of canons and communities of monks that had proliferated during the previous 150-odd years.[6] The distinction between the two had been blurred by the mass ordination of monks following Charlemagne's reforms and the situation was slow to change. The early tenth-century reforming monastics would seek to end the secularization of monks by first removing any canons, and then installing monks bound by the asceticism of the Benedictine Rule, practised in seclusion from the world.

The Reform in Brittany: Redon and Mont-Saint-Michel

In Brittany, Louis found a willing partner in the ancient abbey of Landévennec. Also influenced by the reforms was the new abbey of Redon, founded by Conwoion, a converted layman, in a previously empty space at the junction of four bishoprics, Vannes, Alet, Rennes, and Nantes. Initially opposed by local landholders and denied permission by the emperor, he attracted the support first of the emperor's representative Nominoë, and ultimately of the king himself, in 833.[7] Redon's closeness to the Mont community can be documented from 990 and is likely to have begun far earlier, but understanding it remains elusive.[8]

Until 851 Redon was sited at a point where Brittany abutted the Frankish kingdom of Neustria. As such, Conwoion was able to exploit his contacts among both the Breton and Frankish elites, a particularly important group being the Rorgonids, whose influence extended across Brittany to the English Channel and also to the *ducatus Cenomannensis* in the ninth century, and who were related to the counts of Rennes and Le Mans of the tenth century.[9] A similar liminality pointing in several directions was characteristic of Mont-Saint-Michel. The *Revelatio* author described it as six miles west of Avranches on the borders of Brittany. As part of the diocese of Avranches it was in Carolingian Neustria, but in around 800 the Cotentin peninsula, of which it was part, was run by a *dux* with the Breton name Anowareth.[10] In 851 Charles

---

[6] Gaillard, *D'une réforme à l'autre*, pp. 123–47.

[7] Brett, *The Monks of Redon*, pp. 1–3.

[8] Garault, 'L'abbaye de Redon', pp. 94–96.

[9] See Doumerc, 'Essai de reconstitution'.

[10] Van Torhoudt, 'Les Bretons dans les diocèses', pp. 126–27.

7. *MEMORIA*, MEMORIALIZATION, AND THE MONKS OF MONT-SAINT-MICHEL

the Bald granted the region comprising the counties of Nantes, Rennes, and the Cotentin to the Breton ruler Erispoë, whose successor Salomon held them until his murder in 874. Eventually, the Cotentin, including the dioceses of Avranches, Coutances, and Bayeux, was ceded by Charles the Simple in 933 to William Longsword of Normandy.

During this time, then, any community on Mont-Saint-Michel was under Breton rule. We know little enough about what was there, but there are good indications from the 860s onward that it had become an important place of pilgrimage and as such had an organized religious life of some sort. Although Charles the Bald's grant to Erispoë had specifically reserved to himself the dioceses of Avranches and Coutances, in order to preserve the integrity of the metropolitan see of Rouen, there were no bishops of Avranches between 863 and 989. A regular canon would expect to be subject to a bishop, and bishops were certainly needed for key functions such as ordinations. It is probable, as Florian Mazel has suggested, that the bishop of Rennes initially supplied these functions, before they were taken over by the bishops of Dol.[11] The strong relationship between the Mont community and its close neighbours in the Dolois remained a fact of life for centuries, as did a close relationship with the abbey of Redon.

A letter written by Odo, abbot of Glanfeuil from 862–869, to Bishop Almod of Le Mans, described an encounter with a cleric called Peter from Mont-Saint-Michel, who was journeying to Rome. He purchased five manuscripts from him, all of them Lives of St Benedict and his disciples. One, a Life of St Maur, was so poor that he re-wrote it, in the name of Faustus, a supposed disciple of Benedict. In a classic monastic sleight of hand, Odo was here deliberately recasting the sixth- or seventh-century nobleman Maurus, founder of Glanfeuil, as the older and more shadowy Maurus of Subiaco, disciple of St Benedict. The fact that Peter had all these Lives associated with St Benedict, and that Odo used the phrase *de loco* to describe Mont-Saint-Michel might suggest at least a proto-Benedictine community was then present.[12] Just a few years, later, c. 867–870, a pilgrim monk named Bernard visited Mont-Saint-Michel where he found *abbas Phinimontius Brito*.[13] The interest here is that the abbot is a Breton. His name, evidently a fusion of a personal name with

---

[11] Gaillard, *D'une réforme*, pp. 123–47, esp. 126–29. Mazel, *L'évêque et le territoire*, pp. 184, 215–16; see also Musset, 'Pélerinages', 129.

[12] Discussed in Dimier, 'Le mot *locus*'; Bouet and Desbordes, *Chroniques latines*, pp. 78–79.

[13] Printed in *Chroniques latines*, pp. 371–74.

a location, recalls the *Abbas Finoes* who attested a document in the Redon Cartulary with Conwoion's successor Abbot Ritcand in 868. In all probability this man was the priest Finoës, a favourite of King Salomon.[14] This is likely to mean that he was acting as an *abbas basilicae*, in charge of a community of canons serving a basilica.[15]

The Tenth-century Reform: The Canons

There are indications of the Mont's importance as a place of pilgrimage and penitence in the *Vita Frodoberti* in the 870s, when Pope Adrian sent matricide Ratbert there, but there are no further references until around 920, when Odo of Cluny, in the third book of his *Collationes*, mentioned John *praepositus* of Mont-Saint-Michel, in the Avranchin, also in connection with a penitent.[16] Again, although the terminology is not clear-cut, as it could refer to both a monastic prior, and also to the head of a college of canons, overall the latter is more likely. According to Dudo of St Quentin, writing in the early eleventh century, when Rollo was baptized (as Robert) in 912, he asked Archbishop Franco which were the most important churches in his province. The answer included Mont-Saint-Michel. The same author relates that, following the defeat of his enemies in the early 960s, Richard rebuilt the church at the Mont, and compelled monks there to follow a rigorous way of life. The single sentence describing this event is, again, ambiguous.[17] A rather fuller narrative of events was given in the much later *Introductio Monachorum*, written at the Mont *c.* 1073–1082, and informed by eleventh-century Gregorian currents in general and the fraught contemporary conditions in his monastery in particular. According to the author, the quality of service provided by canons at this prestigious sanctuary displeased the newly confident ruler, who required first they that reform, and second that they be replaced by monks. Archbishop Hugh of Rouen and the count's half-brother Ralph took matters in hand and

---

[14] Keats-Rohan, 'Histoire sécrète', p. 144; *Cartulaire de l'abbaye Saint-Sauveur de Redon*, fols 51ᵛ, 69ʳ, 75ʳ, 122ᵛ; *Cartulaire de l'abbaye de Redon*, XXI, p. 19 (868); LXXXVI, p. 65 (862); CV, p. 80 (*c.* 857/858); CCXLVII, p. 199 (871).

[15] See Pietri, 'Les abbés de basilique'; Bouet and Desbordes, *Chroniques latines*, pp. 164–65.

[16] Adso, *Vita Frodoberti*, CXXXVII, col. 616; Odo de Cluny, *Collationes*, CXXXIII, cols 570–71.

[17] Dudo, *De moribus*, 30, pp. 170–01; 126, p. 290; trans. pp. 50, 164.

7. *MEMORIA*, MEMORIALIZATION, AND THE MONKS OF MONT-SAINT-MICHEL   147

began a search for monks suitable for the endeavour.[18] Unusually, though, canons remained to serve the sanctuary, alongside the monks.

Although there is much that is unsatisfactory in the *Introductio*'s account, the forged papal bull of John XIII being the most obvious, it is a Montois text that offers us at least a later-eleventh-century perspective on an obscure but important tenth-century event. There is a vagueness of detail — 'the noble personage sent by the duke', that may mask a lack of recorded detail available to the author — there is certainly none in Dudo, his main source. This is a memorializing text that can be usefully controlled by the evidence of the Mont's memorial texts. The liturgy of the dead and the liturgy of saints, as reflected in both necrologies and the earliest witnesses to the sanctoral in use at the Mont, combine to offer revealing light on obscure phases in the abbey's history. Some of the material was discussed for the first time in the still useful *Millénaire Monastique* volumes, produced in 1966, on the anniversary of the reform of the monastery in 966 under the aegis of Richard I of Normandy. A full edition is required to make the best use of these texts, work I am in the process of completing for publication, and which forms the principal basis for the observations made here.[19]

Norse Invasions: The Exodus of Clergy and their Saints, 860–935

As already noted, the gap between the *Revelatio* of *c.* 820 and the *Introductio Monachorum* of *c.* 1075 is a very long one. If there are glimpses of communal life on the Mont in the late ninth century, and into the period *c.* 920 when Odo of Cluny made reference in his *Collationes* to John *praepositus* of Avranches, there is nothing concrete for the next thirty years or so. During the period 860–930 the Norse invasions had badly disrupted religious life throughout northern France and elsewhere. Already by the 880s some communities had sent their most precious relics to other places for safe-keeping. Both in Brittany and what became Normandy, whole monasteries were destroyed and their communities displaced. Several sources, including the so-called Annals of Redon copied much later into a manuscript of the Mont, state that Breton clergy went

---

[18] *Chroniques latines*, pp. 212–23.

[19] The necrologies and martyrology are in the Chapter Book, Avranches, Bib. pat. MS 214; Keats-Rohan, 'Testimonies of the Living Dead', pp. 168–83; Keats-Rohan, '*Pretiosa est*'; Laporte, 'Les obituaires', pp. 725–41; Lecouteux, 'Réseaux', I, pp. 364, n. 3 and 507, n. 4.

into exile in some numbers around 920.[20] Redon was among them, eventually heading south to Saint-Maixent in Poitou. Saint-Jouin des Marnes in Poitou was reputedly the refuge of the monks of Saint-Méen de Gaël. The monks of Landévennec also left, with the relics of St Winwaloe, making the longest journey of all to Montreuil-sur-Mer near Boulogne, in the hope of crossing to England.[21] A later text, the *Translatio Sancti Maglorii*, a thirteenth-century copy of which survives in a Mont manuscript, is very informative.[22] Salvator, bishop of Alet, and his clergy left with the relics of St Malo, and went to the monks of St Maglorius at Léhon, who were preparing to leave. On the road they joined a caravan of clergy from Dol and Bayeux. Among the relics the Dol clergy were carrying were those of St Samson, St Exuperius founding saint of the diocese of Bayeux, and the Avranchin saints Senator, Paternus (Pair), and Scubilio. The Dol clergy arrived in Paris, where they were received by Hugh the Great. In May 930, just before Bishop Agan of Dol and his clergy returned, Hugh gave them the church of St Symphorian at Orléans as dependents of St Samson, and from his chapel of St Bartholomew in Paris he created a new monastery of Saint-Magloire, endowed with many Breton relics.[23]

Later documents reveal that Mont-Saint-Michel had relics of St Exuperius, bishop of Bayeux, some of which had ended up at Corbeil, not far from Paris. The Martyrology of Usuard, a monk of Saint-Germain-des-Prés in Paris, was composed, and then amended, at the monastery in the 850s and became one of the most commonly used in Benedictine monasteries. Many communities used it as a basis for their own cult of saints, influenced as that was by their individual locations and preoccupations. One of the distinctive features of the Mont's Usuard martyrology was that it added saints of Corbeil, in the case of Exuperius making a specific reference to the exodus from the diocese of Rennes.[24] These relics were identified by Hubert Guillotel as from the monastery of Saint-

---

[20] Avranches, Bib. pat. MS 213, fols 173ʳ–75ᵛ.

[21] Guillotel, 'L'exode', pp. 283–87.

[22] Avranches, Bib. pat. MS 210, fly-leaves 3ᵛ–4; edited in Guillotel, 'L'exode', pp. 301–16.

[23] Guillotel, 'L'exode', pp. 293–300.

[24] 1 August, Avranches, Bib. pat. MS 214, p. 113, 'Item castro Corboilo; Sancti Exuperii episcopi et confessoris. cuius corpus persecutione Danorum a Redonis ciuitate fugatum. atque a Galliarum incolis honorifice receptum' (Item, at Corbeil, Saint Exupery bishop and confessor, whose body fled the city of Rennes on account of persecution by the Danes, and was received honourably by the inhabitants of Gaul).

Exupère de Gahard (Ille-et-Villaine), later a priory of Marmoutier.[25] The considerable number of Breton relics that were circulating at this time, whether as the result of the 'exodus of clergy', or a shadier black market in stolen relics, is amply demonstrated in the twelfth-century list of relics held by Saint-Magloire de Paris and analysed by Jean-Luc Deuffic.[26] Hugh the Great was a noted connoisseur of relics, as was King Æthelstan of England. Many Breton exiles, including Matuedoi of Poher and his infant son Alan, had taken refuge at the court of Æthelstan, who became godfather to Alan. He also sheltered his nephew, the future Louis IV d'Outremer, son of the deposed Carolingian Charles III the Simple. At this time Hugh sought a marriage that would neutralize the effects of his own father Robert I's role in Charles's downfall. He sent an embassy in 926 to Æthelstan, led by Adelolf of Flanders, who was the English king's nephew, named for his great-grandfather King Æthelwulf. Dol clerics bearing relics were probably included in the party. Their dean Radbod is known to have written to the king about relics of Senator, Paternus (Pair) and Scubilio, recalling that Æthelstan's father Edward the Elder (d. 924) had been a *confrater* of Dol. Æthelstan founded Milton Abbey in Dorset, dedicated to St Mary, St Samson, and St Branwallader (Broladre). Abingdon Abbey had a large collection of Breton relics: Winwaloe (Guénolé), Samson, Malo, Corentin, Judoc. Restoration and renewal in religious life was as much in evidence in England in the tenth century as it was across the Channel, and influences moved in both directions, with the abbey of Fleury playing a key role.[27]

Although the documentary silence from Redon is complete between 924 and 990, many of the exiled Breton clergy returned during the 930s. Conditions had gradually stabilized after 933, when the Cotentin was given to William Longsword of Normandy, following defeats inflicted on the Normans by Judicael Berenger of Rennes in 931, which provoked William's invasion of Brittany and seizure of Dol and Saint-Brieuc. Now adult, Alan Barbe-Torte of Poher returned to Brittany in 936 determined to fight back, and inflicted a major defeat on the Normans in 937, killing their garrisons in both places. With the help of Abbot John of Landevénnec as mediator, Charles III's son Louis IV d'Outremer had also returned, as king, at the instance of Hugh the Great.[28] It would be Louis

[25] Guillotel, 'L'exode', p. 281.

[26] Deuffic, 'L'exode', pp. 366–67, 374–415.

[27] *Historia Ecclesie Abbendonensis*, II, 222–23; Brett, 'A Breton Pilgrim', p. 47; Foot, *Æthelstan*, pp. 103–04, 190–92.

[28] Foot, *Æthelstan*, pp. 167–69; Guillotel, 'L'exode', p. 299.

that would act as guardian of the child Richard I of Normandy, following his father's assassination by agents of Arnulf I of Flanders in 942.

What of the Mont itself? It is clear from later charters that the Avranchin, like the Dolois, was attacked by the Norse, and that the holdings of the community were affected.[29] But was the community forced into exile as well? We simply do not know. Such a marked break in documentary continuity does, however, suggest a form of disjunction that goes beyond that related by the *Introductio* author, which is a significant elaboration of a basic narrative found in the earlier work of chronicler Dudo of St Quentin. What we can say is that some form of religious life must have been in evidence at the Mont at the time a number of pennies were dropped there. Six of them were English, five of them coins of Æthelstan, minted between *c.* 930 and 939, mainly in the north-east midlands; one came from York, minted probably *c.* 941. Three others were pennies struck by the abbey of Saint-Ouen de Rouen in the period 942–945. Another was a silver penny that might refer to William Longsword as ruler of Brittany.[30] Taken together with the later community's evident interest in the exodus, one might plausibly wonder whether some or all of the Mont canons had joined the caravan of Dol clergy in 920, returning by *c.* 935/40.

The Revival of Norman Monasticism, 942–989

Major changes were now afoot. Alan Barbe-Torte, newly returned from exile in England in 936, began to turn the tide with victories against the Norse in 937 and 939.[31] Another factor in the unfolding story was the continuing lack of unity in Brittany itself, where several comital families were vying for hegemony. Alan Barbe-Torte was grandson of the last Breton king Alan the Great, and son of Matuedoi count of Poher, who had taken refuge with King Æthelstan of England. His second wife was a daughter of Count Theobald of Blois, but their children were minors at his death in 954. They soon died in the guardianship of Fulk 'the Good' of Anjou, who had married their mother. This situation was of concern to Richard I of Normandy, who was already a seasoned campaigner by 950, aged just eighteen. His mission was to stabilize his borders and build his nascent duchy into a viable and powerful entity on the Frankish model, a mission in which he was to prove entirely successful. He was himself the son

[29] *Cartulary of Mont-Saint-Michel*, no. 26, pp. 108–10, at p. 109.

[30] Dolley and Yvon, 'A Group of Tenth Century Coins', pp. 7–11.

[31] For Alan Barbe-Torte, see Quaghebeur, 'Alain', pp. 109–40 above.

of his father's union with a Breton concubine, but his stepmother Liutgarde of Vermandois married Theobald of Blois after William Longsword's death. Theobald had retaken her dower of the county of Évreux in alliance with the king. Richard comprehensively repelled his invasion in 962, with the king, Lothar, stepping in to ensure a final peace treaty in 965.[32]

This was the moment, according to Dudo, that Richard sought the 'reform' of Mont-Saint-Michel. In terms of its location, at the border of his duchy and Brittany in a region where the power of the Norman ruler would not be assured until the following century, and its importance as a sanctuary and place of pilgrimage, which it presumably had continued to enjoy, this move made sense. It also forms a piece with the work of restoration of the ancient monasteries of the archdiocese of Rouen which had tentatively begun in 918 with the refoundation of Saint-Ouen in Rouen.[33] That community was sufficiently important around the time of William Longsword's murder in 942 to have been granted short-lived minting rights by the Carolingian king Louis. In the same year, Hugh, a former monk of Saint-Denis, had been appointed as archbishop of Rouen. As was traditional, he became *ex officio* lay abbot of Saint-Ouen de Rouen. This did not sit well with reform trends in the tenth century, which sought not only to restore ancient monasteries, but also to establish a well-disciplined religious life that stood apart from the world. Doubtless on Hugh's initiative, by *c.* 960/70 Saint-Ouen had a regular abbot, Hildebert, who died in 1006 and who may also have been a monk of Saint-Denis.[34]

The restoration of the monastery of St Peter at Jumièges was begun on the initiative of two of the monks, still in their exile at Haspres. It was aided by monks of Saint-Cyprien de Poitiers with the approval of William Longsword, given a few months before his death. Its second abbot, Anno, became abbot of Micy in 950 and ruled Jumièges from there until his death in 973, when he was succeeded by Roderic, who died in 1000.[35] The monks of Saint-Taurin of Évreux had fled Normandy between 858 and 876 and eventually taken refuge at Gigny, founded around 988, by Bernon, first abbot of Cluny *c.* 909.[36] Sometime after Richard I's success at Évreux, Saint-Taurin was refounded and

---

[32] Dudo, *De moribus*, pp. 264–88; trans. pp. 138–63.

[33] Fauroux, *Recueil des actes*, p. 20, n° 2.

[34] Gazeau, *Prosopographie*, I, 8–9; Le Maho, 'Jumièges', p. 15.

[35] Dudo, *De moribus*, 58, pp. 200–03; trans. pp. 176–78; Gazeau, *Prosopographie*, I, 9; Le Maho, 'Jumièges', pp. 15–16.

[36] Lecouteux, 'Réseaux', II, 506 and n. 4.

furnished with an abbot, Fulcran, who was succeeded by Fromund before 989.[37] Fontanelle, exiled in 858, had suffered the loss of its primary relics of saints Wandrille, Ansbert, and Wulfran, to the acquisitive Arnulf I of Flanders, who gave them to his foundation of St Peter's, Ghent, along with some of their properties. It was refounded as the monastery of Saint-Wandrille during the 960s.[38] Richard refused to allow a refoundation from Flanders, though a monk Mainard began the work *c.* 960.[39] This was the least successful of the reinstallations, as is revealed by the account of the second translation of St Ouen in 989, attested by Richard I, Archbishop Hugh, and abbots Hildebert of St Ouen, Mainard of Mont-Saint-Michel, and Fromond of Saint-Taurin. This text was a confection of the reign of Richard II, as Mathieu Arnoux has shown, but the absence of abbots of either Jumièges or Saint-Wandrille from the witness list is anyway revealing.[40] As Lecouteux's rehearsal of the evidence concludes, the restoration of monastic life in tenth-century Normandy was due to monastic and episcopal initiatives, with the ruler giving his approval.[41] Late in his life, in 990, he revived Fécamp — a former nunnery — by installing canons. By this late stage in his reign Richard I had firmly grasped the importance of ecclesiastical structures and how to control them. When Archbishop Hugh died in 989 he replaced him with his own son Robert. Robert was given the task of restoring the diocesan structure of the archdiocese of Rouen, over all of which Hugh had held sway, and his father further ensured that one of the new bishops was his own nephew.

In matters of personal religion Richard's credentials are thoroughly unconvincing, though, thanks to Dudo, he and his son were the objects of local cults in the eleventh century. All the texts relating to the restoration of ecclesiastical structures in Normandy belong to the reign of his son Richard II, and all were influenced by the vision of Richard created in the *Gesta* of Dudo.[42] Nonetheless, Richard I had understood the importance of the work and its significance for the status and security of his duchy and had allowed Archbishop Hugh to foster the restoration movement in Normandy, tapping into reform-

---

[37] Gazeau, *Prosopographie*, II, 93–94.

[38] Trân-Duc, 'Une entreprise hagiographique', pp. 2–12.

[39] According to *Inventio S. Vulfranni*, pp. 28–35.

[40] Arnoux, 'Before the *Gesta Normannorum*', pp. 36–37; *De beati Audoeni translatione et ejus sacratissimi corporis integritate*, CLXII, cols 1160–63, at col. 1162.

[41] Lecouteux, 'Réseaux', II, Annexe 8, pp. 337–38.

[42] Arnoux, 'La conversion des Normands', translation of the text, pp. 275–78.

ing currents inspired by religious visionaries such as Odo of Cluny (d. 942). Hugh was himself both a former monk and the sort of worldly cleric who would be anathema to the Gregorian eleventh century, and his memory was duly traduced by the histories of that era. He is never mentioned by Dudo. Nonetheless, the movement could not have succeeded in Normandy without the direction and support of the metropolitan. He was a man well connected to reforming circles, with links to the school of Reims, and acquainted with the leading reformers from the abbey of Fleury in the diocese of Orléans. This is an important thread that connects the reform as it came to be manifested at the Mont and in Brittany.

Nature of the Tenth-century Monastic Reform

Recent scholarship has reappraised the monastic reform movements of the tenth and eleventh centuries and has suggested that understanding of them has been hampered by an undue concentration on a handful of leading reformers such as Gerard de Brogne (d. 959) and Odo of Cluny (d. 942). Stephen Vanderputten has put the study of reforms in Flanders on a new footing by talking about 'reform as a process' rather than a series of flashpoint events.[43] In the case of early tenth-century Flanders, the movement was directed by the ambitious count Arnulf I, who aimed, very successfully, to control the new or revived monasteries as a means of bolstering his own power and prestige. He gave up lay abbacies but became lay advocate instead, which allowed him fully to exploit the community's resources. Gerard de Brogne found himself employed in the creation of a number of prayer factories for the count and his family, with limited room for the exercise of religious idealism. In fact, in a separate publication, Vanderputten and Meijns have shown that Gerard's achievements as a reformer were fairly limited and that the main engine for reform was mediated by monks of Gorze, reformed by Einald of Toul at the request of Archbishop Adalbero of Toul in 933, and, especially, of Saint-Evre of Toul, where the abbot Gauzilo had introduced the customs of Fleury in 934.[44] Although several communities probably noticed little change, for others like the two abbeys in Ghent, St Peter and St Bavo, all this was a new start. The situation changed after Arnulf's death in 965, but by then other reforming currents were gaining in importance.

[43] Vanderputten, *Monastic Reform*, pp. 1–13.

[44] Vanderputten and Meijins, 'Gérard de Brogne', pp. 293–95.

Isabelle Rosé has distinguished several phases, starting in the first half of the tenth century with Flanders, Lotharingia, and Burgundy, described as 'autonomous movements, in the sense that they were not linked to one particular monastery, but to the dynamism of certain milieux and the personalities of certain men', men who were well-connected aristocrats acting with passion and zeal, often at the request of someone with rights over a community, whether a founder, lay abbot or bishop. Some of them had originally been canons, such as Odo of Cluny, and it was the zeal of such converts that was turned against collegiate communities. Such men included Archbishop Adalbero of Metz, who reformed the monastery of Gorze in Lotharingia.[45] Archbishop Adalbero of Reims (969–989), schooled at Gorze, subsequently initiated reforms at Reims, continuing the reform of Saint-Rémy, begun by his predecessor Hugh in 945 with the help of Archembald of Fleury, for which he obtained a bull from John XIII. He sent a monk from Saint-Rémy to reform Saint-Thierry de Reims in 972. In 966 monks from Saint-Rémy refounded the abbey of Saint-Aubin in Angers, though there too the counts controlled the abbey as advocates into the eleventh century. Adalbero enriched the reputation of Reims as a centre of learning, finally attracting Gerbert of Aurillac, the future Pope Sylvester II.

One of these 'autonomous movements' began in Burgundy, where a small community, founded in 909/10 by William of Aquitaine and subject only to the pope, would in time become the powerhouse of Cluny under the inspirational leadership of St Odo and his successors. Odo himself had started out as a canon of Saint-Martin de Tours before he became a monk aged about thirty. He found himself abbot of Cluny and two other monasteries by 927, some years before he reformed Fleury. Cluny had a special devotion to St Michael — promulgated as the patron saint of the Christian empire in 813 by Charlemagne — which Odo used to justify his visits to Italy, home of Monte Gargano and more recent Michelian centres. Maiol of Cluny (d. 994) would later reform thirty monasteries, including Marmoutier of Tours, and he would recruit as a reformer William of Volpiano, future abbot of Fécamp in Normandy, whom he sent as abbot-reformer to Saint-Bénigne de Dijon. Fleury is an example of what Rosé sees as a 'foyer réformatrice', widening the reformist circle from Burgundy and Lotharingia to Neustria.[46]

This picture of an autonomous, essentially idealistic movement that happened to chime quite nicely with the more secular concerns of the new territo-

---

[45] Rosé, 'Réforme', p. 135.

[46] Rosé, 'Réforme', p. 141.

7. *MEMORIA*, MEMORIALIZATION, AND THE MONKS OF MONT-SAINT-MICHEL   155

rial princes of the age, is far more plausible than its precursors, which tended to see reform in terms of flashpoints and clashes. Often the reason for that is the way it was all re-interpreted by the writers of the eleventh century, influenced by the very different norms of the Gregorian reform.

The absence of monks at the prestigious sanctuary of Mont Tumba inspired the monk Mainard, with the support of Archbishop Hugh, to introduce Benedictinism there. Purely political considerations of defence of borders and making firm statements to Breton and Blésois rivals, as well as personal prestige, most plausibly explain Richard's motives for supporting the reform. In this case, the papal bull of John XIII is certainly forged, and the diploma of Lothar interpolated, but the introduction of Benedictinism certainly occurred at this time, a particularly busy one for reformers. Genuine papal bulls were issued for St Peter's, Ghent at this time, which coincided with the reform of Saint-Aubin d'Angers by monks of Saint-Rémi de Reims in 966. Abbot Wulfald of Fleury (948–962) introduced reform at Saint-Père de Chartres in 951, becoming bishop of Chartres in 963 (d. 967). In turn, his pupil Herbert would take the Fleury customs to Lagny *c.* 1000, where the monk Gerard took up the baton and passed them first to the abbey of Crépy, and then to Saint-Wandrille in 1008.

Saint-Wandrille: 'un besoin d'histoire'

Pierre Bauduin has described Dudo's *De moribus* and the texts deriving from it as manifesting 'un besoin d'histoire'.[47] Nowhere was this need more acute than the unfortunate community at Saint-Wandrille. Divested of its relics by Arnold I in 944, it had to be refounded from scratch in post-Rollo Normandy. Although the refounded monasteries eventually succeeded in recreating much of their patrimonies, this was often a painful process of extracting 'grants' — restitutions — from the Norman rulers. The prestigious abbey of Saint-Ouen in the ducal capital, notionally refounded in 918, found things heavy going until the 940s, when it came under the patronage of Archbishop Hugh and King Louis during Richard's minority.[48] For Saint-Wandrille, starting from scratch without its primary relics was always going to be harder. It made little progress until the appointment in 1008 of Gerard, abbot of Crépy, who

---

[47] Bauduin, 'Autour d'une construction identitaire', pp. 77–91.

[48] Musset, 'Ce qu'en enseigne l'histoire d'un patrimoine monastique', pp. 119–22; Le Maho, 'Jumièges', p. 15.

oversaw the transformation of the abbey's fortunes until his murder in 1031. About twenty years later, one of his monks wrote a text called *Inventio Sancti Wulfranni*. It is now well established that the author invented the discovery of the relics of the saint during building works in the time of Abbot Gerard.[49] The complication is that the author also alleged that it had been first refounded by a certain Mainard, from St Peter's Ghent, who having allegedly provided certain relics to the new foundation, including, with the help of Richard I, those of Maximin and Venerandus, then disappeared from the story in 964 and went to Mont-Saint-Michel.

Véronique Gazeau, in her prosopography of the Norman abbots, has cast strong doubt on the association of the two Mainards, citing the evidence of the still unedited Annals of Saint-Wandrille, the early annals of Mont-Saint-Michel (written around 1048) and the *De immutatione ordinis monachorum* of Robert of Torigny.[50] Saint-Wandrille may have been a dependency of St Peter's, Ghent, until 1008, as suggested by Stéphane Lecouteux, or of Jumièges, as very plausibly suggested by Gazeau. Certainly, we know that it was run by three custodians, of whom the first, *Enfulbert* (probably Engelbert), was a monk of Jumièges who died on 22 September 993 and was buried at Jumièges.[51] Detailed comparative studies of the liturgies of Norman monasteries have begun in recent years and it may be hoped that a greater understanding of how these communities re-established themselves and interacted with each other subsequently may emerge. Already it appears that the tenth-century abbeys and those that were founded in the eleventh century formed three broad liturgical groups. One, the Dijon-Fécamp group, into which Mont-Saint-Michel falls, adopted the liturgical innovations of William of Volpiano and some of the older Dijonnaise liturgies. A Fleury-Chartres group includes Saint-Ouen de Rouen and Saint-Wandrille.[52]

Very little survives of the Mont's liturgy before it fully adopted the changes introduced by William of Volpiano after 1001. Its magnificent mid-eleventh-century Sacramentary, with its many striking features, including several liturgies replicating those in the Sacramentary of Saint-Thierry de Reims, discussed by Henri Tardif in 1966, is now believed to be essentially the same Dijon-based

---

[49] Trân-Duc, 'Une entreprise hagiographique', pp. 4–16.

[50] Gazeau, *Prosopographie*, I, 201–11.

[51] Gazeau, *Prosopographie*, I, 203–04; Lecouteux, 'Réseaux', I, 267–68.

[52] The third was a Bec/St Etienne de Caen group: Lecouteux, 'Réseaux', I, 486–97.

7. *MEMORIA*, MEMORIALIZATION, AND THE MONKS OF MONT-SAINT-MICHEL 157

sacramentary as used at Fécamp, which does not survive.[53] There are a few over-laps with the sacramentary of Saint-Wandrille, but the differences are greater; the one is from the Gelasian tradition of Angoulême, the other from the Gregorian Hadrianum.[54] If one compares the sanctoral of each abbey — those saints whose feasts were observed in the abbey — the similarities outweigh the differences. Such differences as there are mainly relate to special observances in honour of patron saints, or saints whose relics were held. There are a handful of striking cases though.

The feast of St Gerald of Aurillac on 13 October was observed in Normandy only by Mont-Saint-Michel; it was observed at Saint-Aubin d'Angers and Saint-Denis de Paris. Only the Mont had a feast of St Basolus on 15 October. On that day Fécamp and Saint-Wandrille honoured St Wulfran, who was added to the martyrology at Saint-Ouen. The translation of Wandrille, Ansbert, and Wulfran by Bishop Bain at Fontenelle on 31 March, a feast at Saint-Wandrille, is noted in the martyrologies of Saint-Ouen and Saint-Taurin. All the mon-asteries have a double feast on 22 July for St Wandrille (*Wandregisilus*) and Mary Magdalene. Saint-Ouen and Saint-Wandrille have St Valery (*Walaric*) on 1 April. Jumièges celebrated Wolmar of Boulogne on 20 July, and Saint-Ouen celebrated St Swithun of Winchester on 2 July. On 1 October, from the feast of Germanus, Remigius, Vaast (*Vedast*) and Bavo, the Mont had dropped both Vaast and Bavo by the early thirteenth century, Saint-Wandrille had Amand in place of Bavo, Saint-Ouen omitted Bavo, and Fécamp observed Remigius and Germain.[55] On the 26 April, Mont-Saint-Michel shared with Redon the feast and the liturgy of St Marcellinus, pope and martyr, whose relics were given to Redon in 848 by Pope Leo IV.[56] If nothing else, the shunning by Mont-Saint-Michel of the cult of St Wulfran, launched at Saint-Wandrille in the mid-eleventh century, emerges clearly, but the memory of their period in exile for Jumièges, Saint-Ouen and Saint-Wandrille seems to emerge as well.

---

[53] Tardif, 'La liturgie de la messe', pp. 367–77; Lecouteux, 'Réseaux', i, 486–87, 591–92.

[54] Gazeau, *Prosopographie*, i, 208–10.

[55] Information compiled from various calendars and martyrologies. For the Mont, see the synoptic table in Lemarié and Tardif, 'Le calendrier', pp. 290–301, with special reference to the Sacramentary, and Avranches, Bib. pat. MS 42, fols 2ᵛ–8ʳ.

[56] Deuffic, 'L'exode', pp. 365–66. The *Vita* and office of St Marcellin are found in the Mont's copy of Anselm of Bury's Marian collection in Vatican, MS Vat. Lat 9668.

Memoria *and the Chapter Book*

At this point we turn to *memoria* as the liturgy of the dead. The primary texts are contained in the Mont's Chapter Book, Avranches, Bibliothèque patrimoniale MS 214, which contains a second-edition Martyrology of Usuard and associated obits — the Martyrology-Necrology — a lectionary, the Rule of St Benedict, and a Necrology, containing the names of the community's *confratres*. A necrology is a calendared list of names of the dead attached to the day on which they died. By the end of the tenth century the old *libri memoriales*, containing the names of those in confraternity with the community, were giving way to formal necrologies. In many cases these documents were divided into columns separating the *confratres*, ecclesiastic and lay, from the monks of the abbey itself. In a few cases the latter were kept separately, added to each day's entry in the monastery's Martyrology, as was the case at the Mont. Some individuals with a more personal dimension of confraternity also earned a privileged place in this Martyrology-Necrology. The two lists formed the basis for the remembrance of the dead by the reading of their names at the office of Chapter, which at Mont-Saint-Michel took place after the mass which followed the office of Prime, according to the Ceremonial which is now bound in with the Chapter Book texts.[57] At the Mont, novices were assigned the task of preparing each day's list on a rota basis. As names accumulated over time, the lists became untidy and were sometimes rewritten. Those that survive in Avranches 214 were written just before the death of abbot Jordan on 6 August 1212. There are many later additions, often poorly legible, but the first-hand text is good and clear. Analysis of the entries, still ongoing, is very revealing. It is abundantly clear that the order of first-hand entries is hierarchical: bishop, abbot, monk, canon, cleric, layman, laywoman.

The Fleury List

The earliest such material to survive is, however, somewhat different. Between 1000 and 1009, the talented Mont scribe Heriward wrote the names of fifty living monks, and a calendared list of forty deceased monks, onto a blank folio in a sacramentary written in Winchcombe and intended for use at Fleury during its brief sojourn at Mont-Saint-Michel *en route*, perhaps coinciding with a

[57] Avranches, Bib. pat. MS 214, pt. II, pp. 216–20. Printed in Keats-Rohan, 'Testimonies', pp. 187–89.

7. *MEMORIA*, MEMORIALIZATION, AND THE MONKS OF MONT-SAINT-MICHEL 159

visit to the Mont by Abbot Abbo of Fleury.[58] The survival of 'the Fleury list' is a rare and valuable insight into the community at this time. This is presented in Table 7.1 overleaf. Obit dates have been provided for the living monks where they can be easily identified in the Martyrology-Necrology text. These names were written down under Abbot Mainard II (991–1009) and were copied into necrologies in use in the eleventh and twelfth centuries, and into the final re-copying of the early thirteenth century.[59] We could forgive a number of omissions or cacographies, but what we see is a remarkably faithful rendition in almost all cases, although sometimes an initial awaiting artwork was subsequently completed incorrectly or not at all. In sixteen cases the personal names are homonyms and they cannot be certainly identified in the larger texts. It can be said that none of them is identifiable as anything other than a monk. The Mont canons must have had their own necrologies.

Looking first at the names of the dead, we see that the community that flourished under Mainard I (*c.* 966–991) was an eclectic mix, reflecting the 'assembled monks most suited to holy religion from all parts' of the *Introductio* account.[60] The only certainly Breton name is Gleuloes [*recte* Gurloes] — could he have been originally a monk of Redon?[61] The living Englishman Godwin was perhaps a compatriot of the dead monks Sedeman, and *Adelulfus*, whose name could represent English Æthelwulf. Several of the names were normal in the Neustria of the early tenth century, such as Berengar, Roger, Albuin, Theoderic, Drogo, Fulco, Mainer, Mainard, Maur, Stephen, and Ernold. Fastulf, Ansketill, Ansfrid, and Osmund are Scandinavian names. The two Hildeberts, whose name recalls the Childebert of 708, an abbot of Fontanelle in 730, and a dean of Marmoutier in 947, became abbots of the Mont; a homonym was abbot of Saint-Ouen at the same date and the name continued to be common in these and related necrologies. Another of the living monks, Almodus, was a future abbot of the Mont, whose name, like that of Bertrann, *Rotgerius*, and *Guasbertus*, was associated with Neustria, especially the *ducatus Cenomannicus* (Maine). Robert [Ratbert], Grimo, Mainard, Franco, Gilbert, Riculf, and Wido were all names of archbishops of Rouen. Twenty-seven of the names occur

---

[58] Plausibly dated 1005–1009 by Lecouteux, *Réseaux*, I, 184.

[59] Traced in detail in Keats-Rohan, '*Pretiosa est*', pp. 16–19.

[60] *Aggregatis undecumque idoneis in sancta religione monachis*, in *Chroniques latines*, pp. 212–13.

[61] Found in the Martyrology-Necrology as *Gleuloes episcopus*; Avranches, Bib. pat. MS 214, pt. I, p. 143.

160 K. S. B. Keats-Rohan

Table 7.1. 'The Fleury List', Orléans, Bib. mun., MS 127 (103), p. 361

Haec nomina uiuorum fratrum

Domnus abba Mainardus.* [14.vii]. Hildebertus.* [7.i]. Vualcherius [28.vi]. Rainaldus.* [27. ix]/ Gualterius. Herimarus [31.viii]. Frotmundus [23.viii]. Heldemanus.* [14.iii] Mainardus francus.*/ Mainardus.* Vitalis [15.x]. Ansfridus [5.viii]. Harduinus [17.iv]. Almodus.* [17.v] Bona fides / Riculfus.* [16.ii] Hermenulfus. [11.vii] Heruardus. [4.iv] Drocus.* [11 vi] Bernardus.* [24.iii]. Gauzbertus.* [21.vii]/ Gislebertus. [15.i]. Teudo.* [31.x]. Dauid [1.xi]. Hodo.*[28.xii?] Aiulfus.* [8.xii] Vualdricus. [31.x] Algerius. [4.vi]/ Gauffredus/ Burcardus.* [27.ix]/ Anschetellus. [19.x] Mainardus.* Vuascelinus. [?14.x] Heldebertus.* [30 ix]/ Ansgerius. Goduinus. [1.iv] Hosmundus. Drocus.* Rotgerius. Richardus [?22.iv]./ Franco.* [3.ii] Rotgerius.* Rainaldus.* Ebremarus. [5.ix] Goscelmus. Martinus./ Hosbernus.[13.ii] Bertrannus.*[10.xi] Vitalis. Burnincus.* [19.i]

Et haec nomina defunctorum/	
vii Kal. Ian. [26 Dec.] obiit Sedemanus.	xvi kal. August. [17 July] obiit Vuatso.
Nonis Ianuar. [5 Jan.] obiit Uuiddo.	et Ernaldus.
xvii Kal. Feb. [16 Jan] Obiit Stephanus.*	viii kal. August. [25 July] obiit Albuinus.
v kal. Febr. [28 Jan.] obiit Henmenulfus.	iiii id. Aug. [10 Aug.] obiit Vualtelmus.
ii idus Febr. [12 Feb.] obiit Maurus.	xviii kal. Sept. [15 Aug.] obierunt Durandus.
x kal. Mar. [20 Feb.] obiit Berengarus.*	et Gerardus.
xvii kal. April. [16 Mar.] obiit Teodericus.*	xvi kal. Sept. [17 Aug.] obiit Garulfus.
viii kal. April. [25 Mar.] obiit Berengarus.*	x kal. Sept. [23 Aug.] obiit Tetulus.
xvi kal. Mai. [16 April] obiit Mainardus abba*	Nonis Sept. [5 Sept.] obiit Riboldus.
xi kal. Mai. [21 April] obiit Fulredus*	vii idus Sept. [7 Sept.] obiit Fulco.*
iiii kal. Mai. [28 April] obiit Heldemanus.*	xi kal. Oct. [21 Sept.] obiit Gleuloes.
ii kal. Mai. [30 April] obiit Fulco.*	xvii kal. Nov. [16 Oct.] obiit Grimoldus.*
kal. Mai. [1 May] obiit Mainerus.	xiiii kal. Novem. [19 Oct.] obiit Benedictus.*
v nonas Mai. [3 May] obiit Heruardus abba.	xiiii kal. Decemb. [18 Nov.] obiit Adelulfus.
xvi kal Iunii. [16 May] obiit Otbertus.	xii kal. Decemb. [20 Nov.] obiit Uuarinus.*
xv kal. Iunii. [17 May] obiit Balfridus.	v kal. Decemb. [27 Nov.] obiit Uuiddo.
xiiii kal. Iunii. [18 May] obiit Framericus.	iiii nonas Decemb. [2 Dec.] obiit Radulfus.
vi idus Iunii. [8 June] obiit Rainaldus.*	iii nonas Decemb. [3 Dec.] obiit Vuitbertus.
xii kal. Iulii. [20 June] obiit Fastulfus.*	vii idus Decemb. [7 Dec.] obiit Berneherius
vii kal. Iulii. [25 June] obiit Rotgerius.*	
ii idus Iulii. [14 July] obiit Amalbertus.	

* Name occurs in the early ninth century at Saint-Denis

7. *MEMORIA*, MEMORIALIZATION, AND THE MONKS OF MONT-SAINT-MICHEL   161

among ninth-century monks of Saint-Denis (see Table 7.1).[62] Otbert of Redon and Glanfeuil, d. 834, was grand/father of Count Otbert of Maine *c.* 858/68. A ninth-century Redon charter was attested by Otbert *scriptor*. Other charter witnesses include Baldefred, Grimold, and reference to the 'fee of the sons of Teodulus [*Tetulus?*] of Saint-Melaine'.[63]

Some of these names are first encountered in the eastern empire, former Austrasia and Lotharingia. Grimoldus is one example. Like many of these names it was introduced into Neustria by the followers of Robert the Strong in the ninth century.[64] The lands of a Grimold in Bretteville, in the Avranchin, were restored to the Mont by Richard II. The same passage also mentions the land of Bernard, father of Abbot Hildebert at *Rotoloi*, so there is quite probably a connection between the two Grimolds, who may even have been the same person.[65] Clearly, these names amply represent the regions visible to the archangel on his eminence. The men who brought Benedictinism to the Mont were predominantly men who lived in the saint's extensive shadow.

There are only two names that indubitably reflect a more easterly connection than Neustria or West Francia, and those are the two Heriwards, uncle and nephew. A third may be Fraimeric, name of an abbot of Saint-Vaast (*c.* 961–970) and a bishop of Therouanne (974–989), though one of the names occurs once in the early twelfth-century necrology of Saint-Serge d'Angers.[66] The elder Heriward was brother of Erluin, a monk of Gorze and reformer working with Count Rainald of Hainault, who became first abbot of SS Peter and Exuperius at Gembloux. If Sigebert of Gembloux's information is accurate, they were relatives of Bishop Erluin of Cambrai (996–1012). Sent to reform the abbey of Lobbes, Erluin was attacked and blinded by its monks in 947. His abbacy of Gembloux continued with the assistance of a co-adjutor, initially the Aletran who succeeded him at Lobbes in 959, but subsequently, as chronicler Sigebert of Gembloux indicated, his brother and successor Heriward, abbot from 987 until his death in 991. According to Sigebert, in his earlier life, Heriward had been a monk of St Michael in Peril of the Sea.[67] The younger Heriward became

---

[62] Wilmart, 'Les frères défunts', pp. 245–57.

[63] *Cartulaire de l'abbaye de Redon*, fols 58[r], 63[v], 161[v]: XLII, p. 34 (October 850); LIX, p. 48 (18 February 849); CCCXXXV, pp. 285–86 (1084).

[64] Werner, 'Untersuchungen' (1959), pp. 146–93.

[65] *Cartulary of Mont-Saint-Michel*, no. 2, pp. 76–79, at p. 77.

[66] Angers, Bib. mun., ms. 837 (753), fol. 36[r].

[67] Sigebert, *Gesta abbatum Gemblacensium*, col. 614. The name is specific to Mont-Saint-Michel.

the most outstanding of the stellar cast of scribes and illustrators working at the Mont in the late tenth century. The story also suggests that 966 marks the date at which the new sanctuary church was completed for the already settled Benedictines, rather than the date of the first arrivals.

Confraternity

The necrologies offer revealing insights into the nature of monasticism at the Mont in the tenth and early eleventh centuries. Fairly unfriendly documents at first glance, because they mostly consist of a date and a simple name, on further study patterns emerge. The entries are arranged hierarchically, starting with bishops or abbots. The following monks' names are entered in chronological order by the first hand, though later annotations do not respect the original layout. We know this thanks to William of Volpiano, reformer of Saint-Bénigne de Dijon and eventually of Fécamp. Fécamp was refounded by Richard I as a community of canons at the end of his life in 990. Richard II had this refounded for Benedictines under William of Volpiano in 1001, and then extended the reform more widely, starting in 1015. Towards the end of his life, William required that the forty or so monasteries he had reformed or founded should share their obits in confraternity after his death. This practice was kept up to varying degrees. In cases where there was no genuine impulse to confraternity, such as between the Mont and Gorze, the practice lapsed in one or two generations. In other cases, it lasted centuries, the most notable cases being Redon, Saint-Bénigne de Dijon, and Jumièges. By comparing the necrologies of all these abbeys one can identify the monastery a monk named in the Mont necrology came from; importantly, it is these names, combined with those of the Fleury list, that show that the entries are roughly in date order.

Each abbey had an individual confraternity circle which evolved over time. Occasionally ties were allowed to lapse; more often the act of confraternity was renewed or renegotiated as the burden of prayers for individuals, rather than whole communities, increased. Three confraternity lists survive for the abbey; one written shortly after 1411 is now bound into the Chapter Book. The list is headed by the abbey of Cluny, followed by Saint-Bénigne de Dijon.[68] The significance of this relates primarily to the more or less complete adoption of the liturgical reforms of William of Volpiano at Mont-Saint-Michel, and ulti-

---

[68] Avranches, Bib. pat. MS 214, pt. i, p. 198; printed Keats-Rohan, 'Testimonies', pp. 184–86.

7. *MEMORIA*, MEMORIALIZATION, AND THE MONKS OF MONT-SAINT-MICHEL

Table 7.2. Abbots evidenced in the Necrology and Martyrology-Necrology of Mont-Saint-Michel.

Redon

Conwoion 5.i.868 [833–868]
[Thebaud *c.* 992–1005/8] ?Theudo 27.xii
Mainard (abbot of Mont-Saint-Michel 991–1009)
14.vii. *c.* 1005/8–*c.* 1017
Cadwallo 16.i. *c.* 1029–1040
Perenesius 18.v. (*c.* 1041–1060)
Almod 5.ix. (1060–1083)
Robert 20.iv. (1086–1092)
Justin 10.x.(1092–1105/8)
Herve, 2.ix? [1108–1140]
Ivo 18.xi. (1144 – *post* 1157)
Silvester 23.vi. (1164–1169)
Vivian 10.i. (1169–1199)

Saint-Germain-des-Prés

Morard 1.iv. *c.* 1014
William of Volpiano 1.i.1031
Adrald (prob) 5.x.1060
Herbert 18.ix.1066
Robert [of Saint-Wandrille] 24.i.1072
Hugh 20.x.1132?

Saint-Aubin d'Angers

Hubert 28.vii.1020
Walter 30.xii.1054
Theoderic 26.xii.1059
Gerald II, 9.i.1109
Hamelin died as bishop of Rennes 2.ii.1141
Robert 28.iv.1154

Saint-Pierre-de-la-Couture au Mans

Gausbert 28.viii.1007
Ingelbald 28.xi. *c.* 1010
?Laurence 20.xii. *post* 1071
Richard 15.i.1184
Warin 11.ix.1213

Saint-Ouen de Rouen

Hildebert 13.iv.1006 [*c.* 960/970–1006]
Henry 18.vii.1032/3 [1006–1033]
Nicholas 19.ii.1092 [1042–1092]
Hilgod, 20.xi.1112 [1092–1112]
William 7.xii.1126 [possible.]

Jumièges

Roderic 18.ii. *c.* 1000 [possibly *c.* 938/943]
William of Volpiano 1.i.1031 [1001–1028]
Theoderic (also MSM) 17.v.1027
?William 26.iv.1037 [obit date unknown]
Robert 26.v.1045 [1037–1045]
Godfred 23.xii.1048
Roger of Bec, 16.viii.1176 [1169–1176]
Robert 10.vi.1190 [1177–1190]
Roger II 30.x.1190/1
Alexander 24.ix.1213 [1198–1213]

Fécamp

William of Volpiano 1.i.1031 [1001–1028]
John 22.ii.1078 [1028–1078]
Roger 20.iii.1139 [1107–1139]
Henry 10.i.1187 [1140–1187]

Saint-Wandrille

Gerard 28.xi.1031
Gradulf 6.iii.1047
Robert 24.i.1072 [Saint-Germain]
Walter 13.viii.1150
Roger 19.vi.1165
Anfrid 27.iv.1178
Walter 3.xi.1187
Reginald 24.ix.1207
Robert II 28.iv.1194
Geoffrey 20.v.1193

continued overleaf

Table 7.2. *cont.*

Saint-Taurin of Évreux	Fleury
Fulcran 1.vi.? before 989	Odo 22.i.942
Frotmund 8.i. *c. a.* 989–*c.* 1035	Wulfald? 18.iv.967 [obit 1.x]
[shadowy Restald – possibly 7.xi]	Abbo 13.xi.1005
Touo 15.vii.mid-eleventh century [Mont monk]	Gauzlin 16.vi.1030
Ralph 12.vi. (*a.* 14 July 1080–1104)	William 11.ii.1080
Arnoul 2.vi. forced out 1106	Joscerann 7.iv.1095
Paul 27.vi. p. 1122–*a.*1128	?Simon 24.viii.1107
Philip 20.iii. *c.* 1146/54	Macharius 16.iv.1162
Ranulf 23.vi *c.* 1146–1157	Adrald 13.xi.1181
Lambert 14.iii 1159?	
Matthew 24.v., before 1205	**Marmoutier**
	Gausbert 28.viii.1007 (1000)
Saint-Bénigne de Dijon	Richard? 26.viii. *post* 1008
William of Volpiano 1.i.1031 [990–1031]	Albert 19.vi.1064 (1032)
Philip 24.iv.1177 [1145]	Bernard 7.iv.1100 (1084)
John, 16.vii. *post* 1182	William 25.v.1124 (1104)
Haimo 21.iii.1188	Garnier 23.v.1155 (1137)
	Peter 21.iv.1172

mately to the links between the Mont communities, Fleury and the monasteries of the Touraine, as will be seen.

Table 7.2 shows the names of some of the identifiable abbots whose obits occur in either necrology. Note, first of all, that the strongest and most enduring connection of Mont-Saint-Michel was with the abbey of Redon, starting with Conwoion, who died in 868.

Mont-Saint-Michel as 'un foyer réformatrice'[69]

Information about the successors of Conwoion is at best patchy until the late tenth century. A charter of Conan, count of Rennes, making a grant to the Mont in 990, was witnessed by *Arufus* abbot of Redon.[70] Unfortunately, the charter does not survive in an authentic version and is merely indicative

---

[69] See above, p. 154.

[70] Guillotel, *Actes*, no. 6, pp. 161–67; *Cartulary of Mont-Saint-Michel*, Appendix II.1, pp. 192–93.

7. *MEMORIA*, MEMORIALIZATION, AND THE MONKS OF MONT-SAINT-MICHEL 165

of what was an important relationship between the counts of Rennes and the Mont, and between the Mont and Redon. The Cartulary of Redon shows an Abbot Theobald from *c.* 992 – *c.* 1000.[71] If he was the Teudo said by André of Fleury to have been sent by Abbot Gauzlin of Fleury to bring reform to *abbatia Redonensis* (either Redon or Rennes), then the chronicler erred, for it must have been Abbot Abbo.[72] No Teudo is known for the other candidate, Saint-Melaine de Rennes, which seems to have been revived somewhat later. The monk Felix, reformer of Saint-Gildas-de-Rhuys, said to have been sent at the same time, occurs in the necrology. The next known abbot of Redon was none other than Mainard II of Mont-Saint-Michel, brought in by Conan's son Geoffrey of Brittany to revive Redon *c.* 1000.[73] Mont monks helped re-establish Saint-Jacut-de-la-Mer a few years later. Around 1024, Hinguethen, abbot of Saint-Jacut, revived the abbey of Saint-Méen de Gaël, which he re-located to Saint-Méen-le-Grand.[74] He appears twice, on consecutive days, in the necrology. Saint-Jacut and Saint-Méen have each been found to have adopted the liturgical reforms introduced by William of Volpiano.[75] The most obvious route was via Mont-Saint-Michel. A charter of Alan III of Brittany, dated by Guillotel 1009–1019, was attested by three abbots, in order, Hildebert I of Mont-Saint-Michel (d. 1017), Mainard of Redon, and Hinguethen of Saint-Jacut.[76] This suggests that Hildebert I was spearheading William's reforms rather earlier than has been suspected hitherto.

Mainard II had been abbot of Mont-Saint-Michel since 991. By 1009, when he was living permanently at Redon, he wished to appoint a co-adjutor. Richard II of Normandy found that unacceptable and ensured that instead he was replaced at the Mont by Hildebert I, who was doubtless the monk Hildebert whose name followed Mainard's in the Fleury list and was therefore prior at that time.[77] Mainard died at Redon before 1019, soon after Hildebert I in 1017. Redon abbots in an unbroken succession were remembered in the necrologies, with some of them in the Martyrology-Necrology (abbacies of less

---

[71] *Cartulaire de l'abbaye Saint-Sauveur de Redon*, fol. 160[r], 171[v]; *Cartulaire de l'abbaye de Redon*, CCCXXIX, p. 281; CCCLVI, p. 309.

[72] *Vie de Gauzlin*, pp. 64–66.

[73] Avranches, Bib. pat. MS 213, fol. 173[r] (Annales de Redon).

[74] *Actes des ducs*, no. 26, pp. 218–24.

[75] See Lecouteux, 'Réseaux', I, 491–92.

[76] *Actes des ducs*, pp. 174–75.

[77] *Cartulary of Mont-Saint-Michel*, no. 9, pp. 87–88.

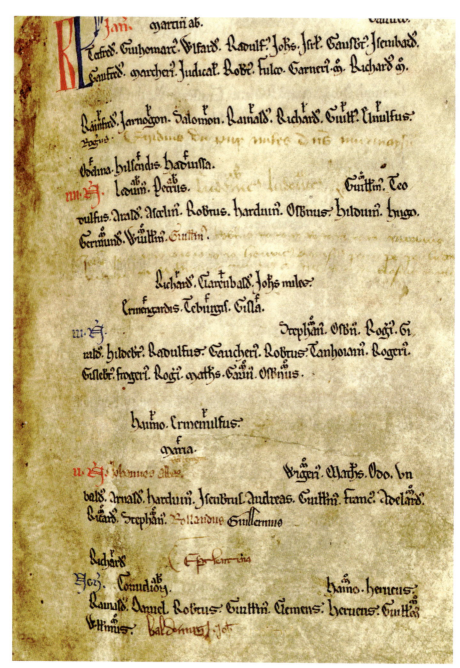

Figure 7.1. Opening page of the Mont's Necrology. Abbot Conwoion of Redon occurs on the Nones of January at the foot of the page, Avranches, Bib. pat., MS 214, pt. 1, p. 109 (image freely available at *Bibliothèque virtuelle du Mont Saint-Michel*).

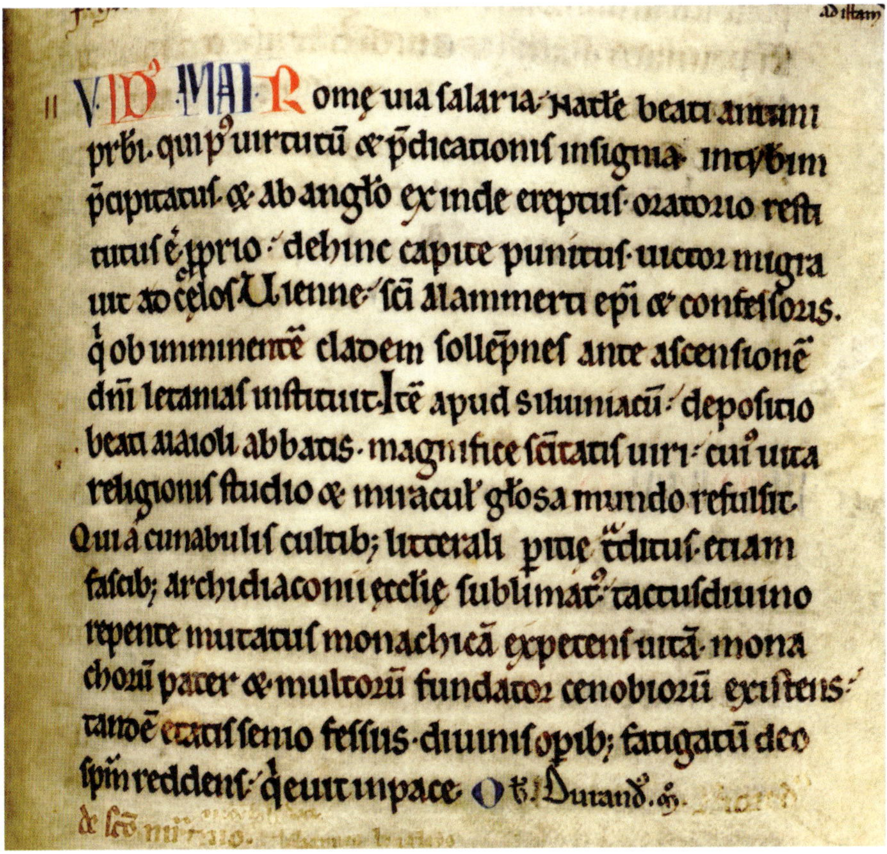

7. *MEMORIA*, MEMORIALIZATION, AND THE MONKS OF MONT-SAINT-MICHEL

Figure 7.2. Eulogy of Abbot Maiol of Cluny, died 11 May 994, in the
Mont Martyrology-Necrology, Avranches, Bib. pat., MS 214, pt. 1, p. 70
(image freely available at *Bibliothèque virtuelle du Mont Saint-Michel*).

than five years are normally not recorded, so are not included in this discussion). These were Almod, doubtless a relative of the Mont's own abbot of that name, and the abbot responsible for part of the Cartulary of Redon; as well as Vivian, Ivo, and Silvester, in the twelfth century.

Both Redon and the Mont had close links with Fleury, which appears in the confraternity lists. The Mont obits include the great reformer and scholar, Abbot Abbo, as well as Abbot Gauzlin, who appears twice in what Stéphane Lecouteux has identified as *in vitam* entries, perhaps marking the occasion of two visits to the abbey, close to which, at Saint-Hilaire, Fleury had a priory.[78]

---

[78] Lecouteux, 'Réseaux', I, 181.

It is possible that the formal confraternity was established on one of these visits — when he could have collected the Winchcombe sacramentary and its inscribed 'Fleury list'. Lecouteux has suggested that when the confraternities were first formalized, by a written agreement between two abbots, an obit was recorded of an illustrious predecessor of the signatory abbot, either a founder or reformer. This would account for the appearance both of Conwoion of Redon on 5 January (Fig. 7.1), and Abbo of Fleury.[79] There are other early links, with Saint-Germain-des-Prés in Paris and Saint-Aubin d'Angers and La Couture nearer home. The obits also include two Gausberts, the reformer of Marmoutier and La Couture, first abbot of Bourgueil and Maillezais, who died in 1007, and his nephew and successor. Gausbert I, a natural son of Hugh Capet, was the leading reformer of the time in the region. Oury has speculated that monks of Saint-Julien de Tours, reformed as a monastery by Odo of Cluny around 933/35, might have been used in the ultimately successful attempt by Gausbert I at reforming Marmoutier for monks.[80] The obits for Odo and Maiol of Cluny, as befitted their status as saints, occur as entries in the Martyrology, where there is an exceptionally fulsome eulogy of Maiol, far exceeding anything so far found in a Cluniac martyrology (Fig. 7.2).[81]

A charter of *c*. 982–986 shows Abbot Mainard I of the Mont seeking a grant of a vineyard from Marmoutier and Abbot Maiol. There are several difficulties regarding the interpretation of this charter.[82] Laurent Morelle has suggested that a phrase referring to the transaction as a first grant — *prima donationis* — given at Mont-Saint-Michel — *ad locum sancti Michaelis* — may be an interpolation. It is perhaps indicative of a reciprocal transaction, at Marmoutier, now lost. The transaction can be understood as an act of mutual support between reformers and their communities. The fact that Mainard is said to have asked for the land, for a render of 12d annually, is reminiscent of other early Mont charters, in which a requested grant of land, whether in Brittany, Normandy, or Maine, reveals an attempt to reconstitute or enhance a disrupted patrimony. Lecouteux has suggested that the Benedictines' link with the reformed abbey of Marmoutier continued an earlier relationship of the canons of the Mont with

---

[79] Lecouteux, 'Réseaux', I, 186–91. In both cases links preceding formal confraternity are highly likely.

[80] Oury, 'Le rôle du monastère', pp. 202–03.

[81] Avranches, Bib. pat. MS 214, p. 69 (11 May), p. 174 (18 November). See Neiske, '*Transitus sancti Maioli*', especially pp. 265–67.

[82] Morelle, 'Notule', pp. 466, 472.

the canons of Tours.[83] We might therefore wonder whether some of Mainard's community may have come from the Touraine. It is worth noting that the name Mainard occurs frequently in necrologies and other texts from this region.[84]

In addition, there are the obits of the abbots of the major Norman abbeys. Particularly striking is the list for Saint-Taurin of Évreux. Overall, the obits of Saint-Taurin's abbots were kept more fully at the Mont than they were at Saint-Taurin itself, to judge from the latter's surviving necrologies of *c.* 1238. Nothing is known of the first abbot, Fulcran, who had been succeeded by Abbot Fromund by 989; both were remembered only in the necrologies of Saint-Taurin and the Mont. Fromund (d. aft. 1035) was named in the Mont Martyrology, as was Tovo (d. bef. 1080) who was a monk of the Mont.[85] It was under him that Saint-Taurin became a dependency of Fécamp in 1034, a situation that lasted until 1247, when Innocent IV restored its autonomy. Olivier Diard has suggested that up until then, the Mont and Saint-Taurin had shared much of their liturgy.[86] Hildebert and Fromund were names that linked the Mont, Saint-Taurin, and Saint-Ouen. It is very likely that these men were connected, probably related. Saint-Ouen, as well as perhaps Saint-Denis and possibly Fleury, may have provided some of the monks 'from all over' who formed the new Benedictine community. Equally, it seems likely that when Saint-Taurin was refounded, some time after the Mont, but in the wake of the same events in Évreux, they were closely supported by the Mont community, some of whom may have been among the first monks of Saint-Taurin.

Collating with Necrologies from Other Abbeys

The picture is equally interesting when reversed. Necrologies survive for Jumièges and Saint-Taurin, and we have fragments from Fécamp (February and November). Also important are the survivals of early necrologies from Saint-Bénigne de Dijon and Saint-Germain-des-Près, both major witnesses from the Volpiano-era confraternity which preserve the names of monks from Fécamp

---

[83] Lecouteux, 'Réseaux', I, 183.

[84] On the origins of a family using this name in this area in the ninth century see Doumerc, 'Essai de reconstitution', I, 228–29, 236 n. 893, 271, 345, 357–60, and Arbre 39, II, 929.

[85] Saint-Taurin included their names in mortuary rolls for Matilda of Caen and Vital of Savigny; Gazeau, *Prosopographie*, II, 93–95.

[86] Diard, 'Histoire et chant liturgique', pp. 196–97, though this will not have lasted as long as he suggests.

and Saint-Wandrille.[87] The only one to record the obit of both Mainard I and Mainard II is Saint-Taurin.[88] Both Hildeberts were remembered at Saint-Taurin, as also at Saint-Bénigne. Saint-Germain remembered Hildebert II as *abbas sancti Taurini episcopi*, an error, but perhaps a revealing one.[89]

Finally, in 1008, Gerard, abbot of Crépy, was appointed to restore Saint-Wandrille. A monk of Lagny, he had studied at Reims at the same time as Fulbert, future bishop of Chartres, and Gerbert of Aurillac. Both Gerard and Fulbert are remembered in the Martyrology-Necrology of Mont-Saint-Michel.[90] From this time until the Mont necrologies were recopied *c.* 1212, a substantially complete list of Saint-Wandrille's abbots were recorded at the Mont, though here, as in a number of cases not including Redon and Saint-Taurin, there was a prolonged gap in recording in the second half of the eleventh century, going into the twelfth. This may have been related to the upheavals of the period after 1030 and may have also been related to a change in recording practice.[91]

When Hildebert II died in 1023 he was replaced by William of Volpiano's protegé Thierry of Fécamp. This was a breach of the right of election, and demeaning for an abbey with such a pedigree, but these were troubled times. Thierry died in 1027 and the monks elected the Almodus of the Fleury list, in rejection of the duke's candidate Suppo of Fruttaria. Almodus was removed during 1032 and sent as abbot to the new monastery of Saint-Vigor de Cerisy. Suppo, at that point a monk of the abbey, was elected in his place. He was driven out by internal factionalism in 1048. Things were no easier for his ducally-appointed replacement Ralph (*c.* 1048–1058), who died on the way back from a pilgrimage, though they stabilized somewhat under Abbot Ranulf (1060/61–1083/84).[92] The trouble may have started under Hildebert II, a period when Alan III of Brittany confiscated a grant

---

[87] Rouen, Bib. mun., MS 1220 (U50); Dijon, Bib. mun. MS 634; BnF, MS nouv. acq. lat. 1899; for Fécamp, BnF, MS nouv. acq. lat. MS 2389, fols 33–34; edited Lecouteux, 'Deux fragments', pp. 61–79. Saint-Germain was edited in Decker-Hauer, *Studien zur Memorialüberlieferung*, pp. 297–352.

[88] BnF, MS nouv. acq. lat., MS 1899, fols 201^r, 212^r.

[89] BnF, MS nouv. acq. lat. 1899, fols 188^v (Saint-Taurin), 222^r; Rouen, Bib. mun., MS 1220 (U50) (Jumièges), fols 161^v, 196^v; Decker-Hauer, *Studien zur Memorialüberlieferung*, p. 340.

[90] Avranches, Bib. pat. MS 214, pp. 51, 180.

[91] Discussed in Keats-Rohan, '*Pretiosa est*'.

[92] Lecouteux, 'Réseaux', II, pp. 323–36.

by his father on grounds of neglect by the abbot, though he restored it in 1032.[93] Relations with Duke Robert and Archbishop Robert of Rouen were also strained, partly because of the monks' closeness to the Breton rulers. More seriously, relations with the canons deteriorated. The restoration of the bishopric in 990 soon led to tensions between the bishops, a revitalized college of canons, and the monks, which were the subject of an accord in 1061 when the abbot became an archdeacon of Avranches.[94] The monks seem to have had no difficulty in adopting the *Revelatio* as a lectionary for the feast of St Michael, or the *Liber de apparitione*, relating the origins of Monte Gargano, or the angelology based on Gregory the Great's synthesis of Pseudo-Denis in his Homily 34: all are evidenced in the *Revelatio* author's text, and all are preserved in late-tenth-century copies in a Mont manuscript.[95] According to *Introductio*, under Hildebert II they also adopted the relics of St Autbert for a monastic cult. The turbulence of the period is well captured by the author of the *Introductio monachorum* and his *De translatione et miraculis sancti Autberti*.

Conclusion: The Value of Memorial Liturgy as a Historical Source

A monastic Chapter book enshrines one of the most central and intimate liturgies of Benedictine life: the remembrance of their dead and the saints most revered by their community, identified by the additions to the basic text of their chosen martyrology. Its potential to reveal much about the community is obvious and well known to historians.[96] In this case, the Mont necrologies go back to the mid-tenth century and continue, at least sporadically, into the sixteenth; additionally, they can be collated against other sources, both internal and external, liturgical and literary. Where such rich prosopographical keys exist to allow a probing examination, the potential for this liturgy to become an important historical source can be revealed, as it has been here. Indeed, any hope of a true understanding of the tenth-century community lies in the necrologies, rather than the narrative texts. They may even help in the matter of Mainard I of Mont-Saint-Michel and Mainard of Saint-Wandrille.[97]

---

[93] *Cartulary of Mont-Saint-Michel*, no. 23, pp. 104–05.

[94] Printed in *Chroniques latines*, pp. 375–78.

[95] Avranches, Bib. pat. MS 211, fols 156–210, copied by Heriward.

[96] For example, see Lemaître, '*Liber capituli*', and Wollasch, 'Les obituaires'.

[97] See above, pp. 155–56.

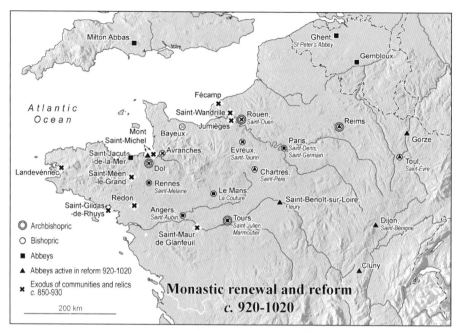

Figure 7.3. Monastic renewal and reform *c*. 920–1020 (Don Shewan, City Cartographic).

It seems that two Mainards were establishing communities at the same time, in the early 960s. One was very successful, the other not. Nearly a century later, a monk establishing a new cult with a fictional *inventio* at Saint-Wandrille chose to merge its founder Mainard with the person of his illustrious contemporary, Mainard I of the Mont.[98] The Mont Martyrology-Necrology has a double entry on November 29 for *Mainardus et Gerardus abbates*, of whom the second is certainly the abbot of Saint-Wandrille. Significantly, only Saint-Taurin, of all the extant Norman necrologies, has Mainard on this date, increasing the likelihood that he was Gerard's predecessor.[99]

Mainard I's is a career with echoes in that of his putative nephew Mainard II, abbot of the Mont and reformer of Redon. Indeed, there surely lies in all these obits the clear evidence that the Montois monks were extremely well connected in reformist circles. Their struggles with the dukes of Normandy ultimately curtailed their ambitions, but there are suggestions here that Montois monks

[98] Eventually, this revised history made its way to the Mont, seen in a fifteenth-century copy of annals in Avranches, Bib. pat. MS 213, fols 170–72.

[99] As suggested by Gazeau, *Prosopographie*, I, 210–11; Lecouteux, 'Réseaux', I, 271. Avranches, Bib. pat. MS 214, p. 180.

established by *c.* 960 had strong reforming credentials and in fact assisted with the restoration and reform of Norman monasticism in the tenth century, as they did in Brittany in the early eleventh. Mainard I's importance was recognized at the Mont by the later attribution of the appellation *primus abbas*, emphasizing that he represented a new beginning. Rosé has pointed to well-connected aristocratic abbots with personal charisma who reformed or assisted reforms in other monasteries in the early tenth century, the final wave of reform emanating from smaller, more regional centres such as Fleury in the second half of the century.[100] Mont-Saint-Michel, it must now be recognized, easily fits into this pattern, probably associated with Cluny and Fleury initially, and later with Saint-Bénigne and Fécamp. This was a community that occupied the centre ground of the tenth-century religious renewal, not the side-lines to which it has too long been confined.

Katharine S. B. Keats-Rohan, PhD (Lond), FSA, FRHistS, Faculty of History, Oxford. Author of 57 papers and editor or co-editor of fourteen books, mainly on north-west France and England ninth to thirteenth centuries, as well as the texts of John of Salisbury, the castle and honour of Wallingford, and a prosopography of English Catholic nuns in exile 1600–1800. An edition of the necrologies and early cartulary of Mont-Saint-Michel is being prepared for the Sources médiévales de l'histoire de Bretagne series, Presses universitaires de Rennes.

[100] Rosé, 'Les réformes', p. 146.

Works Cited

Manuscripts

Angers, Bibliothèque municipale, MS 837 (753)
Avranches, Bibliothèque patrimoniale, MS 42
Avranches, Bibliothèque patrimoniale, MS 210
Avranches, Bibliothèque patrimoniale, MS 211
Avranches, Bibliothèque patrimoniale, MS 213
Avranches, Bibliothèque patrimoniale, MS 214
Dijon, Bibliothèque municipale, MS Dijon 634
New York, Morgan Library and Museum (formerly Pierpont Morgan Library), MS 641
Paris, Bibliothèque nationale de France, MS nouv. acq. lat. 1899
Paris, Bibliothèque nationale de France, MS nouv. acq. lat. 2389
Rouen, Bibliothèque municipale, MS 1226 (U50)
Vatican, MS Vat. Lat. 9668

Primary Sources

Actes des ducs de Bretagne (944–1148), ed. by H. Guillotel, P. Charon, P. Guigon, C. Henry, M. Jones, K. Keats-Rohan, and J.-C. Meuret, Sources médiévales de l'histoire de Bretagne, 3 (Rennes: Presses Universitaires de Rennes, 2014)

Adso Dervensis, *Vita Frodoberti Abbatis*, ed. by J.-P. Migne, Patrologia Latina, CXXXVII (Paris: Garnier, 1879), cols 599–620

André de Fleury, *Vie de Gauzlin, abbé de Fleury*, ed. by R. H. Bautier and G. Labory (Paris: Éditions du Centre national de la recherche scientifique, 1969)

Bibliothèque virtuelle du Mont Saint-Michel <https://emmsm.unicaen.fr/emmsm/bvmsm/> [accessed 25 June 2020]

Cartulaire de l'abbaye Saint-Sauveur de Redon, ed. by H. Guillotel, A. Chédeville, and B. Tanguy, 2 vols (Rennes: Association des Amis des Archives historiques du diocèse de Rennes, Dol et Saint-Malo, 1998–2004)

Cartulaire de l'abbaye de Redon en Bretagne. ed. by A. de Courson (Paris: Imprimerie Impériale, 1863)

The Cartulary of Mont-Saint-Michel, ed. by K. S. B. Keats-Rohan (Deddington: Shaun Tyas, 2006)

Chroniques latines du Mont Saint-Michel (IXᵉ-XIIᵉ siècle), ed. by P. Bouet and O. Desbordes (Caen: Presses Universitaires de Caen, 2009)

De beati Audoeni translatione et ejus sacratissimi corporis integritate, ed. by J.-P. Migne, Patrologia Latina, CLXII (Paris: Garnier, 1854), cols 1160–63

Dudo de Saint-Quentin, *De moribus et actis primorum Normanniae ducum*, ed. by J. Lair, Mémoires de la Société des Antiquaires de Normandie, 23 (Caen: Le Blanc Hardel,

1865); *Dudo of St Quentin: History of the Normans*, trans. by E. Christiansen (Woodbridge: Boydell, 1998)

Historia ecclesie Abbendonensis: The History of the Church of Abingdon, ed. by J. Hudson, 2 vols (Oxford: Clarendon Press, 2002–2007)

Inventio et miracula Sancti Vulfranni, ed. by D. J. Laporte, Société d'Histoire de Normandie. *Mélanges*, 14 (1938), 7–87

The Monks of Redon: Gesta sanctorum Rotonensium and Vita Conuuoionis, ed. by C. Brett, SCH, 10 (Woodbridge: Boydell, 1989)

Odo de Cluny, *Collationes*, ed. by J.-P. Migne, Patrologia Latina, CXXXIII (Paris: Garnier, 1881), cols 517–638

Studien zur Memorialüberlieferung im frühmittelalterlichen, Paris, ed. by A. Decker-Hauer, Beihefte der Francia, 40 (Sigmaringen: Thorbecke, 1998)

Secondary Works

Arnoux, M., 'Disparition ou conservation des sources et abandon de l'acte écrit: quelques observations sur les actes de Jumièges', *Tabularia Études*, 1 (2001), 1–10

Bauduin, P., 'Autour d'une construction identitaire: la naissance d'une historiographie normande à la charnière des x^c–xi^c siècles', in *Conquête, acculturation, identité: des Normands aux Hongrois. Les traces de la conquête*, ed. by P. Nagy, Cahiers du Groupe de Recherche d'Histoire, 13 (Rouen: Presses Universitaires de Rouen, 2001), pp. 79–91

Brett, C., 'A Breton Pilgrim in the Time of King Æthelstan', in *France and the British Isles in the Middle Ages and Renaissance*, ed. by G. Jondorf and D. N. Dumville (Woodbridge: Boydell, 1991), pp. 43–70

Deuffic, J.-L., 'L'exode des corps saints hors de Bretagne: des reliques au culte liturgique', *Pecia*, 8–11 (2005), 355–423

Diard, O., with V. Gazeau, 'Histoire et chant liturgique en Normandie au xi^c siècle: les offices propres particuliers des diocèses d'Évreux et de Rouen', *Annales de Normandie*, 53 (2003), 195–223

Dimier, M.-A., 'Le mot *locus* employé dans le sens de monastère', *Bulletin de la Société Nationale des Antiquaires de France*, 1971 (1973), 221–24

Dolley, M., and J. Yvon, 'A Group of Tenth-Century Coins Found at Mont-Saint-Michel', *British Numismatic Journal*, 40 (1972), 1–16

Doumerc, F., 'Essai de construction d'un espace princier: l'exemple des Rorgonides dans le monde franc puis dans le royaume de France et ses marges (vers 600–vers 1060)', 2 vols (unpublished doctoral thesis, Université du Maine, 2010)

Dubois, D. J., 'Le martyrologe du l'abbaye de Mont Saint-Michel', in *Millénaire monastique du Mont Saint Michel I: histoire et vie monastiques*, ed. by J. Laporte, Bibliothèque d'histoire et d'archéologie chrétiennes (Paris: Lethielleux, 1967), pp. 489–99

Fauroux, M., ed., *Recueil des actes des ducs de Normandie*, Mémoires de la Société des Antiquaires de Normandie, 36 (Caen: Caron, 1961)

Foot, S., *Æthelstan the First King of England* (New Haven, CN: Yale University Press, 2012)

Gaillard, M., *D'une réforme à l'autre (816–934): les communautés religieuses en Lorraine à l'époque carolingienne* (Paris: Publications de la Sorbonne, 2006)

Garault, C., 'L'Abbaye de Redon, entre horizon locale et ouverture culturelle (IXe–XIIe siècle)', in *Histoire de Redon*, ed. by D. Pichot and G. Provost (Rennes: Presses Universitaires, 2015), pp. 83–115

Gazeau, V., *Normannia monastica (X[e]-XIIe siècle). Princes normands et abbés bénédictins. Prosopographie des abbés bénédictins*, 2 vols, Publications du Centre de Recherches Archéologiques et Historiques Médiévales (Turnhout: Brepols, 2008)

Guillotel, H., 'L'exode du clergé breton devant les invasions scandinaves', *MSHAB*, 59 (1982), 301–16

Laporte, D. J., ed., *Millénaire monastique du Mont-Saint-Michel, I: Histoire et vie monastiques*, Bibliothèque d'histoire et d'archéologie chrétiennes (Paris: Lethielleux, 1967)

——, 'Les obituaires du Mont Saint-Michel', in *Millénaire monastique du Mont Saint Michel I: histoire et vie monastiques*, ed. by J. Laporte, Bibliothèque d'histoire et d'archéologie chrétiennes (Paris: Lethielleux, 1967), pp. 725–41

Lecouteux, S., 'Deux fragments d'un nécrologe de la Trinité de Fécamp (XIe–XIIe siècles). Étude et édition critique d'un document mémoriel exceptionnel', *Tabularia* (2016), 2–89

——, 'Réseaux de confraternité et histoire des bibliothèques: l'exemple de l'abbaye bénédictine de la Trinité de Fécamp', 2 vols (unpublished doctoral thesis, Université de Caen, 2015)

Lemaître, J.-L., '*Liber Capituli*: le Livre du chapitre, des origines au XVIe siècle. L'exemple français', in *Memoria: Der geschichtliche Zeugniswert des liturgischen Gedenkens im Mittelalter*, ed. by K. Schmid and J. Wollasch, Bestandteil des Quellenwerkes SOCIETAS ET FRATERNITAS, Münstersche Mittelalter-Schriften, 48 (Munich: Fink, 1984), pp. 635–48

Lemarié, D. J., and H. Tardif, 'Le calendrier du Mont Saint-Michel', in *Millénaire monastique du Mont Saint Michel I: histoire et vie monastiques*, ed. by J. Laporte, Bibliothèque d'histoire et d'archéologie chrétiennes (Paris: Lethielleux, 1967), pp. 287–301

Keats-Rohan, K. S. B., 'Testimonies of the Living Dead: The Martyrology-Necrology and Necrology in the Chapter Book of Mont-Saint-Michel (Avranches, Bibliothèque municipale, MS 214', in *The Durham Liber Vitae and its Context*, ed. by D. Rollason, A. J. Piper, M. Harvey, and L. Rollason, Regions and Regionalism in History, 1 (Woodbridge: Boydell, 2004), pp. 165–90

——, 'Histoire secrète', in *Culte et sanctuaires de saint Michel dans l'Europe médiévale*, ed. by P. Bouet, G. Otranto, and A. Vauchez (Bari: Edipuglia, 2007), pp. 139–59

——, '*Pretiosa est in conspectu Domini mors sanctorum eius*: the Chapter Book Necrologies of Mont Saint-Michel, Avranches, Bib. pat., ms 214', *Tabularia* (2022), 1–55

Mazel, F., *L'évêque et le territoire. L'invention médiévale de l'espace (V[e]–XIIIe siècle)* (Paris: Éditions du Seuil, 2016)

Morelle, L., 'Notule montoise: la charte de l'abbé Maieul de Cluny pour le Mont Saint-Michel', in *Sur les pas de Lanfranc du Bec à Caen. Recueil des études en hommage de Véronique Gazeau*, ed. by P. Bauduin, G. Combalbert, A. Dubois, B. Garnier, and C. Maneuvrier, Cahiers des Annales de Normandie, 37 (2018), pp. 465–74

Musset, L., 'Ce qu'en enseigne l'histoire d'un patrimoine monastique: Saint-Ouen de Rouen du IXe au XIe siècle', in *Sept essais sur des aspects de la société et de l'économie dans la Normandie médiévale (X[e]–XIIIe siècles)*, ed. by L. Musset, J.-M. Bouvris, and V. Gazeau, Cahiers de Normandie, 22 (Caen: Annales de Normandie, 1988), pp. 15–29

——, 'Recherches sur les pèlerins et les pèlerinages en Normandie jusqu'à la Première Croisade, *Annales de Normandie*, 12 (1962), 127–50

Neiske, F., '*Transitus sancti Maioli*: la mémoire de Saint Mayeul dans les nécrologes et les martyrologues du Moyen Âge', in *Millénaire de la mort de Saint Mayeul 4e abbé de Cluny 994–1994: Actes du Congrès International, Valensole 12–14 Mai 1994* (Digne-les-Bains: Société scientifique et littéraire des Alpes de Haute-Provence, 1997), pp. 259–71

Oury, G.-M., 'Le rôle du monastère de Saint-Julien de Tours après sa restauration par Odon de Cluny (peu av. 942–1042)', in *Pays de Loire et Aquitaine de Robert le Fort aux premiers Capétiens: Actes du colloque scientifique international tenu à Angers en septembre 1997*, ed. by O. Guillot and R. Favreau, Mémoires de la Société des antiquaires de l'Ouest et des musées de Poitiers (Poitiers, 1997), pp. 191–213

Pietri, L., 'Les abbés de basilique dans la Gaule du VIe siècle', *Revue d'Histoire de l'Église de France*, 69 (1972), 5–28

Rosé, I., 'Les réformes monastiques', in *Pouvoirs, église et société dans le royaume de France, de Bourgogne et de Germanie aux Xe et XIe siècles (888–vers 1110)*, ed. by P. Bertran, B. Duméil, S. Joye, C. Mériaux, and I. Rosé (Paris: Ellipses, 2008), pp. 135–61

Tardif, H., 'La liturgie de la messe au Mont Saint-Michel aux XIe, XIIe, et XIIIe siècle', in *Millénaire monastique du Mont Saint Michel I: histoire et vie monastiques*, ed. by J. Laporte, Bibliothèque d'histoire et d'archéologie chrétiennes (Paris: Lethielleux, 1967), pp. 353–77

Trân-Duc, L., 'Une entreprise hagiographique au XIe siècle dans l'abbaye de Fontenelle: le renouveau du culte de saint Vulfran', *Tabularia Sources Écrits*, 8 (2008), 1–25

Van Torhoudt, E., 'Les Bretons dans les diocèses d'Avranches et de Coutances (950–1200) environ: une approche onomastique de la question de l'identité', in *Bretons et Normands au Moyen Âge*, ed. by J. Quaghebeur and B. Merdrignac (Rennes: Presses universitaires de Rennes, 2008), pp. 113–44

Vanderputten, S., *Monastic Reform as a Process: Realities and Representations in Medieval Flanders, 900–1100* (Ithaca, NY: Cornell University Press, 2013)

——, and B. Meijns, 'Gérard de Brogne en Flandre. État de la question sur les réformes monastiques du Xe siècle', *Revue du Nord*, 385 (2010), 271–95

Werner, K. F., 'Untersuchungen zur Frühzeit des französischen Furstentums (9.-10. Jahrhundert)', *Die Welt als Geschichte*, 18 (1958), 256–89; 19 (1959), 146–93; 20 (1960), 87–119; trans. by B. Saint-Sorny as *Enquêtes sur les premiers temps du principat français (IXe–Xe siècles)*, Instrumenta hrsg. vom Deutschen Historischen Institut Paris, 14 (Ostfildern: Thorbecke, 2004)

Wilmart, A., 'Les frères défunts de Saint-Denis au déclin du IXe siècle', *Revue Mabillon*, 15 (1925), 241–57

Wollasch, J., 'Les obituaires, témoins de la vie clunisienne', *Cahiers de civilisation médiévale*, 22 (1979), 139–71

8. Présence d'une culture celtique insulaire chez les anciens hagiographes bretons

Joseph-Claude Poulin

RÉSUMÉ Peut-on dire que l'hagiographie bretonne du ixe siècle porte des marques de la culture d'origine des immigrants gallois ? L'essor de l'hagiographie en Bretagne carolingienne arrive trop tard pour refléter directement les premiers temps de l'acculturation des migrants bretons sur le continent. Tant les schémas de composition que les sources d'inspiration (formelles et spirituelles) des hagiographes sont marqués bien plus fortement par une influence continentale qu'insulaire, sauf pour l'origine personnelle des saints eux-mêmes. Il est vrai que les Vies de saints bretons les plus anciennes possèdent un air de famille, mais cet apparentement leur vient du rayonnement du dossier de s. Samson de Dol. Finalement, c'est à Alet et surtout à Landévennec que des traces de culture celtique sont les plus explicites ; mais le dossier hagiographique dans son ensemble illustre plutôt les progrès d'une acculturation des Bretons à la civilisation du monde romano-franc déjà bien avancée.

ABSTRACT Can it be said that ninth-century Breton hagiography is marked by the culture of the homeland of its British immigrant population? The flowering of hagiography in Carolingian Brittany came too late to show a direct reflection of the earliest times of the British migrants' assimilation on the Continent. Both the structure and the sources of inspiration of the hagiographers (stylistic and spiritual) are more strongly marked by Continental than by Insular influence, except with regard to the origins of the saints themselves. While it is true that the oldest Breton saints' Lives seem to form a coherent group, this relationship is due to the influence of the Lives of St Samson of Dol. It is at Alet and especially at Landévennec where the traces of Celtic culture are clearest, but the hagiographical corpus as a whole tends to illustrate the progress of integration of the Bretons to the civilization of the Romano-Frankish world, already well advanced.

MOTS-CLÉS Bili, Brendan, civilisation celtique, Gildas, Guénolé, Gurdisten, hagiographie, hyperbates, Irlande, Landévennec, Malo, *opus geminum*, Samson

Multi-disciplinary Approaches to Medieval Brittany, 450–1200: Connections and Disconnections, ed. by Caroline Brett, Fiona Edmonds, and Paul Russell, TCNE 36 (Turnhout: Brepols, 2023) pp. 179–206　　BREPOLS ⚓ PUBLISHERS　　10.1484/M.TCNE-EB.5.132313

Introduction

Depuis longtemps, la question des rapports de la Bretagne armoricaine avec le monde celtique insulaire a retenu l'attention des chercheurs et l'intérêt des lecteurs. L'objet du présent essai est d'essayer de comprendre comment s'exprimait, chez les Bretons du IXᵉ siècle, la conscience de leurs racines celtiques insulaires. Quelle mémoire ont-ils conservée de leur affiliation à la patrie de leurs ancêtres? Quels traces ou symptômes révèlent un sentiment continué d'appartenance à une civilisation distincte de celle du continent? Ces questions peuvent aussi se poser à rebours: où en était le processus d'acculturation qui les a éloignés — ou pas — de leur milieu d'origine après quelques siècles d'enracinement sur le continent? L'état de la documentation narrative en Bretagne ne permet guère de chercher des réponses qu'à partir du IXᵉ siècle, grâce à une floraison remarquable de la production hagiographique consacrée à des saints bretons.[1]

La Vie ancienne de saint Samson de Dol (BHL 7478–79) — quelle que soit la date qu'on lui attribue (entre la fin du VIIᵉ et la fin du VIIIᵉ siècle, selon les derniers travaux) — permet de poser un premier jalon.[2] La partie insulaire de la Vie du saint y occupe une place prépondérante, d'un simple point de vue quantitatif: 51 chapitres sur 61 au livre I et les chap. 7 à 9 au livre II. Au milieu du IXᵉ siècle, une *Vita II* (BHL 7481, 7483) rééquilibre le récit au profit de la phase continentale de la carrière du saint: 20 chapitres avant la traversée de la Manche, contre 26 après.[3] Déjà un glissement des priorités ou une évolution des sensibilités? Cette marginalisation relative du volet insulaire de l'histoire du saint est confirmée par une réécriture abrégée (inédite) de la *Vita II* avant la fin du IXᵉ siècle: sur les 18 chapitres conservés, 7 seulement concernent la période insulaire.[4] Qu'en est-il ailleurs dans l'hagiographie bretonne de l'époque carolingienne?

---

[1] Cette question a déjà été étudiée, d'un point de vue linguistique, par Kerlouégan, 'Les Vies de saints bretons'.

[2] *Vie ancienne de Samson*, éd. Flobert. Pour un bilan récent de la discussion, cf. Poulin, 'L'hagiographie bretonne avant l'an mil'. Voir aussi, dans ce volume, Jankulak, 'Cross-Channel Intercourse', pp. 209–10.

[3] 'Vita antiqua'.

[4] Cette réduction de la *Vita II* est connue par un manuscrit unique de la fin du IXᵉ siècle (Vatican, BAV Reg. lat. 479, fol. 9–24ᵛ), mutilé à la fin par perte matérielle: Poulin, *L'hagiographie bretonne*, pp. 335–36.

8. PRÉSENCE D'UNE CULTURE CELTIQUE INSULAIRE   181

Un observatoire privilégié permettant de prendre le pouls de la situation est fourni par les dossiers des saints Malo d'Alet (BHL 5116a et b) et Guénolé de Landévennec (BHL 8957–58). L'un et l'autre ont en commun d'avoir été dressés au même moment, vers 870, par des auteurs qui se sont donné le mal de composer des ensembles documentaires de longueur exceptionnelle par comparaison avec le reste de la production hagiographique de leur époque.

Afin de répondre aux questions posées, une approche en trois étapes sera suivie. D'abord, comment caractériser le corpus sélectionné comme moyen d'accès au processus historique concerné? Ensuite, que nous apprennent les méthodes de travail et les sources formelles des auteurs en lien avec leur entreprise mémorielle? Enfin, quels éléments de contenu font de cette documentation hagiographique un exercice conscient de valorisation du passé celtique ou de définition d'une identité bretonne originale, sinon déjà métissée? Sous tous ces aspects, l'ancienne hagiographie bretonne peut se lire comme une chambre d'écho; mais de quoi est-elle l'écho?

Caractérisation du corpus documentaire

Les deux saints ici mis en vedette sont bretons d'origine: Malo est né dans une famille noble du Gwent (au sud du Pays de Galles), Guénolé est né en Armorique, de parents eux-mêmes venus de Grande Bretagne. Leurs biographes respectifs sont également des Bretons, s'il faut en croire leur nom: le diacre Bili pour Malo, l'abbé Gurdisten pour Guénolé. Nous avons donc affaire à des Bretons qui s'adressent au premier chef à d'autres Bretons, à propos de ce qui peut être considéré comme une page de leur histoire commune.

Un décalage temporel important pèse cependant sur la représentation ou la construction d'une mémoire des origines. L'existence de traditions orales susceptibles d'alimenter une rédaction au IXe siècle à propos d'événements survenus au VIe siècle ne fait pas de doute; mais leur contenu est incertain et leur fiabilité historique sujette à caution, à notre avis.[5] Quelques éléments factuels ont pu survivre à la succession des générations, comme le dit Bili pour saint Malo;[6] mais il faut tenir compte du fait que nos auteurs n'en ont mis en forme

---

[5] On trouve une bien meilleure confiance dans des traditions orales relayées par les hagiographes chez Fleuriot, 'Brittonnica et Gallica I'. Aussi chez Merdrignac, *Recherches sur l'hagiographie armoricaine*, I, 37–39; ou Merdrignac, *Les Vies de saints bretons*, pp. 49–52.

[6] 'Ut fideles viri de generatione in generationem narrant' (comme des hommes dignes de foi le racontent de génération en génération): Bili, *Vita S. Machutis*, I.15, pp. 362. Dans le même sens, chez Gurdisten: 'ex maiorum relatione venerabilium dictis elucidare, prout potui-

qu'une relecture hagiographique, c'est-à-dire stylisée et stéréotypée. Au total, nous sommes sans doute plus proche de la création d'une tradition que de sa simple transmission; vers 870, il est assurément trop tard pour refléter sur le vif le processus de première acculturation des Bretons sur le continent. Il s'agira plutôt d'un passé recomposé. Ni Malo ni Guénolé ne bénéficiaient d'une célébrité ou d'un culte déjà établis Outre-Manche et susceptibles d'inspirer des hagiographes du continent.

L'utilisation possible de sources écrites — maintenant perdues — est également problématique. Nous accordons peu de crédit à Bili, quand il prétend disposer d'une version anonyme (par un *alius sapiens* [un autre sage]) plus ancienne; il est vrai que l'oscillation entre deux états du nom de Malo (*Machutes / Machlovus*) pourrait faire croire à l'existence de deux versions — ou deux saints — amalgamés. Gurdisten, de son côté, fait allusion à ce qui pourrait être une version brève (*vita brevis*, au premier vers de la préface métrique du premier livre); il en va de même des prétentions habituelles à disposer d'une documentation écrite dans la préface du deuxième livre (*ex antiquis recolligentes scriptis*). Gurdisten pouvait du moins récupérer quelques données biographiques dans l'hymne alphabétique du défunt moine Clément (BHL vacat).

L'utilisation de la langue latine laisse ouverte la question de savoir si cette latinité est plus ou moins ornée de celtismes et si de telles résurgences constituent un trait délibéré, un marqueur conscient d'appartenance au monde celtique. Rien n'impose de voir dans l'expression *sancti atque electi* (les saints et les élus; *V. Winwaloei*, II.28) un marqueur typique de la latinité irlandaise, comme l'a fait A. B. Kuypers;[7] elle se rencontre aussi chez Ambroise Autpert ou Raban Maur, par exemple. L'identification et l'interprétation de rémanences linguistiques éventuelles sont compliquées par l'écart temporel qui sépare les manuscrits les plus anciens de la date de composition des œuvres: cette tradition ne commence guère avant l'an mil. Il s'ensuit un risque de dilution des traces celtiques possibles, par méprise de lecture du modèle ou par incompréhension.[8]

---

mus, curavimus' (nous nous sommes efforcé, autant que nous l'avons pu, de mettre en lumière ce que nous avons appris par la relation de vénérables Anciens); ou 'a sanctissimis viris referentibus auditum est eosdem audisse apud praedecessores suos et vidisse qui verissime vidissent' (on a entendu dire par des témoins très saints ce qu'ils avaient entendu de leurs prédécesseurs et vu en vérité): Gurdisten, *Vita S. Winwaloei*, II Préface et II.26, pp. 210, 242.

[7] Kuypers, éd., *The Prayer Book of Ædelwald the Bishop*, pp. 243–45, corrigé sur ce point par Martin, éd., *Homiliarium Veronense*, p. xxi. Voir les références dans Poulin, 'L'intertextualité', p. 179.

[8] Ainsi *dicumbitiones*, glosé *donationes* dans Bili, *Vita S. Machutis*, I.44, p. 380: Fleuriot,

8. présence d'une culture celtique insulaire 183

Un essai d'inventaire des tournures bretonnes disséminées dans l'expression latine a été tenté par Léon Fleuriot et poursuivi par François Kerlouégan et Catherine Le Hénaff-Rozé.[9] Les notations répertoriées par ces linguistes n'ont rien d'étonnant, compte tenu du fait que nos auteurs sont sans doute de langue maternelle bretonne. La possibilité de reconnaître chez eux des symptômes d'une latinité qu'on pourrait dire celtique ne se rencontre toutefois que de façon faiblement résiduelle.[10] Les emprunts ou échos de vieux-breton ne semblent pas servir à donner un relief particulier à une manière celtique de manier l'expression hagiographique; au contraire, ils peuvent s'interpréter comme un signe d'assimilation au monde latin, qui ne laissait plus apparaître, au IXe siècle, que des vestiges épars de vieux-breton.

Le traitement de l'onomastique bretonne montre que nos hagiographes conservaient une connaissance active de leur langue maternelle, quand ils donnent des équivalents latins de noms bretons. Ainsi, dans la Vie de s. Guénolé:

– en 1.2: *Alba Trimammis = Gwen Teirbron* (Blanche aux trois mamelles) ou

– en 1.14: *Chreirbia = puella pulcherrima* (la plus belle fille).

Adolfo Tura se demande si les mots bretons traduits en latin pourraient correspondre à l'incorporation dans le texte de ce qui fut d'abord des gloses.[11] Mais nous n'attribuons pas de valeur proclamatoire particulière à ces jeux linguistiques.[12]

Il serait intéressant de savoir jusqu'à quel point les manuscrits porteurs d'œuvres hagiographiques bretonnes adoptent ou prolongent des usages typiquement insulaires. Mais l'analyse de cette facette matérielle de la transmission hagiographique est encore une fois handicapée par l'absence de manuscrits bretons d'âge carolingien. Il est en effet impossible de remonter plus haut que le XIe

Dictionnaire des gloses en vieux-breton, p. 138.

[9] Fleuriot, 'La vie intellectuelle dans la Bretagne ancienne', pp. 66–68; Kerlouégan, 'La littérature latine religieuse et profane', p. 91; Le Hénaff-Rozé, 'Les brittonismes au crible des concordances'; Poulin, *L'hagiographie bretonne*, pp. 162–63 et 166, pour la Vie de S. Malo par Bili.

[10] Ainsi *albigantes* (= oies sauvages) dans Bili, *Vita S. Machutis*, II.18, p. 429 (mais est-ce une occurrence inspirée par la *Vita II S. Samsonis*, II.12, 'Vita antiqua', pp. 133–34?): Harvey, 'Technical Vocabulary and its Identification', p. 381.

[11] Tura, 'Essai sur les *marginalia* en tant que pratique et documents', p. 363.

[12] Voir les recommandations à la prudence pour l'identification d'hispérismes dans le latin celtique du haut Moyen Âge chez Herren, *The Hisperica Famina*. I, *The A-Text*, pp. 45–47. On en trouve pourtant en Bretagne au IXe siècle, sous la plume de Lios Monocus: 'Lios Monocus', p. 277.

siècle par deux manuscrits de la grande Vie de s. Guénolé, vraisemblablement copiés à Landévennec.[13] Ces derniers portent certains symptômes graphiques ou esthétiques apparentés à des usages insulaires; mais il est impossible de décider s'il s'agit de la survivance d'un art du livre pratiqué continûment depuis l'arrivée des Bretons sur le continent, ou d'une recherche plus ou moins délibérée d'archaïsme.[14]

Henri d'Arbois de Jubainville croyait déceler des caractéristiques graphiques typiquement irlandaises dans le manuscrit de Quimper de la *Vita S. Winwaloei*;[15] mais l'esthétique des pages décorées se laisse plutôt rapprocher de modèles aussi utilisés à Jumièges au milieu du XIe siècle.[16] Il n'est donc nullement certain que de telles particularités aient été considérées comme des marqueurs intentionnels de l'originalité bretonne sur le continent. Si le témoignage contemporain de l'épigraphie et du rameau breton de la tradition manuscrite de la *Collectio canonum Hibernensis* peut être appelé ici en renfort, on peut croire à la coexistence d'usages insulaires et d'une forte empreinte de pratiques continentales.[17]

Questions de forme et méthodes de travail

En l'absence de revendication explicite d'affiliation à une civilisation celtique insulaire, est-ce que la structure des œuvres ou la méthode de travail de Bili et Gurdisten permettent de détecter un attachement aux origines celtiques? L'analyse de l'organisation générale des œuvres fournira un premier volet à cette enquête; la gestion des pratiques d'intertextualité, si prégnantes en hagiographie générale, en fournira un second.

[13] Paris, BnF lat. 5610A et Quimper, BM 16.

[14] Pour le manuscrit de Quimper, voir Barret, 'Le manuscrit: codicologie et paléographie', pp. 18–19.

[15] Son analyse est recopiée par Leclercq, 'Landévennec', col. 1241, qui l'attribue par erreur à Émile Ernault. La préface de Jubainville se trouve en tête de l'édition du Cartulaire de Landévennec par Le Men et Ernault, *Cartulaire de Landévennec*, pp. 538–39. Un autre exemple de graphie mixte au IXe siècle à Landévennec est signalé par Ineichen-Eder, 'Theologisches und philologisches Lehrmaterial aus dem Alkuin-Kreise'; Smith, *Province and Empire*, pp. 14 et 167–68.

[16] Selon l'avis de Vergnolle, 'De Jumièges à Landévennec'.

[17] Ainsi chez Handley, 'La paléographie des inscriptions', pp. 67–69; Ambrose, 'The Codicology and Palaeography of London, BL Royal 5 E.xiii', p. 5.

8. PRÉSENCE D'UNE CULTURE CELTIQUE INSULAIRE

A : Plusieurs chercheurs ont cherché à vérifier la présence, dans l'hagiographie du monde celtique, de modèles ou règles de composition.[18] Cette question en cache une autre : si ces schémas existent, dans quelle mesure nos deux auteurs les ont-ils adoptés ou volontairement imités ? De tels schémas, avec leur développement en trois, neuf ou dix étapes, ne peuvent de toute façon pas être appliqués tels quels aux dossiers de Malo ou Guénolé.[19] Il en va de même, à notre avis, des tentatives de discerner des analogies avec un développement en sept étapes de la vie du Christ,[20] ou de reconstituer une structure de composition en forme d'hexagone logique.[21]

Le point extrême des tentatives d'attribution d'un schéma numérique précis considéré comme caractéristique du savoir-faire des écrivains celtiques a été atteint par David Howlett : ses reconstitutions appliquées aux Vies de s. Malo et de s. Guénolé ne nous ont pas convaincu.[22] Son traitement du dossier de Bili sur s. Malo est particulièrement révélateur des limites de l'exercice. Howlett essaie d'abord d'appliquer sa méthode numérologique au *titulus* de l'œuvre, sans réaliser que ce lemme initial est en fait démarqué de la *Vita S. Paterni* de Fortunat.[23] Ensuite, il tisse un lien entre les 64 mots du poème *Vitales qui cupis* et le table des 64 titres de chapitres du livre I qui suit immédiatement.[24] Or le nombre total de chapitres est une affaire qui est loin d'être entendue ; le manuscrit de Londres visé par Howlett donne, en effet, une séquence de chapitres très différente du manuscrit d'Oxford (et son parent de la traduction en vieil-anglais). Enfin, Howlett prolonge sa mise en parallèle en constatant que l'hymne *Benedicite Dominum* compte à son tour 64 strophes. Mais ici encore, la structure de cette section pose des problèmes non résolus : une hymne, ou plusieurs hymnes amalgamées ?

---

[18] Bray, 'Some Aspects of Hagiography in the Celtic Church', p. 123 ; Bray, 'Heroic Tradition in the Lives of the Early Irish Saints'. Dans la même veine : Henken, *The Welsh Saints*.

[19] Picard, 'Structural Patterns', p. 75.

[20] Sellner, 'Songs of Praise', pp. 164–65.

[21] Pour la Vie de s. Guénolé : Merdrignac, 'Folklore and Hagiography', pp. 83–86.

[22] Howlett, *The Celtic Latin Tradition*, pp. 259–62, 266–67 et 394 ; Poulin, *L'hagiographie bretonne*, pp. 164, 404 et 425.

[23] BHL 6477. C'est sans doute parce qu'il a utilisé l'édition de Le Duc, *Vie de saint Malo*, où les emprunts à Fortunat ne sont pas identifiés à leur place dans le texte, comme ils le sont dans l'édition de Lot, *Mélanges*. Pour une comparaison de ces deux éditions, voir Poulin, *L'hagiographie bretonne*, pp. 154–55.

[24] Pour une approche critique des tables de chapitres en hagiographie, voir Poulin, 'Un élément négligé'.

Le découpage éventuel des anciennes Vies bretonnes en sections prédéterminées logiquement ou numériquement est rendu aléatoire par l'état dans lequel les œuvres nous sont parvenues. Bien que la grande Vie de s. Guénolé soit attribuable à un auteur unique, nous avons essayé de montrer ailleurs que ce vaste dossier fut constitué par l'assemblage de pièces composées à des moments différents et dans des buts variés.[25] La liberté d'action de Gurdisten est encore bien illustrée par son montage improvisé d'une version très abrégée de sa Vie de s. Guénolé (BHL 8960): des extraits de sa Vie longue sont complétés par une transcription de son Homélie.[26]

L'usage de structurer une Vie de saint comme un *itinerarium*, c'est-à-dire en suivant les étapes des déplacements successifs du saint, était connu en Irlande: ainsi la *Vita I* de s. Brigitte (après le chap. 20) ou la *Vita S. Columbae*, probablement à l'instar de la *Vita S. Hilarionis* de Jérôme.[27] Les Vies de Malo et Guénolé s'approchent peu ou prou de cette formule, sans qu'il y ait pour autant apparence ou nécessité d'une influence irlandaise en l'occurrence.

Diverses caractéristiques structurelles ont parfois été considérées comme des procédés typiquement celtiques, prolongés au IXe siècle par des hagiographes bretons du continent; par exemple, la présence d'une préface double. Ce trait est en effet observable en tête de la célèbre *Vita S. Columbae* d'Adomnán; mais il ne s'ensuit pas pour autant que la même caractéristique en tête de la Vie de s. Malo par Bili doive s'interpréter comme une marque insulaire sur le travail du diacre d'Alet. En effet, cette pratique fait partie depuis longtemps des usages de l'hagiographie latine, comme l'a montré J.-M. Picard.[28]

Dans les Vies de s. Malo et de s. Guénolé, F. Kerlouégan a cru déceler des traces d'une mode stylistique (les hyperbates doubles) très en faveur dans le monde celtique.[29] Mais outre le fait qu'on ne voit pas par quel canal une telle influence aurait pu s'exercer jusqu'en Petite Bretagne, il faut tenir compte du fait que ce type de construction entrecroisée se rencontre bien ailleurs, comme l'a fait observer Michael Winterbottom.[30]

---

[25] Poulin, 'L'intertextualité', pp. 165–221.

[26] BHL 8959: Poulin, *L'hagiographie bretonne*, p. 434.

[27] Stalmans, *Saints d'Irlande*, pp. 68 et 78; Picard, 'Structural Patterns', p. 80.

[28] Picard, 'Structural Patterns', p. 75. Il est possible que la grande Vie de saint Guénolé ait aussi possédé deux préfaces, la première étant maintenant perdue: sur ce point, voir Poulin, *L'hagiographie bretonne*, pp. 422–23.

[29] Kerlouégan, 'Une mode stylistique', pp. 283–84 et 287.

[30] Winterbottom, 'A "Celtic" Hyperbaton?', pp. 207–12; Winterbottom, 'Aldhelm's Prose

8. PRÉSENCE D'UNE CULTURE CELTIQUE INSULAIRE

Inversement, on observe de façon éclatante dans le dossier de s. Guénolé l'adoption de la formule de l'*opus geminum*, dans le monastère le plus occidental de Bretagne, qu'on aurait pu croire le moins exposé aux influences du monde franc. La pratique de l'*opus geminum* était déjà connue dans l'île de Bretagne — mais pas attestée dans sa partie celtique; pourtant, c'est vraisemblablement par voie continentale que son existence et sa valeur exemplaire sont parvenues jusqu'à Landévennec. Le monument dédié à saint Willibrord par Alcuin à la fin du VIIIe siècle (BHL 8935/39: *Vita* + conversion métrique + sermon) a certainement contribué à populariser cette formule en hagiographie; il est attesté par ailleurs que d'autres œuvres d'Alcuin furent connues de nos deux hagiographes.[31]

D'autres traits, moins spectaculaires mais bien réels, pourraient aussi être attribués à une influence continentale sur Bili et Gurdisten. Ainsi l'utilisation de notes marginales comme méthode de référencement des citations dans le corps du texte.[32] Ou la combinaison des narrations biographiques avec des hymnes, et l'adjonction de sermons aux *vitae*. Un exemple célèbre — et peut-être influent — de cette conception élargie d'un dossier hagiographique à l'époque carolingienne est représenté par l'ensemble documentaire (*gesta* + hymnes + prières de l'office) commandé en 834 par Louis le Pieux à Hilduin de Saint-Denis en l'honneur de saint Denis de Paris.[33]

B: Du point de vue de l'intertextualité, nos auteurs ont utilisé des ressources qui ressemblent par beaucoup de côtés à celles que maniaient déjà les plus anciens hagiographes irlandais, ou même Gildas.[34] Mais ces traits communs — outre les innombrables contacts avec la Bible — ne s'expliquent pas nécessairement par une dépendance directe des hagiographes continentaux à l'égard de leurs pairs insulaires ou par un désir de leur ressembler; la plupart du temps, les sources citées ou démarquées peuvent aussi bien être parvenues en Armorique par voie terrestre et non transmarine.

Style and its Origins', pp. 50–51. Réponse de Kerlouégan dans son article '"Faire" suivi d'un infinitif', p. 120.

[31] On reconnaît des emprunts au sermon d'Alcuin pour saint Vaast chez Bili; à son *Liber de virtutibus et vitiis* chez Gurdisten. Poulin, *L'hagiographie bretonne*, p. 158 pour le premier cas; Poulin, 'L'intertextualité', pp. 170–72 pour le second.

[32] Gurdisten annonce le recours à cette méthode dans la *nota* préliminaire de la *V. Winwaloei* (éd. De Smedt, p. 174). Pour un exemple célèbre de cette pratique bien établie à l'époque carolingienne: Steckel, 'Von Buchstabe und Geist'.

[33] BHL 2172/76: *Hilduin of Saint-Denis*, p. 198.

[34] Ainsi que l'a démontré Picard, 'Structural Patterns', p. 69.

Une exception — et elle est d'importance — concerne Gildas. Gurdisten indique expressément qu'il connaît le *De excidio Britanniae* et y renvoie son lecteur (en 1.1). Certains vocables latins peu courants du vocabulaire gildasien apparaissent çà et là dans la Vie de Guénolé.[35] Mais l'élément le plus significatif se trouve dès l'ouverture, au premier chapitre du premier livre: non seulement parce que la mémoire des origines insulaires s'y trouve affirmée dès les premiers mots,[36] mais aussi par la présence, tout au long de cet alinéa, d'un véritable pastiche du style gildasien.

À notre avis, il s'agit là d'un signal fort d'affiliation culturelle au monde celtique, donné au moment de rappeler les causes de la migration des Bretons vers le continent. Les premiers lecteurs de Gurdisten ont dû décoder l'allusion d'autant plus facilement que Gildas est identifié nommément. Dans ce cas, il est légitime de penser que le *De excidio Britanniae* a pu arriver à Landévennec directement à travers la Manche, illustrant ainsi le maintien de liens vivants avec le monde celtique insulaire.

Faut-il faire la même hypothèse pour expliquer l'utilisation par Gurdisten de la *Vita S. Brigidae* de Cogitosus (BHL 1457)? Le fait que Gurdisten soit le seul hagiographe breton du IXe siècle à remployer cette œuvre insulaire[37] ne signifie pas nécessairement qu'elle soit parvenue à sa connaissance directement d'Irlande; en effet, elle a connu un grand succès sur le continent, où elle s'est largement répandue dès le IXe siècle.[38]

En même temps, et avec une vigueur bien assumée, Gurdisten s'est appuyé sur de très nombreuses sources d'inspiration, d'origine continentale ou méditerranéenne, qui lui sont parvenues directement, sans intermédiaire insulaire; à fortiori pour des auteurs aussi récents que Defensor de Ligugé, Alcuin ou Smaragde de Saint-Mihiel.[39] L'abbé de Landévennec se positionne alors au point d'articulation de deux mondes culturels, celtique et carolingien, qu'il cultive conjointement. Sa maîtrise des usages continentaux en matière de com-

---

[35] Comme par exemple le terme nautique *cyulis* (= quille) dans une partie versifiée de Gurdisten, *Vita S. Winwaloei*, II.15, vers 8, p. 228: voir Harvey, 'Cambro-Romance?', pp. 190–91.

[36] Gurdisten, *Vita S. Winwaloei*, I.1, p. 174: 'Britannia insula, de qua stirpis nostri origo olim, ut vulgo refertur, processit' (L'île de Bretagne, qui fut jadis, selon l'opinion commune, à l'origine de notre race').

[37] Certainement en 1.14; peut-être en 1.19: Kerlouégan, 'Les citations d'auteurs latins chrétiens', pp. 226–27.

[38] Sharpe, *Medieval Irish Saints' Lives*, pp. 13–14; Sharpe, 'Books from Ireland', p. 18.

[39] Pour un bilan détaillé des sources formelles employées par Gurdisten, voir Poulin, 'L'intertextualité'.

8. PRÉSENCE D'UNE CULTURE CELTIQUE INSULAIRE

position hagiographique ne lui fait pas oublier complètement le capital culturel celtique.

Mais au total, il faut reconnaître que le bagage référentiel de Gurdisten est beaucoup plus romano-franc que celtique. Par exemple, les *Disticha Catonis* se sont répandus en Gaule au IXᵉ siècle, d'abord à partir de Lyon; qui plus est, la circulation des *Disticha* s'est parfois faite de concert avec des poèmes d'Eugène de Tolède. Or Gurdisten a utilisé l'un et l'autre pour sa Vie de s. Guénolé, ce qui suggère l'existence d'un canal de communication commun, plus vraisemblablement continental qu'insulaire.[40]

L'intensité et la variété de la tactique intertextuelle de Gurdisten permet une comparaison avec celle d'un auteur emblématique de la latinité bretonne insulaire, Gildas;[41] il en ressort que l'abbé de Landévennec pratique son métier d'écrivain de manière bien personnelle, absolument pas dans la dépendance ou l'imitation de Gildas, bien qu'il en manifeste une connaissance intime.[42]

Toujours au chapitre de l'intertextualité, le dossier de saint Malo illustre des tendances assez différentes de celui de saint Guénolé, mais néanmoins riches d'enseignements. Outre les origines personnelles (galloises) du saint, ce qui le rattache au monde celtique de façon spectaculaire, c'est sa participation à la Navigation de saint Brendan. Il est difficile de décider si cette tradition célèbre circulait à Alet au troisième quart du IXᵉ siècle sous forme écrite, par tradition orale seulement, ou sous des formes plurielles déjà instables;[43] en effet, les trois hagiographes alétiens du IXᵉ siècle qui ont raconté cette aventure en lien avec saint Malo (le diacre Bili et deux [moines?] anonymes en BHL 5117 et 5118a) divergent suffisamment sur ce point pour faire hésiter à départager les trois possibilités.[44] Quoi qu'il en soit, le résultat est le même: une exaltation des racines insulaires du saint patron d'Alet par rattachement à une figure emblématique.

---

[40] Van Büren, '*Membra disiecta*', pp. 340–46. Cet auteur classique est le mieux représenté après Virgile au IXᵉ siècle, d'après les calculs de Munk Olsen, *L'étude des auteurs classiques*, p. 31.

[41] Pour un bilan des emprunts formels dans le *De excidio Britanniae*, voir Wright, 'Gildas's Reading', p. 152.

[42] Poulin, 'Alet, Landévennec, Redon'.

[43] Pour un résumé commode des ultimes positions de Giovanni Orlandi sur la datation et la localisation de la première version écrite de la *Navigatio S. Brendani*, voir Guglielmetti, 'Quando l'"auctor" non serve', pp. 2–3.

[44] Mac Mathúna, 'Contributions to a Study of the Voyages of St Brendan and St Malo', pp. 44–45 et 52; Poulin, *L'hagiographie bretonne*, p. 178. Le classement des premières Vies de saint Malo par Guglielmetti (dans son introduction à l'édition d'Orlandi, *Navigatio Sancti Brendani*, pp. xciv–xcv) ne correspond pas à l'état actuel de la discussion. La *Navigatio Sancti*

Quant aux autres moyens utilisés pour construire ou orner le récit, Bili se distingue de Gurdisten par une absence complète d'emprunts à des auteurs profanes et une variété amoindrie d'auteurs chrétiens (pas même Gildas!).[45] Ces deux hagiographes se rapprochent néanmoins par leurs remplois des mêmes écrivains carolingiens Alcuin et Smaragde.[46] En outre, l'un et l'autre ont eu recours à des œuvres hagiographiques continentales, mais avec plus d'intensité chez Bili — à moins qu'il ne faille ranger séparément une rafale de prélèvements concentrés de 1.51 à 1.75, suspects d'interpolation au xe siècle en milieu parisien.[47]

Un document important d'origine irlandaise assurée, comme la collection canonique dite *Hibernensis*, a certainement circulé dans la péninsule armoricaine au ixe siècle;[48] mais on n'en trouve aucune trace dans l'ancienne hagiographie bretonne, car l'hypothèse d'une dépendance de Gurdisten à l'égard de cette collection canonique n'est pas encore démontrée.[49]

Au total, le bagage référentiel (intellectuel et spirituel) de nos deux auteurs est donc massivement continental et non pas insulaire, même pour raconter les origines bretonnes en Armorique. Et pourtant, ils ont ignoré des sources d'inspiration habituellement bien représentées dans l'hagiographie continentale du haut Moyen Âge, comme les Vies de saint Éloi ou de saint Colomban.[50]

Brendani aurait été mise par écrit une première fois en latin sur le continent vers la fin du viiie siècle; elle aurait donc pu parvenir à Alet par écrit avant 870, même s'il faut en retarder la composition après 825, comme le pense Stifter, *Philologica Latino-Hibernica*, pp. 109–10; Stifter, 'Brendaniana, etc.', p. 204.

[45] Pour un bilan détaillé des sources formelles employées par Bili, voir Poulin, *L'hagiographie bretonne*, pp. 156–63.

[46] Le *Liber in partibus Donati* de Smaragde était certainement connu en Bretagne carolingienne, car il en subsiste un témoin du milieu du ixe siècle copié en Bretagne et glosé en breton (Paris, BnF lat. 13029): Holtz, 'Introduction', p. xv; Lambert, 'Les gloses en vieux-breton à la grammaire de Smaragde'; Bischoff, *Katalog der festländischen Handschriften. III. Padua-Zwickau*, n° 4866, le date du quatrième quart du ixe siècle. Et plus récemment: Dubreucq, 'La "Grammaire" de Smaragde', pp. 117–51.

[47] Poulin, *L'hagiographie bretonne*, p. 281.

[48] L'abbé Conwoion de Redon († 868) en aurait-il ramené un exemplaire de Rome, comme le suggère Flechner, '*Libelli et commentarii aliorum*', p. 109 n. 35?

[49] Malgré Keskiaho, *Dreams and Visions*, pp. 92 et 128.

[50] Bilan de l'influence formelle de la Vie de s. Éloi par Bayer, 'Vita Eligii', pp. 514–16. Sur le rayonnement sur l'hagiographie du viie siècle de la *Vita S. Columbani* de Jonas de Bobbio, voir O'Hara, 'The *Vita Columbani* in Merovingian Gaul'; *Jonas of Bobbio*, trad. O'Hara et Wood, p. 79.

Éléments de contenu

Par delà les aspects de forme ou d'organisation des récits hagiographiques, Bili et Gurdisten ont-ils cherché à mettre particulièrement en valeur des éléments de contenu destinés à donner du relief aux liens qui les unissent au monde celtique? Jusqu'à quel point la création hagiographique fut-elle pour eux le moyen ou l'occasion d'enregistrer, imaginer ou célébrer une affiliation privilégiée à la civilisation des ancêtres gallois?

Les chercheurs ont dépensé beaucoup d'énergie à chercher chez les anciens hagiographes bretons des traces ou symptômes typiquement celtiques qui illustreraient leur attachement à une culture insulaire originelle, sinon une volonté de garder bien vivant le souvenir de leurs origines celtiques. Si l'hagiographie irlandaise fait régulièrement place à des éléments folkloriques ou mythologiques,[51] est-il possible d'inscrire le travail de Bili et Gurdisten dans une même perspective de fidélité délibérée aux mêmes traditions? De nombreux éléments de contenu ont été invoqués à ce titre, mais il faut reconnaître que leur valeur probatoire est très inégale. Parmi les éléments les moins convaincants, nous comptons les propositions suivantes:

- une réminiscence possible de Virgile au début de la *Vita S. Winwaloei* (*stirpis nostrae origo* [origine de notre race], à l'incipit de I.1) suffit-elle à démontrer la présence d'une allusion consciente au mythe de l'origine troyenne des Bretons, comme l'estime Bernard Merdrignac?[52]

- le personnage d'*Alba Trimammis* comme mère de s. Guénolé (en I.2) pourrait correspondre à la *Gwen Teirbron* de la mythologie galloise.[53] Mais faut-il aller jusqu'à reconnaître une affiliation délibérée au monde celtique dans la présentation de Corentin, Gradlon, Guénolé et Tugdual — dans cet ordre (*V. S. Winwaloei*, II.19) — comme une transposition bretonne de la tradition irlandaise des quatre Grands Sages, comme le fait Claude Sterckx?[54]

---

[51] Ó Ríain, 'Celtic Mythology and Religion', pp. 250–51; Sellner, 'Songs of Praise', p. 166.

[52] Merdrignac, 'L'Énéide et les traditions anciennes des Bretons', pp. 199–200 et 205; Merdrignac, *Les Vies de saints bretons*, p. 43. J. Rio est tenté de le suivre sur ce point: *Mythes fondateurs de la Bretagne*, pp. 39–43. Ce contact avec Virgile n'est pas retenu par Wright, 'Some Further Vergilian Borrowings'.

[53] Koch, 'Hagiography. 4 – Breton', p. 880.

[54] Sterckx, 'De Fionntan au Tadig Kozh', p. 9.

- la place des animaux a attiré l'attention, par exemple des prodiges mettant des porcs en scène dans la Vie de s. Malo (1.35). Karen Jankulak y voit un motif particulièrement prisé de l'hagiographie celtique, de préférence à une influence de l'*Énéide*.[55] L'élimination de serpents (*V. S. Winwaloei*, 1.15) fait-elle écho au fait que saint Patrice avait débarrassé l'Irlande de ces animaux?[56] Même si les animaux occupent une place importante dans la tradition celtique,[57] il faut se souvenir qu'ils sont aussi bien présents dans l'hagiographie générale.[58]

- la Vie de s. Guénolé peut-elle servir à illustrer la transposition sur le continent d'un modèle insulaire d'éducation?[59] L'utilisation de tablettes de cire pour apprendre à écrire (*V. S. Machutis*, 1.2) ne peut certainement pas être revendiquée comme une spécificité du monde celtique.

- une première installation de Guénolé et de ses moines sur l'île de Tibidy, aux confins de la Domnonée et de la Cornouaille, correspond-elle à une imitation de la pratique celtique de fondation de monastères entre deux royaumes, comme le pense B. Merdrignac?[60]

Dans d'autres cas, des vestiges du patrimoine culturel celtique sont encore reconnaissables, mais de façon ponctuelle et isolée; nous hésitons à en faire des éléments tactiques d'une stratégie globale de mise en valeur d'une culture spécifique. Ainsi:

- dans la mesure où les œuvres hagiographiques peuvent aussi servir à documenter les droits fonciers d'une abbaye ou d'un siège épiscopal, les auteurs

---

[55] Jankulak, 'Alba Longa in the Celtic Regions?', pp. 271–73 et 278. La question avait déjà été abordée plus largement par Merdrignac, 'Truies et verrats'; Alexander, *Saints and Animals in the Middle Ages*, p. 91.

[56] C'est l'avis de Simon et autres, 'Traduction de la Vie longue de saint Guénolé', p. 148 n. 132.

[57] Lambert, 'Le monde celtique', p. 21; Boekhoorn, *Bestiaire mythique*, pp. 374–75 et 382–83 (à propos de la Vie de saint Malo par Bili). Voisenet pense que l'importance attachée aux animaux s'est estompée rapidement quand les insulaires sont passés sur le continent: *Bestiaire chrétien*, pp. 154–55.

[58] Boglioni, 'Il santo e gli animali nell'alto medioevo'; et encore, Boglioni, 'Les animaux dans l'hagiographie monastique'.

[59] Ainsi chez Dubreucq, 'Le monachisme insulaire armoricain', p. 41.

[60] Gurdisten, *Vita S. Winwaloei*, II.3, p. 216; Merdrignac, 'La mystérieuse "Terre du roi Catovius"', pp. 140–41.

8. PRÉSENCE D'UNE CULTURE CELTIQUE INSULAIRE

utilisent parfois un vocabulaire emprunté aux transactions courantes de leur milieu. C'est ainsi que le vocable *dicumbit* (ou l'équivalent) de la Vie de s. Malo par Bili (en I.43 et 44; II.8, 9 et 11) a attiré l'attention sur un type de charte que Wendy Davies voyait comme propre au monde celtique, à la fois insulaire et continental.[61]

- le géant *Mildu* ressuscité par s. Malo (en I.16) appartient-il à la légende arthurienne?[62]

- les épisodes de navigation merveilleuse (*V. Winwaloei*, I.4; *V. Machutis*, hymne, strophe 10 et I.26/27) sont-ils à mettre au compte d'un substrat celtique?[63]

- la pratique de la tonsure irlandaise à Landévennec au début du IXe siècle correspond-elle à un élément factuel correctement rapporté, ou à une description arbitraire par l'autorité franque, sur la base d'une idée préconçue ou stéréotypée?[64] Quoi qu'il en soit, le passage du mode dit scotique au mode bénédictin de la vie monastique fut peut-être un processus plus progressif que ne le laisse penser l'injonction officielle de Louis le Pieux à l'abbé Matmonoc de Landévennec en 818.[65]

- la psalmodie quotidienne de s. Guénolé dans des positions inconfortables (en II.9 et 14 de la Vie en prose; en II.5, vers 5/6 de la récapitulation en vers) révèle-t-elle un désir d'imitation des prouesses ascétiques de saints insulaires? De la part de Guénolé ou de Gurdisten?

- l'utilisation du vocable *caelicola* dans la Vie de S. Guénolé (II.28) peut-elle être considérée comme une influence du mouvement des Culdées?[66]

---

[61] Davies, 'The Composition of the Redon Cartulary', p. 75; ou encore Lemoine, *Recherches sur l'enseignement et la culture*, pp. 334–36. Position nuancée de Garault, 'Les rapports entre récits hagiographiques et matériel diplomatique', pp. 312 et 319–22.

[62] Proposition de Boekhoorn, *Bestiaire mythique*, p. 361.

[63] Scepticisme sur ce point de Milin, 'La traversée prodigieuse', pp. 20–21.

[64] Gurdisten, *Vita S. Winwaloei*, II.13, p. 227; Davies, 'The Myth of the Celtic Church', p. 21 n. 4. Voir dernièrement sur ce point Picard, *Conversatio Scottorum*, qui y voit un usage breton plus armoricain qu'insulaire.

[65] Une suggestion déjà présente chez Morice, *L'abbaye de Landévennec*, I, 412–14.

[66] Ainsi chez Morice, *L'abbaye de Landévennec*, I, 193–94 et 410–11. Le terme *caelicola* se trouve déjà dans l'hymne alphabétique de Clément (strophe Q, vers 4): De Smedt (éd.), 'Vita S. Winwaloei', p. 264.

Mais enfin, la valeur probatoire de quelques éléments de contenu semble tout de même acceptable, sinon même certaine, dans quelques passages plus éloquents:

– la Navigation de s. Brendan constitue un élément typiquement celtique. Mais sous la plume de Bili, elle devient un matériau narratif éminemment malléable; à telle enseigne que Brendan l'Irlandais devient un abbé gallois (en I.1 et passim). Malo lui paraît même supérieur à bien des égards.[67]

– saint Patrice constitue assurément une figure emblématique pour s. Guénolé comme pour Gurdisten.[68] Mais Guénolé se voit dissuadé de partir en pèlerinage en Irlande par s. Patrice lui-même;[69] l'Irlande n'est donc pas envisagée comme un lieu de perfectionnement spirituel plus désirable que le continent.[70] Sous la plume de Gurdisten, la *patria* des Bretons est désormais continentale, pas insulaire.[71]

Conclusion

Au terme de cette enquête, on ne peut certainement pas voir dans les dossiers imposants de s. Malo et de s. Guénolé une construction mémorielle porteuse d'une revendication assumée d'origine celtique comme trait distinctif d'une identité bretonne. La conscience des origines insulaires est certes présente, ne serait-ce que du fait de l'origine personnelle des saints; mais les moyens formels

[67] Le Duc, 'La Bretagne, intermédiaire entre l'Aquitaine et l'Irlande', pp. 182–84.

[68] Le nom de S. Patrice apparaît dans la *V. Winwaloei* aux articles 19 et 20 de la table des chapitres du premier livre, ainsi qu'aux chapitres I.11, 19 et 20 (pp. 173–74, 190, 205–09). J.-C. Cassard interprète un peu vite ce détail comme l'indice d'un renforcement vers 880 des relations de la Bretagne avec l'Irlande: 'Les navigations bretonnes', p. 30. En I.11, la dernière phrase possède cependant un statut incertain (une ancienne glose marginale?), car elle crée un doublon avec le vers 11 de ce chapitre; cette phrase ultime est absente du manuscrit de Quimper, BM 16, fol. 33ᵛ. En I.20 et dans son Homélie, leçon 8 (*Cartulaire de l'abbaye de Landévennec*, p. 132), Gurdisten présente Patrice comme le maître à penser de Guénolé.

[69] Keskiaho, *Dreams and Visions*, pp. 48–49, comprend à tort que Patrice (en I.19) encourage Guénolé à le rejoindre en Irlande, alors qu'il l'en dissuade.

[70] Dubreucq, 'Le monachisme insulaire armoricain', pp. 37–38. F. Kerlouégan en conclut néanmoins à l'existence de liens particuliers entre Landévennec et l'Irlande: 'Landévennec à l'école de Saint-Sauveur de Redon?', p. 321. Gurdisten attribue à Guénolé l'intention de se rendre en Irlande par l'intermédiaire de marchands assurant une liaison maritime avec l'Irlande (Gurdisten, *Vita S. Winwaloei*, I.19, p. 206).

[71] Comme l'a bien vu Morice, *L'abbaye de Landévennec*, I, 352–54.

déployés sont à dominante nettement continentale par la structure des récits et surtout par les pratiques d'intertextualité. L'horizon culturel vers lequel se tournent Bili et Gurdisten est bien plus continental qu'insulaire. Le capital culturel sur lequel ils s'appuient possède certes des traits communs avec celui des hagiographes irlandais, mais ils y ont un accès généralement direct, sans passer par un intermédiaire insulaire — sauf peut-être pour Gildas à Landévennec et l'aventure brendanienne à Alet.

Ce résultat est corroboré, pour le IXe siècle, par des observations convergentes dans d'autres domaines d'activité eux aussi ancrés dans la vie continentale, sans couleur celtique particulière; comme par exemple l'incorporation de Nominoé dans le système institutionnel franc, à titre de *missus*,[72] la frappe de monnaies imitées du monnayage de Charles le Chauve,[73] ou l'art de l'architecture.[74] On peut donc parler d'une acculturation consentie, plutôt que d'une attitude de résistance, du moins chez les élites ecclésiastiques.[75] Cette ouverture s'explique peut-être en partie par l'incorporation dans l'espace contrôlé par les Bretons, à partir de la seconde moitié du IXe siècle, d'importantes zones non bretonnes (la *nova Britannia*); cette expansion a pu favoriser un métissage culturel croissant.[76]

Là où les marques d'appartenance à la civilisation celtique sont les plus nettes, à Landévennec, se trouve aussi le témoignage le mieux documenté d'un élargissement, typiquement carolingien, de l'éventail des auteurs classiques inclus dans le canon scolaire.[77] De l'avis de Stéphane Lebecq, l'implantation de Landévennec au bord de la mer ne semble pas avoir induit une relation maritime particulièrement dynamique ou privilégiée de la Cornouaille armoricaine avec l'outre-mer celtique.[78] Et quand les auteurs classiques sont complètement

---

[72] Ainsi chez Quaghebeur, 'Lieux de pouvoir', p. 240.

[73] Salaün, 'Pour en finir avec Charles le Chauve en Bretagne', pp. 184–85. Un trésor monétaire à Rennes (vers 920) montre le réseau résolument continental dans lequel s'inscrit l'économie bretonne: Devailly, 'Rennes au Moyen Âge', pp. 72–74 (avec une carte).

[74] Guigon, 'The Archaeology of the So-Called "Celtic Church in Brittany'; Gallet, 'Art et architecture en Bretagne', pp. 74–75.

[75] Voir le bilan historiographique de Mazel, 'L'Église et la société dans la Bretagne', pp. 91–92.

[76] Observation en ce sens de Smith, *Province and Empire*, pp. 150–51.

[77] Munk Olsen, *L'étude des auteurs classiques*, IV, 372–73. J. M. H. Smith se demande si cette acceptation des usages carolingiens n'aurait pas connu une accélération sous le règne de Salomon († 874): *Province and Empire*, pp. 169–73.

[78] Lebecq, 'Guénolé, Landévennec, la mer', p. 95.

ignorés, chez Bili d'Alet, le choix est fait de privilégier un appui formel sur la littérature hagiographique continentale et non insulaire. Nos deux auteurs ne cherchent donc pas à exprimer une nostalgie d'un monde perdu, ni à dresser un corpus protestataire contre une intrusion jugée indésirable d'influences ou de valeurs continentales.[79]

Mais ce bilan ne doit pas faire oublier que l'hagiographie ne peut pas, à elle seule, fournir une 'photographie aérienne' complète de l'état de la Bretagne carolingienne. L'art du livre breton, par exemple, a donné naissance à des évaluations diverses et contrastées: esthétique essentiellement irlandaise pour les uns,[80] protestation anti-carolingienne pour d'autres,[81] ou encore amalgame d'influences orientales, celtes et tourangelles.[82]

Le sort des œuvres normatives pourrait aussi nous instruire. La Bretagne semble en effet avoir joué un rôle dans le maintien et la diffusion de la collection canonique de l'*Hibernensis*, en résistance au mouvement continental de romanisation du droit canon.[83] D'autre part, l'arrivée par la Bretagne des pénitentiels irlandais pourrait attester d'une circulation directe bien active au IXe siècle.[84] Le plus raisonnable est sans doute de reconnaître en Bretagne un carrefour d'influences, avec un ascendant croissant des usages continentaux au IXe siècle. À notre avis, c'est trop dire que de mettre sur un pied d'égalité influences

---

[79] Ainsi chez J.-C. Cassard, qui attribue une vocation défensive à l'hagiographie bretonne: *Les Bretons de Nominoë*, pp. 183–84 (pp. 189–90 de la seconde édition en 2002). Il est suivi sur ce point par Merdrignac, 'Quelques interrogations', p. 132.

[80] Micheli, *L'enluminure du haut Moyen Âge*, pp. 96–101; Mussat, 'Naissance et épanouissement d'un art', p. 220.

[81] Alexander, 'La résistance à la domination culturelle'. Et encore Besseyre, 'Une iconographie sacerdotale', p. 25. Dans la même ligne de pensée: Riché, 'Rapports', pp. 177–78.

[82] Besseyre, 'Une iconographie sacerdotale', pp. 16–17. Le texte biblique en usage à Landévennec paraît s'apparenter, au moins en partie, à la révision alcuinienne de la Bible: Guillotel, 'Recherches sur l'activité des *scriptoria* bretons', p. 21.

[83] Reynolds, 'Unity and Diversity', pp. 103 et 134. Et, plus récemment, les travaux de Flechner, 'Aspects of the Breton Transmission of the *Hibernensis*', pp. 32–39; ce chercheur interprète la popularité de l'*Hibernensis* en Bretagne du IXe siècle comme un acte de résistance culturelle (p. 39; p. 12 de la version numérique). Nous n'avons pas pu voir son édition récente de l'*Hibernensis* (*The Hibernensis*, éd. Flechner). La composition et l'influence de cette collection sont commodément esquissées par Fowler-Magerl, *Clavis canonum*, pp. 46–54. Mais pour J.-M. Picard, la diffusion continentale de l'*Hibernensis* s'est plutôt faite à partir de la France du Nord (Péronne?): 'L'Irlande et la Normandie avant les Normands', pp. 21–23.

[84] Sharpe, 'Books from Ireland', pp. 27–28.

insulaires et continentales pour cette époque.[85] Mais des liens plus nets de continuité entre la Petite Bretagne et la chrétienté celtique insulaire sont peut-être à chercher dans des catégories documentaires autres que l'hagiographie.[86]

Joseph-Claude Poulin, médiéviste, spécialiste d'hagiographie latine du haut Moyen Âge. Codirecteur (avec François Dolbeau et Martin Heinzelmann) de l'entreprise de recherche SHG (Sources hagiographiques de la Gaule) patronnée par l'Institut historique allemand de Paris. Chercheur invité au Département d'histoire de l'Université de Montréal.

[85] C'est ce que suggère C. Brett dans son bilan historiographique, 'Brittany and the Carolingian Empire'.

[86] C'est du moins l'avis de Lambert, 'Les chrétientés celtiques. III. L'Armorique bretonne', p. 835.

Bibliographie

Manuscrits et sources d'archives

Paris, Bibliothèque nationale de France, ms. lat. 13029
Quimper, Bibliothèque municipale, ms. 16
Vatican, Bibliotheca apostolica vaticana, ms. reg. lat. 479

Sources

Bili, *Vita s. Machutis*, in *Mélanges d'histoire bretonne*, éd. F. Lot (Paris: Champion, 1907), pp. 331–430

Cartulaire de l'abbaye de Landevenec. Première livraison: texte du cartulaire, avec notes et variants, éd. A. de La Borderie (Rennes: Catel, 1888)

Cartulaire de Landévennec, in *Mélanges historiques. Choix de documents*, éd. R. Le Men et É. Ernault, Collection de documents inédits sur l'histoire de France, 5 (Paris: Imprimerie Nationale, 1886), pp. 533–600

Gurdisten, *Vita s. Winwaloei*, éd. Ch. De Smedt, 'Vita S. Winwaloei primi abbatis Landevenecensis auctore Wurdestino', *Analecta Bollandiana*, 7 (1888), 167–264; trad. M. Simon, L. Cochou, et A. Le Huërou, 'Traduction de la Vie longue de saint Guénolé par l'abbé Gurdisten', in *Cartulaire de Saint-Guénolé de Landévennec*, éd. S. Lebecq, Sources médiévales d'histoire de Bretagne, 6 (Rennes: Presses universitaires, 2015), pp. 111–50

The Hibernensis. Book 1: A Study and Edition; Book 2: Translation, Commentary, and Indexes, éd. R. Flechner, Studies in Medieval and Early Modern Canon Law, 17.1 et 2 (Washington, DC: The Catholic University Press of America, 2019)

Hilduin of Saint-Denis: The Passio S. Dionysii *in Prose and Verse*, éd. M. Lapidge, Mittellateinische Studien und Texte, 51 (Leiden: Brill, 2017)

Jonas of Bobbio, Life of Columbanus, Life of John of Réomé, and Life of Vedast, trad. A. O'Hara et I. Wood, Translated Texts for Historians, 64 (Liverpool: Liverpool University Press, 2017)

Lios Monocus, 'Incipit Libellus Sacerdotalis quem Lios Monocus heroico metro composuit', éd. P. von Winterfeld, in *Poetae Latini aevi Carolini IV*, MGH, Poetae Latini medii aevi, 4.1 (Berlin: Weidmann, 1899), pp. 276–95

Navigatio sancti Brendani: alla scoperta dei segreti meravigliosi del mondo, éd. G. Orlandi et R. E. Guglielmetti, Per verba, 30 (Florence: Edizioni del Galuzzo, 2014)

Vie ancienne de Samson de Dol (BHL 7478), éd. et trad. P. Flobert, Sources d'histoire médiévale (Paris: CNRS, 1997)

Vie de saint Malo, évêque d'Alet. Version écrite par le diacre Bili (fin du IXe siècle). Textes latin et anglo-saxon avec traductions françaises, éd. G. Le Duc (Rennes: CeRAA, 1979)

'Vita antiqua sancti Samsonis Dolensis episcopi', éd. F. Plaine, *Analecta Bollandiana*, 6 (1887), 77–150

Études

Alexander, D., *Saints and Animals in the Middle Ages* (Woodbridge: Boydell, 2008)

Alexander, J., 'La résistance à la domination culturelle carolingienne dans l'art breton du IXe siècle: le témoignage de l'enluminure des manuscrits', in *Landévennec et le monachisme breton dans le haut Moyen Âge*, éd. M. Simon, Colloque de Landévennec, 1985 (Bannalec: Association Landévennec, 1986), pp. 269–80

Ambrose, S., 'The Codicology and Palaeography of London, BL Royal 5 E.xiii and its Abridgement of the *Collectio Canonum Hibernensis*', *Codices Manuscripti*, 54–55 (2006), 1–26

Barret, S., 'Le manuscrit: codicologie et paléographie', in *Cartulaire de Saint-Guénolé de Landévennec*, éd. S. Lebecq, Sources médiévales d'histoire de Bretagne, 6 (Rennes: Presses universitaires, 2015), pp. 17–24

Bayer, C. M. M., 'Vita Eligii', *Reallexikon der Germanischen Altertumskunde (Nachträge und Ergänzungen)*, 35 (2007), 461–524

Besseyre, M., 'Une iconographie sacerdotale du Christ et des évangélistes dans les manuscrits bretons des IXe et Xe siècles', *Pecia 12: La Bretagne carolingienne. Entre influences insulaires et continentales*, éd. J.-L. Deuffic (2008), 7–26

Bischoff, B., *Katalog der festländischen Handschriften des neunten Jahrhunderts (mit Ausnahme der wisigotischen)*. III. *Padua-Zwickau* (Wiesbaden: Harrassowitz, 2014)

Boekhoorn, D. N., 'Bestiaire mythique, légendaire et merveilleux dans la tradition celtique: de la littérature orale à la littérature écrite' (thèse de doctorat, Université de Rennes 2, 2008); disponible sur <https://tel.archives-ouvertes.fr/tel-00293874> [consulté le 13 mars 2022]

Boglioni, P., 'Les animaux dans l'hagiographie monastique', in *L'animal exemplaire au Moyen Âge (V[e]–XVe siècles)*, éd. J. Berlioz, M.-A. Polo de Beaulieu, et P. Collomb, Colloque d'Orléans, 1996 (Rennes: Presses universitaires, 1999), pp. 51–80

——, 'Il santo e gli animali nell'alto medioevo', in *L'uomo di fronte al mondo animale nell'alto medioevo*, Congrès de Spolète, 1983, Settimane, 31, 2 vols (Spoleto: Presso la sede del Centro, 1985), II, pp. 935–93

Bray, D. A., 'Heroic Tradition in the Lives of the Early Irish Saints: A Study in Hagio-Biographical Patterning', in *Proceedings of the First North American Congress of Celtic Studies*, éd. G. W. MacLennan, Congrès d'Ottawa, 1986 (Ottawa: University of Ottawa, 1988), pp. 261–71

——, 'Some Aspects of Hagiography in the Celtic Church', *Records of the Scottish Church History Society*, 21 (1982), 111–26

Brett, C., 'Brittany and the Carolingian Empire', *History Compass*, 11 (2013), 268–79

Cassard, J.-C., *Les Bretons de Nominoë*, Les bibliophiles de Bretagne, 7, 2e éd. aug. (Rennes: Presses universitaires, 2002)

——, 'Les navigations bretonnes aux temps carolingiens', in *L'Europe et l'Océan au Moyen Âge. Contribution à l'histoire de la navigation*, Congrès de Nantes, 1986 (Nantes: CID éditions, 1988), pp. 19–36

Davies, W., 'The Composition of the Redon Cartulary', *Francia*, 17 (1990), 69–90; réimpr. in W. Davies, *Brittany in the Early Middle Ages: Texts and Societies* (Farnham: Ashgate, 2009), pt I, pp. 69–90

——, 'The Myth of the Celtic Church', in *The Early Church in Wales and the West. Recent Work in Early Christian Archaeology, History and Place-Names*, éd. N. Edwards et A. Lane, Oxbow Monographs, 16 (Oxford: Oxbow, 1992), pp. 12–21

Devailly, G., 'Rennes au Moyen Âge (v^e–xiiie siècles)', in *Histoire de Rennes*, éd. J. Meyer (Toulouse: Privat, 1972), pp. 72–74

Dubreucq, A., 'La "Grammaire" de Smaragde et la culture bretonne à l'époque carolingienne', *Britannia Monastica*, 19 (2017), 117–51

——, 'Le monachisme insulaire armoricain d'après les textes hagiographiques', *Hortus Artium Medievalium*, 19 (2013), 35–46

Flechner, R., 'Aspects of the Breton Transmission of the "Hibernensis"', *Pecia*, 12: *La Bretagne carolingienne. Entre influences insulaires et continentales*, éd. J.-L. Deuffic (2008), pp. 27–44

——, '*Libelli et commentarii aliorum*: The *Hibernensis* and the Breton Bishops', in *Approaches to Religion and Mythology in Celtic Studies*, éd. K. Ritari et A. Bergholm (Newcastle: Cambridge Scholars, 2008), pp. 100–19

Fleuriot, L., 'Brittonnica et Gallica. I. Tradition orale et textes brittoniques du haut Moyen Âge', *ÉC*, 22 (1985), 225–33; réimpr. in L. Fleuriot, *Notes lexicographiques et philologiques (langues celtiques)*, éd. G. Le Menn (Saint-Brieuc: Skol, 1997), pp. 167–77

——, *Dictionnaire des gloses en vieux-breton*, Collection linguistique, 62, réimpr. (Toronto: Prepcorp, 1985)

——, 'La vie intellectuelle dans la Bretagne ancienne. I. Le latin dans l'ancienne société bretonne', in *Histoire littéraire et culturelle de la Bretagne. I. Héritage celtique et captation française. Des origines à la fin des États*, éd. L. Fleuriot et A.-P. Ségalen, réimpr. (Paris: Champion, 1997), pp. 61–70

Fowler-Magerl, L., *Clavis canonum. Selected Canon Law Collections before 1140*, MGH Hilfsmittel, 21 (Hanover: Hahn, 2005)

Gaillard, M., 'La lettre de Louis le Pieux de 818 et l'introduction de la règle de saint Benoît à Landévennec', in *Landévennec 818–2018. Une abbaye bénédictine en Bretagne*, éd. Y. Coativy, Colloque de Landévennec, 2018 (Brest: Éditions du CRBC, 2020), pp. 55–66

Gallet, Y., 'Art et architecture en Bretagne à l'époque carolingienne: l'exemple de Landévennec', in *Landévennec, les Vikings et la Bretagne. En hommage à Jean-Christophe Cassard*, éd. M. Coumert et Y. Tranvouez (Brest: Centre de recherche bretonne et celtique, 2015), pp. 61–78

Garault, C., 'Les rapports entre récits hagiographiques et matériel diplomatique à travers le dossier hagiographique de saint Malo (ixe–xiie siècle)', in *Normes et hagiographie dans l'Occident latin (vi^e–xiie siècle)*, éd. M.-C. Isaïa et T. Granier, Colloque de Lyon, 2010, Hagiologia 9 (Turnhout: Brepols, 2014), pp. 309–27

Guglielmetti, R. E., 'Introduction', in *Navigatio sancti Brendani: alla scoperta dei segreti meravigliosi del mondo*, éd. G. Orlandi et R. Guglielmetti, Per Verba, 30 (Florence: Edizioni del Galluzzo, 2014), pp. i–ccc

——, 'Quando l'"auctor" non serve: la leggenda del viaggio di Brendano', *Filologia mediolatina*, 33 (2016), 1–22

Guigon, Ph., 'The Archaeology of the So-Called "Celtic Church" in Brittany', in *The Archaeology of the Early Medieval Celtic Churches*, éd. N. Edwards, Colloque de Bangor, 2004, The Society for Medieval Archaeology Monographs, 29 (London: Maney, 2009), pp. 173–90

Guillotel, H., 'Recherches sur l'activité des *scriptoria* bretons au ixe siècle', *MSHAB*, 62 (1985), 9–36

Handley, M., 'La paléographie des inscriptions', in *The Inscriptions of Early Medieval Brittany/Les Inscriptions de la Bretagne du Haut Moyen Âge*, éd. J. Graham-Campbell, M. Handley, P. Kershaw, J. T. Koch, G. Le Duc, et K. Lockyear, Celtic Studies Publications, 5 (Aberystwyth: Celtic Studies Publications, 2000), pp. 88–101

Harvey, A., 'Cambro-Romance? Celtic Britain's Counterpart to Hiberno-Latin', in *Early Medieval Ireland and Europe: Chronology, Contacts, Scholarship. A Festschrift for Dáibhí Ó Cróinín*, éd. P. Moran et I. Warntjes, Studia Traditionis Theologiae, 14 (Turnhout: Brepols, 2015), pp. 179–202

——, 'Technical Vocabulary and its Identification in Medieval Celtic Latinity', *Archivum latinitatis medii aevi*, 71 (2013), 377–88

Henken, E. R., *The Welsh Saints. A Study in Patterned Lives* (Cambridge: Brewer, 1991)

Herren, M. W., *The Hisperica Famina. II. The A-Text: A New Critical Edition with English Translation and Philological Commentary*, Studies and Texts, 31 (Toronto: Pontifical Institute of Mediaeval Studies, 1974)

Holtz, L., 'Introduction', in *Smaragdus. Liber in partibus Donati*, éd. L. Holtz, B. Löfstedt, et A. Kibre, *CC CM*, 68 (Turnhout: Brepols, 1986), pp. vii–xcv

Howlett, D., *The Celtic Latin Tradition of Biblical Style* (Blackrock: Four Courts Press, 1995)

Ineichen-Eder, C. E., 'Theologisches und philologisches Lehrmaterial aus dem Alkuin-Kreise', *Deutsches Archiv*, 34 (1978), 192–201

Jankulak, K., 'Alba Longa in the Celtic Regions? Swine, Saints and Celtic Hagiography', in *Celtic Hagiography and Saints' Cults*, éd. J. Cartwright (Cardiff: University of Wales Press, 2003), pp. 271–84

Kerlouégan, F., 'Les citations d'auteurs latins chrétiens dans les Vies de saints bretons carolingiennes', *ÉC*, 19 (1982), 215–57

——, '"Faire" suivi d'un infinitif en ancien français et en latin médiéval: un cas de substrat celtique?', *BSAF*, 110 (1982), 113–21

——, 'Landévennec à l'école de Saint-Sauveur de Redon?', in *Haut Moyen Âge. Culture, éducation et société. Études offertes à Pierre Riché*, éd. M. Sot (La Garenne-Colombes: Éditions Publidix, 1990), pp. 315–22

——, 'La littérature latine religieuse et profane', in *Histoire littéraire et culturelle de la Bretagne. I. Héritage celtique et captation française. Des origines à la fin des États*, éd. L. Fleuriot et A.-P. Ségalen, réimpr. (Paris: Champion, 1997), pp. 71–95

——, 'Une mode stylistique dans la prose latine des pays celtiques', *ÉC*, 13 (1972), 275–97

——, 'Les Vies de saints bretons les plus anciennes dans leurs rapports avec les Îles britanniques', in *Insular Latin Studies. Papers on Latin Texts and Manuscripts of the British Isles, 550–1066*, éd. M. Herren, Papers in Medieval Studies, 1 (Toronto: Pontifical Institute of Mediaeval Studies, 1981), pp. 195–213

Keskiaho, J., *Dreams and Visions in the Early Middle Ages. The Reception and Use of Patristic Ideas, 400–900*, Cambridge Studies in Medieval Life and Thought, 99 (Cambridge: Cambridge University Press, 2015)

Koch, J. T., 'Hagiography, Breton', in *The Celts. History, Life, and Culture*, éd. J. T. Koch et A. Minard, 2 vols (Santa Barbara, CA: ABC-CLIO, 2012), pt I, pp. 406–07

——, 'Hagiography in the Celtic Countries. 4. Breton', in *Celtic Culture. A Historical Encyclopedia*, éd. J. T. Koch, 5 vols (Santa Barbara, CA: ABC-CLIO, 2006), iii, 879–81

Kuypers, A. B., éd., *The Prayer Book of Ædelwald the Bishop. Commonly called the Book of Cerne* (Cambridge: Cambridge University Press, 1902)

Lambert, P.-Y., 'Les chrétientés celtiques. III. L'Armorique bretonne', in *Histoire du christianisme des origines à nos jours. III. Les Églises d'Orient et d'Occident (432–610)*, éd. L. Pietri (Paris: Desclée, 1998), pp. 830–38

——, 'Les gloses en vieux-breton à la grammaire de Smaragde', en note additionnelle à l'article de L. Holtz, 'La tradition ancienne du *Liber in partibus Donati* de Smaragde de Saint-Mihiel', *Revue d'histoire des textes*, 16 (1986), 201–07

——, 'Le monde celtique', in *Le merveilleux, l'imaginaire et les croyances en Occident*, éd. M. Meslin (Paris: Bordas, 1984), pp. 17–23

Le Duc, G., 'La Bretagne, intermédiaire entre l'Aquitaine et l'Irlande', in *Aquitaine and Ireland in the Middle Ages*, éd. J.-M. Picard (Blackrock: Four Courts Press, 1995), pp. 173–87

Le Hénaff-Rozé, C., 'Les brittonismes au crible des concordances. La préposition "cum" dans les "vitae" composées à Landévennec au IXᵉ siècle', in *Corona Monastica. Mélanges offerts au père Marc Simon*, éd. L. Lemoine, B. Meredrignac, et A. Richard-Calarnou, Britannia Monastica, 8 (Rennes: Presses universitaires, 2004), pp. 227–38

Lebecq, S., 'Guénolé, Landévennec, la mer et l'outre-mer', in *Landévennec 818–2018. Une abbaye bénédictine en Bretagne*, éd. Y. Coativy, Colloque de Landévennec, 2018 (Brest: Éditions du CRBC, 2020), pp. 87–95

Leclercq, H., 'Landévennec', in *Dictionnaire d'archéologie chrétienne et de liturgie*, éd. F. Cabrol et H. Leclercq, 15 vols (Paris, Librairie Letouzey et Ané, 1928) viii, 1, col. 1237–56

Lemoine, L., 'Recherches sur l'enseignement et la culture dans la Bretagne du haut Moyen Âge' (thèse de doctorat, Rennes, Université de Rennes 2, 1986)

Mac Mathúna, S., 'Contributions to a Study of the Voyages of St Brendan and St Malo', in *Irlande et Bretagne. Vingt siècles d'histoire*, éd. C. Laurent et H. Davis, Colloque de

Rennes, 1993 (Rennes, Terre de Brume, 1994), pp. 40–55; réimpr. in *The Otherworld Voyage in Early Irish Literature. An Anthology of Criticism*, éd. J. M. Wooding, réimpr. (Dublin: Four Courts Press, 2014), pp. 157–74

Martin, L. T., éd., *Homiliarium Veronense, CC CM*, 186 (Turnhout: Brepols, 2000)

Mazel, F., 'L'Église et la société dans la Bretagne du premier Moyen Âge. Actualité de la recherche historique', in *Les élites et leurs résidences en Bretagne au Moyen Âge*, éd. P.-Y. Laffont et Y. Pellerin, Colloque de Guingamp/Dinan, 2010 (Rennes, Presses universitaires, 2014), pp. 85–96

Merdrignac, B., 'L'Énéide et les traditions anciennes des Bretons', *ÉC*, 20 (1983), 199–205

——, 'Folklore and Hagiography: A Semiotic Approach to the Legend of the Immortals of Landevennec', *CMCS*, 13 (1987), 73–86

——, 'La mystérieuse "Terre du roi Catovius"', in B. Merdrignac, *D'une Bretagne à l'autre. Les migrations bretonnes entre histoire et légendes?* (Rennes: Presses universitaires, 2012), pp. 125–42

——, 'Quelques interrogations sur la référence aux origines antiques dans les "Vitae" de saints bretons du haut Moyen Âge', in *La mémoire de l'Antiquité dans l'Antiquité tardive et le haut Moyen Âge*, éd. M. Sot et P. Bazin, Centre de recherches sur l'Antiquité tardive et le haut Moyen Âge, 8 (Nanterre: Université de Paris X, 2000), pp. 131–48

——, *Recherches sur l'hagiographie armoricaine du VIIe au XVe siècle. I. Les saints bretons, témoins de Dieu ou témoins des hommes?*, Dossiers du CeRAA, Supplément n° H (Saint-Malo: Centre régional archéologique d'Alet, 1985)

——, *Recherches sur l'hagiographie armoricaine du VIIe au XVe siècle. II. Les hagiographes et leurs publics en Bretagne au Moyen Âge*, Dossiers du CeRAA, Supplément n° I (Saint-Malo, Centre régional archéologique d'Alet, 1986)

——, 'Truies et verrats, cochons et sangliers, porcs et porchers dans les "Vitae" des saints bretons du Moyen Âge', in *Mythologies du porc*, éd. P. Walter, Colloque de St-Antoine-l'Abbaye, 1998 (Grenoble: Millon, 1999), pp. 123–53

——, *Les Vies de saints bretons durant le haut Moyen Âge. La culture, les croyances en Bretagne (VIIe–XIIe siècle)*, De mémoire d'homme: l'histoire (Rennes: Éditions Ouest-France, 1993)

Micheli, G. L., *L'enluminure du haut Moyen Âge et les influences irlandaises. Histoire d'une influence* (Bruxelles, Éditions de la Connaissance, 1939)

Milin, G., 'La traversée prodigieuse dans le folklore et l'hagiographie celtiques: de la merveille au miracle', *ABPO*, 98 (1991), 1–25

Morice, Y., 'L'abbaye de Landévennec, des origines au XIe siècle, à travers la production hagiographique de son "scriptorium": culture monastique et idéologies dans la Bretagne du haut Moyen Âge', 2 vols (thèse de doctorat, Université de Rennes 2, 2007), I, disponible sur <http://www.academia.edu/3538710> [consulté le 13 mars 2022]

Munk Olsen, B., *L'étude des auteurs classiques latins aux XIe et XIIe siècles, IV. 2. La réception de la littérature classique. Manuscrits et textes*, IRHT, Documents, études et répertoires (Paris, Éditions du CNRS, 2014)

Mussat, A., 'Naissance et épanouissement d'un art', in *Histoire de la Bretagne*, éd. J. Delumeau (Toulouse: Privat, 1969), pp. 217–50

O'Hara, A., 'The *Vita Columbani* in Merovingian Gaul', *Early Medieval Europe*, 17 (2009), 126–53

Ó Ríain, P., 'Celtic Mythology and Religion', in *Geschichte und Kultur der Kelten. Vorbereitungskonferenz. Vorträge*, éd. K.-H. Schmidt et R. Ködderitzsch, Congrès de Bonn, 1982 (Heidelberg, C. Winter, 1986), pp. 241–51

Picard, J.-M., '*Conversatio Scottorum*. Une mise au point sur les coutumes monastiques irlandaises du haut Moyen Âge (vɪᵉ-vɪɪɪᵉ siècle)', in *Landévennec 818–2018. Une abbaye bénédictine en Bretagne*, éd Y. Coativy, Colloque de Landévennec, 2018 (Brest: Éditions du CRBC, 2020), pp. 113–24

——, 'L'Irlande et la Normandie avant les Normands (vɪɪᵉ-ɪxᵉ siècles)', *Annales de Normandie*, 47 (1997), 3–24

——, 'Structural Patterns in Early Hiberno-Latin Hagiography', *Peritia*, 4 (1985), 67–82

Poulin, J.-C., 'Alet, Landévennec, Redon: trois ateliers d'écriture hagiographique vers 870', in *Monastères, convergences, échanges et confrontations dans l'Ouest de l'Europe au Moyen Âge*, éd. C. L. Evans et P. Evans, Colloque de Toronto, 2016, Haut Moyen Âge, 45 (Turnhout: Brepols, 2023), pp. 55–86

——, 'Hagiographie bretonne ancienne (avant 1100)', in *Histoire de la Bretagne. Église, religion, croyances*, éd. F. Morvan, Encyclopédie de la Bretagne (Pietraserena [Corse]: Éditions Dumane, 2018), pp. 13–32

——, 'Un élément négligé de critique hagiographique: les titres de chapitres', in *"Scribere sanctorum gesta". Recueil d'études d'hagiographie médiévale offert à Guy Philippart*, éd. É. Renard, M. Trigalet, X. Hermand, et P. Bertrand, Hagiologia, 3 (Turnhout: Brepols, 2005), pp. 309–42

——, 'L'hagiographie bretonne avant l'an mil', in *Hagiographies. Histoire internationale de la littérature hagiographique latine et vernaculaire en Occident des origines à 1530*, éd. G. Philippart, M. Gaillard et M. Goullet, CCHAG, 8 vols (Turnhout: Brepols, 2020), vɪɪɪ, 189–242

——, *L'hagiographie bretonne du haut Moyen Âge. Répertoire raisonné*, Beihefte der Francia, 69 (Ostfildern: Thorbecke, 2009)

——, 'L'intertextualité dans la Vie longue de saint Guénolé de Landévennec', *ÉC*, 40 (2014), 165–221

Quaghebeur, J., 'Lieux de pouvoir, symbolique et mémoire institutionnelle en Cornouaille (ɪxᵉ-xɪɪᵉ siècle)', in *Les lieux de pouvoir au Moyen Âge en Normandie et sur ses marges*, éd. A.-M. Flambard Héricher, Colloque de Caen, 2003, Tables rondes du CRAHM, 2 (Turnhout: Brepols, 2006), pp. 227–41

Reynolds, R. E., 'Unity and Diversity in Carolingian Canon Law Collections: The Case of the *Collectio Hibernensis* and its Derivatives', in *Carolingian Essays. Andrew W. Mellon Lectures in Early Christian Studies*, éd. U. R. Blumenthal (Washington, DC: Catholic University of America Press, 1983), pp. 99–135; réimpr. in R. E. Reynolds, *Law and Liturgy in the Latin Church, 5ᵗʰ-12ᵗʰ Centuries* (Aldershot: Variorum, 1994), n° ɪv

8. PRÉSENCE D'UNE CULTURE CELTIQUE INSULAIRE

Riché, P., 'Rapports entre la spiritualité des moines celtiques et celle des moines d'Orient', *Britannia Monastica*, 19 (2017), 173–83

Rio, J., *Mythes fondateurs de la Bretagne. Aux origines de la celtomanie* (Rennes: Éditions Ouest-France, 2000)

Salaün, G., 'Pour en finir avec Charles le Chauve en Bretagne', *Bulletin de la Société française de numismatique*, 58 (2003), 184–85

Sellner, E. C., 'Songs of Praise: Early Celtic Hagiographies and their Spirituality', *Cistercian Studies Quarterly*, 31 (1996), 153–80

Sharpe, R., *Medieval Irish Saints' Lives: An Introduction to Vitae Sanctorum Hiberniae* (Oxford: Oxford University Press, 2010)

——, 'Books from Ireland, Fifth to Ninth Centuries', *Peritia*, 21 (2010), 1–55

Smith, J. M. H., *Province and Empire. Brittany and the Carolingians*, Cambridge Studies in Medieval Life and Thought, 18, réimpr. (Cambridge: Cambridge University Press, 2006)

Stalmans, N., *Saints d'Irlande. Analyse critique des sources hagiographiques (VIIe–IXe siècles)* (Rennes: Presses universitaires, 2003)

Steckel, S., 'Von Buchstabe und Geist. Pragmatische und symbolische Dimensionen der Autorensiglen (*nomina auctorum*) bei Hrabanus Maurus', in *Karolingische Klöster. Wissenstransfer und kulturelle Innovation*, éd. J. Becker, T. Licht, et S. Weinfurter, Materiale Textkulturen, 4 (Berlin: De Gruyter, 2015), pp. 89–129

Sterckx, C., 'De Fionntan au Tadig Kozh: figures mythiques d'Irlande et de Bretagne', in *Irlande et Bretagne. Vingt siècles d'histoire*, éd. C. Laurent et H. Davis, Colloque de Rennes, 1993 (Rennes: Terre de Brume, 1994), pp. 7–13

Stifter, D., 'Brendaniana, etc.', *Keltische Forschungen*, 1 (2006), 191–214

——, *Philologica Latino-Hibernica: Navigatio sancti Brendani,* Diplomarbeit (Vienna: Université de Vienne, 1997); disponible sur <http://othes.univie.ac.at/73> [consulté le 13 mars 2022]

Tura, A., 'Essai sur les *marginalia* en tant que pratique et documents', in Scientia in margine. *Études sur les* marginalia *dans les manuscrits scientifiques du Moyen Âge à la Renaissance*, éd. D. Jacquart et C. Burnett, ÉPHÉ, Hautes études médiévales et modernes, 88 (Geneva: Librairie Droz, 2005), pp. 261–387

Van Büren, V., '*Membra disiecta*: Paris, BnF lat. 8093 (VIII) + Paris, BnF lat. 8318 (III). Un témoin complet des *Disticha Catonis*', *Aevum*, 90 (2016), 333–50

Vergnolle, É., 'De Jumièges à Landévennec. Remarques sur la circulation des modèles au milieu du XIe siècle', *Bulletin monumental*, 175 (2017), 211–20

Voisenet, J., *Bestiaire chrétien: l'imagerie animale des auteurs du Moyen Âge V^e–XIe s.* (Toulouse: Presses universitaires du Mirail, 1994)

Winterbottom, M., 'Aldhelm's Prose Style and its Origins', *Anglo-Saxon England*, 6 (1977), 39–76; réimpr. in M. Winterbottom, *Style and Scholarship. Latin Prose from Gildas to Raffaele Regio. Selected Papers*, éd. R. Gamberini, MediEVI, 26 (Florence: SISMEL, 2020), pp. 101–38

——, 'A "Celtic" Hyperbaton?', *BBCS*, 27 (1977), 207–12; réimpr. in M. Winterbottom, *Style and Scholarship. Latin Prose from Gildas to Raffaele Regio. Selected Papers*, éd. R. Gamberini, MediEVI, 26 (Florence: SISMEL, 2020), pp. 35–40

Wright, N., 'Gildas's Reading: A Survey', *Sacris Erudiri*, 32 (1991), 121–62; réimpr. in N. Wright, *History and Literature in Late Antiquity and the Early Medieval West. Studies in Intertextuality* (Aldershot: Variorum, 1995), n° v

——, 'Some Further Vergilian Borrowings in Breton Hagiography of the Carolingian Period', *ÉC*, 20 (1983), 161–75; réimpr. in N. Wright, *History and Literature in Late Antiquity and the Early Medieval West. Studies in Intertextuality* (Aldershot: Variorum, 1995), n° ix

9. CROSS-CHANNEL INTERCOURSE IN THE EARLIEST BRETON *VITAE*

Karen Jankulak

ABSTRACT In light of the probable travels of the author of *Vita I S. Samsonis* in order to gather information (written and oral) about his subject, this paper investigates the earliest hagiographical texts from Brittany in terms of their use of information gathered on both sides of the Channel. This is not in order to investigate the historicity of such texts but to consider what their use of sources has to say about the existence of such sources, and about the expectations of hagiographers and their audiences with respect to connections between Wales (and Cornwall) and Brittany. The texts at issue are *Vita S. Maglorii*, Wrdisten's *Vita S. Winwaloei*, Bili's *Vita S. Machutis*, Wrmonoc's *Vita S. Pauli Aureliani*, and *Vita I S. Winnoci*, all dating from the Carolingian era, with additional reference to several later texts, Lifris of Llancarfan's *Vita S. Cadoci* and *Vita S. Gurthierni*. It is clear that these texts can indirectly show that information travelled in both directions, and that connections were made between saints and their stories on both sides of the Channel, with Llancarfan and Llanilltud Fawr probably being central to this process.

RÉSUMÉ À la lumière des voyages entrepris (à ses dires) par l'auteur de la première Vie de saint Samson pour recueillir de l'information (orale et écrite) à propos de son sujet, cette intervention examine l'usage d'informations recueillies des deux côtés de la Manche dans les premiers textes hagiographiques de la Bretagne. Le but du travail n'est pas d'évaluer l'historicité de ces textes, mais d'enquêter sur leur dépendance de sources antérieures, et sur les liens entre le Pays de Galles, le Cornwall et la Bretagne tels qu'ils furent compris par les hagiographes et leurs publics. Les textes qui fournissent la matière de la discussion sont la *Vita S. Maglorii*, la *Vita S. Winwaloei* de Gurdisten, la *Vita S. Machutis* de Bili, la *Vita Pauli Aureliani* de Gurmonoc et la *Vita I S. Winnoci* (tous datant de l'ère carolingienne), avec quelques textes plus tardifs — la *Vita S. Cadoci* de Lifris de Llancarfan, et la *Vita S. Gurthierni* — à titre de comparaison. Ces textes montrent clairement, quoique indirectement, que les informations traversèrent la mer dans les deux directions, forgeant des connections entre les saints et leurs histoires, processus où les abbayes de Llancarfan et Llanilltud Fawr jouèrent probablement un rôle central.

KEYWORDS hagiography, migration, exchange, St Samson, St Maglorius, St Winwaloe, St Paternus, St Malo, St Cadog, St Paul Aurelian

---

Multi-disciplinary Approaches to Medieval Brittany, 450–1200: Connections and Disconnections, ed. by Caroline Brett, Fiona Edmonds, and Paul Russell, TCNE 36 (Turnhout: Brepols, 2023) pp. 207–238   BREPOLS 🔲 PUBLISHERS   10.1484/M.TCNE-EB.5.132314

The *Vitae* of saints in Britain, Ireland, and Brittany refer repeatedly to voyages by saints between these lands. Although we no longer expect to read early medieval hagiographical and pseudo-historical texts for accurate information about the period in which they are set it is apparent that these stories of travel reflect exchanges of information between the nations. More methodological reflection is needed; having rejected uncritical approaches to these texts it is not clear that we have fully rehabilitated them with respect to what they *can* tell us, either about the period of their composition or any earlier phases of activity. If we no longer believe that we can trace the travels of saints by using hagiographical texts and place-name and cult evidence in combination, we should still consider the strong likelihood that hagiographers themselves might have travelled, taking written or oral information from Britain to Brittany, and vice versa.

Caroline Brett has thoroughly revisited the complicated and still highly debated issues surrounding the foundation of Brittany and in particular the role of the 'saints' in that process.[1] Casting a very large shadow over medieval and modern discussions of the foundation of Brittany is the immensely powerful model found in pseudo-historical texts, in particular *Historia Brittonum*, stating unequivocally that the Britons went to Armorica, founded Brittany, and never returned: 'Hi sunt Brittones Armorici, et nunquam reversi sunt hucusque in hodiernum diem' (these are the Armorican British and they never came back, even to the present day).[2] Both medieval and modern writers have constructed saints into anachronistic roles as monastic founders and missionaries, with many cults of British saints cast in Brittany as a mission of the British church to the Continent.[3] The rejection of these models has not always been accompanied by a rejection of their migrationist overtones. Having rejected the reading of these texts for early travels of the saints, and for accounts of the foundation of Brittany, we need to appreciate the story they tell of regular, if not continuous, intellectual exchanges across the later first millennium.

---

[1] See Brett, 'Soldiers'.

[2] *Historia Brittonum*, ch. 27, trans. pp. 24–25 and 65. We can put to one side Bede's somewhat unaccountable, and certainly unique, assertion that the insular British came originally from Armorica (*Historia ecclesiastica* 1.1, pp. 16–17). This, suggested Magali Coumert, may well have been a deliberate choice on his part to rid Britain of indigenous inhabitants, in order to counter the implicit suggestion that those who later dispossessed the Britons were invaders (*Origines des peuples*, p. 406). We can at the very least note that Bede's statement has no precedent nor subsequent iteration or elaboration.

[3] Wooding, 'The Representation of Early British Monasticism', p. 140.

9. CROSS-CHANNEL INTERCOURSE IN THE EARLIEST BRETON *VITAE*   209

In the current study, I am confining myself to the Breton Lives that contain British episodes composed before the displacement of people and relics in the face of Viking raids of the tenth century, a period which, in the words of François Kerlouégan, 'correspond en gros à la fin de la période carolingienne'.[4] These are *Vita S. Maglorii*, Wrdisten's *Vita S. Winwaloei*, Bili's *Vita S. Machutis*, and Wrmonoc's *Vita S. Pauli Aureliani*, with additional reference to several later texts, Lifris of Llancarfan's *Vita S. Cadoci*, *Vita S. Gurthierni*, as well as a *Vita S. Winnoci*.[5] Pre-dating these texts, and with a huge influence in terms of style, information, and equally, historiographical significance, is *Vita I S. Samsonis*.

Vita I S. Samsonis

We can say, without controversy, that Samson himself led his early life in Wales before travelling to Brittany via Cornwall.[6] This journey seems to have been reconstructed, and then retraced, by the author of *Vita I S. Samsonis*, who was a member of the community of Dol in Brittany.[7] The author states that he gathered sources along his journey: it has been argued that one written source referred to in the text may have been a more or less fully elaborated **vita primigenia S. Samsonis*, and that this text might have formed the basis for much of the first part of the extant *Vita*.[8] Such arguments are inherently speculative. There is no evidence that such a text circulated in Britain (nor, in this form, in Brittany), and it was, apparently, not found at Llanilltud Fawr where we might expect given its subject matter, but at Samson's Cornish monastery.[9] However, the extremely uneven emphasis in *Vita I S. Samsonis* Book I between Samson's British and Continental activities (including a remarkable lack of attention paid to Samson's foundation of Dol) as well as the notably different concerns

---

[4] Kerlouégan, 'Les vies de saints bretons', p. 195.

[5] Brett, 'Soldiers', pp. 23–24 provides a useful, if necessarily brief, summary of the texts at issue; cf. as well Kerlouégan, 'Les vies des saints bretons'. See also now the comprehensive discussion of this group of texts in Brett, Edmonds, and Russell, *Brittany and the Atlantic Archipelago*, pp. 119–42.

[6] Brett, 'Soldiers', p. 23; Poulin, *L'hagiographie bretonne*, especially Annexe B, pp. 69–70.

[7] See, most recently, Olson, ed., *St Samson of Dol*.

[8] *Vita I S. Samsonis*, Prologue.2, I.1, I.42, pp. 142–43, 146–47, 206–07; Sowerby, 'The Lives', esp. p. 30; Poulin, 'La circulation', pp. 49–52; cf. Olson, 'Introduction', pp. 3–10. For further discussion of the text, see Poulin, 'Présence d'une culture celtique', p. 180 above.

[9] Poulin, 'La circulation', pp. 57–58.

underlying the British and Continental sections (leaving aside the entirely separate nature of Book II) supports the argument that the author had access not only to information that he then used when writing his own text but perhaps also to information already 'composed' in a more or less coherent form, and illustrating its own distinctive concerns.[10] Whether one envisages such a text being composed in Wales or in Cornwall (or in both), or even in Brittany where Henoc supposedly found it (but surely using abundant information from both Wales and Cornwall in that case), for our purposes here it is useful to question the long-held supposition that there was little or no hagiographical writing in pre-Norman Wales and/or Cornwall.[11] *Vita I S. Samsonis* and its possible underlying sources clearly represent information moving across the Channel at an early period.

This investigation into other possible movement of information across the Channel will consider the influence of the Samson texts as a given, and will not be documenting it in detail except where relevant to specific issues. In particular, whenever we look for information that might have come from Britain to Brittany (or *vice versa*) in the pre-Viking period, we need to first determine if it is or is not derived from *Vita I S. Samsonis*.

Vita S. Maglorii

Vita S. Maglorii was composed *c.* 860 by a monk of Léhon, in the medieval diocese of Dol (Côtes-d'Armor).[12] The Life is heavily reliant on *Vita II S. Samsonis* (*c.* 850 × 860), which is not surprising given that it makes its subject the cousin of Samson, with Maglorius made his successor in the see of Dol. Dol is securely an archbishopric in *Vita S. Maglorii*, and Samson is elevated to archiepiscopal rank even before leaving Britain: all of these point to *Vita II S. Samsonis*.[13] Its minor elaborations to the British episodes in *Vita II S. Samsonis* contribute almost nothing to what we already know from the Samson texts. *Vita I S. Samsonis* describes how Samson's parents, Amon and Anna, had, respectively, a brother and sister who also married and had three sons (1.1–2).[14] *Vita S. Maglorii* names one of these sons as Maglorius, thus making Maglorius into

[10] See Jankulak, 'Present and yet Absent', pp. 175–76.

[11] See Guy, 'The *Life* of St Dyfrig', pp. 2–4.

[12] Poulin, *L'hagiographie bretonne*, p. 207; *Vita S. Maglorii*.

[13] Poulin, *L'hagiographie bretonne*, p. 208.

[14] *Vita I S. Samsonis*, pp. 146–49.

9. CROSS-CHANNEL INTERCOURSE IN THE EARLIEST BRETON *VITAE*   211

a cousin of Samson, and includes Maglorius with those said to have studied under Illtud (chs 1–2).[15] The text's co-opting of Samson's British past is entirely unremarkable given its political and hagiographical agenda with respect to Dol and Léhon and its further information, such as it is, reflects exclusively Breton concerns. The text has, arguably, nothing particular to tell us about contacts between Britain and Brittany apart from the fact that the Samson material was available, something we already know from the fact of the rewriting at Dol of *Vita I S. Samsonis* as *Vita II S. Samsonis*.

Wrdisten, Vita S. Winwaloei

The earliest extant Life of Winwaloe, leaving aside hagiographical references in several hymns, is a text in verse and prose by Wrdisten and has been dated to 860 × 884. It has been argued, most recently by Poulin, that a lost Life could be posited as the source Wrdisten describes as a *vita brevis* (*Praefatio rhythmica*, line 1).[16] Poulin, along with Bernard Merdrignac, argued that it was not necessary to attribute the numerous British features of Wrdisten's Latin to a lost text, but that the archaic Breton onomastics in Wrdisten's text might be evidence for an underlying source.[17] The prose element of the Life, which is at issue here, forms part of a larger whole: an *opus geminatum* with a verse text covering the same ground. Wrdisten clearly relied in part on the Samson *vitae* (*Vita II S. Samsonis* probably) for his larger themes and models; its subject matter does not at all overlap.[18]

Vita S. Winwaloei begins with a description of Britain taken from Gildas, *De excidio Britanniae* (ch. 3) and then introduces *Fracanus*, a cousin (*consobrinus*) of *Catovius*, king of the Britons (1.1).[19] Fracanus, we are told, crossed the sea from Britain because of a pestilence taking his sons *Weithnocus* and *Jacobus*. Their mother, *Alba*, was known as *trimammis* because she had three

---

[15] *Vita S. Maglorii*, pp. 782–83.

[16] Wrdisten, *Vita S. Winwaloei*, p. 172; Poulin, while remaining ambivalent about the text's existence, nonetheless assigned it a number in his list: *L'hagiographie bretonne*, p. 406; see also, Poulin, 'Présence d'une culture celtique', p. 182 above.

[17] Merdrignac, *Les saints bretons, témoins de Dieu*, p. 35; Poulin, *L'hagiographie bretonne*, p. 406.

[18] Poulin, *L'hagiographie bretonne*, p. 421.

[19] Gildas, *De excidio Britanniae*, pp. 16–17, 89–90; Wrdisten, *Vita Winwaloei*, pp. 174–76.

breasts and three children (1.2).[20] The text's editor identified a British place-name, *Domnonia*, from the text's apparent reading *Nomniae*, but Arthur de la Borderie quashed this reading convincingly, arguing that the text should instead read *nomine* (so *terra nomine dicta* rather than *terra Nomniae dicta*) that is, that Catovius's realm took its name from him, as is entirely unremarkable.[21] The metrical version has a similar construction (*locum ... cujus nomine dictum*) although it says this with respect to Fracanus's settlement in Brittany taking its name from him (ch. 2, line 8, see further below for Fracanus).[22] The parallel use of the construction serves to strengthen the argument against the reading *Nomniae* in the prose Life.

Those figures presented as Winwaloe's relatives in *Vita S. Winwaloei* appear, or were understood to appear, in later British sources. The connections, or at times more tellingly the lack of connections, can suggest sources available to Wrdisten; they can also illuminate the sorts of identifications made, or partly made, as cults developed. Wethinoc and Jacutus are the subjects, jointly, of an eleventh- or twelfth-century text *Vita SS. Guethenoci et Iacuti*, that is heavily derivative of *Vita S. Winwaloei*, in particular repeating its familial relationships.[23] Jacutus himself does not have a cult in Cornwall, but is relatively well-known in Brittany, being the patron and eponym of the abbey of Saint-Jacut-de-la-Mer which is where *Vita SS. Guethenoci et Iacuti* was composed. Michel Debary has argued that Winwaloe's brother *Jacobus* was identified with Jacutus after the tenth-century Viking raids; this identification was influenced, in particular, by the assembling of the Cartulary of Landévennec.[24] However, Wethinoc, or a saint of that name, clearly was the object of an earlier Cornish cult. He appears as *Geuedenoc* in a tenth-century list of Cornish saints as well as in an alternative, earlier, place-name for Padstow, *Languihenoc* (1086), *Lanwethenek* (1350); not surprisingly, Wethenec also appears in the *Vita Petroci*

---

[20] Wrdisten, *Vita S. Winwaloei*, p. 176.

[21] De la Borderie, *Le Cartulaire de Landévennec*, pp. 15–16, n. 3; Wrdisten, *Vita S. Winwaloei*, p. 176: 'Cujus etiam praedicti regis erat, terra Nomniae dicta' (the region called Nomnia, of which the aforesaid [Catovius] was king), *recte* 'the region taking its name from him'? Cf. Merdrignac, *D'une Bretagne à l'autre*, pp. 134–41. I am indebted to Caroline Brett for pointing out to me the divergence between the prose and metrical Lives.

[22] Wrdisten, *Vita S. Winwaloei*, p. 250: 'Coepit habere locum, modo cujus nomine dictum' (the place began to take its name from him [Fracanus]).

[23] *Vita SS. Guethenoci et Iacuti*, ed. by De Smedt, pp. 98–102.

[24] Debary, 'Saint Jacut', p. 156.

as Petroc's predecessor at the site (ch. 7).[25] It is difficult to argue from silence, but the early attestation of Wethinoc in Cornwall as well as the fact that the Petroc texts (the earliest dating from the eleventh century, composed in Britain but found now only in relatively late Breton manuscripts)[26] give Wethinoc no particular family connections (and do not mention Winwaloe or Jacutus) suggest that at the very least a connection with Winwaloe was not known, or made, at this point in Cornwall, at least among the Cornish. There is a further complication, in that if my model for the transmission of the cult of St Petroc to Brittany before the twelfth-century theft of that saint's relics is credited, Bretons in exile in Cornwall recognized Wethinoc as Winwaloe and Jacutus's brother, despite Wethinoc not having much of a cult in Brittany (and arguably none as a distinctly separate saint, as opposed to being a member of Winwaloe's family).[27] This, I have argued, sufficed to introduce Petroc into a 'local', Breton milieu otherwise not given to the introduction of non-local saints, with Jacutus playing a further part in the expansion of the cult into Brittany.[28] If we credit this, then, we envisage in, say, eleventh-century Padstow, a Cornish audience to whom Petroc and Wethinoc were thought of as local Cornish saints, without obvious family ties to any Bretons, and a Breton audience to which at least one was recognizable or at least able to be interpreted as a local Breton saint on the strength of the family connection between Wethinoc and Winwaloe (and perhaps Jacutus).[29] No texts, British or Breton, mention Petroc in the context of Wethinoc, Jacutus, and Winwaloe: the only connection made in texts is between Petroc and a Wethinoc devoid of familial context. This may serve either to undermine the argument as to the significance of Wethinoc and Petroc being culted at Padstow or Bodmin to the process by which Petroc's cult was introduced to Brittany, or, perhaps more arguably, it highlights the possibility that connections and identifications can be made locally that are not reflected in written texts.

Fracanus is not known from any extant earlier text and seems not to have been the object of any further British interest apart from specifically being Winwaloe's father. The existence of a place-name Ploufragan in Brittany

---

[25] Olson and Padel, 'A Tenth-Century List', p. 53; *Vita I S. Petroci*, ed. by Grosjean, pp. 491–92.

[26] Jankulak, *The Medieval Cult*, p. 2.

[27] Jankulak, *The Medieval Cult*, pp. 98–101.

[28] Jankulak, *The Medieval Cult*, pp. 106–14.

[29] Jankulak, *The Medieval Cult*, p. 109.

(Côtes-d'Armor) is one of several indications that Wrdisten had access to information about its locality which is clearly where he had the family land once in Brittany. Bernard Tanguy rather sceptically commented that it is impossible to know if Wrdisten selected this name because of existing traditions, or merely because of the place-name, but in this case it is hard to disagree with Doble's conclusion that the author knew the district well. It less clear that, as Doble argued, Wrdisten 'had reasons for associating his hero with this district' and impossible to know what those reasons might have been.[30] This question, of course, is a useful reminder that people and information travelled not just across the Channel but within regions on either side of it, although that is not our main purpose here.

Fracanus's cousin Catovius has been identified by Peter Bartrum as a reasonably well-attested Welsh figure (or perhaps figures?) with Arthurian connections, named Cadwy ap Geraint.[31] The 'Cadwy' figures hang together quite well, with Arthurian and west-country implications, but the further identification of Catovius with them probably puts too much weight on the very probably mistaken insertion by the text's modern editor of *Domnonia* into Wrdisten's *Vita S. Winwaloei* (as above). A second Life of St Winnoc (tenth- or eleventh-century) includes a genealogy that names *Catovi filii Gerentonis* as an ancestor of Riwal who himself, the genealogy explains, conquered Brittany from Britain (Riwal also appears in Wrdisten's *Vita S. Winwaloei* as a local ruler in dispute with Winwaloe's father Fracanus, ch. 1.18, as well as elsewhere in later Breton Lives and genealogies: he is clearly a bit of a stock figure).[32] Neither Winwaloe nor Fracanus are mentioned in connection with Catovius in any other context.

Winnoc's genealogy clearly falls into the rather large category of later elaborations of genealogical connections which often throw up multiple and quite different versions of genealogical settings.[33] What makes this worth mentioning in this context, however, is that the earlier Life of St Winnoc (eighth- or ninth-century) who is himself a saint culted in Flanders, says that he came from Britain with three named companions, *Quadanocus, Ingenocus*, and *Madocus*

---

[30] Tanguy, *Dictionnaire*, p. 209; Doble. *The Saints of Cornwall*, II, p. 79.

[31] Bartrum, *A Welsh Classical Dictionary*, p. 86.

[32] *Vita II S. Winnoci, genealogia*, pp. 267–68; Doble, *The Saints of Cornwall*, V, p. 134; Wrdisten, *Vita S. Winwaloei*, pp. 202–05; Bartrum, *A Welsh Classical Dictionary*, p. 571; Brett, Edmonds, and Russell, *Brittany and the Atlantic Archipelago*, pp. 193–96.

[33] Bartrum, *A Welsh Classical Dictionary*, p. 86.

but gives no other detail (ch. 1).[34] Winnoc's name (which could be a hypocoristic form of Winwaloe) has led to confusion as to the identity of the patron saint of the Cornish parish, St Winnow (*San Winvec* and *San Winnuc* in Domesday Book) both in terms of its original founder and its subsequent iterations, and it is possible that Winnoc of Flanders was one of several candidates at different times.[35] All this is suggestive, but ultimately unilluminating; the list of Winnoc and his companions would be the only connection relevant in the context of this discussion, but it is not sufficiently detailed to make anything more of it, other than to say it exists.

Winwaloe's mother, *Alba trimammis*, on the other hand, seems much more solidly identified with a figure appearing in later medieval Welsh texts. The Life of Wethenoc and Jacutus says of her, 'lingua patria Guen appellata, quod Latine sonat Candida' (named Guen in her native language, which in Latin means 'the white') (ch. 2).[36] A *Gwen teirbron* (whose name translates as Alba) appears in the Welsh genealogical text *Bonedd y Saint* (? twelfth-century) with specific Breton connections: she is the daughter of Emyr Llydaw and wife of Eneas Ledewig of Llydaw as well as being mother of St Cadfan of Enlli (19).[37] This Cadfan would seem to be the same as that named in *Vita S. Paterni* as *Catman*, one of the leaders of a company of monks from *Let(avia)* to the west coast of Wales (the other two leaders are *Ketinlau* and *Titechon*, i.e. Cynllo and Tydecho?, ch. 4).[38] *Bonedd y Saint* adds to Cadfan's Breton connections, giving his confessor as Hywyn ap Gwyndaf Hen of Llydaw, and names nine other saints coming with them to Enlli (20).[39] Bartrum commented, in this connection, that 'there seems to be little doubt that Cadfan and all his company really came from a forgotten place in Britain called Llydaw, not the better known Llydaw, that is Brittany'.[40] A large part of the reasoning behind this argument, which he makes several times, runs as follows:

---

[34] *Vita I S. Winnoci*, p. 263; Orme, *The Saints of Cornwall*, p. 256; Doble, *The Saints of Cornwall*, v, p. 130.

[35] Orme, *The Saints of Cornwall*, p. 256; Padel, *A Popular Dictionary*, p. 180.

[36] *Vita SS. Guethenoci et Iacuti*, p. 98.

[37] *Bonedd y Saint*, Early Welsh Genealogical Tracts, p. 57; Bartrum, *A Welsh Classical Dictionary*, p. 312.

[38] *Vita S. Paterni*, pp. 254–55.

[39] *Bonedd y Saint*, Early Welsh Genealogical Tracts, p. 57; Bartrum, *A Welsh Classical Dictionary*, p. 75.

[40] Bartrum, *A Welsh Classical Dictionary*, p. 75.

It seems improbable that these descendants of Emyr Llydaw came to Wales from Armorica: the traffic was almost exclusively the other way. This and other considerations have led to the belief that there was a place called Llydaw in south-east Wales.[41]

Bartrum was, of course, assessing the events described in these texts for a presumed historicity; he also assimilated the older model, most particularly espoused by E. G. Bowen, that saints travelled primarily from Wales to Brittany as part of a secondary Christian mission, via specific routes, at specific times.[42] In the case of genealogy and hagiography, while it is true that what we might consider plausibility can easily be sacrificed to the demands of the genre to accomplish its ends in terms of illustrating truths that in effect lie outside of the text's purported relationship to a historical record, it is also true that we must ourselves examine our own notions of 'plausibility' in interpreting these texts, as well as keeping an open mind about how medieval authors and audiences approached this as a concept. While it is arguable that Breton texts, including the earliest ones, did not know or use the names Llydaw or Letavia (which will be discussed below), it is a different matter for Welsh and Cambro-Latin texts (which are the ones Bartrum is most concerned with).[43] *Vita S. Paterni*, for example, does not consistently use the form *Letavia* (chs 2, 4), but it says clearly that the saint is *gente ... Armoricus* (ch. 2).[44] This surely is all of a piece with the wider descriptions of Cadfan's activities.

With respect to Winwaloe and his family, it will suffice to say that the identification of *Alba trimammis* (or Candida) with *Gwen teirbron* seems relatively well-evidenced and does seem to appear in its Welsh and Breton texts independently. Although *Gwen teirbron* is given a securely Breton setting (for surely Llydaw is Brittany in these texts) it is to be noted that Winwaloe and Fracanus are not mentioned in connection with her in the Welsh texts: these give her a completely different set of (mostly Breton) relations. It is interesting, then, to speculate on the precise sharing of tradition that might give the Welsh Gwen teirbron a Breton ambit without including (indeed, while replacing) her earlier and very notable Breton connections. From the Breton side of things, we might argue that Wrdisten did not know or use a genealogy originating in Wales, unless we admit that the existing,

[41] Bartrum, *A Welsh Classical Dictionary*, p. 250.

[42] Bowen, *Saints, Seaways and Settlements*; cf. Bartrum, *A Welsh Classical Dictionary*, p. 420.

[43] See now Brett, Edmonds, and Russell, *Brittany and the Atlantic Archipelago*, pp. 332–34.

[44] *Vita S. Paterni*, pp. 252–55.

quite consistent, genealogies were only one strand of a larger, contradictory, no longer extant whole (this would not be impossible in the world of genealogical texts). On the other hand, he knew a character with distinctive attributes and the names of her husband, husband's cousin, and two other children. This is not dissimilar to what we can posit lay behind the absence of textual evidence for a known connection between St Petroc and the saints of Wethinoc's Breton family. It is clear that identifications and family connections are being made, sometimes, it would seem, taking on board some aspects of identity, but not all, and many of these only implied rather than made explicit in our narrative texts.

Bili, Vita S. Machutis

The Life of St Malo by Bili, deacon of Alet (Ille-et-Vilaine) is the next text under consideration. It provides some brief, but potentially very important glimpses of hagiographical transmission through South Wales before the main flourishing of Welsh hagiography at the end of the millennium. There are complex arguments about the date of the Life vis-à-vis another Life of Malo, the *vita anonyma brevior*. Here we shall consider Bili's text as the earliest, assigning it to between 865–872, the episcopal floruit of its dedicatee Ratwili.[45] The textual tradition of Bili's Life is also complicated, as no manuscripts are complete and a tenth-century version in Old English is used to reconstruct and supplement Bili's text.[46] It is worth stressing the English provenance of four of the six extant manuscripts (and of two of the three known or surmised lost manuscripts), as well as the fact of its rendering into Old English, probably at Winchester, for all that the composition clearly took place in Brittany.[47] This speaks not just to the movements of texts between Brittany and Britain, but also, in this case, a specific interest in Breton texts and saints in Anglo-Saxon England following on the tenth-century migration of Bretons and texts due to the Viking raids. Saints Samson, Malo, and Judoc are especially prominent; clearly, Bili's *Vita S. Machutis* can be listed among the texts imported into Britain at this

---

[45] Poulin, *L'hagiographie bretonne*, pp. 155–56; Merdrignac, *Les saints bretons entre légendes et histoire*, pp. 98–104. *Vita anonyma brevior S. Machutis*, at any rate, has little to add to the British episodes (it makes Malo's father the founder of the city of *Guinnicastrum*, ch. 14, p. 145): cf. Poulin, *L'hagiographie bretonne*, p. 173.

[46] Poulin, *L'hagiographie bretonne*, p. 147.

[47] Yerkes, *The Old English Life*, pp. xxxix–xlii; Rauer, *Beowulf and the Dragon*, p. 115.

time.[48] The inclusion of material relating to St Brendan in the Life, and its clear concern with Llancarfan (Vale of Glamorgan), set the Malo material apart from the otherwise relatively homogeneous group of texts under consideration here.

Bili claims, repeatedly and at some length, to have revised (*emendare*) an earlier anonymous text which itself was informed by at least oral sources ('sicut ab aliis sapientibus audivit ac didicit' (just as he had heard and learned from other wise men), Prologue) and had been corrupted by numerous copyings.[49] Poulin did not find this claim sufficiently convincing to include a lost *vita primigenia* in his list of texts for Malo, seeing Bili's text as very much the product of its time and circumstances of composition.[50] He argued, moreover, that the references to Bili having recourse himself to oral tradition are limited and generic (Prologue, 1.1, 1.15).[51] However one additional reference of Bili to his source is far more striking: with respect to a miraculous tree grown from a bramble gathered on an otherworld voyage and planted at Llancarfan on their return, Bili says that it is well-known among Bretons visiting Wales: 'multi ex nostris regionibus ad illam patriam euntes viderunt' (many from our regions travelling to that country have seen it) (1. 25).[52] This statement can be seen as a generic statement of authority for a miracle story (and proof of its existence at an early stage), but it is, in addition, an explicit comment about the fact, surely, that Bretons travel, regularly and in reasonable numbers, to Britain. This is supported by Bili's knowledge of material that clearly had a significant (written?) tradition even by this early stage, the Brendan material, and, one might well argue, accessed it via Llancarfan, a church with an undoubtedly significant if mostly lost archive of written material (see below).

The complexity of the early Brendan legend is usefully explored by James Carney, Séamus Mac Mathúna, and Jonathan Wooding, in a series of mostly short studies.[53] A detailed reconsideration of the Malo material with respect

---

[48] See Rauer, *Beowulf and the Dragon*, pp. 95–97.

[49] Bili, *Vita S. Machutis*, ed. by Lot, pp. 351–52; cf. ed. by Le Duc pp. 4–5, 24, 27.

[50] Poulin, *L'hagiographie bretonne*, p. 157; cf. pp. 313–20 (*vita primigenia S. Samsonis*) and 406 (*vita deperdita S. Winwaloei*).

[51] Bili, *Vita S. Machutis*, ed. by Lot pp. 352, 353, 362; cf. ed. by Le Duc, pp. 27, 30–31, 64–65 — the Old English retains these more by implication than by direct statement.

[52] Bili, *Vita S. Machutis*, ed. by Lot, p. 638; cf. ed. by Le Duc, pp. 85–87; again, the Old English text understates this to the point of losing its original point, saying that the tree was a wonderful spectacle to all that saw it, without specifying who the observers were or where they might have come from.

[53] Carney, review of Selmer; Mac Mathúna, 'The Structure and Transmission'; Mac

9. CROSS-CHANNEL INTERCOURSE IN THE EARLIEST BRETON *VITAE*

to the Brendan tradition, in particular in the context of Llancarfan's links with both Ireland and Brittany, would be beyond the scope of the current exercise, but we can make several relevant generalizations. In particular, it is worth noting that while the extant Lives of St Brendan postdate the material here, entries in the 'Litany of Pilgrim Saints' (*c.* 800–900) and the episodes in Bili's *Vita* itself are evidence for an earlier *Vita S. Brendani* that was also the source of the more famous *Navigatio* of Brendan, which is probably of around the same date as Bili's *Vita*.[54] Hence it is most likely that Bili's *Vita*, the extant *Vitae* of Brendan and the *Navigatio* all derive from an older version of the extant *Vita S. Brendani*.[55]

Bili's Life begins with an extremely brief summary of Malo's early life: he was born in Gwent 'in Britannia quadrangula, quae regio Uuenti dicitur' (in four-sided Britain, the region which is called Gwent) to Deruel (a sister of Hamon [Amon], Samson's father), and Uuen, then raised in a valley called Nantcarfan, a form also appearing in Lifris's *Vita S. Cadoci*, as another name for Llancarfan. Bili states that Nantcarfan is near (*prope*) the sea (1.4): Llancarfan is approximately four kilometres from the Bristol Channel as the crow flies and there seems little reason to doubt that Bili meant this site.[56] Malo is ordained a priest by Brendan (1.14). A dove miracle echoes the dove miracles accompanying Samson's three ordinations in *Vita I S. Samsonis* (1.13, 1.15, 1.44).[57] In 1.15 Malo and Brendan set off on an otherworld voyage, clearly derived from the Brendan tradition. They search for the island of Ima, but though they find several miraculous islands, the implication is that Ima itself goes undiscovered. The name, Ima, is unknown outside of the Malo texts, but aspects of it in the *anonyma* tradition of Malo relate to paradise islands in the wider Brendan tradition.[58]

Mathúna, 'Contributions'; Wooding, 'The Medieval and Early Modern Cult'; see also Jonathan M. Wooding, 'Rhygyfarch's *Vita S. Dauid*'. I would like to thank Jonathan Wooding for much detailed discussion of the Brendan material.

[54] Mathúna, 'Contributions' includes a useful tabulation of the episodes in some of the versions of *Vita* tradition, pp. 167–68.

[55] I note here that the *Navigatio* is often referenced in manuscripts as *Vita S. Brendani*, but the *Navigatio* is a discrete text.

[56] Bili, *Vita S. Machutis*, ed. by Lot, p. 355; cf. ed. by Le Duc, p. 39.

[57] Bili, *Vita S. Machutis*, ed. by Lot, p. 361; cf. ed. by Le Duc, pp. 60–61; *Vita I Samsonis*, pp. 166–69, 170–71, 210–11.

[58] *Vita anonyma brevior S. Machutis* makes explicit mention of Ima's paradisiacal nature (ch. 7) as well as it being inhabited by angels (ch. 9, ed. De la Borderie, pp. 139–40). This is reminiscent of *Navigatio S. Brendani*'s Paradise of Birds, an island that has birds that are incar-

Although the Malo material is the earliest written evidence of what would become the Brendan material, we can confidently make several assertions. First, it is clear that the broad outline of the voyage story existed — there is no reason to argue that Bili invented this. Second, this material was firmly attached to Brendan, who is not unknown to the Breton hagiographical tradition but is certainly not prominent in it.[59] Finally, it is surely arguable that the choice of Llancarfan for the setting of this connection is deliberate and significant: it is not explainable as a borrowing from a common theme (in medieval Breton *vitae* if there is a British setting for a saint's formative years, it is with Illtud at his monastery, following the standard set by *Vita I S. Samsonis*).[60] The setting at Llancarfan is surely not explainable as an echo of what the Brendan material might, hypothetically, have contained. In the Brendan *Vitae* Brendan makes a visit to Britain where he encounters Gildas, but that is the extent of the detail and it would be a stretch to see this as implying Llancarfan, though Gildas was later associated with that site.[61] The logical inference is that Bili accessed this Brendan material directly or indirectly via Llancarfan. That Llancarfan itself shows no sign of this material in any of its archive is a salutary warning about how material can exist but almost entirely disappear.

Bili uses several forms of his subject's name: he uses Machutes ninety-one times, Machu ninety-two times and Machlou three times (the other texts about Malo behave similarly). For our purposes this is relevant to the discussion of Bili's sources, if we can trace them, as opposed to a search for the original historical figures lying, or not, behind the text.[62] Bartrum, inspired not only by the different names but by various chronological difficulties (and keeping in

---

nations of angels and who sing the canonical hours (ch. 11, pp. 28–39). *Vita S. Brendani* has no comparable episode, but *Immram Brain* has birds (not angels) that sing canonical hours (ch. 7, pp. 6–7). For birds see Wooding, 'The Date of *Nauigatio S. Brendani abbatis*' as well as Wooding 'Saint and Beast'.

[59] Wooding, 'The Medieval and Early Modern Cult of St Brendan', pp. 183, 197–200.

[60] This material was covered, in part, by Caroline Brett at the 2017 Leeds International Medieval Congress, 'The Life of St Malo: Covering all the Bases' and I am grateful to Dr Brett for additional discussion. It is worth noting, as well, Christopher Brooke's argument that Lifris's inclusion of the story of the conversion of Illtud in *Vita S. Cadoci* (ch. 19, pp. 62–65) shows Lifris 'disposing of a dangerous rival to St Cadog, by attributing the foundation of Llanilltud Fawr to a miracle performed by the founder of Llancarfan', *The Church and the Welsh Border*, p. 85.

[61] Wooding, 'The Medieval and Early Modern Cult of St Brendan', p. 201.

[62] Poulin, *L'hagiographie bretonne*, p. 174.

mind that chronological difficulties are extremely common and in theological terms quite unremarkable in hagiographical texts) argued that three different saints were conflated in the Malo texts, with the British-set episodes reflecting traditions about a 'Machutes, Machudd, Machu', a south Wales saint who is represented in 1.1–15, 25–26 to which was added voyages with St Brendan (1.16–24).[63] Bartrum described this south Wales saint as the founder and/or eponym of several churches in Gwent named in *Liber Landavensis*: Llanllwyd (*Lann Liuit Machumur*) and Llanfannar (*Lann Vannar de Machumur*), as well as St Maughan's or Llanfocha (*Lan Mocha* or *Bocha* and *ecclesia de S. Machuto*).[64] This may or may not be the case, and at any rate there is no evidence of texts or clear path of literary transmission from this saint or saints to Bili. The names of Malo's parents do not help here: his father is merely 'Gwent' and his mother, Dervel, is obscure.[65] Whether or not Bili has conflated several saints (and this is not at all impossible), for our purposes does not matter. What we would like to know is where, if anywhere, Bili found his information about Malo's life in Wales, and surely Llancarfan is an obvious source. Brendan is known from other Welsh sources: he is mentioned in Rhygyfarch's *Vita S. David* (ch. 40), and a fragmentary version of *Navigatio S. Brendani* (called there *Vita S. Brendani*) is found in the main manuscript collection of Cambro-Latin Lives, BL Cotton Vespasian A.xiv.[66] Rhygyfarch, also, seems to have access to a Brendan text.[67] Bili's attribution of Brendan himself to Llancarfan, however, suggests that Llancarfan was the main point of contact for the transmission of Brendan material to Brittany.

[63] Bartrum, *A Welsh Classical Dictionary*, p. 446. The other two saints, he argued, were 'Maclovius, Maclou, Malo, the saint of St Malo' and 'Machutus, a saint of Saintonge', whose stories informed the episodes set on the Continent.

[64] Bartrum, *A Welsh Classical Dictionary*, pp. 447, 240–41; *Liber Landavensis*, pp. 240–41, 74, 320.

[65] Bartrum's speculations (*A Welsh Classical Dictionary*, p. 643) on an identification between Malo's father and several figures collected under the rubric 'Ynyr Gwent' are surely over-elaborate (a trap that Bartrum falls into much less often than he might have done, to his credit). A reasonably well known 'Arthurian' saint, a male Derfel, has his earliest attestation in additions to a late fourteenth-century calendar (the additions 'slightly later' than the main text), London, BL Additional MS 14,912: see Luft, 'Locating the British Library Additional 14912 calendar', pp. 110 and 125.

[66] Rhygyfarch, *Vita S. David*, pp. 134–37; Wooding, 'The Medieval and Early Modern Cult of St Brendan', pp. 201–03.

[67] See Wooding, 'Rhygyfarch's *Vita S. David*'.

Llancarfan, Vita S. Cadoci *by Lifris, and Brittany*

Llancarfan was, as John Reuben Davies described it, 'by the end of the eleventh century, the most powerful ecclesiastical community in Glamorgan'; soon after this it seems to have entirely lost its prominence, arguably due to the overweening influence of Llandaf. Davies speculated, entirely reasonably, that it might have 'emerged in the context of a post-Roman secular administration' but this cannot be substantiated due to the entirely unremarkable lack of evidence.[68] *Liber Landavensis* mentions Llancarfan in its notionally earliest charters, but we await the ninth century for more secure evidence of its existence.[69] It produced a large archive, much of which is known both from *Liber Landavensis* as well as from material appended to Lifris' Life of its founder.[70] Llancarfan produced two known hagiographers, Lifris and Caradog, the latter possibly very prolific as author not only of a (rewritten) *Vita S. Cadoci* but also perhaps, Lives of Gildas, Cyngar, Illtud, Gwynllyw, and Tatheus, and perhaps even *Liber Landavensis* itself.[71] Lifris' *Vita S. Cadoci* (the earliest Life) is one of the two earliest extant Cambro-Latin Lives dating to the late eleventh century (Rhygyfarch's *Vita S. David* is the other). It is a lengthy and somewhat chaotic text, in which its subject travels around north and south Wales, and visits Ireland (chs 10–11), Scotland (ch. 26), Cornwall (ch. 31) the Middle East (this pilgrimage is disposed of in one extremely brief chapter, ch. 32), Brittany (ch. 35) and Beneventum (chs 37–39).[72] There are good reasons to see in Llancarfan an important point of contact for both southern Ireland and Brittany.

Bernard Tanguy has considered Lifris' account of Brittany and argued, very persuasively, that Lifris must have seen Breton charters at Quimperlé during a very specific period of time.[73] Chapter 35 describes a visit to Brittany (just in case there is any doubt, Lifris calls it by three different names: 'Armorica, deinde Lettau, nunc uero Brittannia Minor uocatur' (formerly Armorica, then Llydaw, but now called Lesser Britain) where Cadog finds an unin-

---

[68] J. R. Davies, *The Book of Llandaf*, p. 15 n. 47.

[69] J. R. Davies, *The Book of Llandaf*, p. 15.

[70] W. Davies, 'Property Rights'; J. R. Davies, *The Book of Llandaf*, pp. 91–94.

[71] J. R. Davies, *The Book of Llandaf*, pp. 136, 142.

[72] Lifris, *Vita S. Cadoci*, pp. 46–49, 80–85, 90–95, 96–99.

[73] Tanguy, 'De la vie de saint Cadog'; see also Guy, 'Explaining the Origins', pp. 251–53 below.

9. CROSS-CHANNEL INTERCOURSE IN THE EARLIEST BRETON *VITAE*

habited island, builds a basilica, and a stone bridge, appoints one of his disciples, *Catgualader*, as prior, and leaves.[74] The stone bridge collapses but is miraculously restored. The chapter concludes by saying that Cadog is called by the Bretons *Catbodu* and that the island takes its name from him, that is *inis Catbodu*. This clearly refers to an island in the River Étel, in Morbihan on which was a medieval priory attached to the abbey of Sainte-Croix de Quimperlé, connected by a stone causeway to the village of Saint-Cado. A chapel dating from the eleventh century remains on the island.[75] There are important differences from Lifris' description: the causeway is not a bridge, it is an estuary island rather than a sea island, and the distance from the shore is considerably less than Lifris says.[76] The fact and forms of the names *Catbodu* and *Catgualader* strongly support the theory that Lifris or his informant was working from written sources, a group of charters in the Cartulary of Sainte-Croix.[77] These charters begin with an explanation that a man called *Catuodus* lived on an island in the River Étel, that there is local testimony about him and his miracles, and that a priest called *Judhuarn* stole a written Life, so that nothing else is known about him (CI).[78] Seven charters concern Saint-Cado, the earliest dating to the early eleventh century up to 1089; in one (CIII) is found the name of a *presbiter*, *Catgualadr*.[79] Tanguy argued that Lifris or his informant seem not to have visited Île-Cado itself — the charters must then have been seen at Quimperlé. But these charters would not have been located at Quimperlé until after 1089 when Alain Fergant donated *Sancti Catuodi confessoris de Brouerec monasterium* to Sainte-Croix (CVII); for this reason Tanguy argued that the composition of Lifris' *Vita S. Cadoci* must postdate 1089.[80] Between 1124 and 1128 Gurheden, a monk of Sainte-Croix, compiled the abbey's Cartulary and composed, for inclusion in it, *Vita S. Gurthierni*.[81] This text includes the saint's genealogy, a confusing and composite text with

---

[74] Lifris, *Vita S. Cadoci*, pp. 96–99.

[75] Tanguy, 'De la vie de saint Cadoc', p. 162.

[76] Tanguy, 'De la vie de saint Cadoc', p. 163.

[77] Tanguy, 'De la vie de saint Cadoc', p. 164.

[78] *Cartulaire de l'abbaye de Sainte-Croix de Quimperlé*, p. 255.

[79] *Cartulaire de l'abbaye de Sainte-Croix de Quimperlé*, p. 259.

[80] *Cartulaire de l'abbaye de Sainte-Croix de Quimperlé*, pp. 262–63; Tanguy, 'De la vie de saint Cadoc', pp. 164–65.

[81] *Vita S. Gurthierni*, pp. 42–46; Jankulak, 'Breton *vitae* and Political Need' including pp. 244–48 for translation of the text.

obvious links to Welsh genealogical texts as well as British pseudo-historical tradition as exemplified by, among others, *Historia Brittonum* and *Breuddwyd Macsen*. The genealogy is ascribed to 'Iuthael son of Aidan': Ben Guy has argued, compellingly, for the identification of Aidan with an Aidan appearing as a priest of Llancarfan in its charters.[82] Gurthiern's paternal lineage shows significant overlap with that of Cadog in the fourteenth-century Jesus College manuscript (but, significantly, there is far less overlap between the genealogies of *Vita S. Gurthierni* and the genealogies of Cadog found in Lifris' *Vita S. Cadoci*).[83] Gurthiern's maternal line resembles that of Kentigern as found in that saint's fragmentary anonymous Life (chs 1 and 8): here as well there is a connection (albeit indirectly) with Llancarfan as Jocelyn's twelfth-century *Vita S. Kentigerni* has Kentigern found *Nantcharfan* after it has been donated to him by King Cathwallaun (ch. 23).[84]

It does not seem to be the case that there is a significant cult of St Cadog in Brittany. The name itself is relatively common, but the cult sites commemorating a saint of this name, including in the place-name Pleucadeuc (Morbihan, *Plebs Cadoc* in 826),[85] are better explained with respect to another saint with a different feast day.[86] St Cadog was commemorated in Cornwall with a chapel and well in Padstow parish: Lifris seems to have had good information about both (chs 31–32) and they are reasonably well-attested in medieval sources.[87] This location in Cornwall close to Petroc dedications is further evidence of a link having been established between the two saints at some point. According to Lifris' *Vita S. Cadoci* Petroc son of Glywys was Cadog's uncle (a brother of Cadog's father Gwynllyw, Prologue, ch. 45).[88] *Vita II S. Petroci* (twelfth-cen-

---

[82] See Guy, 'Explaining the Origins', pp. 252–54 below.

[83] *Vita S. Gurthierni*, p. 42; *Early Welsh Genealogical Tracts*, pp. 24–25 (*Vita S. Cadoci*), p. 44 (Jesus College genealogies); Tanguy, 'De la vie de saint Cadoc', p. 174; Jankulak, 'Breton *Vitae* and Political Need', pp. 231–33; Fleuriot. 'Old Breton Genealogies', pp. 2–3. See Guy, 'Explaining the Origins', pp. 250–54 below for a more detailed discussion of the genealogies.

[84] *Vita S. Gurthierni*, p. 42; *Early Welsh Genealogical Tracts*, pp. 27–28; Jocelyn of Furness, *Vita S. Kentigerni*, pp. 200–01.

[85] *Cartulaire de l'abbaye de Redon*, CCLV, p. 205.

[86] Tanguy, 'De la vie de saint Cadoc', p. 165.

[87] Lifris, *Vita S. Cadoci*, ed. and trans. by Wade-Evans, pp. 92–95; Orme, *The Saints of Cornwall*, 81; Orme is mistaken, however, in dating the mention of the well to the twelfth-century *Vita II Petroci*: it appears in a separate text, a genealogy found in the same manuscript, which may be of later date.

[88] Lifris, *Vita S. Cadoci*, ed. by Wade-Evans, pp. 24–29, 116–19.

tury) gives minimal genealogical information but does name one of Petroc's brothers as Winleus (ch. 1).[89] A genealogy appended to the Petroc material in the same manuscript clearly attempts to incorporate Welsh and Cornish traditions, and states that Petroc's father was Glywys, Petroc's brother was Winleus, and Cadog was the son of Winleus; it adds that there was a miracle-giving fountain of St Cadog at what is certainly Padstow.[90] Some of the later Welsh genealogical texts give Petroc a specifically Cornish provenance, and one assumes that this is what lies behind later Welsh texts that give Glywys himself a Cornish origin, even in texts where Petroc is not mentioned.[91] This is a bit rich considering that the whole point of Glywys was to be an eponymous ancestor of a sub-kingdom in south-east Wales (Glywysing), an extremely common reflex of genealogy — but it is also an extremely common reflex of pseudo-historical texts to adapt and re-adapt to different versions of things.

To sum up: while Lifris was arguably drawing upon known material already connecting the Cornish Cadog sites to the Welsh saint, in the case of the Breton material in his Life he seems to have taken an existing site connected to a saint with a similar (but not the same) name, incorporating its story into his narrative and making this connection for the first time. If we were looking for a historical saint, this would be frustrating, but as we are looking for evidence of contact and sharing of written texts, it is extremely revealing. Moreover, in light of the probability that the composition of *Vita S. Gurthierni* (and its inclusion in the Quimperlé cartulary) was inspired by the discovery of relics having labels but no other information, Tanguy speculated, quite reasonably, that perhaps Quimperlé had applied to a Welsh abbey, such as Llancarfan, for a biography of its subject, about which it knew nothing, hence Gurthiern's significantly Welsh aspect. Perhaps, Tanguy ventured, one of Llancarfan's monks, perhaps even Lifris, was sent to Quimperlé with this information and with the donation of Saint-Cado took the opportunity to gather information about that site as well (although not to visit it), eventually incorporating it into his own text.[92] This is extremely speculative, but it rests on the solid foundation of Lifris or his informant having visited, clearly, Quimperlé (as well as Cornwall); if we are looking for a model of

[89] *Vita II S. Petroci*, ed. by Grosjean, p. 146.

[90] *Vita II S. Petroci*, ed. by Grosjean, p. 188.

[91] Bartrum, *Early Welsh Genealogical Tracts*, pp. 24, 29–30, 60, 71.

[92] Tanguy, 'De la vie de saint Cadoc', p. 179; the abbey of Sainte-Croix was extremely active in seeking to invent and document founders in this period: see Jankulak, 'Breton *Vitae* and Political Need', esp. pp. 228–30.

how written information might have passed from one region to another, this is an entirely reasonable one. In avoiding the need to ask whether individual saints travelled between the Brittonic lands, we should not omit to ask whether individual hagiographers, and their information, did indeed so travel.

Wrmonoc, Vita S. Pauli Aureliani

The final text to be discussed here is Wrmonoc's *Vita S. Pauli Aureliani*, dated to 884.[93] In its Prologue Wrmonoc claims to be revising an older life (ch. 2) and identifies himself as a former monk of Landévennec (now it would seem at Léon, Paul's monastery), a pupil of Wrdisten's, and mentions the latter's *Vita S. Winwaloei* as an inspiration (ch. 3).[94] The text shows the significant influence of *Vita S. Winwaloei* but equally, of *Vita I S. Samsonis*. Wrmonoc also signals, apparently, oral sources using *ut dicitur, ut fertur*, and *ut vocitatur*, most often when he is providing onomastic explanations, of which he is extremely fond.[95] He twice attributes his information to *transmarini* (chs 32 and 35), although elsewhere he states that he does not know the names of Paul's other siblings, as the distance in time and place from his writing is too great (ch. 4).[96] There is no reason to argue that Wrmonoc himself visited Britain.[97] Poulin has argued that Wrmonoc's otherwise visible and highly literary borrowings suggest that the supposed earlier text which he claims to have used as a source did not in fact exist.[98] Given the number of names, surnames, place-names, explained and translated, it is easy to agree that Wrmonoc had informants, if not necessarily a written source in the form of an earlier Life. This can be argued most strongly in the case of the extra information he provides for David, whom he presents as one of Paul's fellow pupils.

Wrmonoc says that Paul studied at Illtud's monastery. This is here conflated with *insula Pyrus*, which is a separate site in the Samson tradition (*Vita S.*

---

[93] Poulin, *L'hagiographie bretonne*, p. 274.

[94] Wrmonoc, *Vita Pauli Aureliani*, pp. 209–11.

[95] Poulin, *L'hagiographie bretonne*, p. 274.

[96] Wrmonoc, *Vita Pauli Aureliani*, pp. 232, 234, and 212.

[97] Olson, *Early Monasteries*, p. 20.

[98] Poulin, *L'hagiographie bretonne*, pp. 276–77; Doble, on the other hand, commented 'in many passages it is easy to distinguish between this older Life and Wrmonoc's additions to it' (*The Saints of Cornwall*, I, p. 30).

9. CROSS-CHANNEL INTERCOURSE IN THE EARLIEST BRETON *VITAE*

Samsonis, 1.20).[99] It is mistakenly placed here, albeit vaguely, in a location in Dyfed, well west of Llanilltud Fawr (*Demetiarum patriae in finibus sita*, ch. 6), most likely Caldey Island. Here Samson is found studying alongside Paul, along with Gildas and David (ch. 8);[100] this is our earliest augmentation of the list of pupils studying under Illtud.[101] At this point Wrmonoc does something characteristic: he adds extra information, in this case in the form of David's nickname, *aquaticus*, along with its explanation, that is being due to David's austere habits. This nickname also appears in Rhygyfarch's *Vita S. David* (ch. 1) but it is striking that its earliest appearance is in a Breton text.[102] There is no obvious evidence of a reliance by Rhygyfarch on Wrmonoc's text, but this could be explained by the very different trajectory of David's life and career presented by Rhygyfarch.[103] The simplest explanation is that this is something known in Wales, and in Brittany, about David by the ninth century, probably having made its way from Wales to Brittany rather than vice versa.[104] The epithet is not startlingly original as applied to someone of austere habits, and David is not the only Welsh saint to be called *dyfrwr*, 'water-man' (i.e. *aquaticus*) but neither is the epithet widely occurring.[105] As with Bili, it may be that there was an Irish dimension to this transmission of information: of the other three sources mentioning St David before the late ninth or tenth century (in which period David is mentioned by Asser and dominates the poem *Armes Prydein Vawr*), one is from Wales (the 'Idnert' inscription at Llanddewi Brefi) and two are from Ireland (*Catalogus sanctorum Hiberniae*, 2.e; *Martyrology of Óengus*, main text, 1 March).[106]

Wrmonoc's text also shows strong similarities to the twelfth-century *Vita S. Iltuti*, raising the question of the existence of an earlier written Welsh source for

---

[99] Wrmonoc, *Vita Pauli Aureliani*, p. 213; *Vita I Samsonis*, pp. 178–79.

[100] Wrmonoc, *Vita Pauli Aureliani*, p. 215.

[101] The eleventh-century *Vita S. Gildae* repeats this information but omits David (ch. 3, ed. by Lot, pp. 435–36; *Vita S. Iltuti* incudes David, also calling him Dewi (ch. 11, pp. 208–09). Rhygyfarch's *Vita S. David* does not have anything resembling this, does not mention Samson, or Illtud, and Gildas appears in an entirely different context (ch. 5, pp. 112–15).

[102] Rhygyfarch, *Vita S. David*, pp. 108–09; Dumville, *Saint David of Wales*, pp. 12–13, 22.

[103] Poulin, *L'hagiographie bretonne*, p. 275.

[104] Dumville, *Saint David of Wales*, p. 25, n. 109.

[105] Henken, *Traditions of the Welsh Saints*, p. 72.

[106] *Catalogus sanctorum Hiberniae*, p. 206; *Martyrology of Óengus*, p. 80; cf. Wooding, 'The Figure of David', p. 11.

both texts, but as Poulin pointed out, it is equally possible that Wrmonoc's text was known in Britain, especially considering that one of its two manuscripts, apparently of Landévennec provenance, seems to have gone to Fleury-sur-Loire in the tenth-century flight from Viking raids (the saint's relics were also taken) and, easily, from there to Britain.[107] A comparison of a story (the herding of birds as if they were sheep) appearing in Wrmonoc's text (ch. 11) to an episode in the *Liber Landavensis* version of *Vita S. Samsonis* as well as to an episode in *Vita S. Iltuti* (ch. 14) shows significant correspondences between the two latter texts but not significant correspondences between these and Wrmonoc's version.[108] John Reuben Davies's subsequent inclusion of Wrmonoc's *Vita S. Pauli Aureliani* as one of the sources available to the compiler of *Liber Landavensis* is surely over-stretching the available evidence.[109] That being said, Davies is on firm ground in highlighting the prevalence of Breton sources in *Liber Landavensis*, including not only the Samson and Paul Aurelian material, but also a Life of St Turiau and, possibly, charters of Landévennec.[110]

Before Paul leaves Britain he encounters a ruler, Mark, who, Wrmonoc says, was called *alio nomine Quonomorus* (ch. 22).[111] Oliver Padel suggested that Wrmonoc used local knowledge from Cornwall, specifically a prominent inscription on a routeway, the Castle Dore inscribed stone.[112] The stone could be read as linking the names Tristan and Cunomor, and of course the wider Tristan legendary material links Tristan and Mark. Mark 'is a true pan-Brittonic character of folklore' as Padel described him, known from Breton as well as British material and located in both regions in the relevant tales, but here, suggestively, Wrmonoc placed him in Britain rather than, as one might expect, Brittany. But he also identified him, uniquely, with a figure (or figures) by the name of Conomor, who appears in Gregory of Tours's *Libri Historiarum X* (iv.4) as well as in *Vita I S. Samsonis* (i.59) and subsequently in numerous medi-

---

[107] Poulin, *L'hagiographie bretonne*, pp. 268–71, 281; Smith, 'Oral and Written', pp. 324–25; cf. Mostert, 'Relations between Fleury and England', pp. 197–99.

[108] Wrmonoc, *Vita S. Pauli Aureliani*, pp. 217–18; *Vita S. Samsonis (Liber Landavensis)*, pp. 9–10; *Vita S. Iltuti*, pp. 212–15.

[109] J. R. Davies, *The Book of Llandaf*, pp. 112, 128–30. This is mainly based on the appearance of a pig-related onomastic tale which is of significantly wide distribution, not at all dependent on *Vita S. Pauli Aureliani* as a source, as well as the abovementioned story also shared by *Vita S. Iltuti*; cf. Jankulak, 'Alba Longa'.

[110] J. R. Davies, 'The Cults of Saints', p. 51; J. R. Davies, *The Book of Llandaf*, p. 130.

[111] Wrmonoc, *Vita S. Pauli Aureliani*, p. 226.

[112] Padel, 'The Cornish Background', pp. 72–73, 77–79.

eval Breton Lives as a stock figure of an evil ruler.[113] The fact that Wrmonoc situated this episode in Britain, and that the most obvious link for these two, quite common, names is via the Cornish inscribed stone, is immensely suggestive.[114] It is perhaps a distraction that Wrmonoc also describes him as ruling over people of four languages, in a phrase surely derived from Bede, *Historia Ecclesiastica* I.1, but arguably with a fairly unspecific application. It is perhaps more telling that Wrmonoc specified that Mark/Cunomor's place of burial is in Britain (ch. 23), in an aside more commonly found with respect to saints than to rulers, but locating him firmly on that side of the Channel.[115] Wrmonoc's pains to make this episode as British as possible surely speak to his British sources, very possibly several different sources cobbled together by him.

Wrmonoc also includes an episode that describes the place of residence of Paul's sister, Sitofolla, on the shores of the Channel (chs 27–32).[116] It includes an aetiological story explaining how a natural feature known to *transmarini* as *semita Pauli* and visible in Wrmonoc's time (ch. 32), a version of a miracle performed earlier in the same text at Illtud's monastery (ch. 10) and a variant of which also appears in *Vita S. Iltuti* (ch. 13).[117] This story does not appear in the Samson texts, and it is reasonable to argue, as did Lynette Olson, that its source was a local legend.[118] Sitofolla herself is harder to place, and the existence at Exeter of a cult of St Sidwell does not help matters.[119] We are once again left with an impressive quantity of information, of uncertain quality in terms of accuracy and our ability to locate its referents (either regarding time of composition or time of its supposed setting). It does not follow that *transmarini* did not convey information (of whatever quality), of course.[120] The specific setting of Paul's British doings, apart from his sojourn at Illtud's monastery, is not

[113] *Vita I S. Samsonis*, pp. 230–33; Gregory of Tours, *Libri Historiarum X*, pp. 137–38; Padel, 'The Cornish Background', pp. 73, 77.

[114] See also Guy, 'The Breton Migration', pp. 142–43.

[115] Bede, *Historia ecclesiastica*, pp. 16–17; Poulin, *L'hagiographie bretonne*, pp. 278, 286, is mistaken in saying that ch. 9 gives the place of burial for Illtud: it includes the place-name *Iltuti monasterium* but does not mention Illtud's death or burial.

[116] Wrmonoc, *Vita S. Pauli Aureliani*, pp. 230–33.

[117] Wrmonoc, *Vita S. Pauli Aureliani*, pp. 217 and 232–33; *Vita S. Iltuti*, pp. 208–09.

[118] Olson, *Early Monasteries in Cornwall*, pp. 23–24.

[119] Olson, *Early Monasteries in Cornwall*, pp. 25–26; Orme, *The Saints of Cornwall*, p. 234.

[120] I am indebted to Lynette Olson for the suggestion that Wrmonoc's *transmarini* may well echo those of *Vita I S. Samsonis* which cites *litterae transmarinae* as a source for information (I. 38, pp. 200–03).

located in any terms that we might easily recognize or believe Wrmonoc or his audience to recognize. Julia Smith has argued that Wrmonoc probably had access to 'a few charters in the cathedral archives and conceivably also a list of the names of the companions who crossed from Britain to Armorica with him'; he may also have had access to Cornish and Welsh topographical tales but he is not at pains to site them in specific locations, even assuming he knew these.[121] The only easily locatable church in the British section is that of Illtud (the location of which however is incorrect if we consider it to be Llanilltud Fawr rather than Piro's island); another church is founded and left to his family, his brothers, Notolius and Potolius (ch. 20; compare *Vita I S. Samsonis* which shows Samson's family founding unnamed churches, I. 29–31, I. 40).[122]

There are suggestive links to dedications and textual traditions that appear later (inevitably, considerably later given the relatively early date at which Wrmonoc is composing) in Welsh material. These have been exhaustively listed by Doble and his argument that Wrmonoc was working from oral and written sources concerning two Welsh figures, Paul of Penychen from Glamorgan and St Paulinus from Carmarthenshire, endorsed by Bernard Merdrignac, is entirely reasonable and relatively convincing in its accumulation of detail (although cumulative detail can be a false friend in these matters).[123] Again, because we are looking for evidence of literary transmission rather than historical accuracy, we can acknowledge the strength of the argument, but for questions of where Wrmonoc might have found this material, we can only fall back on his own text, with its archaic spelling of sometimes poorly-understood names and translations, the amplitude of the information, and the explicit reference to *transmarini* as sources.[124] Doble argued, strongly, on this basis, that Wrmonoc must have had recourse to a written Life of St Paulinus, one also available to the

---

[121] Smith, 'Celtic Asceticism', p. 57; Smith 'Oral and Written', p. 323 and n. 57.

[122] Wrmonoc, *Vita S. Pauli Aureliani*, pp. 225–26; *Vita I S. Samsonis*, pp. 188–93, 204–05; cf. Sowerby, 'A Family and its Saint'.

[123] Doble, *The Saints of Cornwall*, I, pp. 31–42. esp. p. 36; cf. Bartrum, *A Welsh Classical Dictionary*, pp. 530–32; Merdrignac, 'Des origines insulaires', p. 71; it is perhaps worth mentioning, in this connection, the inclusion of a saint *Paulennanus* among the relics claimed to have been found with those of Gurthiern (*Vita S. Gurthierni*, p. 46).

[124] As Poulin comments, although Wrmonoc is clearly a Breton, he has trouble with Brehat Dincat (ch. 11), Plebs Lapidea (ch. 40): Wrmonoc, *Vita S. Pauli Aureliani*, pp. 218, 238; Poulin, *L'hagiographie bretonne*, p. 286; cf. Jackson, *Language and History*, pp. 41–42, for the dating of the form Tigernmaglus to the sixth century, for example.

9. CROSS-CHANNEL INTERCOURSE IN THE EARLIEST BRETON *VITAE*

author of *Vita S. Iltuti*.[125] Doble's strongly reasoned argument, even shorn of its supporting 'evidence' of local networks of church dedications or supposed dedications, would suit our written evidence nicely, but remains unprovable.

One final aspect of Wrmonoc's text remains to consider: a story about the saint's bell says that it is known by name *per cunctos Latinorum populos* (ch. 51), or *Lativorum* in another manuscript.[126] Tanguy saw this as one of several examples of the insular terms for Brittany, *Letavia* in Latin or *Llydaw* in Welsh, being unfamiliar to Breton authors, citing the Life of St Brieuc (*Latium trans mare*, ch. 35, eleventh-century) and the Life of St Goulven: 'in partes Letaniae quae pars est Armoricae sive Britanniae Minoris' (in the region of Letania, which is Armorica or Britannia Minor) (ch. 1), thirteenth-century.[127] Later still, he dismissed the form *Lativorum* entirely, on the quite reasonable grounds that Wrmonoc was probably echoing his teacher Wrdisten's phrase *per cunctos Latinorum fines* occurring in a homily to St Winwaloe (*lectio* ix).[128] It is worth repeating, however, that even if this place-name was unfamiliar to our Breton authors, it does not follow that when it appears in Welsh texts it refers to a place in Wales rather than in Brittany.

Conclusion

If we look for particular centres of transmission of information between Britain and Brittany (and Ireland) in Wales, the early medieval evidence suggests that the two main ones are Llancarfan and Llanilltud Fawr. Both were, by the time our written record starts to bring significant light onto the subject, far less prominent than they were previously, even somewhat obscure. Both are also themselves almost completely devoid of texts which show these Breton connections. Llanilltud Fawr did not produce any known texts (although surely a significant part of *vita primigenia S. Samsonis* came from there), despite its wealth and reputation as a seat of learning in the earlier period, as exemplified in its collection of inscribed stones.[129] Llancarfan's clearly copious archive

---

[125] Doble, *The Saints of Wales*, pp. 96–99, 153.

[126] Wrmonoc, *Vita S. Pauli Aureliani*, p. 245.

[127] Tanguy, 'De la vie de saint Cadoc', p. 175; *Vita S. Brioci*, p. 177; *Vita S. Golveni*, p. 176.

[128] Tanguy, 'La cloche', p. 619; *Cartulaire de l'abbaye de Landévennec*, p. 133.

[129] J. R. Davies, 'The Saints of South Wales', pp. 379–80; Jankulak, 'Present and yet Absent', pp. 179–80. It is perhaps worth noting, here, that the *mirabilia* of *Historia Brittonum* include a story about Illtud's floating altar, apparently attached to a church on the Gower Peninsula (71,

makes no reference to Malo, Alet, or Brendan, despite showing signs of contact with Sainte-Croix de Quimperlé at a later period, and only Lifris's Life of St Cadog shows a Breton connection. The Brendan material outside of Brittany, likewise, does not mention Llancarfan, Cadog, or Malo. Bili's *Vita S. Machutis* gives undeniable evidence that these connections existed at an earlier period; that these connections left no other trace is a salutary *caveat*. Similarly, the associations arguably made between St Petroc and Wethinoc's Breton family in Cornwall and then Brittany but entirely absent from any *vitae* should also sound a cautionary note in terms of our sense that our extant written texts must be the overriding, or even sole, evidence of what sorts of information might have been exchanged. Wrmonoc, it can be argued, put two separate bits of British information together, one of which was not in the form of a narrative but in the form of an inscribed stone, to assemble his composite Mark/Cunomor figure. Again we see the exchange of information surely due to travel between Wales and Brittany (and, as well, within these regions); again we see the difficulty of detecting this solely in terms of what the extant texts can tell us directly.

Vita I S. Samsonis has usually been viewed as a bit of an outlier in the British tradition, which seems otherwise not to have produced hagiographical narratives until the Norman period. The detail in the Breton texts examined here, however, suggests that information, oral and probably written, existed and was conveyed across the Channel throughout the period between the composition of *Vita I S. Samsonis* and the appearance of our earliest Welsh hagiographical texts, Lifris of Llancarfan's *Vita S. Cadoci* and Rhygyfarch's *Vita S. David*.[130] There is no good reason to assume that the direction of this travel was only, or mainly, in the one direction, despite the strength of the medieval aetiological tradition as found in our pseudo-historical texts.[131] If we read our texts in light of what we know of the Samson author's travels and paths of transmission of

---

trans. by Morris, pp. 41–42 and 82), a version of which is also found in *Vita S. Iltuti* (ch. 22, trans. pp. 224–27; cf. Evans, 'The Levitating Altar'.

[130] See also, now, Brett, Edmonds, and Russell, *Brittany and the Atlantic Archipelago*, especially pp. 290–91.

[131] A small group of Welsh saints said to be of Breton origin, Illtud, Padarn, Euddogwy, and Justinian, appear in relatively late Cambro-Latin texts, and two others, Cadfan and Tydecho, fall into the same category but with much less textual evidence. It would be outside the scope of the current paper to discuss these in any detail, but see now Jankulak, 'Models of Cross-Channel Migration'. We should probably also mention a small category of British saints with Latin Lives, who are said to have visited Brittany temporarily: Brynach, Cadog, and Teilo.

information, we enable a more nuanced appreciation of their own manners of working. This more nuanced view means that we must grapple with the way our own presuppositions colour our expectations of medieval authors and, more importantly although less accessibly, medieval audiences.[132]

Karen Jankulak specialises in the history of the early British churches. Her major works include *The Medieval Cult of St Petroc* (Boydell, 2000) and *Geoffrey of Monmouth*, in the Writers of Wales Series (University of Wales Press, 2010). A graduate of the Centre for Medieval Studies at the University of Toronto (Canada), she was formerly a Senior Lecturer at the University of Wales, Trinity Saint David.

[132] I am extremely grateful to Lynette Olson, Oliver Padel, and Jonathan Wooding for generous and detailed discussion of aspects of this paper, and to the editors, in particular Caroline Brett, for patience, encouragement and above all careful and helpful editing.

Works Cited

Manuscripts and Archival Sources

London, BL, MS Cotton Vespasian A.xiv, part i

Primary Sources

Bartrum, P. C., ed., *Early Welsh Genealogical Tracts* (Cardiff: University of Wales Press, 1966)

Bede, *Historia ecclesiastica gentis Anglorum*, ed. by B. Colgrave and R. A. B. Mynors, *Bede's Ecclesiastical History of the English People*, Oxford Medieval Texts (Oxford: Clarendon Press, 1969)

Bili, *Vita S. Machutis*, ed. by F. Lot, '*Vita S. Machutis* par Bili', in F. Lot, *Mélanges d'histoire bretonne* (Paris: Honoré Champion, 1907), pp. 331–430

——, *Vita S. Machutis*, ed. by G. Le Duc, *Vie de Saint Malo, évêque d'Alet. Version écrite par le diacre Bili (fin du IXe siècle). Textes latin et anglo-saxon avec traductions françaises* ([Saint-Malo]: Dossiers du Centre régional archéologique d'Alet, 1979)

Bonedd y Saint, in *Early Welsh Genealogical Tracts*, ed. P. C. Bartrum (Cardiff: University of Wales Press, 1966), pp. 51–67

Cartulaire de l'abbaye de Landevenec, ed. by A. de la Borderie (Rennes: Catel, 1888)

Cartulaire de l'abbaye de Redon en Bretagne, ed. by A. de Courson (Paris: Imprimerie Impériale, 1863)

Cartulaire de l'abbaye de Sainte-Croix de Quimperlé, ed. by L. Maître and P. de Berthou, 2nd edn (Rennes: Plihon et Hommay, 1904)

Catalogus sanctorum Hiberniae, ed. by P. Grosjean, 'Édition et commentaire du *Catalogus Sanctorum Hiberniae secundum diversa tempora* ou *De tribus ordinibus sanctorum Hiberniae*', *AnBoll*, 73 (1955), 197–213 and 289–322

Gildas, *De excidio Britanniae*, in *Gildas. The Ruin of Britain and other Works*, ed. and trans. by M. Winterbottom (London: Phillimore, 1978)

Gregory of Tours, *Libri Historiarum x*, ed. by B. Krusch, *MGH SS RM*, I (Hanover: Hahn, 1942)

Historia Brittonum, in *Nennius. British History and the Welsh Annals*, trans. by J. Morris (London: Phillimore, 1980), pp. 9–43, 50–84

Immram Brain, ed. and trans. by K. Meyer, *The Voyage of Bran, son of Febal, to the Land of the Living: An Old Irish Saga* (London: Nutt, 1895)

Jocelyn of Furness, *Vita Kentigerni*, in *The Lives of St Ninian and St Kentigern*, ed. by A. P. Forbes (Edinburgh: Edmonston and Douglas, 1874), pp. 159–242

Lifris of Llancarfan, *Vita S. Cadoci*, in *Vitae Sanctorum Britanniae et Genealogiae*, ed. and trans. by A. W. Wade-Evans (Cardiff: University of Wales Press, 1944), pp. 24–141

Martyrology of Óengus, ed. by W. Stokes (London: Henry Bradshaw Society, 1905)

Navigatio sancti Brendani, ed. and trans. by G. Orlandi and R. E. Guglielmetti, *Navigatio sancti Brendani: Alla Scoperta del Segreti Meravigliosi del Mondo* (Florence: Edizioni del Galluzzo per la Fondazione Enzio Franceschini, 2014)

Rhygyfarch, *Vita S. David*, ed. and trans. by R. Sharpe and J. R. Davies, in *St David of Wales: Cult, Church and Nation*, ed. by J. Wyn Evans and J. Wooding, SCH, 24 (Woodbridge: Boydell, 2007), pp. 107–55

The Old English Life of Machutus, ed. by D. Yerkes (Toronto: University of Toronto Press, 1984)

The Text of the Book of Llan Dâv: Reproduced from the Gwysaney Manuscript, ed. by J. Gwenogvryn Evans and J. Rhŷs (Oxford: Clarendon Press, 1893; Aberystwyth: National Library of Wales, 1979)

Vita anonyma brevior S. Machutis, ed. by A. de la Borderie, in A. de la Borderie and F. Plaine, *Vie inédite de saint Malo écrite au ixe siècle par Bili; autre Vie de saint Malo écrite au ixe siècle par un anonyme* (Rennes: Librarie bretonne de Plihon, 1994), pp. 131–57

Vita S. Brioci, ed. by F. Plaine, 'Vita S. Brioci episcopi et confessoris', *AnBoll*, 2 (1883), 161–90

Vita S. Gildae, ed. by F. Lot, 'Gildae vita et translatio', in F. Lot, *Mélanges d'histoire bretonne* (Paris: Honoré Champion, 1907), pp. 431–60

Vita S. Golveni, ed. by Y. Morice, 'La vie latine de saint Goulven: nouvelle édition', in *À travers les îles celtiques. Mélanges en mémoire de Gwénaël Le Duc*, ed. by G. Buron, H. Bihan, and B. Merdrignac (Rennes: Cirdomoc and Klask, 2008), pp. 173–84

Vita SS. Guethenoci et Iacuti, ed. by C. De Smedt, *AASS* November III, 1910, pp. 98–102

Vita S. Gurthierni, in *Cartulaire de l'abbaye de Sainte-Croix de Quimperlé*, ed. by L. Maître and P. de Berthou, 2nd edn (Rennes: Plihon et Hommay, 1904), pp. 42–54

Vita S. Iltuti, in *Vitae Sanctorum Britanniae et Genealogiae*, ed. and trans. by A. W. Wade-Evans (Cardiff: University of Wales Press, 1944), pp. 194–233

Vita S. Maglorii, ed. by J. Van Hecke, *AASS* October X, 1861, pp. 722–93

Vita S. Paterni in *Vitae Sanctorum Britanniae et Genealogiae*, ed. and trans. A. W. Wade-Evans (Cardiff: University of Wales Press, 1944), pp. 252–69

Vita I S. Petroci, ed. by P. Grosjean, 'Vies et miracles de S. Petroc II. Le dossier de Saint-Méen', *AnBoll*, 74 (1956), 470–96

Vita II S. Petroci, ed. by P. Grosjean, 'Vies et miracles de S. Petroc I. Le dossier du manuscrit de Gotha', *AnBoll*, 74 (1956), 131–88

Vita I S. Samsonis, in *La vie ancienne de saint Samson de Dol*, ed. and trans. by P. Flobert (Paris: Éditions du CNRS, 1997), pp. 133–269

Vita S. Samsonis (Liber Landavensis), in *The Text of the Book of Llan Dâv: Reproduced from the Gwysaney Manuscript*, ed. by J. Gwenogvryn Evans and J. Rhŷs (Oxford: Clarendon, 1893, 1979), pp. 6–24

Vita I S. Winnoci, ed. C. De Smedt, *AASS* November III, 1910, pp. 263–67

Vita II S. Winnoci, ed. C. De Smedt, *AASS* November III, 1910, pp. 267–74

Wrdisten, *Vita S. Winwaloei*, ed. by C. De Smedt, 'Vita S. Winwaloei primi abbatis Landevenecensis auctore Wurdestino', *AnBoll*, 7 (1888), 167–264

Wrmonoc, *Vita S. Pauli Aureliani*, ed. by F. Plaine, 'Vita sancti Pauli episcopi Leonensis in Britannia minori, auctore Wormonoco', *AnBoll*, 1 (1882), 208–58

Secondary Works

Bartrum, P. C., *A Welsh Classical Dictionary* (Aberystwyth: National Library of Wales, 1993)

Bowen, E. G., *Saints, Seaways and Settlements in the Celtic Lands*, 2nd edn (Cardiff: University of Wales Press, 1977)

Brett, C., 'Soldiers, Saints, and States? The Breton Migrations Revisited', *CMCS*, 61 (2011), 1–56

——, with F. Edmonds and P. Russell, *Brittany and the Atlantic Archipelago, 450–1200: Contact, Myth and History* (Cambridge: Cambridge University Press, 2021)

Brooke, C. N. L., *The Church and the Welsh Border in the Central Middle Ages*, ed. by D. N. Dumville and C. N. L. Brooke, SCH, 8 (Woodbridge: Boydell, 1986)

Carney, J., review of C. Selmer *Navigatio Sancti Brendani abbatis*, *Medium Aevum*, 32 (1963), 37–44; reprinted in *The Otherworld Voyage in Early Irish Literature. An Anthology of Criticism*, ed. by J. Wooding (Dublin: Four Courts Press, 2000), pp. 42–51

Coumert, M., *Origines des peuples: les récits du Haut Moyen Âge occidental (550–850)* (Paris: Institut d'Études Augustiniennes, 2007)

Davies, J. R., *The Book of Llandaf and the Normal Church in Wales*, SCH, 21 (Woodbridge: Boydell, 2003)

——, 'The Saints of South Wales and the Welsh Church', in *Local Saints and Local Churches in the Early Medieval West*, ed. by A. Thacker and R. Sharpe (Oxford: Oxford University Press, 2002), pp. 361–95

Davies, W., 'Property Rights and Property Claims in Welsh *Vitae* of the Eleventh Century', in *Hagiographie, cultures et sociétés IVe–XIe siècles. Actes du Colloque organisé à Nanterre et à Paris (2–5 mai 1979)* (Paris: Études Augustiniennes, 1981), pp. 515–33

De la Borderie, A., *Le Cartulaire de Landévennec*, extrait de *Annales de Bretagne*, 4 (1888–1889), 295–364, with renumbered pagination. Online at <https://gallica.bnf.fr/ark:/12148/bpt6k91128q/f1.item> [accessed 18 November 2022]

Debary, M., 'Saint Jacut et les origines de l'abbaye de Saint-Jacut-de-la-Mer', *MSHAB*, 49 (1969), 149–57

Dumville, D. N., *Saint David of Wales* (Cambridge: Department of Anglo-Saxon, Norse, and Celtic, 2000)

Doble, G. H., *The Saints of Cornwall*, I: *Saints of the Land's End District* repr. (Felinfach: Llanerch Press, 1997–1998)

——, *The Saints of Cornwall*, II: *Saints of the Lizard District* repr. (Felinfach: Llanerch Press, 1997–1998)

——, *The Saints of Cornwall*, V: *Saints of Mid-Cornwall* repr. (Felinfach: Llanerch Press, 2010)

Evans, A., 'The Levitating Altar of Saint Illtud', *Folklore*, 122 (2011), 55–75

Fleuriot, L., 'Old Breton Genealogies and Early British Traditions', *BBCS*, 26 (1974), 1–6

Guy, B., 'The Breton Migration: A New Synthesis', *Zeitschrift für celtische Philologie*, 61 (2014), 101–56

——, 'The *Life* of St Dyfrig and the Lost Charters of Moccas (Mochros), Herefordshire' *CMCS*, 75 (2018), 1–37

Henken, E. R., *Traditions of the Welsh Saints* (Cambridge: Brewer, 1987)

Jackson, K., *Language and History in Early Britain* (Edinburgh: Edinburgh University Press, 1953)

Jankulak, K., 'Alba Longa in the Celtic Regions? Swine, Saints and Celtic Hagiography', in *Celtic Hagiography and Saints' Cults,* ed. by J. Cartwright (Cardiff: University of Wales Press, 2003), pp. 271–84

——, 'Breton *Vitae* and Political Need in the Cartulary of Sainte-Croix de Quimperlé', in *Literature and Politics in the Celtic World. Papers from the Third Australian Conference of Celtic Studies, University of Sydney, July 1998*, ed. by J. M. Wooding and P. O'Neill (Sydney: University of Sydney Celtic Studies Foundation, 2000), pp. 218–47

——, *The Medieval Cult of St Petroc*, SCH, 19 (Woodbridge: Boydell, 2000)

——, 'Models of Cross-Channel Migration in Latin Lives of British and Breton Saints', CMCS, 84 (2022), 13–39

——, 'Present and yet Absent: The Cult of St Samson of Dol in Wales', in *St Samson of Dol and the Earliest History of Brittany, Cornwall and Wales*, ed. by L. Olson, SCH, 37 (Woodbridge: Boydell, 2017), pp. 163–80

Kerlouégan, F., 'Les vies des saints bretons les plus anciennes dans leurs rapports avec les îles britanniques', in *Insular Latin Studies. Papers on Latin Texts and Manuscripts of the British Isles: 550–1066*, ed. by M. W. Herren, Papers in Medieval Studies, 1 (Toronto: Pontifical Institute of Mediaeval Studies, 1981), pp. 195–213

Luft, D., 'Locating the British Library Additional 14912 calendar', *Studia Celtica*, 53 (2019), 103–32

Mac Mathúna, S., 'Contributions to a Study of the Voyages of Saint Brendan and Saint Malo', in *Irlande et Bretagne, vingt siècles d'histoire*, ed. by C. Laurent and H. Davis (Rennes: Terre de Brume, 1994), pp. 40–55; reprinted in *The Otherworld Voyage in Early Irish Literature. An Anthology of Criticism*, ed. by J. Wooding (Dublin: Four Courts Press, 2000), pp. 157–74

——, 'The Structure and Transmission of Early Irish Voyage Literature', in *Texte und Zeittiefe*, ed. by H. L. C. Tristram, *ScriptOralia*, 58 (Tübingen: Narr, 1994), pp. 313–57

Merdrignac, B., 'Des origines insulaires de Paul Aurélien', in *Sur les pas de Paul Aurélien*, ed. by B. Tanguy and D. Tanguy (Brest: Centre de recherche bretonne et celtique and Société archéologique du Finistère, 1997), pp. 67–77

——, *Les saints bretons entre légendes et histoire. Le glaive à deux tranchants* (Rennes: Presses universitaires de Rennes, 2008)

——, *Les saints bretons, témoins de Dieu ou témoins des hommes* ([Saint-Malo]: Centre régional archéologique d'Alet, 1985)

Mostert, M., 'Relations between Fleury and England', in *England and the Continent in the Tenth Century: Studies in Honour of Wilhelm Levison (1876–1947)*, ed. by D. Rollason, C. Leyser, and H. Williams, Studies in the Early Middle Ages, 37 (Turnhout: Brepols, 2010), pp. 185–208

Olson, L., and O. Padel, 'A Tenth-Century List of Cornish Parochial Saints', *CMCS*, 12 (1986), 33–72

Olson, L., *Early Monasteries in Cornwall*, SCH, 11 (Woodbridge: Boydell, 1989)

——, 'Introduction', in *St Samson of Dol and the Earliest History of Brittany, Cornwall and Wales,* ed. by L. Olson, SCH, 37 (Woodbridge: Boydell, 2017), pp. 1–18

——, ed., *St Samson of Dol and the Earliest History of Brittany, Cornwall and Wales*, SCH, 37 (Woodbridge: Boydell, 2017)

Orme, N., *The Saints of Cornwall* (Oxford: Oxford University Press, 2000)

Padel, O. J., 'The Cornish Background of the Tristan Stories', *CMCS*, 1 (1981), 53–81

——, *A Popular Dictionary of Cornish Place-Names* (Penzance: Hodge, 1988)

Poulin, J.-C., 'La circulation de l'information dans la Vie ancienne de s. Samson de Dol et la question de sa datation', in *St Samson of Dol and the Earliest History of Brittany, Cornwall and Wales*, ed. by Lynette Olson, SCH, 37 (Woodbridge: Boydell, 2017), pp. 37–82

——, *L'hagiographie bretonne du haut Moyen Âge. Répertoire raisonné* (Ostfildern: Thorbecke, 2009)

Rauer, C., *Beowulf and the Dragon: Parallels and Analogues* (Woodbridge: Brewer, 2000)

Smith, J. M. H., 'Celtic Asceticism and Carolingian Authority in Early Medieval Brittany', *Studies in Church History*, 22 (1985), 53–63

——, 'Oral and Written: Saints, Miracles, and Relics in Brittany, *c.* 850–1250', *Speculum*, 65 (1990), 309–43

Sowerby, R., 'A Family and its Saint in the *Vita Prima Samsonis*', in *St Samson of Dol and the Earliest History of Brittany, Cornwall and Wales*, ed. by L. Olson, SCH, 37 (Woodbridge: Boydell, 2017), pp. 19–36

——, 'The Lives of St Samson: Rewriting the Ambitions of an Early Medieval Cult', *Francia*, 38 (2011), 1–31

Tanguy, B., 'La cloche de Paul Aurélien', in *Mélanges François Kerlouégan,* ed. by D. Conso, N. Fick, and B. Poulle (Paris: Annales littéraires de l'université de Besançon, 1994), pp. 611–21

——, *Dictionnaire des noms de communes, trèves et paroisses des Côtes-d'Armor. Origine et signification* (Douarnenez: ArMen, 1992)

——, 'De la vie de saint Cadoc à celle de saint Gurtiern', *ÉC*, 26 (1989), 159–85

Wooding, J., 'The Date of *Nauigatio S. Brendani abbatis*', *Studia Hibernica*, 37 (2011), 9–26

——, 'The Figure of David', in *St David of Wales: Cult, Church and Nation*, ed. by J. Wyn Evans and J. Wooding, SCH 24 (Woodbridge: Boydell, 2007), pp. 1–19

——, 'The Medieval and Early Modern Cult of St Brendan', in *Saints' Cults in the Celtic World,* ed. by S. Boardman, J. R. Davies, and E. Williamson, SCH, 25 (Woodbridge: Boydell, 2009), pp. 180–204

——, 'The Representation of Early British Monasticism and *Peregrinatio* in *Vita prima S. Samsonis*', in *St Samson of Dol and the Earliest History of Brittany, Cornwall and Wales,* ed. by L. Olson, SCH, 37 (Woodbridge: Boydell, 2017), pp. 137–61

——, 'Rhygyfarch's *Vita S. Dauid, Félire Óengusso*, and the Cults of Irish Saints in Wales', in *Celebrating the Saints,* ed. by N. Volmering (Turnhout: Brepols, forthcoming)

——, 'Saint and Beast in *Nauigatio S. Brendani abbatis*', in *À travers les îles celtiques. Mélanges en mémoire de Gwenaël Le Duc,* ed. by G. Buron, H. Bihan, and B. Merdrignac (Rennes: Cirdomoc and Klask, 2008), pp. 287–96

10. EXPLAINING THE ORIGINS OF BRITTANY IN THE TWELFTH CENTURY: ST CADOG'S SOLUTION

Ben Guy

ABSTRACT This chapter examines the various attempts made in the twelfth century to explain the origins of Brittany. This period saw the emergence of new elements in the story of Brittany's settlement, such as the role played by a certain Cynan son of Eudaf as leader of the Brittonic settlers. It is argued that these new elements arose in south-east Wales, where interest in the origins of Brittany had been generated by the appearance of Breton settlers in the region of Monmouth in the wake of the Norman conquest of England in 1066. All accounts of the origins of Brittany written at this time, including the famous version by Geoffrey of Monmouth, can be traced back to south-east Wales, and to the major centres of the cult of St Cadog in particular.

RÉSUMÉ Dans ce chapitre, nous interrogeons les tentatives, faites au cours du XIIᵉ siècle, d'expliquer les origines de la Bretagne armoricaine. C'est à cette époque qu'apparaissent de nouveaux éléments de l'histoire du peuplement de la Bretagne, par exemple le rôle d'un certain Cynan fils d'Eudaf comme chef des émigrés bretons. Nous proposons que ces nouveaux éléments émanassent du sud-est du Pays de Galles, où l'arrivée de colons bretons dans les environs de Monmouth résultante de la conquête de l'Angleterre par les Normands en 1066 avait suscité l'intérêt aux origines bretonnes. Tous les récits des origines bretonnes écrits à cette époque, y compris la fameuse histoire de Geoffroy de Monmouth, remontent à cette région du Pays de Galles et particulièrement aux grands centres du culte de saint Cadog.

KEYWORDS Brittany, St Cadog, Geoffrey of Monmouth, Caradog of Llancarfan, origin legends, Breton migration, Monmouth Priory, Cynan Meiriadog, Eudaf Hen, Magnus Maximus

---

Multi-disciplinary Approaches to Medieval Brittany, 450–1200: Connections and Disconnections, ed. by Caroline Brett, Fiona Edmonds, and Paul Russell, TCNE 36 (Turnhout: Brepols, 2023) pp. 239–262   BREPOLS 🖳 PUBLISHERS   10.1484/M.TCNE-EB.5.132315

Stories about origins arose throughout the Middle Ages as a natural response to a natural question: why are things the way they are? Such stories could be used to explain the smallest details, such as the names of holy wells, or phenomena of much wider significance, such as the formation of ethnic groups. Even questions of cosmological significance could be addressed with recourse to that most important repository of origin stories, the Bible. It was usually the case that those who attempted to answer such questions had very little to go on. They seldom had more than place-names, local folk traditions, and a few old texts, all liable to be understood (or misunderstood) in a host of different ways. When we study accounts of origins surviving from the Middle Ages, we are not, therefore, studying 'historical' narratives as we would now conceive them; rather, we are studying the erudite speculations of those who sought to rationalize the unfathomable.

The existence of Brittany was one such puzzle that piqued the interest of medieval enquirers, especially among the Britons. In the early Middle Ages, the Britons did not distinguish ethnically between those of their number who lived in northern Britain, Wales, Cornwall, Brittany, or elsewhere: they were all Britons, Latin *Brittones*, or, to use the vernacular term appearing in the tenth-century poem *Armes Prydein Vawr*, *Kymry*.[1] Since the Britons shared their name with the island of Britain, it would have been obvious to learned enquirers (whatever we might think now) that Britain was their 'original' homeland, the crucible that formed them as a distinct people. Such a view is expressed in the *Historia Brittonum*, written in North Wales in 829/30. In that text, various stories from various sources are reproduced to explain the symbiotic relationship between Britain and the Britons. In the early Middle Ages, an obvious way to explain an onomastic relationship between a country and a people was to posit that the country had been named after the founding ancestor of the people. For exactly this reason, one finds that the *Historia Brittonum* contains several origin stories about *Britto* or *Brutus*, first of the Britons and erstwhile founder of *Brittannia*: some said he was a Roman consul, others the grandson of Aeneas, others still the grandson of Alanus, the first descendant of Japheth in Europe.[2] The common denominator is that Britto/Brutus established the Britons *in Britain*. According to the early medieval understanding of the his-

---

[1] *Armes Prydein*, l. 9 (pp. 2–3). For ethnic identity among the early medieval Britons, see Pryce, 'British or Welsh?', pp. 776–80.

[2] *Historia Brittonum* (Harley 3859), §§ 7, 10, and 17–18 (pp. 7, 9, 15, and 17). For the latter story, deriving from the so-called 'Frankish Table of Nations', see Wadden, 'Frankish Table of Nations'.

10. EXPLAINING THE ORIGINS OF BRITTANY IN THE TWELFTH CENTURY

tory of the Britons, it was Brittany on the Continent that was anomalous; it was Brittany that required a subsidiary story of origins to explain its existence.

The earliest surviving attempts by Britons to explain the origins of Brittany belong to the ninth century. Differing accounts survive from Wales and Brittany. These accounts have two features in common: firstly, a dim awareness that Brittany arose as a consequence of the ending of Roman power in Britain; and secondly, an almost total reliance on the intractable testimony of Gildas's sixth-century work *De Excidio Britanniae*, presumably due to Gildas's by-then unassailable authority, coupled with the absence of any alternative sources. It is salutary to realize that several interested parties read Gildas's work with an eye to discovering the origins of Brittany but deduced different explanations from it.

An account from Wales, preserved in the *Historia Brittonum*, attributes the founding of Brittany to a certain *Maximianus*, a character based on Gildas's *Maximus* (the Magnus Maximus who usurped the Western Roman Empire between 383 and 388). Gildas states that Maximus (who is implied to have been a Briton) usurped imperial power with the help of the army of Britain. But the army never returned home, rendering the island vulnerable to external attack.[3] From these bare bones, the following story in the *Historia Brittonum* was adduced:[4]

> Septimus imperator regnauit in Brittannia: Maximianus. Ipse perrexit cum omnibus militibus brittonum a Brittannia et occidit Gratianum regem romanorum et imperium tenuit totius Europę. Et noluit dimittere milites qui perrexerunt cum eo ad Brittanniam ad uxores suas et ad filios suos et ad possessiones suas. Sed dedit illis multas regiones a stagno quod est super uerticem montis Iouis usque ad ciuitatem que uocatur Cantguic et usque ad cumulum occidentalem (id est Cruc Ochident). Hii sunt brittones armorici, et nunquam reuersi sunt huc usque in hodiernum diem. Propter hoc Brittannia occupata est ab extraneis gentibus et ciues expulsi sunt, usque dum Deus auxilium dederit illis.

> A seventh emperor reigned in Britain: Maximianus. He proceeded from Britain with all the soldiers of the Britons and killed Gratianus, king of the Romans, and held the empire of all Europe. But he did not want to send the soldiers who had come with him back to Britain to their wives and their sons and their properties. Instead, he gave them many districts from the pool on the summit of Mount Jupiter

[3] Gildas, *De Excidio Britanniae*, §§ 13–14 (pp. 20–21 and 93).

[4] *Historia Brittonum* (Harley 3859), § 27 (pp. 19 and 21). I have corrected the text against the manuscript: BL, MS Harley 3859, fol. 178ᵛ. Punctuation and translation are my own. For the *Historia Brittonum*'s use of Gildas at this point, see Dumville, 'Sub-Roman Britain', pp. 179–81.

[i.e. in the Alps][5] as far as the town which is called Quentovic and as far as the western mound (that is, *Cruc Ochidient*). They are the Armorican Britons, and up to this day they have never returned here. For this reason, Britain has been seized by foreign peoples and its citizens have been expelled, until such time that God should grant them help.

The author of the *Historia Brittonum* seems to have taken this story from a discrete source. Other passages relating to the Magnus Maximus of history, based on Prosper's *Epitoma Chronicon* and Sulpicius Severus's *Vita Sancti Martini*, call him *Maximus* rather than *Maximianus*.[6] Only the quoted chapter (27), relaying the story of the founding of Brittany by Maximus's soldiers, uses the form *Maximianus*.[7] Intriguingly, this same chapter shares verbal phrasing with two other early Welsh sources that mention Magnus Maximus: the inscription on the Pillar of Eliseg and the Harleian genealogies.[8] All three of these sources may have drawn on the same account of the founding of Brittany, an account inspired by nothing more than Gildas's statement that Maximus's army never returned home to Britain.

Some forty years later, a Breton writer intimately familiar with Gildas adduced a different explanation for the origins of Brittany.[9] Wrdisten, Abbot of Landévennec, writing around 870, began his *Life* of St Winwaloe with the following summary of the settlement of Brittany:[10]

> Et ne eius antiqua profundius repetam facinora, qui haec plenius scire voluerit, legat sanctum Gildam, qui de eius situ et habitatione scribens et eius mira in Christo conversione statimque ritu pene paganico apostatione et divina lugubriter insecuta ultione et eius iterum, ne penitus in favillam et cineres redigeretur, miseratione, multa ex eiusdem actibus congrua bene et irreprehensibiliter disputat [...] Sed longe ab huius quoque moribus parvam distasse sobolem suam non opinor, quae quondam ratibus ad istam devecta est citra mare Britannicum terram. Tempore

[5] For *mons Iovis* as a synonym for a mountain in the Alps, see Williams, 'Nodiadau', pp. 96–98; Bromwich ed. and trans., *Trioedd Ynys Prydein*, p. 144.

[6] For the sources, see Guy, 'Constantine', p. 387 n. 30.

[7] The form *Maximianus* also appears at the start of chapter 29, but only in reference to the subject of chapter 27.

[8] Guy, 'Constantine', pp. 386–87.

[9] For the importance of the Breton branch of the textual tradition of Gildas's *De Excidio Britanniae*, see Dumville, 'Sub-Roman Britain', pp. 183–84. For more detail, see now Larpi, *Prolegomena*.

[10] Wurdisten, *Vita S. Winwaloei*, ed. by de Smedt, I.1 (pp. 175–76). Translation is my own. For the date of the Life, see Joseph-Claude Poulin's chapter in this volume.

non alio, quo gens barbara, dudum aspersa in armis, moribus indiscreta, Saxonum maternum possedit cespitem, huic se cara soboles in istum conclusit sinum; quo se tuta loco magnis laboribus fessam, ad oram concessit sine bello quietam. Interea miserorum, qui paterna incolebant rura, peste foeda repente exorta, catervatim et absque numero et absque sepultura miseranda sternuntur corpora. Ex hac lue magna ex parte antiqua desolatur patria; tandemque pauci et multo pauci, qui vix ancipitem effugissent gladium, aut Scoticam quamvis inimicam, aut Belgicam, natalem autem patriam linquentes, coacti acriter alienam petivere terram.

And so that I need not repeat Britain's ancient crimes at greater length, let he who would wish to know more about these things read St Gildas, who wrote about the establishment and inhabitation of Britain, and about its wonderful conversion to Christ and its immediate apostasy through its almost pagan behaviour, and about the divine vengeance that sorrowfully followed, and again about its misery, lest it should return completely to cinders and ashes; and he examined well and blame-lessly many such things concerning Britain's deeds [...] But indeed I do not consider its small offshoot, which was conveyed on rafts in former times to this land on this side of the British sea, to be far removed from its habits. At the same time at which the barbaric Saxon people, once cruel in arms and imprudent in habits, possessed the maternal turf, the precious offshoot shut itself up here in this refuge; in this safe place, wearied by great labours, it withdrew itself to a peaceful shore free from war. Meanwhile, since a foul pestilence had suddenly arisen, the pitiable bodies of the wretched who still inhabited the paternal lands were scattered in droves with-out number and without burial. Due to this plague, the great, ancient country was partly abandoned; and at length, a few, indeed very few, of those who had scarcely escaped the swords' edges, forsaking their native country, gathered together bit-terly to strive for a foreign land, either Ireland, however hostile, or Belgica.

Like the author of the *Historia Brittonum*, Wrdisten had clearly read Gildas's work, but he does not identify Maximus's lost soldiers as the first settlers of Brittany. Instead, he fastens upon Gildas's famous portrayal of the Saxon assault on Britain as the explanation for the settlers leaving Britain. According to Gildas, some of the survivors of the Saxon invasion 'transmarinas petebant regiones' (made for lands beyond the sea); for Wrdisten, these were the first set-tlers of Brittany.[11] Others, apparently afterwards, fled from a plague in different directions, including to Ireland and north-eastern Gaul.[12] Whether Wrdisten's reading of Gildas is any more authoritative than that of the *Historia Brittonum*'s

[11] Gildas, *De Excidio Britanniae*, § 25 (pp. 27 and 98).

[12] Wrdisten places the plague *interea* (at this time, in the meantime), but Gildas's plague precedes the invitation to the Saxons to act as mercenaries on behalf of the Britons: Gildas, *De Excidio Britanniae*, § 22.2 (pp. 25 and 96).

source, by virtue of having come from a Breton, is unknown; one suspects not, given the obvious reliance on a single source.

During the ninth century, there was evidently no standard explanation for the origins of Brittany, even among the Britons. There was general agreement that Britons migrated from Britain to Brittany following the ending of Roman power in Britain, but the only source of further information about the period then available was Gildas, who does not mention Brittany specifically. With such disagreement matters were left, until the re-emergence of the topic as a source of interest and controversy in the first half of the twelfth century. The remainder of this chapter addresses questions arising from the twelfth-century accounts of the origins of Brittany. In these accounts, two new ideas emerge: that the *Historia Brittonum*'s *Maximianus* belonged to the family of Constantine the Great, and, more importantly, that the king of the Britons at the time of *Maximianus*'s conquest of Rome and the settlement of Brittany was a certain Cynan son of Eudaf. Such ideas occur in genealogies connected to St Cadog, in the Breton *Life* of St Gurthiern, and in Geoffrey of Monmouth's *History of the Kings of Britain*. It is argued that these ideas emerged due to interactions between the Britons of Wales and the Britons of Brittany in the environs of Monmouth, and subsequently entered the literary record in the important Welsh *clas* church of Llancarfan.

St Cadog of Llancarfan

By the second half of the eleventh century, the *clas* church of Llancarfan (now located roughly between Barry and Cowbridge in the Vale of Glamorgan), dedicated to St Cadog, had become one of the most important ecclesiastical institutions in south-east Wales.[13] During this time, the community of Llancarfan dominated the upper ranks of the diocesan clergy, and regularly accompanied the bishop of Glamorgan as he was undertaking his official duties.[14] One such clergyman, St Cadog's hagiographer Lifris of Llancarfan, is described in a charter witness list as 'filius episcopi archidiaconus Gulat Morcant et magister sancti Catoci' (son of the bishop, archdeacon of Glamorgan, and master of St Cadog [i.e. of Llancarfan]); Lifris was the son of Herewald, Bishop of

[13] Davies, *Book of Llandaf*, pp. 15–16. For *clas* churches, with special reference to Llancarfan, see Charles-Edwards, *Wales and the Britons*, pp. 602–14.

[14] The most detailed account of the Llancarfan community in this period is Davies, *Episcopal Acts*, II, 506–37.

10. EXPLAINING THE ORIGINS OF BRITTANY IN THE TWELFTH CENTURY

Glamorgan (1056–1104), and as such had been promoted to high office.[15] The same remained true in the first half of the twelfth century, following the rebranding of the diocese as the 'bishopric of Llandaf' in 1119 by Bishop Urban (1107–1134).[16] Despite the church of Llancarfan having been given to St Peter's Abbey, Gloucester, by Robert fitz Hamo, the Norman conqueror of Glamorgan, sometime between 1095 and *c.* 1100, the community of Llancarfan continued to dominate the local diocese.[17] In 1134, as many as five members of the Llancarfan community accompanied Bishop Urban on his final visit to the Roman curia prior to his death.[18] One of these five was a certain Caradog, who can probably be identified with Caradog of Llancarfan, the famous hagiographer and 'contemporary' of Geoffrey of Monmouth. In these years, the community of Llancarfan practically ran the diocese of south-east Wales.

We see interest in the origins of Brittany re-emerging in this milieu. Around the time that Robert fitz Hamo gave Llancarfan to St Peter's Abbey in Gloucester, Lifris of Llancarfan composed the *Life* of St Cadog.[19] This is by far the longest saint's *Life* surviving from medieval Wales, which is itself a testament to the significance of Llancarfan. In the surviving manuscript (on which more below), Lifris's authorship colophon is followed immediately by a series of genealogies tracing the ancestry of St Cadog.[20] The placement of the genealogies after the colophon prompted Hywel Emanuel to suggest that the genealogies had not been composed by Lifris but had instead been added to Lifris's text at some point following its composition.[21] This view is supported by the existence of a blatant and significant contradiction between the genealogies and the main text of Lifris's *Life* of St Cadog.[22] Embedded in these genealogies is an account of the settlement of Brittany, based on the version in the *Historia Brittonum*:[23]

---

[15] *Text of the Book of Llan Dâv*, p. 274 (cf. pp. 271 and 273). For these charters, see Davies, *Llandaff Charters*, pp. 129–30.

[16] Davies, *Book of Llandaf*, p. 38.

[17] For the dating of the gift, see Brooke, *The Church and the Welsh Border*, pp. 64–65.

[18] Davies, *Episcopal Acts*, II, 516–17; Davies, *Book of Llandaf*, pp. 105–06.

[19] Brooke, *The Church and the Welsh Border*, pp. 72–73 and 89.

[20] *Vita S. Cadoci*, §§ 45–47 (pp. 116–19).

[21] Emanuel, 'Analysis', p. 20. Christopher Brooke agreed: *The Church and the Welsh Border*, p. 70.

[22] Guy, *Medieval Welsh Genealogy*, pp. 83 and 142–43.

[23] *Vita S. Cadoci*, § 45 (pp. 116–19). I have corrected the text against the manuscript: BL,

[...] Galerius genuit Constantinum magnum filium Helene. Constantinus genuit Constantium. Constantius genuit Maximianum, cum quo milites brittonum exierunt a Brittania, et occidit ipse Gratianum inperatorem [*sic*] romanorum tenuitque imperium totius Europę. Et non dimisit pugiles quos secum a Brittannia adduxit repatriare propter strenuitatem illorum; sed tribuit eis plures prouincias et regiones: quippe a stagno quod est super uerticem montis Iouis usque ad ciuitatem nomine Cantguic et usque ad cumulum occidentalem (id est Cruc Ochideint). Atque ex illis equitibus orta est gens que uocatur Lettau.[24] Maximianus itaque genuit Ouguein. Ouguein genuit Nor. Nor genuit Solor. Solor genuit Gliuguis. Gliuguisus genuit Gundleium. Gundleius genuit beatissimum Cadocum.

[...] Galerius begot Constantinus the Great son of Helena. Constantinus begot Constantius. Constantius begot Maximianus, with whom the soldiers of the Britons left Britain, and he killed Gratianus, emperor of the Romans, and held the empire of all Europe. But he did not send the fighters that he had brought with him from Britain back to their own country, on account of their strength; instead, he granted them many provinces and districts: namely, from the pool on the summit of Mount Jupiter as far as the town called Quentovic and as far as the western mound (that is, *Cruc Ochideint*). And from those horsemen was born the nation which is called *Lettau* [i.e. Llydaw, 'Brittany']. And so Maximianus begot Ouguein. Ouguein begot Nor. Nor begot Solor. Solor begot Gliuguis. Gliuguisus begot Gundleius. Gundleius begot the most blessed Cadocus.

The passage is inserted following a list of Roman emperors that has been converted into a linear pedigree; this is why Constantine the Great (d. 337) is made the son, rather than the successor, of Galerius (d. 311). This list-cum-genealogy has been taken from a text related to the Harleian genealogies.[25] What then follows is a rendition of the *Historia Brittonum*'s story about Maximianus and the settlement of Brittany, with one crucial difference: Maximianus is provided with a genealogical background that is lacking in the *Historia Brittonum*. On the one hand, he is made the son of Constantius (d. 361) and grandson of Constantine the Great; on the other, he is made the father of a certain 'Owain' and ancestor of St Cadog.

The purposes of these innovations in the context of the twelfth century are readily discernible. On one level, they provide St Cadog, the patron saint of Llancarfan, with an illustrious (albeit preposterous) Roman pedigree, traced

---

MS Cotton Vespasian A.xiv, part i, fol. 37[r–v]. Punctuation and translation are my own.

[24] *Lettau* glossed *id est brittones*.

[25] See Guy, 'Constantine', pp. 390–91; Guy, *Medieval Welsh Genealogy*, pp. 81–82 and 272–73.

10. EXPLAINING THE ORIGINS OF BRITTANY IN THE TWELFTH CENTURY

back through Maximianus, the founder of Brittany, through Constantine the Great, the first Christian emperor, and on to Augustus Caesar, 'in cuius tempore natus est Christus' (in whose time Christ was born). However, the emphasis on the foundation of Brittany might be understood as having arisen more specifically from the situation pertaining in the diocese of Glamorgan/ Llandaf in the late eleventh and twelfth centuries. Following the Norman conquest of England, many of the Bretons in William I's army acquired lands in Britain.[26] So prominent were the Bretons in the kingdom that references to *Brittones* in Anglo-Norman documents almost invariably relate to Bretons rather than indigenous Britons.[27] One important site of Breton settlement was Monmouth, where Wihenoc of La Boussac was made lord after the revolt of Earl Roger of Hereford in 1075.[28] Following the Norman conquest in 1066, Monmouth castle was initially one of the most westerly outposts of direct Norman lordship along the borders of South Wales.[29]

Although Monmouth became part of the diocese of Hereford, there were good reasons for the diocesan clergy of Glamorgan, and more specifically those associated with the *clas* church of Llancarfan, to maintain a keen interest in Monmouth's ecclesiastical affairs. Monmouth's new Benedictine priory, founded by 1086, held as many as seven properties that were claimed for Llandaf in the charters recorded in the Book of Llandaf (written *c.* 1132).[30] One pair of char-

---

[26] In general, see Keats-Rohan, 'Bretons and Normans'; Keats-Rohan, *Domesday People*, ch. 3.

[27] Cf. Keats-Rohan, *Domesday People*, p. 38; Pryce, 'British or Welsh?', pp. 792–94.

[28] So Keats-Rohan, *Domesday People*, pp. 54–55, following the evidence of *The Text of the Book of Llan Dâv*, pp. 277–78. Guillotel, however, has cast doubt upon the latter record, suggesting instead that Wihenoc was a follower of William I who was established in Monmouth prior to Roger's revolt, perhaps in 1070 or 1071: 'Une famille bretonne', pp. 362–64.

[29] Davies, *Book of Llandaf*, pp. 20–21 and 30; Crouch, 'Slow Death of Kingship', pp. 24–26; Crouch, 'Transformation', pp. 3–6.

[30] Davies, *Book of Llandaf*, pp. 48 (and n. 19), 171–72, 180, 183–84, and 188–89. Llandaf's claims are documented in the following charters (numbered according to the pages on which they appear in *Text of the Book of Llan Dâv*): 72a, 74/171b, 183a, 201, 210a, 240, and 246. Although these charters were edited to varying degrees in the interests of Llandaf in the early twelfth century, it is probable that they are all (with the possible exception of 240) based on original documents, dating from between the early seventh century (72a) and *c.* 1020 (246): see Davies, *Llandaff Charters*, pp. 92–94, 107, 110–11, 116, 118, and 125–26. For the date and probable authenticity (*pace* Davies) of 72a, see Guy, '*Life* of St Dyfrig', pp. 21–22 and 28–30. For a recent restatement of the view that the essential details of the charters in the Book of Llandaf (principally the names of the donors, beneficiaries, properties, and witnesses) derive from original records of the seventh to eleventh centuries, see Sims-Williams, *Book of Llandaf*.

ters, probably deriving from a record made around 733, even claims that the old church of Monmouth itself had been given to Llandaf.[31] The first abbatial witness listed in these documents is *Dagan*, abbot of Llancarfan, raising the possibility that it was really Llancarfan, rather than Llandaf, that had originally been given the church at Monmouth (the idea that the bishop of Llandaf was the beneficiary of so early a gift is a later conceit).[32] Significantly, the early church of Monmouth was dedicated to St Cadog, and had formed the most important component of the endowment given to Monmouth Priory at its foundation.[33] In this context, the portrayal of St Cadog in the genealogies as the direct descendant of the founder of Brittany may have been a subtle ploy to encourage mutual respect between the new Bretons of Monmouth and the old clergy of the diocese of Llandaf, led by the community of Llancarfan. Since the text of the genealogies is preserved in a manuscript written in Monmouth Priory, as is discussed further below, the ploy presumably did not fall on deaf ears.

Cynan son of Eudaf

The story embedded in the genealogies of St Cadog discussed above was not the only attempt by the community of Llancarfan to wed their patron saint to traditions about the settlement of Brittany. Other attempts sought to incorporate a new element into the story, one that is absent from the *Historia Brittonum*. This is the idea that a certain Cynan son of Eudaf was king of the Britons at the time of Maximianus's expedition to Rome, and was thereby responsible for the settlement of Brittany.[34] A somewhat garbled example of this story in

[31] Charter 186b specifically states that the church of Monmouth was given to the bishop of Llandaf, whereas an apparent doublet of the same record, charter 175, merely claims that Monmouth was the location of a transaction involving an unnamed church. See Charles-Edwards, *Wales and the Britons*, pp. 261–64; Sims-Williams, *Book of Llandaf*, pp. 96–97; cf. Davies, *Llandaff Charters*, pp. 108 and 112; Davies, *Book of Llandaf*, pp. 179 and 181.

[32] *Text of the Book of Llan Dâv*, pp. 175 and 187. Sims-Williams maintains that the original beneficiaries of the charters were bishops, albeit bishops whose sees were not necessarily located at Llandaf: *Book of Llandaf*, ch. 7. For an alternative view, see my review of Sims-Williams, *Book of Llandaf*, pp. 226–27. Even if the church of Monmouth had originally been given to Llancarfan in the eighth century, it is probable that the community of Llancarfan was content to accept Llandaf's claim to it in the twelfth century, given the close involvement of the Llancarfan community in Llandaf.

[33] See further below, pp. 257–58.

[34] Some have claimed that Cynan appears earlier in two texts from Brittany, the *Livre des faits d'Arthur* and the *Life* of St Goeznovius, but the dating of these texts is hotly disputed. For

10. EXPLAINING THE ORIGINS OF BRITTANY IN THE TWELFTH CENTURY

a Llancarfan context appears as part of another genealogy of St Cadog, found among the genealogies in Oxford, Jesus College, MS 20. Although this manuscript was written around 1400, the genealogy itself was probably constructed in the twelfth century:[35]

> Catt6c m. Gwynlli6 m. Gli6s m. Filur m. Nor mab Owein mab Maxen. Maxen Wledic brenhin y Brytanyeit, a gwedy hynny yn amhera6dyr yn Rufein, a Chynan yn vrenhin yn y le. Kynan m. Eudaf *m. Custenin m. Maxen* m. Maximianus m. Constantinus m. Custeint. Mam Constantinus oed Elen Luedya6c, yr hon a enilla6d y groes yg Karusalem, ac a duc rann genthi y Gonstantinobyl, a ran arall a anuones y'r Brytanyeit.

> Catt6c son of Gwynlli6 son of Gli6s son of Filur son of Nor son of Owein son of Maxen. Maxen Wledic [was] king of the Britons, and after that emperor in Rome, with Cynan as king [of the Britons] in his place. Kynan son of Eudaf *son of Custenin son of Maxen* son of Maximianus son of Constantinus son of Custeint. The mother of Constantinus was Elen Luedya6c, who obtained the cross in Jerusalem, and brought a part with her to Constantinople, and another part she sent to the Britons.

I have argued elsewhere that the words *m. Custenin m. Maxen* (italicized) were inserted into this text at a late stage.[36] Those words aside, one can see that this genealogy of St Cadog agrees closely with that inspected above. Cadog's ancestor Owain is again made the son of a 'Maximus' character, here called *Maxen Wledic*, a name for Maximus that became customary in Wales from the late twelfth century onwards.[37] Nevertheless, the form *Maximianus* appears later in the text, as the son (rather than grandson) of Constantine the Great, showing the persistent influence of chapter 27 of the *Historia Brittonum*. Although the text does not specify that Maximus's army settled in Brittany, there is a clear allusion to the same story, with the addition that Cynan son of Eudaf became king of the Britons once 'Maxen Wledic' was emperor of Rome. Moreover, discounting the two probably intrusive generations, Cynan son of Eudaf is made the grandson of 'Maximianus'.

A less corrupt and more certainly early example of the same story appears in the *Life* of St Gurthiern. This text appears at the beginning of the cartulary

---

references to the debate, see Guy, 'Constantine', p. 392 n. 60 (cf. p. 397 n. 85).

[35] Guy, *Medieval Welsh Genealogy*, p. 340 (§ 4).

[36] Guy, 'Constantine', pp. 393–94; Guy, *Medieval Welsh Genealogy*, pp. 150–53.

[37] Guy, 'Constantine', pp. 400–01; cf. Sims-Williams, *Rhai Addasiadau Cymraeg Canol*, pp. 6–9.

of Sainte-Croix de Quimperlé, a Benedictine abbey situated in the *département* of Finistère in the west of Brittany. The cartulary was probably compiled in the 1120s and early 1130s in order to safe-guard the possessions of the abbey, following a dispute with the abbey of Saint-Sauveur de Redon over possession of the estate of Belle-Île.[38] It is likely that the *Life* of St Gurthiern was assembled at the same time by the cartulary's main scribe, Gurheden (probably d. 1131 × 1133).[39] St Gurthiern became important for Sainte-Croix when his relics were 'discovered' for the abbey on the Île de Groix, apparently during the time of Abbot Benedict (1066–1079).[40] A chronicle in the cartulary records that a church was dedicated to Gurthiern in 1089, though the location of the church is not specified.[41]

Of present interest is the short genealogical statement with which the *Life* begins:[42]

Haec est genealogia sancti Gurthierni, nobilis genere, incliti officio, quam quidam laicus fidelis nomine Iuthael filius Aidan demonstrauit, non pro terreno munere sed pro celesti. Igitur Gurthiern filius Boni filii Glou filii Abros filii Dos filii Iacob filii Genethauc filii Iudgual filii Beli filii Outham senis filii Maximiani filii Constantii filii Constantini filii Helenę, quę crucem Christi habuisse refertur [...] Beli et Kenan duo fratres erant, filii Outham senis. Ipse Kenan tenuit principatum quando perrexerunt Britones ad Romam. Illic tenuerunt Lęticiam, et reliq[...][43] Beli filius Annę, quam dicunt esse consobrinam Mariae, genetricis Christi.

This is the genealogy of Saint Gurthiern, noble in birth and renowned in office, which a certain faithful layman called Iuthael son of Aidan has revealed, not for earthly but for heavenly reward. Thus, Gurthiern son of Bonus son of Glou son of Abros son of Dos son of Iacob son of Genethauc son of Iudgual son of Beli son of Outham the Old son of Maximianus son of Constantius son of Constantinus son

---

[38] Cyprien Henry in *Cartulaire de Sainte-Croix de Quimperlé*, ed. by Henry, Quaghebeur, and Tanguy, pp. 24–25 and 28–29; cf. Jankulak, 'Breton *vitae*', pp. 225–26.

[39] Jankulak, 'Breton *vitae*', p. 231; Poulin, *L'hagiographie bretonne*, pp. 456–57.

[40] *Cartulaire de l'Abbaye de Sainte-Croix de Quimperlé*, p. 45. Cf. Tanguy, 'De la vie de saint Cadoc', pp. 168–69; Jankulak, 'Breton *vitae*', pp. 238–40.

[41] *Cartulaire de l'Abbaye de Sainte-Croix de Quimperlé*, p. 105.

[42] Text taken from BL, MS Egerton 2802, fols 4ᵛ–5ʳ; see the facsimile edition in *Cartulaire de Sainte-Croix de Quimperlé*, ed. by Henry, Quaghebeur, and Tanguy, and cf. *Cartulaire de l'Abbaye de Sainte-Croix de Quimperlé*, ed. by Maître and de Berthou, p. 42. Punctuation and translation are my own. For full translations of the *Life* into French and English, see respectively Tanguy, 'De la vie de saint Cadoc', pp. 169–72 and Jankulak, 'Breton *vitae*', pp. 244–48.

[43] The end of this word is illegible.

10. EXPLAINING THE ORIGINS OF BRITTANY IN THE TWELFTH CENTURY

of Helena, who is said to have had the Cross of Christ [...] Beli and Kenan were two brothers, sons of Outham the Old. This Kenan held dominion when the Britons went to Rome. From there they took *Lęticia* [i.e. *Letauia*, 'Brittany'] and [...] Beli [was] son of Anna, whom they say was cousin of Mary, mother of Christ.

The genealogy of St Gurthiern offered in this passage is undoubtedly fictional and has been assembled from various earlier sources, especially the *Historia Brittonum* and a text resembling the Harleian genealogies.[44] More notable, however, is the appearance of the two new elements in the story of the settlement of Brittany that have been identified in texts originating in Llancarfan. The *Historia Brittonum*'s Maximianus has been inserted into the same genealogical context as is found in the genealogies appended to Lifris's *Life* of St Cadog: he is the son of Constantius and grandson of Constantine the Great. Moreover, one finds here the story of Cynan son of Eudaf (*Outham* in Old Breton or Old Welsh), who ruled the Britons during the expedition to Rome and the subsequent settlement of Brittany. Here, Cynan is made the grandson of Maximianus, just as in the genealogy in Oxford, Jesus College, MS 20 once the two probably interpolated generations are discounted.

The spellings of some of the names in the Gurthiern genealogy, including the name *Kenan*, clearly imply that the genealogy derives from Welsh sources.[45] The links with the St Cadog material examined above would seem to implicate Llancarfan as the most obvious place for such sources to have originated. Intriguingly, there is further evidence for a connection between Llancarfan and Sainte-Croix de Quimperlé. Bernard Tanguy has drawn attention to an episode in Lifris's *Life* of St Cadog where Cadog is said to have travelled to an island off the coast of Brittany called 'Inis Catbodu', and there founded a monastery.[46] As Tanguy pointed out, this story concerns the Île de Saint-Cado, an island in the estuary of the River Étel in the south of Brittany.[47] The real priory on the Île de Saint-Cado was donated to Sainte-Croix by Alain Fergant, Duke of Brittany, in

---

[44] Guy, 'Constantine', p. 393; Guy, *Medieval Welsh Genealogy*, p. 88; Tanguy, 'De la vie de saint Cadoc', p. 174; cf. Chadwick, 'Note on the Name Vortigern', pp. 39–43 and (more dubiously) Fleuriot, 'Old Breton Genealogies', pp. 3–4.

[45] Thus, the *e* in *Kenan* represents a distinctively Welsh sound change (/ən/ < /ön/ < /un/ in pretonic syllables) that did not occur in Breton. Similarly, the *au* in *Genethauc* represents another distinctively Welsh sound change (/au/ < /ɔː/ in stressed syllables). See Tanguy, 'De la vie de saint Cadoc', p. 175; Bernard Tanguy in *Cartulaire de Sainte-Croix de Quimperlé*, ed. by Henry, Quaghebeur, and Tanguy, p. 84.

[46] *Vita S. Cadoci*, § 35 (pp. 96–99); Tanguy, 'De la vie de saint Cadoc', pp. 161–67.

[47] See too Doble, *St Cadoc*, pp. 15–22.

1089.[48] This may suggest that it was the monks of Sainte-Croix who were Lifris's source of information about the Île de Saint-Cado. That Lifris had acquired genuine information about the island is implied not only by his evocative (though not entirely accurate) description of the island's topography, but also by his specification that Cadog appointed a prior called Cadwaladr to govern the priory following Cadog's departure. An undated (but probably early-eleventh-century) charter in the cartulary of Sainte-Croix shows that there had indeed been a prior of the Île de Saint-Cado with that name.[49] Furthermore, the charter calls the saint of the island 'sanctus Catuodus', just like Lifris. Since Lifris was writing after the donation of the priory to Sainte-Croix, it is most probable that he or his informant took the names from a document deriving from Sainte-Croix. All these factors prompted Tanguy to suggest that there had been an exchange of information between Llancarfan and Sainte-Croix: Lifris received information about the 'sanctus Catuodus' of the Île de Saint-Cado, whom he equated with St Cadog, and Sainte-Croix received the first part of the Life of St Gurthiern, with its Welsh name forms.[50] It may be significant that Sainte-Croix was given the priory of the Île de Saint-Cado in 1089, the same year in which a church was dedicated to St Gurthiern. Was this the year in which the exchange took place, a decade or so before Lifris completed his *Life* of St Cadog? Or did Gurheden receive Gurthiern's genealogy at a later time, following the establishment of a relationship between the two houses by Lifris a generation earlier?

There is a further complication. The *Life* of St Gurthiern states that Gurthiern's genealogy was revealed not by Lifris of Llancarfan, but by 'a certain faithful layman called Iuthael son of Aidan'. Some have speculated that Iuthael son of Aidan was a professional genealogist.[51] However, given the nature of the genealogical material incorporated into the *Life* of St Gurthiern, a more compelling identification can be proposed. Tanguy noted that the *Life* of St Gurthiern contains the only instance of the name *Aidan* in extant Breton documents.[52] In origin, the name is Irish (OI *Áedán*), but it was also borrowed

---

[48] *Cartulaire de l'Abbaye de Sainte-Croix de Quimperlé*, ed. by Maître and de Berthou, § CVII (pp. 262–63).

[49] *Cartulaire de l'Abbaye de Sainte-Croix de Quimperlé*, ed. by Maître and de Berthou, § CIII (pp. 258–59).

[50] Tanguy, 'De la vie de saint Cadoc', pp. 164–65, 175, and 179.

[51] Fleuriot, 'Old Breton Genealogies', p. 6; Brett, 'Breton Latin Literature', p. 8; Jankulak, 'Breton *vitae*', p. 232.

[52] Tanguy, 'De la vie de saint Cadoc', p. 173; Bernard Tanguy in *Cartulaire de Sainte-Croix de Quimperlé*, ed. by Henry, Quaghebeur, and Tanguy, p. 84.

10. EXPLAINING THE ORIGINS OF BRITTANY IN THE TWELFTH CENTURY

from Irish by the Britons of Wales. This is significant considering the unambiguously Brittonic name of Aidan's son Iuthael. One might therefore look for Iuthael son of Aidan in Wales.

Strikingly, a certain Aidan appears as a priest of Llancarfan in three charters in the Book of Llandaf dating from the 1070s. The clerical witness lists in the three charters read as follows:[53]

> Charter 267 (*c.* 1070): De clericis testes sunt Hergualdus episcopus, Moruarch et Merchuiu canonici, Gulbrit et Tutnerth et Selis, Ioseph lector Catoci, Aidan presbiter Catoci, Catguaret presbiter sancti Docunni.

> Charter 271 (*c.* 1075): De clericis testes sunt Heruualdus episcopus, Mormarch presbiter, Merchuiu presbiter, Tutnerth, Lifris filius episcopi archidiaconus et magister sancti Catoci, Ionas presbiter, Aidan presbiter sancti Catoci, Gurci presbiter sancti Catoci, Gurcinnif presbiter sancti Ilduti, Iohannes presbiter sancti Docunni.

> Charter 272 (*c.* 1072): De clericis testes sunt Heruualdus[54] episcopus, Lifricus filius suus, Mormarch presbiter sancti Teliaui, Merchbiu presbiter, Aidan presbiter sancti Catoci, Ioseph doctor Catoci, Gurci presbiter sancti Catoci, Benedictus presbiter Bassalec.

> Charter 267 (*c.* 1070): From the clergy the witnesses are Bishop Hergualdus, the canons Moruarch and Merchuiu, Gulbrit and Tutnerth and Selis, Ioseph the teacher of Cadog [i.e. of Llancarfan], Aidan the priest of Cadog, Catguaret the priest of St Dogwyn [i.e. of Llandochau Fach/Llandough].

> Charter 271 (*c.* 1075): From the clergy the witnesses are Bishop Heruualdus, Mormarch the priest, Merchuiu the priest, Tutnerth, Lifris the son of the bishop, archdeacon, and master of St Cadog, Ionas the priest, Aidan the priest of St Cadog, Gurci the priest of St Cadog, Gurcinnif the priest of St Illtud [i.e. of Llanilltud Fawr/Llantwit Major], Iohannes the priest of St Dogwyn.

> Charter 272 (*c.* 1072): From the clergy the witnesses are Bishop Heruualdus, Lifricus his son, Mormarch the priest of St Teilo [i.e. of Llandaf], Merchbiu the priest, Aidan the priest of St Cadog, Ioseph the teacher of Cadog, Gurci the priest of St Cadog, Benedictus the priest of Basaleg.

---

[53] *Text of the Book of Llan Dâv*, pp. 268 and 271–73. For the dates, see Davies, *Llandaff Charters*, p. 129.

[54] *uual* is repeated at the end of one line and the beginning of the next.

These three witness lists provide an insight into the composition of the episcopal household of the bishop of Glamorgan during the 1070s. The relative prominence of the clergy of Llancarfan is immediately apparent: alongside the bishop, two canons of Llandaf (Mormarch and Merchbiu), two priests of Llandochau Fach (Catguaret and Iohannes), a priest of Llanilltud Fawr (Gurcinnif), and a priest of Basaleg (Benedictus), one regularly finds two priests of Llancarfan (Aidan and Gurci), the teacher of Llancarfan (Ioseph), and the archdeacon and master of Llancarfan (Lifris), himself the son of the bishop. Here Lifris, the author of the *Life* of St Cadog, is seen to be a regular companion of a fellow Llancarfan clergyman called Aidan. Is this the father of the layman Iuthael who 'revealed' Gurthiern's genealogy to the monks of Sainte-Croix, cobbled together from various pseudo-historical and genealogical records available in Llancarfan? The genealogy certainly seems to derive from Llancarfan sources. In addition to the material concerning Maximianus and Cynan son of Eudaf, which is known to have been circulating in Llancarfan, the Gurthiern genealogy has been constructed from the *Historia Brittonum* and a text related to the Harleian genealogies, both of which were available in Llancarfan, as shown by the genealogy of St Cadog appended to Lifris's *Life* of the saint. The example of Herewald and his son Lifris suggests that clerical offspring were common in this environment. Herewald's other son, Mai, was a layman.[55] Indeed, a family of laymen probably descending from Lifris held Llancarfan property into the twelfth century.[56] There would be few men better placed to convey the genealogical material found in the *Life* of St Gurthiern than a lay son of Aidan, priest of Llancarfan and known associate of Lifris of Llancarfan.

Geoffrey of Monmouth

There is another, much better-known story about the settlement of Brittany belonging to the twelfth century: that found in Geoffrey of Monmouth's *History of the Kings of Britain*, completed in or shortly before 1138.[57] Compared with the rather sparse sources examined above, Geoffrey tells his story much more coherently and at greater length. He found ways to incorporate both of the new elements of the story associated with Llancarfan sources. But, as is ever the case with Geoffrey, he chose to reshape rather than simply reproduce his

[55] Davies, *Episcopal Acts*, II, 515.

[56] Davies, *Episcopal Acts*, II, 517–19; Davies, *Book of Llandaf*, pp. 106–07.

[57] Geoffrey of Monmouth, *The History of the Kings of Britain*, v. 80–88.

sources for greater narrative effect.[58] Thus, he adopts the *Historia Brittonum*'s Maximianus into the family of Constantine the Great, but not as the son of Constantine or Constantine's son Constantius; instead, Geoffrey makes his Maximianus the cousin of Constantine's mother Helena, through an invented father Loelinus, Helena's uncle. Similarly, he incorporates the idea that Cynan (his Conanus Meriadocus) was the leader of the Britons who settled in Brittany during Maximianus's assault on the Continent; but Conanus Meriadocus is now the nephew, rather than the son, of Octavius, Geoffrey's Eudaf. Octavius is no longer the son of Maximianus, as in the *Life* of St Gurthiern and in the genealogy in Oxford, Jesus College, MS 20, discounting the two interpolated generations. Rather, he becomes Maximianus's father-in-law, once Maximianus marries his unnamed daughter and inherits the kingdom of Britain. Contrary to what has sometimes been supposed, these genealogical variations do not indicate that Geoffrey drew on some early, now-lost variant of the story.[59] The genealogical re-arrangement was contrived by Geoffrey himself, since it allowed him to narrate a succession dispute between Maximianus (Octavius's son-in-law) and Conanus (Octavius's nephew). Succession disputes of this type, often involving female heiresses, were of great interest to Geoffrey.[60]

The parameters of Geoffrey's story indicate that he was familiar with the ideas circulating in Llancarfan. One of these ideas, the genealogical reorienta-tion of Maximianus, pertains specifically to St Cadog's genealogy, and one might suppose that Geoffrey learned about it from the community of Llancarfan. The other idea, concerning the supposed role of Cynan son of Eudaf in the settle-ment of Brittany, is more general, but there are nevertheless two reasons for thinking that Geoffrey learned about it in the context of interaction with the community of Llancarfan.

Geoffrey informs us that he was an associate of Caradog of Llancarfan.[61] It has already been noted that Caradog of Llancarfan is probably to be identi-fied with the Caradog in the entourage of Bishop Urban of Llandaf in 1134. Caradog of Llancarfan is known to have written at least two saints' *Lives* (a *Life* of St Gildas and a revised version of Lifris's *Life* of St Cadog), and it has been argued that he was responsible for several more.[62] It is possible that

---

[58] Cf. Guy, 'Geoffrey of Monmouth's Welsh Sources'.

[59] As discussed in Guy, 'Constantine', pp. 395–96.

[60] Cf. Tolhurst, *Geoffrey of Monmouth*, pp. 118–22.

[61] Geoffrey of Monmouth, *The History of the Kings of Britain*, XI. 208. 601–02.

[62] Most recently by Davies, *Book of Llandaf*, pp. 133–36.

Geoffrey was sent source material by Caradog.[63] Geoffrey made extensive use of the *Historia Brittonum* and a text related to the Harleian genealogies.[64] It has already been noted that the same sources were used to compile the genealogies appended to Lifris's *Life* of St Cadog and the genealogy of St Gurthiern that was probably sent to Sainte-Croix from Llancarfan. Other notable instances of these sources being used in the twelfth century can be linked specifically to Caradog of Llancarfan. Both sources were used during the compilation of the Book of Llandaf.[65] It has been suggested that Caradog of Llancarfan was the author of the Book of Llandaf, and in any case he must have been aware of its production.[66] A genealogy of St Petroc found in Gotha, Forschungsbibliothek, MS Mm.I.81, fol. 148ᵛ was constructed using a combination of elements drawn from St Cadog's genealogy and from a version of a pedigree found in the Harleian genealogies.[67] The same manuscript contains the only surviving copy of Caradog's *Life* of St Cadog.[68] Lastly, the *Historia Brittonum* and a text like the Harleian genealogies were used in Glastonbury Abbey to augment William of Malmesbury's *De antiquitate Glastonie ecclesie*, probably late in the twelfth century.[69] Earlier in the century, Caradog of Llancarfan had written a *Life* of St Gildas for Glastonbury Abbey.[70] If it were Caradog who supplied Geoffrey with copies of the *Historia Brittonum* and the Harleian genealogies, it may also have been Caradog who informed him about stories circulating in Llancarfan concerning the settlement of Brittany.

But there may have been more complicated factors at work. Geoffrey's self-declared epithet, *Monumutensis*, implies that he came from Monmouth. The Breton influence on Monmouth, instigated by Wihenoc of La Boussac, has already been discussed. It was exactly this Breton influence in the place of

---

[63] The following summarizes an argument made in Guy, *Medieval Welsh Genealogy*, pp. 79–100.

[64] Guy, 'Geoffrey of Monmouth's Welsh Sources', pp. 42–58.

[65] Cf. Guy, '*Life* of St Dyfrig', pp. 2 n. 3 and 10.

[66] Davies, *Book of Llandaf*, pp. 136–42.

[67] *De Progenie Sancti Petroci*; cf. Jankulak, *Medieval Cult of St Petroc*, pp. 10–13.

[68] Caradog of Llancarfan, *Vita S. Cadoci*; cf. Grosjean, 'De Codice Hagiographico Gothano', pp. 98–99.

[69] *The Early History of Glastonbury*, § 4 (pp. 52–53, and see pp. 187–88, nn. 22 and 24); cf. Gransden, 'Growth of the Glastonbury Traditions', pp. 356–57; Thornton, 'Glastonbury and the Glastening', pp. 195–96 and 200–02.

[70] Caradog of Llancarfan, *Vita S. Gildae*.

10. EXPLAINING THE ORIGINS OF BRITTANY IN THE TWELFTH CENTURY

Geoffrey's origin that originally led J. E. Lloyd to suggest that Geoffrey himself might have been Breton.[71] Whatever the case about Geoffrey's ethnic background, his origin in Monmouth remains significant. Geoffrey probably received his earliest schooling in the newly founded Monmouth Priory. The Breton influence on the early years of Monmouth Priory is clear. The priory was founded by Wihenoc sometime before 1086 as a house of Saint-Florent-de-Saumur.[72] At that time, the abbot of Saint-Florent-de-Saumur was William of Dol (abbot 1070–1118), who, like Wihenoc himself, was a member of a prominent family from the region of Dol in Brittany. Many of the earliest monks of Monmouth Priory were no doubt from Brittany.[73]

As mentioned above, the primary endowment for the new priory in Monmouth was the old church of St Cadog, which in early times had allegedly been a possession of Llandaf, though perhaps had really been a possession of Llancarfan. The importance of the church of St Cadog to the first monks of the priory is mentioned in the priory's foundation charter:[74]

> Notum sit diligentiae vestrae quod ego Wihenocus [...] struxi in castro meo de Monemue ecclesiam, eamque in perpetuam elemosinam dedi monachis sancti Florentii de Salmuro, unde evocavi monachos ad praedictam ecclesiam meam inhabitandam; et ut ibi Deo servituri regulariter viverent dedi eis diversas possessiones, tam in agris, quam in ecclesiis et decimis; videlicet, ecclesiam sancti Cadoci iuxta castrum meum sitam in fundo, et dominio meo, ubi primum monachi praefati, antequam ecclesia Monemue perficeretur, aliquandiu inhabitaverant [...]

> May it be known to your diligence that I, Wihenoc, [...] built in my castle of Monmouth a church, and I gave it in perpetual alms to the monks of Saint-Florent-de-Saumur, from where I summoned monks to dwell in my aforesaid church; and so that they might live there serving God in accordance with the monastic rule, I gave them various properties, as much in land as in churches and tithes: namely, the church of St Cadog, sited in an estate next to my castle in my lordship, where the aforementioned monks first lived for a while before the church of Monmouth was completed [...]

---

[71] Lloyd, 'Geoffrey of Monmouth', pp. 466–68.

[72] Burton, 'Transition and Transformation', pp. 22 and 33.

[73] Cf. Harris, 'Kalendar of the *Vitae Sanctorum Wallensium*', pp. 14–16.

[74] *Monasticon Anglicanum*, IV, 596, no. 1; *Chartes anciennes du prieuré de Monmouth*, p. 15, no. 1. Translation is my own. Guillotel has suggested that this charter is a fabrication of the twelfth century, especially because of the anachronistic mention of Wihenoc's seal: 'Une famille bretonne', p. 365 n. 26. If so, this only emphasizes the perceived importance of the church of St Cadog to the monks of Monmouth.

Not only was Monmouth's old church of St Cadog given to the new priory, but the monks of the priory actually lived in the church of St Cadog for the first twenty years or so of the priory's existence (the new priory building was consecrated in 1101/02).[75] The cult of St Cadog must have left a lasting impression upon the monks of Monmouth, for even a century later they chose to copy out a major collection of saints' *Lives* dominated by Lifris's *Life* of St Cadog, which fills most of five of the manuscript's fourteen quires.[76] This manuscript is now BL, MS Cotton Vespasian A.xiv, part i. Kathleen Hughes once suggested that most of its contents had been collected initially in St Peter's Abbey, Gloucester, which, as mentioned above, had been given the church of Llancarfan sometime between 1095 and *c.* 1100.[77] Be that as it may, the Monmouth scribes copying the manuscript clearly had more than a passive interest in St Cadog. They expanded Lifris's text on two fronts: a different scribe from the one responsible for the main text inserted a series of documents derived from the archive of Llancarfan,[78] while a further scribe added various passages from Caradog of Llancarfan's version of the *Life* of St Cadog.[79] The monks of Monmouth remained adherents of St Cadog long after they abandoned the old church of St Cadog in Monmouth in favour of the newly constructed priory. That Caradog's work should be known in a priory that would certainly have been familiar to Geoffrey in his youth might cause us to wonder whether Caradog was Geoffrey's *contemporaneus* in quite a literal sense; did the two know each other from their early days, having perhaps spent time together in the Breton-influenced priory of Monmouth?

It is difficult not to believe that the renewed interest in the origins of Brittany witnessed in the twelfth century arose from the new political and cultural cir-

---

[75] Harris, 'Kalendar of the *Vitae Sanctorum Wallensium*', pp. 12 and 16.

[76] The manuscript is conventionally dated to *c.* 1200, but recent reanalysis of its palaeography by Professor Teresa Webber (pers. comm.) has suggested that it should be dated a little earlier, to sometime in the last third of the twelfth century: cf. Guy, '*Life* of St Dyfrig', p. 6 n. 17. The manuscript was first attributed to Monmouth Priory by Harris, 'Kalendar of the *Vitae Sanctorum Wallensium*', p. 20.

[77] Hughes, *Celtic Britain*, pp. 58–64. Gloucester's role might have been less fundamental than Hughes supposed: see Guy, 'Vespasian Life of St Teilo'.

[78] *Vita S. Cadoci*, §§ 48–68 (pp. 118–37); cf. Charles-Edwards, *Wales and the Britons*, pp. 256–61 and 272–73; Sims-Williams, *Book of Llandaf*, pp. 39–41.

[79] *Vita S. Cadoci*, §§ 18, 20, and 32 (pp. 62–67 and 94–95), in addition to various shorter passages silently incorporated into Lifris's text by Wade-Evans. Cf. Emanuel, 'Analysis', pp. 223–26.

cumstances pertaining in what is now south-east Wales, where it was given literary form thanks to the connections between the *clas* church of Llancarfan, the episcopal centre of Llandaf, and the Benedictine priory of Monmouth. It was here that all the major players, including Lifris of Llancarfan and the contemporaries Caradog of Llancarfan and Geoffrey of Monmouth, originated. It was here that the most informative early texts circulated, including the *Historia Brittonum* and a version of the Harleian genealogies. Perhaps most significantly, it was here that countless unrecorded interactions took place between the Britons of Wales and the Britons of Brittany, who often found themselves aligned with opposing political factions despite their evident common cultural heritage. Well might these Britons have wondered how it all began.

Dr Ben Guy is a Research Associate in the School of Welsh at Cardiff University. His interests range across early Insular history, medieval historical writing, manuscript studies, and medieval Welsh literature. He is the author of *Medieval Welsh Genealogy: An Introduction and Textual Study* (Woodbridge: Boydell, 2020).

Works Cited

Manuscripts and Archival Sources

Gotha, Forschungsbibliothek, MS Mm.I.81
London, BL, MS Cotton Vespasian A.xiv, part i
London, BL, MS Egerton 2802
London, BL, MS Harley 3859
Oxford, Jesus College, MS 20

Primary Sources

Armes Prydein: The Prophecy of Britain, from the Book of Taliesin, ed. by I. Williams, English version by R. Bromwich, Medieval and Modern Welsh Series, 6 ([Dublin]: Dublin Institute for Advanced Studies, 1972)

Caradog of Llancarfan, *Vita S. Cadoci*, ed. by P. Grosjean, 'Vie de Saint Cadoc par Caradoc de Llancarfan', *AnBoll*, 60 (1942), 35–67

Caradog of Llancarfan, *Vita S. Gildae*, in *Two Lives of Gildas: By a Monk of Ruys, and Caradoc of Llancarfan*, trans. by H. Williams (Felinfach: Llanerch, 1990), pp. 80–103 (repr. from *Gildas*, ed. by H. Williams, 2 pts, Cymmrodorion Record Series, 3 (London: Nutt, 1899–1901), ii: *Gildae De Excidio Britanniae / Gildas: The Ruin of Britain* (1901), pp. 315–420 (pp. 390–413))

Cartulaire de l'abbaye de Sainte-Croix de Quimperlé, ed. by L. Maître and P. de Berthou, 2nd edn (Rennes: Plihon et Hommay, 1904)

Cartulaire de Sainte-Croix de Quimperlé, ed. by C. Henry, J. Quaghebeur, and B. Tanguy, Sources médiévales d'histoire de Bretagne, 4 (Rennes: Presses universitaires de Rennes, 2014)

Chartes anciennes du prieuré de Monmouth en Angleterre, ed. by P. Marchegay (Vendée: Les Roches-Baritaud, 1879)

De progenie sancti Petroci, in P. Grosjean, 'Vies et miracles de S. Petroc i. Le dossier du manuscrit de Gotha', *AnBoll*, 74 (1956), 131–88, at p. 188

Geoffrey of Monmouth, *The History of the Kings of Britain: An Edition and Translation of* De gestis Britonum [Historia Regum Britanniae], ed. by M. D. Reeve, trans. by N. Wright, Arthurian Studies, 69 (Woodbridge: Boydell, 2007)

Gildas, *De Excidio Britanniae*, in *Gildas: The Ruin of Britain and Other Works*, ed. and trans. by M. Winterbottom (London: Phillimore, 1978)

Historia Brittonum (Harley 3859), in E. Faral, *La légende arthurienne: études et documents*, 3 vols (Paris: Champion, 1929), iii, 5–62

Monasticon Anglicanum: A History of the Abbies and Other Monasteries, Hospitals, Frieries, and Cathedral and Collegiate Churches, with their Dependencies, in England and Wales [...] Originally Published in Latin by Sir William Dugdale, Kᵗ·, Garter Principal King at Arms, new ed. by J. Caley, H. Ellis, and B. Bandinel, 6 vols in 8 (London: Longman, Harding, and Harding, 1817–1830; repr. London: Bohn, 1846)

The Early History of Glastonbury: An Edition, Translation and Study of William of Malmesbury's De Antiquitate Glastonie Ecclesie, ed. and trans. by J. Scott (Woodbridge: Boydell, 1981)

The Text of the Book of Llan Dâv: Reproduced from the Gwysaney Manuscript, ed. by J. G. Evans with J. Rhys, repr. (Aberystwyth: National Library of Wales, 1979)

Vita S. Cadoci, in *Vitae Sanctorum Britanniae et Genealogiae*, ed. and trans. by A. W. Wade-Evans (Cardiff: University of Wales Press, 1944), pp. 24–141

Wrdisten, *Vita S. Winwaloei primi abbatis Landevenecensis*, ed. by C. de Smedt, *AnBoll*, 7 (1888), 167–264

Secondary Works

Brett, C., 'Breton Latin Literature as Evidence for Literature in the Vernacular, A.D. 800–1300', *CMCS*, 18 (1989), 1–25

Bromwich, R., ed. and trans., *Trioedd Ynys Prydein: The Triads of the Island of Britain*, 4th edn (Cardiff: University of Wales Press, 2014)

Brooke, C. N. L., *The Church and the Welsh Border in the Central Middle Ages*, ed. by D. N. Dumville and C. N. L. Brooke, SCH, 8 (Woodbridge: Boydell, 1986)

Burton, J., 'Transition and Transformation: The Benedictine Houses', in *Monastic Wales: New Approaches*, ed. by J. Burton and K. Stöber (Cardiff: University of Wales Press, 2013), pp. 21–37

Chadwick, N. K., 'A Note on the Name Vortigern', in *Studies in Early British History*, ed. by N. K. Chadwick (Cambridge: University Press, 1954), pp. 34–46

Charles-Edwards, T. M., *Wales and the Britons 350–1064* (Oxford: Oxford University Press, 2013)

Crouch, D., 'The Transformation of Medieval Gwent', in *The Gwent County History*, II: *The Age of the Marcher Lords, c. 1070–1536*, ed. by R. A. Griffiths, T. Hopkins, and R. Howell (Cardiff: University of Wales Press, 2008), pp. 1–45

Crouch, D., 'The Slow Death of Kingship in Glamorgan, 1067–1158', *Morgannwg*, 29 (1985), 20–41

Davies, J. C., *Episcopal Acts Relating to Welsh Dioceses 1066–1272*, 2 vols (Cardiff: Historical Society of the Church in Wales, 1946–1948)

Davies, J. R., *The Book of Llandaf and the Norman Church in Wales*, SCH, 21 (Woodbridge: Boydell, 2003)

Davies, W., *The Llandaff Charters* (Aberystwyth: The National Library of Wales, 1979)

Doble, G. H., *St Cadoc in Cornwall and Brittany*, Cornish Saints Series, 40 (Truro: Netherton and Worth, 1937)

Dumville, D. N., 'Sub-Roman Britain: History and Legend', *History*, 62 (1977), 173–92 (repr. with the same pagination in his *Histories and Pseudo-Histories of the Insular Middles Ages* (Aldershot: Variorum, 1990), ch. 1)

Emanuel, H. D., 'An Analysis of the Composition of the "Vita Cadoci"', *National Library of Wales Journal*, 7 (1952), 217–27

Fleuriot, L., 'Old Breton Genealogies and Early British Traditions', *BBCS*, 26 (1974–1976), 1–6

Gransden, A., 'The Growth of the Glastonbury Traditions and Legends in the Twelfth Century', *The Journal of Ecclesiastical History*, 27 (1976), 337–58 (repr. in *Glastonbury Abbey and the Arthurian Tradition*, ed. by J. P. Carley (Cambridge: Brewer, 2001), pp. 29–53)

Grosjean, P., 'De Codice Hagiographico Gothano', *AnBoll*, 58 (1940), 90–103

Guillotel, H., 'Une famille bretonne au service du Conquérant: les Baderon', in *Droit privé et institutions régionales: Études historiques offertes à Jean Yver* (Paris: Presses universitaires de France, 1976), pp. 361–67

Guy, B., 'Constantine, Helena, Maximus: On the Appropriation of Roman History in Medieval Wales, c. 800–1250', *JMH*, 44 (2018), 381–405

——, 'Geoffrey of Monmouth's Welsh Sources', in *A Companion to Geoffrey of Monmouth*, ed. by J. B. Smith and G. Henley, Brill Companions to European History (Leiden: Brill, 2020), pp. 31–66

——, 'The *Life* of St Dyfrig and the Lost Charters of Moccas (Mochros), Herefordshire', *CMCS*, 75 (2018), 1–37

——, *Medieval Welsh Genealogy: An Introduction and Textual Study*, SCH, 42 (Woodbridge: Boydell, 2020)

——, review of P. Sims-Williams, *The Book of Llandaf as a Historical Source*, *Morgannwg*, 64 (2020), 225–29

——, 'The Vespasian Life of St Teilo and the Evolution of the *Vitae Sanctorum Wallensium*', in *Seintiau Cymru, Sancti Cambrenses: Astudiaethau ar Seintiau Cymru / Studies in the Saints of Wales*, ed. by D. Parsons and P. Russell (Aberystwyth: Canolfan Uwchefrydiau Cymreig a Cheltaidd Prifysgol Cymru, 2022), pp. 1–30

Harris, S. M., 'The Kalendar of the *Vitae Sanctorum Wallensium*', *Journal of the Historical Society of the Church in Wales*, 3 (1953), 3–53

Hughes, K., *Celtic Britain in the Early Middle Ages: Studies in Scottish and Welsh Sources*, ed. by D. N. Dumville, SCH, 2 (Woodbridge: Boydell, 1980)

Jankulak, K., 'Breton *Vitae* and Political Need in the Cartulary of Sainte-Croix de Quimperlé', in *Literature and Politics in the Celtic World: Papers from the Third Australian Conference of Celtic Studies, University of Sydney, July 1998*, ed. by J. M. Wooding and P. O'Neill, Sydney Series in Celtic Studies, 4 (Sydney: University of Sydney Celtic Studies Foundation, 2000), pp. 218–47

——, *The Medieval Cult of St Petroc*, SCH, 19 (Woodbridge: Boydell, 2000)

Keats-Rohan, K. S. B., 'The Bretons and Normans of England 1066–1154: The Family, the Fief and the Feudal Monarchy', *NMS*, 36 (1992), 42–78

——, *Domesday People: A Prosopography of Persons Occurring in English Documents, 1066–1166. I. Domesday Book* (Woodbridge: Boydell, 1999)

Larpi, L., *Prolegomena to a New Edition of Gildas Sapiens "De excidio Britanniae"* (Florence: Edizioni del Galluzzo, 2012)

Lloyd, J. E., 'Geoffrey of Monmouth', *EHR*, 57 (1942), 460–68

Poulin, J.-C., *L'hagiographie bretonne du haut Moyen Âge: Répertoire raisonné* (Ostfildern: Thorbecke, 2009)

Pryce, H., 'British or Welsh? National Identity in Twelfth-Century Wales', *EHR*, 116 (2001), 775–801

Sims-Williams, P., *The Book of Llandaf as a Historical Source*, SCH, 38 (Woodbridge: Boydell, 2019)

——, *Rhai Addasiadau Cymraeg Canol o Sieffre o Fynwy* (Aberystwyth: Canolfan Uwchefrydiau Cymreig a Cheltaidd Prifysgol Cymru, 2011)

Tanguy, B., 'De la vie de saint Cadoc à celle de saint Gurtiern', *ÉC*, 26 (1989), 159–85

Thornton, D. E., 'Glastonbury and the Glastening', in *The Archaeology and History of Glastonbury Abbey: Essays in Honour of the Ninetieth Birthday of C. A. Ralegh Radford*, ed. by L. Abrams and J. P. Carley (Woodbridge: Boydell, 1991), pp. 191–203

Tolhurst, F., *Geoffrey of Monmouth and the Translation of Female Kingship* (Basingstoke: Palgrave Macmillan, 2013)

Wadden, P., 'The Frankish Table of Nations in Insular Historiography', *CMCS*, 72 (2016), 1–31

Williams, I., 'Nodiadau ar Eiriau', *BBCS*, 17 (1956–1958), 93–98

11. Generic Place-Name Elements in the Three Brittonic Regions

O. J. Padel

Abstract: Some Brittonic words are shared as generic place-name elements between all three regions of Wales, Cornwall, and Brittany, while other such elements are restricted to one or two of those regions. Eight of the commonest such elements are examined here, four secular (*trev, *bod, *cair and *lis) and four ecclesiastical (*lann, *pluiv, *log and *egluis). In several respects the usage seen in Brittany differs from that of Cornwall and Wales more than those two regions differ from each other. The differences seem likely to reflect distinctive administrative or social conditions at an early stage in Breton history.

Résumé: Quelques mots britonniques sont partagés, comme éléments génériques de noms de lieu, entre toutes les trois régions de langue britonnique, le Pays de Galles, le Cornwall et la Bretagne, tandis que d'autres éléments sont restreints à une ou deux de ces régions. Ici sont examinés huit des éléments les plus répandus, quatre de caractère séculier (*trev, *bod, *cair et *lis) et quatre ecclésiastiques (*lann, *pluiv, *log et *egluis). À plusieurs égards, l'usage de ces éléments en Bretagne se distingue de celui au Cornwall et au Pays de Galles plus nettement que ne se distinguent ces deux régions l'une à l'autre. Ces différences réfléchissent probablement des conditions caractéristiques administratives ou sociales dans les premiers temps en Bretagne.

Keywords: place-names; Wales, Cornwall, Brittany; settlement; migration; early Church.

Multi-disciplinary Approaches to Medieval Brittany, 450–1200: Connections and Disconnections, ed. by Caroline Brett, Fiona Edmonds, and Paul Russell, TCNE 36 (Turnhout: Brepols, 2023) pp. 263–310   BREPOLS PUBLISHERS   10.1484/M.TCNE-EB.5.132316

nyone comparing the maps of Brittany, Cornwall, and Wales will be struck by similarities and differences among the place-names of the three regions. Some of these similarities, especially in names referring to natural features of the landscape, are due simply to the closeness of the three languages; and some of the differences are similarly due to divergence between the languages, especially in the later-medieval and modern periods. But some of both, particularly in names which refer to administrative structures (including those of the Church) or to other aspects of land-settlement, enticingly seem to impart potential historical clues about the early medieval period, for which direct documentary evidence is so scarce. The purpose here is therefore to examine similarities and differences in the use of certain elements which were common in the period before about 1100. The particular aim is to see what light such a comparison may perhaps cast upon the Insular settlement in Brittany, by examining the extent to which Brittonic naming-practices were transferred, or not, to the new land. In their use of some types of name, notably those with *trev, *bod and *lann, all three Brittonic regions are similar to one another. In other types Wales and Cornwall are similar to each other, but differ from what is observable in Brittany. These latter types suggest that the migrants adopted some new naming practices in Brittany, changing from those used in their homeland. One possible reason for this change, especially the use of *pluiv, could be that they were adapting their practices to new conditions which they encountered when they arrived; in other cases, especially the increased use in Brittany of *cair, *lïs, and *log and the lack of names in *egluis, the differences arose probably from later developments within Brittany, still within the earlier medieval period down to the twelfth century.

Because of the differing available documentation, as well as differing states of scholarship in the three regions, it is not possible to give full or precise comparisons. The distribution maps offered here are derived from the work of others in the cases of Brittany and Wales, and some of them are necessarily provisional and/or partial. So the present exercise is itself a provisional one, and its findings may be altered by future work. But even as a preliminary exercise the comparison is instructive. While examining these three regions, it will be wise also to keep an eye on the incidence of the same elements in a fourth one, north-west England and southern Scotland, where the number of Brittonic place-names is significantly higher than in most of England. However, the Brittonic place-names in those areas, though more numerous than elsewhere, nevertheless constitute such a small proportion of the overall toponymy of the region, and the documentation is mostly so much later than in Wales, Cornwall, and Brittany, that the distributions cannot be directly compared with our three regions where

11. GENERIC PLACE-NAME ELEMENTS IN THE THREE BRITTONIC REGIONS

the early names are overwhelmingly Brittonic. For this reason that northern region can provide only occasional data, not sustained comparisons such as can be attempted between the three Brittonic regions themselves.

Eight elements are examined here, considered under two categories, secular and ecclesiastical names; but in some cases the distinction is an uncertain one, as will be seen. According to the context, they are here cited primarily in 'Common Neo-Brittonic' form, the unattested parent-language after it had undergone the momentous changes of the fifth and sixth centuries, but before it gradually separated into its three daughter-languages, starting in about the eighth century. (These forms are necessarily qualified by an asterisk since they are hypothetical ones.) But where appropriate they are also cited in forms of the individual later languages (for example, Welsh *caer*, Breton *ker*), or in the forms that they frequently take when occurring as the first (generic) elements of modern place-names (for example, as *Tre-*, *Plou-*). Naturally some of these various forms are identical over time and/or across the languages.[1]

Secular Elements: (1) *trev*

The element *trev* (Common Neo-Brittonic) 'farmstead, estate, farming hamlet' (Modern Welsh *tref*, Middle Cornish *tre*, Modern Breton *trev*, Old Breton *Treb-*) is considered first, since it is common in all three regions, and in Cornwall at least it has provided a significantly large proportion of the toponymy.[2] It is found over almost all of the county, except for moorland areas and two areas on the eastern boundary with Devon, where there had been extensive Anglo-Saxon settlement probably by about AD 900, and anyway long before the time of Domesday Book in 1086 (Fig. 11.1, overleaf).[3] Altogether there are about 1300 known place-names in Cornwall containing the element. It is well represented among the earliest place-names recorded in Cornwall, in char-

---

[1] My warm thanks to Caroline Brett, Graeme Kirkham, David Parsons, and Ann Preston-Jones for their advice, information, and helpful comments on this article; particularly to Caroline Brett for the opportunity to read before publication her chapter, '"Saints and Seaways": the Cult of Saints in Brittany and its Archipelagic Links', in Brett and others, *Brittany and the Atlantic Archipelago*, pp. 231–91; it has greatly informed parts of the present article. Also to the participants in the conference in Cambridge in November 2017 for similar help and stimulation; and to Pete Joseph for the maps.

[2] Padel, *Cornish Place-Name Elements*, pp. 223–32; Le Moing, *Noms de lieux bretons*, pp. 190–98.

[3] Padel, 'Place-Names and the Saxon Conquest'.

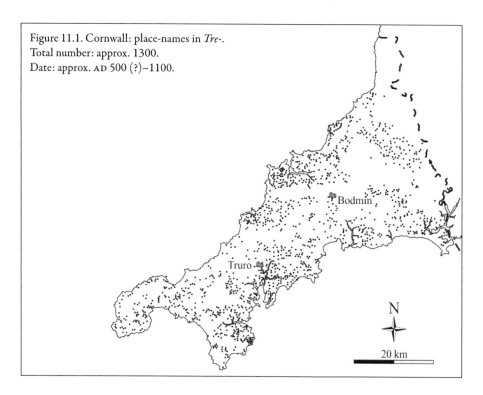

Figure 11.1. Cornwall: place-names in *Tre-*.
Total number: approx. 1300.
Date: approx. AD 500 (?)–1100.

ters of the tenth and eleventh centuries, and in Domesday Book itself, where ninety-three of the 347 (approximately) manors have a name containing it as the generic element.

Several pieces of evidence indicate that *tre* was little used to form place-names in Cornwall after about AD 1100. First, it is evenly distributed across most of the county, except for the areas mentioned above. By contrast, words which continued to serve as formative elements into the later Middle Ages show a westward increase in density across the county, because of the later survival of the language in the western half, contrasted with the death of the language in the east by about the thirteenth century; a situation somewhat comparable with that seen between the two parts of Brittany.[4] (With the map of **trev* contrast those of the elements **cair* and **egluis*, below.) Second, *Tre-* is often qualified by a Brittonic personal name, and in Cornwall such personal forenames were giving way to Old English ones in the tenth century and had largely gone out of use by about 1100, as far as the evidence goes.

[4] Padel, 'Where was Middle Cornish Spoken?'; Tanguy, 'Limite linguistique'.

11. GENERIC PLACE-NAME ELEMENTS IN THE THREE BRITTONIC REGIONS

Occasionally *Tre-* is qualified by an Old English personal name (for instance, Tredundle, *Tre- + Denewold*, and Trebursye, *Tre- + Beorhtsige*), again suggesting formative use before about 1100, when Old English personal names had themselves begun to be replaced by Norman ones all over England; on the other hand, Middle English forenames do not occur in the same role with *Tre-*, nor do Middle English surnames, except in a very few cases, for example Tresemple in St Clement parish, attested as *Tresempel* 1278, with a William *le Symple* living nearby in 1287.[5] These few later *Tre-* names could have been created analogically, so were not necessarily formed using the element in its pre-Conquest sense. Third, the element occurs combined with certain vocabulary that had become obsolete in Middle Cornish, notably *perveth* (Welsh *perfedd*, Old Breton *permed*) in the sense 'middle', for which Middle Cornish used the word *cres*, Breton *kreiz*. These three factors all indicate that *Tre-* was no longer a formative element in Cornwall after about 1100, though still current as a word in the language, in various senses. In the later Middle Ages the standard word for a minor 'house' or 'dwelling' in Cornwall was *chy* (Modern Welsh *tŷ*, Modern Breton *ti*), found in many place-names in the western half of the county (and none in the eastern half).[6]

Unfortunately most farms with names in *Tre-* are still inhabited, so there have not been many archaeological investigations at their sites, which could have given some indication of the dates when such farms were created and occupied, although the farms could anyway have been already old when their names were created. There are reasons for thinking that the element was in use from the earliest post-Roman times, say the fifth or sixth century. First, the fact that it is common to all three main Brittonic regions, and is also found among the Brittonic names of southern Scotland and northern England, suggests an element that was used for forming place-names at the period when the languages were little differentiated, and at the time of the migrations to Brittany. Second, a few *Tre-* place-names in Devon also show the element to have been in use when Brittonic language and society were flourishing there sufficiently to create place-names, hardly later than the seventh century.[7] However, its inci-

---

[5] Early spellings of Cornish place-names are taken from my collection of forms for the English Place-Name Society. The modern forms of names under discussion are not italicized, unlike early spellings.

[6] Padel, *Cornish Place-Name Elements*, pp. 77–80; Padel, 'Where was Middle Cornish Spoken', pp. 4–7 (including map, p. 6).

[7] Padel, 'Place-Names and the Saxon Conquest', p. 217 and map (p. 216) showing the three names.

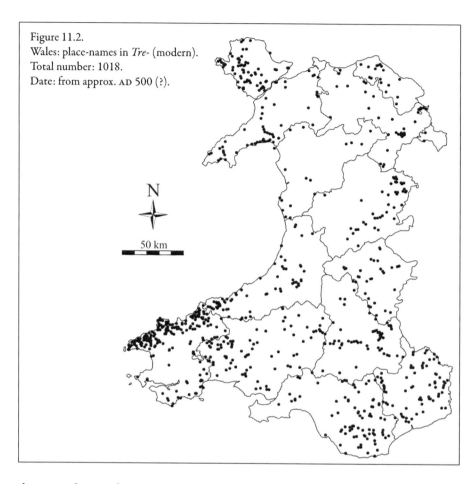

Figure 11.2.
Wales: place-names in *Tre-* (modern).
Total number: 1018.
Date: from approx. AD 500 (?).

dence in the northern region, as in Devon, is not on the scale of its frequency in the three main Brittonic regions; so we may surmise that its frequency as a generic element subsequently increased differentially in the various areas, and particularly in Cornwall.

The distribution of Welsh *tref* is at first glance similarly even (see Fig. 11.2, which I owe to the kindness of David Parsons; he emphasizes its provisional nature).[8] The element is well attested in the earliest Welsh toponymy, with one example, *Treb guidauc*, in the Chad Memoranda (ninth century) and about forty in the charters copied into the twelfth-century Book of Llandaf,

---

[8] This map shows names appearing on the Ordnance Survey Six-Inch map, without verification from early spellings or adding lost names; but its overall picture is likely to be broadly correct.

some potentially as early as the sixth or seventh century; in these charters it is sometimes rendered into Latin as *villa*, for example *Trefret* (title) = *uillam ret* (text), and *villa procliuii* = *Tref ir isceiauc* (both in the title).[9] As in Cornwall *Tre-* is evenly distributed over most of Wales, except for upland areas, and with slightly greater density in areas of better farmland. One area in the south-west has a notably greater density, namely the coastal strip of north Pembrokeshire, extending into south-western Cardiganshire.

However, when the comparative sizes of Cornwall and Wales are taken into account, the similarity is lessened. The element is significantly less numerous in Wales than in Cornwall, with about 1000 names over the whole country, compared with the total of about 1300 names in the single county of Cornwall, a sixth of the area. So the density across Cornwall is in fact much greater even than that in south-west Wales, let alone that of the rest of that country. In Wales the element may have continued longer in use than in Cornwall, for it occasionally appears in combination with forenames of the type used in England after the Norman Conquest, and hence current in Wales under Anglo-Norman influence (a pattern unknown in Cornwall), perhaps through being used as an equivalent of Middle English *toun*: for example, Trephilip in Breconshire (*Philippeston* 1380, *Tre ph'* 15th), and Treglemais in Pembrokeshire (*Trefclemens* 1326 (16th), *Clementiston* 1332).[10] But in Wales the element seems not to occur in combination with surnames (as in Tresemple and one or two other names in Cornwall), unsurprisingly since surnames proper were so late in being generally adopted in Wales.[11]

In Brittany, too, the element is common and evenly spread, at least in the east, although there somewhat denser in the south than the north (Fig. 11.3).[12]

---

[9] *Book of Llan Dâv*, p. xlv, and Jenkins and Owen, 'Welsh Marginalia', pt i, pp. 52–54 (Chad 3); p. 224 (*Trefret*); and p. 204 (*Tref ir isceiauc*); compare W. Davies, *Llandaff Charters*; and, for *isceiauc = proclivium*, Williams, 'ysgi, ysgai, Ysgeiawc, Ysgeifiog'.

[10] Morgan and Powell, *Breconshire Place-Names*, p. 149 (Trephilip); Charles, *PN Pembrokeshire*, i, 230 (Treglemais); my thanks to David Parsons for these examples and for discussion about them.

[11] Morgan and Morgan, *Welsh Surnames*, pp. 15–24; nineteenth-century place-names in which *Tre-* is combined with a surname, such as Treharris and Trelewis, both in Glamorgan, are probably due to a conscious revival of the element rather than a natural continuation of its medieval usage.

[12] Based on Tanguy, 'Limite linguistique', p. 460, with discussion, pp. 458–59; and compare Le Moing, *Noms de lieux bretons*, pp. 190–98 and maps 9–10 (pp. 453–54), covering independently the same area as Tanguy's map.

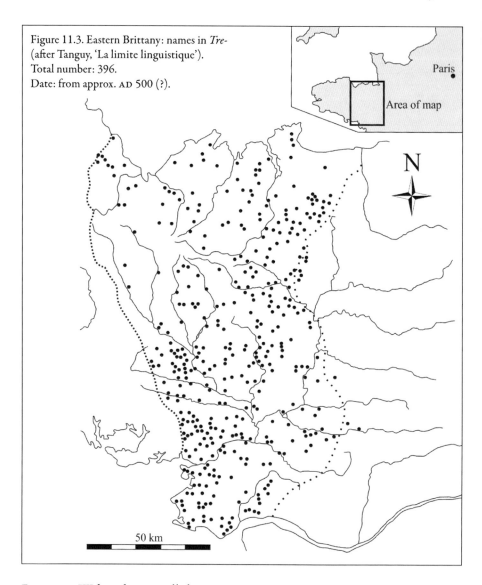

Figure 11.3. Eastern Brittany: names in *Tre-* (after Tanguy, 'La limite linguistique').
Total number: 396.
Date: from approx. AD 500 (?).

But, as in Wales, the overall density in eastern Brittany is much lower than in Cornwall, with just under 400 instances across a considerably larger area, compared with the 1300 examples in Cornwall. The element is well attested in the earliest recorded toponymy, with some thirty-five examples in the charters copied into the Cartulary of Redon (ninth to eleventh centuries),[13] where it was

---

[13] Tanguy, 'De la treb à la trève', p. 238, gives the figure as nineteen only; but his analytical

sometimes translated with Latin *villa*, for example *Treb arail = uilla Arhael*, *Treb etuual = uilla Etuual*, as in the Book of Llandaf;[14] Bernard Tanguy has pointed out that a surprising proportion of names in *Treb-* in the Cartulary of Redon have failed to survive into later times; and also that a high proportion of them have a personal name as second element, with only a few having a descriptive word.[15] In the slightly later material copied into the smaller Cartulary of Landévennec (eleventh century) there are twenty-three examples; in that source there are also a further sixteen places named (in Latin) as *Tribus X*, where *tribus* seems to have been a Latin rendering of Old Breton *treb* [**tre:v**]. This translation with Latin *tribus* introduces a complication, for the meaning of Breton *trev* has changed significantly. The word has gained an ecclesiastical sense, and in the standard Breton dictionary is translated 'trève (division de paroisse), succursale' ('*trève* (division of a parish), chapel-of-ease'), a sense attested from the fifteenth century but thought to have developed rather earlier, in about the twelfth century.[16] French *trève* is itself unknown to most French-speakers, being borrowed from Breton; another word used to translate Breton *trev* has been 'frairie', but the meaning of that French word itself ('division of a parish') seems slightly obscure; Tanguy has affirmed that it is not the same as 'confrairie' ('confraternity, guild').[17] The development of the meaning of *trev* was presumably from an original sense 'hamlet' to 'hamlet with a (sub-parochial) chapel' to 'sub-parish'.[18] The use of Latin *tribus* to translate it in the Cartulary of Landévennec may suggest that this development was already under way in the eleventh century. In Fig. 11.3, therefore, in any given instance it is uncertain whether it shows *Tre-* in its secular, Common-Brittonic, sense, or in its later ecclesiastical one. In its ecclesiastical sense, Tanguy does not say that it is particularly liable to be qualified by the names of saints, nor does he suggest any formal means by which the two meanings can be distinguished. Probably only detailed work on individual instances can achieve that.

---

index to the Cartulary lists a larger number: *Cartulaire de Redon*, II, 61–128 (at pp. 120–21), and Tanguy may have been counting only the lands specifically granted in the charters, not other places named incidentally in them.

[14] *Cartulaire de Redon*, fols 71ʳ (*Treb arail, uilla Arhael*), 88ᵛ, 104ᵛ (*Treb etuual*), and 94ᵛ (*uilla Etuual*), and index, II, 120b; compare Tanguy, 'De la treb à la trève', p. 238.

[15] Tanguy, 'De la treb à la trève', pp. 238–39.

[16] Tanguy, 'De la treb à la trève'.

[17] Tanguy, 'De la treb à la trève', pp. 237–38.

[18] Largillière, *Les Saints*, pp. 23 n. 23, 29–30, and 182–84 (= pp. 33, 42–43, and 234–36).

Apart from its attestation in all three regions, the early use of the element is supported by its occurrence also in Scotland and north-west England, where similarly it is one of the commoner generic elements. In that region Alan James has listed seventy-four possible examples altogether, of which forty-six show it as a generic element in phrasal names, comparable with the hundreds of instances in Wales, Cornwall, and Brittany, and twenty-eight as generic element in a compound name, for instance Ochiltree, comparable with Welsh Ucheldref.[19] However, many of these names, of both types, are very uncertain, partly for lack of early documentation. The proportion of compounds among the Scottish names containing generic *trev, more than a third, is much higher than in Wales, Cornwall, and Brittany, but no reason for that discrepancy has been suggested, to my knowledge. At any rate the use of this element in the northern region as well as in Wales, Cornwall and Brittany suggests that its role in forming place-names goes back to the earliest post-Roman centuries, in all areas.

Margaret Gelling has suggested, in conversation, that the use of habitative place-name elements with a personal name in the Celtic languages was due to Anglo-Saxon or Anglo-Norman influence. She was thinking especially of the word *baile* in the Gaelic languages, where her particular interest was the Isle of Man; but her suggestion is worth bearing in mind in considering the exceptional frequency of *Tre-* names in Cornwall and (to a lesser extent) in south-west Wales, both areas of greater English influence than Brittany and the rest of Wales. However, it would be chronologically awkward to separate instances of *Tre-* plus personal name from those qualified by a topographical term; and the ninth-century examples (qualified by personal names) in Chad and the Redon Cartulary can hardly be due to English influence. Nonetheless her suggestion should not be entirely dismissed; it is a possible factor in considering the exceptional frequency of the element in Cornwall, and perhaps in south-west Wales. The density in Cornwall is so markedly different from that in Wales and Brittany that some particular explanation seems required.

Another idea which has been proposed in recent years is that the increased use of *trev* was associated with a thorough reorganization of the whole landscape and settlement-pattern in Cornwall, consequent on the introduction of

---

[19] James, 'Brittonic Language in the Old North', *s.v.* **treβ**; also James, 'Cumbric *Trev* in Kyle, Carrick, Galloway and Dumfriesshire'; Richards, *Units*, p. 218, lists seven instances of Ucheldref.

11. GENERIC PLACE-NAME ELEMENTS IN THE THREE BRITTONIC REGIONS

Christianity in about the fifth century.[20] The idea, though not explicitly articulated in this form, seems to be that society, being now Christian, became more cooperative and egalitarian, so settlements did not need to be fortified: the enclosed settlements or 'rounds' (see *cair, below) were abandoned, and the unenclosed farming hamlet (*trev) became the norm.[21] It has been suggested that *trev farms were created particularly around major ecclesiastical centres;[22] but that does not seem to account for its equal frequency in most other parts of Cornwall. I have previously suggested that names in *trev had a special place in the structure of land-tenure in the pre-Saxon south-west.[23] In fact, although Tre- names are prominent both among the names of Domesday manors and in the names of the later tithings (areas of law-enforcement), this prominence may be due simply to its overall prominence in the toponymy of the county. Whatever the reason for the frequency of *trev in Cornwall, and the date of its increased use, it does not seem to have applied to the migrants who went to Brittany, since its role there was less significant than it was to become in Cornwall. That might suggest, in turn, that the distinctive increase in the use of *trev in Cornish toponymy could date from a slightly later period than that of the migrations (perhaps from that of Saxon influence, starting in the eighth century?), which could explain the greater density of such names in Cornwall, compared with that in Brittany and Wales.

Secular Elements: (2) *bod

Common Neo-Brittonic *bod 'dwelling' is less numerous than *trev, in all three regions.[24] In Cornwall there are about 230 examples in total, of which sixteen appear in Domesday Book, compared with the 1300 *trev names, with ninety-three in Domesday Book, a strikingly similar proportion of about one in fourteen. Bod- names also are evenly distributed over most of the county, with the predictable exceptions of the two Anglo-Saxon areas on the boundary with Devon and the moorland areas, but with the added and notable discrepancy of

[20] Turner, *Making a Christian Landscape*, especially pp. 71–98.

[21] Turner, *Making a Christian Landscape*, pp. 78–79; Herring, 'Cornish Strip Fields', especially p. 73; and see further below, pp. 278–79, ***cair**, and 284–86, ***lis**.

[22] Turner, *Making a Christian Landscape*, pp. 83–98.

[23] Padel, *Cornish Place-Name Elements*, pp. 224–26.

[24] Padel, *Cornish Place-Name Elements*, pp. 23–26; Le Moing, *Noms de lieux bretons*, pp. 120–28.

a particular density in the Land's End peninsula, which contains over a quarter of the total (Fig. 11.4).[25] This density existed as early as the tenth century, when a charter of lands granted to St Buryan church, within that peninsula, already had five names in *Bod-* alongside two in *Tre-*.[26] These examples, plus one other tenth-century one, also suggest a generally early date for such names; and that impression is reinforced by its occurrence with Brittonic personal names, and none with Anglo-Saxon or later English ones. The discrepancy of its geographical distribution is curiously paralleled in Wales, where the element is almost entirely restricted to the northern half of the country, and, even odder, with an exceptional density in the Llŷn peninsula, an area of similar size and geography to the Land's End peninsula in Cornwall.[27] In Wales there are no examples in the Book of Llandaf, but that is because the lands named there are all in the south.

It is difficult to suggest any explanation for this curious parallel between Wales and Cornwall. One relevant point may be a general impression that places with *Bod-* names in Cornwall were of lower status than ones in *Tre-*, and seem to occur more readily in marginal areas, including those with poorer farmland such as uplands, whereas *Tre-* names tend to occupy good agricultural sites; such a sense would accord with its use in the compound **havos* 'summer-dwelling, shieling' (Welsh *hafod*).[28] This general impression of lower status would apply only at the earliest period, for by the time of Domesday Book, as already seen, a similar proportion of places named with *Bod-* and *Tre-* had attained the status of manors, as had even some of the names in **havos* 'shieling'.[29] Similarly in Devon English names in *-cott*, presumably naming places of lower status, often appear as manors in that text. Northern Wales is, overall, less agriculturally rich than the south, but that would hardly explain so complete a contrast between north and south Wales; and the frequency of the element on Anglesey, regarded as the granary of northern Wales in medieval times, is also at odds with that interpretation.[30] Whether this tendency towards lower-quality sites

[25] Padel, *Cornish Place-Name Elements*, p. 25.

[26] Birch, no. 785; Sawyer, no. 450; Della Hooke, *Pre-Conquest Charter-Bounds of Devon and Cornwall*, pp. 22–27.

[27] See the list in Richards, *Units*, pp. 15–18: names in the counties of Anglesey, Caernarfonshire, Denbighshire, Flintshire, Montgomeryshire, and Merioneth, but not further south.

[28] Padel, *Cornish Place-Name Elements*, p. 127.

[29] Compare Johnson and Rose, *Bodmin Moor*, I, 79.

[30] Carr, *Medieval Anglesey*, p. 18.

11. GENERIC PLACE-NAME ELEMENTS IN THE THREE BRITTONIC REGIONS

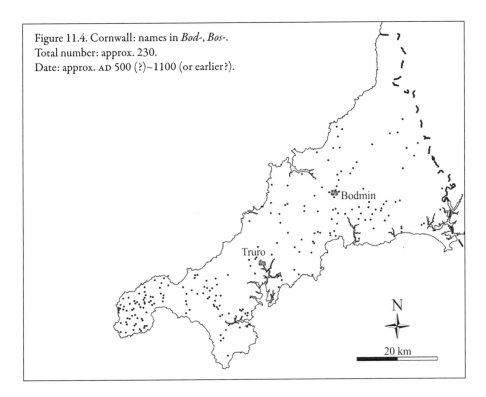

Figure 11.4. Cornwall: names in *Bod-*, *Bos-*.
Total number: approx. 230.
Date: approx. AD 500 (?)–1100 (or earlier?).

can also be used to explain the exceptional frequencies in the wind-swept peninsulas of Llŷn and Land's End is uncertain.

In Brittany the element is well represented in the Cartulary of Redon, with twenty-four instances in Tanguy's index, but only two in that of Landévennec. As in Cornwall, one such place was of high status by the mid-ninth century, for it was the location of an 'aula quae dicitur Botnumel' (hall called *Botnumel*) where an envoy was sent on a mission to the Breton ruler Nominoe at that period.[31] The incidence of the element in Brittany does not seem to have been studied in detail, so it is not possible to state here its frequency and distribution; there seem to be occasional instances where the element is qualified by a saint's name, as occasionally in Cornwall, or other hints of an ecclesiastical association.[32] Overall it seems likely that in Brittany, as in Cornwall, names in

---

[31] *Monks of Redon*, ed. Brett, p. 209; my thanks to Caroline Brett for pointing this out to me.

[32] Padel, *Cornish Place-Name Elements*, p. 26; compare the ecclesiastical sense detected for its Gaelic cognate **both* (normally a secular word, 'hut, bothy') in eastern Scotland, perhaps under Pictish influence: Taylor, 'Place-Names and the Early Church', pp. 95–98.

bod in the sense 'dwelling' date from an early period, and that it may later have dropped out of use as a formative element. Uniquely among the Brittonic languages, Breton has retained the use of the word as a common noun, with the sense 'shelter, refuge'; in later toponymy a meaning 'clump of trees' is also recognized, treated as the same word etymologically though with different gender.[33]

In Scotland, James lists twelve possible names in *Bod-*, but half of these are north of the Forth-Clyde line, and may be Gaelic names created under Pictish influence; and of the remaining six, several are very uncertain.[34] So there may be no unequivocal examples in southern Scotland of this element, of which the distribution is uneven all over the Brittonic world.

Secular Elements: (3) *cair*

The element *cair* (Common Neo-Brittonic; Old Welsh *cair*, Modern Welsh *caer*, Modern Breton *kêr*; Old Cornish *Caer-*, *Car-* in place-names)[35] is the most problematical of the secular elements, because of the variation and uncertainty in its meaning. In Welsh its meaning varies from 'hill-fort' (as an antiquity) to 'city', a meaning attested as early as the ninth-century *Historia Brittonum* formerly attributed to Nennius.[36] In Cornwall there are about 130 instances of the element in names of settlements (with further ones in field-names), mostly with the assumed meaning 'a round', that is a fortified hamlet of the Iron-Age, Roman or early post-Roman periods. Graeme Kirkham kindly informs me that there is some correlation between place-names in *Car-* (derived from *Caer-*) and some of the known rounds or similar structures. At present there is no evidence that 'rounds' continued to be used as settlements after about the sixth century, although the scarcity of excavated examples makes generalization difficult; some became disused rather earlier.[37] The date when such habitations were used is important in considering the formative use of the element referring to them. Even in the more restricted sense of the word as used in Cornwall, there is an uncertainty whether it was used, in any particular case, to refer to a 'round'

---

[33] Tanguy, *Noms de lieux bretons*, p. 99; Tanguy, *Dictionnaire du Finistère*, p. 28; Hemon, *s.v. bod*.

[34] James, 'Brittonic Language in the Old North', *s.v.* **bod**.

[35] Padel, *Cornish Place-Name Elements*, pp. 50–54; James, 'Brittonic Language in the Old North', *s.v.* ***cajr**; Le Moing, *Noms de lieux bretons*, pp. 139–47 and 278–79.

[36] Jackson, 'Nennius and the Twenty-Eight Cities'.

[37] Quinnell, *Trethurgy*, pp. 240–44.

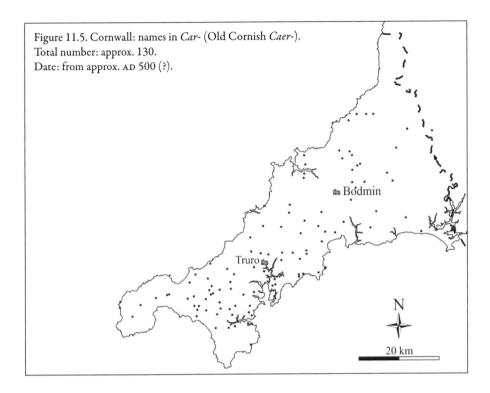

Figure 11.5. Cornwall: names in *Car-* (Old Cornish *Caer-*).
Total number: approx. 130.
Date: from approx. AD 500 (?).

while it was actually occupied as a settlement, or as an antiquity. In Cornwall its currency as a formative element at some time in the period 500–1100 is shown by its use with Brittonic personal names, but not with English ones of any date, though a single example, Carzise (*Carseys* 1303, 'English-speaker's fort, Englishman's fort'; in Crowan parish), shows its formative use continuing into the English-speaking period in the far west, tenth century or later. Its density increases slightly in the western third of the county (Fig. 11.5), which could suggest that some of the names there were created in the later Middle Ages, when Cornish was no longer a living language in the east. However, rounds themselves seem also to be commoner in that western area, so the increase in names may merely reflect one on the ground.[38] A farm might have been named *Caer-X* merely from being located close to a round (as an antiquity), so their names do not necessarily indicate the currency of the rounds as a settlement-type at the date when those names were created. On the other hand, the fre-

[38] Johnson and Rose, 'Defended Settlement in Cornwall', Figure 1 (p. 189); this map shows all types of ramparted enclosures but predominantly rounds.

quency of place-names in *Caer-* qualified by a Brittonic personal name suggests, as in southern Scotland (below), that some rounds were in use during at least some of the period when such personal names were current, from the fifth to the eleventh centuries in Cornwall.

In Brittany, habitations similar to Cornish rounds are well known from the Iron Age through to the central Middle Ages; one excavated example, on the Île Guennoc off the north-west coast of Finistère near Landéda, was built around AD 450–750 and was still inhabited around 700–950.[39] The element **cair* appears in about fifteen names in the Cartulary of Redon, seven of them in a single eleventh-century charter, though a few are ninth-century;[40] and in as many as forty-four in the smaller Cartulary of Landévennec. However, the word has changed its meaning in Brittany, where it now means any 'house' or other dwelling. This semantic change is exemplified in contrasts between the three languages, where the standard phrases meaning 'at home' are in Modern Welsh *adre* (from *tref*), in Middle Cornish *agy* (from *chy* 'house') and in Modern Breton *e-ger* (from *kêr*). The Breton usage has been explained (on this side of the Channel) by reference to the idea that rounds, having been the standard type of habitation during the Roman period, were replaced at some time in about the sixth or seventh century by the (unfortified) **trev*; at the period of the migrations to Brittany Neo-Brittonic **cair* could therefore have been the standard word current in the language for any habitation.[41] The problems with this explanation are the uncertainty of the date of the migrations and whether they came from an area in southern Britain where rounds were a standard type of habitation, and the uncertainty about when the unfortified **trev* replaced the round as the standard type of dwelling, and even whether there was such a replacement at all, or whether the two types of settlement were in use concurrently. Moreover, the toponymic use in early Brittany of **trev* and **bod*, combined with the additional currency there in the language of *ti* 'house' (corresponding to Middle Cornish *chy*, mentioned above, which came to serve the same toponymic function as *kêr* did in Brittany) means that the full range of

[39] Giot and others, *British Settlement of Brittany*, pp. 209 (rounds generally) and 210–11 (Ile Guennoc).

[40] *Cartulaire de Redon*, index, at II, 70b and 95a.

[41] Classically expounded by Thomas, 'Character and Origins of Roman Dumnonia', pp. 97–98; since that article was published in 1966, archaeological information and interpretation have naturally progressed; its legacy may still be present in recent theories about *Tre-* place-names in Cornwall, discussed above.

elements used later in Britain for 'dwelling' (*trev, *bod and *tï) was also available alongside *cair in early Brittany.

Instead Tanguy has suggested convincingly that the reason for the frequency of Ker- in Breton place-names is that its meaning was extended, from the eleventh century onwards, to fill the gap in the toponymicon created by the shift of trev to an ecclesiastical sense.[42] Among other points his suggestion explains the much greater frequency of the element Caer- in the charters of Landévennec (eleventh-century) than in those of Redon (predominantly ninth-century): most name-elements are better represented in the Redon texts, because the Landévennec Cartulary contains many fewer charters, and thus fewer names, than that of Redon. But in the case of this element, and also of Lann- (see below), the position is reversed. Tanguy's suggested date for the increased use of Caer- well explains this discrepancy in numbers, since the Landévennec material is later in date than that of Redon. Correspondingly, it follows from Tanguy's explanation for the later importance of Ker- in Breton toponymy that the discrepancy in the use of *cair between Cornwall and Brittany has no chronological implications for the archaeology of rounds in Cornwall, as formerly suggested. However, it remains to be established what the Breton meaning of *cair was, in referring to habitations, during the intervening centuries between the migrations and the change of meaning around the eleventh century; just as its meaning in Cornwall is also uncertain, although it did apparently refer to rounds in some cases at least.

For Scotland James lists no fewer than sixty possible names containing *Cair- as generic element.[43] However, this number may be inflated by names where the early spellings are inadequate to distinguish *cair from other phonologically similar elements, notably Common Neo-Brittonic *cadeir 'seat (= hill?)', *carn 'rock-pile', *carreg 'rock' and *crüg 'tumulus', or indeed (in Scotland) Gaelic cognates of all those words. In Cornwall Caer- had become confused with some of these words by the thirteenth century, sometimes earlier still; so to distinguish between these elements with assurance, forms of that date or earlier are needed. James has also noted that in several of his examples the word is qualified by a personal name, implying that *cair was used for inhabited sites, parallel to names in Wales and Cornwall where it is similarly qualified. If the element is indeed significantly more numerous in this region than in Wales or Cornwall, the frequency is presumably independent of its frequency in Brittany, since that

---

[42] Tanguy, 'De la treb à la trève', p. 240.

[43] James, 'Brittonic Language in the Old North', *s.v.* **cajr**.

Breton usage seems to have arisen in about the eleventh century, under particular circumstances. Kenneth Jackson has suggested that the element in Cumbric developed 'the same secondary meaning that it did in Breton — simply a small hamlet or a manor-house and farm, originally protected by some kind of defensive stockade';[44] but he evidently thought this development independent in Cumbric and Breton, and considered that the Cumbric names (or some of them) were among the latest Brittonic names in north-west England, which might make their date not very different from the period when such names started to become frequent in Brittany.[45]

Secular Elements: (4) *līs

The Common Neo-Brittonic element *līs 'court' (Modern Welsh *llys*, Modern Breton *les*; Old Cornish *Les-, Lis-* in place-names) also has several different meanings, but they are more readily separated than those of *cair*.[46] In both Wales and Cornwall, the element is much less numerous than the three elements examined already, and its importance lies in its administrative significance rather than its frequency. Cornwall has only about fifteen examples in total of the word as a generic element (Fig. 11.6; one or two uncertain, late-attested, examples have been omitted). One category of meaning which can be readily separated is the use of *līs to refer to antiquities, in the names of places which have never had any administrative role in historic times. In Wales, Melville Richards has identified, though without going into further detail, its 'satirical' or 'scornful' use referring to ruins or antiquities, such as Llys-y-fran (two instances, 'crow's court') and Llys-y-dryw ('wren's court'), both in Pembrokeshire.[47] In Cornwall, seven of the names are of this type, about half the overall total; they belong to minor settlements having no administrative significance, but mostly situated close to known antiquities, to which the word presumably referred. The clearest example is the farm-name Leskernick 'rocky court' on Bodmin Moor, adjacent to a hill covered in Bronze-Age remains (including dozens of hut-circles) amidst natural granite outcrops and scree,

[44] Jackson, 'Angles and Britons', p. 80.

[45] Jackson, 'Angles and Britons', pp. 81–82.

[46] Padel, *Cornish Place-Name Elements*, pp. 150–51; Le Moing, *Noms de lieux bretons*, pp. 171–75.

[47] Richards, *Enwau Tir a Gwlad*, p. 86; Charles, *PN Pembrokeshire*, I, 261 and II, 427–28 (Llys-y-fran), and I, 177 (Llys-y-dryw).

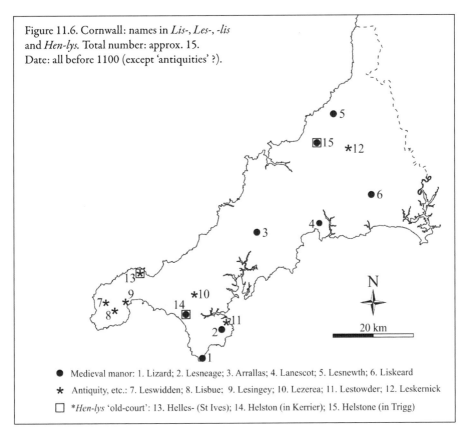

Figure 11.6. Cornwall: names in *Lis-*, *Les-*, *-lis* and *Hen-lys*. Total number: approx. 15. Date: all before 1100 (except 'antiquities' ?).

● Medieval manor: 1. Lizard; 2. Lesneage; 3. Arrallas; 4. Lanescot; 5. Lesnewth; 6. Liskeard
* Antiquity, etc.: 7. Leswidden; 8. Lisbue; 9. Lesingey; 10. Lezerea; 11. Lestowder; 12. Leskernick
□ *Hen-lys* 'old-court': 13. Helles- (St Ives); 14. Helston (in Kerrier); 15. Helstone (in Trigg)

the whole site extending over twenty-one hectares.[48] In other names of this type the element *Les-* refers to a hill-fort or a round; and in one or two others, not near any known antiquity, the element is qualified by a word referring to livestock, including Lezerea (Old Cornish **gre* 'flock, herd') and Lisbue (Old Cornish **byu* 'cattle').[49] In these names the element may simply refer to a practical use, or may be a romantically-tinged reference to a disused antiquity.[50] In addition there is a minor fortification, of unknown date, at Lestowder, where

---

[48] Illustration in Johnson and others, *Bodmin Moor*, I, 42–43 and Figure 4 (p. 10); Bender and others, 'Leskernick'.

[49] Padel, *Cornish Place-Name Elements*, pp. 112 (**gre*) and 22 (**byu*); the element may also refer to antiquities in one or two compounds, such as **cad-lys* 'battle-court': Padel, *Cornish Place-Name Elements*, pp. 35–36 and 150.

[50] Compare Llys-y-defaid 'the court of the sheep', Charles, *PN Pembrokeshire*, I, 68.

the element is qualified by a personal name from saints' legends, King Teudar;[51] and one of the three Cornish examples of the compound *Hen-les 'old-court', the minor double settlement of Hellesvean and Hellesvear (*Hellesmur* 1284) outside St Ives, respectively 'little' and 'great' *Hen-les 'old-court', seems to refer to an antiquity, a building (part of a larger settlement?) which has been dated by pottery-finds to about the ninth to eleventh centuries.[52]

However, the more significant type of *Les-* names is those applied to places which were of administrative importance in the Saxon period and later, having presumably been inherited as centres when Saxon governance was established in Cornwall in the ninth to tenth centuries. Melville Richards has again identified a number of such places in Wales, together with historical contexts for some of them;[53] but, inevitably, some major royal or administrative centres did not have names in *Llys-*, such as Aberffraw, the seat of the medieval princes of Gwynedd on Anglesey, reminding us that for other periods and areas where documentation is more sparse, toponymic evidence may necessarily be an incomplete guide. Several of these Cornish places bear a relation to the administrative hundreds (divisions of the county), which themselves also give every appearance of having been inherited from Cornwall's Brittonic past, being anomalously large in comparison with hundreds elsewhere in southern England.[54] Liskeard lies at the boundary between the two hundreds of Eastwivelshire and Westwivelshire (originally Old English *Twifeald-scīr 'twofold-shire'), while Helston (in Kerrier), a second *Hen-les 'old-court' plus Old English *tūn* 'manorial centre', is close to the boundary between the two westernmost hundreds of Penwith and Kerrier (Fig. 11.7). In north Cornwall, the village and parish of Lesnewth 'new court' lies at the centre of the great Domesday hundred comprising the three later hundreds of Trigg, Lesnewth, and Stratton (the pre-Saxon district of 'greater Triggshire'), and gave its name to the middle one of those hundredal sub-units. The earlier administrative centre which Lesnewth had presumably replaced to become the 'new' court was the manor of Helstone (in Trigg), six miles away, the third Cornish *Hen-les 'old-court'. Helstone lies at the boundary between two of these three sub-units, those called Trigg and Lesnewth in

[51] Tangye, 'Lestowder'.

[52] Russell, *West Penwith Survey*, p. 70 (St Ives, Post-Roman, nos 1–2), and references; but Richards, *Enwau Tir a Gwlad*, p. 86, assumes that Welsh Henllys always refers to a place of former administrative significance.

[53] Richards, *Enwau Tir a Gwlad*, pp. 81–85.

[54] Padel, 'Ancient and Medieval Administrative Divisions'.

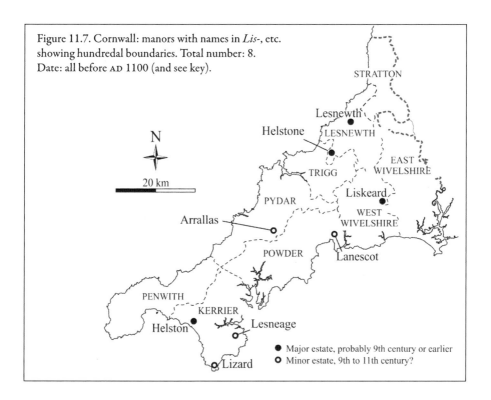

Figure 11.7. Cornwall: manors with names in *Lis-*, etc. showing hundredal boundaries. Total number: 8. Date: all before AD 1100 (and see key).

● Major estate, probably 9th century or earlier
○ Minor estate, 9th to 11th century?

the later Middle Ages. All four of these manors retained their significance in 1086 and later, Helston and Liskeard being exceptionally large estates. Another **les* name lying on a hundredal boundary is the manor of Arrallas, formerly *Arganlis* 1086 'silver court', on the boundary between the mid-western hundreds of Powder and Pydar (Fig. 11.7); but in 1086 and later Arrallas had no special importance, being only an ordinary manor, unlike Liskeard, Helston, Helstone, and Lesnewth.

But some of the *Les-* names in Cornwall do not refer to places of special significance such as these five which can be related to the hundredal structure of the later county, but to manors of minor importance. They had been estates in the Saxon period, as reflected in Domesday Book (1086), but were of no greater significance. There are three such names, all near the south coast of Cornwall (Fig. 11.7): Lizard ('court on a height'), Lesneage ('court of the Meneage', a small district) and Lanescot (*Lisnestoch* 1086, probably 'court of one **Nestöc*'). These names can be explained by looking to Brittany.

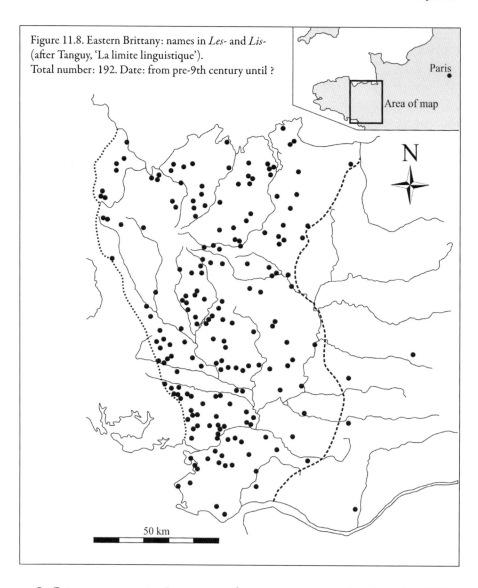

Figure 11.8. Eastern Brittany: names in *Les-* and *Lis-* (after Tanguy, 'La limite linguistique').
Total number: 192. Date: from pre-9th century until ?

In Brittany, names in *Les-* are much more numerous than in either Wales or Cornwall, and evidently have a different significance (Fig. 11.8).[55] Broadly their distribution in eastern Brittany is similar to that of *Tre-* names there (cf. Fig. 11.3), but they are about half as frequent, with 192 in the area that contains 396 *Tre-* names. The element is well represented in the early documentation: in

[55] Based on Tanguy, 'Limite linguistique', p. 461, with discussion, p. 459.

the Cartulary of Redon there are about twenty instances, and it tends to be translated with Latin *aula* 'court', for example *Liscolroet = aula Colroit*;[56] the smaller Cartulary of Landévennec contains some six instances. This frequency of the element, striking from an Insular point of view, seems likely to be connected with the unusual historical situation that Wendy Davies has identified, where local lords in Brittany, at about the level of the parish, seem to have led a semi-autonomous existence in the ninth century, with little input from higher authority, even though such authority did exist.[57] The administrative centres of these minor lords also served a local public function, and it is easy to envisage such settlements being called 'courts';[58] so the frequency of the element *Les-* in Brittany accords with that unusual social situation. This would not be to imply that there was no stratification in eastern-Breton society at this period. Its existence is demonstrated by the high-status sites identified archaeologically from their finds, such as window glass and silver coins;[59] and the place-names in *Les-* are themselves evidence of places which were considered to have a certain status (and probably authority). But in Brittany (at least in the east), status and authority were apparently more evenly-spread and operated at a more local level than in other Brittonic or neighbouring societies at this period, and the greater frequency of *Les-* place-names seems to reflect that situation.

In Cornwall and Wales, on the other hand, authority was so much more centralized that fewer administrative centres existed, but those had greater importance, and held sway over much larger areas. So the different social and administrative conditions visible in Brittany in the ninth century provide an explanation for the distinctive Breton use of this element. It remains uncertain, for lack of historical evidence, how much earlier than the ninth century these unusual administrative conditions had arisen, and therefore how much older the distinctive place-names in *Les-* may have been.

This frequency in Brittany of minor estates with names in *Les-* suggests an explanation for the three small estates in Cornwall with the same type of name. Two of them, Lizard and Lanescot, appear in Domesday Book, while one, Lesneage, existed as the object of a grant in the tenth century, but is not mentioned in 1086, evidently being subsumed within a larger estate at that date,

---

[56] *Cartulaire de Redon*, I, fols 68ʳ and 75ʳ; and index, II, 97.

[57] W. Davies, *Small Worlds*, especially pp. 134–60 and 208–10.

[58] W. Davies, *Small Worlds*, pp. 138–42.

[59] See the chapter by Catteddu and Le Gall, 'Archaeology of Early Medieval Rural Societies in Brittany', pp. 57–80 in this volume.

although it is named in charters around the same period.[60] The names of these three estates, all close to the south coast (Fig. 11.7), seem to use Old Cornish *Les-* in the distinctive Breton sense, to mean the centre of a small estate belonging to a minor local lord. This Breton-type usage in three Cornish place-names may be due to small-scale reverse migration, perhaps in the tenth century, or more broadly to cross-channel linguistic influence. Comparable names, the single examples of Cornish *Plu-* and *Loc-* used in a Breton sense, will be seen below. This explanation would not imply that the owners of these three estates in Cornwall enjoyed similar semi-autonomy to their counterparts in Brittany, only that their three estates were named in imitation of the Breton usage. The presence of just these three names of a type so frequent in Brittany, and no more, serves to emphasise that over most of Cornwall the secular administration was sufficiently different from that of Brittany not to encourage the use of *Les-* in this minor local sense. This toponymic difference between the two regions can be compared with the lack, until recently, of archaeological evidence for high-status sites in Brittany in the early Middle Ages, as observed by Caroline Brett, in contrast with Cornwall and elsewhere in Britain; recent discoveries of higher-status goods (glass and silver coins) at sites in Brittany may change this understanding, though they may still be still compatible with the idea of a society that was 'flattish', less sharply-stratified, than others at the period.[61]

Six possible names in southern Scotland with **Lïs-* as generic (first) element are cited by James;[62] but in two of them Gaelic *Lios-* seems more likely to be present than the Brittonic element, and the others are all doubtful; some may be English names, for example.

Ecclesiastical Elements: (1) **lann*

In Insular scholarship the Common Neo-Brittonic word **lann* (Modern Welsh *llan*) 'church-site' has long been considered central to understanding the early Church in Brittonic areas, particularly in Wales and Cornwall.[63] Formerly

---

[60] *Lesmanaoc* 967 (11th) Birch, *Cartularium*, no. 1197 (S 755); *Limanech c.* 1070 (14th), *Cartulary of St Michael's Mount*, ed. by Hull, no. 1, etc.

[61] Brett, 'Soldiers, Saints and States?', pp. 47–48, and references; and Catteddu and Le Gall, 'Archaeology of Early Medieval Rural Societies in Brittany', pp. 57–80 in this volume.

[62] James, 'Brittonic Language in the Old North', *s.v.* **lï:s[s]*.

[63] Among other work: Taylor, *Celtic Christianity*, pp. 70–71 and 120–21; Largillière, *Les*

the word was often translated 'monastery', but more recently archaeological emphasis has been laid upon the curvilinear enclosed cemeteries often present at sites with names containing the word. In Wales the element is very frequent, with nearly 200 examples in the Book of Llandaf alone, where it is often represented by Latin *ecclesia* or *podum*, the latter word thought to be a variant of *podium*, from the raised ground of the enclosure which it denoted.[64] The particular frequency of *Llan-* in Wales, with hundreds of place-names in total,[65] may be partly due to its having remained a formative element later than in Cornwall and Brittany, having become a general word signifying 'church' generally. John Davies has suggested that its use qualified by a saint's name (which he regards as a later usage within the life of the element) was at its height in the eighth to tenth centuries, being associated particularly with a shift of lay burial into ecclesiastical cemeteries in the eighth and ninth centuries; accordingly he has suggested the meaning 'church-complex plus cemetery' for the word.[66] The corollary would be that the element itself was in use (albeit perhaps not qualified by a saint's name) rather earlier than the eighth century, for its use to change then. One unique aspect of its Welsh usage is its frequent occurrence in combination with the names of certain universal saints, principally Mary, Peter, and Michael (Llanfair, Llanbedr, Llanfihangel); there are so many places with those names that they subsequently had to be distinguished from one another by affixes, often using nearby secular place-names; unfortunately it is unclear when these dedications are likely to have arisen in such large numbers. The element may have continued to be formative perhaps as late as the twelfth century (and see below), although the formalization of the parish-system at that period may make it unlikely that many new examples would have been created later than that.

Saints, pp. 27–33 (= 39–46); Thomas, *Early Christian Archaeology*, pp. 85–87; Padel, 'Cornish Names of Parish Churches'; Le Moing, *Noms de lieux bretons*, pp. 166–71; Brook, 'Early Christian Church'; James, 'Early Medieval Cemeteries'; Preston-Jones, 'Decoding Cornish Churchyards'; John Davies, 'Saints of South Wales'; Parsons, *Warning: May Contain Saints*; and Padel, 'Brittonic *lann* in Place-Names'.

[64] *Dictionary of Medieval Latin from British Sources, s.v. podium* 3, 'monastic settlement, sometimes with appurtenant land, originally with reference to elevated site or raised boundary'. But if the reference is to raised ground, was it raised from the start, or did it rise because of burials? If the latter, then a reference to raised ground could only have developed later.

[65] About 870 examples are listed in Richards, *Units*, pp. 100–43, which would not claim to be complete.

[66] J. Davies, 'Saints of South Wales', pp. 393–94; and compare p. 386.

In Cornwall names in *Lann-* probably date from the sixth or seventh century to about the tenth; it is perhaps unlikely that conditions would have favoured the creation of new examples after the county was incorporated into the Anglo-Saxon ecclesiastical system in the ninth to tenth centuries. There are about fifty examples referring to parish churches or parochial chapels, and probably about as many again referring to non-parochial sites, although the latter number is very uncertain owing to confusion of the element with other words, particularly *Nant-*, *Nans-* 'valley', for example Lanteglos, originally *Nanteglos* 'valley with a church (*eglos*)'. This confusion, also seen in Wales and Brittany, could occur at least as early as the eleventh century.[67] The fifty or so *Lann-* names referring to parish churches constitute about a quarter of all the parish churches in the county. They also include eighteen named in Domesday Book, where parish-names are otherwise poorly represented; the high number of such names in that text is due to the prominence of the element in the names of pre-Saxon monastic churches.[68] Parish churches with names in *Lann-* are situated mainly towards and on the coast, especially around estuaries, and inland up river-valleys; but their east-west distribution is fairly even across the county (Fig. 11.9; names of parish churches in *Eglos-* show a different distribution, below). This even east-west distribution shows that such names had ceased to be formed by about 1200 at the latest, since otherwise they would show a greater density towards the west, where the language lasted longer; but that evidence leaves open the question of how much earlier than 1200 the element may have ceased to be used. Two places in Cornwall have a name in *Lann-* qualified by the name of a universal saint, of the type frequent in Wales but seemingly unknown in Brittany: Launceston (**Lann-Stefan* plus Old English *tūn* 'manorial centre'), which was in existence by the late tenth century (below), and St Michael Caerhays, called *Lanuyal* 1396, *Lanvyhayll* 1473–7, *Lavihale* 1576.[69] If such dedications to universal saints in the Brittonic world are later in date than ones to native saints (see below), then these two places may con-

---

[67] Examples in Padel, *Cornish Place-Name Elements*, p. 143; compare Llancarfan and other places in Wales, from *Nant-*: Morgan, *Place-Names of Glamorgan*, p. 118.

[68] Olson, *Early Monasteries*, pp. 93–97.

[69] Respectively in manorial account rolls, Cornwall Record Office (Redruth) AR2/840 m.1 (1396) and British Library, Additional Charter 32,963 (1473–77), and the Inquisition Post Mortem of Edward Trevanion, National Archives, C142/173 (16); there may have been another, lost, place called *Leveals* in Padstow parish, but its documentation and status are late and uncertain.

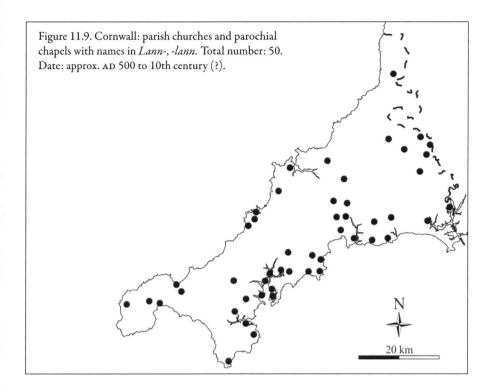

Figure 11.9. Cornwall: parish churches and parochial chapels with names in *Lann-*, *-lann*. Total number: 50. Date: approx. AD 500 to 10th century (?).

stitute the only evidence that *Lann-* may have continued to be formative in Cornwall perhaps as late as the tenth century.

In Brittany the element has long been recognized as belonging to the earliest period, but there does not seem to have been much recent discussion of its meaning, which is generally assumed to be 'monastery' or 'hermitage', referring to sites that were not central to the system of 'paroisses primitives' denoted by names in *Plou-* (below), which have tended to receive greater attention.[70] The same confusion of *Lann-* with *Nant-* occurs as in Wales and Cornwall, and in Brittany there is the additional difficulty of distinguishing place-names containing **lann* 'church-site' from those containing *lande* 'moorland', borrowed from French.[71] Names containing *Lann-* are well represented in the earliest

---

[70] Tanguy, 'Gloses toponymiques', p. 234; Vallerie, 'Grandes paroisses', p. 80; Giot and others, *British Settlement of Brittany*, pp. 136–38 and 250; Largillière also gave an additional meaning, 'une simple chapelle, un oratoire', *Les Saints*, p. 27 (= 39), as it were a precursor of the later *Loc-* (below).

[71] Well discussed by Largillière, *Les Saints*, pp. 75–79 (= 99–104).

documentation, including five examples (three of them ninth-century) in the Cartulary of Redon, and no fewer than thirty-two in the smaller Cartulary of Landévennec. Because of their occurrence all over Brittany (including areas where Breton ceased to be spoken quite early), and because of their being qualified, in place-names, by the same saints' names as names in *Plou-*, Largillière considered these names to be of the same broad period as those in *Plou-* and *Tre-*, therefore 'ancient', meaning presumably from the fifth century to about the tenth.[72] The total number of such names in Brittany is uncertain, partly because of the difficulty in identifying examples, as noted above. Vallerie suggests a figure of about 1000 in total, of which some ninety are names of ancient parishes. The latter figure constitutes a very small proportion of the total compared with Cornwall and Wales, presumably because the parish-system in Brittany was dominated instead by names in *Plou-*.[73]

No likely examples of the element have been found in southern Scotland and north-west England, except in one or two (secular) compound names.[74] The absence is striking when compared with the prominence of the element in all the three main Brittonic regions.

In recent archaeological writing the early importance of the word has been questioned, on the grounds that one aspect of its likely meaning, 'enclosed cemetery', is incompatible with archaeological evidence showing unenclosed cemeteries in use in the early post-Roman period; also on the grounds that the early use of the word in place-names is inadequately attested.[75] These reservations can both be answered, the first by suggesting that unenclosed and enclosed cemeteries could have co-existed, perhaps with enclosed ones used specifically by explicitly-Christian communities;[76] and as for the second, some of the earliest charters in the Book of Llandaf, likely to date from the sixth or seventh centuries, imply the word in toponymic use at that period, often translated as Latin *ecclesia* or *podum*, as noted above. If the occasional use of *Lann-* in the names of churches in eastern Ireland is due to Brittonic influence, as has been suggested, then its appearance in eighth-century names of Irish churches is

[72] Largillière, *Les Saints*, pp. 27–33 (= 39–46).

[73] Giot and others, *British Settlement of Brittany*, p. 138; but they give a figure of fifty ancient parishes rather than ninety.

[74] James, 'Brittonic Language in the Old North', *s.v.* **lann**.

[75] Turner, *Making a Christian Landscape*, pp. 5–8; Petts, *Church in Wales*, pp. 123–26.

[76] Compare J. Davies, 'Saints of South Wales', p. 393, the 'shift of lay burial into ecclesiastical cemeteries'; and Preston-Jones, 'Early Medieval Church', pp. 272–73.

11. GENERIC PLACE-NAME ELEMENTS IN THE THREE BRITTONIC REGIONS

further evidence that the word was well established in Welsh toponymy rather earlier than that.[77] A third indication of its early use in Brittonic is the four *Lan*- place-names in Dorset, Somerset, and Devon, which, as Brittonic place-names in those counties, can hardly have been created later than about the seventh century.[78] A fourth indication of its early use appears in the First Life of St Samson, probably written in the seventh century, where the phrase 'monasterium quod Docco uocatur' (the monastery called *Docco*), with *Lann*- rendered as Latin *monasterium*, implies that the Cornish name recorded in the tenth century as *Landochou* was known to the writer at that earlier date.[79] Four or five other *Lann*- names are attested in Cornwall in the tenth century: *Lannmoren* (now Lamorran), *Lanlouern* (now Lanlawren, in Lanteglos by Fowey parish), *Lannaled*- (St Germans), *Lanstf* (Launceston, on a coin), and uncertainly *Lankinhorn* (now Linkinhorne);[80] and many more in Domesday Book (above). The lack of attested examples in Cornwall before the tenth century is of course due to the almost complete lack of documentation providing any place-names at all there before that date. Thus there is good evidence both from southern England east of Cornwall and from Cornwall itself that place-names in *Lann*- were being formed at least as early as the seventh century, and probably earlier, as in Wales. Naturally its meaning at that earliest period is uncertain. It is even theoretically possible that it could refer to an unenclosed burial-site, of the type that has become noticeable through recent studies. But in compounds the word could designate secular enclosures, of various types, so the basic sense of the word seems to have been 'enclosure'. The uncompounded word does not seem to have been used in a secular sense, so at present there is no evidence that it ever meant other than an enclosed ecclesiastical site.[81]

---

[77] Mac Mathuna, 'Observations on Irish *lann*', especially p. 156; *Lann Leri* (now Dunleer, Co. Louth) is attested in 721, and *Lann Ela* (now Lynally, Co. Offaly) in 740: *Annals of Ulster*, pp. 174 and 194.

[78] Landkey and Landcross, north Devon; *Lanprobi* (= Sherborne, Dorset); *Lantokai* (= Leigh near Glastonbury, Somerset): all in Coates and Breeze, *Celtic Voices*, pp. 290–91, 294 and 331, with further references.

[79] *Vita I S. Samsonis*, p. 212 (§ 1.45); Picken, 'Landochou charter'; Sawyer, no. 810.

[80] S 770 (Lamorran) and S 1207 (Lanlawren); for Lanlawren see also Padel, 'Charter of Lanlawren'; the coin minted at *Lanstf* and dated 978 × 1016 has been published by P. Carlyon-Britton, 'Cornish Numismatics', pp. 107–08; for further details of *Lannaled*- (St Germans) and *Lankinhorn* (Linkinhorne, in a late copy of an uncertain charter, Sawyer, no. 838) see Padel, 'Brittonic *lann* in Place-Names'.

[81] For example, Roberts, 'Welsh Ecclesiastical Place-Names', pp. 43–44.

Archaeologically, the lack of demonstrably early excavated examples of *Lann-* sites, in Wales as well as Cornwall, is largely due to the general lack of excavations at sites with such names, partly because many of them are still in use as churchyards. One likely example is the parish church of Mullion, where imported Mediterranean pottery of the fifth or sixth century has been found; the adjacent farm is Lafrowder (*Lanffroudr'* 1299).[82] Another is Helland in Mabe parish (**Hen-lann* 'ancient, former church-site'). Here the site itself was presumably superseded by its nearby church, Mabe (itself originally **Lann-vaba*), which in turn was taken over by what was to become its parochial mother-church, Mylor (itself **Lann-wythek* 'wooded *lann'*), all before the parochial system became fully formalized in the twelfth century. Helland thus is clearly a strong candidate for a very early, but minor, *lann* site, which never became a church; but unfortunately its excavation took place too early for modern dating-methods to have been used.[83] Ann Preston-Jones has pointed out that the curved, raised enclosure at Helland is significantly smaller than that of any parish church in Cornwall.[84] It may also be suggested that an earlier overemphasis by archaeologists upon the cemetery as a central aspect of the meaning of **lann* may itself have caused an overreaction, also in archaeological writing.[85] We could perhaps envisage **lann* as primarily a settlement-term, denoting a settlement that was explicitly Christian, and perhaps having a cemetery for the families of the inhabitants but not serving the wider community of an area until parish administration started to become more formalized, perhaps in about the tenth century, when some such sites gained a place in the parochial system.[86]

The Brittonic names in *Lann-* still need further study, particularly from an onomastic and historical perspective but also taking archaeological aspects into account, and especially in Brittany and in the context of comparable names in Wales and (all of) south-west England, and the discrepant proportions of them which have become names of later parishes. Overall the lack of close correspondence between names in *Lann-* and the parochial system, especially

---

[82] Preston-Jones, 'Early Medieval Church', p. 273 (with minor caveats); Assize Roll of 1299, National Archives, Kew, Just1/1315 m. 18.

[83] Henderson, *Mabe Church and Parish*, pp. 2 and 30, and plate IV.

[84] Preston-Jones, 'Decoding Cornish Churchyards', pp. 117–18 (= 85–86).

[85] As suggested in 1988: Padel, *Popular Dictionary*, p. 191; and Preston-Jones, 'Decoding Cornish Churchyards', p. 108 (= 76).

[86] Compare Preston-Jones, 'Decoding Cornish Churchyards', pp. 122–23 (= 91).

in Brittany, but to some extent in Cornwall and Wales as well (compare the remarks about Helland in Mabe parish, above), may suggest that these names belong predominantly to a period well anterior to the advent of parochial organization. In Brittany the *Lann-* places appear to have been almost independent of the system of 'paroisses primitives' implied by the *Plou-* names (below), while belonging to the same period; and in Cornwall and Wales, too, only a proportion of the *Lann-* sites became later parish churches, perhaps only half in Cornwall, although that necessarily remains a guess. Preston-Jones has convincingly suggested that by about the tenth century new churches in Cornwall tended to be given a name in *Eglos-* rather than *Lann-*; and this likelihood further suggests that *Lann-* might already have declined in use by that date in Cornwall. It may be that the main period of creation of names in *Lann-* in Cornwall was very early, say from the fifth century to about the eighth, and that only some of those places survived as ecclesiastical sites to the period when parishes were being formed.

In Wales the word seems to have been in use equally early, but there it continued in use perhaps to the twelfth century, and was combined with the names of universal saints at the many churches called Llanfair, Lanfihangel, and Llanbedr. One useful example of the later creation of a name in *Llan-* is the parish church of Llanfihangel-y-traethau (Merionethshire, SH5935, north of Harlech), where an inscription states that the church, and therefore presumably the place-name too, was first created in the mid-twelfth century during the reign of Owain Gwynedd (1137–1170): 'QuI PrIMVM EDIFICAVIt HANC ECLesiAm IN TEMPoRe EWINI REGIs' ('who first built this church [*scil. Llanfihangel*] in the time of King Owain').[87] David Parsons has recently reexamined the category of Welsh place-names in *Llan-* qualified by the name of a universal saint:[88] Names containing 'Michael' may be the earliest, being possibly as early as the tenth century, while ones involving the 'Mary' are later, though with a possible hint of a single one before the Norman Conquest. These findings fit well with the Cornish data: if Cornish usage was similar to Welsh, then the two examples of *Lann-* plus 'Michael' and the lack of any with 'Mary' would reflect the obsolescence of the element in about the tenth century. Similarly the lack of any such examples in Brittany is also compatible with the element having gone out of use there at an early date.

---

[87] Nash-Williams, *Early Christian Monuments of Wales*, pp. 168–69 and plate LX (no. 281); Edwards, *Corpus: North Wales*, p. 473; my thanks to an anonymous referee for pointing this out.

[88] Parsons, *Warning: May Contain Saints*, pp. 7–8 and 27–32.

294   O. J. Padel

At the earliest period one would expect the element to have been used similarly on both sides of the Channel, and the question of *Lann-* as an early settlement-term, whether 'monastic' (in a broad sense) or for wider Christian communities, deserves examination across the three Brittonic regions.

Ecclesiastical Elements: (2) **pluiv*

The second ecclesiastical element to be considered is Common Neo-Brittonic **pluiv* 'people, populace' (Modern Welsh *plwyf* 'parish', Middle Cornish *plu* 'populace', Modern Breton *ploue* 'countryside').[89] This word is absent as a generic element in medieval Welsh place-names, though it does occur as a specific (qualifying) element in names such as Blaenplwyf 'end of the parish'.[90] The vocabulary providing specific elements in place-names is much broader than that providing generic elements, it should be noted, and it can include adjectives and personal names as well as a greater range of common nouns. By contrast, *ploue* is very important in early Breton toponymy, and has been much discussed, particularly because of its possible significance in relation to the colonization of Brittany from Britain. Names in *Plou-* (etc.) occur all over Brittany, but particularly across northern Brittany and at its western extremity (Fig. 11.10).[91] The element is normally qualified by a personal name, sometimes but not always one independently known as a saint.[92] Names in *Plou-* are usually thought to have been created from about the fifth century; Brett has summarized the consensus that most of them were probably formed 'in the ninth century or earlier'.[93] Its toponymic meaning is uncertain, however. Etymologically the Brittonic word means 'populace' (derived from Latin *plēb-* 'people'); the development of meaning to 'parochial flock' was already beginning in

[89] Padel, *Cornish Place-Name Elements*, p. 187; Le Moing, *Noms de lieux bretons*, pp. 180–81.

[90] Several examples in Cardiganshire: compare Owen and Morgan, *Place-Names of Wales*, p. 36; occasional instances where *plwyf* does appear as generic element, such as *Plwyv y Groes* 1736 'the parish of the cross' (= Whitchurch, Pembrokeshire; Charles, *PN Pembrokeshire*, I, 338), seem all to be modern names (post-Reformation), often nonce-formations denoting a parish in its new role of civil administration.

[91] Based on Tanguy, 'Paroisses bretonnes primitives' (1988), p. 22; this map includes a few names in Old Breton *Guic-* 'churchtown' (see below).

[92] Tanguy, 'Paroisses primitives en *plou-*' (1981), p. 153: he has about a third (35%) qualified by names of known saints, a third (34%) by names of 'saints inconnus mais attestés', and a third (30%) by names unknown as saints; but he emphasizes that these figures are approximate.

[93] Brett, 'Soldiers, Saints and States?', p. 31.

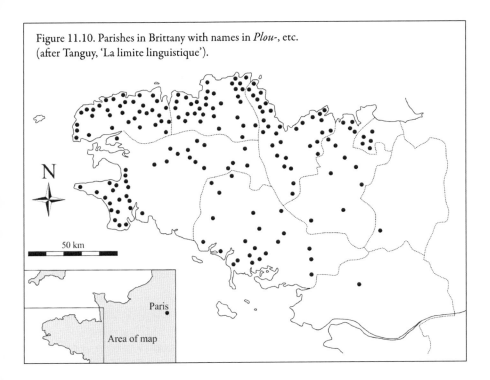

Figure 11.10. Parishes in Brittany with names in *Plou-*, etc. (after Tanguy, 'La limite linguistique').

Latin in the early Middle Ages.[94] In Breton historical scholarship the element is translated 'parish'.[95] However, in western Europe, parishes in the later ecclesiastical sense are generally considered to have been only beginning to take shape by the ninth century, and in fact this meaning given to the Breton place-name element seems to be a scholarly extrapolation from Welsh, for it does not seem to occur in Breton texts at any period. By the fifteenth century, Breton had borrowed from French the word *parroes* 'parish', presumably because it lacked a word with that meaning,[96] and in medieval and modern Breton *ploue* means 'countryside, the rural part of a parish', as contrasted with the churchtown (Old Breton *Guic-*, from Latin *vicus*); in a few cases *Guic-* and *Plou-* can be seen to be used interchangeably as generic elements in the name of a single parish, so

[94] W. Davies, 'Priests and Rural Communities', pp. 177–78.
[95] Largillière, *Les Saints*, chs 10 'La toponymie paroissiale', pp. 191–203 (= 245–60) and 11 'La constitution des paroisses', pp. 205–23 (= 261–84).
[96] Piette, *French Loanwords*, p. 153; the word may actually have been borrowed earlier, but that is the date of its earliest attestation.

the two elements are often considered together.[97] The compromise in Breton scholarship has been to refer to the *Plou-* units in the early period as 'paroisses primitives', though it has not been clear precisely what is envisaged by that term — perhaps a unit of secular as much as ecclesiastical administration.[98] Because this transition in meaning from 'people' to 'countryside' occurred too early for texts to show its course, it is uncertain whether it came first to denote the 'rural population', retaining its reference to the people but restricting it to rural areas, or through changing to denote the territory occupied by the parish flock.

At first sight it is not obvious why the element has been considered an ecclesiastical one in Brittany. If its early date is considered to relate directly to the settlement from Britain, then one might have supposed that its etymological meaning 'people' would have been emphasized, with the qualifying personal name being envisaged as the leader of a group of people who settled a particular district, much as Anglo-Saxon place-names composed of a personal name plus *-ingas* have been considered to denote the territories of early settlers in eastern England.[99] However, Tanguy's figures, cited earlier, suggest that in a fair proportion (between one-third and two-thirds) of such place-names the qualifying personal name is that of a known saint,[100] and indeed these names have been enlisted to serve the narrative of early Christian missionary-settlers with their bands of devotees.[101] It can be accepted that *Plou-* in Brittany has long played a role in the 'parochial' toponymy, even if we are not sure what we mean by 'parishes' in this context.[102] The element is well attested in the earliest documentation, with eleven examples in the Cartulary of Redon, and seven in the smaller Cartulary of Landévennec. In the Redon charters its Latin equivalent was the ancestral Latin *plebs*, though that word was also used for 'parishes' which did not have *Plou-* in their names. Wendy Davies considers that in these ninth-century texts the word (both Latin and Old Breton) still had its meaning 'populace, community', but could also have a territorial sense; she has emphasized that the civil functions of these communities were at least as prominent as

---

[97] Tanguy, 'Paroisses bretonnes primitives' (1981), pp. 27–29, with map; and see note 91, above.

[98] W. Davies, 'Priests and Rural Communities', pp. 178–79.

[99] For example, Parsons, 'Churls and Athelings', pp. 47–53.

[100] Largillière, *Les Saints*, pp. 47–74 (= 63–97).

[101] Brett, 'Soldiers, Saints and States?', especially pp. 28–34.

[102] Useful discussion of its meaning, with examples, in Tanguy, 'Paroisses primitives en *plou-*' (1981), pp. 124–26; W. Davies, 'Priests and Rural Communities', especially pp. 180–82; and Vallerie, *Communes bretons*.

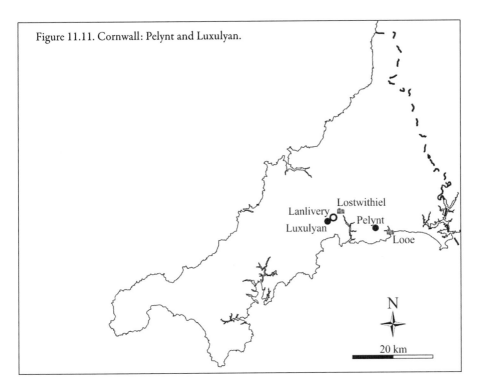

Figure 11.11. Cornwall: Pelynt and Luxulyan.

their ecclesiastical ones,[103] though that could be partly due to the secular nature of the documents showing the communities in action.

For present purposes the significant point is the large number of *Plou-* names in Brittany, contrasted with their virtual non-existence in Britain. The sole example in the whole of Britain of this word as the generic element in a medieval place-name is the parish of Pelynt, near to the port of Looe on the south coast of Cornwall (Fig. 11.11). The name is first attested in Domesday Book as *Plunent* 1086, and the manor (and therefore presumably its name) already existed in 1066. It consists of Cornish *Plu-* plus a saint's name, though the precise form of the latter is uncertain, let alone the identity of the saint.[104] It seems legitimate to consider this single example in Cornwall an outlier of the distribution in Brittany, possibly created as a result of small-scale reverse migration from Brittany to Cornwall, or simply by cross-channel linguistic influence, as with the three comparable names discussed under *lĭs (above). The Breton

---

[103] W. Davies, *Small Worlds*, pp. 63–67.

[104] Jacobs, '*Non, Nonna, Nonnita*'.

diaspora in the early tenth century, caused by Viking attacks there, provides an obvious possible context, and would be a very plausible period for this name to have been created; but in Brittany that date might be considered rather late for the creation of a *Plou-* name, and the intercourse between Cornwall and Brittany has been so constant over the centuries that it is possible to envisage the name having been created at any date from (say) the sixth century down to the eleventh when it is first attested.

The great contrast between Brittany and mainland Britain in the use of this Brittonic name-element suggests that the settlers needed to create a new type of name in Brittany. Presumably they used the word to name territories or settlements of a different kind from those existing in Britain. These territories or settlements could have been either ones that they encountered and adopted when they arrived; or ones that they developed themselves after arriving, in the context of different conditions there. In either case the distinctive vocabulary seems to imply different administrative units, perhaps (though not certainly) different ecclesiastical structures, while the names in *Les-* reflect different secular ones; and, in the case of *Plou-* at least, these different administrative conditions seem likely to be due to structures which the settlers found already in place when they arrived in Brittany, and which were different from what they had known at home in Britain.[105]

*Ecclesiastical Elements: (3) *log*

The Old Breton element **log* 'chapel' (Modern Breton *log* 'hut, cabin'; Modern Welsh *llog* '(consecrated) place') is, like **pluiv*, prominent in Breton toponymy and almost unknown in Britain, but for different reasons. In this case the reason is that the element came into use in Brittany at a date well after the settlement-period. It denoted chapels, subsidiary sites within the parochial system, and was current from the eleventh century to the thirteenth, perhaps later.[106] Accordingly it is also restricted, in Brittany, to the western zone where Breton was current at that period (and later), not to the eastern zone where Breton was current in the ninth to tenth centuries but died out thereafter; and it tends to be qualified, in place-names, by the name of a universal saint, not a Brittonic one.

---

[105] Compare W. Davies, 'Priests and Rural Communities', pp. 178–79, and Brett, 'Soldiers, Saints and States?', p. 53.

[106] Largillière, *Les Saints*, pp. 17–27 and 175–79 (= 25–39 and 225–30).

The cartularies of Redon and Landévennec each show a single example, the Redon one in an eleventh-century charter.

As with *pluiv*, there is a single example of this common Breton element in Cornwall, likewise the only medieval example of the word as a place-name generic in the whole of Britain, and again near the south coast (Fig. 11.11). The single Cornish example, Luxulyan, accords with Largillière's analysis of the much more ample Breton material. It too was not a parish church in the Middle Ages but a chapelry, in this case within the contiguous parish of Lanlivery, significantly with a name in *Lann-*; the qualifying saint's name, *Sulien*, in this case a Brittonic one, is also found in one *Loc-* name in Brittany (Lossulien, at Le Relecq-Kerhuon, near Brest, Finistère). As with Pelynt as the sole example of a *Plu-* name in Cornwall, this single Cornish example of *log* 'chapel' constitutes an outlier of the Breton distribution, though in this case it may have been created later, since the place-name is not attested until 1282. The Norman Conquest might therefore provide a possible context for this Breton-type name to have been given, particularly since a few Breton landholders are known to have acquired lands in Cornwall after 1066;[107] but, as with Pelynt, other contexts are also possible for this name near to the south-coast port of Lostwithiel.

Thomas Clancy has tentatively suggested that three names in southern Scotland, Lochwinnoch (Ayrshire), *Lochkindeloch* (lost, Kirkcudbrightshire) and Lochmaben (Dumfriesshire) may contain a generic element *login* which may have had an ecclesiastical sense; and that a fourth name, Loquhariot (Midlothian) may contain Cumbric *log* itself;[108] however, he points out that other derivations are possible for these names (including *loch* for some of them), and leaves the possibility very open.

Ecclesiastical Elements: (4) *egluis*

The Common Neo-Brittonic element *egluis* 'church' (Modern Welsh *eglwys*, Middle Cornish *eglos*, Modern Breton *iliz*) shows a marked contrast with *pluiv* and *log*, since it is well attested as a generic element in both Wales and Cornwall but unknown in Brittany. However, the reason for its uneven occurrence between the regions is different, since it does not reflect distinctive administrative structures, nor correspond in meaning to either of those two elements which

---

[107] Padel, 'Where was Middle Cornish Spoken?', pp. 28–29.

[108] Clancy, '*Logie*: An Ecclesiastical Place-Name Element'; he rightly discounts numerous other Scottish place-names containing *logie* of Gaelic or English derivation.

are (almost) unique to Brittany. In Cornwall the reason is that its use was later in date, perhaps starting in about the tenth century, particularly for a new type of church, ones founded to serve (pre-Norman) manorial centres, which tended to have rectilinear churchyards rather than curvilinear ones.[109] These churches were evidently not thought suitable for names in *Lann-*, whether because the word had already gone out of use at the period when they were being created (probably the tenth to twelfth centuries), or because they were seen as a different kind of site. As generic element *Eglos-* thus appears in the names of only two parishes in Cornwall today, Egloskerry and Egloshayle. Five other parish churches have a name in *Eglos-* surviving for an adjacent farm, but not as the name of the church or parish: Phillack (a second Egloshayle), Philleigh (Eglosrose), St Issey (Egloscrow, from *-cruc*), Merther (Eglosmerther) and Budock (Eglos Budock); and a further three farm-names in *Eglos-* do not refer to their parish churches but presumably were named from chapels, Egloshayle in Maker parish, Eglarooze in St Germans parish, and Eglosderry in Wendron parish. Apart from these ten modern names, the majority of *Eglos-* names were seemingly transient phrases used in the Middle Ages, at attested dates ranging from the eleventh century to the sixteenth, for twenty-two other parish churches and two non-parochial chapels, and occasionally for land-holdings named from the churches (Fig. 11.12). Three of these were church estates named in Domesday Book (1086), *Ecglosberrie* (St Buryan), *Hecglosenuder* (St Enoder) and *Hecglostudic* (St Tudy). In nearly all of these lost names *Eglos-* was followed by the name of the patron saint of the church, always a local, Brittonic one.

These names have a western bias in their distribution within the county, reflecting where the language was alive at the date when the various names were recorded. Most of these lost names in *Eglos-*, particularly those where the element was qualified by a saint's name, do not seem to have been true place-names but phrases within the language, remaining current only while that still survived in the western half of the county. This is not the place to discuss the problem of distinguishing between a phrase in the language and a formal name. The boundary will sometimes be blurred or subjective; but it is particularly the transience of many of these names, and their currency only in areas where Cornish was still alive, that are crucial factors in this case. Of the six names in *Eglos-* in the eastern half, two were transient names of that kind, recorded in the eleventh and twelfth centuries respectively; and the other four have become fossilized as names, two being the modern parishes with *Eglos-* in their names,

---

[109] Preston-Jones, 'Decoding Cornish Churchyards', pp. 111–13 (= 79–81).

11. GENERIC PLACE-NAME ELEMENTS IN THE THREE BRITTONIC REGIONS

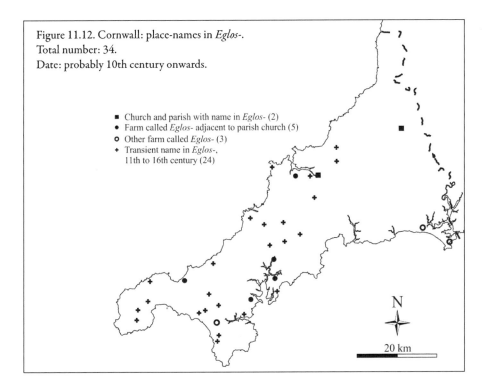

Figure 11.12. Cornwall: place-names in *Eglos-*.
Total number: 34.
Date: probably 10th century onwards.

- ■ Church and parish with name in *Eglos-* (2)
- ● Farm called *Eglos-* adjacent to parish church (5)
- ○ Other farm called *Eglos-* (3)
- + Transient name in *Eglos-*, 11th to 16th century (24)

and two being farms where the name presumably referred to a lost chapel. The remaining, western, names are mostly of the transient type, names such as *Egloserm* 1345 (St Erme), *Egloslagek* 1354 (Ladock), and *Eglosnyulin* 1415 (Newlyn East), mostly not true place-names but simply the way that Cornish-speakers referred to (some of) their parish churches, and occasionally to land-holdings named from the churches. It was mainly through becoming the name of a secular land-holding that such names were recorded at all, and sometimes survived to modern times.

In Wales names in *Eglwys-* are quite common, though not remotely approaching the frequency of those in *Llan-*, and given the comparative sizes of the two regions they seem to be less common than in Cornwall, although that may be because nonce-phrases containing the element have not yet been systematically published. The standard list shows some thirty-nine examples, of which at least nine are obsolete, including ones where *Eglwys-* has been replaced by *Llan-*, or has been dropped altogether leaving only the saint's name.[110]

---

[110] Richards, *Units*, pp. 64–65; compare Richards, 'Ecclesiastical and Secular', pp. 10–11.

There are a few examples of such names in the Book of Llandaf, for example *Eccluis Santbreit*, now Caldicot, Monmouthshire,[111] but seemingly not in the texts of early charters in that collection, only in the rubrics or in later material; and these names too have been lost or replaced. This similar tendency in Wales as in Cornwall for names in *Eglwys-* to become obsolete or be replaced is probably due, at least in part, to the same reason, namely that some of them were phrases in the language rather than formal place-names. For this conclusion about names in *Eglwys-* and *Eglos-* one may compare the similar explanation for nonce-formations in Welsh *Plwyf-* in the early modern period (above), and, less closely, David Parsons's suggestion that Welsh names in *Merthyr-* plus saint's name were originally simplex place-names, *Merthyr* alone, and that the addition (in these names) of the saint's name itself was secondary and transient;[112] his explanation may account for the Cornish names in *Merther-* as well.[113]

Breton *iliz* does not appear as generic element at all, though it can appear as the qualifying (specific) element, just as **pluiv* can appear as qualifier in Welsh and Cornish place-names. Breton names incorporating it as qualifying element include Ker ilis and Tref an ilis, corresponding to Cornish Treveglos and Treneglos, Welsh Trefeglwys.[114] Even within the language generally, phrases such as *Iliz-X* (where X is a saint's name) seem to be rare: Grégoire de Rostrenen, in 1732, translated 'Église de saint Paul' into Breton as *Ilis Paul*, *lan-Baul*,[115] in which the second phrase at any rate appears to be artificially created, using *lan*, a word not normally current in the language. Overall, therefore, it seems that the disparity in the use of **egluis* as a generic element between Wales and Cornwall on the one hand, and Brittany on the other, rather than reflecting any significant difference in ecclesiastical structures as names in *Plou-do*, or arising in the central Middle Ages as those in *Lok-* do, is instead a function of the way the word was used at later periods in the languages, or of the way in which places (rather than their actual names) were recorded at different periods in the respective regions.

---

[111] *Book of Llan Dâv*, p. 235; W. Davies, *Llandaff Charters*, p. 123.

[112] Parsons, *Martyrs and Memorials*, pp. 34–35, 40–41 and 47–48.

[113] Padel, 'Local Saints and Place-Names in Cornwall', pp. 314–15, with map.

[114] Largillière, *Les Saints*, p. 193 (= 248).

[115] Rostrenen, *Dictionnaire*, p. 325b.

11. GENERIC PLACE-NAME ELEMENTS IN THE THREE BRITTONIC REGIONS

This selection of eight generic elements serves to indicate how much difference, as well as similarity, there is between Brittany, Cornwall, and Wales in the place-names. The differences between Brittany and the two Insular regions are significantly greater than those within Britain between Cornwall and Wales. The similarities between Brittany and the Insular regions occur particularly in elements thought to have been used at earlier dates, most obviously, *trev, *bod, and *lann; while some of the differences arise from divergences in meaning or usage from about the tenth century, notably in *trev (again), *ker, *egluis, and *log. But other differences seem to go back much earlier, notably in the use of *pluiv and perhaps of *lis. It is hard to avoid the conclusion that the use of *pluiv, in particular, arose from the use of different administrative structures from the time of the settlement or soon afterwards, and that the distinctive use of *lis can be associated with the unusual social conditions of the small independent-seeming secular administrative units identified by Wendy Davies, although it is unclear how long before the ninth century that situation may have arisen.

The question then arises whether this use of different administrative structures was due to the adoption, by the settlers, of existing arrangements which they found in Armorica when they arrived, or whether they created these structures afresh. Wendy Davies has considered this problem, specifically concerning the origin of the distinctive *plebs* units so prominent in the ninth century: 'Were they a result of British migration into Brittany, or of subsequent developments, or even some reflection of pre-migration structures?'[116] The use of some of the same elements, notably *lann, *trev and *bod, shows that the migrants did sometimes continue to use naming-patterns current in the homeland, so the use of a fresh one, *pluiv, which had not had (nor was later to have) any such use in Britain suggests that the settlers were adopting a type of structure which had not existed in Britain. Caroline Brett has anticipated the suggestion which is made here on toponymic grounds: 'the *plebes* or *plous* look suspiciously organized, and as though they may pre-date the Breton settlements in some form'.[117] If this conclusion is accepted, it brings in turn implications for the scale of the migrations and the nature of the interaction between the settlers and the existing population which they found there. And if so, then the *lann* churches or settlements which the migrants presumably did introduce must somehow have fitted alongside this existing structure. It would seem that, in Brittany, the

---

[116] W. Davies, 'Priests and Rural Communities', p. 178.

[117] Brett, 'Soldiers, Saints and States?', p. 53.

places with names in *Lann-* were not part of the parochial system but existed almost independently of it. This independence might accord with the situation described in the sixth-century 'Letter to Lovocat and Catihern', where priests with Brittonic names, and their groups of followers (including women) were apparently serving the countryside in a manner which ran counter to expected practices on the Continent in various ways, such as to incur the disapproval of the bishops.[118] In Cornwall and Wales, on the other hand, where there had not been a parochial system in the early Middle Ages (whether ecclesiastical, 'civil', or both), some, though not all, of the *Lann-* churches were pressed into service when ecclesiastical parishes did develop in the central-medieval period, and hence came to have a greater role than in Brittany in the parochial system as it has continued to the present day.

As for the secular elements, the migrants arrived with a full range of vocabulary referring to farmsteads, houses, and other secular dwellings: **trev* 'farmstead, farming hamlet'; **bod* 'dwelling'; **ti* or **tï* 'house'; **cair* presumably (at that period) still meaning 'a round'; and **lïs* 'ruler's court'. Of these elements, **trev* was not used as intensively as in Cornwall, and only detailed work at the local level will show what proportion of the names in Brittany use the element in its older, secular, sense, and how many use its later ecclesiastical one. The elements used and their expected meanings will also be affected by the question of where within Britain the migrants came from.[119] Here the only toponymic guidance within Britain comes from Wales and Cornwall, since so few place-names survive containing any of these habitative elements from southern England east of that county.[120]

The element **bod* 'dwelling' seems to have been little studied in its own right in Brittany; it probably dropped out of use there at an early date, as in Cornwall. The greatest secular difference from Insular usage in Brittany is the frequency of **cair*, as Breton *Ker-* 'house, dwelling', which Tanguy has explained by suggesting that its use was extended to fill the gap left by the change in meaning

---

[118] Jülicher, 'Ein gallisches Bischofsschreiben des 6. Jahrhunderts'; Labriolle, *Sources de l'histoire du montanisme*, pp. 226–30 (no. 187); compare Giot and others, *British Settlement of Brittany*, pp. 136–38.

[119] Guy, 'Breton Migration', argues for the area of the *civitas* of the *Durotriges* (chiefly modern Dorset).

[120] Padel, 'Place-Names and the Saxon Conquest', maps on pp. 216 and 218, shows the few instances of **trev* and **bod* in Devon; all the secular elements discussed here are virtually unknown further east, except for a single instance of **lis* as Leece (Hampshire): Coates and Breeze, *Celtic Voices*, p. 302.

of *trev to an ecclesiastical sense, in about the eleventh century. Although that explanation is convincing, it leaves open the question of what the meaning of *cair was during the centuries between the migration and this extension of its use. Finally, the distinctive frequency of *Les-* 'court' in Brittany can be attractively explained, as noted by Brett, by the comparative lack of centralized secular authority there, compared with Cornwall and Wales.[121]

O. J. Padel [ojp21@cam.ac.uk] formerly Reader in Cornish and Celtic, University of Cambridge; former president of the Society for Name Studies in Britain and Ireland, and of the English Place-Name Society.

[121] Brett, 'Soldiers, Saints and States?', especially pp. 41–44.

Works Cited

Manuscripts and Archival Sources

London, British Library, Additional Charter 32,963
London (Kew), National Archives, C142/173 (16), Inquisition post mortem of Edward Trevanion
Redruth, Cornwall Record Office, AR2/140, manorial account roll

Primary Sources

The Annals of Ulster (to A.D. 1131), ed. by S. Mac Airt and G. Mac Niocaill (Dublin: Institute for Advanced Studies, 1983)

Cartulaire de l'abbaye Saint-Sauveur de Redon, ed. by H. Guillotel, A. Chédeville, and B. Tanguy, 2 vols (Rennes: Association des Amis des Archives historiques du diocèse de Rennes, Dol et Saint-Malo, 1998–2004)

The Cartulary of St Michael's Mount (Hatfield House MS. no. 315), ed. by P. L. Hull, Devon & Cornwall Record Society, n.s., 5 (1962)

Cartularium Saxonicum, ed. by W. de G. Birch, 3 vols and index (London: Phillimore & Co., 1885–99)

Dictionary of Medieval Latin from British Sources, ed. by R. E. Latham, D. R. Howlett and R. K. Ashdowne, 17 fascicules (Oxford: University Press, 1975–2013)

The Monks of Redon: Gesta Sanctorum Rotonensium and Vita Conuuoionis, ed. by C. Brett, SCH, 10 (Woodbridge: Boydell, 1989)

The Text of the Book of Llan Dâv: Reproduced from the Gwysaney Manuscript, ed. by J. G. Evans with J. Rhys, repr. (Aberystwyth: National Library of Wales, 1979)

Vita I S. Samsonis, in *La Vie ancienne de saint Samson de Dol*, ed. and trans. by P. Flobert (Paris: Éditions du CNRS, 1997), pp. 133–269

Secondary Works

Bender, B., S. Hamilton, and C. Tilley, 'Leskernick: the Biography of an Excavation', *Cornish Archaeology*, 34 (1995), 58–73

Brett, C., 'Soldiers, Saints and States? The Breton Migrations Revisited', *CMCS*, 61 (2011), 1–56

Brett, C., with F. Edmonds, and P. Russell, *Brittany and the Atlantic Archipelago, 450–1200. Contact, Myth and History* (Cambridge: Cambridge University Press, 2022)

Brook, D., 'The Early Christian Church East and West of Offa's Dyke', in *The Early Church in Wales and the West*, ed. by N. Edwards and A. Lane (Oxford: Oxbow, 1992), pp. 77–89

Carlyon-Britton, P. W. P., 'Cornish Numismatics', *British Numismatic Journal*, 3 (1907), 107–16

Carr, A. D., *Medieval Anglesey* (Llangefni: Anglesey Antiquarian Society, 1982)

Charles, B. G., *The Place-Names of Pembrokeshire*, 2 vols (Aberystwyth: National Library of Wales, 1992)

Clancy, T. O., '*Logie*: An Ecclesiastical Place-Name Element in Eastern Scotland', *Journal of Scottish Name Studies*, 10 (2016), 25–88

Coates, R., and A. Breeze, ed., *Celtic Voices, English Places: Studies of the Celtic Impact on Place-Names in England* (Stamford: Shaun Tyas, 2000)

Davies, J. R., 'The Saints of South Wales and the Welsh Church', in *Local Saints and Local Churches in the Early Medieval West*, ed. by A. Thacker and R. Sharpe (Oxford: Oxford University Press, 2002), pp. 361–95

Davies, W., *The Llandaff Charters* (Aberystwyth: The National Library of Wales, 1979)

——, 'Priests and Rural Communities in East Brittany in the Ninth Century', *ÉC*, 20 (1983), 177–97

——, *Small Worlds: the Village Community in Early Medieval Brittany* (London: Duckworth, 1988)

Edwards, N, *A Corpus of Early Medieval Inscribed Stones and Stone Sculpture in Wales*, III: *North Wales* (Cardiff: University of Wales Press, 2013)

Edwards, N., and A. Lane, ed., *The Early Church in Wales and the West* (Oxford: Oxbow, 1992)

Giot, P.-R., P. Guigon, and B. Merdrignac, *The British Settlement of Brittany: The First Bretons in Armorica* (Stroud: Tempus, 2003)

Guy, B., 'The Breton Migration: A New Synthesis', *Zeitschrift für celtische Philologie*, 61 (2014), 101–56

Hemon, R., *Geriadur Istorel ar Brezhoneg: Dictionnaire historique du Breton*, 36 parts (Brest: Preder, 1958–1979)

Henderson, C., *Mabe Church and Parish, Cornwall* (Long Compton: King's Stone Press, [1930])

Herring, P., 'Cornish Strip Fields', in *Medieval Devon and Cornwall: Shaping an Ancient Countryside*, ed. by S. Turner (Macclesfield: Windgather, 2006), pp. 44–77

——, A. Preston-Jones, C. Thorpe, and I. Wood, 'Early Medieval Cornwall', *Cornish Archaeology*, 50 (2011), 263–86

Hooke, D., *Pre-Conquest Charter-Bounds of Devon and Cornwall* (Woodbridge: Boydell, 1994)

Jackson, K., 'Nennius and the Twenty-Eight Cities of Britain', *Antiquity*, 12 (1938), 44–55

——, 'Angles and Britons in Northumbria and Cumbria', in *Angles and Britons*, ed. by H. Lewis, O'Donnell Lectures (Cardiff: University of Wales Press, 1963), pp. 60–84

Jacobs, N., '*Non, Nonna, Nonnita*: Confusions of Gender in Brythonic Hagiography', *Transactions of the Honorable Society of Cymmrodorion*, 23 (2017), 19–33

James, A., 'The Brittonic Language in the Old North', Scottish Place-Name Society, online at <https://spns.org.uk/resources/bliton> [accessed 1 November 2018]

——, 'Cumbric *Trev* in Kyle, Carrick, Galloway and Dumfriesshire', *Transactions of the Dumfriesshire and Galloway Natural History and Antiquarian Society*, 88 (2014), 21–42

James, H., 'Early Medieval Cemeteries in Wales', in *The Early Church in Wales and the West*, ed. by N. Edwards and A. Lane (Oxford: Oxbow, 1992), pp. 90–103

Jenkins, D., and M. Owen, 'The Welsh Marginalia in the Lichfield Gospels', *CMCS*, 5 (1983), 37–66; and 7 (1984), 91–120

Johnson, N., and P. Rose, 'Defended Settlement in Cornwall: An Illustrated Discussion', in *Studies in Rural Settlement and Economy*, ed. by D. Myles, 2 vols, British Archaeological Reports, British Series, 103 (1982), i, 151–207

——, P. Rose, and D. Bonney, *Bodmin Moor: An Archaeological Survey*, 2 vols (London: English Heritage, 1994–2008)

Jülicher, A., 'Ein gallisches Bischofsschreiben des 6. Jahrhunderts als Zeuge für die Verfassung der Montanistenkirche', *Zeitschrift für Kirchengeschichte*, 16 (1896), 664–71

Labriolle, P. de, *Les Sources de l'histoire du montanisme* (Paris: Leroux, 1913)

Largillière, R., *Les Saints et l'organisation chrétienne primitive dans l'Armorique bretonne* (Paris: Plihon, 1925); new edition with additions (Crozon: Armeline, 1995); page-references are to both editions, thus: 27–33 (= 39–46)

Le Moing, J.-Y., *Les Noms de lieux bretons de Haute-Bretagne* (Spezed: Coop Breizh, 1990)

Mac Mathuna, L., 'Observations on Irish *lann* "(piece of) land; (church) building" and Compounds', *Ériu*, 48 (1997), 153–60

Morgan, R., *Place-Names of Glamorgan* (Cardiff: Welsh Academic Press, 2018)

——, and R. F. Peter Powell, *A Study of Breconshire Place-Names*, Welsh Heritage Series, 9 (Llanrwst: Gwasg Carreg Gwalch, 1999)

Morgan, T. J., and P. Morgan, *Welsh Surnames* (Cardiff: University of Wales Press, 1985)

Nash-Williams, V. E., *The Early Christian Monuments of Wales* (Cardiff: University of Wales Press, 1950)

Olson, L., *Early Monasteries in Cornwall*, SCH, 11 (Woodbridge: Boydell, 1989)

Owen, H. W., and R. Morgan, *Dictionary of the Place-Names of Wales* (Llandysul: Gomer, 2007)

Padel, O. J., 'Ancient and Medieval Administrative Divisions of Cornwall', *Proceedings of the Dorset Natural History and Archaeological Society*, 131 (2010), 211–14

——, 'Brittonic *lann* in Place-Names', in *Names, Texts and Landscapes in the Middle Ages: a Memorial Volume for Duncan Probert*, ed. S. Bassett and A. J. Spedding (Donington: Shaun Tyas, 2022), pp. 123–50

——, 'The Charter of Lanlawren, Cornwall', in *Latin Learning and English Lore: Studies in Anglo-Saxon Literature for Michael Lapidge*, ed. by K. O'Brien O'Keeffe and A. Orchard, 2 vols (Toronto: University Press, 2005), ii, pp. 74–85

——, 'Cornish Names of Parish Churches', *Cornish Studies*, 4/5 (1976–1977), 15–27

——, *Cornish Place-Name Elements*, English Place-Name Society, 56/57 (Nottingham: English Place-Name Society, 1985)

——, 'Local Saints and Place-Names in Cornwall', in *Local Saints and Local Churches in the Early Medieval West*, ed. by A. Thacker and R. Sharpe (Oxford: Oxford University Press, 2002), pp. 303–60

——, 'Place-Names and the Saxon Conquest of Devon and Cornwall', in *Britons in Anglo-Saxon England*, ed. by N. Higham (Woodbridge: Boydell, 2007), pp. 215–30

——, *A Popular Dictionary of Cornish Place-Names* (Penzance: Hodge, 1988)

——, 'Where was Middle Cornish Spoken?' *CMCS*, 74 (2017), 1–31

Parsons, D., 'Churls and Athelings, Kings and Reeves: Some Reflections on Place-Names and Early English Society', in *Perceptions of Place: Twenty-First-Century Interpretations of English Place-Name Studies*, ed. by J. Carroll and D. N. Parsons (Nottingham: English Place-Name Society, 2013), pp. 43–72

——, *Martyrs and Memorials: Merthyr Place-Names and the Church in Early Wales* (Aberystwyth: Canolfan Uwchefrydiau Cymreig a Cheltaidd Prifysgol Cymru, 2013)

——, *Warning: May Contain Saints: Place-Names as Evidence for the Church in Early Wales* (Cambridge: Department of Anglo-Saxon, Norse, and Celtic, 2019)

Petts, D., *The Early Medieval Church in Wales* (Stroud: History Press, 2009)

Picken, W. M. M., 'The "Landochou" Charter', in W. G. Hoskins, *The Westward Expansion of Wessex*, Occasional Papers, 13 (Leicester: Leicester University Press, 1960), pp. 36–44

Piette, J. R. F., *French Loanwords in Middle Breton* (Cardiff: University of Wales Press, 1973)

Preston-Jones, A., 'Decoding Cornish Churchyards', in *The Early Church in Wales and the West*, ed. by N. Edwards and A. Lane (Oxford: Oxbow, 1992), pp. 104–24; reprinted in *Cornish Archaeology*, 33 (1994), 71–95; page-references are to both editions, thus: 104 (= 71)

——, 'The Early Medieval Church', in P. Herring, A. Preston-Jones, C. Thorpe, and I. Wood, 'Early Medieval Cornwall', *Cornish Archaeology*, 50 (2011), 263–86, at pp. 269–76

Quinnell, H., *Trethurgy: Excavations at Trethurgy Round, St Austell: Community and Status in Roman and Post-Roman Cornwall* ([Truro]: Cornwall County Council, 2004)

Richards, M., 'Ecclesiastical and Secular in Medieval Welsh Settlement', *SC*, 3 (1966), 9–18

——, *Enwau Tir a Gwlad*, ed. by B. Lewis Jones (Caernarfon: Gwasg Gwynedd, 1998)

——, *Welsh Administrative and Territorial Units* (Cardiff: University of Wales Press, 1969)

Roberts, T., 'Welsh Ecclesiastical Place-Names', in *The Early Church in Wales and the West*, ed. by N. Edwards and A. Lane (Oxford: Oxbow, 1992), pp. 41–44

Rostrenen, G. de, *Dictionnaire françois-celtique ou françois-breton* (Rennes: Vatar, 1732)

Russell, V., *West Penwith Survey* (Truro: Cornwall Archaeological Society, 1971)

Sawyer, P., *Anglo-Saxon Charters: an Annotated List and Bibliography* (London: Royal Historical Society, 1968); updated edition at 'The Electronic Sawyer', <www.esawyer.org.uk> (accessed 1 July 2019)

Tanguy, B., *Dictionnaire des noms de communes, trèves et paroisses du Finistère* (Douarnenez: Le Chasse-Marée, 1990)

——, 'La limite linguistique dans la péninsule armoricaine à l'époque de l'émigration bretonne (IV^c–VI^c siècle) d'après les donnés toponymiques', *ABPO*, 87 (1980), 429–62

——, *Les Noms de lieux bretons*, I, *Toponymie descriptive* (Rennes: Centre Régional de Recherche et de Documentation Pédagogique, 1975)

——, 'Les paroisses bretonnes primitives', in *Histoire de la paroisse: actes de la onzième Rencontre d'histoire religieuse tenue à Fontevraud les 2. et 3. octobre 1987* (Angers: Presses de l'université d'Angers, 1988), pp. 9–32

——, 'Les paroisses primitives en *plou*- et leurs saints éponymes', *BSAF*, 109 (1981), 121–55

——, 'De quelques gloses toponymiques dans les anciennes vies de saints bretons', in *Bretagne et pays celtiques: langues, histoire, civilisation: mélanges offerts à la mémore de Léon Fleuriot*, ed. by G. Le Menn and J.-Y. Le Moing (Rennes: Presses universitaires de Rennes, 1992), pp. 227–35

——, 'De la treb à la trève ou de l'origine des frairies et des trèves', in *Chrétientés de Basse-Bretagne et d'ailleurs: mélanges offers au chanoine Jean-Louis le Floc'h*, ed. by Y. Celton, T. Daniel, and Y. Tranvouez (Brest: Société archéologique du Finistère, 1998), pp. 237–44

Tangye, M., 'Lestowder, St Keverne: a Previously Unidentified Stronghold', *Cornish Archaeology*, 34 (1995), 176–81

Taylor, S., 'Place-Names and the Early Church in Eastern Scotland', in *Scotland in Dark Age Britain*, ed. by B. Crawford (St Andrews: Scottish Cultural Press, 1996), pp. 93–110

Taylor, T., *The Celtic Christianity of Cornwall* (London: Longman, 1916)

Thomas, C., 'The Character and Origins of Roman Dumnonia', in *Rural Settlement in Roman Britain*, ed. by C. Thomas, CBA Research Report, 7 (London: Council for British Archaeology, 1966), pp. 74–98

——, *The Early Christian Archaeology of North Britain* (London: Oxford University Press, 1971)

Turner, S., *Making a Christian Landscape: The Countryside in Early Medieval Cornwall, Devon and Wessex* (Exeter: Exeter University Press, 2006)

Vallerie, E., *Communes bretons et paroisses d'Armorique* (Brasparts: Beltan, 1986)

——, 'Origine des grandes paroisses en Lan-', in *Les Débuts de l'organisation religieuse de la Bretagne armoricaine, Britannia Monastica* 3 (1994), 72–83

Williams, I., 'ysgi, ysgai, Ysgeiawc, Ysgeifiog', *BBCS*, 11 (1941–44), 83

12. Facing Different Ways: The Onomastics of People in Medieval Brittany

Paul Russell

ABSTRACT This paper considers the personal-name patterns of medieval Brittany from a number of different directions: it first focuses on the changes and developments in naming patterns in Brittany broadly in the early and high medieval periods; secondly, in order to maintain an element of comparison, it takes a particular category of names, the witness lists to charters, and sets them against comparable bodies of material from early medieval Wales and Cornwall; thirdly, it examines some specific groups of names of varying levels of status, some of which come from outside Brittany and so have the added benefit of allowing us to see how Breton names could be transmitted outside Brittany. It argues that, to gain a clearer sense of how the onomastics of medieval Brittany worked, all these approaches need to be brought together.

RÉSUMÉ Cet article présente une enquête en plusieurs dimensions sur les noms d'hommes en Bretagne médiévale. D'abord sont décrites les grandes lignes de développement de l'anthroponymie en Bretagne au Moyen Âge haut et classique. Ensuite, les noms qui apparaissent dans une catégorie particulière de sources, à savoir les listes de témoins des actes, en Bretagne, au Cornwall et au Pays de Galles, sont comparés. L'article présente enfin une étude plus détaillée de quelques groupes de noms à divers niveaux sociaux, dont quelques-uns émanent d'au-delà de la Bretagne, ce qui nous laisse voir comment les noms bretons purent se propager par ailleurs. Pour comprendre plus clairement comment fonctionnèrent les pratiques d'onomastique de la Bretagne médiévale, il faut réunir toutes ces approches.

KEYWORDS Clohars, 'condensation' of names, Cornwall, Gurheden, patronymy, personal names, Prüm, Quimperlé, St Yves, Salomon, Wales

---

Multi-disciplinary Approaches to Medieval Brittany, 450–1200: Connections and Disconnections,
ed. by Caroline Brett, Fiona Edmonds, and Paul Russell, TCNE 36 (Turnhout: Brepols, 2023)
pp. 311–358   BREPOLS ᴪ PUBLISHERS   10.1484/M.TCNE-EB.5.132317

312 *Paul Russell*

Just after 1084 Count Alan reaffirmed a grant relating to land at Clohal (Cluthgual; modern Clohars-Carnoët, between Quimperlé and the coast to the south) which had been made by his father and his grandfather to the abbot and monks of the Holy Cross of Quimperlé.[1] The main body of the charter is unremarkable but the witness list has some striking features: together with the bishops of Nantes and Cornouaille the list includes the abbot, the deacon, the scribe, and the chaplain, and then a list of presumably lay individuals, Tanki mab Guegun, Derian mab Tanki, and Tanki Mab, at which point (bottom of fol. 80ʳ) the main scribe of this manuscript, Gurheden, breaks off with the assertion that the 'rustic imbecility' of the names prevented him writing any more of them:[2]

> Cum his hi etiam idonei testes affuerunt. Iungomarius abbas. Guigonus decanus. Aldroenus grammaticus. Coriou capellanus. Tanki mab guegun. Derian mab tanki. Tanki mab cognomine. et alii plurimi quorum nomina eorumdem rustica imbecillitas hic notari prohibuit.

> Together with these, these suitable witnesses were also present: Iungomarius the abbot, Guigonus the deacon, Aldroenus the scribe, Coriou the chaplain, Tanki mab Guegun, Derian mab Tanki, and Tanki Mab, and many others; the rustic stupidity of their names prevented them from being noted here.

This passage offers a useful starting point for thinking about personal names in medieval Brittany as it makes us consider what names are for and why these names in particular should have generated such disapproval. After all, it is relatively rare for scribes and writers at any period to comment on the form of personal names; names are usually seen simply as designators of individuals and therefore not always fully meaningful in their own right.[3] Where comments are made, then, it is worth asking why. It may depend on very personal circum-

---

[1] Facsimile of London, British Library, Egerton 2802: *Cartulaire de Quimperlé*, ed. by Henry and others, fol. 79ᵛ–80ʳ; edition: *Cartulaire de Quimperlé*, ed. by Maître and de Berthou, pp. 177–78.

[2] *Cartulaire de Sainte-Croix de Quimperlé*, ed. by Henry and others, fol. 80ʳ14–19; edition: *Cartulaire de l'abbaye de Sainte-Croix de Quimperlé*, ed. by Maître and de Berthou, p. 178, ll. 20–24. For a full text and translation, see Appendix 1 below (pp. 347–48).

[3] Nicknames are a different matter as their force depends precisely on them being meaningful; for discussion, see Wilson, *Means of Naming*, pp. 118–23, 280–88; also McClure, 'Nicknames and Petnames'; McDowell, 'Towards a Semiotics of Nicknaming'; Morgan and others, *Nicknames*; Holland, 'The Many Faces of Nicknames'; Skipper and Leslie, 'Towards a Theory of Nicknames'.

stances which are only occasionally enunciated; a rare example is Abelard about Saint-Gildas-de-Rhuys: 'the country was wild and the language unknown to me, [...] the natives were brutal and barbarous'.[4] In medieval sources generally, a common circumstance is when the vernacular forms of names are Latinized. The comments can sometimes be explicit; for example, William of Malmesbury is prone to mutter darkly about Latinizing Anglo-Saxon names: 'ne uocabulorum barbaries delicati lectoris sautiaret aures'.[5] Occasionally, the comment is implicit in how a name is represented: in mid-twelfth-century Wales, the biographer of Gruffudd ap Cynan, though he does not say what he is doing or why, Latinizes Welsh names in such a way as to avoid non-Latinate sounds, thus *Griffinus*: *Gruffudd*, etc., and in doing so hints at something of his view about the Latinization of Welsh names; thirteenth-century Welsh writers, on the other hand, are much more comfortable with Welsh fricatives in their Latin.[6] But here in this charter it does not seem to be a question of foreign sounds or not knowing how to spell certain names or needing to Latinize them; the scribe is after all Breton and the matrix language of the charters is Latin. We return to the issues raised by Gurheden and his names later in this paper.

But we may begin by stepping back from this specific case. The study of personal names, like that of place-names, forms an important part of any study of a society, and especially of medieval Brittany where other forms of evidence are not always easily to hand or evenly distributed over time and place. Personal names and place-names tell us about different things. Place-names are by usually fixed to a place and, if traced over time, can be used to trace the distribution not only of land-holdings, by which social change might be detected, but also of linguistic change.[7] There is of course overlap with personal names in that place-names can incorporate the names of people (often that of the landowner), but generally the names of places do not change very quickly (except insofar as they are subject to the usual linguistic changes). We can also learn something different depending on whether we examine them at a macro-level, such names of regions, of landscape features, or of large settlements, etc., or at various levels

---

[4] Abelard, *Historia Calamitatum* (*The Letters of Abelard and Eloise*, trans. pp. 44–45).

[5] *Vita Wulfstani*, I. 16. 5 (*Saints' Lives*, ed. by Winterbottom and Thomson); cf. Winterbottom, 'The Language of William of Malmesbury', pp. 130–31.

[6] *Vita Griffini*, pp. 125–26; cf. also Pryce, 'Uses of the Vernacular'.

[7] Place names can also be imported by migrants; for example, there is a striking similarity in the regional names in Brittany and in south-west Britain, such as Cornouaille: Cornwall; see Brett, Edmonds, and Russell, *Brittany and the Atlantic Archipelago*, pp. 79–85.

down to the micro-toponymy of, for example, field-names. At the latter level the historian can learn much about local land-holdings and how or why they might change over time.[8] But the level of detail is not uniform and varies hugely depending on source material available for any area; for example, areas which figure in the surviving cartularies are always more heavily documented that others. By contrast people move about but we are still only introduced to them if they figure in surviving documents or are of sufficiently high status to be commemorated in some lasting way at their death. Like place-names, personal names are always carriers of linguistic evidence but can be difficult to interpret; naming is not a straightforwardly linguistic process in the sense that it is difficult to be clear about the semantics of name-elements (insofar as they have any) and the phonology does not always follow the usual lines of development.[9] But, as nowadays, they also involve important extra-linguistic factors, such as social and political determinants (for example, being named after an ancestor, or following the dictates of a fashion of a given period); all of this can give rise to interesting features, such as the surprising conjunctions of names, e.g. a father with a Frankish (Germanic) name having a son with a Breton name, or the persistence of a small number of particular, high-status names in noble families.[10] Personal names are also inherently conservative, both linguistically and socially, and that is particularly the case in the kinds of texts which survive the vagaries of transmission. Since the nature of the source material inevitably ensures that the data are socially loaded towards the upper echelons (for example, witness lists of charters only contain local landowners and clerics), we have to be very careful about what can be said and deduced on the basis of such evidence.[11]

We therefore need to consider the forms and types of personal names used in medieval Brittany and what they might contribute to our understanding of Brittany in this period. The evidence is very patchy and uneven: in date it can range from the scattered inscriptions of the fifth and sixth centuries onwards.[12] In terms of quantity we find single names in some inscriptions but thousands of

---

[8] See, for example, W. Davies, *Small Worlds*.

[9] On the former, see pp. 316–17 below; and on the latter, see Russell, 'Old Welsh *Dinacat, Cunedag, Tutagual*', pp. 447–48.

[10] See, for example, the use of the name Arthur in a charter of Salomon dated to 860 (p. 350 below).

[11] For some rare evidence about lower-status onomastics, see Davies, *Small Worlds*, pp. 87–89.

[12] These have been collected in Davies and others, *The Inscriptions of Early Medieval Brittany*.

names in some of the larger cartularies which can vary in date from the eighth century to the fourteenth or fifteenth. Such corpora of names, such as can be found in witness lists to charters, are often most informative in that they offer us a group of names from a single place at a single (often very precise) date, or at least within a clear date range, and so can provide a broad sense of how the names might have worked in context and over time. The recent new facsimiles of several of the Breton cartularies (together with excellent introductory discussions and complete indices of names) have now made this material much more accessible, not least so that the accuracy of the readings in the older printed editions can be checked.[13] Other lists can also be helpful, such as the list of individuals providing witness statements for the canonization of Yves in 1330.[14] However, all such materials present considerable problems of interpretation and raise awkward methodological questions about how names were used and how we can legitimately compare names from different types of sources. Even the simplest of questions can be extremely hard to answer; for example, how can we know whether the Guegon (father of Tanki) in the charter quoted above is to be identified with the Guegon noted elsewhere in the Cartulary of Quimperlé as *dominus Hennebont*?[15]

Methodologies

Recent work on Breton personal names of the medieval period has tended to fall into one of two categories which can be broadly characterized as historical and anthropological. A historical approach tends to consider these names as forms which can be analysed philologically and tell us something about the origins of the name-forms. This has been very much the traditional approach

[13] For Quimperlé, see *Cartulaire de Sainte-Croix de Quimperlé*, ed. by Henry and others (1904 edition: *Cartulaire de l'abbaye de Sainte-Croix de Quimperlé*, ed. by Maître and de Berthou); for Redon, *Cartulaire de Redon* (1863 edition: *CR*); and for Landevenec *Cartulaire de Landevenec*, ed. by Lebecq (editions: *CL* (1866); *Cartulaire de l'abbaye de Landevenec*, ed. by de la Borderie (1888)). For an introduction to Breton cartularies, see also Guillotel, 'Cartulaires bretons médiévaux'. Editions of, or at least extracts from, other cartularies can be found in, for example, *Anciens évêchés de Bretagne*, ed. by Geslin de Bourgogne and de Barthélemy, and *Cartulaire générale*. ed. by Rosenzweig, Cf. also *L'abbaye cistercienne de Bégard*, ed. by Evans; *Cartulaire de Sainte-Melaine de Rennes*, ed. by Reydellet and others.

[14] *Monuments originaux*, ed. by de la Borderie and others.

[15] *Cartulaire de l'abbaye de Sainte-Croix de Quimperlé*, ed. by Maître and de Berthou, p. 51; and implied in the indices to *Cartulaire de Sainte-Croix de Quimperlé*, ed. by Henry and others, p. 455.

to these names dating back to Loth's *Chrestomathie* and beyond. The concern has been with their Celtic origins and so the tendency has been to look across the English Channel to Welsh and Cornish names or to look back in time and compare them with Gaulish ones.[16] A consequence is that such studies focus on two features: first, the dithematic form of many early names, e.g. *Cathoiarn* (*cat* 'battle' + *hoiarn* 'iron'), *Artmael* (*art* 'bear' + *mael* 'prince'), *Uuethencar* (*uuethen* 'battle, warrior' + *car* 'friend'), thus matching a common pattern in other Brittonic languages, and secondly, the patronymic structure of longer name forms which is perceived as a particularly Celtic way of forming complex names.[17] Thus a recent interesting study by German, after surveying the different types of complex-name patterns found in Brittany which may variously refer to ancestry (patronyms), place of origin, occupation, physical or moral traits, focused on what he calls 'type 5', dithematic names 'which can generally be traced back to the oldest Brythonic sources and are numerous in the saints' lives and the monastic cartularies [...]'.[18] Typically the semantics of such names revolve around the core themes of warriors, warbands, warlike animals, warrior-like qualities, etc. and can be paralleled in early Welsh verse. His conclusion is that such names may well in origin have been epithets rather than names as such and that they attest to a literary as well as a linguistic culture shared with the Brittonic-speaking world.[19] While one might question a clear-cut distinction between names and epithets, such studies are important and useful, but they are only a small part of the narrative and very much a backward-looking part. Though they offer us very little about individuals bearing those names and lack any kind of chronological framework, they can tell us something about the factors governing the choice of names by proud parents wishing to give their offspring a good onomastic start in life. For example, the person, and it is probably a single individual, who crops up in several witness lists in the Cartulary of

---

[16] Loth, *Chrestomathie*; Evans, 'Comparison'; German, 'Breton Patronyms'; and for a wide-ranging discussion, the two theses by Cane, 'Personal Names of Women', and 'Personal Names of Men'.

[17] German, 'Breton Patronyms', pp. 62–75; for names based on place-names, pp. 59–60 (cf. also Gourvil, *Noms de familles bretons*); for occupation names, pp. 60–61, and physical characteristics, pp. 61–62. More generally, see Divanach, *5000 patronymes bretons*; Gourvil, *Noms de famille Basse-Bretagne*.

[18] German, 'Breton Patronyms', p. 62.

[19] German, 'Breton Patronyms', pp. 86–87; cf. also discussion of these name-elements in Cane, 'Personal Names of Women', and 'Personal Names of Men'; on the earlier names, see also Sims-Williams, *The Celtic Inscriptions of Britain*.

Redon in the mid-ninth century called *Arthur* is a strikingly early owner of that name, perhaps influenced by the narrative of *Historia Brittonum*.[20]

The other categories distinguished by German are at least as important because they remained productive within the history of medieval Brittany. But several interesting points which remain implicit in his discussion still need to be brought out. First, and in some ways most importantly, for such a discussion even to make sense, it has to be underpinned by an assumption that such names have some sort of meaning. Here we touch on an extremely complex subject: as noted above, names are often thought of simply as signs; they may be made up of elements that in the past were meaningful (and may still be depending on the extent to which phonological changes have preserved or obscured the form of these elements), but it is not clear that names retain their full semantic load. That said, nor are they semantically empty, made up of random segments of language; otherwise there would be no reason why most name elements are semantically positive. This is why it is problematic to make a clear-cut distinction between names and epithets, as German does. It is important to acknowledge, however, that there might be a difference between what might be called 'first' names and other additional name elements; the former are more likely to be semantically opaque, while the latter only work precisely because they convey some semantic information which serves to distinguish this person from someone else, defining them by reference to another person (often, but not always, a father), a place, occupation, or physical characteristic. Secondly, it is highly likely that individuals in the medieval world had more than one name, with those names being used in different contexts; it is well known that many saints had more than one name over their careers and that clerics may have taken another name on ordination, sometimes a hypocoristic version of a previous name.[21] As will be suggested later, it is not clear that patronymy was necessarily quite as important a naming-pattern in medieval Brittany as it appears. They are perhaps frequent in witness lists for two reasons: first, some of the witness are high status and they tend to hold on to patronymy rather longer than other classes since their status depends on ancestry; secondly, these charters are often dealing with land transactions (often in the form of donations by a family to

---

[20] *Cartulaire de l'abbaye Saint-Sauveur de Redon*, 11.65, *s.v. Arthur*. The date-frame of the occurrences (861–868) suggests that he may also be the same person who witnessed the charter now preserved in Prüm (see below, pp. 335–36 and 350). He is not, however, the oldest known owner of this name; that is currently Artur mac Áedáin of Dál Riata at the end of the sixth century.

[21] On this, see Russell, 'Patterns of Hypocorism'.

the local monastery) where ancestry was a significant element in the collective memory of what land belonged to whom. Other types of names are of a different order; for example, those based on place-names generally seem to have one of two functions:[22] either among aristocrats as a way of marking a claim to hereditary ownership (often implying the exclusion of others), or when people have moved away from their home territory and settle in towns where it made sense to be able to distinguish 'person A from place X' from 'person A from place Y'.[23] In view of the context where such names are found in our sources, it is far less likely that we are dealing with aristocratic naming practices; such names rather offer important evidence for the movement of people away from their ancestral lands.

It is also worth pointing out that such studies, backward-looking as they are, tend to be most interested in the earlier evidence for naming patterns in Brittany. One of the more useful areas where a historically and philologically orientated approach is useful is in gauging and analysing the proportions of Breton (Celtic) names as against Frankish (Germanic) names. These are usually provided in the discussion of names in the introductions to the new editions of the cartularies.[24] It is not surprising that the proportions shift in favour of Frankish names over time nor that this shift is more marked in what became eastern Brittany (but which was not part of Brittany in the early medieval period). This emerges particularly from a comparison of the two parts of the Cartulary of Redon: the earlier section dating to the ninth century is predominantly Breton, while the later, much shorter section is very heavily Frankish in its range of personal names.[25] Two observations, however, are worth making: first, the scant evidence of the early medieval inscriptions from Brittany shows that Frankish names are already attested in inscriptions dated by their script to the sixth or seventh centuries, though admittedly such names are from eastern Brittany, e.g. *Turtoualdus, Berthildis*.[26] Secondly, while a Breton name, especially in a cartulary where we have a Breton name with a Breton patro-

---

[22] For discussion of these different ways of interpreting names based on place-names, see Hanks and others, *Oxford Dictionary of Family Names*, p. xvii.

[23] For such names in Brittany, see Gourvil, *Noms de familles bretons*; German, 'Breton Patronyms', pp. 59–60.

[24] For example, Tanguy, 'Les noms d'hommes', pp. 49–60; *Cartulaire de Sainte-Croix de Quimperlé*, ed. by Henry and others, pp. 88–89; Lambert, 'Les noms de personnes', pp. 39–52.

[25] Tanguy, 'Les noms d'hommes', pp. 51–60.

[26] Davies and others, *Inscriptions of Early Medieval Brittany*, pp. 81–82 (inscriptions I3 and I5).

nymic, is a reasonable guide to identity, Frankish names with Breton patronymics (cf. Theuderic, son of Bodic (probably imitating Theuderic, the oldest son of Clovis[27])), or indeed Breton names with Frankish patronymics, or a mixed Breton and Frankish family tree, all suggest more complex patterns of identity. Names may also reveal issues of status; for example, it is striking that the Breton names which occur in the charters of the cartulary of Saint-Melaine in Rennes, dating from 1136 to 1323, are all to be found in the lower end of the clerical ranks.[28] Another feature to bear in mind is the use of classical and biblical names, and especially the latter, among the clergy.[29]

A different approach which has become popular in the last few decades takes us in a different direction. The long-term project (and numerous publications) under the broad title of *Genèse médiévale de l'anthroponymie moderne*, under the auspices of Monique Bourin and Pascal Chareille, has sought to study the development of personal names in France and western Europe in the framework of a broad, wide-ranging longitudinal model;[30] it enables us to see Breton developments in that broader context of developments in naming. Within that broader framework, the work of André Chédeville on Breton names has provided a range of statistics which can be used to inform more detailed work;[31] one weakness (which relates to the distribution of viable evidence across other geographical regions) is that his statistics start at *c.* 1000 and so do not include the important data from the earlier charters of the Cartulary of Redon. Such work tends to be interested in the development of names over time and the origins of modern naming patterns, and thus much of its impetus arises from the comparative aspects of the work. One effect of that perspective is that much of the discussion is driven by considerations that may only be of marginal application to Brittany and, as noted above, can be skewed chronologically towards the

---

[27] Gregory of Tours, *Libri Historiarum X*, v.16.

[28] Cf. the charters in *Cartulaire de Saint-Melaine de Rennes*, pp. 433–38.

[29] On this, see Sharpe, 'The Naming of Bishop Ithamar'; J. R. Davies, 'Old Testament Personal Names'; for medieval Scotland, J. R. Davies, 'Old Testament Personal Names in Scotland'; Chédeville, 'L'anthroponymie bretonne', pp. 14–15; and below, pp. 320 and 326.

[30] See, for example, Bourin, 'Intérêt et faiblesse des cartulaires'; Beech and others, *Personal Names Studies of Medieval Europe*; Bourin and Chareille, *Noms, prénoms, surnoms au moyen âge*, and the series of volumes under the general title of *Genèse médiévale de l'anthroponymie modern*. For a similar approach applied to early English naming, see Chetwood, 'Re-evaluating English Personal Naming'. For other ways of approaching personal names, see, for example, Wilson, *Means of Naming*.

[31] Chédeville, 'L'anthroponymie bretonne'.

later medieval period when more evidence is available elsewhere.[32] Moreover, the nature of the evidence from Brittany for this period is problematic; cartularies by their nature tend to privilege certain types of name forms and so distort the data; if we focus just on witness list, two types of name can be problematic: first, for reasons noted above, patronymics may be more common, and secondly, among the clerical witnesses single names are very frequent. Arguably, neither of these patterns is necessarily a very reliable guide to the normal patterns of naming outside these specialized contexts and that is why it is worth trying to look elsewhere. Another factor which can be pursued is that of status; some of the charters in the Cartulary of Redon are very high status productions involving royal grants, while others are more local and literally parochial, and it may be among the latter group that a comment about 'rustic imbecility' was intended to bite.

The two approaches outlined above can sometimes seem, then, to be facing in different directions, both chronologically and geographically. While there is some danger in over-polarizing such approaches, there is something to be said for taking several different, more detailed, snapshots of how these names work; it is, after all, this kind of detail which underpins the broad-brush discussion of Chédeville and others. In what follows, three aspects are considered. First, we focus on the changes and developments in naming patterns in Brittany broadly in the early and high medieval periods. Secondly, in order to maintain an element of comparison, we take a particular category of names, the witness lists to charters, and set them against comparable bodies of material form early medieval Wales and Cornwall. Thirdly, we examine some specific groups of names of varying levels of status, some of which come from outside Brittany and so have the added benefit of allowing us to see how Breton names could be transmitted outside Brittany. By that route we shall eventually return to thinking about the names from Clohars and why they might have incurred such displeasure.

Taking the Long View

The onomastic evidence from medieval Brittany, ranging from late antiquity onwards, allows us to take an extended view of how personal names might have developed. The evidence is uneven both chronologically and geographically; there are dense patches of evidence during the date-range of a particular car-

---

[32] On this, and the more general trend towards the 'Europeanization' of personal-name usage, see Bartlett, *Making of Europe*, pp. 270–80.

12. FACING DIFFERENT WAYS

tulary or several chronologically overlapping cartularies, but the earlier period before the ninth century is much more thinly evidenced as we are restricted to epigraphic evidence. Geographically, eastern Brittany with the data of the Cartulary of Redon is much better covered, as are certain areas controlled by other monasteries, mainly for the earlier period along the south coast, such as Quimperlé, Quimper, and Landévennec (though the last has a very small surviving cartulary). Other cartularies are available but for the purposes of the present discussion we restrict ourselves to the ones with modern editions or facsimiles which allows for more nuanced discussions.[33]

The earliest sustained body of evidence is the earlier section of the Cartulary of Redon (fols 1–135). According to Tanguy (and this body of material was not incorporated in Chédeville's statistics) there are some 1300 Breton names (ninety per cent of all the Breton names in the cartulary) beside 420 Frankish names in the ninth-century charters, most of the latter relating to land-holdings east of the Vilaine.[34] By contrast, the later section of the cartulary (which is much shorter — only thirty folios long) shows a quite different pattern in several respects. First, the range of names is much narrower; only ten per cent of the name-forms irrespective of origin attested in the earlier section are found in the later (eleventh- and twelfth-century) section.[35] This widespread and increasing feature of the development of personal names is known in the French-speaking scholarship as 'condensation', the tendency for more and more people to share the same name, and has consequences for other aspects of naming.[36] In particular, it would have encouraged the use of additional naming elements in order to distinguish individuals with the same name; indeed Tanguy notes that, whereas patronymy is very common in the earlier period, there was

---

[33] Thus, for example, Peyron's edition of the cartulary of Quimper, which only provides a selection of charters, is only used in passing.

[34] Tanguy, 'Les noms d'hommes', p. 52; many of these names of course occur multiple times, some referring to the same individual more than once, some to different indiviuals, though it is often difficult to tell unless more onomastic details are provided.

[35] Tanguy, 'Les noms d'hommes', p. 57; he notes also that there are some Breton names which are found in the later sections, but that does not affect the general trend towards a narrowing of the corpus of names in use.

[36] See, for example, Chédeville, 'L'anthroponymie bretonne', pp. 12–14; this was particularly common with Norman and Angevin names at this period (Wilson, *Means of Naming*, pp. 109–11, and on the comcomitant growth in hypocoristic versions of these names, pp. 111–14); for a comparable situation, cf. for Anglo-Saxon England, Chetwood, 'Re-evaluating English Personal Naming', and for Wales, Cane, 'Personal Names of Men', pp. 252, 301.

a significant increase in the use of 'soubriquets' in the later period, e.g. adjective, occupational terms, place-name references, etc.[37] As noted above, the last are important as they are suggestive of movement away from one's native soil.[38] Another point of contrast and interest involves the use of Breton and Frankish names within kin-groups: kin-groups where all the names are Breton are common, but less frequent are cases, such as a charter of 867 in which a father, Standulf, with a Frankish name has a son with a Breton name, Haeluuocon;[39] we might infer that Standulf's wife might have been Breton. A particularly interesting example of this is another charter of 867 which contains the only example of a *Ran* place-name containing a Frankish name:[40] Arthuiu granted his wife, Maginsin, two *rannou* called *Ranriculf* and *Ranbudhoiarn* for her use and which she subsequently donated to Redon. If we assume that such place-names reflect an earlier stratum of personal names, one wonders whether there is any connection between the fact that these two *rannou* contain one Frankish name and one Breton name and that Arthuiu's wife has a Frankish name or whether this is merely a function of the location, east of the Vilaine. Such cases are more common in the later charters where we also see small groups of names (both Breton and Frankish) alternating within the same family line; for example, in a group of charters dated 1008–1031 the names in the family of the lords of La Roche-Bernard alternate between Bernard, Riuallon, and Simon.[41] By this period there was presumably a sufficient level of intermarriage between Breton- and Frankish-speakers that the onomastic distinctions gradually became less significant, though there is no obvious reason why this should be more prevalent in the eleventh century than the ninth. Another factor may well have been the growing 'Europeanization' or 'metropolitanization' of the Breton upper classes who, as part of that process, were adopting French names.

The Cartulary of Redon presents us with the earliest corpus of names but it may be instructive, now that we have some context, to look back to the epi-

---

[37] Tanguy, 'Les noms d'hommes', pp. 53, 58–59; only about fifteen different 'soubriquets' are used in the earlier period.

[38] We assume here, as noted above (p. 318), a largely non-aristocratic use of names based on place-names.

[39] *Cartulaire de l'abbaye Saint-Sauveur de Redon*, ed. by Guillotel and others, fol. 72ʳ9 (dated 867).

[40] *Cartulaire de l'abbaye Saint-Sauveur de Redon*, ed. by Guillotel and others, fol. 99ᵛ22–4 (dated 867); cf. Tanguy, 'Les noms d'hommes', p. 55; and generally, Davies, *Small Worlds*.

[41] *Cartulaire de l'abbaye Saint-Sauveur de Redon*, fols 149 and 177; Tanguy, 'Les noms d'hommes', p. 58.

graphic evidence of the preceding century or so, before looking at the other cartularies. There is a small and thinly spread corpus of inscriptions, both upright stones and grave-slabs, from Brittany dating from the fourth to the eleventh century which offer a body of evidence which partly predates and partly overlaps with the evidence of the cartularies.[42] The corpus consists of some twenty-six inscriptions containing thirty-five names; nineteen of them are probably Celtic, e.g. *Bodognous* (C1), *Uenomaili* (F5), etc. (and another eight are possibly Celtic);[43] three are Latin and three or four Germanic, e.g. *Turtoualdus* (I3). There is an interesting group of inscriptions from Morbihan (M1–10) which share a number of features (in terms of both content and palaeography) with inscriptions from Wales and Cornwall.[44] Unsurprisingly, the Germanic names occur on stones from eastern Brittany (Ille-et-Vilaine and also Guernsey) and date from the sixth–seventh century or later. In general terms the corpus is so small that relatively little can be gleaned from it, though it is worth noting that the distribution and proportions of names is broadly consistent with what we see later.

While the inscriptions are too few and scattered to offer much of significance, at least the types of names and indeed the proportions of Breton to Frankish names broadly match the later patterns. When we turn to the Cartulary of Landévennec, and its very brief collection of charters preserved at the end of the manuscript after the hagiographic dossier of St Winwaloe, we find just over 320 names, most of which are Breton and very few are Frankish (under three per cent), e.g. *Berduualt, Rodaldus*, etc.[45] This is strikingly different to what we see further east and is presumably related to the western location of Landévennec.

Moving a little further east to Quimper, we are at more of a disadvantage as we do not have a clear and easy access to the charters; Peyron's edition of the charters is a selection from three gatherings of material and not even based on the original manuscript but on copies.[46] Most of the collection dates

---

[42] They have been collected and studied in Davies and others, *The Inscriptions of Early Medieval Brittany*; see in particular p. 80 (the collected texts of the inscriptions), p. 40 (a distribution map), pp. 48–69 (discussion of their palaeography); for a useful overview, see Charles-Edwards, *Wales and the Britons*, pp. 169–73.

[43] References are to the editions in Davies and others, *The Inscriptions of Early Medieval Brittany*.

[44] Brett with Edmonds and Russell, *Brittany and the Atlantic Archipelago*, p. 26.

[45] For discussion, see Lambert, 'Les noms de personnes'.

[46] Guillotel, 'Cartulaires', p. 337; *Cartulaire de l'église de Quimper*, p. vi.

from between the thirteenth and fifteenth centuries. On the other hand, the Cartulary of Quimperlé is rather easier to deal with as we have a recent facsimile with up-to-date discussion.[47] The main body of charters dates from the mid-eleventh century until the early twelfth (with additions up to the mid-thirteenth). Breton names account for about a fifth of the name-forms in the whole cartulary. There are just over a thousand different individuals mentioned but many with the same name (thus *Riuallon* occurs forty-five times, *Even* thirty-three, *Eudo* twenty-eight, *Guegun* twenty-five, etc.), a clear example of the 'condensation' of names.[48] Although there are some sixty instances of Germanic names in the cartulary, the range of names is very narrow; most are *Uuilhelmus*, *Bernardus* and *Gaufridus*, and most of the individuals so named are clerics. It is also noteworthy that, as with the later sections of the Cartulary of Redon, Breton and Germanic names are intermingled in family groups presumably through intermarriage, thus, for example, Ansger father of Prigent, Gaufridus son of Aldroen and father of Brient, etc.[49] The majority of cases where the father has a Germanic name and the son has a Breton name date from the last decades of the eleventh century into the twelfth century. By that stage it is likely that some of the very common Germanic names might simply have been part of the general name-stock.

The charters of the abbey of Bégard offers us a snapshot from a later period (1130 × 1471) and a different geographical area, Trégor in northern Brittany.[50] Up to the early fourteenth century the matrix language was Latin but changed to French even though the spoken language of Trégor throughout this period was Breton.[51] Almost all the place-names in the charters are Breton, e.g. *Ker-*, *Maes*, *Prat*, *Luorz*, etc. and these are subject to pluralization and derivation so that it is clear that they form part of a living language. On the other hand, the 'surnames' of witnesses are occasionally Breton, thus *en Gouff*, *Guern Bihan*, but often use the French definite article, e.g. *Pierre le Cozic*, *Roland Le Floch*,

---

[47] *Cartulaire de Sainte-Croix de Quimperlé*, ed. by Henry and others; the older edition is *Cartulaire de l'abbaye de Sainte-Croix de Quimperlé*, ed. by Maître and de Berthou.

[48] Chédeville, 'L'anthroponymie bretonne', pp. 12–14.

[49] *Cartulaire de Sainte-Croix de Quimperlé*, ed. by Henry and others, fol. 75ᵛ, 118ᵛ, 132ᵛ, 93ʳ.

[50] *L'Abbaye cistercienne*; on the personal names and the Breton features, see pp. 87–92; the cartulary has not survived but Evans has brought copies of charters together from a range of sources.

[51] *L'Abbaye cistercienne*, p. 87.

12. FACING DIFFERENT WAYS

325

and occasional French names, e.g. *Pierre le Mignon*.[52] By contrast in most of these charters relatively few first names are Breton, though there are some significant exceptions; for example, in a charter dated 20 October 1350 from Lannion the names of some 250–300 tenants are listed who had agreed to pay double rent if they left their land without permission.[53] Of these almost all are Breton, and many list a patronymic, though usually without a filiation marker, e.g. *Prigent Jahan*. There is some filiation but it is marked with *fi(l)z* or *fille*, though without *de*, which might reflect a straightforward replacement of (*m*) *ab* by the French term in official documents. We might conclude therefore that the naming patterns in these charters do not necessarily reflect local naming patterns or practice but rather an establishment which was more acculturated to a world beyond Brittany than to its local area.[54]

Most of the evidence for personal names we have considered so far is based on the lists of names in cartularies. Such corpora have the advantage of size and thus they are amenable to statistical analysis, but for the reasons noted above — single names in the witness lists, the relationship of patronymy to land-holding, etc. — the disadvantage is that they are restricted in range. A further issue with cartularies is that their language matrix is always Latinate (except for one Old Breton boundary clause in the Cartulary of Redon where personal names are not involved[55]), and this makes it more difficult to identify adjectival or occupational elements of personal names; in later cartularies they are often in Latin and so it is not clear whether they are name elements or descriptive terms (in so far as it is possible to distinguish the two). In the earlier part of the Cartulary of Redon epithets are only occasionally in Breton and sometimes marked by *qui et* 'who is also (*sc.* called) ...', e.g. *Haeluuocon Sqrenic*, *Cumael qui et Bonic*;[56] but in the later, smaller section they are more common, e.g. *Alfredus Bluch*, and also often in Latin, e.g. *Moises barbatus, Lambert par-*

---

[52] *L'Abbaye cistercienne*, pp. 131, 125, 105, 148, 155 respectively.

[53] *L'Abbaye cistercienne*, pp. 186–88.

[54] This view might be supported by noting where the charters end up (widely distributed and many in England).

[55] See fol. 87ʳ where the same boundary clause is described in Old Breton at ll. 10–14 and in Latin at ll. 27–29 (*CR*, CXVI and CXLIII); see Tanguy, 'Les noms d'hommes', p. 67 where the two clauses are edited and translated. We might wonder whether other original single-leaf charters had boundary-clauses in both languages (or perhaps a mixture) and that the Old Breton version was later edited out.

[56] Respectively fols 71ʳ and 121ᵛ (*CR*, XCIII, CCXLV, and CCXLVI), dated 860–871; Tanguy, 'Les noms d'hommes', p. 53 for discussion.

vus, etc. A feature of the later tranche of the Cartulary of Redon (but not the earlier) is the use of occupational terms, e.g. *Rivalonius carpentarius, Gaufridus molendarius*, etc., though, as with all social designators, it is not clear that we should understand them as names as such or simply as ways of noting their profession.[57] Likewise the later section also sees the appearance of names based on place-names, sometimes prefixed by the preposition *de*, e.g. *Rioco Gledenni filio de Arsal* beside *Riocus Arsal* in the main text of a charter.[58] A particularly striking example of how these additional onomastic elements could be treated as secondary markers is a charter towards the end of the Cartulary of Redon, dated 20 July 1141, where the witness list of twenty-five individuals consisted originally of single names, but the same scribe has added secondary designations to almost all of them (glosses are enclosed in < >), e.g. Robertus <prior de Iouine>, Gaufridus <de Moia>, Gaufridus <filius Ernalt>; clerical posts, adjectives, place-names, professions, all figure in the list.[59]

Another feature of cartularies of all periods is the relatively high number of names derived from Greco-Latin and Hebrew sources, e.g. *Daniel, Sim(e)on, Abraham, Salomon*, etc. but also *Beatus, Donatus, Missus, Omnis*, etc. It would appear that the relatively high frequency of such names (approximately ten per cent in the Cartulary of Redon) is due to their popularity in several different contexts: they were traditionally very common in Wales and Cornwall (especially in hagiography) and so likely to have been so in Brittany as well before the twelfth century at least.[60] From then on, the use of such names is probably part of the more general 'Europeanization' of naming we have already noted.[61] The range of names is relatively small but it is clear that they were popular; for example, *Daniel* appears some forty-six times in the Cartulary of Redon, some thirty times in the Cartulary of Quimperlé, only five times in the very few charters in the Cartulary of Landévennec (two of whom are Counts of Cornouaille), and twenty-seven times in the selection of charters edited by Peyron from the Cartulary of Quimper. Some of the Latin names of this type

---

[57] This raises the editorial question of whether they should be printed with a capital letter or not.

[58] Respectively fols 185[r]48, and 164[v]7 (*CR*, CCCLXXXVIII and CCCXLII) dated to the first half of the twelfth century.

[59] Fol. 183[v] (*CR*, CCCLXXXI).

[60] Davies, 'Old Testament Personal Names'; Sharpe, 'The Naming of Bishop Ithamar'; Chédeville, 'L'anthroponymie bretonne', pp. 14–15.

[61] On this, see Mitterauer, *Ahnen unde Heilige*, pp. 230–40; Bartlett, *Making of Europe*, pp. 270–80.

also appear in a Breton form, e.g. *Benedic*, *Custentin*, or in a Romance form, e.g. *Martin*, *Saturnan*. The presence of such forms should not be surprising, but they add another dimension to the dossier of names.

Cartularies then provide a series of corpora of personal names which cannot be ignored, but they also present difficulties. Other than in cartularies, corpora of personal names are rather harder to come by; but there is at least one collection which, although rather late for our purposes, can act as a counter-balance to the weight of evidence provided by the cartularies.

In early 1330 an inquest was opened in Trégor to enquire into the evidence for the canonization of Yves (to become eventually in June 1347 St Yves of Kermartin). Depositions and witness statements were provided by some 243 witnesses whose names and affiliations were provided in the dossier;[62] they provide a somewhat different distribution of names from the cartularies. By the early fourteenth century the distinction between Breton and Germanic names is probably of no real significance in signalling people's ethnic identity, but the list provides some interesting data: of the 243 witnesses forty-nine (approximately twenty per cent) are women, most of whom are designated as *uxor*, *relicta* or *filia* of a husband or father.[63] Of the 192 men, fifty-one are clerics, most of whom have a single name and their clerical status is also indicated. Of the remaining 128, more than half (approximately eighty) are labelled by their patronymic; however, of these, unlike cartularies, the most (sixty-four out of the eighty) do not use *filius* but rather the second name is in the genitive (if Latin) or simply unmarked (if Breton). The latter pattern is very common in Breton (apart from certain areas where reflexes of *mab* (usually *ab*) seem to have been retained in surnames[64]), and effectively takes over from the more fully marked filiation pattern. By contrast professional markers are not very common (twelve examples), e.g. *Oliuerius Le Maczon, parochie de Plouclevec*; *Alanus Le Cervesier, civitatis Trecorensis*, etc., and that may have to do with the purpose of the list;[65] many of the witnesses are part of small family groups, father/husband, mother/wife, son, daughter, where relationships and location seem to be the primary validating criteria. Trying to work out how many individuals use a location marker as part of their name is more complicated as everyone's parish is noted

---

[62] See *Monuments originaux*, and for a summary list of names, pp. 492–96 (to which the numbers refer).

[63] Two are designated as *soror*, and one as *alumna*.

[64] Le Brun and le Menn, 'La répartition géographique'.

[65] *Monuments originaux*, p. 495 (with references to the full text of their statements).

as a standard part of the process (as it confirmed their right to give evidence), but this tends to be the final piece of information provided, e.g. *Guillielmus filius Aymonel, parochie de Trievelevron*.[66] But examples such as *Rollandus de Plechec, parochianus de Puec* (63), or *Hamo de Regen, parochie de Ploeymiam*, where the location comes earlier in the list of information (often when this differs from the parish) might suggest that they are being treated as an onomastic element which would be possible if they came from a different place;[67] their place of origin could then function as a differentiating marker.

Another interesting feature of this list is that it is possible to see how family groups name themselves; for example, *Margellia, filia Guillelmi Yrundinis, parochie de Prato; Pleysou, uxor Guillelmi de Venello, mater illius Margillie; Guillelmus de Prato dicte parochie*.[68] This is a confusing but interesting example; it is not clear whether Guillelmus de Prato is the same person as *Guillemus Yrundo/Venellus*; indeed their depositions could be read to suggest that they were not, though in that case the ordering of the list is oddly coincidental.[69] But, if he is, it shows how flexible the naming patterns could be: Guillemus may have been known locally as *Yrundo* (corresponding to Breton *guennel* 'swallow' (*Venellus*)) and perhaps further afield as *de Prato*, though the force of the former is not clear.

The following example allows us to track a family through distinctive names, though the relationships are not easy to disentangle: *Panthouda, relicta Rivallonis joculatoris, de parochia Plebis Prisiac; Amicia, filia Panthode supradicte; Jaquetus filius quondam Rivallonis, parochie S. Petri de Lohannec; Gaufridus, filius Panthouade, relicti Rivallonis joculatoris; An Quoantha, soror dicti Gaufridi*.[70] The father, Rivallon, the *joculator*, perhaps 'musician, entertainer', died and left his wife with what appears to be a son and daughter, Jaquetus and Amicia. It is possible, however, that Jaquetus was the son of Riwallon by a different mother, or that all except Jaquetus were her children from a previous marriage.[71] Furthermore, it is also not clear is who the father of Gaufridus and An Quoantha is;[72] it is not Rivallon, but there is no indication

---

[66] *Monuments originaux*, p. 493.

[67] *Monuments originaux*, pp. 493 and 495.

[68] *Monuments originaux*, p. 494.

[69] The Index (p. 507) suggests he is the same person.

[70] *Monuments originaux*, p. 493 (items 40–41, 43, 48–49).

[71] I am grateful to one of the reviewers for suggesting this to me.

[72] *An Quoantha* seems to be a Latinized version of Middle Breton *coant* 'pretty, kind' (Modern Breton *koant*).

12. FACING DIFFERENT WAYS

that Panthouda has remarried since she is still designated as *relicta*. Again we are bound by our sources; they only tell us what is necessary for them to be able to provide a witness statement.

Although the body of names is relatively late, it provides an alternative way of looking at Breton personal names which is not so dependent on cartularies. Set alongside them it offers a somewhat less ecclesiastically focused list (even though it relates to a canonization) where naming by location is almost as important as filiation. We have seen that the cartularies do offer a sense of chronological development from the very Breton witness lists of Redon in the ninth and tenth centuries to the markedly less Breton lists in the later part of the Cartulary of Redon. Further west, as one might expect, Germanic names were slower to catch on, but gradually certain names became more embedded, as also do certain biblical names.

This broadly corresponds to what we see in Chédeville's statistical analysis of Breton names from the year 1000 onwards with the rise of various versions of 'surnames' whether paternal names (often without explicit filiation), location names, or professional names, etc. It may be the nature of the evidence but it is certainly clear that patronymy remains more clearly marked in Brittany for longer than in other parts of France.

Witnessing to Names

The backward-looking comparative approach to Breton personal names has over the years proved very attractive to many scholars as a way of using names as evidence which can consolidate our understanding of Brittonic phonological and morphological developments;[73] personal names in our Breton sources are seen to share name-elements, and indeed names, with comparable sources in medieval Wales and Cornwall to the extent that the possibility of a shared name-stock seems a likely possibility. Such research can be tracked back into the nineteenth century in the work of Loth and has remained productive in the last few decades in the work of Cane and German.[74] Cane's wide-ranging surveys of both male and female names are an extremely useful starting point for thinking about these issues, though perhaps too wide-ranging to be entirely useful without further sharpening. Her discussion is divided into two large

---

[73] Loth, *Chrestomathie*; Evans, 'Comparison'; German, 'Breton Patronyms'.

[74] Cane, 'Personal Names of Women' and 'Personal Names of Men'; German, 'Breton Patronyms'.

periods, up to 1100 and then 1100–1400; for Brittany she uses the evidence of the cartularies of Redon, Quimperlé, and Landevennec;[75] for Cornwall the Bodmin Manumissions (*c.* 950–1100);[76] and for Wales a wide range of sources including genealogies, subsidy-rolls, the Book of Llandaf, etc.[77] In addition she also includes the early epigraphic evidence from each area. It is, however, immediately obvious that these corpora are not easily comparable whether in terms of size, date, or geographical distribution. That said, her findings for the earlier of her two periods are very interesting for our purposes; she concludes:

> Comparing Breton elements to Welsh and Cornish elements, we see that the Breton elements that are most common in names are not those common in Wales and Cornwall. Only *con* 'hound' and *uur* 'man'/*uuor* (intensive prefix) reach a similar level of use in Brittany to that in Wales and Cornwall. It is clear that the use and distribution of elements in Brittany is very different to that in Wales and Cornwall.[78]

Elsewhere she notes what quickly becomes clear when working with Breton cartularies, that there are numerous name elements in Breton, e.g. *wethen, bresel, maen, louuen, hoiarn*, etc. which are at best rare, and often non-existent, in names in Wales and Cornwall.[79] These findings are important and need testing more rigorously for several reasons: first, as noted above, the evidence of Breton cartularies is very patchy and uneven in its distribution both chronologically and geographically, but in addition a differently uneven distribution is found in the Welsh evidence, and then in addition the Cornish evidence is very thin. Secondly, the concentration on name-elements rather than on names themselves is potentially misleading. Unlike many languages where the elements of names have become obscured through phonological change, the name-elements in Brittonic languages usually remain as comprehensible lexical items and so could be deployed as part of a compound name at any time; a full compound name attested in Wales, Brittany, and Cornwall would at least suggest that they were thinking along these lines in terms of name formation,

[75] Cane, 'Personal Names of Men', pp. 257–300.

[76] Cane, 'Personal Names of Men', pp. 236–52.

[77] Cane, 'Personal Names of Men', pp. 158–227.

[78] Cane, 'Personal Names of Men', p. 300. Generally it is impossible to tell forms of *uur* 'man' and the intensive prefix *uuor* apart, and the conjunction of form may in part explain its apparently high frequency; that is, we are dealing with two name-elements.

[79] Cane, 'Personal Names of Men', p. 299; for elements common to Welsh, Breton, and Cornish, see pp. 312–19.

12. FACING DIFFERENT WAYS

331

even if it may be risky to suppose that the name belongs to the ancestral name-bank of Common Brittonic. The fact that, as noted by Cane, there is considerable variation in the onomastic resources drawn upon in Wales, Cornwall, and Brittany suggests that that dithematic names continued to be coined as a living process throughout the early Middle Ages: accordingly, a statistically insignificant preference for certain elements would over time be reinforced by the weight of examples and give rise to the different frequencies visible in the evidence.[80]

Moreover, the concentration on elements tends to push the discussion towards thinking about meaning, even though that is precisely one of the problems. Names, then, rather than name elements, may therefore provide clearer evidence as we see the names already formed; to focus on the elements only is to deal with the raw material of name-formation but not with the names themselves. Thirdly, the breadth of the source material makes it difficult to compare like with like; names from genealogies may have quite a different rationale from those found in witness lists to charters or in Anglo-Norman surveys of medieval Wales.[81] We might take one example to highlight the problem: a name *Ana(u)oc* is attested in all three countries: in the Bodmin Manumissions dating from the tenth to eleventh centuries, in the Cartulary of Redon in a charter datable to 843–845, and in the Book of Llandaf in a charter datable to *c.* 620;[82] given the chronological range (of perhaps up to some four hundred years) it is not clear what we should conclude beyond the fact that in all three areas a derivative based on the element *Ana(u)*- was used to form names.

What follows, then, offers a test of Cane's findings though necessarily on a much narrower range of evidence. It takes as its starting point the name-forms found in the Cartulary of Redon in charters datable to 850–1050; the date-range essentially amounts to the latter part of the earlier but bigger section of the cartulary (thus excluding the more Frankish second part) but, as will emerge, these dates are also useful for other reasons. These were compared with names dating from approximately the same period attested in the witness lists of the Book of Llandaf.[83] Wendy Davies' ground-breaking work on the witness lists of the Book of Llandaf, in which she demonstrated that it is pos-

[80] I am grateful to one of the reviewers for encouraging me to think harder about this.

[81] For a specific instance of data from the surveys, see below, pp. 345–46.

[82] On dating the Llandaf charters, see below, pp. 332–33.

[83] For the text, see *The Text of the Book of Llan Dâv*; the data has been extracted from the indices of Davies, *Llandaff Charters*, pp. 145–87.

sible to rearrange the charters from their textual order into their chronological order on the basis of the membership of the witness lists (and thus *inter alia* to detect which charters might be forgeries), now allows us to identify at least in general terms chronological blocks of charters.[84] For our purposes the time-frame proposed above for the sample from the Cartulary of Redon corresponds approximately to Davies' 'third sequence' of charters and so provides a convenient match for comparison.[85] By focusing the discussion in this way we avoid the problems of both chronological mismatches and geographical variation; we have a time-slot of two hundred years in both places. Furthermore, we shall focus on names (mainly compound but with some suffixed forms), not name-elements.

In charters from this period in the Cartulary of Redon, there are 725 name-forms (many of which occur more than once during this period).[86] There are 320 name-forms in the Book of Llandaf in Davies' 'third-sequence' datable 850–1050 (again some, but not many, occur multiple times). In her broader-based survey of some 1500 names in each of Wales and Brittany Cane identified eighty-seven 'name-element combinations or single element names that are recorded in both the Welsh and Breton evidence', amounting to 5.8% overlap.[87] Our briefer, more focused, survey found thirty-three name-forms common to both sources (amounting to 4.5% overlap with the names in the Cartulary of Redon and 10.3% with those in the Book of Llandaf, averaging out at 7.4%).[88] Furthermore, there are six biblical or at least Latinate names common to both, *Abraham, Alexander, Clemens, Gedeon, Ioseph*, and *Sim(e)on*; these may not

[84] For an important study of how useful this approach can be in studying phonological change, see Sims-Williams, 'Emergence of Old Welsh, Cornish and Breton Orthography'; cf. also Russell, '*Rowynniauc, Rhyfoniog*'.

[85] Davies, *Llandaff Charters*, pp. 59–73 (for the 'third sequence'), 73–82 (for the absolute chronology); it is worth pointing out too that this sequence of charters seems to be the most reliable in terms of its ordering. The dates used here are those provided in the Index of Persons in Davies, *The Llandaff Charters*, pp. 145–87. See also now the recent discussion by Sims-Williams, *The Book of Llandaf as a Historical Source*.

[86] The same forms are also attested before and after this period but for the reasons given above, we are focused on this date-range. The numbers here are based on the index to *Cartulaire de l'abbaye Saint-Sauveur de Redon*, II.61–128.

[87] Cane, 'Personal Names of Men', p. 307.

[88] The more precise criteria for inclusion of course tend to exclude some obvious pairs but the pay-off is greater chronological precision. Six names do not figure in Cane's list: *Birran* (CR): *Birran* (Llandaf), *Catuuocon: Catguocaun, Glueu: Gloiu, Uuoletec: Goleiduc, Iudon: Iudon, Merchion: Meirchiaun*; more doubtful are *Congen: Cincenn, Elmoin: Eluen*.

be significant as some of them are very common but they should probably be taken into account, since biblical names are more strongly preferred in Wales.[89] Proportionally, then, the period 850–1050 seems to include more common names than Cane's broader time-span, but it broadly matches and confirms her results; nevertheless, the overlap of name-forms remains relatively low.

In order to triangulate these findings, however, it is useful to compare what is happening in Cornwall. Here the only body of names which is even minimally useful is that in the Bodmin Manumissions, a series of manumission notes added to a gospel book associated with St Petroc between 950 and 1100.[90] There are about 250 named individuals in the collection and they seem to share some 155 names, of which fifty-five are unsurprisingly Anglo-Saxon and twenty-six biblical, leaving some seventy-five names; apart from a handful of uncertain cases, most are Celtic and almost all Cornish. Of these, twenty are shared with the Book of Llandaf sample and eighteen with the sample from the Cartulary of Redon, while only three are found in all three: *Freoc, Morcant*, and *Wincuf* (forms from the Bodmin Manumissions). Again, although one might quibble over the precise numbers, these figures broadly correspond to Cane's statistics. Around a quarter of the names in the Manumissions are shared with the Book of Llandaf and a quarter with the Cartulary of Redon, but there is minimal overlap between these categories. As Cane notes, and it is confirmed here, while the number of examples is very small, the evidence of the names in the Bodmin Manumissions seems to locate it between the Breton and Welsh corpora.

What emerges from this brief discussion is that, while more or less the same inherited body of name-elements was probably available in Brittany, Cornwall, and Wales, the choices of name-formation made in Brittany were rather different from those made elsewhere; this is perhaps most noticeable in the number of name-elements used in Breton names, e.g. *hitr, uuethen, louuen, presel*, which are hardly, if ever, used in Cornwall and Wales. All of this would seem to point to Brittany's cultural as well as geographical distance. But there does seem to be some variation over time. We noted that, while Cane's figures produced an overall percentage overlap of name-elements between Brittany and Wales (400–1100) of 5.8%, our more focused study of names (rather than name-ele-

[89] J. R. Davies, 'Old Testament Personal Names'.

[90] For a text, see Förster, 'Die Freilassungsurkunden des Bodmin-Evangeliars'; for a recent discussion, Padel, *Slavery in Saxon Cornwall*, and for the names themselves, Lowe, 'Personal Names in the Bodmin Manumissions'; cf. also Stokes, 'Manumissions in the Bodmin Gospels', pp. 333–38 (text), 338–45 (list of names).

ments) in the period 850–1050 produced an overlap of names amounting to 10.3% of the names in the Book of Llandaf and 4.5% of those in the Cartulary of Redon; the difference between the two is not significant as it is a function of the number of names in each corpus, but the average 7.4% is slightly higher than Cane's overall figure. Now if that figure is significant, it implies that elsewhere in the chronological range the overlap would be smaller. To check this, we can compare the Book of Llandaf figures against a smaller set of charters (and witness-lists) appended to the Life of Cadog (preserved in BL Cotton Vespasian A xiv); they come from the same region (Llancarfan) but probably from an earlier period, c. 650–765;[91] the witness lists contain just over a hundred distinct names (several individuals witness multiple charters). Of these, nineteen (eighteen per cent) are also found in the Book of Llandaf and thirteen (twelve per cent) find correspondences in the earlier part of the Cartulary of Redon (though twelve of the names are also attested in the period 850–1050). Although the sample is very small and it is difficult to be sure whether there is anything significant going on here, the overlap seems to be somewhat greater in the earlier period. That would not be surprising though the explanation may be as much the distorting effect of the later addition of Frankish names in the Breton material and English names in Wales and Cornwall.

Names and Status

So far we have paid relatively little attention to status, or the lack of it, and its relevance to personal name formation.[92] Chédeville has already noted the problem: 'la nature de la documentation rend souvent en Bretagne plus difficile qu'ailleurs la distinction entre nobles et roturiers'.[93] He notes, however, that the drop in the use of single names among nobles between 1000 and 1100 was followed in the next century by an arguably imitative abandonment of single names among the 'roturiers'.[94] Chédeville's statistics only begin in 1000 and, when we turn to the earlier period, high-status charters tend to have a higher proportion of single names than later charters of a similar status.

---

[91] For these charters, see *Vitae Sanctorum Britanniae et Genealogiae*, pp. 125–44; for discussion, Koch, 'When was Welsh Literature First Written Down?', p. 45; Sims-Williams, 'Emergence of Old Welsh, Cornish and Breton Orthography', pp. 29–30; Russell, '*Rowynniauc, Rhufoniog*', pp. 35–36; Charles-Edwards, *Wales and the Britons*, pp. 245–67, 272–73.

[92] For an excellent detailed discussion, see Davies, *Small Worlds*, pp. 86–104.

[93] Chédeville, 'L'anthroponymie bretonne', p. 32.

[94] Chédeville, 'L'anthroponymie bretonne', pp. 32–33.

A good example, which also leads in other directions, is a charter which has not survived in Brittany. On 7 October 860 at *Bedulcampus* (identified as Bouchamps-lès-Craon) on the eastern borderlands of Brittany, Salomon agreed to restore to Ansbald, abbot of Prüm, at his request monastic lands which had fallen into Salomon's hands;[95] at this period, Prüm had held extensive estates in eastern Brittany which were used as a way of establishing Frankish influence in this frontier zone.[96] The charter is preserved in the Golden Book of Prüm (Stadtbibliothek Trier, Hs 1709) fol. 91^v–92^v, in the section dating to the first half of the twelfth century.[97] For our purposes the most important aspect of this charter is the witness list which begins with Salomon and his wife, Winbrit, and their close family. The names are all single except for two disambiguating patronymics, *Ruuali filii eius* and *Irispoi filii Galuei*; in the former the *eius* refers to Salomon so as to distinguish him from the other witnesses called Ruualus and Ruualon, while in the latter case Irispoe was also the name of a son of Salomon. Given the high status of these individuals we may assume that most of them were well enough known not to require further elaboration.[98] Comparison with the witness lists of the Cartulary of Redon for the period 850 × 870 reveals most of the witnesses in the list from the Prüm charter, thus providing strong evidence that the charter is genuine. However, there is some variation in forms. Some can be explained as copying error: for example, *Alfinit* for *Alfrit*,[99] *Burthuuant* for *Bertuualt*, *Heligar* for *Helugon*,

[95] On the identification of *Bedulcampus*, see Meuret, *Peuplement, pouvoir et paysage*, pp. 231, 263–64; Chédeville and Guillotel, *Bretagne des saints et des rois*, pp. 326–27; on the more general geographical and historical context, see Brunterc'h, 'Géographie historique'.

[96] Smith, *Province and Empire*, pp. 56–57, 131. On Ansbald's travels in Francia, see the letter from Lupus of Ferrières to Ansbald (*Loup de Ferrières, Correspondance*, II.166–68 (no. 116), dated 862).

[97] For the text and translation, see Appendix below (pp. 349–52). For images of the charter and the list of witnesses, see Nolden, *Das 'Goldene Buch'*, fol. 91^v–92^v with a German translation, pp. 318–20; Nolden, *Das goldene Buch*, p. 98 is an image of the witness list on fol. 91^r. For earlier editions of the charter, see *Mémoires*, I.314–16; *Urkundenbuch*, I.99–100; on the manuscript, Lamprecht, *Deutsches Wirtschaftsleben im Mittelalter*, II.737–43; Franz and Nolden, *Kostbare Bücher und Dokumente*, pp. 77–78.

[98] Two witnesses appear to be called *Lagu*, but they, or one or other of them, may be an error for *Iagu* (cf. *CR* fol. 58^v (dated 860–863), 85^r, etc.). That said, an inscription from Locoal-Mendon (Morbihan) dated to the eighth–tenth centuries contains the single name *LAGU* (Davies and others, *Inscriptions*, M7 (pp. 230–36)).

[99] Cf. for spellings of *Altfrid*, etc., see *Cartulaire de l'abbaye Saint-Sauveur de Redon*, II.63, s.v. *Altfrid*. Alternatively, this may be miscopying of a name like *Finit* by eyeskip from a name beginning in *Al-*.

Hedrimelich perhaps for *Hedrimerch*, *Anacocart* for *Anauhocar* (perhaps with a *t* added by analogy with Germanic names in *-rt*); there is some variation between *-och* and *-oc*, and misreading of *-oe* as *-oc(h)*, e.g. *Edrebedoch* for *Hi(d)rbidoe*. Occasional names suggest that a different Old Breton spelling was in the exemplar: *Laguern* may perhaps correspond to *Louen* (containing also a *r/n* error) but it uses the later Old Breton *-gu-* spelling for */w/-*; *Uuiomaro* may be an earlier spelling for *(G)uiomarch*; and *Presel-* certainly corresponds to the element *Bresel-* in the Cartulary of Redon. Some variation is more complex: for example, *Canathedri* is probably an error for the name which in the Cartulary of Redon is spelt *Anauhidr*; either the scribe mis-segmented a list of names and separated off a final *-c* (or perhaps *-t*) from the preceding word, or miscopied *c-* from the beginning of a different name. If so, such mis-segmentation suggests that the exemplar (or an exemplar further back in the line of transmission) was structured like a Breton witness list from the Cartulary of Redon where the names follow each other in close succession; it would be very hard to make the same kind of error with an exemplar like the Prüm charter itself where the names are set out in columns. In terms of chronology, two spelling features suggest an exemplar broadly contemporary with the event: first, the suffix *-oc* or *-och* spelt with *-o-* is the older spelling (later *-uc*); secondly, apart from *Laguern*, */w/* is consistently spelt *uu* both initially and internally.[100]

The evidence of this charter's witness list is useful as a guide to how Frankish scribes might misread Breton names; crucially the evidence of this charter suggests miscopying. However, there are also occasional examples of names which can only be explained by assuming that they were transmitted in a spoken form and then written down at a later stage. Julia Smith has recently discussed an important group of relic labels which preserve names of saints from the seventh and eighth centuries.[101] Among them is an eighth-century example from Chelles (near Paris) which is almost certainly Breton in origin, *Uurgonezlo*. The only philological discussion of this name is that of Léon Fleuriot.[102] However, his discussion raises as many problems as it solves. He analysed is as *uur-* + *-gon-* + *-ezl* (with a Latin case ending *-o*). The first two elements are relatively unproblematic in that they can be paralleled elsewhere: *uur-* is a very

[100] Cf. Lambert's useful discussion of the variation in spelling in his discussion of the names in the Cartulary of Landévennec ('Les noms de personnes', p. 39).

[101] Smith, *Relics and the Insular World*, p. 24, and for an image of the relic label in a script characteristic of Chelles, p. 44.

[102] Fleuriot, 'Britonnica et Gallica', pp. 194–97.

common Breton element: either the prefix *uuor-*, later *gur-*, *gour-* 'over, above' (cf. Welsh *gor-*) or alternatively *uur-*, *gur-*, *guur-* 'man' as the first element of a compound; *-gon-* is found as a name element: there is a bishop of Senlis (*c.* 550) called *Gonothigernus*, later the same name appears as *Gondiernus* and *Gundiernus* in the *Cartulaire de Redon*. More usefully these first two elements seem to occur in Welsh in the name *Goronwy*, Old Welsh *Guorgonui* (Book of Llandaf).[103] Fleuriot listed some other possible examples of *-gon-* and suggested that it is related to the **gen-* root 'born'. The real problem, however, lies with *-ezlo*. Fleuriot assumed it is a suffix but then quoted a series of Old Breton words, *banadl* 'broom' (plant), *kenedl* 'people', *dadl* 'debate', *hoedl* 'age, period', *odl* 'ode' (all of these have clear Welsh correspondences), and a personal name *Gradlon*, but in none of these is *-(e)dl* a segmentable and generalizable suffix.[104] In other words, whatever we might think about the other issues, *-gonezl(o)* should be a recognizable item by itself (that is, it cannot be suffixed), but there is no lexical item it can be identified with, as it stands. Further problems arise with the spelling of this *-/ð/-*: in Old Breton it was usually spelt as *-d-* but from the eleventh century onwards it was often spelt with *-z-* (in modern Breton it is pronounced *-/z/-* but in Middle Breton it was probably spelt *-z-* but pronounced *-/ð/-*).[105] In other words, if this were Old Breton, the spelling with *-z-* for *-/ð/-* is entirely unexpected and unparalleled.[106] There is a case of *-z-* in Old Breton but it stands for *-/tˢ/-* in *puz* (< French *puits* 'well').[107] On that basis it might be thinkable that the *-z-* stands for /tˢ/ or /st/, and although there are Brittonic words in *-stl*, again it is not a segmentable suffix nor is there any form in *gonestl* or the like.

Fleuriot's analysis then is difficult to sustain, and one might be tempted to think that it is not Breton at all. There is, however, a way of extracting something Breton from this.

---

[103] Davies, *The Llandaff Charters*, p. 169 (date *c.* 950).

[104] As a philological aside, in early Brittonic there was a suffix **-tlo-* (which has a good Indo-European pedigree) which lenited to **-/dlo-/* in Brittonic. Within the early Brittonic languages (after the loss of final syllables) this either remained as *-/dl/* or assimilated to *-/ðl/*, the latter happening (as far as we can tell) in Breton, Cornish, and southern Welsh, the former arguably in north Wales; for discussion, see Russell, 'Welsh *anadl*/*anaddl*'.

[105] On this, see Fleuriot, *Le vieux breton*, pp. 104–05; Jackson, *Historical Phonology*, pp. 643–67 (esp. 645–49).

[106] Fleuriot, *Le vieux breton*, pp. 101–05; Jackson, *Historical Phonology*, pp. 645–48.

[107] Fleuriot, *Le vieux breton*, pp. 104–05; Jackson, *Historical Phonology*, p. 769, n. 3.

Fleuriot's discussion is predicated on the assumption that the spelling system being used is that of Old Breton, but that in fact might be an obstacle to thinking clearly about this. If we assume that the name is Breton but it is being spelt away from Brittany, somewhere in France (perhaps at Chelles itself), what did they think they might have been spelling? Because Fleuriot was thinking in Old Breton terms, he was trapped into thinking that -*g*- was original (i.e. it was not the product of a -/g/- from a lenited -/k/- which in Old Breton would have still been spelt as -*c*- or -*k*-). But if we suppose that this name was being spelt further east and being spelt by ear with other spelling conventions rather than according to Old Breton spelling rules, it is possible that originally the name being spelt was /wurgeneðl/ with the second element being /keneðl/ 'race, tribe, people'. If so, the first element is more likely to be 'man' rather than 'over', as the initial element of the second element of compounds is lenited in all insular Celtic languages, while after the prefix *uur*- (or the like) lenition is sporadic. One drawback to this is that the *cenedl* word is very rare in names: there is one clear case in Welsh genealogies, *Cenedlon* (where it is a female name), and there is another one in Brittany, a priest called *Cenetlor*.[108] One of the variant spellings, *Kenethlur*, is striking as it might be argued that this consists of *cenedl* + *gur* 'man', possibly our proposed elements in the reverse order. If this is the name, we would have to assume two things; first, that at Chelles, or somewhere else in Francia, /ð/ was spelt *z*, and secondly that in the process of scribal copying -*gen*- was miscopied as -*gon*-. Both of these would be quite possible.[109]

The cases discussed in this section offer an interesting insight into what happened to Breton names when they fall into the hands of Frankish scribes or were pronounced by Frankish speakers. Moreover, these names are likely to come from different social strata; while we have no idea who Saint *Uurgonezl* was, the Prüm charter, like many of the charters in the Cartulary of Redon,

---

[108] *Early Welsh Genealogies*, p. 45 (§ 10), corresponding to Guy, *Medieval Welsh Genealogy*, p. 341; *Cartulaire de l'abbaye Saint-Sauveur de Redon*, II.95, *s.v. Kenetlor* (variously spelt); the name appears several times and given the date range of 833–852 they may well refer to the same person.

[109] There are other possibilities, though requiring a greater degree of scribal mis-copying. For example, if we think that the *z* represents /st/, then the -*gonezl*- might be a corruption of Old Breton *guuistl* 'hostage' (cf. Old Cornish *guestl*, Welsh *gwystl*) Although *guistl* vel sim. is rather more common as a name element (cf. Welsh *Tangwystl*), the required degree of corruption is greater. Another possibility (though even less likely) is a version of the name *Guenngustl(e)*, as it would require *r*/*n* confusions as well; that said, it is a name associated with St Ninnoc in the cartulary of Quimperlé (*Cartulaire de Sainte-Croix de Quimperlé*, ed. by Henry and others, fol. 109ʳ).

12. FACING DIFFERENT WAYS   339

deals with high-status business. But not all charters dealt with such lofty transactions, and we can now return to the charter in the Cartulaire de Quimperlé
with which we began in which the scribe, Gurheden, apparently declines to
continue to copy a list of witnesses on account of the *rustica imbecillitas* of the
names.

Rustica imbecillitas

We may approach Gurheden's dilemma in different ways. One possibility is that
this was just a more elaborate and pointed way of saying that the witness-lists
are too long and that, since this is only the cartulary copy and so perhaps not
necessarily legally binding, not all the names need be copied. In the Cartulary of
Quimperlé itself the scribe twice curtails lists on the grounds that they are too
long: '[...] et alii quos perlongum est enumerare';[110] '[...] et alii plures quorum
nomina subnotare perlongum est'.[111] Likewise in the Cartulary of Redon there
are several examples of a similar truncation or in one instance at least a redirec-
tion to where the names can be found in the *liber vitae*: '[...] et alii quamplures
quorum nomina longum est enarrare';[112] 'et alii quam plures testes';[113] 'et multi
alii qui aderant testes';[114] 'et aliis multis quorum nomina sunt in libro uite'.[115]
In the Cartulary of the Abbey of Notre-Dame de Beauport a witness list ends
with the statement that it would be superfluous to add more names: '[...] et alii
quamplures quos quia enumerare videtur superfluum preterimus'.[116] Elsewhere

---

[110] *Cartulaire de Sainte-Croix de Quimperlé*, ed. by Henry and others, fol. 104^r; *Cartulaire de l'abbaye de Sainte-Croix de Quimperlé*, ed. by Maître and de Berthou, p. 218 (dated
1107–1112); 'and others whom it would be too long to list'.

[111] *Cartulaire de Sainte-Croix de Quimperlé*, ed. by Henry and others, fol. 141^v; *Cartulaire
de l'abbaye de Sainte-Croix de Quimperlé*, ed. by Maître and de Berthou, p. 269 (dated 1088):
'and many others whose names it would be too long to note'.

[112] *Cartulaire de l'abbaye Saint-Sauveur de Redon*, fol. 175^v; *CR*, p. 320 (dated 20 June
1101): 'and others whose names it would be too long to list'.

[113] *Cartulaire de l'abbaye Saint-Sauveur de Redon*, fol. 143^r; *CR*, p. 247 (dated 1026): 'and
many other witnesses'.

[114] *Cartulaire de l'abbaye Saint-Sauveur de Redon*, fol. 177^r; *CR*, p. 324 (dated 1112): 'and
many other witness who were present'.

[115] *Cartulaire de l'abbaye Saint-Sauveur de Redon*, fol. 182^v; *CR*, p. 336 (dated 1095); 'and
many others whose names are in the *Liber Vitae*'.

[116] *Anciens évêchés de Bretagne*, iv.280; 'and many others whom we have omitted because it
would be superfluous to list them'.

the omission of a list of burgesses is accounted for by a scribe (writing in the first plural) as '[...] quorum nomina brevitate gaudentes pretermittendo diu exagitatam hoc modo terminavimus [...]'.[117] Even more prosaically again, some of the shortening-phrases occur towards the bottom of a page and it is tempting to suspect that the scribe wanted to round a charter off at the bottom of the page in order to start a new charter at the top of the next page and so avail himself of the top margin for the rubricated heading.

But while that may be part of the story, the unusual vehemence of *imbecillitas* should press us to think harder. We might begin by wondering whether the simple fact that the names were in Breton was the problem; Bernard Tanguy seems inclined to this view: 'Les anciennes anthroponymes trouvaient-ils pas grâce à ses yeux?'[118] As we have noted above, in the Cartulary of Redon, Breton names are common in the ninth- and tenth-century sections of the cartulary, though far less so in later sections. The names mentioned in this charter are admittedly repetitive but that it is probably because they form a family group. In other words, Breton names by themselves seem unlikely to have triggered this response by Gurheden as they are sufficiently common throughout the cartulary that they would not probably have caused offence.

What might have been more problematic is the use of patronymics, and more specifically the use of patronymics using Breton *mab* 'son'. In the Cartulary of Quimperlé as a whole there are over two thousand different combinations of names in the Latin form 'X *filius* Y', and many of those are repeated over and again. But there are only forty-two instances of 'X *mab* Y', and only thirty of these are found in witness lists (the others being in lists of land-holders providing food-renders and so on) of which twenty-one are copied by Gurheden. The Breton forms are also not spread throughout the cartulary but are restricted to a period of some eighty years (1057 × 1140 with only one charter dating from after 1128) within a cartulary of a date spread of 1029 × 1237. Even then there is a tendency to move into Latin to form the plural; thus in the *Cartula Loc Deui* (Lotivy) from Quiberon, nine individuals are designated with patronymics in *mab* but then we find *Rudalt et Loeshoarn filii Altfret*.[119] This is sugges-

---

[117] *Anciens évêchés de Bretagne*, IV.279.7–9: 'rejoicing in brevity we have ended this long drawn-out list in this way by omitting these names'.

[118] Tanguy, 'Les noms d'hommes', p. 88.

[119] *Cartulaire de Sainte-Croix de Quimperlé*, ed. by Henry and others, fol. 86[r–v] (dated 1069); *Cartulaire de l'abbaye de Sainte-Croix de Quimperlé*, ed. by Maître and de Berthou, pp. 188–89.

12. FACING DIFFERENT WAYS

341

tive: it may be that *mab* was not really being used as a fully functioning lexical item which could be pluralized with its full semantic force of 'son'. Support for the idea that *mab* was not at this period fully lexical may come from another charter from the end of the eleventh century or early in the twelfth concerning Moguel, in which at the end of a list names in which *filius* is used Guihomarch mab Guegant makes an appearance;[120] it could be argued that, as the last in the list, the scribe had been changing all the earlier instances of *mab* into *filius* but failed to do so in the last instance, but on the other hand the use of *mab* might be understood as a very specific personal choice perhaps because he simply saw it as part of his name rather than as a statement of patronymy.

Two other points are worth making at this stage. The charter in which the scribe breaks off from the witness list is dated to 1084 but Gurheden was writing in the 1120s some thirty or more years later and it may be that the time-lag is significant; was Gurheden looking back and seeing these names in *mab* as in some sense old-fashioned? It also worth focusing briefly on the 'rustic' element of Gurheden's complaint. None of the charters containing *mab* relates to places in Quimperlé itself; from the urban perspective of Gurheden such names may not only have seemed old-fashioned but they may have been literally 'rustic' (i.e. from the country) and so triggered a negative value judgement, and what we are seeing here is a distinction between naming patterns in Quimperlé and out in the countryside.

The more specific target, then, may be the patronymics which employ Breton *mab*. As noted, they are rare in this cartulary and virtually non-existent elsewhere; the use of Latin as the matrix-language usually triggers *filius* rather than *mab*. Chédeville has also noted the steady use of patronymics between 1000 and 1280, though it is beginning to drop off by *c.* 1250.[121] In other words patronymy *per se* seems not to be the problem, since we also find numerous names such as Walter fitz Alan from Dol. The Cartulary of Redon, the earlier charters of which are not used by Chédeville, suggests that patronymic patterns seem to be being used in the first half of the eleventh century, while prior to that there is a strong preference for single names. Since the charters of this period tend to be markedly higher status than the ninth-century ones, this may reflect the rise of new aristocratic naming patterns. But, as has been noted already, charters

---

[120] *Cartulaire de Sainte-Croix de Quimperlé*, ed. by Henry and others, fol. 100ʳ–101ᵛ; *Cartulaire de l'abbaye de Sainte-Croix de Quimperlé*, ed. by Maître and de Berthou, pp. 214–16; at p. 216, n. 1 it is suggested that Moguel was located between Bannalec and Quimperlé.

[121] Chédeville, 'L'anthroponymie bretonne', pp. 255–56.

may not be a reliable guide to more general naming patterns: names in witness lists have to be distinctive within quite a long list of names, many often belonging to the same family. On the other hand, more general naming patterns may have had other concerns such as identifying individuals by reference to where they live or how they earn their living. Such forms do also occur in cartularies but, as already noted, the frequency of patronymics may be artificially high in the witness lists of charters and perhaps give a misleading sense of how names functioned.

One hint of this lies in our charter. The last name on the list, before Gurheden gives up, is *Tanki mab cognomine*; a similar form of name occurs twice in charters in the same cartulary from a decade or so earlier: *Altfrit mab cognomento/cognomine*.[122] In both cases, *mab* looks as it is being treated as a surname by itself; that appears to be the import of *cognomen/cognomentum*.[123] It might just be possible to read *mab* here as equivalent to 'young' or 'junior' in contrast to a father also called *Tanki* or *Altfrit* comparable to the use of *Fychan* (anglicized as Vaughan) 'small, junior' in Wales, but the presence of *cognomen/ cognomentum* makes that less likely, and such a usage would only be restricted to cases where father and son have the same name.[124] The fact that this term had to be used in two cases indicates that using *mab* by itself was ambiguous and vulnerable to being misinterpreted; if so, then the patronymic system may not have been defunct but perhaps fading in salience.

There is, however, another way to think about such names. In 1997 David Thornton argued that the name *Maccus*, common in northern England and southern Scotland between the tenth and thirteenth centuries, rather than being derived from Old Norse *Magnús*, as had previously been argued, was a Hiberno-Scandinavian form based on the Irish patronymic element *mac* 'son'.[125] He also drew attention to Welsh instances, notably Walter Map, as well as cases of the anglicized surnames *Mab* and *Mabe*, one Cornish instance, *Godric Map*, and the later Breton surname *Le Map* or *Le Mab* (the use of the article being

---

[122] *Cartulaire de Sainte-Croix de Quimperlé*, ed. by Henry and others, fols 70ʳ (*cognomento*) and 71ʳ (*cognomine*); *Cartulaire de l'abbaye de Sainte-Croix de Quimperlé*, ed. by Maître and de Berthou, pp. 151 and 155.

[123] On the sense of these terms, see Billy, 'Glossaire des formules de dénomination', pp. 227–28.

[124] Smith, *Walter Map and the Matter of Britain*, pp. 13–15, suggests this possibility for the name of Walter Map.

[125] Thornton, 'Hey, Mac!'.

12. FACING DIFFERENT WAYS

343

characteristic of Breton names taken over into French).[126] The interesting point for our purposes was made tentatively by Thornton:[127]

> It is not impossible therefore that the Irish patronymic construction encountered by the Scandinavians and perhaps used by a minority of the Hiberno-Scandinavian settlers could even have lost its functionality. That would mean that the noun *mac* — the non-onomastic and functionally genealogical element in the construction — was subsequently regarded by the predominantly non-Gaelic-speaking population simply as part of the overall naming-system and came to be employed by them as a personal name in its own right, independent of Irish usage.

Thornton goes on to draw a parallel with the use of Irish *gilla* 'servant, boy', derived probably from names like *Gilla Pátraic* (lit.) 'the servant of Patrick', which seems to follow a similar trajectory towards being used in medieval English and Icelandic sources as a simple name, *Gille* or *Gilli*.[128] In such cases it looks very much as if *map* and *mac* have become names in their own right and so could be used both as a name and as a *cognomen*.[129] But, Thornton's suggestion that the patronymic element could have lost its functionality does not necessarily follow. The onomastic context in which *maccus* and *mab* became simple names was one in which patronymy was a very common naming pattern, and one which would have been entirely familiar in a Norse or Anglo-Norman context as well as in Irish or Welsh ones. But it might still be possible that, for example, *mac* and *mab* were not seen as part of a patronymic naming pattern by French or Norse speakers but simply as name elements. But we are not talking about that kind of linguistic context in Quimperlé, though such conditions may have pertained in the eastern parts of Brittany, nor is it a context where we might imagine that patronymics were falling out of use at this period; the statistics and graphs provided by Chédeville (which incidentally

---

[126] Thornton, 'Hey, Mac!'; note that in an appendix to Thornton ('Hey, Mac!', pp. 95–98) Padel provides another Cornish example, *Talkarn Mackus*. Cf. also Divanach, *5000 Noms Bretons*, pp. 74 and 76; Morgan and Morgan, *Welsh Surnames*, p. 155, *s.v. Mab*. On Walter Map, see now Smith, *Walter Map and the Matter of Britain*, pp. 13–15. On the absence of name forms of the type 'X *mab* Y' in the Bodmin Manumissions, see Padel, *Slavery in Saxon Cornwall*, pp. 12–13. For similar developments in medieval Scotland, see Hammond, 'The Development of *mac* Surnames in the Gaelic World'.

[127] Thornton, 'Hey, Mac!', pp. 80–81.

[128] Thornton, 'Hey, Mac!', p. 81.

[129] Note that by this period the derivative *maban* was already being used as a name and this may have helped in the development of *mab* into a name; for *Maban* as a name, cf. *CR* fol. 67^r (*Cartulaire de l'abbaye de Redon en Bretagne*, LVIII, dated to the mid-ninth century).

do not distinguish between *mab* and *filius*) suggest that in general terms the use of patronymics seems to drop off in the thirteenth to fourteenth centuries but not earlier. But we need not suppose that the loss of patronymy was evenly spread across Brittany. It may well have been very variable and dependent very much on local record-keeping preferences; for example, we have seen that in Kermartin (Trégor) no word for 'son' was used.[130] On the other hand, we know that (perhaps fossilized) reflexes of patronymic usage, e.g. in names such as *Abgrall*, *Abivin*, survived until the nineteenth century in parts of Léon in the records of the arch-deaconry of Kemenet-Ili;[131] however, such forms are only reflexes of earlier usage, just as are names such as Pritchard, Pryce, Bevan in Wales, and that is no guarantee that a full patronymic pattern (where 'A son of B' was still widespread and productive) survived as late as the nineteenth century.[132]

It is not clear then that these instances of a 'surname' *mab* arose in circumstances where the vernacular marking of patronymy by using a word for 'son' was fading; there is little evidence of that. However, we might think about form: where patronyms survived long enough to be fixed in surnames, the form of the 'son' element (or indeed other relationship markers which occupy that same position) tended to be reduced in articulation, mainly because they were unstressed (and in Irish at least were pretonic, that is, immediately preceding the stressed syllable);[133] thus in Welsh beside *mab* 'son, boy', the lenited form *vap/vab* was used in patronymic constructions, and this was gradually reduced to *ap/ab* (whence anglicized forms like *Pryce* < *ap Rhys* where the loss of the *a* shows that it was unstressed).[134] On the Isle of Man the reduction of *mac* (in genitives and vocatives lenited to *mhic*) was so advanced that in anglicized forms of names only the final velar survived, e.g. *Quiggin* < *mac Uiginn*, *Kermode*

---

[130] See above, pp. 327–29.

[131] Le Brun and le Menn, 'La repartition géographique'; cf. German, 'Breton Patronyms', p. 59. The restriction of these forms to one arch-deaconry in Léon is striking and may be an artefact of record-keeping; perhaps the record-keepers or local priests preserved forms which were in use but not recorded in the same way elsewhere, for example, by writing *ab-* as part of the name while elsewhere it was disregarded.

[132] Morgan and Morgan, *Welsh Surnames*, pp. 17–18.

[133] On these phonological reductions in unaccented elements, see Russell, '*Gwas, Guos-, Gos-*', esp. pp. 82–84.

[134] The accommodation of the final -/b/ to -/p/ before unvoiced consonants at the beginning of the father's name, e.g. *ap Cynan* beside *ab Einion* suggests the same.

12. FACING DIFFERENT WAYS

< *mhic Dhiarmait*.[135] If the phonology of patronymics markers in southern Brittany had developed in a similar way, it may already have been marked by *ab* rather than *mab* and this may have been the pattern that Gurheden was familiar with. Bearing in mind that Gurheden was copying a document thirty years later, it is possible then that forms in *mab* were unfamiliar and to him were redolent of rusticity. We also have to allow for the in-built conservatism of the spelling of names: even at Clohal in the 1050s they may not have been saying *mab* but that is how they spelt it. But for Gurheden such names were a marker of rusticity (and tainted with all kinds of connotations of rusticity and old-fashionedness) and by the early twelfth century perhaps the naming patterns of a town like Quimperlé were rather different from the surrounding countryside. We can only guess at this as the evidence is lacking, but it is conceivable that, as the population of Quimperlé grew by inward migration from the country, the patronymic naming pattern became less and less useful; in part this may be because it was so closely linked to family and local land-holding, but we also need to bear in mind the 'condensation' of names over this period which might have resulted in several people with the same first name and the same patronymic. Names elements based on professions or places of origin might have proved much more distinctive and useful designators, the former offering a possible advertisement for the services or wares an individual could provide, and the latter maintaining a link to somewhere else.

In compiling their statistics Chédeville and others rightly distinguish between patronymy and other secondary naming patterns, the addition, for example, of a 'soubriquet', or of a place-name, of another name (sometimes that of the father), of a profession, etc., or various combinations of these. But it is important to keep in mind that the same person could be designated in different ways depending on the context or in none: that is, there could be an inverse relation between the use of patronymy (or occupation terms) to extend a name and the context presumed by the writer to be known to his readers; the more familiar an individual is the less likely it would be that the extra onomastic markers would be needed. So in different contexts different onomastic markers might be appropriate; and that brings us back to the question of whether patronymy was more common in the legal context of witness lists than elsewhere.

---

[135] The initial of the father's name would have been standardly lenited in a genitive or vocative. Similar reductions results in anglicized names in *Gil-* (< *Gilla*), *Macle-* (< *mac gilla*), and *Gos-* (< *gwas*) (especially in Scotland); for last of these, see Russell, '*Gwas, Guos-, Gos-*'.

A parallel from Wales may be useful: if we look at native sources, such as chronicles, one could be forgiven for thinking that Welsh society was relentlessly patronymic in its naming patterns. However, if we turn to the earliest of the Norman surveys of Wales, the Merioneth lay-subsidy roll of 1292–1293, a different picture emerges:[136] taking into account all the male names attested more than ten times (of which the most common are Adda, Dafydd, Einion, Gronw, Iorwerth, and Madog) which in total are used by over 2500 individuals, in a third of cases the primary name is not followed by a patronymic but by some other marker, an adjective, a place name, or professional designator, etc. It is likely that the Anglo-Norman surveyors and their local representatives were using whatever identifiers locals offered them; in other words, a third of the taxable population were not self-identifying by using patronymics (even though presumably they had fathers, though not all might have known who they were). That is a higher rate of retention of patronymics than in the St Yves canonization case where only half of names include a patronymic. But even so, presumably patronymy was still one of the naming-patterns available even if it was not everyone's first choice of self-identification.

What this excursion into the detail of Breton onomastic practices suggests is that different approaches can tell us different things; all are useful, the broad quasi-teleological analyses which track developments into the early modern period, those that look back into the origins of these names and compare the distribution of name-forms, and then finally close micro-studies of a specific feature. But without the detail of particular cases, the broader studies have no basis in the reality of the evidence. Drilling down into the detail can show how complex and nuanced matters of naming were at the level of the individual name-holders and, if nothing else, should make us think harder about the generalizations we make.

---

[136] *Merioneth Lay Subsidy Roll*, ed. by Williams-Jones; these figures were extracted from the Indices (pp. 102–36).

12. FACING DIFFERENT WAYS

Appendix 1

Facsimile: *Cartulaire de Quimperlé*, ed. by Henry and others, fol. 79ᵛ–80ʳ; edition: *Cartulaire de Quimperlé*, ed. by Maître and de Berthou, pp. 177–78

[fol. 79ᵛ] **Cartula de Clohal**

Quoniam summorum astucię philosophorum haut irrationabiliter placuit digna quęque memoria uocum articulatarum permanentibus commendari signis ne nostri posteri plurium reuolutione annorum preteritorum[137] obliti donorum nostrę negligentię culpa detrimentum incurrerent.[138] quę alanus comes filius hoeli comitis sanctę crucis kemperelegiensis abbati et monachis concessit et donauit. his lituris[139] tradere curauimus. Patre enim suo hoelo uidelicet comite defuncto. atque eius consulatus regimine ab eo suscepto. omnia quę ad abbatię sanctę crucis constructionem et ad cotidiana ipsius monachorum stipendia auus suus cornugalliensium comes donauerat. et pater suus hoel consul confirmauerat. abbati atque congregationi eiusdem crucis in perpetuum concessit. Vt uero pro anima patris sui scilicet hoeli in eodem monasterio perpetua dicatur oratio. terre numenoe de cluthgual dominium quod suum tunc erat [fol. 80ʳ] illud quidem quod ad consulatus principatum attinebat eidem abbatię donauit. Vt autem posterorum noticię manifestum sit quos census ipsa terra sancte cruci debeat quod quidem consuli prius debebat; illud huic cartę commendauimus. In unoquoque anno hęc debet sanctę cruci Vaccam unam. et unum porcum. et duos multones. et quatuor gallinas. et octo annonę sextarios. quatuor quidem frumenti atque totidem auenę. Pastum quoque tot hominibus quot eiusdem monasterii abbas uoluerit. et fures et quoslibet alios scelestos in suis forisfactis in ea deprehensos. Hęc autem duobus episcopis uidentibus et audientibus concessa sunt, benedicto quidem nannetensi episcopo qui eiusdem abbatię tunc abbas existebat. et benedicto corisopitensi episcopo. Cum his hi etiam idonei testes affuerunt.

Iungomarius abbas. Guigonus decanus. Aldroenus grammaticus. Coriou capellanus. Tanki mab guegun. Derian mab tanki. Tanki mab cognomine. et alii plurimi quorum nomina eorumdem rustica imbecillitas hic notari prohibuit.

---

[137] prestitorum ed.

[138] incurrunt ed.

[139] litteris ed.

'Since not unreasonably it pleased the astuteness of great philosophers that everything worthy of memory be commended by the permanent indications of articulated words, so that our descendants should not get into difficulties by the passing of many years and forget past gifts by the fault of our negligence, we have ensured to preserve in these words that which Count Alan, son of Count Hoel granted and donated to the abbot and monks of the Holy Cross of Quimperlé. For when his father, namely count Hoel died and he took over as ruler, he granted to the abbot and to the congregation of the Holy Cross in perpetuity everything which his grandfather, the count of Cornouaille, had donated for the building of the abbey of the Holy Cross and for the daily allowances of the monks, and which his father Hoel, the lord, had confirmed. So that a perpetual prayer be said for the soul of his father, namely Hoel, in that monastery, he donated to that abbey rule over the land of Numenoe of Clohal which at that time was his and which related to the rule of the princes. Moreover, so that it might be clearly known by our descendants what rents that land owes to the Holy Cross (which previously it used to owe to the lord) we have included that in this charter. In any single year this land owes to the Holy Cross one cow, and one pig, and two sheep, and four hens, and eight measures of grain, four of wheat and as much again in oats; food for as many men as the abbot of that monastery wants; and that thieves and any other wicked people causing trouble there be apprehended. Moreover these were granted in the sight and in the hearing of the two bishops, Benedict, bishop of Nantes who was at that time abbot of that abbey, and Benedict, bishop of Cornouaille. Together with these, these suitable witnesses were also present: Iungomarius the abbot, Guigonus the deacon, Aldroenus the scribe, Coriou the chaplain, Tanki mab Guegun, Derian mab Tanki, and Tanki Mab by name, and many others; the rustic stupidity of their names has prevented them from being noted here.'

12. FACING DIFFERENT WAYS

Appendix 2

The Bedulcampus charter in Trier Stadtbibliothek, Hs 1709[140] (*Das goldene Buch von Prüm*), fol. 91^v–92^v

Prestaria Tradit*a* Salemonis

[91^{v}1] In nomine d*omi*ni n*os*tri Ih*e*su Chri*st*i Salomon gra*tia et* beneficio Dei dux et princeps Brittonu*m*. Om*n*ibus ep*iscop*is abb*at*ibus *et* comitib*us*. centenariis ac uicariis. om*n*ibusque qui sub n*os*tra dominatione *et* regno in iudicaria c*on*sistunt potestate. Notu*m* sit itaq*ue* uob*is* qualit*er* quida*m* abba nomine Ansbaldus de monasterio qui d*ici*tu*r* Prumia qu*od* e*st* in honore d*omi*ni et saluatoris mundi Ih*e*su Chri*st*i consecratu*m et* constructu*m*. ueniens ad n*os*tram mansuetudine*m*. peciit ut res memorati d*omi*ni saluatoris qu*ę* in n*os*tra potestate et regno uidentu*r* esse. in ei*us* potestate*m* et dominatione*m* redderem*us* ad utilitate*m* uidelic*et* monachor*um* qui in iam dicto monasterio Deo saluatori nos*t*ro deseruiunt. Igit*ur* libentissime ei*us* annuentes peticionib*us* prop*ter* amore*m* Dei *et* saluatoris mundi Ih*e*su Chri*st*i *et* remissione*m* peccator*um* n*os*tror*um*. om*n*ia qu*ę* petiit illi c*on*cessim*us*. atq*ue* procerum n*os*tror*um*[141] ante reliquias *san*c*t*i saluatoris de om*n*ibus rebus qu*ę* ad memoratu*m* monasteriu*m* p*er*tinent qu*ę* sub n*os*tra scilic*et* erant potestate p*er* uuadium n*os*tru*m* reuestim*us*. ut tam ipse qua*m* successores ei*us* libera*m* in omnib*us* habeant potestate*m* faciendi qu*ę*cunque uoluerint ad utilitate*m* seruo*rum* Dei qui in memorato loco c*on*sistunt. Petiit *etiam* ut memoratas res sub n*os*tra tuitione et defensione haberem*us*. atq*ue* om*n*ia qu*ę* antecessores n*os*tri reges uidelic*et* et principes ad iam dictu*m* locu*m* de eisdem rebus c*on*cesserunt. *pro* remedio anim*ę* n*os*tr*ę* sicut gr*ati*am saluatoris mundi uoluissem*us* hab*er*e *et* uita*m* *ę*terna*m* ex n*os*tra quoq*ue* parte indulgeremus. Q*u*od et fecim*us* cu*m* magna deuotione. Precipim*us* itaq*ue* ex auctoritate d*omi*ni et saluatoris mundi Ih*e*su Chri*st*i qui e*st* creator om*n*ium uisibilium et inuisibiliu*m*. ut nullus iudex publicus *u*el alia qu*ę*lib*et* potestas aut ministri n*os*tri tam t*em*porib*us* n*os*tris qua*m* successo*rum* n*os*tror*um* aliqua*m* inquietudine*m* aut inpedime*n*tum aut dampnu*m* in rebus memorati saluatoris mundi audeat inferre. nec freda exigere. nec fideiussores tollere. nec scaras *u*el mansionaticos. seu co*n*iectos. nec teloneu*m*. siue de carrigio. siue de naui-

---

[140] For discussion, see pp. 335–36 above; for an image of the text, see Nolden, *Das 'Goldene Buch'*, fol. 91^v–92^v (with a German translation on pp. 318–20); for an image of the witness list on fol. 91^r, see Nolden, *Das goldene Buch*, p. 98. The text is transcribed from Nolden's manuscript image; the translation is mine.

[141] presentia *add. Urkundenbuch zur Geschichte*, ed. Beyer, p. 99.

gio *uel* de quacu*n*que re exquirere nec fodru*m*. nec parafredos tollere. homines
quoq*ue* ta*m* liberi qua*m* ecclesiastici *uel* deseruientes qui infra agros uel sup*er*
*t*erram memorati monasterii commanent, quieti resideant. ut neq*ue* in hoste*m*
p*er*gant. neq*ue* heribannum soluant. s*ed* om*n*ia h*ę*c aut qu*ę*cu*n*que ad *nost*ram
parte*m* poterat [92r1] deue*n*ire ex *nost*ra indulgentia ad utilitate*m* suprascripti
monasterii *con*cedim*us*. *et* q*uo*d nos p*ro*pt*er* nom*en* d*omin*i *et* remedio *nost*r*ę*
anim*ę* ad ia*m* dictu*m* monasteriu*m* concedim*us*. *con*testam*ur* *et* adiuramus
p*er* terribile nom*en* d*omin*i et saluatoris mundi ta*m* p*re*sentes qua*m* futuros ut
nec regalis potestas nec cuiuslib*et* iudicu*m* s*ę*ua cupiditas audeat infringere aut
contradicere. s*ed* inuiolabilit*er* p*er* futura sec*u*la conseruet*ur*; si quis uero q*uo*d
futuru*m* *ess*e *non* credimus. contra hanc auctoritatem *nost*ram et p*ro*cerum *nos*-
*tro*rum q*uo*d in honore d*omin*i et saluatoris mundi fecim*us* aliquid uoluerit
facere aut ea*m* infringere ira*m* D*e*i om*n*ipotentis incurrat. atq*ue* in die iudicii
cora*m* saluatore mundi reddat ratione*m*. et inter dampnatos anathema depute-
t*ur*. Et ut h*ę*c auctorita\ti/s *nost*r*ę* p*ro*cerumq*ue* *nost*rorum preceptio firma et
inuiolabilis p*er* futura maneat te*m*pora. manu p*ro*p*ri*a p*ro*cerumq*ue* *nost*rorum
manib*us* firmauim*us*. et anuli *nost*ri impressione subt*er* firmare fecim*us*. Si quis
u*er*o hanc auctoritate*m* *nost*ram uiolauerit. sexaginta libra\s/ auri purissimi sol-
uat. *et* q*uo*d repetit euindicare *non* ualeat.

Signu*m* salamonis principis.	Signu*m* + Winbrit. coniugis eius.	
Signu*m* + riuuali filii eius.	Signu*m* + Pasquithan.	Signu*m* + Hoernian.
Signu*m* + Bodoan.	Signu*m* + Bran.	Signu*m* + Uuiomaro.
Signu*m* + Alan.	Signu*m* + Spreuui.	Signu*m* + Artur.
Signu*m* + Moruuithan.	Signu*m* + Irispoi filii galuei.	Signu*m* + Matuedoi.
Signu*m* + Frutgaudi.	Signu*m* + Uuaranton.	Signu*m* + Canathedri.
Signu*m* +Heligor.	Signu*m* + ruulin.	Signu*m* + Fines.
Signu*m* + Beruualt.	Signu*m* + Alfinit.	Signu*m* + Catmonoch.
Signu*m* + Anagogert.		
Signu*m* + Damarcoc.	Signu*m* + Commesnen.	Signu*m* + Iagu.
	Signu*m* + Felix.	Signu*m* + Laguern.
	Iter*um* Signu*m* + Iagu.	Signu*m* + Bernehart.
Signu*m* + Penna.	Signu*m* + Uuinoch.	Signu*m* + Burtuuant.
Signu*m* + Hedrimelich.	Signu*m* Matfredi.	Signu*m* + Conani.
Signu*m* + Catbudich.		Signu*m* + Riodoch.
Signu*m* + Preselmarcoc.		Signu*m* + Bertuualt.
Signu*m* + Sabioch.		Signu*m* Ratuuili.
Signu*m* + Heluuithen. Signu*m* + Edrebedoch. Signu*m* + Finon.		

[92v1] Actu*m* uilla publica sedis *nost*r*ę* Bedulcampo sub die non*as* Oct*o*bris.
Anno dominic*ę* incarnationis. Octogentesimo. Saexagesimo. Indictione VII*ima*.
In D*e*i nomine felicit*er*. regni u*er*o *nost*ri tercio.

12. FACING DIFFERENT WAYS

351

In the name of our Lord Jesus Christ, Salomon by the grace and kindness of God, duke and prince of the Bretons, to all bishops, abbots, and counts, leaders of hundreds, and deputies, and to all who under our power and rule hold judicial powers, let it be known to you that an abbot called Ansbald from the monastery called Prüm which has been consecrated and constructed in honour of our Lord and Saviour of the world, Jesus Christ, came to our graciousness and asked that we return to his control and rule for the use of the monks who serve God, our Saviour, in the aforementioned monastery the property of our remembered Lord and Saviour which are under our control and rule. Gladly assenting therefore to his request on account of the love of God and the Saviour of the word, Jesus Christ, and for the remission of our sins we have granted all that he requested, and [in the presence] of our nobles before the relics of the holy Saviour we restore everything which belongs to the aforementioned monastery which was under our control by our promise so that both he and his successors might have unlimited power in every respect to so whatever they wish for the benefit of the servants of God who are in that aforementioned place. He also requested that we hold the aforementioned property under our protection and defence. And everything which our predecessors, both kings and princes, granted to the aforementioned place with regard to the same things, just as we would have wanted to have the grace of the Saviour of the world for the remediation of our soul and would enjoy eternal life for our part too, we also have done with great devotion. And so we command, on the authority of the Lord and Saviour of the world, Jesus Christ, who is the creator of all things visible and invisible, that no public judge or any other power of our servant, whether now or among our successors, should dare to inflict any disquiet or impediment or damage upon the possessions of our aforementioned Saviour of the world, nor demand fines, nor demand sureties nor military service, or lodging, or taxes, nor customs-dues, whether relating to land transport of shipping, or make any other demand, nor demand fodder-rights, nor requisition horses. Men also, whether free or in holy orders or in service who dwell within the agricultural land or on the land of the aforementioned monastery, should remain at peace so that they are not drafted for war nor make a payment in place of military-service, but we grant by our indulgence all these things or whatever could come down as our share to the benefit of the aforementioned monastery. We declare and swear by the fear-inspiring name of the Lord and Saviour of the world that neither royal power or the greed of any judge should dare to infringe or contradict it both in the present and in the future, but that it be preserved inviolate in future ages; but if anyone should desire to do anything — which we do not believe will happen — against this authority of ours and our nobles which we have done in honour of the Lord and Saviour of the world and infringe it, let him incur the wrath of the almighty God. And on the day of judgement let him render account to the Saviour of the world, and let him be reckoned as an anathema among the damned. And so that this command of our authority and that of our nobles remain firm and inviolate in the future, we have confirmed it by our own hand and that of our descendants, and we have had it confirmed by the seal of our ring. If anyone should violate our authority, let him pay a fine of sixty pounds of the purest gold and let him not be able to achieve what he seeks.

[witness list]

Enacted at our public dwelling of Bedulcampus (Bouchamps-lès-Craon) on 7 October in the year of our Lord 860, happily in the name of God, in the third year of our reign.

Paul Russell [pr270@cam.ac.uk] is Professor of Celtic in the Department of Anglo Saxon, Norse and Celtic in the University of Cambridge. His research interests include learned texts in Celtic languages (especially early Irish glossaries), Celtic philology and linguistics, early Welsh orthography, Middle Welsh translation texts, grammatical texts, medieval Welsh law, hagiography, and Latin texts from medieval Wales.

12. FACING DIFFERENT WAYS   353

Works Cited

Manuscript and Archival Sources

London, British Library, MS Egerton 2802
Trier Stadtbibliothek, Hs 1709

Primary Sources

L'abbaye cistercienne de Bégard des origines à 1476: histoire et chartes, ed. by C. Evans,
Atelier des Recherches sur les Textes Médiévaux, 16 (Turnhout: Brepols, 2012)
Anciens évêchés de Bretagne, ed. by J. Geslin de Bourgogne and A. de Barthélemy, 4 vols
(Paris: Dumoulin, 1855–1859)
Bartrum, P. C., ed., *Early Welsh Genealogical Tracts* (Cardiff: University of Wales Press,
1966)
Cartulaire de l'abbaye de Redon en Bretagne, ed. by A. de Courson (Paris: Imprimerie
Impériale, 1863)
Cartulaire de l'abbaye de Sainte-Croix de Quimperlé, ed. by L. Maître and P. de Berthou,
2nd edn (Rennes: Plihon et Hommay, 1904)
Cartulaire de l'église de Quimper, ed. by Abbé Peyron (Quimper: Kerangal, 1909)
Cartulaire de l'abbaye de Landévennec publié pour la Société archéologique du Finistère,
ed. by A. de la Borderie (Rennes: Catel, 1888)
Cartulaire de Landévennec, Collection des documents inédits sur l'histoire de la France,
ed. by R.-F.-L. Le Men and É. Ernault, Mélanges historiques, 5 (Paris: Bibliothèque
nationale, 1886)
Cartulaire de Sainte-Croix de Quimperlé, ed. by C. Henry, J. de Quaghabeur, and
B. Tanguy, Sources médiévales de l'histoire de Bretagne, 4 (Rennes: Presses universi-
taires de Rennes, 2014)
Cartulaire de Saint-Guénolé de Landévennec, ed. by S. Lebecq, Sources médiévales de
l'histoire de Bretagne, 6 (Rennes: Presses universitaires de Rennes, 2015)
Cartulaire de Saint-Melaine de Rennes, ed. by C. Reydellet, M. Chauvin-Lechaptois, and
J. Bachelier, Sources médiévales de l'histoire de Bretagne, 5 (Rennes: Presses universi-
taires de Rennes, 2015)
Cartulaire de l'abbaye Saint-Sauveur de Redon, ed. by H. Guillotel, A. Chédeville, and
B. Tanguy, 2 vols (Rennes: Association des Amis des Archives historiques du diocèse
de Rennes, Dol et Saint-Malo, 1998–2004)
Cartulaire générale du Morbihan, ed. by L. Rosenzweig (Vannes: Lafolye, 1895)
Gregory of Tours, *Libri Historiarum X*, ed. by B. Krusch, *MCH SS RM*, 1 (Hanover:
Hahn, 1942)
The Letters of Abelard and Eloise, trans. by B. Radice (Harmondsworth: Penguin, 1974)
Loup de Ferrières, Correspondence, ed. by L. Levillain, 2 vols (Paris: Champion, 1927–1935)
Mémoires pour server de preuves à l'histoire de Bretagne, ed. by H. Morice, 3 vols (Paris:
Osmont, 1742)

The Merioneth Lay Subsidy Roll 1292–3, ed. by K. Williams-Jones (Cardiff: University of Wales Press, 1976)

Monuments originaux de l'histoire de Saint Yves, ed. by A. de la Borderie, Abbé J. Daniel, R. P. Perquis, and D. Tempier (St Brieuc: Prudhomme, 1887)

Saints' Lives: Lives of SS. Wulfstan, Dunstan, Patrick, Benignus and Indract, ed. by M. Winterbottom and R. M. Thomson, Oxford Medieval Texts (Oxford: Oxford University Press, 2002)

The Text of the Book of Llan Dâv, ed. by J. G. Evans and J. Rhŷs (Oxford: Clarendon Press, 1893)

Urkundenbuch zur Geschichte der Mittelrheinischen Territorien, ed. by H. Beyer, L. Eltester, and A. Goerz, 3 vols, repr. (Aalen: Scienta, 1974)

Vita Griffini filii Conani. The Medieval Latin Life of Gruffudd ap Cynan, ed. and trans. by P. Russell (Cardiff: University of Wales Press, 2005)

Vitae Sanctorum Britanniae et Genealogiae, ed. by A. W. Wade-Evans (Cardiff: University of Wales Press, 1944)

Secondary Works

Bartlett, R., *The Making of Europe: Conquest, Colonization, and Cultural Change 950–1350* (London: Allen Lane, 1993)

Beech, G. T., M. Bourin, and P. Chareille, eds, *Personal Names Studies of Medieval Europe: Social Identity and Familial Structures*, Studies in Medieval Culture, 43 (Kalamazoo: Medieval Institute Publications, 2002)

Billy, P.-H., 'Glossaire des formules de dénomination dans les sources médiévales', in *Genèse médiévale de l'anthroponymie modern, Tome IV: Discours sur le nom: normes, usages, imaginaire (VIe–XVIe siècles)*, ed. by P. Beck, Études d'anthroponymie médiévale VIIe rencontres, Azay-Ferron 1995 (Tours: Publications de l'Université de Tours, 1997), pp. 223–37

Bourin, M., 'Intérêt et faiblesse des cartulaires pour l'étude de l'anthroponymie médiévale', in *Les Cartulaires. Actes de la Table ronde, organisée par l'École nationale des chartes, et le G.D.R. 121 du C.N.R.S. (Paris, 5–7 décembre 1991)*, ed. by O. Guyotjeannin, L. Morelle, and M. Parisse, Mémoires et Documents de l'École de Chartes, 39 (Paris: École des chartes, 1993), pp. 105–14

——, and P. Chareille, eds, *Noms, prénoms, surnoms au moyen âge*, Les médiévistes français, 12 (Paris: Picard 2014)

Brett, C., with F. Edmonds, and P. Russell, *Brittany and the Atlantic Archipelago, A.D. 450–1200: Contact, Myth and History* (Cambridge: Cambridge University Press, 2021)

Brunterc'h, J.-P., 'Géographie historique et hagiographie: la vie de Saint Mervé', *Mélanges de l'École française de Rome. Moyen Âge, Temps modernes*, 95 (1983), 7–63

Cane, M., 'Personal Names of Men in Wales, Cornwall and Brittany, 400–1400 A.D.', 2 vols (unpublished doctoral thesis, University of Wales, Aberystwyth, 2003)

—, 'Personal Names of Women in Wales, Cornwall and Brittany, 400–1400 A.D.' (unpublished M.Phil. thesis, University of Wales, Aberystwyth, 1999)

Charles-Edwards, T. M., *Wales and the Britons 350–1064* (Oxford: Oxford University Press, 2013)

Chédeville, A., 'L'anthroponymie bretonne', in *Genèse médiévale de l'anthroponymie moderne, Tome II.1: Persistances du nom unique. Le cas de la Bretagne. L'anthroponymie des clercs*, ed. by M. B. and P. Chareille, Études d'anthroponymie médiévale IIIᵉ et IVᵉ rencontres, Azay-Ferron 1989–1990 (Tours: Publications de l'Université de Tours, 1992), pp. 9–40

—, and H. Guillotel, *La Bretagne des saints et des rois vᵉ–xᵉ siècle* (Rennes: Ouest-France, 1984)

Chetwood, J., 'Re-evaluating English Personal Naming on the Eve of the Conquest', *Early Medieval Europe*, 26 (2018), 518–47

Davies, J. R., 'Old Testament Personal Names among the Britons: Their Occurrence and Significance before the Twelfth Century', *Viator*, 43 (2012), 175–92

—, 'Old Testament Personal Names in Scotland Before the Wars of Independence', in *Personal Names and Naming Practices in Medieval Scotland*, ed. by M. Hammond, SCH, 39 (Woodbridge: Boydell, 2019), pp. 187–212

Davies, W., *The Llandaff Charters* (Aberystwyth: National Library of Wales, 1979)

—, *Small Worlds. The Village Community in Early Medieval Brittany* (London: Duckworth, 1988)

—, J. Graham-Campbell, M. Handley, P. Kershaw, J. T. Koch, G. Le Duc, and K. Lockyear, *The Inscriptions of Early Medieval Brittany/Les Inscriptions de la Bretagne du Haut Moyen Âge* (Oakville, CN: Celtic Studies Publications, 2000)

Divanach, M., *5000 Patronymes bretonnes francisés* (Brest: Éditions du Vieux meunier breton, 1975)

Evans, D. E., 'A Comparison of the Formation of Some Continental and Early Insular Celtic Personal Names', *BBCS*, 24 (1970–1972), 415–34

Fleuriot, L., 'Britonnica et Gallica: 24. *Samsoni, Uurgonezlo*, noms des saints bretons dans les reliques de Chelles', *Études celtiques*, 24 (1987), 194–97 (repr. in L. Fleuriot, *Notes lexicographiques et philologiques*, Bibliothèque bretonne, 4 (Spézet: Skol, 1997), pp. 196–99)

—, *Le vieux breton. Éléments d'une grammaire* (Paris: Klincksieck, 1964)

Förster, M., 'Die Freilassungsurkunden des Bodmin-Evangeliars', in *A Grammatical Miscellany offered to Otto Jespersen*, ed. by N. Bøgholm, A. Brusendorff, and C. A. Bodelsen (Copenhagen: Munksgaard, 1930), pp. 77–99

Franz, G., and R. Nolden, *Kostbare Bücher und Dokumente aus Mittelalter und Neuzeit. Katalog der Ausstellung er Stadtbibliothek und des Stadtarchivs* (Trier: Stadtbibliothek Trier, 1984)

German, G. D., 'Breton Patronyms and the British Heroic Age', in *Regards croisés sur la Bretagne et le Pays de Galles. Cross-cultural Essays on Wales and Brittany*, ed. by A. Hellegouarc'h-Bryce and H. Williams (Brest: University of Wales Centre for Advanced Welsh and Celtic Studies, 2013), pp. 53–88

Gourvil, F., *Noms de familles bretons d'origine toponymique* (Quimper: Société archéologique du Finistère, 1970)

——, *Noms de famille de Basse-Bretagne. Matériaux pour servir à l'étude de l'anthroponymie bretonne* (Paris: Éditions d'Artrey, 1966)

——, *Noms 'héroïques' dans l'anthroponymie bretonne* (Salamanca: Universidad de Salamanca, 1958)

Guillotel, H., 'Cartulaires bretons médiévaux', in *Les cartulaires. Actes de la Table ronde, organisée par l'École nationale des Chartes, et le G.D.R. 121 du C.N.R.S. (Paris, 5–7 décembre 1991)*, ed. by O. Guyotjeannin, L. Morelle, and M. Parisse, Mémoires et documents de l'École de Chartes, 39 (Paris: École de Chartes, 1993), pp. 325–42

Hammond, M., 'The Development of *mac* Surnames in the Gaelic World', in *Personal Names and Naming Practices in Medieval Scotland*, ed. by M. Hammond (Woodbridge: Boydell, 2019), pp. 100–43

Hanks, P., R. Coates, and P. McClure, ed., *The Oxford Dictionary of Family Names in Britain and Ireland* (Oxford: Oxford University Press, 2016)

Holland, T. H., Jr., 'The Many Faces of Nicknames', *Names*, 38.4, ed. by J. K. Skipper and P. L. Leslie (1990), 254–72

Jackson, K. H., *A Historical Phonology of Breton* (Dublin: Dublin Institute for Advanced Studies, 1967)

Koch, J. T., 'When was Welsh Literature First Written Down?', *SC*, 20/21 (1985–1986), 43–66

Lambert, P.-Y., 'Les noms des personnes dans le Cartulaire de Landévennec', in *Cartulaire de Saint-Guénolé de Landévennec*, ed. by S. Lebecq, Sources médiévales de l'histoire de Bretagne, 6 (Rennes: Presses universitaires de Rennes, 2015), pp. 39–52

Lamprecht, K., *Deutsches Wirtschaftsleben im Mittelalter. Untersuchungen über die Entwicklung der materiellen Kultur des Platten Landes auf Grund der Quellen zunächst des Mosellandes*, 3 vols (Leipzig: Dürr, 1885–1886)

Le Brun, B., and G. le Menn, 'La répartition géographique des noms de famille dans le Finistère en 1836', *MSHAB*, 64 (1987), 365–88

Loth, J., *Chrestomathie bretonne (armoricain, gallois, cornique), première partie Breton-armoricain* (Paris: Bouillon, 1890)

Lowe, J. M., 'The Personal Names in the Bodmin Manumissions' (unpublished M.A. thesis, University of Wales, Aberystwyth, 1980)

McClure, P., 'Nicknames and Pet Names', *Nomina*, 5 (1981), 63–76

McDowell, J. H., 'Towards a Semiotics of Nicknaming: the Kamsa Example', *Journal of American Folklore*, 94 (1981), 1–18

Meuret, J.-C., *Peuplement, pouvoir, et paysage sur la marche Anjou-Bretagne*, La Mayenne: Archéologie, Histoire, suppl. 4 (Laval: Société d'archéologie et d'histoire de la Mayenne, 1993)

Mitterauer, M., *Ahnen und Heilige: Namengebung in der europäischen Geschichte* (Munich: Beck, 1993)

Morgan, J., C. O'Neill, and R. Harré, *Nicknames: Their Origins and Social Consequences* (London: Routledge, 1979)

Morgan, T. J., and P. Morgan, *Welsh Surnames* (Cardiff: University of Wales Press, 1985)

Nolden, R., ed., *Das 'Goldene Buch' von Prüm (Liber aureus Prumiensis). Faksimile, Über-setzung der Urkunden, Einband* (Prüm: Geschichtsverein, 1997)

——, ed., *Das goldene Buch von Prüm. Liber aureus Prumiensis (StB Trier, Hs 1709). Ein Kopier mit Urkunden abschriften des 8. Bis 12. Jahrhunderts*, Kostbarkeiten der Stadt-bibliothek Trier, 4 (Trier: Stadtbibliothek Trier, 2013)

Padel, O., *Slavery in Saxon Cornwall: the Bodmin Manumissions*, Kathleen Hughes Memorial Lecture (Cambridge: ASNC, 2009)

Pryce, H., 'Uses of the Vernacular in the Acts of the Welsh Rulers, 1120–1283', in *La langue des actes: actes du XIe congrès international de diplomatique (Troyes, jeudi 11-samedi 13 septembre 2003)*, ed. by O. Guyotjeannin (Paris: École des Chartes, 2003), available online only <http://elec.enc.sorbonne.fr/CID2003/pryce> [accessed 24 November 2022]

Russell, P., '*Gwas, Guos-, Gos-*: the Reflexes of Brittonic **wo*', in *Mélanges en l'honneur de Pierre-Yves Lambert*, ed. by G. Oudaer, G. Hily, and H. Le Bihan (Rennes: Tir, 2015), pp. 77–89

——, 'Old Welsh *Dinacat, Cunedag, Tutagual*: Fossilised Phonology in Brittonic Personal Names', in *Indo-European Perspectives in honour of Anna Morpurgo Davies*, ed. by J. H. W. Penney (Oxford: Oxford University Press, 2004), pp. 447–60

——, 'Patterns of Hypocorism in Early Irish Hagiography', in *Saints and Scholars. Studies in Irish Hagiography*, ed. by J. Carey, M. Herbert, and P. Ó Riain (Dublin: Four Courts, 2001), pp. 237–49

——, '*Rowynniauc, Rhufoniog*: The Orthography and Phonology of /μ/ in Early Welsh', in *Yr Hen Iaith. Studies in Early Welsh*, ed. by P. Russell (Aberystwyth: Celtic Studies Publications, 2003), pp. 25–47

——, 'Welsh *anadl/anaddl, gwadn/gwaddn*', *BBCS*, 31 (1984), 104–12

Sharpe, R., 'The Naming of Bishop Ithamar', *English Historical Review*, 117 (2002), 889–94

Sims-Williams, P., *The Book of Llandaf as a Historical Source* (Woodbridge: Boydell, 2019)

——, *The Celtic Inscriptions of Britain: Phonology and Chronology, c. 400–1200*, Publi-cations of the Philological Society, 37 (Oxford: Oxford University Press, 2003)

——, 'The Emergence of Old Welsh, Cornish and Breton Orthography, 600–800: The Evidence of Archaic Old Welsh', *BBCS*, 38 (1991), 20–86

Skipper, J. K., and P. L. Leslie, 'Towards a Theory of Nicknames: A Case for Socio-onomastics', *Names*, 38.4 (1990), 273–82

Smith, J. B., *Walter Map and the Matter of Britain* (Philadelphia: University of Penn-sylvania Press, 2017)

Smith, J. M. H., *Province and Empire. Brittany and the Carolingians* (Cambridge: Cambridge University Press, 1992)

——, *Relics and the Insular World, c. 600–c. 800* (Cambridge: ASNC, 2017)

Stokes, W., 'The Manumissions in the Bodmin Gospels', *Revue celtique*, 1 (1870–1872), 332–45

Tanguy, B., 'Les noms d'hommes et les nom de lieux', in *Cartulaire de l'abbaye Saint-Sauveur de Redon*, ed. by H. Guillotel, A. Chédeville, and B. Tanguy, 2 vols (Redon: Association des Amis des Archives historiques du diocèse de Rennes, Dol et Saint-Malo, 1998–2004), pp. 49–69

Thornton, D., 'Hey, Mac! The Name *Maccus*, Tenth to Fifteenth Centuries', *Nomina*, 20 (1997), 67–98 (including Appendix II by O. J. Padel, 'Talkarn Mackus', 95–98)

Wilson, S., *The Means of Naming. A Social and Cultural History of Personal Naming in Western Europe* (London: UCL Press, 1998)

Winterbottom, M., 'The Language of William of Malmesbury', in *Rhetoric and Renewal in the Latin West 1100–1540: Essays in Honour of John O. Ward*, ed. by C. J. Mews, C. J. Nederman, and R. M. Thomson (Turnhout: Brepols, 2003), pp. 129–47

INDEX

Abbaretz-Nozay: 48
Abbo, abbot of Fleury: 159, 165, 167–68
Abingdon, monastery: 149
Adalbero, archbishop of Metz: 154
Adalbero, archbishop of Reims: 154
Adalbero, archbishop of Toul: 153
Adelolf, count of Flanders: 149
Adomnán, *Vita S. Columbae*: 186
Aeneas: 240
Æthelred, ealdorman of Mercia: 127
Æthelstan, king of England: 3, 110, 120, 123–31, 134, 149–50
Æthelwold of Wessex: 125
Æthelwulf, king of Wessex: 121, 124, 134, 149
Agan, bishop of Dol: 148
Aidan, priest of Llancarfan: 224, 252–54
Alan (Alain) I, ruler of Brittany: 111–12, 114–19, 122, 124, 132, 150
Alan (Alain) II Barbetorte, duke of Brittany: 3, 110–38, 149–50
Alan III, duke of Brittany: 165, 170
Alan (Alain) IV Fergant, duke of Brittany: 223, 251, 312, 348
Alanus, ancestor of the Britons: 240
Alba Trimammis (Gwen Teirbron), St: 183, 191, 211–12, 215–16
Alcuin of York: 188, 190
    Vita S. Willibrordi: 187
Alet: 16, 144, 148, 181, 186, 189–90, 195, 217, 232
Alfred, king of Wessex: 119–27
Almod, abbot of Redon: 167
Almodus, abbot of Mont-Saint-Michel: 159–60, 170

Ammianus Marcellinus: 13
Angers: 83–84, 86
    Saint-Aubin, monastery: 154–55, 157, 163, 168
    Saint-Serge, monastery: 113n., 161
Anglesey: 274, 282
Anglo-Saxon Chronicle: 33, 120–21, 134
Anowareth, Breton ruler in the Cotentin: 144
Ansbald, abbot of Prüm: 335, 349–51
Ansbert, St: 157–58
Aourken (Orgain), wife of Alan I of Brittany: 119, 132, 133n.
Aquitaine: 14, 37, 110–11, 154
Archembald of Fleury: 154
Armes Prydein Fawr: 227, 240
Armorica (Armorican peninsula): 3, 9, 10–15, 19–23, 27, 35–36, 40, 47–49, 60, 75, 81, 87, 102, 122–25, 190, 193n., 208, 216, 222, 230–31, 303
    see also *Tractus Armoricanus*
Armoricans: 121, 137–38, 242
Arnulf I, count of Flanders: 150, 152–53
Arthuiu, donor: 322
Arthur: 317
Asser of St Davids: 120–23, 135, 227
    De rebus gestis Ælfredi (*Histoire du roi Alfred*): 120–23
Augustus Caesar: 247
Autbert, bishop of Avranches: 143, 171
    De translatione et miraculis sancti Autberti: 171
Avranches: 94–96, 142–45, 147, 171
Avranchin: 118, 137, 143, 146, 148, 150, 161

Bais: 73
Ballon, battle of: 113
Bantham, Devon: 42
Basaleg: 253–54
Bavo, St: 157
    see also St Bavo
Bayeux: 81, 94–95, 145, 148
Beauport, Notre-Dame de, monastery,
    cartulary: 339
Bede, *Historia Ecclesiastica*: 229
Bégard, monastery, cartulary: 324
Belgica, province: 88, 243
Belle-Île: 114, 250
belt-fittings: 10, 20, 36, 38, 45
Benedict of Nursia, St: 145
    Rule of St Benedict: 142, 144, 158
Benedict of Aniane, St: 144
Benedict, abbot of Quimperlé: 250
Benedict, bishop of Nantes: 348
Benedict, bishop of Cornouaille: 348
Berenger (Judicael Berenger), *dux* in
    Brittany: 137, 149
Bifrons, Kent (cemetery): 70
Bili, *Vita S. Machutis*: 181, 183n., 184–87,
    189–96, 209, 217–21, 227, 232
bioscientific evidence: 31, 34
Blavet, river: 115
Bodic *see* Budic
Bodmin: 213
    Bodmin Manumissions: 330–31, 333, 343n.
    Bodmin Moor: 280
Bonedd y Saint: 215
Bourges: 87–89
Bourgogne *see* Burgundy
Braga, councils of: 98–99
Branwallader (Broladre), St: 149
Bréal-sous-Vitré: 73
Breconshire: 269
Brendan, St: 189, 194–95, 218–21, 232
    Navigatio S. Brendani: 189n., 194, 219,
    221
    Vita S. Brendani: 219
Bressilien, Paule, Côtes-d'Armor: 65–69, 75
Brest: 11, 16–19
Breuddwyd Macsen: 224
Brieuc, St:
    Vita S. Brioci: 231
    see also Saint-Brieuc
Brigid, St:

Vita I S. Brigidae: 186
    see also Cogitosus
Britanni, *Brittones*, as ethnic community:
    82–102, 240
Britannia:
    as term for Continental Brittany: 89–91,
    93–97
    as term for Wales: 121
Britonia in Galicia: 98–100
Britto (Brutus), eponymous founder of
    Britain: 240
Brittones see Britanni
brooches: 10, 20, 45
Broweroch (*Brouerec*, *provincia Uuarrodua*):
    116, 118, 223
Budic (Bodic), Breton ruler: 90, 319
Burgundy (Bourgogne): 4, 37, 110–11, 154
burials *see* cemeteries

Cadbury, Somerset: 42
Caden: 116
Cadfan, St: 215, 232n.
Cadog, St: 222–25, 231, 244–59
    Cadog genealogies: 244–59
    charters appended to *Vita S. Cadoci*: 334
    see also Caradog of Llancarfan; Lifris of
    Llancarfan
Cadwaladr (Catgualadr), priest or prior of
    Saint-Cado: 223, 252
Caldey Island: 227
Camp de Péran, Plédran: 66
Caracalla, emperor: 15
Caradog of Llancarfan: 222, 245, 255–56,
    258–59
    Vita S. Cadoci: 222, 255–56
    Vita S. Gildae: 222, 255–56
    possibly author of Lives of Cyngar, Illtud,
    Gwynllyw, and Tatheus: 222
Carausius, emperor: 12
Cardiganshire: 269, 294n.
Carhaix: 19, 63, 69, 71, 84
Carloman, brother of Charlemagne: 121
Carmarthenshire: 230
Carnac, villa: 46
Castle Dore inscription: 228
Catalogus sanctorum Hiberniae: 227
Catgualadr, priest *see* Cadwaladr
Catihern, priest: 83–85, 304
Catovius, king of the Britons: 211–12, 214

INDEX

Caudan, Morbihan: 63
cauldrons, Westland type: 70
cemeteries: 292
  in Brittany: 15, 22–23, 45, 71–73
  in England: 32, 38, 40–45, 70, 72
  in Gaul: 36, 70, 72
  in Wales: 71–72, 287, 290
Chad Memoranda: 268, 272
Chalon, council of, 647 × 654: 96
Chantepie: 62
Charlemagne, emperor: 121, 125n., 126n.,
  128, 144, 154
Charles the Bald, king of the Franks:
  117–18, 121, 124, 134, 144–45, 195
Charles the Fat, king of the Franks: 121–22
Charles the Simple, king of the Franks: 110,
  117, 122, 126, 128–29, 131, 145, 149
Chartres: 155, 156, 170
  Saint-Père de Chartres, monastery: 155
Chasné-sur-Illet, Ille-et-Vilaine: 66, 73
Châteaugiron, Ille-et-Vilaine: 60–62
Châteaulin: 69
Châteauneuf-du-Faou (cemetery): 71
Chavagne, Ille-et-Vilaine: 62, 66
Chelles, monastery: 336, 338
Childebert I, king of the Franks: 95–97
Childebert III, king of the Franks: 143
Chilperic I, king of the Franks: 88–89, 92
Chlothar II (Clotaire), king of the Franks: 92
Chreirbia, sister of St Winwaloe: 183
citizenship, concept: 85–86
Clement, monk of Landévennec: 182
Clohal (Cluthgual, Clohars-Carnoët): 312,
  320, 345, 347–48
Clotaire *see* Chlothar II
Cluny, monastery: 154, 162, 168, 173
Coesmes, Ille-et-Vilaine: 66
Cogitosus, *Vita S. Brigidae*: 188
coinage: 12, 36, 38, 42, 48, 66, 135, 150–51,
  195, 285–86, 291n.
Collectio canonum Hibernensis: 184, 190, 196
Columba, St *see* Adomnán
Columbanus, St: 190
Compiègne: 117
Conan, count of Rennes: 164–65
Conanus Meriadocus, legendary founder of
  Brittany: 255
  see also Cynan son of Eudaf

Conomor (Cunomor), Breton ruler: 96,
  228–29, 232
Constantine, emperor: 36, 128, 244,
  246–47, 249–51, 255
Constantine II, king of Scotland: 127
Constantius Chlorus, emperor: 36, 246,
  250–51, 255
Conwoion, St, abbot of Redon: 144,
  163–64, 166, 168
Corbeil: 148
Corentin, St: 149, 191
corn-drying ovens (kilns): 66–69, 74–75
Cornouaille: 115, 123, 128n., 134–37, 192,
  195, 312–13, 348
Corseul: 19, 84
Courantgen, bishop of Vannes: 114
Cotentin: 118, 137, 144–45, 149
Coutances: 94–95, 97, 145
Cunomor *see* Conomor
Cynan (Kenan) son of Eudaf, king of the
  Britons: 244, 248–51, 254–55
  see also Conanus Meriadocus

Dagan, abbot of Llancarfan: 248
Dagobert, king of the Franks: 125
David, St: 226–27
  see also Rhygyfarch
deditices: 15
Derian mab Tanki, witness: 312
Deruel (Dervel), mother of St Malo: 219, 221
Devon: 42, 265, 267–68, 273–74, 291, 304n.
Dijon: 156
  Saint-Bénigne de Dijon, monastery: 154,
  162, 164, 169–70, 173
Diles, *vicecomes* of Cornouaille: 136
Disticha Catonis: 189
Dol: 84, 126, 129, 145, 148–50, 209–11,
  257, 341
  see also Samson
Domesday Book: 32, 215, 265–66, 273–74,
  282–85, 288, 291, 297, 300
Domnonia, region in Britain: 212, 214
Domnonia (Domnonée), region in Brittany:
  96, 192
Dorset: 36, 43, 149, 291, 304n.
Drogo, son of Alan II of Brittany: 133, 135
Dudo of Saint-Quentin, *De moribus et actis
  primorum Normanniae ducum*: 126,
  146–47, 150–53

Durotriges: 304n.
Dyfed: 120, 227

Eadgifu of Wessex: 128
Eadgyth of Wessex: 128
Eadhild of Wessex: 128
Eastwivelshire, Cornwall: 282
Edward the Elder, king of Wessex: 120,
    124–27, 129, 134, 149
Eligius (Éloi), St: 190
Empingham, Rutland (cemetery): 70
empire, Carolingian: 75, 154, 161
empire, Roman: 1, 10–16, 21, 27–28, 30,
    32, 35–36, 48, 82, 241
empire, Gallic: 36
Emyr Llydaw, Breton ancestor: 215–16
England:
    culture: 38–43, 75
    during Anglo-Saxon period: 33, 35,
        38–39, 57, 62, 71, 120, 128, 217,
        282–83, 296
    language, Old English, influence in
        Cornwall: 272–73
    pottery: 69, 72
    settlement: 33–34, 265
Enlli: 215
Épaone, council of, 517: 86
Ercé-près-Liffré: 62
Erispoe, ruler of Brittany: 114, 116, 118–19,
    127, 132, 145
Ermeland, St:
    Vita S. Ermelandi: 93
Étel, river: 223, 251
ethnogenesis: 34
Étienne *see* Stephen
Eudaf (Octavius, Outham), Breton ancestor:
    244, 248–51, 254–55
Eugenius of Toledo: 189
Eustochius, bishop of Angers: 84
Évreux: 96, 151, 169
    Saint-Taurin d'Évreux, monastery:
        151–52, 157, 169–70. 172
Exuperius, St, bishop of Bayeux: 148

Fécamp, monastery: 152, 154, 156–57,
    162–63, 169–70, 173
Felecan, Scandinavian leader: 137
Finglesham, Kent (cemetery): 70
fish-processing: 14–15

Flanders: 4, 152–54, 214–15
Fleury, monastery: 149, 153–56, 158–70,
    173, 228
Fleury confraternity list: 158–62, 168
Flodoard, *Annales*: 112, 125–26, 129, 137n.
foederati: 36, 37n., 40
Fracanus, father of St Winwaloe: 211–14,
    216
Franks (*Franci*): 28, 36–37, 88, 92–93, 97,
    113, 121, 126
Fredegar (Frédégaire), *Chronique*: 97
Frisia: 30–31, 71
Fromund, abbot of Saint-Taurin: 152, 169
Fulcran, abbot of Saint-Taurin: 152, 164, 169
Fulk the Good, count of Anjou: 150
funerary sites *see* cemeteries

Galerius, emperor: 246
Galicia: 12, 81, 97–101
Garonne, river: 14
Gaul (*Gallia*): 9–21, 28, 35–37, 47, 68–69,
    71–72, 243
Gausbert, abbot of Marmoutier: 164, 168
Gauzilo, abbot of Saint-Evre, Toul: 153
Gauzlin, abbot of Fleury: 165, 167
Geoffrey I, duke of Brittany: 165
Geoffrey of Monmouth: 254–59
    History of the Kings of Britain: 244–45,
        254–59
Gerard de Brogne: 153
Gerard, abbot of Crépy and Saint-Wandrille:
    155–56, 170, 172
Gerbert of Aurillac (Pope Sylvester II): 154,
    170
Ghent:
    St Bavo, monastery: 153
    St Peter's, monastery: 152–53, 155–56
Gildas: 187, 220, 222, 227, 242–44, 255–56
    De excidio Britanniae (*The Ruin of
        Britain*): 40–42, 48, 82, 85, 187–90,
        195, 211, 241–44
    see also Caradog of Llancarfan; Saint-
        Gildas-de-Rhuys
Glamorgan: 218, 222, 230, 244–45, 247,
    254, 269n.
Glanfeuil, monastery: 145, 161
Glastonbury, monastery: 256
Glywys, eponymous king of Glywysing:
    224–25

INDEX

Goas-an-Eyec, Pont-de-Buis-lès-Quimerch, Finistère (burials): 45
Gontran *see* Guntram
Gorze, monastery: 153–54, 161–62
Gouesnac'h, Finistère (cemetery): 71
Goulven, St:
Vita S. Golveni: 231
Gradlon, legendary Breton ruler: 191
Gratian, emperor: 15n., 241, 246
Great Chesterford, Essex (cemetery): 40, 70
Grégoire de Rostrenen: 302
Gregory (Grégoire) I ('the Great'), St, pope: 114–15, 171
Gregory (Grégoire) of Tours: 48
Libri Historiarum X: 89–95, 97, 228, 319n.
Groix, Île de: 114, 250
Grubenhäuser see sunken-featured buildings
Gruffudd ap Cynan, king of Gwynedd: 313
Guénolé, St *see* Winwaloe
Guérande: 116
Guegon, lord of Hennebont: 315
Guerech, son of Alan II of Brittany: 133–34
Guernsey: 323
Guethenoc, St *see* Wethinoc
Guipavas, Finistère: 65, 69
cemetery: 73
Gunhard, bishop of Nantes: 113
Guntram (Gontran), king of the Franks: 90, 92
Gurci, priest of Llancarfan: 253–54
Gurdisten *see* Wrdisten
Gurheden, scribe of Cartulary of Quimperlé: 223, 250, 252, 312–13, 315, 339–42, 345
Gurthiern, St: 230n., 249–52, 254–56
Vita S. Gurthierni: 209, 223–25, 230n., 244, 249–52, 254–56
Gwen Teirbron *see Alba Trimammis*
Gwent: 181, 219, 221
Gwynedd: 282
Gwynllyw, St: 222, 224

Hadrian's Wall: 82
Hakon, king of Norway: 130–31
handbells: 69, 231
Harleian genealogies: 242, 246, 251, 254, 256, 259
Helena, mother of Emperor Constantine: 246, 250–51, 255

Henoc, informant of author of *Vita I S. Samsonis*: 210
Herbert of Vermandois: 129
Hereford: 247
Herewald, bishop of Glamorgan: 244–45, 253–54
Heriward, monk at Mont-Saint-Michel, abbot of Gembloux: 161
Heriward, scribe: 158, 161–62, 171n.
Herstal, capitulary of: 102
Herules: 12
Hildeberts I and II, abbots of Mont-Saint-Michel: 159, 161
Hildebert, abbot of Saint-Ouen: 151, 159
Hilduin of Saint-Denis: 187
hill-forts: 48
Hincmar, archbishop of Reims: 121
Hinguethen, abbot of Saint-Jacut-de-la-Mer: 165
Historia Brittonum: 15, 208, 224, 231n., 240–51, 254–56, 259, 276, 317
Hoel, count of Nantes, son of Alan II of Brittany: 133–35
Hoel, grandson of Alan II of Brittany: 133
Houuel, count of Cornouaille: 135
Hugh, archbishop of Rouen: 146, 151–53
Hugh (Hugues), count of the Franks: 126, 128, 148–49
Hywel Dda, king of Deheubarth: 127, 134–36

Île Cado (*Inis Catbodu*): 223, 251–52
Île Guennoc: 278
Illtud, St: 211, 220, 222, 226–31, 232n.
Vita S. Iltuti: 222, 227–29, 231
see also Caradog of Llancarfan
Ima, miraculous island: 219
Indre, monastery: 93
Inis Catbodu see Île Cado
inscriptions: 5, 43, 47, 228, 314, 318, 321, 323, 335n., 330
Ioseph, teacher at Llancarfan: 253–54
Ireland: 31, 192, 194, 208, 219, 222, 227, 231
Isidore of Seville, *Etymologiae*: 86
Isle of Man: 344
Israel the Grammarian: 128
Iuthael son of Aidan, genealogist: 224, 250, 252–54

Jacobus, St: 211–12
Jacutus, St: 212–13, 215
   Vita SS. Guethenoci et Iacuti: 212, 215
   see also Saint-Jacut-de-la-Mer
Japheth: 240
Jerome, St, *Vita S. Hilarionis*: 186
Jocelyn of Furness, *Vita S. Kentigerni*: 224
John, abbot of Landévennec: 149
John XIII, pope: 147, 154–55
John, *praepositus* of Mont-Saint-Michel:
   146–47
Jordanes, *De origine actibusque Getarum*:
   87–88
Jublains: 84
Judhuarn, priest: 223
Judicaël, king of the Bretons, *fl.* 635: 97,
   125–26
Judicael, Breton ruler, d. 892: 115
Judicael, grandson of Duke Alan II of
   Brittany: 133
Judicael Berenger *see* Berenger
Judith, queen of Wessex: 121, 134–35
Judith, wife of Duke Alan II of Brittany:
   133–35
Judoc, St: 125–26, 149, 217
Judual, Breton ruler: 96
Jumièges, monastery: 151–52, 156–57,
   162–63, 169, 184

Kenan *see* Cynan son of Eudaf
Kentigern, St: 224
   Vita S. Kentigerni: 224
   see also Jocelyn
Kergoutois: 63, 69
Kerran, villa: 16
Kerrier, Cornwall: 282
Kymry: 240

La Cochardière, Rennes (cemetery): 22
laeti: 10–11, 15, 36, 40
La Feuillée: 65
Lagny, monastery: 155, 170
La Mézière, Ille-et-Vilaine (cemetery): 22
Landévennec, monastery: 73, 113–14, 125,
   129n., 135–36, 144, 148–49, 181, 184,
   187–89, 193, 195, 226, 228, 323
   Cartulary of Landévennec: 135–36, 212,
     271, 275, 278–79, 285, 290, 296,
     299, 321, 323, 326, 330, 336n.

Land's End, Cornwall: 274–75
Langobards *see* Lombards
Langoëlan, Finistère: 65, 69
Lanlivery, Cornwall: 299
La Roche-Bernard: 322
La Turballe: 116
Lauto, bishop of Coutances: 95
Léhon, monastery: 148, 210–11
Leo IV, pope: 121
Léon: 344
Leucadius, bishop of Bayeux: 95
Le Mans: 84, 94–96, 144–45
   Saint-Pierre-de-la-Couture, monastery:
     163, 168
Leontianus, bishop of Coutances: 95
Leovigild, king of the Visigoths: 98–99
Letavia see Llydaw
Le Yaudet: 16–19, 48
Liber Landavensis see Llandaf
Licinius, archbishop of Tours: 84
Lincoln: 40
Lifris of Llancarfan: 222–25, 244–45,
   252–54
   Vita S. Cadoci: 209, 219, 222–25, 232,
     244–59
Llancarfan: 218–21, 224–25, 231–32,
   244–49, 251–59
Llandaf: 222, 245, 247–48, 253–54, 257,
   259
   Book of Llandaf (*Liber Landavensis*):
     221, 222, 228, 247, 253, 256, 268,
     271, 274, 287, 290, 302, 330–34, 337
Llanddewi Brefi: 227
Llandochau Fach: 253–54
Llanilltud Fawr: 209, 220n., 227, 230–31,
   253–54
LLydaw, Welsh term for Brittany: 215–16,
   222, 231, 246; latinized as *Letavia*:
   215–16, 231
Llŷn peninsula: 274–75
Locmariaquer: 116
Locronan, ringwork: 69
Loelinus, uncle of Helena: 255
Loire, river: 14, 62, 88, 93, 113, 118, 129,
   137n.
Lombards (Langobards): 28, 115
London: 45, 120
Lostmarc'h, Crozon, Finistère (cemetery): 13
Lostwithiel, Cornwall: 299

INDEX

Lothar, king of the Franks: 151, 155
Lotharingia: 4, 154, 161
Louis d'Outremer, king of the Franks: 126, 130, 149, 151, 155
Louis the Pious, emperor: 83, 113n., 119, 125n., 144, 187, 193
Louis the Stammerer, king of the Franks: 118, 122, 124n.
Lovocat, priest: 83–85, 304
Lugdunensis III (Lyonnaise III), Roman province: 84, 86, 95
Lugo, council of, 569: 98
Lusitania, province: 99

machtierns: 111, 136
Maclou, Breton ruler: 89–90
Maglorius, St: 210–11
    Translatio Sancti Maglorii: 148
    Vita S. Maglorii: 209, 210–11
    see also Saint-Magloire
Magnus Maximus, emperor: 15, 241–42, 249
Mailoc, bishop of Britonia: 99, 101n.
Mainard I, abbot of Mont-Saint-Michel: 152, 155–56, 159, 168–73
Mainard II, abbot of Mont-Saint-Michel and Redon: 159, 163, 165, 170–72
Maiol, abbot of Cluny: 154, 167–68
Malo (Machutes, Machutus, Machu, Machlou, Machlovus, Macloe), St: 148–49, 181–82, 185–86, 189, 192–94, 217–21, 232
    Anonymous *Vitae*: 189
    Vita anonyma brevior: 217
    Old English *Life*: 185, 217
    see also Bili
Mansuetus, bishop of the Britons: 88
manuscripts: 5, 143, 145
    Angers Bibliothèque municipale 837 (753): 161
    Avranches Bibliothèque patrimoniale Avranches 42: 157n.
    Avranches Bibliothèque patrimoniale Avranches 210: 148n.
    Avranches Bibliothèque patrimoniale Avranches 211: 171n.
    Avranches Bibliothèque patrimoniale Avranches 213: 147, 148n., 165n., 172n.

    Avranches Bibliothèque patrimoniale Avranches 214: 142, 147n., 148n., 158–59, 162n., 165–70, 168n., 170n., 172
    Dijon Bibliothèque municipale Dijon 634: 170n.
    Gotha Forschungsbibliothek Mm.I.81: 256
    London British Library Additional 14,912: 221n.
    London British Library Additional Charter 32,963: 288n.
    London British Library Cotton Vespasian A.xiv: 221, 245–46, 248, 258, 334
    London British Library Egerton 2802: 250n., 312n.
    London British Library Harley 3859: 240–41n.
    London (Kew) National Archives Just1/115 m. 18, Assize Roll of 1299: 292n.
    London (Kew) National Archives C142/173 (16), Inquisition post mortem of Edward Trevanion: 288n.
    Madrid El Escorial D.1.2: 100
    New York Morgan Library and Museum (formerly Pierpoint Morgan Library) 641: 142, 156–57
    Oxford Jesus College 20: 224, 249, 251, 255, 259
    Paris Bibliothèque nationale de France latin 3846: 101n.
    Paris Bibliothèque nationale de France latin 4280: 100n.
    Paris Bibliothèque nationale de France latin 5610A: 184n.
    Paris Bibliothèque nationale de France latin 9889: 125n.
    Paris Bibliothèque nationale de France latin 13029: 190n.
    Paris Bibliothèque nationale de France nouv. acq. lat. 1899: 170n.
    Paris Bibliothèque nationale de France nouv. acq. lat. 2389: 170n.
    Quimper Bibliothèque municipale 16: 184n., 323; *see also* Landévennec: Cartulary of Landévennec
    Redruth Cornwall Record Office AR2/140, manorial account roll: 288n.

Rouen Bibliothèque municipale 1266 (U50): 170n.
Trier Stadtbibliothek 1709: 335, 349
Vatican City Bibliotheca apostolica vaticana Reg. lat. 479: 180n.
Vatican City Bibliotheca apostolica vaticana Vat. lat. 9668: 157n.
Marius of Avenches: 93
Mark, legendary British king: 228–29, 232
Marmoutier, monastery: 149, 154, 159, 164, 168
Martianus, abbot of *Scesciacus*: 94
Martyrology of Óengus: 227
Mary, St: 149, 251, 287, 293
Mary Magdalene, St: 157
Matmonoc, abbot of Landévennec: 193
Matuedoi, count of Poher: 110–11, 123–24, 134, 149, 150, 350
Maur, St: 145
Mawgan Porth, Cornwall: 72
Maxen Wledic: 249
Maximianus, alleged founder of Brittany: 15n., 241–42, 244, 246–47, 249–51, 255
Melanius (Melaine), St, bishop of Rennes: 84, 95
Mercia: 123, 124
Mérida, council of, 666: 99
Michael, St: 142, 143, 154, 161, 171, 287, 293
migration: 1–3, 9–23, 27–49, 75, 82–84, 188, 217, 239–44, 264, 267, 278, 286, 296–97, 303–05, 345
Milton Abbey, Dorset: 149
Monmouth: 244, 247–8, 256–59
  Monmouth Priory: 247–48, 257–59
Monte Gargano, Apulia: 143, 154, 171
Montours, Ille-et-Vilaine: 60–62
Montreuil-sur-Mer: 129n., 148
Mont-Saint-Michel (Mont Tumba), monastery: 141–73
  Annals of Mont-Saint-Michel: 156
  Cartulary of Mont-Saint-Michel: 142, 150, 161, 164
  Chapter Book: 142, 158, 162
  Confraternity lists: 162
  Historia: 142
  Introductio Monachorum: 142, 146–47, 150, 159, 171

Martyrology/Necrology: 142, 158, 165–70, 172
Necrology: 142, 158, 162, 166, 169, 170, 171
Revelatio: 142–44, 147, 171
Sacramentary: 142, 156–57
Mont Tumba *see* Mont-Saint-Michel
Morbihan: 323
Mordelles: 62
Morvan, ruler of Brittany: 119
Mucking, Essex: 38–39
name-elements, personal: 328n., 330–33, 335–36, 338
  mab: 340–44
  gilla: 343
name-forms, individual:
  Ana(u)oc: 331
  Gonothigernus: 336
  Uuorgonezlo: 336–38
names, personal: 131–35, 266–67, 311–52
  biblical: 319, 326, 329, 332–33
  classical: 319, 326
  dithematic (compound): 331–32
  Frankish (Germanic): 314, 318–19, 321–24, 327, 329, 334, 336
  in charter of Salomon for Prüm abbey: 335–6, 347–51
  in inquest on the canonization of St Yves of Kermartin: 327–29, 344, 346
  in inscriptions (epigraphic evidence): 321, 323, 335n., 330
  as location markers: 322, 327–29, 342, 345–46
  Old English: 266–67, 274, 313, 321 n., 333, 334
  patronymy: 318–21, 325, 327, 329, 335, 340–46
  in relic-labels: 336–39
  soubriquets (surnames): 321–22, 325–26, 329, 342–46
Nantais: 92, 116, 118, 135, 137
Nantes: 48, 84, 87, 91–94, 96, 113, 116, 119, 129, 135, 138, 144–45, 312, 348
Chronique de Nantes: 109–12, 126, 135
Nennius: 15, 276
  see also Historia Brittonum
Neustria (Neustrie): 96, 129, 144, 154, 159, 161
Nicholas I, pope: 84

INDEX

Nominoe, Breton ruler: 111, 113–14, 119, 123, 138, 144, 195, 275
Normandy: 62, 75, 145, 147, 149–57, 165, 168, 172
North Sea: 11–12, 16, 30–31, 42
Notitia Dignitatum: 36, 83n.
Notitia Galliarum (Notice des Gaules): 86–87
Noyal-sur-Vilaine: 62, 66

oats: 70–71, 74
Octavius *see* Eudaf
Odo, abbot of Cluny: 146–47, 153–54, 168
  Collationes: 146–47
Odo, abbot of Glanfeuil: 145
opus geminum (opus geminatum): 187, 211
Orléans: 88, 153
  church of St Symphorian, Orléans: 148
  council of Orléans, 511: 88
  council of Orléans, 549: 86
Osismi: 10, 14, 71
Otto, emperor: 128
Ouen, St: 152
  see also Saint-Ouen
Oust, river: 90, 93, 95
Outham *see* Eudaf
Oviedo: 98
Owain Gwynedd: 293

Padarn, St:
  Vita S. Paterni: 215–16
Padstow (*Languihenoc, Lanwethenek*): 212–13, 224–25, 288n.
Paris: 88, 148–49, 336
  chapel of St Bartholomew: 148
  council of Paris, 561: 95
  Saint-Denis, Paris, monastery: 151, 157, 161, 187
Parochiale Suevum: 98–100
Pascweten, count of Vannes: 114–19, 132, 136
Paternus (Pair), St: 94–96, 126, 148–49
  see also Venantius Fortunatus: *Vita S. Paterni*
Patrick, St: 192, 194
Paul Aurelian, St: 226–31
  see also Wrmonoc
Paul of Penychen: 230
Paulinus, St: 230

Pays-de-Loire: 62
Pelagius, bishop of Oviedo: 98
Pembrokeshire: 269, 280, 294n.
Penwith, Cornwall: 282
Pépin *see* Pippin
personal names *see* names
Petroc, St: 213, 217, 224–25, 232, 256, 333
  Petroc genealogy: 225, 256
  Vita I S. Petroci: 212–13
  Vita II S. Petroci: 224–25
Phinimontius, abbot of Mont-Saint-Michel: 145–46
Pierre le Baud: 110
Pillar of Eliseg: 242
Pippin (Pépin) of Aquitaine: 111
Piro, St: 226, 230
place-names: 82–83, 95, 263–305, 313–14
place-name elements:
  aula: 275, 285
  baile: 272
  *bod- (bos-): 264, 273–76, 278–79, 303–04
  *both: 279n.
  *byu: 281
  *cadeir: 279
  *cair- (caer, car, kêr): 264–65, 266, 273, 276–80, 304–05, 324
  *carn: 279
  *carreg: 279
  chy (tŷ, ti): 267, 278–79
  -cott: 274
  cres (kreiz): 267
  *crûg: 279
  *egluis (eglos, eglwys, iliz): 264, 266, 288, 293, 299–303
  *gre: 281
  guic- (gui-): 95, 294n., 295
  *havos (hafod): 274
  *hen-les: 282
  *lann-: 264, 286–94, 303–04
  *lis- (les-, lis-, llys): 264, 280–86, 297, 303–05
  lios-: 286
  loch: 299
  *log- (loc-): 264, 286, 298–99, 303
  logie: 299n.
  luorz: 324
  maes: 324
  merthyr (merther): 302

nant-, nans-: 288–89
perveth (perfedd, permed): 267
plou- see *pluiv-
*pluiv- (plou-): 82, 95, 264–65, 286, 290, 293, 294–99, 302–03
podum: 287, 290
prat: 324
ran-: 322
*trev- (tref, tre, treb): 264–73, 278–79, 290, 303–05
trève: 271
tribus: 271
villa: 269, 271
place-name forms:
Aberffraw, Anglesey: 282
Arrallas, Cornwall: 283
Blaenplwyf: 294
Botnumel: 275
Budock, Cornwall: 300
Carsize, Cornwall: 276
Eastwivelshire, Cornwall: 282
Eccluis Santbreit (Caldicot), Monmouthshire: 302
Ecglosberrie see St Buryan
Egloslagek see Ladock
Eglarooze, St Germans, Cornwall: 300
Eglos Budock, Cornwall: 300
Egloscrow, Cornwall: 300
Eglosderry, Wendron, Cornwall: 300
Egloshayle, Maker, Cornwall: 300
Egloshayle, Phillack, Cornwall: 300
Egloskerry, Cornwall: 300
Eglosmerther, Cornwall: 300
Eglosnyulin see Newlyn East
Eglosrose, Cornwall: 300
Hecglosenuder see St Enoder
Hecglostudic see St Tudy
Helland, Cornwall: 292–93
Hellesvean and Hellesvear, near St Ives, Cornwall: 282
Helston, Cornwall: 282–83
Helstone, Cornwall: 282–83
Ladock (Egloslagek), Cornwall: 301
Lamorran, Cornwall: 291
Landcross, Devon: 291n.
Landéda, Finistère: 278
Landkey, Devon: 291n.
Landochou, Cornwall: 291
Lanescot, Cornwall: 283, 285

Lann Ela (Lynally, Co. Offaly): 291n.
Lanlawren, Cornwall: 291
Lann Leri (Dunleer, Co. Louth): 291n.
Lanprobi (Sherborne, Dorset): 291n.
Lanteglos, Cornwall: 288, 291
Lantokai (Leigh near Glastonbury, Somerset): 291n.
Lanuyal, Lanvyhayll see St Michael Caerhays
Launceston, Cornwall: 288, 291
Lavihale see St Michael Caerhays
Leece, Hampshire: 304n.
Leskernick, Cornwall: 280
Lesneage, Cornwall: 283, 285
Lesnewth, Cornwall: 282–83
Lestowder, Cornwall: 280
Lezerea, Cornwall: 280
Linkinhorne, Cornwall: 291
Lisbue, Cornwall: 280
Liscolroet: 285
Liskeard, Cornwall: 282–83
Lizard, Cornwall: 283, 285
Llanbedr: 287, 293
Llanfair: 287, 293
Llanfihangel: 287, 293
Llanfihangel-y-traethau:, Merionethshire: 293
Llys-y-defaid, Pembrokeshire: 281n.
Llys-y-dryw, Pembrokeshire: 280
Llys-y-fran, Pembrokeshire: 280
Lochkindeloch, Kirkcudbrightshire: 299
Lochmaben, Dumfriesshire: 299
Lochwinnoch, Ayrshire: 299
Loquhariot, Midlothian: 299
Lossulien, Finistère: 299
Luxulyan, Cornwall: 299
Mabe, Cornwall: 292–93
Merther, Cornwall: 300
Mullion, Cornwall: 292
Mylor, Cornwall: 292
Newlyn East (Eglosnyulin), Cornwall: 301
Ochiltree: 272
Pelynt (Plunent), Cornwall: 297, 299
Phillack, Cornwall: 300
Philleigh, Cornwall: 300
Plwyv y Groes (Whitchurch, Pembrokeshire): 294n.
Ranbudhoiarn: 322
Ranriculf: 322

St Buryan (*Ecglosberrie*), Cornwall: 274, 300
St Enoder (*Hecglosenuder*), Cornwall: 300
St Erme (*Egloserm*), Cornwall: 301
St Germans, Cornwall (*Lannaled*): 291, 300
St Issey, Cornwall: 300
St Michael Caerhays (*Lanuyal, Lanvyhayll, Lavihale*), Cornwall: 288
St Tudy (*Hecglostudic*), Cornwall: 300
Treb arail: 269
Treb etuual: 269
Treb guidauc: 268
Trebursye, Cornwall: 269
Tredundle, Cornwall: 267
Tref ir isceiauc: 269
Tref ret: 269
Treglemais. Pembrokeshire: 269
Trephilip, Breconshire: 269
Tresemple, Cornwall: 267, 269
Ucheldref: 272
Westwivelshire, Cornwall: 282
Plélan-le-Grand: 117
Plésidy, Côtes-d'Armor: 48
Pleucadeuc, Morbihan: 224
Ploërdur-Mellionnec: 65
Ploudaniel: 69
Plouedern: 65, 69
  cemetery: 72
Plouescat, Finistère (cemetery): 71
Ploufragan, Côtes-d'Armor: 213
Poher: 110, 118–19, 122–23, 128n., 136n., 137n., 149, 150
Poitiers: 93
  Saint-Cyprien de Poitiers, monastery: 151
Pont-de-Buis, Finistère: 22
population: 13, 15, 28–32
pottery: 13–15, 36, 38, 42–43, 66, 69, 71–72
  amphorae: 14, 42
  Anglo-Saxon: 69, 72
  Argonne ware: 13
  black burnished (Dorset) ware: 13, 36, 72
  Cranbeck ware: 72
  marbled wares: 14
  Mediterranean: 42, 47, 292
  New Forest ware: 13, 36
  Oxfordshire pottery: 36
Poundbury, Dorset: 43

Powder, Cornwall: 283
preventive archaeology: 58
Prosper, *Epitoma chronicon*: 242
Prostlon, daughter of Salomon of Brittany: 117, 119, 132
Prüm, monastery: 317n., 335–36, 338, 349–51
  see also Regino
Pydar, Cornwall: 283

Quehelen, Paule, Côtes-d'Armor: 69
Quentovic: 242
Quimper: 321, 323
  Cartulary of Quimper: 321n., 323–24, 326
Quimperlé: 222–23, 225, 232, 312, 315, 321, 343, 345
  Cartulary of Quimperlé: 223, 225, 249–56, 312, 315, 321, 324, 326, 330, 337n., 339–45, 347–48
  Sainte-Croix de Quimperlé, monastery: 223, 250–56, 312
Quoit Brooch Style: 9, 22, 27, 43–47, 72

Radbod, prior of Dol: 126, 129–30, 149
Ralph (Raoul), king of the Franks: 126, 137
Ratwili, bishop of Alet: 217
Reccared, king of the Visigoths: 99
Recceswinth, king of the Visigoths: 99
Redon, monastery: 83, 114–16, 118, 144–49, 157, 159, 161–68, 170, 172, 250
  Annals of Redon: 147–48
  Cartulary of Redon: 116, 117, 118n., 133n., 134n., 136, 146, 165, 167, 193n., 270–72, 275, 278–79, 285, 290, 296, 299, 317, 318–22, 324–26, 329, 330–36, 338–41
Regino of Prüm, *Chronicon*: 115
Reims: 153–56, 170
  Saint-Rémy, monastery: 154
  Saint-Thierry, monastery: 154, 156
Remismond, king of the Sueves: 98
Rennais: 118
Rennes: 46, 62, 83–84, 86, 91–97, 102, 144–45, 148–49, 163–65
  Saint-Melaine de Rennes, monastery: 161, 165, 319
  Cartulary of Saint-Melaine: 319

Rezé: 87

Rhine, river: 14, 19, 37

Rhygyfarch, *Vita S. David*: 221, 222, 227, 232

Richard I, duke of Normandy: 146–47, 150–52, 156, 162

Richard II, duke of Normandy: 152, 161–62, 165

Riothamus (Riotime), 87–88

Riwal, Breton ruler: 214

Robert, archbishop of Rouen: 152, 159, 171

Robert I (Robert of Neustria), king of the Franks: 129, 149

Robert I, duke of Normandy: 171

Robert de Torigny, abbot of Mont-Saint-Michel: 143, 156

    De immutatione ordinis monachorum: 156

Robert fitz Hamo: 245

Robert the Strong, count of Anjou: 161

Roger, earl of Hereford: 147

Rollo: 129, 146

Romacharius, bishop of Coutances: 94

Roman Empire *see* empire

Romania, region in Merovingian Gaul: 96

Rome: 3–4, 19, 115, 119, 121, 145, 244, 248–49, 251

Rorgonid family: 144

Rouen: 87, 145

    see also Saint-Ouen

round, settlement type: 273, 276–79

Saint-Brieuc, Côtes-d'Armor: 149

Saint-Cado, Morbihan: 223, 225, 251–52

Saint-Dizier (cemetery): 70

Saint-Éxupère de Gahard, monastery: 148

Saint-Florent de Saumur, monastery: 257

    Annales Sancti Florentii Salmurensis: 113

Saint-Germain-des-Prés, Paris, monastery: 148, 163, 168–70

Saint-Gildas-de-Rhuys, monastery: 165, 313

Saint-Jacut-de-la-Mer, monastery: 165, 212

Saint-Jouin des Marnes: 148

Saint-Magloire, Paris, monastery: 148–49

Saint-Maixent, Poitou: 148

Saint-Marcel, Morbihan (cemetery): 22–23, 45–47, 72

Saint-Martin-des-Champs, Finistère: 63, 69

Saint-Méen de Gaël, monastery: 125–26, 148, 165

Saint-Ouen de Rouen, monastery: 150–52, 155–57, 159, 163, 169

St Peter's, Gloucester, monastery: 245, 258

Saint-Pol-de-Léon: 226

Saint-Symphorien, Paule, Finistère: 66, 69–70, 73

Saint-Tugdual: 65, 73

Saint-Urnel, Plomeur, Finistère (cemetery): 13

Saint-Wandrille, monastery: 152, 155–57, 163, 170–72

    Annals of Saint-Wandrille: 156

St Winnow, Cornwall: 215

Salomon, ruler of Brittany: 114–19, 122–23, 132, 145–46, 335, 349–51

Salvator, bishop of Alet: 148

Samson, St: 82, 96, 97, 126, 148–49, 209–11, 217, 219, 226–29, 232

    *Vita primigenia S. Samsonis: 209, 231

    Vita I S. Samsonis: 82, 96, 97, 180, 209–10, 219–20, 226–27, 230, 232

    Vita II S. Samsonis: 180, 210–11

Santa Maria de Bretoña, Mondoñedo, monastery: 98

Saxons: 9–12, 19–20, 37, 243

Scotland: 31, 35n., 70n., 222, 264, 267, 272, 275n., 276, 278–79, 286, 290, 299, 319n., 342, 343n., 345n.

Scubilio, St: 126, 148–49

Seine, river: 14, 97, 129

Senator (Senier), St: 126, 148–49

settlement archaeology:

    in Brittany: 59–69

    in Anglo-Saxon England: 62

Shakenoak, Oxfordshire: 38

Sidonius Apollinaris: 12, 21, 48, 88

Sidwell, St: 229

Sigebert of Gembloux: 161

Sihtric Cáech, king of Northumbria: 125, 127n.

Sitofolla, St: 229

Smaragdus of Saint-Mihiel: 188, 190

Somerset: 42, 291

Sparatus, priest: 84–85

Spong Hill, Norfolk (cemetery): 40

Stephen (Étienne) II, pope: 121

Stratton, Cornwall 282

subsidy-rolls: 330

    Merioneth lay subsidy-roll, 1293–1293: 346

INDEX

Sueves: 98
Sulpicius Severus, *Vita S. Martini*: 242
sunken-featured buildings (*Grubenhäuser*):
38, 63, 65, 68–69, 74

Tandderwen (cemetery): 72
Tanki Mab, witness: 312, 342
Tanki mab Guegon, witness: 312, 315
Teudar, legendary British king: 281
Thames, river: 14
Theobald, abbot of Redon: 165
Theobald the Trickster, count of Blois-
Chartres: 133, 150–51
Theodemir, king of the Sueves: 98
Theodesindus, bishop of Britonia: 98
Theodoric II, king of the Visigoths: 98
Theuderic son of Bodic, Breton ruler: 319
Theuderic son of Clovis: 319
Tintagel: 42
Toledo, councils of: 99, 101
Torcé: 62
Tournai: 88
Tours: 83–84, 86–87, 96, 118, 122, 154,
169; *see also* Gregory of Tours
Saint-Julien, monastery: 169
Saint-Martin: 154
council of Tours, 461: 88
council of Tours, 567: 87
Tractus Armoricanus: 16, 87
Translatio Sancti Maglorii see Maglorius
Tredarzec, Côtes-d'Armor: 70
Trégor: 324
Trigg, Cornwall: 282
Tristan: 228
Tugdual, St: 191
Turiau, St: 228

Urban, bishop of Llandaf: 245, 255
Usuard, martyrology: 148, 158
Uurdisten *see* Wrdisten
Uurmaelon, count of Poher: 122
Uurvand, Breton ruler: 115, 117–18

Vaast (Vedast), St: 157
Vannes: 16, 19, 20, 62, 81, 84, 90, 92–93,
95, 97, 102, 114, 116, 118, 136, 144
council of Vannes, 461 × 491: 84
Vannetais: 92, 115, 116, 118, 134, 136

Venantius Fortunatus, *Vita S. Paterni*:
93–96, 185
Veneti: 14
Verdun: 14
Vergil: 191
Aeneid: 192
Vidimaclus, Breton ruler: 92
Vigor, bishop of Bayeux: 95
Vikings (Norse, Scandinavians): 110–38,
147–50, 209–10, 212, 217, 228, 298
Vilaine, river: 90, 93, 95, 97, 321, 322
villas: 16, 19–20, 38–39, 46, 47n., 95
Visigoths (Wisigoths): 28, 98–99, 102
Visseiche: 73
Vita Frodoberti abbatis: 146

Wandrille (Wandregisilus), St: 152, 157
see also Saint-Wandrille
Waroch (Weroc), Breton ruler: 89–90, 92,
133
Wessex, kingdom: 4, 110, 120–21, 123–30,
135, 137–38
Westwivelshire, Cornwall: 282
Wethinoc (Guethenocus, Geuedenoc,
Weithnocus, Wethenec), St: 211–13,
232
Vita SS. Guethenoci et Iacuti: 212, 215
Wihenoc of La Boussac: 247, 256–57
William I, king of England: 247
William of Dol, abbot of Saint-Florent-de-
Saumur: 257
William Longsword (Guillaume Longue-
Épée), duke of Normandy: 129, 137,
145, 149–51
William of Malmesbury: 313
De antiquitate Glastonie ecclesiae: 256
William of Volpiano, abbot of Fécamp: 154,
156, 162–65, 169
Winbrit, wife of Salomon, king of Brittany:
335, 350
Winnoc, St: 214–15
Vita I S. Winnoci: 214
Vita II S. Winnoci: 209, 214
Winwaloe (Guénolé), St: 82, 148–49,
181–82, 185, 191–94, 211–16, 231, 323
see also Wrdisten
Winchester: 125, 157, 217
Wisigoths *see* Visigoths

Wrdisten (Gurdisten, Uurdisten), abbot of
     Landévennec: 114–15, 212, 214, 216,
     242–43
   Vita S. Winwaloei: 114–15, 181–89,
       191–94, 209, 211–17, 226, 242–43
   Homily: 186
Wrmonoc, *Vita S. Pauli Aureliani*: 226–31,
     232
Wulfald, abbot of Fleury, bishop of
     Chartres: 155
Wulfran, St: 156–58
   Translatio Sancti Wulfranni: 156

York: 127, 128, 150
Yves, St, inquest for canonization: 315,
     327–29, 346

Zosimus, *New History*: 36

MEDIEVAL TEXTS AND CULTURES OF NORTHERN EUROPE

All volumes in this series are evaluated by an Editorial Board, strictly on academic grounds, based on reports prepared by referees who have been commissioned by virtue of their specialism in the appropriate field. The Board ensures that the screening is done independently and without conflicts of interest. The definitive texts supplied by authors are also subject to review by the Board before being approved for publication. Further, the volumes are copyedited to conform to the publisher's stylebook and to the best international academic standards in the field.

Titles in Series

Drama and Community: People and Plays in Medieval Europe, ed. by Alan Hindley (1999)

Showing Status: Representations of Social Positions in the Late Middle Ages, ed. by Wim Blockmans and Antheun Janse (1999)

Sandra Billington, *Midsummer: A Cultural Sub-Text from Chrétien de Troyes to Jean Michel* (2000)

History and Images: Towards a New Iconology, ed. by Axel Bolvig and Phillip Lindley (2003)

Scandinavia and Europe 800–1350: Contact, Conflict, and Coexistence, ed. by Jonathan Adams and Katherine Holman (2004)

Anu Mänd, *Urban Carnival: Festive Culture in the Hanseatic Cities of the Eastern Baltic, 1350–1550* (2005)

Bjørn Bandlien, *Strategies of Passion: Love and Marriage in Old Norse Society* (2005)

Imagining the Book, ed. by Stephen Kelly and John J. Thompson (2005)

Forms of Servitude in Northern and Central Europe: Decline, Resistance, and Expansion, ed. by Paul Freedman and Monique Bourin (2005)

Grant risee?: The Medieval Comic Presence / La Présence comique médiévale. Essays in Honour of Brian J. Levy, ed. by Adrian P. Tudor and Alan Hindley (2006)

Urban Theatre in the Low Countries, 1400–1625, ed. by Elsa Strietman and Peter Happé (2006)

Gautier de Coinci: Miracles, Music, and Manuscripts, ed. by Kathy M. Krause and Alison Stones (2006)

The Narrator, the Expositor, and the Prompter in European Medieval Theatre, ed. by Philip Butterworth (2007)

Learning and Understanding in the Old Norse World: Essays in Honour of Margaret Clunies Ross, ed. by Judy Quinn, Kate Heslop, and Tarrin Wills (2007)

Essays in Manuscript Geography: Vernacular Manuscripts of the English West Midlands from the Conquest to the Sixteenth Century, ed. by Wendy Scase (2007)

Parisian Confraternity Drama of the Fourteenth Century, ed. by Donald Maddox and Sara Sturm-Maddox (2008)

Broken Lines: Genealogical Literature in Medieval Britain and France, ed. by Raluca L. Radulescu and Edward Donald Kennedy (2008)

Laments for the Lost in Medieval Literature, ed. by Jane Tolmie and M. J. Toswell (2010)

Medieval Multilingualism: The Francophone World and its Neighbours, ed. by Christopher Kleinhenz and Keith Busby (2010)

The Playful Middle Ages: Meanings of Play and Plays of Meaning. Essays in Memory of Elaine C. Block, ed. by Paul Hardwick (2011)

Emilia Jamroziak, *Survival and Success on Medieval Borders: Cistercian Houses in Medieval Scotland and Pomerania from the Twelfth to the Late Fourteenth Century* (2011)

Normandy and its Neighbours, 900–1250: Essays for David Bates, ed. by David Crouch and Kathleen Thompson (2011)

Historical Narratives and Christian Identity on a European Periphery: Early History Writing in Northern, East-Central, and Eastern Europe (c. 1070–1200), ed. by Ildar H. Garipzanov (2011)

Multilingualism in Medieval Britain (c. 1066–1520): Sources and Analysis, ed. by Judith Jefferson and Ad Putter with the assistance of Amanda Hopkins (2013)

The Social Life of Illumination: Manuscripts, Images, and Communities in the Late Middle Ages, ed. by Joyce Coleman, Markus Cruse, and Kathryn A. Smith (2013)

Stefka Georgieva Eriksen, *Writing and Reading in Medieval Manuscript Culture: The Translation and Transmission of the story of Elye in Old French and Old Norse Literary Contexts* (2014)

Keith Busby, *French in Medieval Ireland, Ireland in Medieval French: The Paradox of Two Worlds* (2017)

Medieval Francophone Literary Culture Outside France: Studies in the Moving Word, ed. by Nicola Morato and Dirk Schoenaers (2019)

Colmán Etchingham, Jón Viðar Sigurðsson, Máire Ní Mhaonaigh, and Elizabeth Ashman Rowe, *Norse-Gaelic Contacts in a Viking World* (2019)

Crossing Borders in the Insular Middle Ages, ed. by Aisling Byrne and Victoria Flood (2019)

The Chronicles of Medieval Wales and the March: New Contexts, Studies, and Texts, ed. by Ben Guy, Owain Wyn Jones, Georgia Henley, and Rebecca Thomas (2020)

Making the Profane Sacred in the Viking Age: Essays in Honour of Stefan Brink, ed. by Irene García Losquiño, Olof Sundqvist, and Declan Taggart (2020)

The Cult of Saints in Nidaros Archbishopric: Manuscripts, Miracles, Objects, ed. by Ragnhild M. Bø and Jón Viðar Sigurðsson (2022)

Crusading and Ideas of the Holy Land in Medieval Britain, ed. by Kathryn Hurlock and Laura J. Whatley (2022)

Celts, Gaels, and Britons: Studies in Language and Literature from Antiquity to the Middle Ages in Honour of Patrick Sims-Williams, ed. by Simon Rodway, Jenny Rowland, and Erich Poppe (2022)